Also by Alan Palmer

A DICTIONARY OF MODERN HISTORY, 1789–1945
YUGOSLAVIA
THE GARDENERS OF SALONIKA
NAPOLEON IN RUSSIA
INDEPENDENT EASTERN EUROPE,
  A HISTORY (with C. A. Macartney)

The Lands Betwee

A History of East-Central Eu
since the Congress of Vienna

Alan Palmer

The Lands Between
A History of East-Central Europe since the Congress of Vienna

The Macmillan Company

The Macmillan Company
866 Third Avenue, New York, N.Y. 10022

Library of Congress Catalog Card Number: 74: 83064

First published in Great Britain in 1970 by Weidenfeld and Nicolson, London
First American Edition 1970

Contents

Illustrations

Maps

Preface

This book is intended as an introductory study of the political development over the last century and a half of the lands between Germany and Italy in the west and Russia in the east. It is therefore primarily concerned with six countries in Eastern Europe as constituted today: Bulgaria, Czechoslovakia, Hungary, Poland, Roumania and Yugoslavia. Since history in the broadest sense is no respecter of frontiers the narrative trespasses at times beyond the strict geographical limits of this region, but events in Germany, Austria and the northern and southern fringe are considered only in relation to the main theme – the fate of the peoples in the central borderland and their response to the recurrent menace to independence offered by their more powerful neighbours.

The principal chapters cover nineteenth- and twentieth-century history since the Congress of Vienna in 1815. The book begins, however, with a topographical survey of the Vistulan, Danubian and Balkan lands and a background sketch indicating the way in which the distant past has created enduring legends for all the nationalities in this area. It was harder to select a point at which to finish. Most of this narrative was written during 1967 and 1968, and as I worked on it the daily press reports made me increasingly conscious that each successive emergency was an instance of continuity in change rather than a distinctive ending to an epoch. I therefore decided to continue the chronicle of events up to November 1968, not because this was a significant date in itself for Eastern Europe but because it marked the fiftieth anniversary of the fall of the old supra-national empires, the only dramatically sharp division in the recent history of this area. It is a sad commentary on the chronic insecurity in East-Central Europe that completion of half a century of nominal independence should be marked not, as one had hoped, by celebrations of progress and achievement but by the presence of an army of occupation in the territory of the one totally new republic founded in 1918.

A foreigner narrating the history of a part of Europe in which patriotism has always cut deep furrows of pride in the national character runs the risk of offending people from these lands by an apparent lack of sympathetic understanding. I write as an Englishman but one who believes that each of these six countries has, like Britain, a heritage worthy of great respect and of occasional censure. Political leaders are neither demi-gods nor demons; they have the virtues and vices of mere mortals but their failings are magnified because of the position which they hold; and it is this occupational hazard which leads to unjust assessment by those who seek to explain their acts. It seems unlikely that I have avoided errors of bias, and for these I apologize.

My debt to the scholars who have specialized in this field of study is enormous and may be gauged by anyone who glances at the bibliographical section. I am especially grateful to Mr A. J. P. Taylor who, when I was a young undergraduate, stimulated my interest in Central Europe during a term in which I was fortunate enough to have him as a tutor. I also remember the patience and kindness with which the late Professor R. W. Seton-Watson allowed me to badger him with questions after one of the last series of lectures he delivered at Oxford. My greatest obligation is to Dr C. A. Macartney, with whom I had the honour of working on *Independent Eastern Europe* in the late 1950s. Without his inspiration I doubt if I would have written anything about this part of the world, even though it has fascinated me for so long. Naturally, I alone am responsible for all judgements and interpretations in the chapters which follow.

I have, of course, a further debt to my friends at Highgate and elsewhere who have encouraged me in writing this book. The only person with whom I have discussed it in detail chapter by chapter has been my wife, Veronica; and I am grateful to her both for critical comments on the manuscript and for the assistance she has given me in journeys down the Danube and to the Balkan lands.

A.W.P.

HIGHGATE
February 1969

I
Borderlands of Europe

The contrasting destiny of Europe's peoples is preordained by the map.
To the west of the continent, sea-coasts and mountains early determined
the framework of national states and, if their formation was delayed, this
was as much the fault of human prejudice as of geography. The Pyrenees
and the Alps are not impassable barriers but, like the English Channel,
they have been crossed only rarely by an invading force. In East-Central
Europe, however, all is different. The lands which separate Germany and
Italy from Russia lack natural frontiers; they are organisms with vertebrae
and arteries but no external shell. Their few mountain ranges are cut by
rivers so that they are incapable of keeping out migratory hordes or of
repelling an all-conquering army; and the only ocean is formed by the
grey-green waves of steppe land rolling endlessly into the Eurasian plain.
Open to wandering races from the east and attracting colonial settlement
from the west, this region became the home of at least fifteen distinctive
nationalities even though it covers, in area, less than two thirds the size of
Western Europe.

Geographically East-Central Europe falls conveniently into three
divisions: the Vistulan basin; the Danubian basin; and the Balkan ranges.
But this pattern is complicated by the existence of transitional zones and
by the great horseshoe of the Carpathian massif which cuts the Danubian
basin in two, although without changing its essential form. Moreover,
there are few other areas in the world where the interplay of geography
and history – and, sometimes, of geography and contemporary politics –
has made it possible for the traveller to meet such sudden changes in
social characteristics between settlements separated by a few miles. All too
often in this part of Europe local variations mock geographical generaliza-
tion and force historical judgement into qualifying parenthesis.

The Vistula rises in the Western Beskid range of the Carpathians and flows
into the Baltic at Gdansk (Danzig), 650 miles to the north. This slow and
meandering river is something greater than a trade route. For the Vistula
has served as the axis of the Polish nation through a thousand years of

political vicissitude, a unifying force linking the cities of Warsaw and Cracow and the great estates of Galicia with the Baltic coast. In a sense it is a mystic river succouring the spirit of Poland when the political state was dead and the hour of resurrection seemed distant. More prosaically, it irrigates the Polish plains, rolling and formless fields of wheat and sugar-beet and rye, stretching for over three hundred miles from north to south, broken here and there by forest and marshland and, in Masuria, by reed-fringed lakes set in sandy soil. The Vistulan basin ends with a belt of gentle hills in Silesia which climb eventually into the Sudeten mountains or, farther east, into the Beskids where knolls of soft rock lie humped over lazy streams and the passes are broad and low. To the southeast of the basin the main tributary of the Vistula, the Bug, taps the resources of the eastern marshlands so that the plain is carried into the rich granary of the Ukraine and down the Dniester to the Black Sea.

Since the Second World War and the conferences of Yalta and Potsdam the Poles have controlled another great navigable river; for in 1945 the right bank of the Oder and the whole of its tributary, the Warta, were incorporated within the boundaries of the Polish Republic, supplementing in character the geographical configuration of the Vistulan area. At the same time, in the east, Poland lost to the Soviet Union nearly half of the territory which had been shown as Polish on the maps of the inter-war period, and the lower Bug became a frontier rather than an interior route of communication. This general westward movement of the borders of the Polish State ran counter to the historical development of the nation in the preceding two hundred years. Yet, painful though its consequences were to both Poles and Germans, it is no more than a recent instance of the tragic burden imposed by geography on Poland's past; for, because of the accessibility of the Vistulan plain to invading armies from both sides, Poland's shifting boundaries have made her, over the centuries, the only amorphous state in Europe. Three hundred years ago her eastern frontier lay beyond Smolensk and barely ninety miles from Moscow; she was, at that time, territorially the largest state on the continent (apart from the inchoate mass of Russia). Today the most eastern salient of Polish land lies 500 miles west of this seventeenth-century boundary, while the advance of her German frontier to the Oder has brought Poland, on an average, 150 miles farther into Europe.

Such translation of the home of a nation is, fortunately, unique in the history of the modern world. Throughout these changes, the Polish character of the Vistulan cities, with their Baroque architecture and intensive religious feeling, has remained constant; for although Poland was wiped off the political map in 1795 and not restored as an independent state until 1918, awareness of a common culture and tradition – Western

~ARTHUR BANKS ~

THE LANDS BETWEEN
Physical

0   400
Miles

- Galati   Towns
BANAT   Geographical regions
Danube   Rivers, lakes, etc.
Pindus   Mountain features
            Land above 6000 feet
            3000 to 6000 feet
            1500 to 3000 feet

GULF OF FINLAND

Leningrad

BALTIC SEA

Dvina

Smolensk

Neman

Vilna

Dnieper

Gdansk

Elbe

Oder

Poznan

Vistula

Bug

Pripet

Warta

Warsaw

Sudetes

BOHEMIA
Prague

Cracow

GALICIA

UKRAINE

MORAVIA

Beskids

Tatra

Danube

Thaya

Morava

SLOVAKIA

CARPATHIANS

Chernovtsy

Dniester

BUKOVINA

BESSARABIA

Odessa

Bratislava

Tisza

Vienna

Budapest

TRANSYLVANIA

Cluj

Pruth

Siret

THE ALPS

Drava

L. Balaton

Szeged

Mures

Galati

Karawanken

Ljubljana

SLOVENIA

Zagreb

Trieste

BANAT

Transylvanian Alps

Ploesti

BLACK SEA

Venice

Rijeka

Fruska Gora Hills

DOBRUDJA

CROATIA

Sava

Belgrade

The Iron
Gate

Bucharest

Constanta

BOSNIA

Dinaric Alps

Sarajevo

SUMADIJA

Danube

Zardar

DALMATIA

Drina

Varna

Mostar

Morava

Nis

Balkan Mts

Dubrovnik

Cetine

Sofia

Plovdiv

Bosphorus

Rome

ADRIATIC

SEA

Durres

MACEDONIA

Skopje

Rhodopes

Edirne

Istanbul

L. Ohrid

Kavalla

THRACE

Salonika

Pindus

Dardanelles

AEGEAN SEA

Athens

MEDITERRANEAN   SEA

and Catholic but Slavonic – preserved the national consciousness despite the enticements of the German Powers or of Russia.

With frontiers which expanded or contracted so remarkably, it is hardly surprising that Poland has never been racially homogeneous. The first Polish state emerged in the middle of the tenth century when six Slavonic tribes, long settled in the plain between the southern Oder and the Vistula, combined for defence against their German and Bohemian neighbours and, in AD 960, accepted Mieszko, the warrior leader of the almost mythical family of Piast as their ruler. The Poles, like other Slav peoples, divided the territories of a dead king among his various sons and this process inevitably weakened the embryonic state, to the advantage of the more organized feudal institutions in the German lands. Germanic settlements were originally established by the Teutonic Knights in the thirteenth century, and although the power of the Knights was broken by the Poles in the first battle of Tannenberg (1410), German infiltration long continued, especially down the lower Vistula and in the areas of Poznan (Posen). Moreover, living around the fringe of the traditionally Polish lands were predominantly peasant peoples – Lithuanians, White Russians, Ukrainians – on whom the Polish aristocracy imposed a largely alien culture. Among these groups, the Lithuanians were readily assimilated: the greatest of Polish dynasties (the Jagiellon, 1386–1572) was itself Lithuanian in origin; and Vilna (Wilno), with its dozen churches and formidable citadel, was a city which, despite its Lithuanian foundation, symbolized the union of the two peoples. The Lithuanian lands were formally, and belatedly, incorporated in Poland in 1569 and it was not until the 1880s that any specifically Lithuanian national sentiment revived. Other peoples, however, fared less well: both the White Russians and the Ukrainians were regarded as inferior stock and were treated accordingly; and the privileges accorded to the Jewish population were derisory.

As so often in Europe's borderlands, national distinctions in the old Poland implied social fragmentation. Thus in eighteenth-century Galicia Polish landowners expected their fields to be tilled by Ukrainian peasants while trading in the towns through Jewish merchants and having their carriages and waggons made and repaired by German craftsmen; and this class pattern survived the Partitions of 1772 and 1795.

The Polish lands of the Vistulan-Oder area are separated in the west from the Danubian basin by the 'Historic Provinces', the basically Czech lands of Bohemia and Moravia. Although Bohemia is a plateau of rolling plain, hemmed in by forests and mountains on three sides, the ridge of hills to the east is low, while in the north-west the valley of the Elbe gives easy access to Saxony and the heart of Germany; and it is largely for this reason that the whole of the outer fringe of Bohemia, the

Sudetenland, was settled overwhelmingly by German peasants from the thirteenth century onwards.

Bohemia had experienced more than 500 years of history before this eastward migration of Germans. A western Slavonic state corresponding to Bohemia appears to have existed in the middle of the sixth century. It was, however, little more than a tribal union, under a chieftain known as Samo, and it disintegrated soon after his death in AD 685. There was a 'Greater Moravian Empire' in the ninth century which under Prince Svatopluk included Bohemia and Slovakia as well as the area corresponding to modern Moravia. This state, too, only survived its principal ruler for a few years, for in 906 the Moravians were defeated by the Magyars in a battle near what is now the city of Bratislava: the western lands of Svatopluk's realm united with Bohemia and Silesia under the saintly head of the House of Premysl, King Wenceslas; but the eastern lands – Slovakia – shared the fate of Magyar Hungary for over a 1,000 years.

Medieval Bohemia was a half-Slavonic and half-Germanic state. With Moravia and Silesia, Bohemia formed the 'Historic Lands of the Crown of St Wenceslas', and the term 'Historic Provinces' survived as an official title for this region until the fall of the Habsburg Monarchy in 1918. Bohemia's 'golden age' was under King Charles I of the House of Luxemburg who, as Charles IV, was also Holy Roman Emperor from 1347 to 1378. The scholarship of Bohemia's university, established in Prague in 1348, placed it in the late middle ages on an equal footing with Paris, Bologna and Oxford; and in John Huss the Czechs found, in the early fifteenth century, a national leader and religious reformer who became, like Luther in Germany a 100 years later, the father of his people's language and literature. The Hussite struggle for religious independence weakened the political structure of Bohemia by accentuating distinctions between the Germanized Catholic landowners and the predominantly Czech-speaking and 'heretical' peasantry. Yet Bohemia maintained an independent existence, at times more illusory than genuine, until the traditional skilful marriage policy of the Habsburgs and the need for a unified defence against the Turkish hordes brought the Historic Lands under the rule of the Emperor Charles V in 1526. Their constitutional liberties perished a century later in the Thirty Years War and by the middle of the seventeenth century the 'Crown of St Wenceslas' had become an integral part of the Habsburg inheritance.

The landscape of Bohemia has more in common with Western Europe than any other region with which this book is concerned (except, perhaps, Slovenia) but the Czech peoples, although highly receptive to the sophistication of the West, have always sought cultural strength from their linguistic affinity with the Slavonic East. Yet, just as the Poles have suffered from the fluidity of their boundaries, so Bohemia's strategic position has condemned the Czechs to become involved, with varying degrees of commitment, in every historical upheaval of both the West and the East since the first stirrings of the Protestant challenge in the early fifteenth century. For Prague, the chief city of Bohemia, lies almost midway between Vienna and Berlin and, indeed – of equal historical significance – midway between the rivers Main and Vistula. 'He who is master of Bohemia is master of Europe,' Bismarck once declared, uncompromisingly; and the implications of his aphorism have all too frequently proved grievous for the Czech peoples.

Moravia, the eastern plateau area of the 'Historic Provinces', has a similar strategic importance, although in modern times a less menacing one. For across Moravia runs the main route between Poland and the Hungarian plain, a key section on one of the great north–south links of Europe. Moravia thus offers a natural gateway through the crescent buttress of the Carpathians, originating with the upper Oder and opening out of a six mile wide valley into a broader plain around the town of Olomouc. The river Morava flows south from Olomouc to join the Thaya and eventually, west of Bratislava, the Danube. To the east of the Morava lies Slovakia, long a backward and remote mountainous region although the valleys sheltered by the Beskids and Tatra are fertile and productive. Slovakia is the threshold of the Danubian basin; its capital, Bratislava, which is only forty miles downstream from Vienna, has played a varied role in the history of the riparian lands, generally as Pressburg (the German name) and occasionally as Pozsony (the Magyar name), but the character of the city, rich in architectural contrasts, has been shaped by the great river beside which it stands

The Danube winds across Central Europe for 1,700 miles, a thread tenuously drawing a diversity of peoples into coalescence although never strong enough to bind them lastingly in unity. The river rises in the Black Forest and for nearly a third of its length flows through foothills of the Alps. But beneath the spur of the Leopoldsberg, the steep wooded cliff standing sentinel west of Vienna, it finally sweeps out into the fertile plain which the Romans called Pannonia. The 100,000 square miles of this middle Danubian plain is soaked with the blood of Europe's invaders from the East; for this was the line of march of the Huns and Avars in the so-called 'Dark Ages', of the Magyars at the end of the ninth century, of the Turks in the sixteenth and seventeenth centuries, and of the Russians in the twentieth century. And it has been the route of the western answer to the challenge – whether the cavalry of Eugene of Savoy, the panzer divisions of Field-Marshal List and General von

Kleist, or the more insidious invasion of Austro-German manufacturers and salesmen 'thrusting to the East' in the last decade of the Habsburg Monarchy. Small wonder that at so many points on this central section of the river – at Esztergom and Budapest, for example, or in Serbia at Belgrade and Smederevo – the relics of citadels continue to brood over the wide plains. Belgrade alone has been taken and re-taken by opposing armies a dozen times in the last two and a half centuries.

The Pannonian Plain proper – to the south of the river as it skirts Slovakia, but west of it when it turns to bisect Hungary – consists of undulating country, rising gently to a ridge of hills around Lake Balaton. The farmers of this region have, quite naturally, followed the agricultural techniques of southern Germany and Austria, and ever since the withdrawal of the Turks in 1685 the Hungarian right bank of the river has been markedly 'West-Central' rather than 'East-Central' in character. In the eighteenth and nineteenth centuries Pannonia was settled far more systematically than other districts along the central Danube, partly because of its proximity to Budapest – and, indeed, to Vienna – and partly because the pattern of relief favoured a greater density of population. Although colonization was encouraged by feudal landowners, of whom many were themselves Magyar, this process added considerably to the ethnic confusion of a racial borderland by mingling German 'Swabians', Slovaks and even South Slavs with the peasantry, who were, at least in part, descendants of the Magyar settlers of the ninth century.

Across the Danube, on the Hungarian left bank, the geographical features are different and so, too, has been the way of life. This is the region known as the Alföld (or 'low field'), a cultivated plain but so featureless that it is in many ways a westward projection of the Asiatic steppes. For some 800 years it was the natural home of wild and nomadic horsemen and in the 'Puszta' areas, where poor soil discourages the growing of crops, there long remained vestiges of the gypsy communities who brought music and colour to create the picturesque image of Hungarian culture.

Like Poland, Hungary is one of the 'historical' nations of Europe, having lost from time to time its independence but never its identity. The Hungarian State was created in the last decade of the ninth century AD when the hitherto wandering Magyars, who had originated on the far side of the Urals, swept through the Carpathians and established themselves in the Alföld, later crossing the Danube where Buda and Esztergom now stand. In two ways the Magyars were early marked off as distinct from the other Asiatic hordes, which flowed into East-Central Europe between the seventh and thirteenth centuries: their language was Finno-Ugrian in form rather than Slavonic; and, in the year 1000, legend says that their leader, Stephen, received from the Pope insignia recognizing

7

his dignity as a Christian and Apostolic King. By the late Middle Ages the 'Holy Crown' had become in itself a mystical symbol of national unity. In the early eleventh century Hungarian power was consolidated to the east in Transylvania and, at the same time, spread southwards into Slavonia and Croatia (which, after a personal dynastic union in 1102, retained institutions of its own). But in 1526 the Hungarian army was defeated in battle by the Turks at Mohács: all the Alföld and part of the territory beyond the Danube up to Lake Balaton was annexed to the Turkish Empire; and the rump of Hungary, with the 'Holy Crown' and Bohemia-Moravia, passed in 1541 into the protection of the Habsburgs, a union which was to endure for four centuries and gain added significance as the Turks were pushed gradually eastwards.

There is no natural Hungarian frontier to the south. The endless plains, fed by the greater river, continue with little change of character into what is now Yugoslavia. There the Danube is joined by two important tributaries, the Drava from the west, and as the river itself turns eastwards the Tisza (or Theiss) from Szeged and the Alföld in the north. The region in which the Drava and the Tisza flow into the Danube is known as the Vojvodina, and contains some of the richest farming land in south-eastern Europe, where there are crops of corn and wheat and sugar-beet as well as a tradition of horse-breeding. The Vojvodina ('Duchy') comprised three districts: the Baranya, a triangle of land on the right bank of the Danube, bounded in the west by the Drava; the Bácksa, the region between the Danube and the Tisza; and the Bánát, a much larger area extending north-eastwards beyond Timisoara (Temesvár) to the river Mures. Today, the term Vojvodina is retained for an administrative unit within Yugloslavia but it does not include the Baranya (which is divided to form a Hungarian county in the north and a district in Croatia in the south) nor most of the Bánát, which was partitioned after the First World War, with Roumania receiving the larger part. The old Vojvodina, and more especially the Bánát, was a region in which historical chance and deliberate policy created an extraordinarily confused pattern of nationalities. When the frontiers were re-drawn after the First World War it was found that there were villages in the Bánát in which peoples of Magyar, Serbian, Roumanian and German stock lived side by side – although, unfortunately, not in harmony. Here, as in so many other regions of East-Central Europe, indigenous tensions outlived the old political order.

South of the Drava the fertile plain of the Danubian basin is known as Slavonia and continues into Croatia proper until it reaches hill country covered with vineyards and eventually the mountains and forests of Bosnia. The boundary between Slavonia and Croatia is formed by the river Sava, which is itself a tributary of the Danube and which runs parallel to the Drava for more than 250 miles. Even though it does not debouch into a seaport, the Sava is, in many ways, to lowland Yugoslavia what the Vistula is to Poland; it rises in the Alpine chain of the Karawanken and tumbles down through rich timber country to pass close to the Slovene capital of Ljubljana and on to the Croatian capital of Zagreb, being united with the Danube beneath the limestone crags of Belgrade itself. Yet although the Sava is today such a vital artery for the Yugoslav lands, it long had another purpose; for more than 200 years it was the eastward moat of the West against the Turk. Early in the eighteenth century the Habsburgs advanced the 'Military Frontier', which they had originally established in 1578 among the foothills of the Alps, so that the new line of defence ran through Slavonia along the Sava and, in due course, down the Danube and across the Bánát. This borderland of watch-towers, guard posts and beacons was inhabited by frontiersmen who were generally hardy refugees from inside Serbia or adventurous German colonists and who were bound in military allegiance to the Imperial government in Vienna. Their descendants remained as privileged holders of estates until the very end of the nineteenth century and continued as loyal servants of the Habsburg Monarchy even later.

To the east, the Danubian Plain is less wide than in Slavonia and Croatia. There are wooded hills, the Fruska Gora, between the Danube and the Sava in the region known as Srem, a Serbian approximation to the Latin name 'Sirmium', bestowed on this outpost of Empire by Domitian's legionaries in the first century AD. And farther east still, in the quadri-lateral formed by the rivers Danube, Sava, Drina and (Serbian) Morava, lies the rolling countryside of the Šumadija, densely forested little more than a century ago but cleared now and given over to the cultivation of cereals and plums and to the raising of pigs. The Šumadija, the cradle of the modern Serbian nation, is geographically a transitional zone between the Danubian basin and the Balkan ranges, whose wooded slopes loom over the upper Drina and the upper Morava.

Eighty miles downstream from Belgrade the mountains begin to converge on the Danube itself, almost meeting in the Kazan defiles where the river narrows to less than two hundred yards wide. Immediately north, on the Roumanian bank, there are summits in the Carpathian chain, or 'Transylvanian Alps', which are as high as Snowdon and, although the Balkan offshoots on the Yugoslav bank are lower, they too have peaks some 2,500 feet above sea-level. Such heights are, of course, not in themselves remarkable, but their proximity to the river and the presence to the east and the west of broad plains gives to them a majesty which is both picturesque and awe-inspiring. In the most eastward defile cliffs of granite force the Danube to pass over rocky rapids; river traffic at this point, the 'Iron Gates', moves slowly through the locks of a canal, only completed in 1896, and work is in progress on a massive barrage to provide Roumania and Yugoslavia with hydro-electric power. The Carpathians have, in reality, never proved such a formidable barrier to communications as the map would suggest; for, as well as the route along the Danube, deep troughs farther north have cut natural passages across which migratory peoples and invading hordes have swept down the centuries. But it was through the Kazan defiles that Trajan's legionaries first brought the civilization of the West to the eastern plains and to the country whose modern name perpetuates this ancient link with Rome.

The Danube is still 620 miles from the sea when it passes the Iron Gates. North-east of it lies the Roumanian province of Wallachia with rich soil on which wheat and maize are cultivated; and, farther north, between Bucharest and the south-eastern curve of the Carpathians there are oil fields around Ploesti ('rainy-town'), where a primitive refinery began to function as early as 1857. The eastern Danubian plain stretches northwards across the lakes and marshes of the lower river Siret into the province of Moldavia and, without any intervening natural barrier, into the steppe-lands which separate the rivers Pruth and Dniester. This is the region known as Bessarabia, possibly after the half-legendary Wallachian family of Basarab who, in the early fourteenth century, tried to establish an independent Roumanian principality at the mouth of the Danube. Since the Second World War the Russian frontier has advanced to the Pruth and Bessarabia forms part of what is, somewhat confusingly, called the Soviet Socialist Republic of Moldavia. Geographically, there is little to distinguish Bessarabia from the great expanses of the Ukraine which adjoin it; and politically the province has been disputed by successive rulers of the Roumanian lands and by the Russians for 200 years. Vini-culture flourished under the tsarist landowners but was neglected by the Roumanians between the wars. Although the province has little economic importance it is strategically of considerable value; for by possessing Bessarabia, Russia becomes a Danubian Power, entitled to participate in all riparian conferences.

The winding course of the Danube seems almost to hold the lowland areas of Roumania in an embrace. After leaving the Iron Gates the river forms a frontier between Wallachia and the northern plain of what is now Bulgaria until it is within fifty miles of the Black Sea coast. There slightly higher contours in the region known as the Dobrudja force the Danube northwards for almost a 100 miles, with the river frequently overspilling into marshland. As the Danube once more approaches the Carpathians, it is joined by the Siret and soon after by its last important tributary, the Pruth. The combined streams turn eastwards and break up into muddy channels before the great river finally reaches the sea.

If this Danubian delta suggests a parallel with the Mississippi, then the river port of Galati, at the confluence with the Siret, is Eastern Europe's New Orleans. But the resemblance is essentially superficial, for Galati began to handle sea-going vessels only in the present century. The Roumanians have never been a maritime people; trade in the Black Sea was long a monopoly of Greeks and Armenians whose ships used, not Galati, but Constanta, which was once the Roman seaport of Tomi and the city where Ovid died in exile. Geographically Constanta is part of the Dobrudja and there is a stretch of marshland twelve miles wide around the Danube between the port and the Wallachian plains. But, partly because the whole of the Dobrudja is more accessible from the northern lowlands of Bulgaria, the rulers in Bucharest have particularly stressed the Roumanian character of Constanta, linking the interior to it by rail and road and pipe-line. The coastal littoral between Constanta and the Bulgarian port of Varna, eighty miles to the south, is an ethnic jumble of Bulgarians, Roumanians, Turks, Greeks and immigrant seafarers from the Caucasus; and this region, the southern Dobrudja, with silver sands beside a hyacinth blue sea, was for long a shuttlecock in the power game of Sofia and Bucharest.

Wallachia and Moldavia are indisputably part of the Danubian basin; they were even known officially as the 'Danubian Principalities' until late in the nineteenth century. But if the river has been the life-blood of Roumania, the Carpathian chain forms its backbone; for the mountains loom over the lowlands in a massive arc, the outer curve of which sweeps across the country for more than 400 miles. Within this arc, geographically compact, lies the plateau of Transylvania, rich in forests, rich in mineral resources, rich in good pasture-land – but for generations spiritually impoverished by the suspicion and resentment of feuding nationalities.

The Transylvanian Question was the archetype of Eastern European internal conflict. Its origins lie in the Middle Ages. Because the passes of the Carpathians were exposed to the great migratory route across the Eurasian plains, the thirteenth-century kings of Hungary invited Germans ('Saxons') to settle in Transylvania and assist the feudal Magyar nobility to preserve Central Europe from fresh invasions. The Saxons, receiving rights of virtual autonomy which they continued to enjoy for more than 600 years, established seven fortified towns as instruments of colonization; it is significant that the German name for Transylvania is still Siebenburgen. There were, however, quite apart from the Magyar overlords, already two other racial groups in the region before the coming of the Saxons: a native peasantry speaking a corrupt form of Latin, who are generally termed Roumanian; and the people who had moved into Transylvania from the Alföld and who were called Szeklers. Like the Magyars, whom they closely resembled, the Szeklers originated in the grasslands beyond the Urals, and, like the Saxons, they were granted privileges of self government in return for duty along the frontier. Although there were occasional clashes between the Magyars, mainly plainsmen, and the Szeklers, mainly mountaineers, both groups of people came in time to think of themselves as Hungarian, determined to preserve a common front against the Roumanian peasantry and generally receiving the support of the Saxons. The union of Transylvania with Roumania after the First World War therefore represented, not only a change of allegiance but a reversal of the social order; and, as in other parts of East-Central Europe, the hostility of the rival nationalities has remained even after the far greater revolution in government which followed in the wake of communism.

There are, however, elements in the Transylvanian Question which few other areas of conflict experienced. For the ethnographical pattern was complicated by the geographical circumstance that the Szekler communities were in the south-eastern districts, along the line of the mountains and therefore adjoining Wallachia, while the western region of Transylvania, bordering on the Hungarian lowlands, was predominantly inhabited by Roumanians. By contrast the German-Saxon families were powerful in almost every urban settlement, although their commercial preponderance began to be challenged after the Napoleonic Wars by a rapidly growing Jewish community. Moreover, social and political rifts in this supremely heterogeneous province have, over the centuries, been deepened by the variety of religious faiths professed by its peoples. Branches of the Orthodox Church, Catholics with the Latin rite, Catholics with the Eastern rite, Calvinists, primitive Baptists and Lutherans all flourished within the region; and, with fortuitous irony, the chief city of Transylvania – which the Roumanians called Cluj, the Hungarians Kolozsvár and the Germans Klausenburg – became an intellectual centre of the sect known as Unitarian.

The north-eastern slopes of the arc of mountains were for long sparsely inhabited. They were mostly covered by thick forests and the chief occupation of the hardy mountain-folk who lived there was felling timber. In the late eighteenth century the Austrians created in this region the province of the Bukovina ('beechwood') with an administrative centre in a town on the upper Pruth which they knew as Czernowitz (Cernauti to the Roumanians and Chernovtsy to the Russians). At that time the population was predominantly Roumanian in origin but there was a strong incursion of Ukrainians – or, as they were called in this part of Europe, Ruthenes – during the nineteenth century, and by 1880 they were the largest single national group. There is little to distinguish the northern areas of the Bukovina from the region known as Ruthenia which was for long a part of 'Austrian Poland' (Galicia); and both the Bukovina and Ruthenia were administered from Vienna until 1918. In the inter-war period, however, the Bukovina was incorporated in Roumania while Ruthenia formed part of the Czechoslovak State. Today the whole area, apart from a small segment of southern Bukovina which remains Roumanian, is within the Soviet Union and it is known as the 'Sub-Carpathian Ukraine', an appellation which emphasizes the ethnical and linguistic similarity between the mountain people and the workers of the Black Earth region at the expense of both the legacy of history and the common-sense of geography.

The third geographical sub-division of East-Central Europe, the Balkan ranges, fills most of the triangle formed by the line of the Sava and the Danube and the peninsula bounded by the Adriatic, Aegean and Black Seas. The Balkan Mountains proper are a chain of summits which cut across Bulgaria from east to west for 370 miles; and it is from them that the whole peninsula takes its name. There are fertile plains in Greece, although they are small in extent, a cultivable plateau in central Bulgaria, and coastal strips along the Adriatic, thin in Dalmatia, but broader in Albania around Durrës. Elsewhere life is dominated by the mountains. Two off-shoots of the Balkan Chain, the Rhodopes and the Pirins, move from north-west to south-east across Bulgaria towards the Aegean in Thrace. Farther west the Dinaric Mountains run the whole length of western Yugoslavia, separated only by a forested and broken plateau in Slovenia (the so-called Ljubljana Gap) from the Alps. The Dinaric line broadens out to envelop most of Bosnia and the whole of Herzegovina; it includes Lovcen, the 'Black Mountain' which has given its name to Montenegro; and it reaches down into the desolation of Albania, the grimness of whose boundaries is relieved by three large lakes, Skutari in the north and Ohrid and Prespa in the south. The chain spills over in the south to form the Pindus range, which cuts northern Greece in half and sends out one spur to house the gods on Olympus and another to shelter the muses on Parnassus. The mountains continue even into the Peloponnese, where there are summits nearly 8,000 feet high on a peninsula which is more properly part of the Mediterranean world than of East-Central Europe.

The Balkan scene varies little in the highland zones of all four countries – Yugoslavia, Bulgaria, Albania, Greece. Under wild slopes, bleak with the chill of limestone or darkened by tumbling scree, a peasant will saddle his donkey with blankets as he drives his herd along a path gashed into the rocky hillside. In full light the mountains themselves look neither black nor grey but colourless, as though defying pigmentation in some puritan assertion of an awful austerity; but at dusk, when even the low-spirited villages show resilience and the air is heavy with the aromatic smoke of charcoal braziers, these same peaks glow with purple, the valleys are sepia and the dun-tanned plains mellow momentarily into the richness of honey. The old market towns cling to crested spurs of land for protection, terraced alleys of low roofs with curved tiles clustering beneath the slim pencil of a minaret or the stuccoed cupola of a church; but the newer urban settlements stalk out defiantly along rutted roads only to seek the shadow of plane-trees or cypresses and find cohesion in an untidy square, where café tables allow private affairs to be lived in public, as they have always been in south-eastern Europe. For changelessness persists: yoked oxen still draw single-furrow ploughs across the cruel soil or haul timber in a caravan of four-wheeled carts; tobacco leaves are still festooned to dry on poles hung from the walls of peasant houses in Macedonia and Bulgaria; and, in much of the peninsula, rich costume and national dances still preserve a folk tradition in all its bitterness and glory.

It would, of course, be misleading to look upon the mountainous regions as nothing more than a petrified curiosity shop. The fast flowing streams were first harnessed for power in the inter-war period and Yugoslavia, Greece and Bulgaria have all undertaken extensive hydro-electric schemes in recent years. Mining and metallurgy began to be developed in the uplands of the South Slav districts and, to a lesser extent, Greece at the start of the twentieth century, and this process, too, continues to bring industry to backward areas. Yet for most of the last century and a half, the Balkan ranges have been a centre, not of economic advancement, but of perpetuated strife, their woods and valleys providing shelter for insurgent bands challenging the rule of empires, the dictated frontiers of statesmen in congress, or the establishment of new authority serving an alien mandate. In some regions, such as Macedonia, the ethnic boundaries are as complex as in Transylvania and a sense of affronted nationalism has kindled the conflict; and in others, such as Bosnia, there have also been distinctions no less deeply felt of culture and of creed. The intolerance of the mountain lands seems at times to have bred in both natives and invaders a cruelty which transgressed with terrifying ease the border between the acceptable and the cynically condoned; and it is this human ugliness which has so often won the moral thunder of distant judges, observing Balkan tensions free from personal commitment.

Yet behind the historical geography of the Balkans there remains a paradox: the peninsula is the only part of East-Central Europe to appear on the map as protected by sea and mountain, but throughout both ancient and modern times it has been not so much a barrier as a bridge between Asia and the West. Indeed its accessibility is the chief reason why the medieval empires established in the tenth and twelfth centuries by warrior rulers of the Bulgars and the Serbs enjoyed only a brief period of primacy in the Balkans. For the simplest routes from the East into the Danubian plains and Central Europe only touch the fringe of the mountains. From Istanbul (Constantinople) westwards the land that still remains Turkish today is flat as far as Edirne (or Adrianople) on the River Maritsa, which can be followed through Eastern Rumelia to beyond Plovdiv (Philippolis) before the first high ground is encountered. Valleys separating the Rhodopes from the Balkans proper lead through Sofia and Slivnitza to the Dragoman Pass and eventually to Niš, on the (Serbian) Morava, from where the land slopes gently northwards to the Danube. The Crusaders passed this way, in reverse, during the thirteenth century and the railway builders in the nineteenth. There are two other ways of entering the Morava valley: from Kavalla, on the Thracian coast, across the Rupel Pass and up the river Struma to the Dragoman; or from Salonika, the prized port for all the Balkan states, up the Vardar to Skopje so as to reach the headwaters of the Morava north of Kumanovo.

It is along these avenues, opening Central Europe to invasion no less effectively than the passes in the Carpathians or the expanse of the Vistulan plains, that the armies have marched through the centuries. But there was also the way followed by the Roman legionaries, the *Via Egnatia*, a road constructed across the top of the peninsula from Durrës (or Durazzo) through the central Albanian plain, across the Pindus to lakes Ohrid and Prespa, and down to Florina, Edessa and Salonika. And there were other routes, too: from Florina to Bitolj (Monastir) and so across the Babuna Pass to Skopje and the Morava; or, a harder way, from Skopje to Pristina and the valley of the Ibar – the region known in Turkish times as the Sanjak of Novipazar – to Kragujevac and the lands of the Šumadija.

In many ways it was – and is – more difficult to cross the Dinaric Alps through Montenegro or Herzegovina to Bosnia and the plains of Croatia-Slavonia. For this reason Mostar, the capital of Herzegovina, and Cetinje, the old capital of Montenegro, appear more remote and backward than many towns farther east. Montenegro remains a genuine mountain fastness which only superb constructional engineering has begun to open up, but there is one river across Herzegovina; the small mountain stream called the Naretva cuts its way from the Adriatic through Mostar and along deep gorges to Konjić, where there is a pass to Sarajevo, the chief town in Bosnia and the most cosmopolitan centre in all the Balkans. From Sarajevo rivers, which are almost dried up ravines in summer, form a route to the Sava and the central plains.

Two regions in the Balkans, Dalmatia and southern Greece, are on the periphery of East-Central Europe, drawn by tradition and geographical position outwards into the Mediterranean world, to Italy or the Levant. And Albania, too, has been linked for brief periods with the politics of the Italian peninsula; for at one point barely eighty miles of sea separate Albania from Italy, and the great port of Brindisi is slightly nearer Durrës (Durazzo) than Southampton is to Le Havre.

The successive inhabitants of the coastal plain of Dalmatia, cut off from the interior by a wall of limestone *karst,* have tended to look across the Adriatic towards the culture of Rome or northwards to the commercial empire of Venice; and it is significant that it was not until 1925, when a Yugoslav State had existed for seven years, that the first effective economic link was completed between the Adriatic coast and the Croatian plain, a railway from the port of Split to Zagreb. Although some of the most far-sighted believers in the Yugoslav Ideal have come from Dalmatia, there has always been a large Italian-speaking minority along the littoral. Moreover, some of the towns have fostered a habit of independence; this is true of Zadar and Kotor, and more especially of Dubrovnik, which as Ragusa was for four centuries and a half virtually an autonomous state challenging Venice in the enterprise and extent of her trading ventures, until – again like Venice – she lost her liberties in the political whirlwind of the Napoleonic revolution.

Southern Greece was never one of Europe's borderlands although the tide of invading armies, from the Crusaders and the Turks to the Axis Powers of the Second World War, overflowed into her plains and valleys. The Greeks, however, are essentially members of the Mediterranean community and their incursions into the affairs of East-Central Europe in modern times have been largely incidental to a grander design, the vision of a Pan-Aegean commonwealth spanning the waters between Europe and Asia as once the colossus of Chares bound the two arms of the harbour of Rhodes. They were the traders and seafarers of the Turkish Empire, with settlements on the mainland of Anatolia and the coast of the Black Sea as well as on the islands. But these maritime activities carried them to Salonika and the much smaller harbours of Kavalla and Alexandroupolis (which, as Dedeagatch, was only founded by the Turks as late as 1860). This line of ports is, however, the natural southern outlet for the trade of Eastern Europe and it was therefore inevitable that the ambitions of the statesmen and rulers of Greece should, from time to time, have involved their countrymen in the general politics of the Balkan hinterland, particularly because of the rival claims of both Serbia and Bulgaria to control Macedonia.

All these areas of south-eastern Europe, from the Peloponnese to the Danube and beyond, are still haunted by the shadow of Byzantium, the Eastern Roman Empire which flourished from AD 330 until the Turks entered Constantinople in 1453. Politically the spectre remained active as late as 1922, tempting the Greeks into disaster in Asia Minor under a king named after the founder of the city on the Bosphorus. Commercially and socially, the 'Phanariot Greeks' long afforded continuity of ideas, and sometimes of family descent, between the Byzantine Empire and the Ottoman administrations which succeeded it. The term 'Phanariot' was originally applied to an inhabitant of the Phanar, the Greek quarter of Constantinople, but in time it came to mean any Greek agent of the Turkish government, either political or commercial. The Phanariot Greeks were particularly influential in Wallachia and Moldavia; and from 1714 to 1821 the sultans chose members of the Phanariot families as governors (*hospodars*) of the two principalities.

The main impact of Byzantium was, however, cultural. From Constantinople the Balkan peoples – like the Russians – received their Church, their art, their music and, in most cases, their alphabet. The medieval civilization of Serbia and Bulgaria was an attempt to superimpose Byzantine principles on a primitive Slavonic society; and the boundary between the Serbs and Montenegrins (whose Christianity and culture came from Byzantium) and the Croats and Slovenes (whose Christianity and culture came from the West) has survived as a deep rooted barrier hampering the unity of the Yugoslav peoples. Significantly this line separating Greek from Latin Christianity followed closely the administrative division made in AD 385 between the eastern and western halves of the Roman Empire. Although with no basis in geography, this is the most enduring of all frontiers in Europe's borderlands.

The ethnographical pattern of East-Central Europe almost defies systematic analysis. Most of the land between the Baltic Sea and the Adriatic was settled by migrating tribes from the East between the seventh and thirteenth centuries AD and it is customary to divide these peoples into four main racial groups: the Western Slavs (Poles, Czechs, Slovaks, Ruthenes); the Southern Slavs (Serbs, Croats, Slovenes, Bulgarians, Macedonians); the Hungarians (Magyars and Szeklers); and the ethnically enigmatic 'Latins' (Roumanians). But to these nationalities must be added the widely dispersed settlements of Greeks and Turks and Albanians (or 'Shqiptars'); and the colonies established from the West, either as highly organized enclaves of Germans or as smaller, and much less influential, trading outposts of Italians. There are also several towns along the Black Sea coast in which minorities from the Caucasus established themselves, especially Armenians. The racial pattern was complicated still further by the establishment of the various Jewish communities, some of whom were assimilated in the life of the country in which they had settled although most retained their own customs, culture and language. There were communities of Ashkenazi Jews in Poland, Hungary, Roumania and Bulgaria; and Sephardic Jews, expelled from Spain at the end of the fifteenth century, found sanctuary in the Balkans, especially, until the coming of Hitler's armies, in Sarajevo and Salonika.

The ultimate origin of most of the nationalities and their early history is uncertain. Much of the evidence is dubious, the 'Dark Ages' being lit at times by the garish beams of chauvinist scholarship. But two peoples, in particular, pose intriguing problems: the Albanians and the Roumanians.

There are settlements of Albanians, not only in the country which since 1913 has borne their name, but in Yugoslavia from Kosovo to Ohrid and Kumanovo and in many parts of Greece, both near the frontier and as far away as Kavalla and Corinth and even on the islands of Hydra and Salamis. Earlier this century there were also isolated Albanian groups in Bucharest, Sarajevo, Srem and the districts around Zadar, but most of these seem to have lost their identity – although the word 'Shqiptar' survives as a pejorative in several regions of the Balkans. Over the centuries the Albanians absorbed the customs and traditions of the Turks, but they possess a distinctive language of Indo-European formation, split into numerous dialects, and it is possible that they are the descendants of the people who lived in Illyria and Thrace during the great age of classical Greece. They retained, however, at least until the Second World War, such a patriarchal sense of clan loyalty that they never asserted a claim to national primacy on the strength of ancient glory, although they have at times rejoiced in the legend of Skanderbeg, a brigand made hero for successfully defying the Turks over a quarter of a century 500 years ago.

The Roumanians, on the other hand, have been acutely conscious of their ancient past even though it was only in 1862 that a Roumanian principality came into existence. For 165 years, in the second and third centuries AD, most of their present territory, including the whole of Transylvania, formed the Roman province of Dacia, and their Latin foundation was for long a cherished legend, to which verisimilitude was given by the character and formation of the language. There is, however, no doubt that all the lands at the mouth of the Danube were overrun by Slavonic tribes during the great migration and that other wandering peoples, moving northwards out of the Balkans, crossed the Danube in the thirteenth century. Moreover, the whole of Wallachia and Moldavia was considerably influenced by cultural missionaries from Byzantium. Hence it is probable that the racial distinction between the Roumanians and their neighbours was never so marked as the publicists of Bucharest maintained (at least until the southward spread of Russian influence in 1945). Yet, whether the claim was true or false, the belief that they were in some way the easternmost champions of a Latin civilization served for many generations as an inspiration to Roumania's statesmen, often for the good – and occasionally for the discreditable.

Dead history long remained present politics for the peoples of Eastern Europe. Glorification of distant episodes of valour, pious evocation of a unique national mission, retrospective quests for a patriot father-figure, all helped to transform the chronicles of the past into living epics. There was much truth behind this romantic exaggeration. During the Middle Ages most of the nationalities did, indeed, produce dynasties whose fame and power flashed as meteors across the borderlands: the Piasts, who extended Poland's frontier to the Oder at the end of the tenth century, and the Jagiellons, who carried them eastwards into Muscovy 500 years later; the Arpáds of Hungary, defending the Danubian plains against the Tartar invasions in the thirteenth century; the Premysls of Bohemia, seeking the mastery of Central Europe from Königsberg on the Baltic to the Karawanken in Carinthia; and the Nemanjids of Serbia who, by the middle of the fourteenth century, had asserted their sovereignty from the eastern Sava to the south of Thessaly. And there were, as well, individual national heroes: great princes like Tsar Simeon of Bulgaria in the tenth century or Mátyás Hunyadi, the Renaissance king of Hungary's Golden Age; and shadowy figures such as Tomislav and Kresimir Peter, the early leaders of Croatia, and Stephen Tvrtko, the ruler of Bosnia in the second half of the fourteenth century, or Michael the Brave who championed the Roumanians in revolt against the Turks 200 years later. Like Skanderbeg of Albania, their reputations as almost mythological beings long outlived their achievements, images compounded as much of hope as of veneration.

During the centuries of foreign rule there was, too, a curious apotheosis of valiant disaster. Nineteenth-century Czech writers, for example, encouraged the people of Bohemia and Moravia to regard the battle of the White Mountain of 1620 as a national martyrdom, when their ancestors perished rather than accept the predatory plundering of a German tyrant. But the most famous of such traditions is the Serbian cycle of folk ballads on the battle of Kosovo of 1389. It was then that Prince Lazar's army of Serbian chiefs, supported by contingents of Albanians, Bulgars, Croats and Hungarians, were defeated by the Turks on the 'Plain of Blackbirds', a place so hallowed in popular myth that when at last the Serbian army liberated Kosovo in 1912 the soldiery removed their boots as they crossed the old battle fields for fear of disturbing the sleep of the warriors of the past.

Kosovo, was, indeed, a historical climacteric, heralding a period of humiliation and paralysis for the peoples of south-western Europe in which only the name and memory of the medieval Balkan states survived. The victory of the Turks in the battle of Mohács of 1526 similarly marked the end of independence for the Danubian peoples. All East-Central Europe south of the Vistulan basin was thereafter divided between the

Habsburgs, with their capital in Vienna, and the Ottomans, reigning in splendour from Constantinople. Twice Habsburg primacy seemed challenged: once by the Bohemian Revolt which precipitated the Thirty Years War and the disaster of the White Mountain; and again by the sudden resilience of Turkish power which carried the Sultan's armies momentarily to the suburbs of Vienna in 1683. Yet within four years fortune was favouring the Habsburgs once more. Buda was in Austrian hands, with the Magyars in gratitude recognizing the hereditary rights of the rulers in Vienna to the lands of the 'Holy Crown'; and a second battle at Mohács reversed the decisions of 1526. But, apart from the unassailable fastness of Montenegro and the line of trading communities along the Dalmatian coast, all the Balkans remained under the Moslem scimitar until the beginning of the nineteenth century.

The most persistent challenge to Ottoman authority came not from the west but from the north, with the growth of the Russian empire. On six occasions between the accession of Peter the Great in 1682 and Napoleon's march on Moscow 130 years later the Russians went to war with the Turks, gradually gaining a foothold in the Crimea, which they annexed in 1783, and on the Black Sea, where they established the port of Kherson in 1778 and the even more valuable grain-port of Odessa in 1794. The outstanding achievement of Russian diplomacy came at the end of Catherine II's first war: this was the treaty of Kutchuk-Kainardji, which took its name from the Bulgarian village in which it was signed in July 1774. By the settlement Russia acquired much of the Black Sea steppe-land, broke the Ottoman monopoly of maritime trade, and was granted the right to erect a 'Russo-Greek Church' in a suburb of Constantinople and to make representations on behalf of 'those who served' the Church, a vague phrase upon which the Russians subsequently claimed a protectorate over Orthodox Christians throughout the Ottoman Empire. At the same time the Turks admitted that the Russians had a right to 'remonstrate' on behalf of the Christian population of Moldavia and Wallachia. These concessions were of major importance to the whole of East-Central Europe and not merely to Russia. Turkish commerce was at last opened to outside competition: the Austrians, for example, were able to benefit from the new trading arrangements and sent the first cargo vessel down the Danube from Vienna to the Black Sea in 1782. Politically, however, Kutchuk-Kainardji was a specifically Russian triumph which, by its very imprecision, provided successive Tsars with pretexts for interference in Ottoman affairs for the next eighty years. Subsequently the Russians gained the frontier of the Dniester by the treaty of Jassy (1792) and the incorporation of Bessarabia by the treaty of Bucharest (1812), but neither of these settlements was so explosive in character as Kutchuk-Kainardji.

Russia's emergence as a major European Power under Catherine II also sealed the fate of the Vistulan lands. The elective monarchy of Poland had continued to flourish throughout the seventeenth century, reaching its apogee with the reign of John Sobieski (1674–96), who commanded the army which relieved Vienna from the Turkish siege, probably the greatest triumph in Poland's 800 years of history. But after Sobieski's death the decline of the Polish State was rapid. A handful of magnates, politically irresponsible, gave themselves up to internal rivalry, having elected to the throne two Saxon rulers for whom none could find respect. 'The King is King in Warsaw, but I am Lord in Neuswiez', boasted an intimidating proclamation fastened over the entrance to Prince Radziwill's estate; and it was a view characteristic of the selfish arrogance of the Polish aristocracy. Yet, at the very moment when the magnates had lapsed into feudal bickering, the Russian State to the east was assuming the full panoply of Tsardom, while Brandenburg to the west had become the Kingdom of Prussia. Liberal writers everywhere subsequently condemned the Partitions of Poland as a crime; but was it murder, or suicide?

The first challenge to the Polish State came, however, not from Russia or Prussia, but from Austria. For in 1769 the Habsburgs seized the trading town of Spiš (Zips in German, and Szepes to the Magyars), a county almost surrounded by Hungarian territory. The partitions began three years later. The Russians acquired lands, predominantly non-Polish, along the Dnieper and to the north-east of Vitebsk; but Prussia and Austria sought compensation in what was essentially Polish territory, in western Pomerania and Galicia respectively. Belated reform of the Polish State leading to a liberal constitution in 1791 prompted Prussia and Russia to undertake a second partition in 1793 'to save Poland from Jacobinism'. When, in the following year, a patriotic revolt under Tadeusz Kosciuzko challenged the new frontiers, all three Powers undertook a fresh invasion, sharing the rump of Poland between them. Only the spectre of Polish nationalism remained, a mightily powerful ghost binding the three autocracies together for 150 years in perpetuation of their deed.

With the Third Polish Partition of 1795 all East-Central Europe, from the sandhills of the Baltic to the rocky peninsula of the southern Peloponnese, passed under the rule of the four supra-national monarchies who were to dominate the region until the First World War – Russia, Prussia, Austria and Turkey. There was, however, at that time little indication that this division of power would endure for so long. Indeed, at first it seemed as if the settlement would prove remarkably short-lived, for there followed twenty years in which the French struck blow after blow against the old system of government. Napoleon himself twice entered

Vienna in triumph. His armies threatened to tear up the map of Eastern Europe in 1805 and 1807 and again in 1809. Moreover, if Russia had sued for peace after the occupation of Moscow in 1812, Borodino might well have proved a battle as momentous in its consequences for the Vistulan lands as Mohács for the Danubian basin. Politically Napoleon offered Europe's borderlands a transformation more rapid and more comprehensive than any they ever experienced in earlier times. He created a puppet-state, the Grand Duchy of Warsaw; he seized the Slovenian lands and the Dalmatian coast; he even despatched a French garrison to Corfu, a stepping-stone to the Balkan peninsula. To the Poles, the South Slavs and the Greeks he held out a faint hope of national independence. If these prospects never came near to realization it was because he lacked a clear or consistent Eastern policy. Was he to champion order or encourage national revolt? Did he wish the Ottoman Empire to be strengthened against Russia or swept away with Russian acquiescence? He posed questions to which the contradictions of his own career prevented an answer. And when his empire crumbled in 1814, the problems remained to confound the statesmen of Europe for more than a century.

2

The Congress of Vienna and the first National Revolts

In September 1814, with Napoleon I on Elba and peace at last breaking out on the continent, a cavalcade of sovereigns and plenipotentiaries descended on Vienna and for nine months met there in congress. Only once before, at Westphalia in 1648, had there been a conference of so many European states. Then, however, neither Russia nor England was invited to attend. Now Tsar Alexander I took over a wing of the Hofburg Palace and the British Foreign Secretary, Lord Castlereagh, moved into the Minoritenplatz. It was a fascinating assembly of the politically eminent and the socially ambitious. Metternich, the Rhinelander who had controlled Austrian foreign policy for five years and was to continue to do so for another thirty-four, presided at committees in the Ballhausplatz; and Friedrich von Gentz, his chief adviser and a Prussian in the Austrian service, acted as Secretary to the Congress, giving select dinner parties at his lodgings in the Seilergasse. Talleyrand, the spokesman for Bourbon France, held receptions in the Johannesgasse, and somewhere in the city the rulers of thirty German states resided with attendant ministers and courtesans. Amid the suburban vineyards of Neussdorf and Cobenzl a covey of Polish counts waited hopefully for a summons which never came. There was a colourful Wallachian representing the Sultan, and a Doctor Bollman from Philadelphia representing no one but himself though accepted into society as the republican freak in a monarchical circus.

The peacemakers of Vienna were primarily concerned with the problems of Germany, Italy and the West. They looked naturally towards Paris as the source of the revolutionary virus and much of their effort was designed to contain France behind her old frontiers. Metternich's social and political background made him assume that France would remain the greatest challenge to peace and order; he was by habit a 'Westerner' rather than an 'Easterner'. But, since the Congress sought the 'general repose' of all Europe, it could not entirely ignore the eastern third of the continent; and here the great changes of the previous century had been the total eclipse of the Polish State and its replacement, as a major power, by the Russian Empire.

Throughout the Vienna Congress the Austrians and Prussians were therefore doubly shell-shocked by the 1812 campaign. Alarmed at the French achievement in marshalling a Pan-European army, they became no less concerned at Russia's ability to pursue it back across the Niemen and beyond. Castlereagh, too, was disturbed by the presence of Russian troops in the heart of Western Europe; for when Tsar Alexander rode triumphantly into Paris in April 1814, he was the first foreign conqueror to enter the city since Henry V of England in 1413. There seemed no greater commentary on the shift in power over Europe's borderlands than the sudden success of Russian arms. The Cossacks were policing the Polish lands and the Tsar's agents had infiltrated into the Danubian Principalities and Serbia. Moreover, as though flaunting the compass of his patronage, Alexander even included in his delegation to the Congress a Polish aristocrat (Adam Czartoryski) and a Corfiote Greek (John Capodistrias). It is small wonder that Gentz wrote to Metternich a warning that Russia was the chief beneficiary from the destruction of Napoleon's power. If the Habsburgs were to retain their primacy in East-Central Europe, it was essential to stem the Russian advance. The long duel for mastery of the Lands Between was beginning; and it was inevitable that the contenders should first face each other over the affairs of Poland.

The Polish question was so serious that it seemed, at one time, to pose the threat of a new war. The march of Napoleon's armies had destroyed the territorial divisions of 1795: Prussia lost her share of the Partitions to the Grand Duchy of Warsaw in 1807; Austria surrendered Galicia in 1809. But by the spring of 1813 the whole of Poland was in Russian hands and ultimately the Tsar, as he bluntly insisted to Castlereagh, was himself the arbiter of Poland's future because his army occupied every Polish city. 'I have conquered the Duchy and I have half a million men to keep it,' he said, 'I will give Prussia what is due to her but not a single village to Austria.' Yet over Poland's status, as over most issues, Alexander's mind was divided. His ministers and generals wished to incorporate the whole of Poland in the Russian Empire, and Alexander 'the Autocrat of All the Russias' agreed with them. But 'Alexander the Blessed,' that unique instrument of the Divine Will, was less sure: he sought some recognition of Polish rights, partly because of his friendship with Czartoryski but also because of the muddled sentimentality that always made him admire resolute opponents – he had even sent a Russian guard of honour to salute the patriot revolutionary, Kosciuszko, in Paris. The Poles themselves would have liked to see the restoration of an independent kingdom under any sovereign, but they could only accept what the Tsar offered them. The Prussians, though in general terms distrustful of the Russian movement westwards, were always prepared to sacrifice Polish territory to the Tsar in return for good German land on the Rhine or in Saxony. The Austrians alone were implacably hostile to Alexander's designs: to them the cynical bargain of 1795 retained the sanctity of a legal contract.

Negotiations over the future of Poland lasted five months, for three of which Tsar Alexander refused even to speak to Metternich. So deep was the rift between the former allies that on 3 January 1815 Metternich and Castlereagh signed a secret military convention with Talleyrand against the Russians and Prussians in case war should be resumed and the Russians march on Vienna. The existence of this alliance soon became known in a highly coloured form to the Tsar and the King of Prussia (who, somewhat ironically, were still the daily dining companions of Metternich's master in the Hofburg). The war scare was, however, fundamentally artificial; and the alliance, which has received an undeserved fame, little more than a bluff to call a bluff. For Alexander knew at heart – and so did Metternich – that a new Polish campaign was beyond the resources of either country. The crisis evaporated with disingenuous rapidity and, within five weeks, an agreement was reached which settled the division of the Polish lands for over a century, apart from a minor variation in 1846.

The Polish protocols, which were later incorporated in the definitive Treaty of Vienna, assigned Poznania to Prussia and Galicia to Austria. Cracow and an area of about 600 square miles became a neutral and independent republic. The rest of the former Grand Duchy, including Warsaw itself, was set up as a kingdom under the sovereignty of the Tsar of Russia who, of course, also retained as part of his empire the lands acquired by the partitions of 1772 and 1793. The agreement thus made two gestures to the spectre of the Old Polish State: Cracow, the first cultural centre of Polish life, was permitted a tenuous freedom; and 'Congress Poland', as the kingdom was generally known, was granted a constitution which provided for a Polish Diet and a Polish army. But the preamble to the constitution made it manifestly apparent that Poland enjoyed her rights only by grace of the Russian Tsar. Favours granted were easily rescinded; the prospect of a distinctively Polish contribution to the political life of the kingdom was largely illusory; and the Romanov dynasty was as firmly in the saddle in Warsaw as in Moscow or St Petersburg.

There was another region in which the Russian advance was ultimately more threatening to Austrian interests than in Poland; and this was Bessarabia. By the Treaty of Bucharest of 1812 the Russian frontier in the south-east was carried to the banks of the Pruth; any farther incursions into the Turkish Empire would enable the Russian Army to cross the Danube near its entry into the Black Sea and thereby establish a stranglehold on Austria's main artery. Metternich himself, a German in body and soul, tended to ignore such questions: there is no evidence that he ever travelled as much as 100 miles downstream from Vienna; and he once declared 'Asia begins at the Landstrasse,' the avenue which gave access to the East from the city. Gentz, on the other hand, though no less a German than Metternich, had a broader vision; he knew the Danubian lands and maintained a daily correspondence throughout the Congress with one of the provincial governors (*hospodars*) of Wallachia. It was Gentz who more than anybody else induced the Habsburgs to abandon their historic role and seek to prop up the Ottoman Empire rather than topple it over; 'The end of the Turkish monarchy could be survived by the Austrian for but a short time,' he wrote prophetically in 1815.

Yet there seemed at the time no acceptable solution for the Eastern Question; and the Austrians for their part wished to ignore it altogether. The matter was, however, raised by the Tsar with Castlereagh when the British Foreign Secretary, ill-advisedly, proposed a comprehensive guarantee by the Great Powers of the integrity of the Ottoman lands. Alexander informed Castlereagh that he hoped Britain, France and Austria would mediate between Russia and Turkey so that all outstanding questions between the two empires might be settled before an international guarantee was drawn up. A memorandum, prepared by Nesselrode (the Russian Foreign Minister), reiterated Russia's claim – first asserted tentatively in Catherine II's reign – to protect all the Christians under the Sultan's rule, although this time it made no distinction between those living in Serbia, in Greece, in the Levant or in Constantinople itself. The Sultan, with good reason, refused to discuss even the possibility of mediation as long as the Russian proposals were so comprehensive. Fortunately the Russians were not yet prepared to force the issue and Metternich and Gentz saw to it that the whole question was hurriedly dropped. It was a simple non-solution. The bear had growled and momentarily opened his claws; there was no reason to suppose that, ignored, he would go away.

The Vienna Settlement was thus in essentials a defeat for Russia. Tsar Alexander arrived at the Congress weighted down with military prestige; he left it assured of Warsaw and of little else; even his nebulous scheme for securing monarchical solidarity reached fruition – if that is not too mundane a noun for a 'Holy Alliance' – only after the Congress had broken up. The treaties offered the Tsar little. The predominantly non-Polish lands acquired by his grandmother in the First Partition (1772) were confirmed in Russian hands and so were the racially mixed areas gained in 1793 and 1795. Finland, which Alexander had seized from

Sweden in 1809 with Napoleon's blessing, was recognized as a Russian province, and so – grudgingly – was Bessarabia, the sole profit from the seven year war with Turkey. But apart from 'Congress Poland', in itself a compromise solution, no new territories acknowledged the Tsar's sovereignty. Terms such as these seemed scant compensation for the losses and devastation of recent campaigns.

By contrast, the gains of the House of Habsburg were impressive. The presidency of the German Confederation brought the Emperor Francis little real political power, for the new institution was only a loosely linked association of thirty-five states and four Free Cities with no central authority; but it afforded a degree of unity to territories as different as Schleswig-Holstein, the Tyrol and Bohemia-Moravia; and all were under Habsburg hegemony. Similarly the creation of dynastic dependencies throughout the Italian peninsula gave the Emperor Francis influence over the central belt of Europe, a hold strengthened by the annexation of Lombardy and Venetia. To the east, the whole of Istria and the Dalmatian coast and islands became Austrian appendages, while Habsburg rule was reimposed on provinces temporarily lost during the Bonapartist transmutations – Slovenia, western Carinthia, a part of Croatia and Galicia. The 'Austrian Empire,' formally proclaimed only in 1804, received at Vienna in 1815 tacit recognition of its reason for existence, the preservation of the integrity of Central Europe. But integrity against what? The double-headed eagle of the imperial coat-of-arms faced both ways: that was to prove Austria's strength and Austria's weakness.

Western historians traditionally regard the settlement of 1815 as the true watershed between the eighteenth and nineteenth centuries, giving to the epoch which separates 'Vienna' from 'Versailles' a natural unity both of time and character. Since all chronological divisions are necessarily arbitrary, there is as much to be said for this viewpoint as for any other: the Congress does, indeed, represent a sharp breach between the twenty-five years of revolution and war and the succeeding decades of external peace and internal unrest which culminated in the unification of Italy and Germany. The affairs of the continent throughout the century were regulated by the diplomatic machinery first oiled at Vienna, with civilized courtesies of ambassadorial procedure enjoying a respect unknown before and ignored since. Even in the eastern borderlands of Europe the terms of the Vienna Treaty achieved a rare permanence: Austrian Dreadnoughts were at anchor off Pula and Kotor in 1917 just as Austrian four-masters had been in 1817; and hostile armies did not transgress the frontiers drawn across Poland for ninety-nine years,

27

despite the fact that at no point did they constitute a militarily defensible barrier. Yet the Congress was essentially an assembly of rulers and its decisions necessarily amplified the voice of the chancelleries rather than the barely articulate aspirations of the peoples. Those who met at Vienna were acutely conscious of 'the Revolution' and the Europe they conceived was conservative and repressive; they failed, however, to see that another challenge, an awareness of national identity which was totally independent of 'Jacobinism' was developing within their own territories. For these subject nationalities the events of 1815 had little significance, apart from confirming which particular monarchical institution was to deny them recognition.

In almost every racial group the earliest consciousness of a communal tradition in the modern world has sprung from a linguistic and cultural revival. This is as true of the eastern third of Europe as of the better known instance of Italy (or, indeed, of Ireland and Wales). The enlightened rationalism of the last decades of the eighteenth century, although itself universalist in character, stimulated throughout Central Europe a spirit of inquiry into the origins of spoken tongues and distinctions of dialect; and the standard-bearers of nationalism were thus not in the first instance romantic revolutionaries disputing barricades but philologists and lexicographers disputing orthography. Farther east, in the lands within the Turkish Empire, the movement assumed a slightly different form because the Orthodox Churches had always cherished the Old Slavonic and Greek languages within their liturgy, although perpetuating ecclesiastical archaisms which were later to offend purist scholars and men of letters. In Poland, of course, there were special circumstances: the tragedy of the Partitions followed a period of literary renaissance, especially in the theatre, but the cult of language helped to broaden the basis of the patriotic struggle, with the Catholic priest Kopczynski publishing a 'Grammar for National Schools' in 1778 and Linde editing a definitive dictionary of Polish during the seven years of the Grand Duchy of Warsaw. The second stage of cultural nationalism, inspired by Romantic poetry, came, however, sooner in Poland than elsewhere in East-Central Europe.

Among some peoples there was a long delay between the earliest stirring of national consciousness and political action. For example, the first grammar of the Roumanian language was published in 1780 by two seminarists of the Transylvanian Uniate Church (Eastern Christians acknowledging papal supremacy): by successfully asserting the primacy of the Latin alphabet over the Cyrillic, they marked off the Roumanians as unique among the peoples of south-eastern Europe. But three more generations were to pass before the Roumanians across the Carpathians in Moldavia and Wallachia demonstrated their sense of nationhood. And although the Bulgarian monk Paisij completed a history of the 'Bulgarian Tsars and Saints' in 1762, it was not printed until 1841 when the Russians had begun to 'educate' the Bulgars from across the frontier. The patriotic pride of a few intellectuals could kindle the flame of nationality, but not keep it burning; in every instance, much depended on the possibility of external support or of influential backing.

Within the Habsburg dominions the linguistic revival of the Western Slavs and Hungarians received, at times, perfunctory imperial patronage. The Empress Maria Theresa, for example, authorized the study of Czech at the University of Vienna in 1775, sixteen years before it was introduced at the University of Prague, and the Emperor Leopold II (1790–92) even sat through performances of plays in the Czech language when he came to Prague for his coronation as king of Bohemia. Emperor Francis in 1792 permitted the study of Magyar to be made compulsory in all higher schools within Hungary proper (but not in the ethnically mixed areas of the Military Frontier, Croatia and Transylvania); and from 1805 he allowed his Hungarian subjects to correspond with the Hungarian Chancellery in Magyar rather than in German or in Latin, which remained the official state language of Hungary until 1844. On the other hand, the ten-year interlude of Joseph II (1780–90) saw rigorous Germanization of both government and public education – thereby provoking in Bohemia and in Hungary an obstinate pride in the vernacular as an expression of the national will to exist. Indirectly and without realizing the political consequences of his action, Joseph also stimulated linguistic patriotism by the Patent of Toleration of 1781, which allowed Protestant and Orthodox believers full religious and civil equality with the Roman Catholics. The Lutheran Lyceum at Bratislava, for example, became a centre of Czech and Slovak literary activity, and among its students were the Pan-Slav poet, Jan Kollár (himself a Lutheran Pastor), and the great Czech historian, František Palacky. The basic laws of Czech grammar and orthography were, however, as in Poland, laid down by a Catholic priest, Joseph Dobrovsky, significantly writing in German.

The Slovene linguistic movement was, in some ways, a false dawn for all the South Slavs. Slovene is an old, but distinctive, form of Slavonic; it was spoken in the eighteenth century by scattered communities living mainly in Carinthia, Styria and the province known as Carniola, the region around Laibach (as Ljubljana was then called). The study of Slovene legend and folklore owed much to the patronage of a dilettante scholar, typical of the 'Age of Enlightenment,' the rich mineowner, Baron Zois (Cojz in Slovene). But it was a Franciscan priest, Valentin Vodnik, who with the financial support of Zois, founded the first Slovene newspaper at Ljubljana in 1797 and published elementary handbooks of the Slovene language as well as more learned works on the principles of grammatical construction. For five years, from 1809 to 1814, most of the Slovene lands (with Dalmatia and the fringe of Croatia) formed part of the French Empire, the 'Illyrian Provinces', and Vodnik was made responsible for fostering education in the new administrative unit, which stretched from Villach to Dubrovnik, with Ljubljana as the provincial capital. Vodnik hailed Napoleon in an ode as the liberator of the Slovenes, 'the great hero' who called on Illyria 'to shake off the dust of fourteen centuries' and 'resting one hand on Gaul, give its other hand to Greece.' Here the poet was showing historical licence as well as anatomical dexterity, for there are no reasons for identifying the Slovenes with the ancient Illyrians; but the sentiments seemed at the time impeccable, if soon out of fashion.

The brief episode of French sovereignty had, however, a double importance for the Slovenes: it considerably improved the material condition of the whole region; and, for the first time, it associated Slovenes with Serbs and Croats in a common political community. But the encouragement shown by the French to Slovene culture forced the Austrians to establish a rival centre for Slovene studies at Graz, across the temporary frontier in Styria (where the Slovenes formed about a quarter of the population). In Graz the linguistic and grammatical analyses of Jernej Kopitar complemented the work of Vodnik. But Kopitar, although interested in the way of speech of all Yugoslav peoples, was in politics a particularist Slovene, hostile to the Illyrian concept for fear that it would swamp the specifically Slovene tradition. It is significant that when Austrian rule was restored in Ljubljana in 1815 Vodnik withdrew from public life, while Kopitar became a government censor. 'Illyrianism' remained an active force in Metternich's Europe although leadership passed from the Slovenes to the Croats, inspired in the 1830s by the brilliant young scholar, Ljudevit Gaj. Slovene literature flourished throughout the century, and yet it was not until the eve of the First World War that the Slovenes again participated in the common Yugoslav movement which Vodnik had championed. This political abnegation was, in part, a consequence of Kopitar's cultural isolationism; it was, however, also favoured by comparatively prosperous living standards and by the accident of geography which had dispersed the Slovenes through no less than six Austrian provinces.

The Serbian cultural awakening had a more enduring political influence than the Slovene. It, too, originated within the Habsburg lands. In 1691 a large emigration of Serbs fleeing from the wrath of the Turks had crossed the Danube and settled in the region which became known as the Vojvodina. These Serbs, *prečani* ('over the border') as they were called, rapidly developed schools and religious institutions of their own, and indeed a middle class which controlled much of the trade of southern

Hungary. The education offered to young Serbs in the Vojvodina was, of course, narrowly clerical in character, but it produced the outstanding Serbian scholar of the Enlightenment, Dositej Obradović, a monk, who, in 1760, lost his vocation under the compulsion of adolescent revolt. For half a century Obradović sought to convince his countrymen of the need to express their spoken language in literate prose, free from the artificially elegant Russian and ecclesiastical forms earlier writers affected. The Church, whether Catholic or Orthodox, seemed to him a divisive force which 'separated the members of one (racial) family' by meaningless barriers of distinctive rites. He fed his craving for South Slav union on rationalistic distrust of Christianity, which – at least in his autobiography – reminds one of his English contemporary, Edward Gibbon.

Obradović was by no means typical of the *prečani* Serbs, let alone his compatriots to the south, who continued to wallow in ignorant bondage. His style has an urban sophistication, which was probably more remote from popular speech than he recognized; his Russophobia was politically inexpedient, and his agnosticism socially eccentric. Nothing could disturb the passionate devotion of the Serbs to their Church. Indeed, in Obradović's lifetime, the Church seemed more than ever before the guardian of a national tradition, within Serbia proper; for in 1722 the Greek Episcopate had induced the Turks to abolish the Serbian Patriarchate thereby imposing on the Serbs a Greek cultural domination which was hardly less pervasive than the political domination of the Turks. Serbian leaders tended to value the patriotic histories of the doctrinally conventional monk Jovan Rajić, more than the critical studies of Obradović. Even as a linguistic reformer his impact was less creative than that of his pupil, Vuk Karadzić. But Obradović's teaching has a twofold significance in the development of the Yugoslav peoples: it turned the Vojvodina into the intellectual power-house of Serbianism; and it asserted against ten centuries of history, the basic kinship of Serb and Croat. There were other men of letters among the *prečani* Serbs, but none of greater importance for the eventual pattern of European politics.

It was across the Sava and the Danube, in Serbia itself, that a consciousness of nationality first challenged the political power of the Ottoman Empire. Turkish rule throughout the Balkan lands in the late eighteenth century was both corrupt and inefficient. The Janissaries, originally the select bodyguard and *corps d'élite* of the Sultan, had become so serious a threat to Ottoman power in Constantinople that successive rulers adopted a policy of despatching them in large numbers to the outlying provinces, especially Serbia. Their commanders (*dahis*) exercised a largely independent authority, as cruel and capricious as any feudal baronage in Western

Europe. They respected neither the Sultan's representative, the Pasha of Belgrade, nor the elected spokesmen of the village communities, who were responsible for maintaining contact between the Serbs and the Ottoman administration. In 1801 the *dahis* executed the Pasha; three years later they ordered the Janissaries to murder seventy-two of the village elders. It was under the shadow of this massacre that the Serbian Revolt began.

At first the Serbian struggle was a movement of protest against the tyranny of the *dahis*. Had it remained so it would have been a passing episode, not a historical event. Peasant rebellions in Turkey's distant provinces were not uncommon: there were five in Bosnia and three in Albania between 1820 and 1840, all swiftly and mercilessly suppressed. The Serbian Revolt was distinguished from other insurrections by the participation of organized bands of well-armed horsemen, by a conscious desire for the apparatus of government, and by the emergence of a natural leader. It also, unfortunately, achieved far less than it promised.

The hills and forests of the Šumadija had long been a lawless area of what was known as hajduk warfare, brigandage retrospectively honoured as nascent patriotism. Among the hajduk leaders was a fifty-two year old pig dealer, Djordje Petrović, who as a young man had crossed to the Vojvodina and enlisted in the Austrian army. Decorated for bravery and promoted sergeant, he subsequently returned to the Šumadija with a reputation for personal bravery and for monumental rages. His experiences with the *prečani* Serbs had given him a greater awareness of government than any of the legendary peasant rebels, although like them he remained illiterate. Partly because of his swarthy appearance and partly because of his thunderous disposition, he was known as 'Black George' (Karadjordje) and he was to give this nickname as a patronymic for the only enduring native dynasty in the Balkans. No one had ever elected him a village spokesman, perhaps understandably for he was neither tactful nor ingratiating, but in February 1804 he was proposed as leader of the insurrection by an assembly of Serbs meeting at Orasac, fifty miles south of Belgrade. It was a natural choice, even though in time he was to quarrel with his earliest supporters.

In the tactics of revolt, but not otherwise, Karadjordje was a prototype Tito. He was a remarkable military leader, capable of linking the hajduk partisan groups together in a series of concerted offensives against the Janissaries which were so successful that by the end of the year he was encamped on the hills around Belgrade. In the next twelve months the fortress towns of northern Serbia fell one by one to the rebels although the citadel of Belgrade did not surrender until November 1806. Karadjordje thought in terms of an independent, or at least autonomous, Serbia very early in the revolt even if for tactical reasons he was prepared to reach temporary accommodations with the Sultan's representatives against the *dahis*. Only nine months after the Orasac meeting a delegation of Serbs, led by Matija Nenadović, arrived in St Petersburg, 1,200 miles away, and in an interview with Czartoryski (who was then deputy foreign minister) sought Russian backing for Serbian self-government. Czartoryski offered little: a small subsidy; sound advice; and a guarded sympathy. But, even if the mission achieved nothing, it was proof that what was taking place in Serbia was something more than peasant unrest. The presence of these ambassadors of rebellion amid the elegant colonnades of St Petersburg was a portent for the rulers of all the supra-national empires. In due course, the Russians did indeed provide munitions and a few detachments of troops, but for the most part Serbia was left to make herself by her own exertions.

For eight years Karadjordje controlled what was virtually an independent principality extending from the Sava and the Danube across the Šumadija down the valley of the Morava. The Sultan rejected a proposed settlement which would have recognized Serbian autonomy, and Karadjordje proceeded to organize a central government with a State Council and a national assembly (Skupština). Obradović, whom Karadjordje appointed Minister of Instruction, and other Serbian scholars hastened to Belgrade from the Vojvodina: the High School which Obradović founded still stands in Belgrade, despite the destructive wars of the last century and a half.

Yet by October 1813 Karadjordje's act of defiance had ended in disaster, his administration crumbling as he himself fled to the Vojvodina in emotional collapse. The Turks re-entered Belgrade, apparently victorious, and ruled once more in terror over all the Serbian lands. Some of the reasons for their success were military: they were more numerous and better led than in 1805–6. Moreover, with Russia, France and Austria all participating in the Leipzig campaign, there was no prospect of outside assistance reaching the Serbs. But much of the blame rests with the Serbs themselves. Karadjordje increasingly allowed his character to dictate his statecraft: he substituted an autocratic and militaristic monarchy for the patriarchal democracy of the first years of the revolt; he vainly sought aid from Napoleon and from Metternich, even offering to cede Serbian fortresses; and, above all, he proved unable to control the army commanders, many of whom became as arbitrary and despotic as any *dahi*. When the Turks resumed the offensive in 1813, the Serbian peasantry were disillusioned by the experience of self-rule: exploited by a black market in the towns and by the exactions of warlords in the countryside, they lacked the will to continue guerrilla resistance, and the insurrection collapsed as suddenly as it had begun. Some twenty-four thousand Serbs escaped to the Vojvodina. Many others hid arms in the hills. Women were sold in the market of Belgrade; their fathers and husbands had stakes driven through their bodies in front of the city gates.

Eighteen months later Serbia rose again. This time the revolt was led by Miloš Obrenović, a man in his early forties, far more devious even than Karadjordje. His military strategy consisted of ingenious out-flanking movements across mountain paths that carried him into virtually undefended towns while a Turkish force, 10,000 strong, moved slowly towards his old position. During the interlude between the insurrections Miloš had given the Turks the impression that he was a willing colla-borator, and once northern Serbia was in his hands he again sought an agreement with the Sultan. A curious compromise was worked out, although not formally acknowledged by the Turks until 1830. The Serbs were allowed a share in the administration of justice and permitted to maintain a militia and summon a national assembly to Belgrade but Serbia remained a Turkish province with Turkish troops in the town and a pasha still representing the Sultan in the citadel of Kalemegdan. Miloš showed patience in negotiating with the Turks for seventeen years before his authority as prince was recognized over all the lands which Karadjordje had controlled but he had no mercy for his rivals among the Serbs. When Karadjordje himself returned from southern Hungary in 1817 he was swiftly murdered, allegedly on the orders of Miloš (who, it should be added, believed that Karadjordje had poisoned his half-brother in 1809). The feud between the Karadjordjević and Obrenović families lasted until 1903, weakening the Serbian State by its intensity and discrediting the monarchy by its bloodiness.

It is difficult to assess the importance of the Serbian struggle for Europe. Many western historians have tended to ignore it, giving pride of place among the liberation movements to the Greeks. The early rulers of Serbia never fulfilled the hopes of the first years of the Karad-jordje regime. Professor Vašo Cubrilović, writing to commemorate the 150th anniversary of the revolt, argued that the collapse of 1813 delayed the development of Serbia for half a century. In 1854 the Turks were still garrisoning eight Serbian towns: they did not finally leave the Kale-megdan citadel in Belgrade until 1867; and even then another eleven years were to elapse before the Great Powers recognized the full independence of the Principality. The growth of Serbia was a far slower process than had seemed likely when Czartoryski received the Nenadović mission in St Petersburg. *Prečani* Serbs, rather than the inhabitants of the Principality, attracted the attention of Europe, notably in 1848–9, and the Vojvodina continued to be the intellectual centre of Serbian culture. The full sig-nificance of the two Serbian revolts became apparent only in the twentieth century: Karadjordje, Miloš and the whole host of legendary hajduk horsemen had set between the lands of two great empires a small but powerful national magnet which in time attracted the loyalty of all of Serbian stock and many kinsmen from the other southern Slav peoples as well. Without the pull of this magnet on the subject nationalities of the Habsburg and Ottoman Empires the history of East-Central Europe – and, indeed, of the whole continent – would have been completely different, conceivably for the better, probably for the worse.

The Serbian revolts illustrate not only the weakness of Ottoman rule but also its resilience and tenacity. The Turks had always shown greater skill in promoting rivalry between factions and clans than in governing the Balkan peoples efficiently. When their adversaries were predatory warlords to whom the concept of nationality meant nothing, the sultans resorted to the simple – and hardly original – policy of playing off jealous beys against their neighbours, although there were often many years of bloodshed and massacre before a settlement was reached. By such methods the Turks disposed of Pasvan-Oglu, the Pasha of Vidin (now a Bulgarian port on the Danube) who, in the first years of the nineteenth century, plundered freely in Wallachia and the fringe of Serbia. Similarly in 1822, after three decades of local conflict and a full-scale military expedition, they at last liquidated Ali Pasha of Janina, the most redoubtable Albanian chieftain since Skanderbeg. But the problems of Greece defied such elementary solution, though the Turks for a time sought it. For the Greek struggle for independence raised questions that concerned the whole of south-eastern Europe and brought into operation the cumbersome apparatus of international power politics.

The ideas which produced the revolts of 1821 had fermented in the Greek commercial colonies of the eastern Mediterranean and the Black Sea for several decades. In origin the movement was radically ambitious. It aimed, not solely at the creation of an independent Greek national state, but at the establishment of a Balkan confederation, a modern Byzantium, administered by Greeks and including within its frontiers the Danubian principalities, Serbia, Albania, Bulgaria, all Macedonia and Thrace, Constantinople and much of the Levant as well as the area generally recognized as constituting Greece. Archbishop Voulgaris of Kherson was typical of the intellectual prophets of this Neo-Hellenism, claiming that the Greeks would recover mastery of the Near East 'by the Gospels and by Homer.' But there were lay writers, too, who were anxious to counter the virtual monopoly of the Orthodox Church in Greek affairs: Constantine Rhigas Pheraios, who became the first great national martyr when the Turks executed him in 1798, wrote fundamentally secularist patriotic poems and showed a sense of Balkan unity; and Adamantios Coraes, a classical scholar in his own right, travelled to Paris in 1804 to seek the sympathy of the French rationalists for a new Greece. The most famous manifestation of the movement was, however, the Philike Hetairia, a secret society set up in 1814 in the rapidly expanding Russian grain port of Odessa by a group of Greek merchants and pledged to liberate the Balkan lands from Ottoman rule.

The Philike Hetairia believed that it could reconcile Slavonic and Greek interests: it enrolled Karadjordje as a member, shortly before his murder; and it looked for support to the Russian government and especially to John Capodistrias, the Corfiote whom Tsar Alexander appointed joint foreign minister (with Nesselrode) in 1816. But the political philosophy of the Hetairia was far too radical for the Russians – or, indeed for the Greek Orthodox hierarchy and the wealthier Phanariots. Capodistrias refused an invitation secretly offered to him in 1817 to become the head of the organization. But three years later General Alexander Ypsilantis, a of the Hetairia was far too radical for the Russians – or, indeed, for the ponsibility Capodistrias had declined, and began to plan a general insurrection in south-eastern Europe which was to erupt in 1825. Hetairia agents established links, not only with influential shipowners in the Greek islands, but with Miloš Obrenović of Serbia, with Ali Pasha of Janina, and with the Ottoman-nominated Hospodar of Moldavia, Michael Sutu. They also contacted Tudor Vladimirescu, a Wallachian peasant by birth and a former tsarist officer who had participated in the first Serbian revolt and had hopes of becoming a Roumanian Karadjordje.

Ypsilantis was by nature impatient and temperamental. He was also genuinely afraid that the Turks would discover too much about his plans. Accordingly, in March 1821, with little preparation, he crossed the Pruth with a battalion of Greek students and marched on Jassy, the main town of Moldavia, where his banner, proclaiming the triumph of the Cross over the Crescent, was solemnly blessed by the Orthodox Metropolitan. The great revolt had begun, four years prematurely. It was to prove a dismal fiasco. Only Michael Sutu supported Ypsilantis; even the Church soon turned against him. The Tsar formally dismissed him from the Russian army and authorized the Turks to take what punitive action they wished. Miloš Obrenović made no move. Vladimirescu, on the other hand, seized Bucharest ahead of Ypsilantis, denounced the invaders as perpetuators of alien Phanariot rule, and countered their leader's appeal for cooperation with the forthright declaration, 'Greece belongs to the Greeks, but Roumania to the Roumanians.' The behaviour of Ypsilantis's troops alienated many potential sympathizers: they slaughtered a group of Turkish merchants in Galati; and Vladimirescu himself was murdered at night by one of Ypsilantis's officers. Eleven days later (7 June) the invading force was defeated by Turkish regular troops at Dragasani, ninety miles west of Bucharest, and Ypsilantis fled into Transylvania (where he was arrested and, on Metternich's orders, imprisoned for the next seven years).

With the flight of Ypsilantis the Philike Hetairia swiftly disintegrated and nothing more was heard of the plan for a general Balkan insurrection. But Hetairist agents in the Peloponnese had already sparked off a revolt against the Turk, the cause of Greek independence being taken up by Archbishop Germanos of Patras and soon spreading to the islands, notably Hydra and Spetsai. This new movement was, however, a specifically Greek revolution, a national and religious act of defiance, limited to the shores and islands of the Aegean and of no direct concern to the peoples of the Danubian Principalities or of Serbia, although both benefited considerably by the subsequent international agreements.

The Greek War of Independence, as distinct from the Hetairist agitation, is more properly an episode in the history of the Mediterranean peoples and of the Near East than of the Lands Between, but its repercussions were so widespread that it cannot be entirely ignored. Fighting between Greeks and Turks lasted from April 1821 to September 1829. At first the war favoured the Greeks, but in 1823 open conflict between rival Greek leaders gave the Sultan the opportunity to re-occupy Athens, and the Turkish position was improved still further in the following year by the arrival of a powerful Egyptian army under Ibrahim Pasha. Only reluctant and confused intervention by the Great Powers – and, in particular, the destruction of the combined Turkish and Egyptian fleets at Navarino in 1827 by British, Russian and French naval squadrons – saved the Greeks from defeat. Curiously enough, the final Greek victory, the routing of a Turkish force near Thebes, was won by Demetrius Ypsilantis, brother of the former Hetairist commander. Decisions on the frontiers and character of the new Greek State were, however, taken not in Athens or even in Constantinople, but in St Petersburg and London, the war itself being no more than a sombre and at times tiresomely irrelevant background to long drawn-out diplomatic negotiation.

The Great Powers, seeking in general terms the tranquillity of Europe, were embarrassed by the Greek Revolt and their policies were irresolute. Only Metternich remained consistently hostile to any new arrangement in the East, fearing that the disintegration of Turkey would jeopardize the delicate balance of nationalities within the Austrian Empire itself, as Gentz had predicted. British public opinion was strongly philhellene but successive governments moved cautiously, and the attitude of the restored French monarchy was similar. Russian policy, too, vacillated. Religion and sentiment linked the Russians and the Greeks, but so long as Alexander I was on the throne disinclination to patronize rebellion checked effective intervention. Capodistrias was so disillusioned by the Tsar's attitude that he left Russia in 1822: he became the first President of

Greece in 1827 and was assassinated by jealous landowners four years later. When Nicholas I succeeded Alexander in 1825 the Russians began to take a stronger line with the Turks. Nevertheless, it is clear that they were more interested in securing influence in the lands between the Danube and Constantinople than in such a remote area as the Peloponnese. Thus the Convention of Akkerman of October 1826, conceded by the Sultan's representatives under threat of war with Russia, virtually ignored the Greek Question: it extended the liberties enjoyed by Miloš Obrenović in Serbia; and it provided that the Turks should evacuate their troops from the Danubian Principalities and should henceforth permit the *hospodars* of Moldavia and Wallachia to be elected by the Roumanian 'boyars' (landowning nobility) rather than appointed directly by the Sultan. These terms were of momentous significance to the peoples of the lower Danube area, but they had no effect on the struggle in Greece.

At last, however, in April 1828 Russia did indeed go to war with Turkey. The Russian army advanced slowly across the Principalities and, for the first time, crossed the Balkan ranges. By September 1829, as the final skirmishes were being fought in Greece itself, Russian cavalry units thrusting south from Adrianople reached the Aegean, less than fifty miles west of Constantinople. The Turks sued for peace and the whole future of the Ottoman Empire was in the balance. But, in the last resort, the Russians shrank from sweeping the Turks out of Europe; they feared that if the Ottoman Empire broke up the other Great Powers would seek territorial compensation and would eventually constitute an even greater menace to Russia's position on the Black Sea than an enfeebled Ottoman regime. Hence the treaty of Adrianople (14 September 1829) merely amplified the Convention of Akkerman: it gave the Russians considerable gains in the Caucasus; it guaranteed the Russian merchant fleet free access through the Straits to the Mediterranean; it permitted the Russians to supervise the political administration of the *hospodars* in the Danubian Principalities; but, as far as Greece was concerned, it limited itself to securing recognition from the Turks of the need to establish an autonomous state south of a line from the Gulf of Arta to the Gulf of Volo.

Negotiations to constitute a fully independent Greek kingdom continued in London for another three years, with the British convinced that the Tsar would make the new state a Russian satellite while the Russians were equally certain that Palmerston, who became Foreign Secretary in November 1830, wished to place some dependent relative of the British royal house on the Greek throne. Eventually, in May 1832, a convention was signed in London which established an independent Greece within the boundaries accepted at Adrianople and under the rule of Prince Otto of Bavaria. The convention mentioned a possible

~ARTHUR BANKS ~

THE BALKAN LANDS
1830-1914

0   250

Miles

—·—·— Boundaries of 1913
1878   Dates of effective ending of Turkish rule from 1830
Territory lost by Turkey as a result of the Balkan Wars, 1912-13
Bessarabia
Southern Bessarabia (ceded by Russia to Roumania,1856 retroceded by Roumania to Russia,1878)
Southern Dobrudja (ceded by Bulgaria to Roumania,1913)

RUSSIA

BESSARABIA

MOLDAVIA
Autonomous 1822

ROUMANIA
1878

Belgrade

BOSNIA
Sarajevo

Bucharest

WALLACHIA
Autonomous 1822

DOBRUDJA
1878

1830

S
E
R
B
I
A

Nis
1878

1878

Sofia

BLACK SEA

BULGARIA
1885

ALBANIA
1913

1913

MACEDONIA

Adrianople

1913

Constantinople

MONTENEGRO
Independent since 1389

Ochrid

Salonika

1913

G
R
E
E
C
E

1913

CORFU
English 1814-63
Greek 1863

1881

TURKEY

AEGEAN SEA

1830

Athens

Smyrna

MEDITERRANEAN SEA

DODECANESE
Italian 1912

CRETE
Greek 1913

39

guarantee of Greece by the three 'Protecting Powers,' Britain, France and Russia. No such guarantee was, in fact, ever given, but the Protecting Powers continued to act as if a bond of this character existed, sometimes to the advantages of Greece (as in 1897) but sometimes no less for their own ends (as in 1915).

Although the London Convention left nearly two million Hellenes outside the new kingdom and therefore recognized only the minimum programme of the Greek patriots, it marked a turning-point in the struggle of the subject nationalities. By securing the independence of Greece the statesmen of Western Europe conceded that, if Turkey disappeared from the map like Poland in the previous century, some more equitable system would be devised than a cynical division of the Ottoman legacy among the surviving autocrats. This was, in itself, an important principle even though the Russians took another quarter of a century to appreciate it. No less significant was the revelation of the interplay of Great Power politics and local aspirations. Without foreign intervention the Greek leaders would have suffered the fate of Ali Pasha and Pasvan-Oglu or, indeed, of Alexander Ypsilantis. Hence the Greek revolt demonstrated, what the Italian Risorgimento was to show even more clearly in the next generation, that a sense of nationality by itself was insufficient to win independence. This need for powerful external backing was a lesson well-learnt by the Roumanians and the Bulgars and, in due course and in another form, by the Czechs and the Poles.

There was, however, another side to the picture. Foreign support was never given in a spirit of altruism. Protecting Powers exersised a considerable right of intervention in internal affairs. For example, from the Greek revolt until the entry into the First World War of the great American republic, it was assumed that new states would necessarily be monarchies and that their rulers would come from established dynasties rather than from native families; the Serbian experience was repeated nowhere else in Eastern Europe, partly no doubt because of the fear that an autochthonous royal house would perpetuate ancient feuds and hamper unity. Moreover, delineation of boundaries was a prerogative claimed by the experienced statesmen of the traditional capitals of Europe: frontiers were compromises drawn by diplomats jealous of each other's interests; it was rare for them to accord with local feeling. By 1830 the national principle had begun to assert itself as a necessity of statecraft; but the crusading appeal of 'self-determination' lay, as yet, far in the future.

3
The Years of the Barricades

In the third of a century which followed recognition of Greek independence the principal threat to the mastery of the eastern autocracies came from the old historic peoples of Central Europe rather than from incipient nationalism in the Balkans. The rapid growth in the Vistulan and Danubian lands of an urban middle class easily thrilled by the seductive irrationality of political romanticism struck at the very heart of the Metternich system. At the same time the spread of a consciousness of nationality among the Germans and Italians menaced the stability of the whole Vienna settlement and provided other subject races both with an example and a potential challenge. It was not, of course, until 1848 that the barricades were to go up in city after city and Metternich himself seek sanctuary in London but the era of national defiance begins much earlier than the 'year of revolutions' and lasts longer. Just as, for the West, the fall of the French Bourbons in 1830 and the riots in Belgium and the German states foreshadowed the disturbances of eighteen years later, so in Eastern and Central Europe the Warsaw rising of November 1830 established a pattern of insurrection for the Polish people and their neighbours. And, with a rare sense of historical tidiness, the era closes where it had begun, with a second abortive Polish revolt in 1863.

The origin of the first Polish rising lies in the disillusionment which followed the proclamation of the Congress Kingdom in 1815. At first all had seemed to go well. The Russians allowed the Poles considerable freedom to develop their economic resources: new mines were opened up, foundries established, a textile industry created in what had been a woodland area to the south-west of Warsaw. Trunk roads linked capital and provinces, and Warsaw itself took on a new appearance as planners and builders thrust their way through the confines of the old burgher city. Even the farmers, although suffering for several years from the aftermath of war, benefited from more scientific methods of agriculture. The population soared rapidly ahead: the kingdom seemed rich with the promise of material progress; and the growth of industry and business enterprise led to the emergence of a specifically Polish middle class, a social revolution of momentous consequence for the whole Polish nation.

Yet by the summer of 1830 the Polish towns, though not the country-side, were seething with unrest. Russian administration had proved both inept and frustrating. In 1815 the Poles had hoped that Tsar Alexander I would entrust the government of the kingdom to his friend, Adam Czartoryski; but the Tsar preferred to appoint his brother, the Grand-Duke Constantine, as commander-in-chief while leaving all political questions to be settled by a nominated Commissioner, the Russian landowner, Nicholas Novosiltsov. A number of Poles held important posts: Czartoryski was, until 1824, Chancellor of the University at Vilna (which was not within the Congress Kingdom); and Drucki-Lubecki, as finance minister, was responsible for the remarkable improvement in the Polish economy; but, for the most part, representation in the Diet was limited to only the greater Polish landowners. The accession of Nicholas I in 1825 made little difference, for although the new Tsar was known to detest everything Polish, he was prepared to maintain the system estab-lished by his brother. He duly came to Warsaw for a solemn coronation in May 1829, although significantly it was a Russian, rather than a speci-fically Polish, crown which was placed on his head. A year later he was once more in Warsaw, attending a meeting of the Polish Diet. Grand-Duke Constantine, who had by now acquired a Polish wife, spoke favourably to the Tsar of the Polish army although, in reality, the officers were constantly intriguing with secret patriotic societies. Nicholas, however, returned to St Petersburg, disturbed by news that revolution had broken out in Paris, but convinced that all was well in the Congress Kingdom. Five months later the Polish army mutinied and by the end of the year patriot hawks in the Diet were calling for a crusade against Russia.

The conspiracy of 29 November 1830 was ill-planned and should, by all reasonable standards, have failed disastrously. It was primarily the work of junior officers of the Fourth Infantry Regiment, who were on guard duty in Warsaw, and of cadets from the military academy. No popular demagogue harangued the crowd, for the revolution was strangely leaderless. The Polish members of the Diet and of the civil administration were taken by surprise and perplexed by the rebels' in-tentions. University students and workers in northern Warsaw broke into the arsenal and rapidly formed themselves into a national guard. So great was the confusion that Grand-Duke Constantine exaggerated the strength of the insurgents; and once he hesitated, he was lost. By 5 December a provisional government of the Kingdom of Poland had been set up and General Jozef Chlopicki, a veteran of Napoleon's Grand Army, was proclaimed dictator. Since Chlopicki was himself a moderate con-servative rather than a radical, Polish regiments in other garrisons rallied to the national cause; but Chlopicki was no Kosciuszko and he was prepared to seek a settlement with the Tsar, rather than risk a war which he felt must end in disaster.

Communications in the Russian Empire were so bad in December that the Tsar did not learn of the military coup until more than a week after it had taken place; and another month was to elapse before he could concentrate a Russian force capable of punishing the rebels and of restoring order. The tardiness of the Russian response helped to transform a Warsaw insurrection into a national rebellion. Chlopicki's moderation rapidly became unfashionable and he was forced out of office on 17 January 1831. A fortnight later the provisional government formally deposed the Tsar-King and entrusted executive authority to a five-man council, with Adam Czartoryski as president. The radicals were demanding not merely independence and the incorporation of Lithuania, but restoration of the old frontiers of 1772; they seemed willing to challenge all three autocracies and not Russia alone. Czartoryski, a reluctant revolutionary, was acutely conscious that his hand was being forced by the urban masses in Warsaw. Some of his fellow councillors – notably the historian, Joachim Lelewel – sought to change the social order; as a minimum concession, they hoped to win the support of the peasantry by a promise of land reform; but the gentry shrank from emancipating their serfs. Czartoryski himself preferred to seek diplomatic action from the European chancelleries, for this was the world in which he had lived and moved. Desperately he hoped for foreign recognition and an initiative by the statesmen of Western Europe in order to achieve a genuine independence for the Polish State. But Poland, not for the first or the last time in her history, was left in tragic isolation.

Yet the Poles continued to defy their Russian masters until the autumn of 1831. They were helped by the death in the great cholera epidemic that summer of both the Russian commander-in-chief, Marshal Diebitsch, and the Grand-Duke Constantine. Much of the credit for the protracted resistance rests, however, with the courage of the Polish officer class and especially with General Zygmunt Skrzynecki, a veteran of the 1812 campaign, who held the Poles together after a reverse at Grochow outside Warsaw in February and who mounted a successful counter-offensive to the north-east of the city in May. But the Polish leaders frequently quarrelled among themselves. Skrzynecki was held to be over-cautious and was dismissed; repeated changes in the civil government and military command were bad for morale. The failure to support risings in Lithuania and the Ukraine exasperated the radical elements in Warsaw. As the main Russian army under Paskievič drew near the city, the mood of the populace became ugly. Rioting in the streets on 15 August was followed by a random slaughter of suspected traitors in the prisons. But, if Warsaw showed the temper of revolutionary Paris, it had no Danton to snatch victory from the gutter. Moreover, Paskiević was an abler commander than the Duke of Brunswick had been thirty-nine years before. Relentlessly, Paskiević kept up the pressure. On 6 September the Russians reached the outskirts of the city. For two days there was grim fighting on suburban barricades with both sides suffering heavy losses; but the Poles could not stand up to the concentrated fire-power of the Russian guns and on 8 September a Polish force of 33,000 men marched wearily out towards the north and the Prussian frontier. By the beginning of October resistance throughout the Congress Kingdom was at an end.

The Polish rebellion anticipated many of the failings of 1848: the excessive nationalistic claims of extremist patriots; the conflict between conservative gentry and urban radicals; the indifference of the peasantry; and the ultimate inability of heroic defenders on the barricades to check the disciplined army of an autocratic state. Nor were all the parallels with 1848 negative ones. The Poles were the first of the subject peoples to stir the conscience of the West. Several thousand defenders of Warsaw reached Paris in 1831 and 1832 and were welcomed to the city that prided itself on being the nursery of liberalism by the legendary Lafayette himself. Some of the Polish exiles subsequently settled in Britain while others crossed the Atlantic to Latin America or the United States. There was genuine sympathy in London and Paris for the plight of the Polish people; in both capitals, in the safe haven of the Swiss cantons, and in such unexpected centres as Glasgow and Newcastle associations sprang up dedicated to friendship with Poland. An annual motion deploring the subjection of Poland to Russian rule crept into the parliamentary ritual of France and the government of Louis Philippe paid pensions to more than 5,000 of the refugees; while in Britain the radicals in the House of Commons saw to it that the Polish exiles received a grant of £10,000 a year until 1852.

Politically the Polish emigration continued to show the divisions which had prevented effective leadership in Warsaw. Czartoryski remained a firm believer in the enlightened rule of the aristocracy until his death in 1861 but he became more and more isolated from the younger generation of émigrés, who responded sympathetically to the appeal of Mazzinianism. Lelewel moved steadily to the left, transferring his activities to the freer environment of Brussels and even striking up an acquaintance with the young Karl Marx. The Polish community in the West, had, however, a far greater influence outside politics; for Polish nationalism both inspired literary romanticism and was, in its turn, inspired by it. The messianic mission of the Polish expatriates was expounded in the poetry of Krasinski and Slowacki; and the finest work of Adam Mickiewicz was published in Paris during the years of emigration. 'For the universal war which shall free the Nations, we beseech thee, O Lord,' Mickiewicz supplicated in 1832. It was not permitted him to receive an answer to his curious litany, for he died in Constantinople during the Crimean War while seeking to raise a Polish Legion to fight beside the Turks against the Russian oppressor; but the prayer remained as part of the émigré ideal for another sixty years after his death.

Although the exiles painted a universally grim picture of their 'martyred nation,' the burden of the Russian rule varied in the different regions of Poland. Within the districts originally acquired by Russia in 1793 – around Vilna, for example – there was stern repression; it was maintained by the authorities in these 'lands of the Empire' that Polish families who sympathized with Czartoryski had been guilty of treason. Congress Poland proper fared less badly. It is true that the Diet was abolished and that Polish educational funds were confiscated in order to pay for a citadel on the banks of the Vistula, with guns trained permanently on the heart of Warsaw. But the Tsar's Organic Statute of 1832 kept in being the separate administration of the kingdom and the lower ranks of the official bureaucracy were staffed by Poles. Naturally the independent status of the Polish army was abolished; and Marshal Paskiević, who had restored order in the capital, was created 'Prince of Warsaw' and appointed Viceroy. Trade and industry continued to develop, especially after the construction of a railway from Vienna to Warsaw, begun in 1839 and completed in 1847. But Polish cultural life suffered as much in the Congress Kingdom as in Lithuania and the other eastern provinces. The University of Warsaw, like the university which Czartoryski had built up in Vilna, was forced to suspend its classes; and from 1839 onwards Polish schools were incorporated in the Russian educational system, such as it was. A strict and incompetent censorship prevented the publication of books on historical subjects and banned the works of Polish writers who had fled to the West. Only the Church saved Congress Poland from becoming a cultural desert, and the activities of the Catholic hierarchy were viewed with suspicion by the Russian administration.

Across the frontier in Prussian Poland government in the 1830s was hardly less oppressive than in the Congress Kingdom although living standards were higher, especially in the countryside. In the years immediately following the Vienna settlement some of the gentry, notably the Radziwills, had worked for Prusso-Polish reconciliation. The peasantry were virtually emancipated from their feudal obligations and use of the Polish language was encouraged in the schools. The Prussian army leaders had, however, always regarded Polish national aspirations with particular distaste. When Warsaw rose in revolt in 1830 Gneisenau, the military commander in the East, and Clausewitz, his chief of staff (who, like Diebitsch, fell a victim to the cholera epidemic of the following

45

year) were deeply conscious of the strategic importance of the Polish provinces, and their attitude induced the Governor-General of Poznania, Erich Flottwell, to introduce a systematic policy of repression, which continued throughout the decade. There was a particularly bitter conflict between the Lutheran Prussian administration and the Roman Catholic clergy, which culminated in the suppression of the religious orders and the confiscation of monastic estates. With the accession of Frederick William IV in 1840 conditions suddenly improved, for the new King was on terms of personal friendship with some members of the Polish aristocracy. In the city of Poznan the Poles were able to set up a centre of national culture based upon the public library established by Edward Raczynski and the 'Bazar' of Marcinkowski, a natural forum for the exchange of political ideas by the Polish middle class. The benevolent attitude of the administration enabled the Poznan liberals to contact the Polish Democratic Society in Paris who sent an agent, Ludwik Mieroslawski, to prepare for a general insurrection in all the Polish lands for the night of 21/22 February 1846. But before the plans were complete, the Prussian secret police arrested Mieroslawski and the other conspirators and, in due course, they were imprisoned in Berlin. Official policy, which had changed so dramatically in 1840, was now once more hurriedly reversed. All Polish societies were closed down and much of the penal legislation of the Flottwell period was brought back; but the Prussians had not heard the last of Mieroslawski.

The vigilance of the police in Poznania was in part a consequence of events in the Habsburg territories. Throughout 1845 there had been a spate of rumours in Galicia, a condition of instability akin to the hysteria of the 'Great Fear' which had swept across France in the summer of 1789: both gentry and peasants believed that they would be attacked at night by brigands, and there were hair-raising tales of outrage for which there seemed, at the time, no basis of fact. It was enough to put the authorities on their guard.

Galicia was an agricultural region, economically and socially backward, in which the large estates of the Polish gentry yielded only a small crop because of antiquated farming methods. The legal obligations of feudalism were as burdensome as anywhere in Central Europe. As in the Austrian lands, the *robot* required the peasant to work for certain hours on his lord's estate but also permitted him to cultivate a strip of land of his own. There was, however, as marked a distinction between the gentry and the tillers of the soil as in pre-revolutionary France. Even where, as in western Galicia, the peasantry was Polish rather than Ruthene in origin, it still lacked all national consciousness. The landowners, on the other hand, were as patriotically proud as in the Congress Kingdom; and they were encouraged by the liberties enjoyed by Polish intellectuals in the 'Free

City' of Cracow. It is significant that Mieroslawski had begun his conspiratorial activities in Cracow, before crossing into Poznania.

Ever since 1833, when an ill-planned insurrection came to nothing, Metternich and the Austrian authorities had anticipated that the Polish gentry would make a further attempt to raise a revolt as soon as the general situation in Europe afforded it some chance of success. The bad harvests and financial uncertainty in the West had, indeed, played a part in determining the despatch of Mieroslawski from Paris to Cracow. But plans for a revolt were by no means complete. Learning, however, of his arrest by the Prussians across the frontier, bands of Polish patriots rose prematurely on 18–19 February 1846. The Austrians, lacking adequate armed forces to restore order, appealed to the peasantry; if they took action against the landowners they were promised the abolition of all the contractual obligations in the *robot*. The peasants needed little bidding; and overnight the fear of the previous twelve months became a reality. A *jacquerie,* which accounted for two thousand dead, spread through western Galicia. Mansions were burned or looted. Polish patriots, dead or alive, were conveyed to the guard posts of the Austrian police or soldiery, and rewards were promptly paid, both in cash and in kind. It was a crude, but devastatingly effective, way of stamping out an insurrection.

Only in Cracow, where the peasants were fully emancipated, was there a genuinely united Polish national movement. For ten days that February a 'Republic of Cracow,' radical and independent, proclaimed in the words of the patriot anthem, 'Poland is not yet dead.' But the Republic could not last. The Austrian army attacked from the south, the Russians from the north. And on 3 March Russian guardsmen lowered the Polish flag over the city. Seven months later Cracow was formally incorporated in the Habsburg Monarchy. The final vestige of Polish independence, the half-real Free City created by the Treaty of Vienna, was wiped off the map.

The Galician disorders and the annexation of Cracow mark the real beginning of the revolution of 1848 for the Habsburg lands even though the improbable alliance of crown and peasantry had silenced the opposition and provided the gentry with a grim lesson in the folly of playing at rebellion. Yet it would be misleading to seek in the Polish question a simple diagnosis of the general malaise. For in Galicia there were no more than two issues at stake: the right of a historic Slav people to preserve its identity; and the instinctive craving of a backward peasantry for social recognition. Both of these problems did, indeed, recur elsewhere in Central Europe but their effects were modified, and sometimes distorted, by three other causes of unrest: a historical myth of national supremacy based upon linguistic exclusiveness; the desire of the bourgeoisie in a number of cities for political acceptance; and the first protests of the artisan class at the burden of industrialism. Fundamentally, as Metternich himself sensed, it was the ill-defined character of the Habsburg State that made revolution virtually inevitable – 'I spend my time propping up a mouldering structure,' he wearily complained after a quarter of a century of service to the dynasty.

To a far greater extent than either Russia or Prussia the Habsburg dominions formed a league of powerful noble families rather than a genuinely autocratic empire. Sometimes the lands of the magnates were concentrated in one area but often they crossed the old administrative boundaries: the Schwarzenberg family, for example, although technically members of the Bohemian aristocracy, also had estates in Lower Austria; and the properties of the Esterházys, the Telekis and the Károlyis were not all in the predominantly Magyar areas. But the Habsburg Empire was so extensive that it permitted the growth and maintenance of distinctive local variations of character, even within this single class. The magnates of Hungary, despite the opposition of the stronger Habsburg rulers, had retained their own system of local administration through county assemblies in which the lesser nobility, 'the gentry,' formed a majority but which they themselves dominated; and in these assemblies they were jealously possessive of their rights, real or imaginary. The magnates of the Czech or Croatian-Slavonian frontier regions, on the other hand, owed their existence to the favours of the ruling dynasty as a reward for services rendered; their outlook was almost wholly Imperial Germanic and they saw to it that the local Diets, where they were permitted to exist, duly reflected their traditional toryism. These deep-rooted distinctions in loyalty help to explain the conflicting attitudes of the great families in the Habsburg Empire to the crisis in government of the 1840s. It was in the Czech lands of Bohemia-Moravia and, above all, in Hungary that the challenge was most sharply defined.

Throughout the eighteenth century Bohemia and Moravia had seemed politically dead and even in the turbulent years of Napoleon the tide of war had swept twice over the provinces without depositing any revolutionary flotsam. But, early in the Metternich era, first Bohemia and Silesia and later Moravia experienced a minor industrial revolution: a textile industry came into being, coal-mines were opened up, ironworks created and the traditional sugar industry revived. These developments began to modify the class structure of both Bohemia and Moravia: a bourgeoisie, originally German or Jewish in composition, settled in Prague and in Brno; and Czech peasants from the fields sought employment in the new urban communities that grew up on the fringe of the old towns. Riots among the Czech artisans at Prague and Pilsen in 1846 were a more significant portent of specifically social revolution than the disturbances in Galicia although, at the time, they passed almost unnoticed.

The most astonishing change in the Czech lands was, however, cultural. Philologists and historians began to arouse a territorial patriotism for the half-legendary Kingdom of Bohemia by their studies. The pioneer linguistic work of Joseph Dobrovsky was followed up by scholars in the Bohemian Museum Society which he had helped establish in 1818 and by Jungmann's great Czech Dictionary which was published between 1835 and 1839. It was, however, František Palacký who emerged as the natural intellectual leader of the Czech peoples; his massive *History of Bohemia*, which began to appear in 1836, evoked hope for the future by chronicling the courage of the past. Palacký saw in the history of his people a continuous conflict between the democratic Slavs and the overbearing Teutons. He felt, however, that it was necessary for him to write his earlier volumes in German, rather than in Czech, so as to reach a wider reading public. Strangely enough, until the spring of 1848, the German-speaking citizens of Prague, influenced by the romantic historical escapism of Johann Herder, were more generous financial backers of Bohemian antiquarianism than the Czechs themselves. Thus, Czech national feeling was revived almost, as it were, by accident and without a conscious awareness among its patrons of the consequences for Central Europe of their actions.

It was otherwise in Hungary. For there a golden age of poetry and drama ran parallel with a determined movement in the Hungarian Diet for constitutional rights based upon a narrow nationalism. Since nearly all educated Magyars were members of the nobility it was natural that, in its earliest years, the cultural renaissance, no less than the political struggle, should assume that the Hungarian landowners were divinely ordained masters of the middle Danube and that, over all this region, the obscure exclusiveness of the Magyar tongue was the only appropriate medium of communication. On the eve of revolution the lyricism of the young poet, Sandor Petöfi, introduced less limiting social tenets to the ideal of the Magyar patriotism he had embraced (for his father was a Serb and his mother a Slovak); but the genius of Petöfi was able to flower only after a bitter political battle had won more enemies than friends by forcing linguistic Magyarization through the Diet. In 1835 Magyar was permitted as an alternative to Latin in the law courts; five years later it superseded Latin as the official language of the Diet; and in 1844 it became the sole language of the administration and commerce in all the Hungarian lands. Small wonder that even before barricades went up in 1848 the Roumanians, the Transylvanian Saxons and the Slovaks should have been thrown into opposition to everything Hungarian by the

Magyarizing hotheads of the Diet; while in Croatia antagonism added a fillip to the 'Illyrianism' of Ljudevit Gaj and his attempt to standardize the different dialects of both Croatia and Serbia in one common Serbo-Croat tongue.

It would, however, be a mistake to assume that every Magyar in the 1830s and 1840s was politically intolerant and impetuous. When the 'Reform Diet' first met in 1832 at Bratislava – or 'Pozsony,' as the Hungarian delegates called the town – the leading spokesman of the magnates was Count István Széchenyi, whom even his rival Kossuth was to call 'the greatest among the Magyars.' Széchenyi was as proud of his descent as any other member of a historic family; he had contributed a year's income from his estates to help found a National Academy of the Sciences in order that the Magyar language, which he so admired, might be purified and standardized. But Széchenyi was convinced that Hungary needed close relations with the other Habsburg lands for her economic development, if not her very existence. He had travelled widely outside the Empire and knew his own class so well that he was prepared to criticize its social blindness and to condemn the folly with which it sought to retain an archaic system based on exemption from taxation. In the 1830s he emphasized the need for land reform and for improved communications but, with the rapid growth of Magyarization in the next decade, Széchenyi began to caution the Hungarian liberals against excessive chauvinism; and, in a historic speech in November 1842, he demanded a policy towards national minorities which would be morally justifiable within the Christian concept of brotherly love. Széchenyi was not alone in opposing extremism: a group of 'Progressive Conservatives,' led by György Apponyi, favoured cooperation with Metternich in a series of limited reforms; and Deák and Eötvös, who were to play a considerable part in making the Ausgleich a generation later, were already preaching moderation in the Diets of the forties. But, by 1848, the Magyar people – especially the lesser nobility – were far too proudly headstrong for political restraint: Széchenyi's protests at Magyarization had destroyed his following; and it was the brilliant orator and journalist, Lajos Kossuth, who voiced such of the national will as was allowed to be articulate.

Kossuth is a historical enigma, a curious mixture of national redeemer and rabble-rousing mountebank whose career was as full of contradictions as his political philosophy. Although believing the nobility to be guardians of the Magyar heritage, he advocated peasant emancipation and extension of the franchise with the fire of a genuine radical; born into a Protestant family originally Slovak in origin, he accepted the mystic symbolism of the 'Hungarian Crown' and, by the power of his pen, piloted the Magyarization laws through the Diet; rating national liberty above all other social progress, his tribunals and gibbets made him as hated among his Slovak kinsfolk as Cromwell in Ireland; and, though retrospectively honoured in the United States as a 'Champion of Freedom,' he scoffed in his days of power at the rights of the Serbs and Roumanians and denied them to the Croats entirely. Yet, if it is all too easy to note the flaws that make the image of Kossuth counterfeit, the achievement remains none the less real. He lifted the Magyar gentry, half a million petty landowners, backward and backward-looking, out of apathy and squalor and transformed them into the vanguard of an army of national liberation. If their myopic insensibility and arrogance were reflected in his cause, it is hardly surprising, for they were the very class from which he himself had climbed. There is no doubt that Kossuth gloried in Magyar independence as Garibaldi did in the name of Italy; he rightly won a reputation on both sides of the Atlantic as a romantic failure, a hero with the gift of expressing himself, even in English, in phrases which seared the memory with their passion. It was a tragedy for all Central Europe, and not least for Hungary, that his love of country should by its intensity have aroused a lasting hatred among those who were its victims. 'Incite every nationality against the Magyars,' declared Széchenyi prophetically in 1847, 'and you fill to the brim the cup of vengeance with your poison.' The warning went unheeded; perhaps it had come too late.

Yet when the Hungarian Diet met at Bratislava – Pressburg, as it then was in September 1847 – there was nothing to show that revolution and civil war were any nearer than in the previous four years. The Diet, indeed, had a closer resemblance to a representative institution than its predecessors since, for the first time, a distinctive party system had emerged. There was a government bloc, led by Apponyi and supported by most of the magnates, including Széchenyi, and an opposition in which Kossuth's 'Liberals', the party of the lesser nobility, formed an uneasy alliance with the moderates of Deák and the 'centralists' of Eötvös. This opposition wanted a responsible Hungarian government with a parliament in Pest elected on a broader franchise than the Diet, and it also pressed for social reform, including abolition of feudal dues and freedom of the press. As the debates dragged on into the new year, it became clear that, while the magnates might concede social reform, there was little chance of securing a responsible government; and by the end of February there was deadlock in the Diet. It was at this point that the tedium of inactivity was relieved by news reaching the Danubian cities from Paris – the Orleanist Monarchy had fallen and France was again a republic.

Metternich had once declared, 'When Paris sneezes, Europe catches cold': now his words were seen to be a metaphorical understatement, for in Hungary the political temperature climbed rapidly from below normal to a fever. In Vienna student demonstrations and rioting by the workers led to Metternich's dismissal on 13 March and to the summoning by the Emperor of a constituent assembly two days later. The Magyars were not far behind. Radical students in Pest – for this was the hour of Petöfi – sent a thrill of panic among the magnates; and Kossuth hurriedly swept the demand for a Hungarian government through the Diet at Bratislava. A series of 'March Laws' gave Hungary an administration of her own and, at the same time, took a big step towards the emancipation of the peasantry by the abolition of the *robot*. By the end of the month Kossuth, Széchenyi, Deák and Eötvös were all sitting in the same Council of Ministers under the presidency of a progressively-minded magnate, Count Batthyány. When on 11 April Emperor Ferdinand duly sanctioned the March Laws it seemed as if the Hungarian Revolution was over. But revolution, like war, is easier to start than to end; and, for the subject nationalities, it had as yet hardly begun.

During 1848 revolutionary barricades went up, sometimes on more than one occasion, in twenty European cities from Seville in the south-west to Poznan in the north-east. Since the first town to rebel was Palermo in Sicily and the first capital Paris, it is slightly misleading to treat the risings in East-Central Europe in isolation from those in the south and the west. Yet, though the intellectual power-house of liberalism might be French, the bastion of the conservative order was in Vienna and it was the flight of Metternich, rather than the flight of Louis Philippe and Guizot, which provided the revolutionary impulse for the peoples of Central Europe. Moreover, while in the west the revolutionaries were primarily concerned with securing democratic reforms, farther east their principal objectives were less politically advanced. Hence, although there is a close connexion between developments in Italy, Germany and the Danubian basin, the specifically nationalistic character of the insurrections in the Habsburg territories give them a certain unity in diversity, despite the conflict of interests.

For a few weeks in the spring of 1848 it seemed as if the fate of Central Europe might well be settled on the plains of Lombardy rather than in the Danubian basin. In the thirty years which followed the Treaty of Vienna the Austrians had used their Lombard and Venetian provinces as a means to indirect mastery of the whole Italian peninsula. The news of Metternich's fall encouraged all the Italian states to seek freedom and unity, and on 23 March the small kingdom of Sardinia-Piedmont declared war on the Habsburg Empire in an attempt to eject the Austrians from Lombardy and Venetia. Milan was duly liberated and the Austrian garrisons withdrew into the four fortresses of Peschiera, Mantua, Verona and Legnano, the famous military 'Quadrilateral'. Until Marshal Radetzky's counter-offensive defeated the Piedmontese at Custozza in the fourth week of July 1848, the Italian front made heavy demands on Austrian resources. Even after Radetzky regained control of the Lombard plains, the 'Republic of St Mark' in Venice continued to champion Italian nationalism until August 1849, when shortage of food and an epidemic of cholera forced its insurgent leaders to resign themselves to the return of Austrian rule. Nowhere else in 1848, apart from Hungary, was defiance so long sustained.

The rapid change in the temper of revolt is clearly shown in the sequence of events in Prague. There, as in Bratislava and Pest, the crowds were in the streets even before the Viennese had driven Metternich into exile on 13 March. But there was, as yet, little sign of urgency about the demonstrations. A meeting of the Bohemian liberals, German-speaking as well as Czech, at the St Wenceslas Baths on 11 March showed caution and restraint; a committee was appointed to consider proposals for constitutional reform which would, in due course, be put into a petition for presenting to the Emperor. The liberals talked of linguistic equality in the courts of law, of freedom of assembly and the press, of peasant emancipation, and possibly – although on this issue they were vague – of a common Diet for the Czech lands, to meet alternately at Prague and Brno. It was only at the end of the week, after the news of two days of riots in Vienna had reached the Czechs, that proposals were made for a representative assembly common to all three provinces in the 'lands of the crown of St Wenceslas' (Bohemia, Moravia and Austrian Silesia). The workers from the new suburbs joined the demonstrations of bourgeoisie and students and forced the liberals to send a more consciously nationalistic delegation to Vienna; and on 8 April the Imperial government accepted the wishes of the Czech representatives; the three provinces would enjoy virtual autonomy.

Within four weeks of Metternich's fall the Emperor Ferdinand had thus made three major concessions: the promise of an Austrian Constitution; acceptance of the Hungarian 'March Laws'; and recognition of the 'rights of the Bohemian Crown'. And all this had been achieved without violence by the revolutionaries, apart from some clashes at the gates of Vienna. But already there were divisions among those who sought reform, and in the Czech lands these had particular significance.

The Moravian Diet, meeting in Brno, resented the way in which the liberals of Prague presumed to speak for all three Czech provinces, and protested to the crown; and the Silesian Diet was no less hostile. In neither of these assemblies had Germans and Czechs worked so closely together as in Bohemia, nor were the Slav delegates – mostly Catholics from the countryside – so politically conscious or so astute as the urbanized Czechs in Prague. In a sense, however, the racial split in Moravia and Silesia merely anticipated by a few days the decision of the most influential of Czech spokesmen, Palacký, who was himself by birth a Lutheran Moravian, though a resident of Prague. On 6 April Palacký had been invited to assist the German liberals at Frankfurt in drafting a democratic constitution for all the territories in the German Confederation, including Bohemia. But on 11 April he despatched to Frankfurt a reply in which he declined to cooperate for three reasons: he was himself of Slav descent, and not a German; the Czech lands were never historically part of Germany, but were merely linked with the old empire in a dynastic union; and, most important of all, the proposed Pan-German Assembly would inevitably weaken the Austrian State, which he regarded as a European necessity in order to defend the Danubian peoples from 'Asiatic elements' in Russia.

Palacký's momentous letter contained the first modern definition of the Czech national point of view. It was far more Habsburg in sympathy than any sentiment which had as yet emanated from the Court in Vienna, but paradoxically it embodied the most revolutionary concept of all: an Austrian Federation of autonomous states which would preserve the natural economic unity of the Danubian basin against the encroachment of both Russia and Germany but which, by its very existence, would be predominantly Slavonic in composition. It is small wonder that Palacký was offered by the Vienna government a ministerial post (which he declined) or that the German liberals, both at Frankfurt and in the Austrian cities, found his argument incomprehensible and sought to damn him as the servant of reaction. This he certainly was not, as his decision to convene a Slav Congress at Prague in June was to show, but there is little doubt that the open breach between Slav and German nationalists in Bohemia encouraged the Imperial Court that summer to revert to the well-tried political tactic of 'divide and rule'.

If the Czechs could prick the bubble of 'Greater German' enthusiasm, then the Croats were in a position to offer a similar challenge to the Magyar Revolution. By chance, the post of Ban (Governor) of Croatia was vacant in March 1848 and, before accepting the Hungarian 'March Laws,' the Emperor Ferdinand filled it by the appointment of Baron Josip Jellačić, a forty-seven year old fanatically Hungarophobe colonel in one of the Military Frontier regiments. Jellačić, a thorough 'Illyrian' in sentiment, refused to acknowledge the authority of the Batthyány government. On 25 March he convened a meeting of representatives of 'the nations of the Triune Kingdom' – Croatia-Slavonia and Dalmatia – in Zagreb, and this assembly duly elected Jellačić as principal officer of State and adopted a thirty-point declaration of rights. The reforms which this National Council sought to impose on the sovereign were remarkably extensive: they included constitutional changes amounting to a recognition of autonomy, and acceptance by the Church of the abolition of

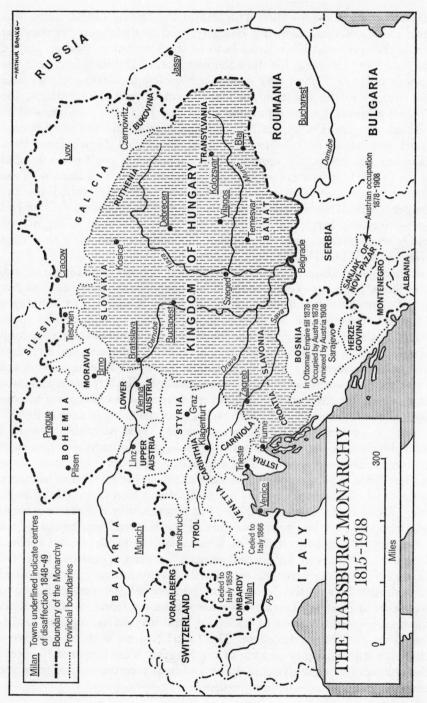

~ARTHUR BANKS~

RUSSIA

Jassy

BUKOVINA

Czernowitz

Lvov

GALICIA

RUTHENIA

Debrecen

KINGDOM OF HUNGARY

TRANSYLVANIA

Kolozsvar

Blaj

Vilagos

Temesvar

BANAT

Maros

Danube

ROUMANIA

Bucharest

BULGARIA

Cracow

Kosice

SLOVAKIA

Tisza

Szeged

Belgrade

SERBIA

Austrian occupation
1878-1908

SANJAK OF
NOVI-PAZAR

MONTENEGRO

ALBANIA

SILESIA

Teschen

MORAVIA

Brno

BOHEMIA

Prague

Plisen

LOWER
AUSTRIA

Vienna

Bratislava

Budapest

Danube

Drava

Sava

Zagreb

CROATIA

SLAVONIA

BOSNIA

In Ottoman Empire till 1878
Occupied by Austria 1878
Annexed by Austria 1908

Sarajevo

HERZE-
GOVINA

Linz

UPPER
AUSTRIA

STYRIA

Graz

CARINTHIA

Klagenfurt

CARNIOLA

Trieste

ISTRIA

Fiume

Munich

BAVARIA

Innsbruck

TYROL

VENETIA

Venice

Ceded to
Italy 1866

VORARLBERG

SWITZERLAND

Ceded to
Italy 1859

LOMBARDY

Milan

Po

ITALY

Milan Towns underlined indicate centres
       of disaffection 1848-49
—·—· Boundary of the Monarchy
······· Provincial boundaries

THE HABSBURG MONARCHY
1815-1918

0   300

Miles

celibacy and the use of the vernacular in the Divine Office. There was little chance of these demands being realized in their entirety: they cut across the territorial boundaries both of the Hungarian counties and of the Austrian provinces, for the administration of Dalmatia had been the responsibility of Vienna ever since the Napoleonic Wars; and they also ran counter to the traditions of the Roman Church. Nevertheless, the Council achieved the main purpose for which Jellačić had summoned it: his authority had the appearance of popular sanction; and the Imperial Court was left in no doubt of the total divorce of Zagreb from Pest. Claiming that he would 'remain a firm supporter of the Crown as head of the South Slav Movement,' Jellačić dramatically cut all links with the Hungarian government on 19 April, and confidently waited for the Emperor to call on his services. To some extent, however, Jellačić had over-played his hand; the Imperial authorities continued to regard the Ban with marked distaste throughout the summer; and for a time they even suspended him from office.

Other nationalities were also protesting against the March Laws. The Serbs from the Vojvodina sent a deputation to Pest in April but found their claims brusquely turned aside by Kossuth. On 10 May a 'National Assembly' of Slovaks at Tepla, in the Tatra Mountains, petitioned both the Emperor and the Batthyány government for recognition of the rights of the non-Magyar peoples within Hungary; and five days later, in Transylvania, a gathering of forty thousand Roumanians on the outskirts of the small town of Blaj sent a message of loyalty to the Emperor and condemned attempts by the Magyar-packed Diet in Kolozsvár to vote for legislative union with the Hungarian National Government in Pest.

But the Imperial authorities, who received these petitions, were in a difficult position. Frequent riots in Vienna led the Court to seek sanctuary at Innsbruck on 17 May. The Emperor's advisers – and they alone mattered, for the Emperor Ferdinand was too feeble-minded to influence policy – still looked with favour on the Czechs, a historic people strategically placed in the heart of Europe; but it was a very different matter to lend support to minority movements in the remote outer fringe of the monarchy. When a deputation of Roumanians from Blaj at last reached Innsbruck it received no encouragement, or even sympathy, from the Court officials. Moreover, as yet, the Batthyány ministry had remained scrupulously loyal to the dynasty; and the Imperial government hoped to secure from Hungary crack troops for the Italian front so as to bolster the hard-pressed divisions of Radetzky, who was defending the Quadrilateral against the Piedmontese. The Court had no wish to provoke a civil war with Hungary so long as the Magyars were prepared to accept the obligations of the dynastic union and help save the empire from the encroachments of an alien nationalism.

Batthyány, who visited Innsbruck in June, was inclined to reach an agreement with the dynasty, and was even prepared to make concessions to Jellačić. Széchenyi and Deák shared his views, but with each day that passed the revolution became more and more identified with the strident voice of Kossuth, and he certainly was never one to compromise. Within eight hours of the opening of the new Hungarian Parliament on 4 July Kossuth declared that the country was in danger from Croatian and *prečani* Serb revolts; and, as minister of finance, he asked the deputies to vote him funds for an army of two hundred thousand men. He favoured cooperation between the old historic master-races – the Germans, Magyars and, to a lesser extent, the Poles – in order to keep the subject nationalities in their place. This attitude made him, of course, more sympathetic to the ideals of the German National Assembly in Frankfurt than to the Austrian Parliament in Vienna, with its Ruthene, Slovene and Czech deputies. But he was, nonetheless, prepared to strike a bargain of a sort with the dynasty: if the Imperial government 'offered its good services for the reduction of Croatia and, at the end of the war, conceded all justified national demands to the Italians,' the Hungarian liberals were willing for Magyar regiments to be despatched for service on the Italian front. It is unlikely that such conditions could have been accepted at any time – and perhaps they were never meant to be – but, coming as they did at that particular moment in July 1848, they seemed totally unrealistic. For, in the same week that Kossuth proposed sending troops to Italy, Radetszky gained his decisive victory of Custozza against the Piedmontese. Autocracy was once more in the saddle; the Court made ready to return from Innsbruck to Vienna; and the prospect of a campaign to discipline the Magyars came appreciably nearer. Time was running out for Kossuth.

By August the revolutionary tide seemed on the ebb throughout Europe. With the 'June Days' the propertied class and the peasantry in France had recoiled in terror at the menace of a social republic: and once again the fevered nerves of Paris evoked a delayed response in distant cities where others, too, preferred a possible Caesarism to a routine of violence. In Vienna, for example, the ominously named Committee of Public Safety, which had been set up in May, was seen to be no more than a phantom threat, and the main achievement of the Austrian Revolution was enacted, in September, by the predominantly middle-class and peasant parliament – the formal abolition of the labour services of the *robot* and all hereditary rights of landowners. Thereafter, the radical intellectuals and the workers became more and more cut off from the mass political movement; hence when the Left in Vienna attempted a second revolution in October, they were as isolated as the Parisian socialists had been four months previously and the guns of the Imperial army made short work of the barricades.

Austrian gunners had already quelled disorders earlier in the year in Cracow and Prague. The revolution in Cracow was half-hearted, probably because of the Galician failure two years before. Demonstrations on 26 April were, however, countered by a steady bombardment. Thereafter, Galicia remained quiet, apart from an insurrection of the workers at Lvov in November which was, again, suppressed by unrestrained use of artillery. On this occasion fifty-five Polish labourers were shot to pieces on the barricades by General Hammerstein's guns.

Events in Bohemia had a special significance because of the paramount position of the Czechs among the Slav nationalities of the empire. Prague was a natural sanctuary for refugees from Prussian persecution of the Poles and Magyar intimidation of the Slovaks; and it was among these exiles that the first proposals were made, during April, for the summoning of a Slav Congress. The idea was taken up by Palacký and by the Slovak, Safarik, but the Czech leaders insisted on limiting the Congress membership to Slav subjects of the Habsburg Empire, although other Slavs were permitted to attend as guests. The Congress opened in Prague on 2 June with pledges of loyalty to the Habsburg dynasty and with a programme of reform which called for the construction of an Austrian Federal Empire. There were radicals among the Slovaks – for only the more daring ones were prepared to risk the wrath of the Hungarian administration by going to Prague – and among the Poles and Ruthenes; but, as the Governor of Bohemia subsequently reported to Vienna, 'The Slav Congress . . . pursued no illegal aims and . . . did not plan anything contrary to the law or incompatible with the interests of the Austrian Monarchy.' Proclamations were prepared proposing that the Slav Congress should become an annual event (though meeting in different cities) and that common Slavonic academic institutions should be set up. These proclamations were, however, never approved. The radical students and, to some extent, the artisans of Bohemia were carried away by the general atmosphere of excitement in Prague. Rioting broke out over trifling incidents during the Whitsun weekend. Prince Windischgraetz, the commander of the Prague garrison, withdrew all troops from the city on 15 June and, two days later, under cover of a bombardment, ordered his men to retake the Bohemian capital hill by hill and street by street. It proved the end of the Slav Congress and, indeed, of the liberties promised to the Czech lands on 8 April. The moderate Czech deputies were permitted to attend the Austrian Parliament until it was dissolved in March 1849; but in Prague, as he himself declared, General Prince Windischgraetz was sole master of Bohemia.

Windischgraetz's punitive bombardment of Prague was celebrated by the Pan-Germans as a major defeat for their Slav rivals, and especially for Palacký. As the summer progressed the German National Assembly in Frankfurt came to rely more and more on the armies of the old dynasties and thereby divorced itself from the revolutionary fervour which had brought it into being. Most of its work was, of course, concerned with the problems of territories which could be considered German historically or linguistically (and is therefore outside the scope of this present study). There were, however, several regions which defied simple classification upon either of these principles; and two of them, Bohemia and Poznania, were inhabited predominantly by people of Slavonic origin. The position of Bohemia had been clarified, to the disgust of the German delegates, by Palacký's famous letter; but there was no one of his stature among the people of Poznania to speak for the Poles. Indeed, since Poznania constituted one of the eight provinces of the Kingdom of Prussia, the attitude of the Frankfurt Parliament to Polish affairs depended, to a large extent, on the whim of whoever was in power in Berlin.

In March 1848 there had been a brief period of Prusso–Polish friendship. During the first days of the revolution Mieroslawski and the other Polish conspirators were released from the Moabit Prison and escorted through the Berlin streets by cheering crowds; even King Frederick William IV greeted them at the Royal Palace. Political concessions soon followed: the Poles were permitted to establish a National Committee in Poznan and to begin training a specifically Polish army. For a time there seemed a real prospect of a Prusso–Polish combination, possibly backed by republican France, against Russia. 'The German nation has spurned the alliance of its Princes with Asiatism, and is ready to carry its flag of Black-Red-Gold together with yours, into the battle of light against darkness,' declared one of the German leaders on 22 March. The new generation seemed to be pursuing the phantom of 1812.

Such a rapturous union could never outlive the honeymoon. For the Poles in Poznania did not share the broad national concept of their émigré leaders nor could the Germans in the province abandon old habits and attitudes. While Mieroslawski was thinking of a war to liberate the Congress Kingdom, the Poznanian peasantry were attacking local 'oppressors' in the Prussian bureaucracy or the Jewish trading community. The Prussian army was traditionally anti-Polish and genuinely alarmed at the spread of anarchy; it had no intention of permitting a Galician-type *jacquerie*. On 10 April, only three weeks after Mieroslawski's release from prison, Prussian regular troops attacked some Polish army units. For a month skirmishes continued between the rival military formations in and around Poznan until finally, on 9 May, the 'insurgents' – as the Poles were now called in Berlin – capitulated, and the German garrisons restored order.

These events influenced the attitude of the German national liberals in Frankfurt. The German Pre-Parliament, which had met at Heidelberg in March to prepare for the subsequent Assembly in Frankfurt, had originally passed a resolution condemning the partitions of Poland as 'a shameful crime' and proclaiming the restoration of a Polish State as 'the sacred duty of the German nation.' These sentiments did not survive the breach between the Prussians and Mieroslawski. The only debate in the Frankfurt Parliament specifically concerned with Poznania was not held until the fourth week of July, and by then the German democrats had outgrown the 'imbecile sentimentality' of earlier resolutions. 'Our right is that of the strongest, the right of conquest,' thundered Wilhelm Jordan, a delegate from Berlin: since history, which looked favourably on the German people, denied the Poles a state in which to express 'healthy national egotism', it was clear that the Poles were not entitled to political independence. By 342 votes to 31, with 188 abstentions, the Frankfurt Parliament decided that Poznania was a province essentially German in character. There was only one Polish member of the Frankfurt Parliament and in the debate he left his German colleagues in no doubt of the consequences of their action: 'The Poles have been swallowed up,' he declared, 'but, by God, it will not be possible to digest them.' In its way, the Assembly's verdict was historic, for it marked the end of any hope of a German solution for the Polish Question, though the possibility was raised once more during the First World War. Enmity between the two races of Poznania was to endure for a century, perhaps longer.

The disavowal of Polish rights, first by the Prussians and subsequently by the Frankfurt Parliament, gratified Tsar Nicholas I who had observed the spread of revolutionary enthusiasm in March with considerable apprehension. Congress Poland remained quiet throughout 1848, partly because of the vigilance of the Viceroy, Paskievič, and partly because there was a slow improvement in living standards, particularly in Warsaw and its suburbs. But the Tsar was constantly alive to the risk of revolution on Russia's borders. In his eyes there was another neighbouring nationality, besides the Poles, which had dangerous links with the French radicals: he was determined not to tolerate a national movement among the Roumanians in the Danubian Principalities. Since he considered that Russia had treaty-rights which were tantamount to a suspended protectorate over the mouth of the Danube, he believed he had every justification to intervene in case of a crisis in government.

In reality, the Tsar had little to fear from the northern principality, Moldavia. It is true that there was a demonstration in Jassy, the principal town, at the end of March 1848, but the leaders of the movement were speedily arrested and the mass of the people remained indifferent to what was happening elsewhere. As a precautionary measure, however, the

Tsar in July ordered his army to cross the Pruth and occupy Moldavia. By then, a more serious revolt had broken out to the south, in Wallachia. It was inspired in part by the example of the Roumanians across the frontier at Blaj in Transylvania and the latent liberal enthusiasm was certainly fanned by the arrival in Bucharest, hot-foot from republican Paris, of the brothers Ion and Dimitrie Bratianu. A provisional government was set up in Bucharest and pledges given of extensive reform. But once again the Tsar intervened. He urged the Sultan, as the ultimate sovereign of the Principalities, to restore the traditional system of administration; and, at the same time, he ordered his own generals to cross the river Sereth into Wallachia and give the Turks assistance. By the end of September the nationalist movement had collapsed: the Roumanian liberals sought sanctuary in the West; and a Russian army of occupation was firmly entrenched in both Principalities. It remained south of the Pruth for two and a half years.

Compared with events in the Habsburg lands and Germany, the Roumanian revolution had gone off at half-cock. Nevertheless, it had two important consequences: Ion Bratianu's activities in Bucharest, however inept, succeeded in placing the Roumanian Question on the agenda of Europe, where it remained for the next thirty years; and the southward movement of the Russians meant that the Tsar's divisions were spread around the arc of the Carpathians, ready to cross the passes into Transylvania should the Habsburgs need any effective demonstration of the principle of conservative solidarity. It was no accident that the entry of Russian troops into Wallachia coincided with a hardening of the attitude of the Imperial authorities in Vienna towards Hungary.

By September 1848 Kossuth was sole ruler of Hungary in everything but name. The Batthyány ministry had been an uneasy coalition from the first, and in the late summer it fell apart. Kossuth and the Liberals argued that they could retain the advantage of a dynastic union with the other Habsburg lands while repudiating all share in the National Debt: Széchenyi, Deák and the moderates knew that no one in Vienna would sanction such a casual evasion of financial obligations. First Deák and then Batthyány resigned; and Széchenyi, who tried desperately to avert civil war, experienced a mental collapse in September and spent the last twelve years of his life in an asylum at Dobling, near Vienna. The political field in Hungary was left clear for Kossuth.

In the first week of September the Imperial Court authorized Ban Jellačić to take action against the recalcitrant Magyar government; and on 11 September he crossed the Drava at Varazdin, with an army of forty five thousand men, and headed north-eastwards towards Balaton and

Budapest itself, 150 miles away. This Croat invasion provided Kossuth with the spark with which he could fire the enthusiasm of the Magyar gentry. He was helped by the brilliance of the thirty-year-old general, Arthur Gorgei, who commanded the Hungarian militia (*Honvéd*) in the south. Görgei not only checked Jellačić, he pushed him back across the border. It was a savage war, with irregulars on both sides committing atrocities; and the general bestiality spread rapidly to Slovakia, Transylvania and the Vojvodina (where the *prečani* Serbs, rising in revolt in October, gave no quarter to the Magyars, and received none).

The Hungarian War lasted in all for eleven months. At first, before winter set in, there was some prospect that the *Honvéd* might march on Vienna; and the October rising in the capital was in part a demonstration of sympathy for Kossuth by the Pan-German radicals. But, even though the Court went on its travels again (to Olmütz, in central Moravia, this time), Windischgraetz saw to it that there would be no more Viennese revolutions; and, by the end of November, the aristocratic and conservative officer-class was firmly in control of the Austrian provinces, and eager to chastise the radicals of Pest. On 2 December the Emperor Ferdinand abdicated in favour of his eighteen-year-old nephew, Francis Joseph. To some extent this constitutional measure was part of the war against Hungary, for the new Emperor was not pledged, as his predecessor had been, to uphold the 'March Laws'. Significantly, Kossuth refused to recognize Ferdinand's act of abdication. To the Magyar constitutional purists Francis Joseph would only become ruler of Hungary when he was crowned in Buda; until then, Ferdinand was King while he lived (and he did not die until 1875, eight years after Francis Joseph's eventual coronation). The regular Hungarian army officers had taken their oath to Ferdinand; so long as the civil war lasted they owed no allegiance to his successor.

Such niceties of conscience did not trouble Windischgraetz or Jellačić. Their two armies marched against Hungary and within a fortnight Pest was in Windischgraetz's hands and the Magyar administration had fled eastwards to Debrecen. It seemed as if Kossuth would soon be trapped, for in Transylvania General Puchner had succeeded in raising a Roumanian legion and the local Saxon community was also in arms against Magyar marauders. But Kossuth kept his hold on Transylvania thanks to the remarkable generalship of the exiled Polish veterans, Bem and Dembinsky. Görgei began a counter-offensive towards the Danube and, for a time, even held Budapest once more. On 14 April 1849 the Hungarian Parliament, meeting in Debrecen, formally deposed the Habsburgs and proclaimed 'Hungary with all its dependencies' an independent state with Kossuth as regent and the future form of government left unspecified.

The deposition of the Habsburgs was an act of political suicide. No foreign power was prepared to recognize Kossuth's authority (except, pathetically, the Venetian Republic which Radetzky's troops were starving into surrender). Even before he heard of the Debrecen proclamation, Francis Joseph asked the Tsar for aid to suppress the Hungarian rebellion. Russian troops had already crossed once into Transylvania in February but had withdrawn again on the advance of General Bem. But the presence of the two Polish generals made Nicholas eager to intervene. In June Russian troops swept across the Carpathians, not only from Wallachia, but from the Congress Kingdom by way of Galicia and the Bukovina. On 31 July Bem's army, outnumbered by more than two to one, was broken at Schassburg, the young poet Petöfi being among those killed. Bem himself escaped to Turkey; and the Russians streamed relentlessly across the featureless steppe of the Alföld.

The last weeks of the Hungarian Revolution were clouded by dis-agreements between Kossuth and Görgei. The Austrians forced Görgei back into south-eastern Hungary and he knew that, with the Russians to the north and Croats and Serbs to the south, his position was hopeless. At first, Kossuth would not accept the inevitability of defeat, but on 11 August he handed over his responsibilities to Görgei and escaped to Turkey, with a small bodyguard. Two days later, at Világos, Görgei capitulated to Paskievič, confident that he would receive from the Prince of Warsaw more generous treatment than from the vindictive Austrian, General Haynau. Görgei was right, for Hungary was subjected to military occupation and court-martial for more than a year: thirteen former officers of the Imperial army who had served with field rank in the *Honvéd*, were hanged at Arad in October; and even Batthyány, who had withdrawn from politics before the split developed between Kossuth and the Crown, was shot; but Görgei, protected by Paskievič, escaped – and indeed, lived on until 1916.

The Világos capitulation ended the cycle of revolutions for all Central Europe. Politically, in retrospect, their successes seem few and their record of action discreditable, for the interplay of national animosity facilitated the restoration of absolutionist rule. But socially their achieve-ment was great: the abolition of the last restraints of serfdom enabled the more enterprising peasants to raise their status considerably, even in devastated Hungary. Moreover, labourers in the fields had, like the town workers, secured freedom of movement: they could seek employment in the new industrial centres; and, of even greater significance, they could emigrate. Ultimately, however, the main historical legacy of the revolu-tions were the legends which they created: a belief, for example, in the common identity of the Slav peoples; a conviction, particularly strong among the English-speaking peoples, that the Magyar gentry were at heart Jeffersonian Whigs; and the certainty that the Russian bogy was real and the tsarist state an evil institution, pledged to repress liberalism wherever it raised its head. None of these assumptions was wholly false; the real error of interpretation lies in the ease with which people over-simplified the complexities of the revolts, seeking a black and white moral clarity out of the inextricably confused. For in a tumbling world of divided loyalties men behave as their natural selves, and it is only the frenzy of the idolaters which turns them into gods.

Throughout the 1850s Europe lived in the shadow of the revolutions. Outwardly the peoples of the Habsburg Empire were soon pacified; for, with the final suppression of the national movements, Francis Joseph imposed a disciplined bureaucratic administration on the monarchy. The Austrian Parliament was dispersed even before the defeat of Hungary, and no attempt was made to summon another. Despite their rich diversity of custom, the Habsburg lands were treated as a single unitary state, centred on Vienna. They were also – and this made more sense – treated as a single free-trade area, for the tariffs which had separated the Austrian provinces from Hungary were abolished in July 1851, a measure which contributed considerably to the prosperity of the Czech lands and, in due course, of the Hungarian Kingdom as well.

Politically, however, it was a dead era. No nationality was favoured, only the bureaucracy. Once the military regime had ended in Hungary, the Magyars found themselves no worse off than the Croats, who had stood by the dynasty in 1848–9; but equally, to their intense chagrin, they were no better off than the Slovaks or the Roumanians or the *prečani* Serbs. By chance, the one section in the community which improved its status was the urban middle class in Bohemia, both German and Czech, for this was the prime recruiting-ground for the Habsburg civil service. There was accordingly some justice in the complaint of the people of Budapest that their city was being run by Czechs, although in Bohemia and Moravia themselves the specifically national revival of the Czech language was halted; a move to try Palacký before a military court was defeated but Karel Havlíček, the doyen of Czech journalists, was arrested and imprisoned. It was a dull decade for all the peoples of the empire; the glamour had gone with the exiled Kossuth to packed meetings in London and Southampton and New York.

It was natural that Kossuth's speeches should have increased the hatred with which liberals on both sides of the Atlantic regarded Russia. Alone of the continental autocrats, the Tsar had survived the two years of revo-lution without an insurrection in his territories and with his authority so secure at home that he could despatch armies to tidy up the Danubian Principalities and settle the civil war in Hungary. He was the gendarme of a Europe which had no desire to be policed by his methods – and which had shown as much as early as 1831 when the Poles crossed into exile. The notion of a general European war against Russia had an ideological appeal in the West long before the absurdities of the Holy Places dispute made it a probability.

The Crimean War was fought primarily over naval power in the Black Sea and potentially, by way of the Straits, in the eastern Mediterranean. It was therefore concerned more with the European Balance than with the fate of the peoples along Russia's borders. But as a side issue – and, at times, a highly important one – it raised the question of Roumania. Indeed, the initial cause of war actually lay in the Danubian Principalities, which the Russians re-occupied in July 1853, as a means of putting pressure on the Turks, and where the first fighting took place between Turks and Russians less than four months later. Moreover, when the British and French sent an ultimatum to Russia in February 1854, their sole demand was for the evacuation of the principalities; and it was the Tsar's failure to withdraw his troops, even though Paskievič as commander-in-chief favoured it on strategic grounds, which provided the two Western Allies with their excuse for sending armies to the Black Sea.

When, in June, the British troops landed at Varna (on what is now the sea-coast of Bulgaria) they could hear the Russian guns thundering at the Turkish positions around Silistria, sixty miles away on the Danube, and it seemed probable that they would have to hold the line of the Balkan Mountains against a Russian thrust to Constantinople. But at the end of the month the Russians raised the siege of Silistria and began to pull back across Wallachia. By the beginning of September the Russians had completely evacuated both Principalities: the Crimea, and not the Balkan Peninsula, was to be the theatre of war. Another sixty-one years were to elapse before the British and French committed their troops to Balkan operations for the first time.

The Tsar's change of heart over the Principalities was a direct consequence of Austrian policy. Buol, Francis Joseph's foreign minister, was determined to safeguard the lower Danube basin. For a time it looked as if he had secured a striking diplomatic triumph. He concluded an agreement with Turkey which permitted Austria to occupy the Principalities for the duration of the war with Russia, and by threatening joint action with Prussia against the Russians he induced the Tsar to give way as well. Hence, from August 1854 until March 1857, Austrian troops stood guard along fourteen hundred miles of the Danube, from its confluence with the Inn at Passau to the marshy channels of the delta. Had the Austrians been able to retain this position once peace was restored the Russians would have been cut off for all time from expansion into the Balkans (except, of course, by defeating the Austrian Empire in yet another war).

Buol may have hoped that he would be allowed to make the temporary occupation permanent, but it was unlikely that the other Powers would have accepted such a major change in the map of Europe. The chief effect of the Austrian move was to make the problems of the Danube figure prominently in the Peace Congress at Paris of 1856. The Treaty of Paris established two international commissions for the river: a 'European Commission' of the Great Powers, with responsibility for clearing the channels of the delta; and – of more lasting importance – the 'Danubian Commission,' on which the riparian states would be represented and which would have the task of determining rules of navigation and police control so that the river could be developed as an international waterway. At the same time, the treaty deprived Russia of an outlet on the Danube by detaching southern Bessarabia and assigning it to Moldavia so that the area was restored to the formal suzerainty of the Sultan of Turkey. The two Principalities themselves remained nominally part of the Turkish Empire, but were permitted 'independent, national administrations' and even national guards. No foreign power was to have any exclusive right of intervention in either Wallachia or Moldavia.

The Danubian Principalities had thus won, through the jealousy of the Great Powers, virtual but distinctive independence. If Napoleon III could have had his way, they would have been unified as a Roumanian State, for the Emperor of the French felt bound to take notice of the claims of a Latin people for national recognition, especially when their leading spokesmen formed an influential pressure group in the French capital itself. The Russians, too, would have preferred a Roumania in which they might have intrigued with freedom rather than two separate provinces which were artificially bolstered up as a barrier against them. But neither Britain nor Austria supported the Roumanian nationalists: Palmerston distrusted both Napoleon III and the new Tsar, Alexander II; and Buol feared that union of the Principalities would increase nationalist feeling among the Roumanians of Transylvania.

The dispute over 'union' or 'division' dragged on long after the delegates to the Paris Congress had dispersed. A special diplomatic conference on this question was held in Paris in the summer of 1858; it produced a Convention which provided that the 'United Principalities of Moldavia and Wallachia' have two separate princes, two separate administrative councils and two separate popular assemblies. The nonsense of this semantic aberration was soon mocked by the good sense of the Roumanian people themselves. For in February 1859 the Wallachian Assembly followed the example of the Moldavian Assembly a fortnight previously and elected Colonel Alexander Cuza as Prince. The divided Principalities thereby secured a common ruler despite the constitutional obstacles which the Paris Convention had sought to impose.

In many ways, Cuza was a strange choice as a national leader: in 1848, although arrested, he had been a sympathetic but cautious observer rather than a leading participant in the movement for liberation; and although his public utterances carried an assuring note of patriotic probity, revelation of his private morals inspired neither respect nor, one hopes, emulation. Eventually, in 1866, a tendency to ape the less endearing characteristics of his patron and mentor, Napoleon III, led the army (with the backing of most political figures) to depose him and choose a German princeling in his place. But, though he lacks the dignified stature of a founding father, the achievements of his seven year reign were not insignificant: land reform freed the peasants from feudal restraints, although the new holdings were so badly distributed that in time emancipation created more burdens than it relieved; and an educational programme, again unfortunately more impressive on paper than in practice, provided a basis for intellectual development. Above all, Cuza was prepared to defy the Great Powers in order to ensure a common government; and when in February 1862, on the third anniversary of his election, he merged the two assemblies into a centralized parliament meeting in Bucharest, the name of Roumania was at last formally assumed by the 'United Principalities'. Hence, by a curious irony, the most ineffectual of the 1848 national revolts was the first in East-Central Europe to gain general acceptance.

The spark of national-liberal insurrection flared up for the last time in the Polish rebellion of 1863. Although the Poles themselves believed that they were, to a large extent, shadow-acting the events of 1830–31, there was little continuity between the two movements and a marked contrast both in the circumstances which prompted the two risings and in their general character. Indeed, it is tempting to suggest that the only real resemblance between 1831 and 1863 lies in the rivalry, intrigue and suspicion among revolutionary leaders.

The deaths in March 1855 of Tsar Nicholas I and in January 1856 of his Viceroy, Marshal Paskievič, removed the two pillars of the old order. The Poles in the Congress Kingdom once more began to hope that they could extract concessions from their Russian masters; and they were duly allowed to set up both an Agricultural Society and institutions of higher education in Warsaw. Tsar Alexander II was intent on modernizing the whole of his empire and favoured reform in Poland as the surest means to stability and effective government: all he sought, in return, was the cooperation of the Polish landowners and their renunciation of the long cherished ideal by which the Lithuanian territories should be merged in a Polish Kingdom. In an attempt to secure reconciliation with the

Poles, the Tsar appointed Alexander Wielopolski in March 1861 to head what was officially called a 'Commission of Religion and Education' in Warsaw, although his terms of reference included land reforms and the establishment of specifically Polish administrative institutions. This was in itself a conciliatory gesture, for the new commissioner had participated in the 1830 revolution.

Wielopolski, an ardent Slavophile, genuinely believed that he could induce his fellow members of the 'White' landowning nobility (*Szlachta*) to share his own faith in the good intentions of Alexander II. He failed, however, for three main reasons: suspicion by the *Szlachta* of his proposals to convert the peasants into tenant farmers paying money rents; an obstinate insistence on the inclusion of the 'lost' borderlands of Lithuania and Ruthenia in any projects for Polish reform; and fear of retributive acts by the radical element (the 'Reds') in the Polish movement against any group which associated itself too closely with the tsarist administration. The Russians behaved, at times, with clumsy ineptitude: thus in October 1861 they allowed themselves to be pushed into conflict with the Catholic hierarchy when they sent troops to clear the Warsaw churches of worshippers who were singing national hymns – at great length and with many repetitions – to commemorate the death of Kosciuszko. Wielopolski himself made two major tactical errors in policy: he secured the dissolution of the Agricultural Society and hustled its moderate 'White' leader, Zamoyski, into exile; and he announced that young men would be conscripted into the Russian army in order to curb the indiscipline of the Polish cities. Both of these actions played into the hands of the 'Reds' who, in so far as they accepted any control at all, followed the principles of the indefatigable Mieroslawski, veteran of 1846 and 1848.

The threat of conscription precipitated the rebellion, which began on 22 January 1863 and lasted for some fourteen months. Its prime supporters were to be found among the urban population under the age of thirty-five, some of them the sons of the gentry or of the professional classes and many of them artisans; but, because of the strength of the Russian garrisons, the rebellion was never able to secure control of any of the larger towns. It was an insurrection rather than a civil war. For a fortnight in March General Marjan Langiewicz, a former member of Garibaldi's Legion, held the small town of Wachock with 1,000 men. He hoped that he could convert this remote mining area, some fifty miles north of the Galician frontier, into a Polish Sicily, from which the rest of the kingdom would be liberated while the European Great Powers would put pressure on the Tsar to yield to a Polish Risorgimento. But, although France and Britain and even Austria petitioned Alexander II to observe the liberties of 1815, the parallel with Italian unification was fundamentally false in a land-locked province and with no 'Cavour' in Warsaw. Two Russian regiments swiftly and brutally repulsed Langiewicz's incursion, forcing those who survived the fighting to cross back into Galicia and accept Austrian internment. Elsewhere the rebellion took the form of un-coordinated guerrilla operations in which the peasants remained either apathetic or positively hostile to the Polish cause; while amid the under-ground movement in the towns, the conflict between 'Whites' and 'Reds' sank to a depth of assassination and betrayal only surpassed by subsequent divisions at the end of the Second World War.

With all Poland and much of Lithuania aflame, no more was heard of Wielopolski's policy of collaboration; disillusioned, he passed into exile and out of history. The Russian authorities stamped out the rebellion by repressive actions, which were particularly severe in Lithuania, and by a successful attempt to turn the peasants against the whole movement by presenting them with a new agrarian settlement. In March 1864 the peasants were granted freeholds for the land they tilled and, at the same time, they were permitted to keep rights for the use of pastures and in the forests. Holdings were even created for landless peasants out of state properties. The peasant was thus put in a far better position than the ex-serfs emancipated three years earlier in Russia itself: the Poles had, in general, larger holdings and paid no redemption dues; and, moreover, they were guaranteed legal equality with the rest of the Polish population, whereas in Russia there was still discrimination against the former serfs. It may, of course, be argued that in time Russian generosity to the Polish peasants was to prove disastrous: for, since the peasants now had no social grievances against the *Szlachta,* all their discontent was crystallized into a positive Polish patriotism which sought liberation from Russian officialdom and from the burdens of an alien culture and language.

For the moment, however, the agrarian reform destroyed any lingering sympathy among the mass of the rural population for the revolutionary movement. The authorities in Warsaw were able to impose an even harsher period of restraint than in the quarter of a century when Paskievic governed from the Citadel. But times were changing in Poland. As industrialism swept across the kingdom with astonishing rapidity, past discontents were forgotten and old loyalties unobtrusively repudiated until, at the turn of the century, the issue of national allegiance was re-phrased in a different environment by a generation which had not yet come into being. For the heir to the tradition of Langiewicz, and indeed of Kosciuszko, was to be Jozef Pilsudski, who was born near Vilna in 1867 at the peak of this economic revolution.

The defeat of the Polish rebellion marked the end of an epoch for all the European peoples. The rising of 1863 was the last occasion in the nineteenth century when deep patriotic enthusiasm prompted an armed revolt in a relatively developed society. Riots and demonstrations still took place from time to time in some of the older cities as youth voiced its impatience with the slowness of change; but the revolutionary barricade had become the exclusive property of the socialist Left. The concept of a heroic struggle for national liberation survived among the comparatively unsophisticated communities in the Balkan lands; elsewhere, however, reason had begun to triumph over emotion in politics. In Italy and Germany the frenzy of 1848 gave way to the ice-cold calculations of diplomatic technique perfected by Cavour and Bismarck; and a similar realism underlies the attitude to the national problem among the subject peoples of Eastern and Central Europe although outwardly its successes appear less impressive. Compromise and accommodation were to be the key to the new politics: the movement for national recognition had become middle-aged.

4
Ferment down the Danube

The 1860s witnessed more radical changes in the structure and composition of Central Europe than any previous decade. The most dramatic upheaval was, of course, caused by the victories of Prussian arms and statecraft under the direction of Otto von Bismarck; for, although Bismarck himself had little interest in the Danubian basin and none at all in south-eastern Europe, the emergence of a united Germany so soon after a united Italy finally drove the Habsburg Monarchy 'to shift its centre of gravity to Hungary' – the phrase, significantly, was Bismarck's own. This 'Danubian mission' of the dynasty was, from the outset, challenged by its Slav subjects and yet the accommodation made between Francis Joseph and the Magyars in 1867 lasted for more than half a century, breaking up only with the collapse of the Bismarckian Reich itself in 1918.

Although it is customary to emphasize the importance of the political developments of the 1860s and to stress their responsibility for the tension of later years, it would, however, be a mistake to ignore the social adjustments forced upon the Central European peoples at the same time by the growth of industrial capitalism. For in this region the 'Age of Bismarck' was also the 'Age of Steam-Power'. The Austrian provinces of the Monarchy had possessed a network of railways even before the 1848 revolutions but now the lines began to link east and west, concentrating first in Bohemia and subsequently penetrating to all the frontiers and sometimes beyond. Nor was steam-power limited to transport. Iron and engineering works in Styria or Bohemia or central Hungary came to rely on steam engines to drive machine tools, to work hammers, to operate cranes. Forests of chimneys shot up around Vienna and Brno or on Csepel Island, south of Budapest. The factories re-shaped the character of civilized life, drawing men in from the countryside and creating both an urban proletariat and a business class that speculated in bonds and stocks, often with irresponsible abandon and sometimes – as in 1873 – with disaster. The proportion of the population engaged in industry multiplied even more rapidly in the last third of the century, but as early as 1870 the contrast in Vienna between the ornate buildings along the new Ringstrasse and the slums beyond the Danube Canal was in itself a social commentary, while in Budapest housing conditions for the workers rapidly became as grim as anywhere in Europe. Hence, although it was not until 1889 in Austria and 1890 in Hungary that the first specifically Marxist political parties were formed, the stresses of industrial society began to make themselves felt almost as soon as the Dual Monarchy was created. In many ways the elaborate ceremonial of Francis Joseph's coronation as King of Hungary in June 1867, with 800 richly caparisoned horsemen clattering through the streets of Pest, was the final gala performance of feudal monarchy. Already the Habsburg Monarchy had become as much a medieval anachronism as the Holy Roman Empire it had sought to supersede little more than sixty years before.

Francis Joseph, though conscientious and painstaking, was neither intelligent nor perceptive but, even before the disastrous war with Prussia in 1866, he had sensed that the fabric of his authority was alarmingly brittle. Between March 1860 and the outbreak of the Prussian war he authorized no less than four constitutional experiments, conscious that each of them, whether federalist or centralist in character, would fail to satisfy more than a handful of political leaders. The inadequacy of the Habsburg system of government demanded a firm grasp of the balance of national forces within the Empire, and to achieve this it was essential to reach an understanding with the Magyars.

In 1864, encouraged by Count Maurice Esterházy, a Magyar aristocrat whose estates were little more than fifty miles down the Danube from Vienna, the Emperor secretly made contact with the Hungarian liberal, Ferenc Deák; and he found in him a statesmanlike quality rare among the public figures of the monarchy. Deák, who had been a moderate in politics even before 1848, did not conceal his intentions: he sought what a later generation would have termed 'Home Rule' for Hungary. At the age of thirty-four Francis Joseph was sufficiently experienced not to reject Deák's proposals out of hand, as he would have done in the earlier years of the reign. When, in the following spring, he suddenly visited Budapest and received an enthusiastic welcome from its inhabitants, it became clear to the other nationalities that the Emperor was preparing to take the Magyars into partnership.

Yet, if it had not been for the menace from Prussia and the subsequent defeat of the Austrian army at Sadowa-Königgrätz, it is probable that his flirtation with the Magyars would have proved as abortive as other constitutional measures in the preceding six years. For the prospect of transforming the monarchy into a Dualist State unleashed furious criticism from almost every political group. Strongest in condemnation were the Czechs, Palacký publishing a book entitled *The Idea of the Austrian State* in which he maintained that in order to fulfil her historic mission Austria needed to treat her German, Magyar and Slav peoples on a basis of equality. The Emperor hesitated: he sent a message to the Czechs assuring them of his desire to be crowned, in Prague, as King of Bohemia; and he seems to have favoured, for a time, a project of the Austrian premier, Count Belcredi, by which the empire would have been divided into five federal states.

The leisurely pace of these domestic wrangles was, however, soon outstripped by the growing crisis beyond Bohemia's northern frontier. For Bismarck and Moltke had determined that if Francis Joseph was not prepared to give up his claim to primacy in Germanic affairs, the Prussian army would have to destroy for all time the Habsburg power to arbitrate in Germany. A six week campaign brought one Prussian army corps to Bratislava and another to Wagram. The Hungarians remained non-belligerent: they welcomed the Empress Elizabeth (who had a romantic enthusiasm for everything Magyar) in Pest; they failed to respond to overtures from Bismarck; but they also sought to forbid recruiting for the Imperial army on Hungarian soil. For Deák the war was an irrelevancy, a squabble over control of the German Confederation, a matter of no moment to any good Magyar. When he told Francis Joseph that Hungary asked no more after Sadowa than before it, Deák was showing not magnanimity but consistency. He had already stated his maximum claims. What had changed was Hungary's position rather than her attitude; for, with the Prussians astride the Danube between Vienna and Budapest, Francis Joseph could no longer afford to parley with the Magyar leaders. The resultant agreement was termed a 'Compromise' (Ausgleich); to the Slav peoples of the empire the word seemed a euphemism for surrender.

The final negotiations for the Ausgleich took place between Ferdinand von Beust, the Saxon whom Francis Joseph appointed Austrian premier, and Count Gyula Andrássy, a Magyar aristocrat, who had been reviled as a rebel only eighteen years before. Deák himself, modest and personally unambitious, had declined political office, but it was on his advice that Francis Joseph appointed Andrássy as the first Hungarian prime minister. Within a short time the Emperor had come to regard Andrássy as indispensable and, as foreign minister of the monarchy from 1871 to 1879, he exercised an influence on European affairs unequalled by any of his predecessors since the days of Metternich.

The Ausgleich – Law XII by Austrian reckoning – was ratified by the newly summoned Hungarian Parliament at the end of May 1867. In form it was a contract between the sovereign and his Magyar subjects although it assumed that there would be a parallel system of government in the other half of the Monarchy. By the terms of the Ausgleich Francis Joseph recognized the unity and integrity of 'the lands of the Crown of St Stephen,' including Transylvania, the Slovakian highlands, the Military Frontier and Croatia-Slavonia, in return for an admission by the

Hungarian Parliament of the Emperor-King's responsibility for foreign affairs and defence and of his right to appoint joint ministers with authority over these matters and over the common financial obligations of the two parts of the monarchy. The Hungarian Kingdom and the 'Imperial Lands' (Austria – including Carniola, Gorz and Istria – Bohemia, Moravia, Galicia, Silesia and the Bukovina) were to have separate bi-cameral parliaments and separate executives, each headed by a prime minister. Every year 'Delegations' of sixty members nominated by each parliament were to meet alternately in Vienna or Budapest to discuss, independently of each other, matters relating to both states. Although there was no provision for common citizenship, so that an 'Austrian' living in Hungary could participate in public affairs only if he became naturalized and vice versa, provision was made for a commercial union, the terms of which were renewed every ten years. The distribution of joint expenditure favoured Hungary: as Andrássy himself once declared, 'If anyone complains that the terms of the Ausgleich are not favourable to Hungary, I reply that we are at present paying thirty per cent of the joint expenditure and are enjoying similar rights to those who are paying seventy per cent.'

Technically this unique constitutional document created the Dual Monarchy of Austria–Hungary, but the advantages gained by the Magyars were so considerable that it seemed at times as if 'Hungary-Austria' might represent a more apt, if less euphonious, description of the relationship. The structure of the Hungarian Kingdom was politically unitary and its spirit predominantly Magyar: the structure of the 'Imperial Lands' was pseudo-federal with the local Diets retaining extensive powers, although never sufficient to counter the centralizing tendencies of the Court or to content the political leaders of the subject nationalities. As Palacký had feared, 'Dualism' in practice limited the freedom of action of any sovereign who might wish to satisfy the demands of another national group. Unwittingly Francis Joseph and Beust had confined the dynasty within a strait-jacket of their own designing. When, in the early 1870s, Andrássy as foreign minister took the lead in securing a reconciliation with Bismarckian Germany, it became clear that the character of the constitutional structure determined, not only the internal affairs of the monarchy, but even the shaping of foreign policy; and so it remained until 1918.

Andrássy detested everything Slav, and there were many other aristocrats both in Budapest and Vienna who shared his convictions. But, quite apart from the moderating influence of Deák, the Andrássy government possessed in the philosopher and novelist Joseph Eötvös a minister of education who sincerely believed that discrimination against the non-Magyar peoples was both inhumane and inexpedient. It was Deák and

Eötvös who secured the passage through the Hungarian Parliament in 1868 of what was, on paper, a liberal and enlightened Nationalities Law promising extensive rights to racial minorities in justice and in educational and local administrative affairs – guarantees which the chauvinistic intransigence of later governments rendered a mockery.

The Hungarians were left to make their own settlements with the Roumanian majority in Transylvania and with the South Slavs in Croatia-Slavonia, the third subservient racial group (the Slovaks) remaining virtually inarticulate and therefore ignored. Transylvania was refused a Diet of its own; the Roumanians were invited to send deputies direct to the parliament in Budapest although the franchise was so rigged that few Roumanians had the vote. Autonomous rights were, however, granted to the Roumanian Orthodox Church which thereafter served as a standard bearer for the movement for unification within the boundaries of the Roumanian State, a patriotic role which has had repercussions in more recent years. But, otherwise, the people of Transylvania could seek comfort only in the rights promised by the Nationalities Law. So long as the Roumanian Kingdom itself remained weak, the main inclination of the people of Transylvania was towards some form of autonomy within the Habsburg Empire; to achieve this objective their leaders looked to Vienna – and especially in later years to the Archduke Francis Ferdinand – but never to Budapest.

Among the Croats the Ausgleich was regarded as tantamount to an act of betrayal by the dynasty. Under Ban Jellačić they had remained loyal during the upheavals of 1848–9 and Croatian soldiers played a large part in putting down the Italian revolutions as well as in helping to oust Kossuth. Yet they had received no material or political advantages as a reward from their sovereign, apart from a statue of Jellačić with his sword pointing towards the heart of Hungary and the transference of the port of Rijeka (which was then known by its Italian name of 'Fiume') from Hungary to the new administrative unit of Croatia-Slavonia. Now they were left to make their own settlement with the Magyars, a people who persisted in regarding them as 'barbarians'.

To Andrássy – and indeed to Deák and Eötvös – the settlement of 1868 with Croatia, the Nagoda, appeared generous: Croatia was accepted as a 'political nation' with the right for its people to be represented in a parliament (Sabor) at Zagreb; a three-man Croatian executive controlled internal affairs, justice and education; and Serbo-Croat was recognized as the official language of the state. But the Croats were far from satisfied, and with good reason. Their viceroy (Ban) was responsible not to Francis Joseph but to a Hungarian minister of state in Budapest; and all relations with other provinces under Habsburg rule were regulated in the Hungarian capital rather than in Zagreb, a serious restraint on the region's commercial and economic development. Moreover, elections for the Sabor were notoriously corrupt, with the franchise almost entirely restricted to large landowners and officials; about one person in fifty had the vote. One of the most flagrant instances of trickery concerned the status of Fiume. The Hungarian text of the Nagoda declared the port restored to Hungary as an integral part of the kingdom: the Croatian text merely recorded that discussions would take place over its future administration. When the Croatian text was presented to Francis Joseph for signature, a Croat translation of the Magyar version was pasted over the original and received the royal assent. Until 1918 Fiume was therefore treated as an exclusively Hungarian possession, an arrangement which it must be admitted considerably benefited the town although the Croats never abandoned their claim that the port should by rights have been administered directly from Zagreb rather than from Budapest.

Had Croatia-Slavonia remained the primitive and backward province of Magyar legend, then the Nagoda would at least have possessed the merit of realism. But in the 1850s there was a remarkable renaissance of Croatian culture, associated in particular with Joseph Strossmayer, Bishop of Djakovo. It was on his initiative that a South Slav academy of the arts and sciences was established at Zagreb in 1867, to be followed in 1874 by a University and a decade later by an Art Gallery. Strossmayer, who held the very wealthy see of Djakovo for fifty-six years, influenced the development of Croatian learning up to his death in 1905, patronizing poets and philologists and historians. He was a firm believer in the ideal of South Slav unity, hoping to attract in time Serbs, Montenegrins and Bulgars to join the Croats in a Yugoslav Federation of which Zagreb would be the spiritual centre, perhaps even the political capital. He was, however, distrusted almost as much by the politicians in Belgrade as by the Hungarian leaders; and, since most Croats tended to regard Serbs inside or outside their frontiers with a similar contempt to that bestowed upon themselves by the Magyars, there was never much prospect of Strossmayer's dream becoming a reality. Yet his work – and the studies of his main collaborator, the historian Franjo Rački – lifted Croatian scholarship to a new level of renown. Through his correspondence with Gladstone and his vigorous opposition to extreme Papal claims at the Vatican Council of 1870, Strossmayer became a European figure. He was, in a sense, the first public relations man of the South Slav movement, and especially of the specifically Slavonic identity of the Croat peoples. Kossuth, the idol of western liberals, had once declared that there was no Croatian nationality and that he could not find Croatia on a map; it was Strossmayer's achievement to have made nonsense of such arrogance.

As a complement to the Ausgleich, formal constitutional rule was introduced into the 'Imperial Lands' in December 1867; and a series of liberal measures followed, limiting the power of the Church, humanizing the criminal code, improving the status of the Jews and providing for public education. But 'Austria', too, was faced with problems of nationality: the relationship of the Poles of Galicia and the Czechs of Bohemia-Moravia to the central administration in Vienna. Both questions carried stormy echoes of the recent past and pressed for solution; but, for the moment, the other national groups – notably the Ruthenes and Slovenes – were no more articulate than the Slovaks in Hungary, and their political existence was ignored.

In 1868 the Galician Diet, meeting in Lvov, voted a number of resolutions which would have assured the province a high degree of self-government. For five years the Polish members of the Vienna Parliament sought to realize this programme. It was, however, almost impossible within the framework of Dualism to accord the Poles such an opportunity of national development, although since they were a 'historic people' their aspirations always received more sympathetic attention from the Magyars than those of other Slav groups whose antecedents were less socially impeccable. The Poles, if denied the full Lvov programme, did secure acceptance by the Vienna Parliament of laws permitting polonization of schools and universities; and they were granted the right to be represented permanently on the Crown Council by a special 'Minister for Galicia'. There could be no doubt that the Poles in Galicia enjoyed a higher degree of independence than their compatriots within the Russian Empire or Prussia; and Polish scholarship continued to flourish in Lvov and in Cracow.

The Czechs had hoped for formal recognition by the dynasty of 'Bohemian State Rights' and they urged Francis Joseph, as they had done before the Prussian invasion, to come to Prague for a formal coronation. On three occasions the Emperor agreed to the ceremony, but each time events forced him to go back on his word. He was not, however, entirely to blame for such apparent breach of faith; the actions of Czech political leaders were remarkably inept. Palacký, with his thunderously prophetic dicta, rightly enjoyed European renown for his scholarship; but politically he was so long-sighted that he constantly blundered over nearer objectives. His son-in-law, František Rieger, the spokesman of the younger generation, assisted Palacký all too well. It was a major error of policy to visit the Panslav Ethnographic Exhibition in Moscow within a few months of Sadowa and emphasize the Slavonic brotherhood that linked Czechs and Russians; nor was it wise to have summoned a Panslav Congress to Prague itself in 1868, ineffective though that oratorical excursion proved to be. Finally, when in 1869 an ill-kept secret revealed that Rieger had gone to Paris and urged Napoleon III to intercede for the Czechs, it is hardly surprising that the attitude of Francis Joseph perceptibly hardened.

The decisive year for the Czechs was 1871. The Bohemian Diet put forward a detailed project for securing national autonomy, the 'Fundamental Articles'. The Emperor accorded the Czechs a hearing and Hohenwart, the Austrian prime minister, was not unsympathetic; but there were noisy demonstrations by the Germans of the Empire against a decision which they believed would eventually lead to home rule for each of the nationalities and so destroy the German hold on Central Europe. Rioting broke out in Vienna and in the Sudetenland. With Hohenwart uncertain how to proceed, Francis Joseph turned almost automatically to Andrássy, who had no legal right to be consulted over Bohemian affairs but on whom the Emperor had come to rely as a friend and forthright counsellor. The Magyars, like the Germans, regarded the Fundamental Articles as the thin end of a Slavonic wedge; and when Andrássy, with a proper show of reluctance, came to Vienna, his advice to Hohenwart was devastatingly simple: 'Are you prepared to carry through the recognition of Bohemian State Rights with cannon? If not, do not begin this policy.' Andrássy's warning was as effective as a formal veto; the negotiations with the Czechs came to an abrupt end. For another eight years the elected Czech deputies would not take their seats in the parliament in Vienna, refusing to take part in the affairs of an assembly which denied them their national rights, but it is questionable whether Rieger and his colleagues gained any advantages by their policy of piqued abstention.

Yet this failure to make a settlement with Prague perpetuated and deepened the antagonism between Germans and Czechs at a crucial moment in the social and economic development of Bohemia and Moravia. The cultural progress of the Czechs in the 1860s had been as remarkable as that of the Croats; these years saw the establishment of a respected Czech daily newspaper and the foundation of a Czech national theatre. A new generation of Czech novelists emerged and the operas of Smetana opened a golden age in Czech music. Pride in patriotism was fostered, too, by the Sokols. This mass gymnastic movement was founded in 1862 in the belief that service to the nation could be attained by training the mind through the rhythm of disciplined physical energy, a philosophy of spiritual education which owed something to German antecedents but which gave to the Czech national movement a unique character although it was in due course imitated – and sometimes abused – in other lands.

The growth of patriotic sentiment came at a time when the Czechs were moving into new industrial areas, forming a proletariat dominated by German-speaking employers. In no other part of the empire was the social question in the towns so closely tied up with national rivalry. With the foundation in 1868 of the first Czech bank – the Zivnostenska Banka – and the penetration of the petty commercial bureaucracy by the Czechs, an even more formidable challenge began to develop to German-Austrian supremacy. The chief struggle between the Czechs and the Germans in the 1880s and the 1890s was not, as earlier, over pseudo-historical rights but over employment and the use of the Czech language. Every year, almost imperceptibly, the Czechs gained a greater hold on the economic life of the monarchy.

South and east of the Danube, beyond the confines of the new Imperial and Royal Monarchy, social and economic conditions remained primitive and the frontier seemed more than a mere boundary between neighbouring states. French and British capital had begun to open up Roumania in the 1860s, concentrating on the export of grain, and there was a rapid growth of sea-borne trade in the lower Danube, much of it in competition with Odessa and the Russian Black Sea ports; but as yet there was little industry in either of the Danubian Principalities. Serbian industrial development too was slow; by 1870 there were barely a dozen factories in the country. Economic growth was hampered both by a Guild Law, passed in 1847, to protect traditional domestic crafts and by the refusal of the Austrians to modify tariffs originally drawn up with the Ottoman government in the early eighteenth century on the assumption that the Serbs would remain a pastoral people. In Bulgaria – still within the Turkish Empire and, like Serbia, restrained by guild laws – there were some textile mills and, at Stara Zagora, one modern factory, but the main changes in economic life were in the countryside where attempts were made to expand feudal estates into large landholdings providing for a wider market. This transformation was assisted by the needs of the Turks to find a replacement for their lost Roumanian granary and by the spread in Western Europe of the habit of smoking cigarettes made of 'Turkish' tobacco.

The age of steam-power was slow in reaching the Balkans; yet although the continuous railway trunk-route linking Constantinople to Central Europe was completed only in 1888, isolated lines had been constructed more than twenty years earlier and some of these were to have considerable strategic and commercial importance. Thus the British built a railway across the Dobrudja from Constanta to Cernavoda thirty years before the massive twelve-mile Cernavoda bridge over the Danubian marshes was opened in 1894; and it was the British, too, who in 1866 laid the first Bulgarian line, running from Varna to Rustchuk (Ruse) where the Danube was also eventually bridged, although in this instance not until 1954. In the 1870s and 1880s railway enterprise in the Balkans proper was promoted for the most part by German and Austrian capital. The existence of a line from Constantinople to Philippopolis (Plovdiv) had a military value for the Turks in the war with Russia of 1877-8 since it enabled troops to be rushed northwards to defend the Balkan passes; but in general the economic development of south-eastern Europe was unrelated to the political problems of the period, except in as much as a decade of protracted confusion was bound to postpone the growth of industry and commerce.

The shadow of Bismarck fell so heavily over Western and Central Europe in the 1860s that the Balkan peoples were for the most part left, for once, to work out their own destiny. Thus, in 1866 the Bucharest politicians were able to get rid of Cuza in a bloodless *coup d'état* and choose Charles of Hohenzollern-Sigmaringen as prince of what was for the first time officially termed 'Roumania'. Since Prince Charles, an energetic Prussian officer of twenty-seven, also had the good fortune to be a cousin of Napoleon III, his election was carried through with the minimum amount of international discord, the dynasties in both Berlin and Paris being gratified at their relative's elevation.

Meanwhile in Belgrade, where the politicians never possessed such an accommodating instinct for monarchical susceptibility, the eight-year reign of Prince Michael Obrenović saw the growth of a modern state-machine. He created an efficient and well-equipped army and became a popular hero in 1867 when he secured the final evacuation of the Turkish garrisons from Belgrade and the other fortresses. Indeed, had not Prince Michael been assassinated at Topčider on the outskirts of the city in 1868 in one of those unsolved mysteries which bedevil Serbian history, it is possible that with Russian backing an anti-Turkish league of Balkan peoples would have come into being while Europe was preoccupied by the conflict of France and Prussia. Michael's successor, his cousin Milan Obrenović, was a mere boy of fourteen, subject for the first four years of his reign to a regency of elderly politicians.

There was certainly a marked change in the political character of the Balkan lands in the fifteen years which followed the Congress of Paris. In part this was due to the creation and consolidation of the new Roumania, and to the subjection of Ottoman administration in Bulgaria, Macedonia and Bosnia to the increasingly capricious whims of Sultan Abdul-Aziz; but it also owed much to the attempts by General Ignatiev, Russian ambassador at Constantinople from 1864 to 1877, to harness resentment at Turkish rule to the chariot of Panslavism. Moreover, independently of both Ignatiev and official Russian policy, there was a growth of sentiment in favour of South Slav (i.e. Yugoslav) unity, under the inspiration of Strossmayer and the Croats – for the word

'Yugoslav' was coined in the Zagreb Diet of 1861 – and through the activities of a Serbian conspiratorial youth movement, the Omladina. This organization, more social revolutionary in character than the Czech Sokols and lacking their spirit of moral enlightenment, was regarded with increasing suspicion in both St Petersburg and Zagreb, and in the end it proved too dangerously revolutionary for the Obrenović rulers in Belgrade as well. In many ways conditions in the early 1870s anticipated the better-known situation on the eve of the First World War when the activities of Russian diplomats and of the Serbian secret society known as the 'Black Hand' set a pace which neither the Russian foreign office nor the Serbian government could control.

It was, however, the national awakening of the Bulgarian people which, more than any other cause, transformed the map of the Balkans in the 1870s and riveted the attention of the Great Powers on south-eastern Europe for over a decade. The cultural renaissance of the Bulgars came far later than that of the other South Slav peoples for four main reasons: geographical isolation; educational backwardness, for the first Bulgarian school – a gift to his native town by a retired vodka merchant from Gabrovo – was only opened in 1835; the absence of trading links with the rest of Europe until the end of the 1850s; and confusion over the form of the Bulgarian literary language through a highly academic dispute between rival philologists over the merits of the western and eastern dialects.

Although the Russian army had occupied Bulgaria in 1828–9 it did nothing to encourage an anti-Turkish movement, largely because, in comparison with the Serbs of the previous generation, the Bulgars lacked any regional organization. Even in the Crimean War the Russian government only contemplated encouragement of the Bulgars as an ineffectual afterthought. During the twenty years which followed the war some five hundred Bulgars were educated in Russia, mainly through the patronage of the Moscow Slavonic Benevolent Committee, a body set up in 1858 and subsequently identified in the minds of foreign observers with Panslavism. The education offered to the Bulgars, first in Moscow and later in Odessa, was religious in character, though many students reacted against their tutors and became tainted with nihilism. Contemporaries, and some historians, exaggerated the degree to which Panslavism created and shaped the Bulgarian risorgimento. There was only one Bulgar, Professor Marin Drinov from Kharkov University, who attended the two Panslav gatherings of 1867 and 1868 in Moscow and Prague; he was, after 1878, to achieve distinction as the first Bulgarian minister of education and, indeed, as the person who suggested that Sofia should be the capital of the new principality; but before the Eastern Crisis of 1877–8 Drinov's influence on the Bulgarian exiles was negligible. The leaders of the movement – men like Lyuben Karavelov, Hristo Botiev and the younger but better known Stefan Stambulov – regarded Russian tsardom as an oppressive tyranny and were far more distrustful of Panslav exuberance than, for example, the Czechs under Palacký and Rieger. It is significant that these Bulgarian patriots had found refuge, not in Kharkov or Odessa, but in Bucharest where they were less dependent on Russian patronage. They sought to use Panslavism but not themselves to be used by the Panslavs, a distinction which eluded the statesmen of Western and Central Europe who long failed to perceive the obstinate independence of the Bulgarian national movement.

This Bulgarian desire to determine their own future was shown as early as the 1860s when the long battle against Greek ecclesiastical and cultural dominance reached its climax. The Russians encouraged the Bulgarian demand for some form of representation in the synods of the Orthodox Church and for the use of the Bulgarian language in the liturgy. But the Bulgarian nationalists, while willing to employ Ignatiev as an intermediary with their Turkish overlords, wanted far more than the Panslavs thought they should obtain: they sought a fully independent church, as free from the control of the Oecumenical Patriarch in Constantinople as Henry VIII's Anglican settlement had been from the Pope; and in 1870 they obtained all that they wished. For in that year the Turkish government authorized the setting up of a Bulgarian Exarchate with fourteen dioceses controlled by a Synod which owed no allegiance to the Patriarch. The Turkish authorities no doubt counted on the religious feud between the Bulgars and the Greeks – and, indeed, between the Bulgars and the Serbs, for two of the dioceses were in regions where the population was overwhelmingly Serbian – as a distraction from the political campaign against Ottoman rule; but within a few years the Exarchate had become the power-house of Bulgarian national sentiment, serving the patriotic cause as the bishops and clergy of Greece had done half a century previously.

Yet, though the Bulgarian leaders might have no intention of acting as Russia's catspaws, the Panslav movement continued to pour money into the Balkans, backed by a press campaign in Moscow. Official Russian policy as laid down by the chancellor, Gorchakov, was far more reserved; but since Gorchakov himself had taken the opportunity of the Franco-Prussian war to announce that Russia could no longer be considered bound to observe the clauses in the Treaty of Paris which had demilitarized the Black Sea, it was natural that the other European statesmen should fail to distinguish between Gorchakov's caution and Panslav impetuosity. There was talk, once more, of 'trouble in the spring when the Balkan snows have melted'. Bismarck dreaded a conflict over a part of the world where Prussia had nothing to gain; and it was partly for this reason that in 1872–3 he encouraged a loose agreement between the Three Emperors of Germany, Russia and Austria-Hungary (the first Dreikaiserbund) as a gesture of monarchical solidarity and a guarantee that diplomacy rather than war would seek a solution of any future crisis. Andrássy, too, as foreign minister of the Dual Monarchy, had no wsih for a general post in the Balkan lands; he was as much a champion of the integrity of Turkey as Metternich and Gentz had been, and for much the same reasons. But – with yet another anticipation of 1914 – the Austrian military party did not share the foreign minister's views. To them the narrow strip of Dalmatia was a militarily indefensible finger. The hinterland comprised the Turkish provinces of Bosnia-Herzegovina; and their occupation by the Imperial and Royal army would safeguard the monarchy in south-eastern Europe. It was an argument with which Francis Joseph, still smarting from the loss of his Italian possessions in 1859 and 1866, had considerable sympathy.

The flame of the Great Eastern Crisis of 1875–8 was, in fact, kindled by the Austrian military party in Herzegovina rather than by the Panslavs in Bulgaria. For Francis Joseph spent the month of May 1875 inspecting his Dalmatian garrisons; he received deputations from the Catholic minority in Herzegovina and paid a visit to Prince Nikita of Montenegro in his capital of Cetinje. The Slav population of Herzegovina, suffering from an inequitable taxation system and backward agrarian conditions, already believed that they could count on sympathetic support from Russia; now they hoped for assistance from the Austrians as well. Within a month of the Emperor's tour the Herzegovinian Christians were in revolt; and by the middle of August the Bosnian Serbs, encouraged by the Omladina, had also risen against their Turkish masters. In Belgrade demonstrators urged Prince Milan to declare war on Turkey and hundreds of Russian volunteers journeyed across Roumania and into Serbia, while in Vienna Andrássy tried, not without success, to hold back the military party and began the slow process of finding a diplomatic settlement acceptable to the Great Powers, to the Sultan and to the rebels.

The Bulgarian Central Revolutionary Committee, with headquarters in Bucharest, was not yet ready for a full-scale insurrection although an abortive rising flared up briefly in September 1875. But as first one side and then the other rejected the proposals of the diplomats, the Bulgarian exiles began to plan for a major rising to take place in the spring of 1876. Agents were ferried across the Danube from Giurgiu to foster discontent among the peasantry. When the revolt broke out the Turks were already on the alert and in six weeks of bloodshed Turkish irregulars known as Bashi-Bazouks ruthlessly suppressed every sign of Bulgarian national life; somewhere between 12,000 to 15,000 men, women and children perished.

These activities of the Bashi-Bazouks and the Circassian irregulars stirred the conscience of the West and thereby changed the character of the crisis. Western journalists had penetrated the Bulgarian lands and reported what they saw and heard; from the end of June onwards the readers of the *Daily News* in Britain and the *New York Times* across the Atlantic were spared few details of massacre, arson and rape. The Russian press, carefully fed by handouts from Ignatiev, fanned Panslav enthusiasm to fever pitch. In Britain Gladstone's famous pamphlet, *The Bulgarian Horrors and the Question of the East*, was published at the beginning of September and over 40,000 copies were distributed in the first week; while a cheap Russian translation issued in the same month sold over 10,000 copies. What Gladstone termed in his diary 'the eastern sky full of storm and underlight' cast a sombre reflection that winter to the west and to the north. No other nationality – not even the Greeks – had won such sympathetic publicity as the Bulgars.

Meanwhile, in Serbia, Prince Milan had run into grave difficulties. For more than twelve months after the first rising he had remained at peace, and official advice from St Petersburg continued to urge restraint. But Milan, who in his twenty-two years of life had acquired an impressive list of vices unredeemed by political understanding, was hardly his own master. Ristić, his chief minister, was a shrewd bully; and the Russian consul-general, an essentially weak man intimidated by the Panslavs, breathed fire and flame with all the insidious bellicosity of a frock-coated civilian. Far more menacing was the crowd in the Belgrade streets, jeopardizing the throne in the fervour of its demonstrations against the Turkish flag which, by an odd dispensation of international law, still flew over the fortress of the Kalemegdan even though the last Turkish troops had left nine years before. At last, on 30 June 1876, Milan joined Prince Nikita of Montenegro in declaring war on Turkey. The crowd delighted the painters of patriotic canvasses by pulling down the hated crescent flag, and the Serbian army, led by Russian volunteers, marched valiantly into battle.

The campaign was a fiasco: from the outset, Russian and Serbian officers failed to cooperate. The Russian general, Mikhail Chernyaev, was so anxious to pose as the Serbian Garibaldi that he ignored strategy and tactics. The Turks gained success after success; and by the middle of September Milan was forced to sue for peace and beseech the Great Powers to save Serbia from Turkish vengeance. The wisdom of Michael Obrenović had won respect for Serbia throughout Europe; the misadventures of his young successor relegated her to an inferior position. Henceforth Russian patronage was bestowed almost exclusively on

Bulgaria, a country which had the strategic advantage for the Russians of lying astride the main land-route to the Straits. On 11 November 1876, Tsar Alexander II, who rarely committed himself to public statements, made a warlike speech in Moscow: he castigated the Serbs, praised the Montenegrins and spoke of 'our volunteers, many of whom have paid with their blood for the cause of Slavdom'. 'I much desire,' he concluded, 'that we shall reach a general agreement. . . . If this is not attained . . . then I firmly intend to act independently. . . . May God help us to fulfil our sacred mission.'

There remained another six months of diplomatic effort although there could be little doubt of the outcome. Already, in the previous July, Gorchakov and Andrássy had met at Reichstadt and reached a verbal agreement for the division of the Balkans, after a Russo-Turkish war, into Austrian and Russian spheres of influence (though there are discrepancies between the two versions of the understanding). Further secret agreements – the so-called 'Budapest Conventions' of January 1877 – were more precise: the Austrians were assured a free hand in Bosnia-Herzegovina in return for benevolent neutrality in a Russo-Turkish war; and, although it was understood that Bulgaria would be set up as an independent state, there was a formal guarantee that 'the establishment of a great compact State, Slav or otherwise, is out of the question.' Meanwhile, Bismarck was using the creaking machinery of the Dreikaiserbund to avoid a clash between his two main partners and secure a peaceful outcome to the crisis; and the Beaconsfield government, though implacably hostile to the Russians and constantly minimizing the reports of atrocities, urged the Turks to satisfy liberal consciences by a pledge of internal reform. But Sultan Abdul-Hamid, who had succeeded the discredited Sultan Abdul-Aziz in the previous September, played a devious game, possibly through a failure to understand the limits of British support: in January 1877 he denied the right of a conference of ambassadors at Constantinople to interfere in Turkey's domestic affairs; and in April he finally rejected an Anglo-Russian settlement which would have permitted international supervision of reform within the Ottoman lands. The Russians thereupon lost patience and on 24 April 1877 went to war with Turkey.

Bulgaria was the main theatre of military operations but there was also a campaign in the Caucasus while to the west the Serbs and Montenegrins once more took the field. The Roumanians, too, had wished to assist the Russians, but since the Russians sought the recovery of Bessarabia as part of the peace settlement, their offers were treated coolly; Prince Charles was told that Roumania might go to war provided that he placed the army under Russian command, a request which he rejected (as he was meant to do).

All seemed at first to go well for the Russians and by the middle of July they controlled the Balkan range, with the advance cavalry astride the vital Shipka Pass. But the Turks held out in the town of Plevna, throwing back three Russian assaults throughout the autumn and early winter. So hard-pressed were the Russians that, swallowing their pride, they had to accept the cooperation of a Roumanian expeditionary force of thirty thousand men under Prince Charles's command. It was not until December that the Russians finally captured Plevna and advanced on Sofia and Plovdiv (which was one of the strongest centres of Bulgarian national sentiment). At last, on 20 January 1878, Russian cavalry entered Adrianople (Edirne); with the road open to Constantinople, the Turks concluded an armistice.

Reports that the Russians were contemplating the occupation of the Turkish capital itself brought Britain and Russia to the brink of war and led the British to send a fleet into the Sea of Marmora. The Russians thereupon sent 10,000 men to occupy the town of San Stefano, which was on the shores of the Sea of Marmora and only eight miles off Constantinople. In London a fickle public opinion, swiftly forgetting the 'Turkish butchers' of 1876, followed Beaconsfield and a music-hall song in an exercise of premature brinkmanship. The atmosphere was far too strained for a lasting solution of the Eastern Question, but no incidents took place between the two Great Powers.

It was at San Stefano that, on 3 March 1878, a Russo-Turkish treaty was signed with Ignatiev and his chief deputy, Nelidov, dictating the terms of peace. The Turks were forced to make far reaching concessions: the complete independence of Roumania, Serbia and Montenegro was formally recognized, each state receiving an additional territorial gain; and, with utter disregard of the Budapest Conventions, an autonomous Bulgaria was created, so large that it straddled the Balkans. This 'Great Bulgaria' was to include not merely the lands where the national revolt had flared up, but all western Thrace and Macedonia, apart from the port of Salonika; the new state stretched so far to the west that it even climbed the foothills of the Albanian Mountains. Ignatiev and the Panslavs appeared to have gained a total victory; but it was one which ignored Austrian ambitions in the western Balkans and British sensitivity over the Aegean seaboard. It was a treaty which would never have been accepted in Vienna or London; and even in St Petersburg Gorchakov felt unable to defend Ignatiev's achievement.

The four months of diplomatic negotiation which separate San Stefano from the Treaty of Berlin belong as much to the general history of international relations as to the Lands Between. By the time the Great Powers gathered in Congress at Berlin all had been settled but the final details. 'Great Bulgaria' was seen as a stillborn child of Ignatiev's ambition. Macedonia remained in Turkish hands while the area around Plovdiv became the semi-autonomous province of 'Eastern Roumelia'. Autonomous Bulgaria was limited to the region between the Danube and the crest of the Balkan range. The Austrians received the right to occupy Bosnia-Herzegovina (which remained technically part of the Ottoman Empire) and to police the corridor separating Serbia and Montenegro, the Sanjak of Novipazar. There was little change in the terms relating to Roumania; a formal recognition of independence and the acquisition of the Dobrudja and the Danube delta in return for the retrocession to Russia of Bessarabia. Serbia and Montenegro, too, received confirmation as independent states: Serbia gained more territory to the south-east of Niš than she had been promised by the San Stefano treaty; and Montenegro, assured three small coastal villages by the terms of San Stefano, did indeed gain an outlet to the Adriatic at Antivari (now called Bar) but only on condition that the harbour there should never be developed as a naval base. The Turks pledged themselves to improve conditions for the Christians remaining in the Ottoman Empire; they also agreed to negotiate frontier rectifications with Greece – an undertaking which the Turks fulfilled only under considerable British pressure but which, in 1881, secured for Greece the richly fertile plain of Thessaly and a small region in Epirus. Apart from these changes in Europe, the Sultan was forced to pay a heavy indemnity to the Russians and to cede considerable territory in the Caucasus; a separate convention, not mentioned in the Treaty of Berlin, permitted Britain to garrison the Turkish island of Cyprus.

Although the Berlin settlement freed the Balkans from major war for over a third of a century, the Congress did not fully satisfy any of the participants – except, perhaps, Bismarck who sought nothing from it but prestige. Tsar Alexander II testily complained that it had been 'a European coalition against Russia'; while to Andrássy and to Salisbury (Beaconsfield's Foreign Secretary) the Berlin Treaty had recognized so many concessions to the principle of nationality that the Ottoman Empire seemed no longer a viable proposition. Each of the smaller powers was discontented. The Roumanians were bitterly angry at the way in which Bessarabia was wrenched from their control and relations between Bucharest and St Petersburg remained cool; Prince Charles – or, as he became in 1881, King Carol I – ostentatiously cultivated his kinsfolk in the German courts and moved gradually into the orbit of Bismarck's diplomacy. The Serbs felt that they had been thrown by the Russians to the Austrians, with whom they were incensed over the occupation of Bosnia-Herzegovina. Even the Montenegrins felt cheated, though

D

Prince Nikita used the opportunity of disorders on his frontier in 1880 to occupy the port of Ulcinj, more or less when the Great Powers were not looking.

But the most important effect was in Bulgaria. The Bulgars were, of course, disappointed that the frontiers of San Stefano received no permanence. Their attainment continued to tempt the more chauvinistic Bulgarian politicians into rash action until the Second World War; and even in communist Bulgaria there are, at times, odd echoes of distant controversies. But the Bulgars did, at least, have a state machine; and at Trnovo in February 1879 their political leaders drafted a remarkably liberal constitution which provided for a parliament (Sobranjie) elected by almost universal manhood suffrage. The example of democratic progress afforded by the Bulgarian Principality to Eastern Roumelia (where the Sultan retained considerable powers) stimulated the growth of a revolutionary movement in Plovdiv which sought unification of the two parts of the country.

The Bulgars themselves were grateful to the Russians. Monuments to the heroes of liberation were erected in most of the Bulgarian towns and on the heights of the Shipka Pass. The Russian army had sustained more than two hundred thousand casualties in the campaign of 1877–8; and the Russians, for their part, considered that they were entitled to take decisions on the future development of the Bulgarian State. Alexander of Battenberg, the German Prince elected to the Bulgarian throne in 1879, was a relative of the Tsarina – his dynastic connexions were as irreproachable as those of his neighbour, King Carol of Roumania. But Alexander had a powerful personality; he sensed that the Bulgarian Liberals would never be content with a passive acceptance of Russian domination. At the same time, Alexander was not willing to allow the politicians the free hand they had gained by the Trnovo Constitution. By 1885 the Prince had become a somewhat isolated figure: distrusted by the members of the former revolutionary movement; and less pliant than the Russian diplomatic service had assumed at the time of his election. He particularly disliked the Russian general who had been forced on the Bulgars as war minister; and, like almost every one of his subjects, he resented the way in which the Russians had secured every command in the Bulgarian army above the rank of captain. 'All the scum of Russia has taken refuge here and tainted the whole country,' he once wrote indignantly from his new capital.

It was at this point, with the Russians regarding Alexander as an enemy and the Bulgarian liberals distrusting him as an autocrat, that the revolutionaries in Plovdiv struck; on 18 September 1885 they declared the union of the two Bulgarias, and the feeble administration in Eastern Roumelia did nothing to check them. Alexander, with Stefan Stambulov pressing him, accepted the *fait accompli*.

The Bulgarian Crisis of 1885–6 is one of the most curious in Balkan history. The Russians promptly withdrew all their officers from the Bulgarian army. The knowledge that the Russians had abandoned their favoured protégé among the Balkan nations was an irresistible temptation for King Milan of Serbia – the royal title had been assumed in 1882. Two months after the Plovdiv coup Milan sent the Serbian army to invade Bulgaria; within a week it had been defeated at Slivnitza by the Bulgars – despite the absence of senior officers – and Niš was in Bulgarian hands. Only threats from Austria dissuaded the Bulgars from advancing even farther into the country and marching on Belgrade itself.

In February 1886 the Turkish government recognized Alexander as governor-general of Eastern Roumelia, thereby making possible a personal union of the two Bulgarias although not, as yet, a full political union. In August a Russian conspiracy led to a palace revolution in Sofia and forced Alexander to abdicate; less than a fortnight later, he returned. But there seemed a strong possibility that he would be assassin-ated by either the Russians or the Bulgarian revolutionaries. The poor man made one last effort to secure a reconciliation with the Tsar, but this gesture made him so unpopular with his subjects that, only eleven days after coming back to his capital, he abdicated for the second time in a month and made an abrupt but positively final departure from the country, which was left under the control of Stambulov. The Russians thereupon broke off diplomatic relations with the principality which they had done so much to create only a few years previously. At last in July 1887 the Sobranjie offered the Bulgarian throne to Prince Ferdinand of Saxe-Coburg, an officer in Francis Joseph's army. It seemed, at the time, improbable that he would be ruler of a united Bulgaria for more than a few months: he was a Roman Catholic; he was faced by the implacable hostility of Russia; and he had come to a country which lacked any institutional permanence. It says much for Ferdinand's shrewdness, if not for his political morality, that he should have remained on the throne until November 1918, and have lived to see his dynasty survive until 1946 (when, for a second time, Russian liberators had swept down from the north).

These events in Sofia, although seeming in an eighty-year-old retrospect like a vintage farce on some Ruritanian stage, form a watershed in the history of south-eastern Europe. Although nothing could destroy the natural sympathy of the Balkan peoples for 'Mother Russia' there is little doubt that the crisis of 1885–7 marked their emancipation from blind allegiance to the Panslav myth. For the first time a newly-created state had insisted that independence must imply full freedom to express national policy. The statesmen of the Great Powers began to modify their views: in St Petersburg it seemed as if only the military occupation of Constantinople and the Straits would secure mastery of the Black Sea; and, conversely, in London it no longer appeared axiomatic to prop up the rotten edifice of the Turkish State as a means of keeping Russia away from the Mediterranean. There were changes, too, in the attitudes of the businessmen of Germany and Austria-Hungary: new states were new clients; the Danube, which had so often served as an invasion route, was now open for commercial competition. If south-eastern Europe was to enjoy two generations of peace, this was as much the achievement of the industrialists and manufacturers as of the wisdom of the politicians. But with nationalism no less divisive than in 1848 and with a new conflict beginning below the surface between the exploited and their economic masters, the prospect for a lasting settlement in these lands remained as elusive as ever.

5
The Heyday of Nationalism

Nationalism in nineteenth-century Europe was always double faced: on one side there were movements of popular insurrection seeking general recognition of patriotic desires; and on the other an introspective identification of virtues which seemed to mark off the inheritors of one tradition from their less fortunate neighbours. Sometimes both aspects were combined in the same act of national self-expression, as for example in the Janus-like patriotism of Kossuth. But more commonly the distinction may be seen in retrospect to lie between generations, separating the young people of the 1880s and 1890s from their fathers and grandfathers. All too frequently the new aggressive exclusiveness seems to have been the product of partial education and social resentment. Confidence in human progress grew side by side with a narrowing of human sympathies: and therein lies, perhaps, the greatest tragedy of modern Europe.

In the West this phenomenon was manifested in two ways: the willing acceptance by the masses of the cross of imperial responsibility; and a belief in the righteousness of state action free from restraints of morality and justice. Thus if Britain had a Rhodes and a Milner, France had a Barrès and a Maurras. In Central and Eastern Europe, however, a similar state of mind produced different ideologies. There, established nationalities demanded loyalty on a basis of discipline and uniformity: hence along the western frontiers of the Tsar's empire 'Russification' served as the chosen instrument of state policy; and in the heart of the continent the new concept of 'Pan-Germanism' challenged the whole character of Habsburg rule. In time a contempt for diversity spread also among the newly recognized nationalities, erecting a glass curtain of incomprehension between Jews and Gentiles, Catholics and Orthodox and even Patriarchate and Exarchate. The favoured epithet of political ambition was 'Greater' – in Linz and Vienna demagogues spoke of 'Greater Germany,' in Bucharest of 'Greater Roumania,' in Belgrade of 'Greater Serbia'. The world was to reap the folly of their words in the new century; for it was into this environment that Adolf Hitler was born in 1889, Ion Antonescu in 1882 and Gavrilo Princip in 1894.

The region in which aggressive nationalism first sought to curb the will of an historic people was Poland. In the 1870s and even more in the 1880s the Poles in the old 'Congress Kingdom' were subjected to a deliberate policy which aimed at turning them into Russians in loyalty and in thought. At the same time their compatriots in the Prussian provinces were in conflict with Bismarck first over religion – for these were the years of the struggle of Church and State in Germany known as the Kulturkampf – and subsequently over the provision of government subsidies to enable Germans to purchase Polish estates, a process of eastward colonization by the Junker landowners. In both Prussian Poland and Russian Poland there were conflicts over education: thus in May 1874 the notorious Prussian minister of education, Falk, insisted that German should be the normal means of instruction, although a curious escape clause in the regulations permitted Polish to be used 'if no other language was understood'; and in 1885 the Warsaw administration promulgated a law insisting that all teaching in primary schools must be in Russian, apart from classes of instruction in Catholicism and lessons in which Polish was studied as a foreign language.

The Catholic hierarchy, always defenders of the Polish heritage, remained a problem for both governments: the Prussians replaced Polish bishops by Germans; and the Russians despatched, somewhat half-heartedly, cultural missionaries in the vain hope of winning, at least among the peasantry, converts to Orthodoxy. The Russians had far more success in their insidious policy of playing off the Poles against other racial groups: it was easy enough to fan Polish resentment of Jewish traders and business-men, and to encourage the Poles in their traditional assumption of superiority over the Lithuanians around Vilna and the Ukrainians in the south-east. Yet restrictions on the press and on rights of assembly fell equally heavily on every national group. In this respect Austrian Galicia, although economically so much more backward than the other two regions, seemed a haven of liberalism; and it was there alone that specifically Polish political parties continued to flourish.

The tragedies of 1831 and 1863 in Congress Poland and of 1846 in Galicia had taught the Polish patriots a new circumspection, a realistic appraisal of what was possible in contrast to the older romanticism of revolt. There was, in consequence, some inclination to accept as a political programme the doctrine of *Trojloyalyzm* ('Triple Loyalty') first advocated by the more conservative landowners in Cracow and Lvov in the 1860s. Triple Loyalty implied obedience to each of the three empires ruling the Polish lands, not as an act of treason to the national cause but in the belief that the contribution made by the Poles to social life would be so much greater than anything their foreign masters could offer that they would themselves in time absorb their oppressors. This argument made good sense in Russian Poland where rapid industrialization guaranteed responsible work for any Pole of intelligence and steady employment for the less able. It made even better sense in Galicia, for there were opportunities for Poles in government and administration within the Austrian Empire whereas the Russians firmly barred all Poles from bureaucratic posts. But it made no sense at all in Prussian Poland, where the superior technical knowledge and administrative efficiency of the Germans assured that the Poles were regarded as natural tillers of the soil or predestined factory fodder.

Curiously enough, Triple Loyalty was accepted as a political tactic by two markedly contrasting revolutionary leaders: Roman Dmowski, who founded the National Democratic Party in 1897, urged reconciliation with Russia as a method of promoting the political education of his people; and Rosa Luxemburg, the outstanding Polish Marxist, argued at exactly the same time that the Polish workers could achieve political mastery solely in cooperation with the socialists of Germany, of Austria-Hungary or of Russia since each of these states possessed a balanced industrial economy and geographically extensive markets. Only a small section of the Polish Marxist intelligentsia was prepared to accept the subtleties of Rosa Luxemburg's logic. Most of the socialists placed Polish independence as a prerequisite of social democracy; this nationalistic wing was led by Jozef Pilsudski, who as a student at Kharkov University had been arrested in 1887 for subversive agitation and exiled to Siberia for five years. His implacable hostility to everything Russian led Pilsudski to advocate cooperation with the Austrians, a policy which gained wide acceptance in the eight years preceding the First World War.

The Russian administration in Warsaw was first puzzled and later reassured by the policy of Triple Loyalty. It was seen as proof of the effectiveness of Russification, an attitude of mind which hardened rather than eased after Nicholas II succeeded his father as Tsar in 1894. Inevitably the Poles participated in the revolutionary agitation of 1905 and in June there was a week of rioting in the textile centre of Lodz, but significantly the actions of the Polish workers formed part of a general wave of strikes throughout European Russia; there was little specifically nationalistic in their demonstrations. For two years the policy of Russification was slightly relaxed: the Poles were allowed to set up private schools in which all instruction was to be in the Polish language. But at the end of 1907 even this meagre concession was withdrawn, and under Stolypin the Poles were once again ordered to turn themselves into dutiful Russian citizens. By 1914 it had become clear that nothing of lasting value could be attained under tsardom; Triple Loyalty was interpreted, not as a gesture of reconciliation, but as a token of surrender.

In Prussian Poland the fall of Bismarck in 1890 at first eased restrictions on the non-German inhabitants but under Bulow conditions became as oppressive as ever. With the turn of the century the Ostmarkverein, an organization which aimed at the attainment of completely German supremacy in the social and economic life of Prussia's 'Eastern Marchlands', secured the passage of irksome regulations limiting the use of the Polish language, not only in schools, but in any public meeting. There were a number of strikes among the Polish school-children, who were punished with savage discipline, notably in 1906. Such an early and vivid introduction to the conflicts of nationalities helps to explain, if not to excuse, the bitterness felt by this generation towards the Germans when it reached manhood after the First World War.

Pan-Germanism in 'Cisleithania' – as the non-Hungarian part of the Dual Monarchy was called – was different in origin and character from the intensive Germanization practised in Prussian Poland. It was first expounded by George von Schönerer, whose father, a Viennese railway baron, had left a considerable fortune for his son to squander on political adventures. Schönerer was elected to the Austrian Parliament as early as 1873 as representative of the frontier area around Linz, the region where Hitler's parents were so soon to settle; but it was not until 1882 that Schönerer achieved wide recognition as the main draftsman of a manifesto of Pan-German policy, the so-called 'Linz Programme'. Schönerer wished all the areas within the Habsburg Empire which had been included in the old German Confederation to unite with the new German Reich under the Hohenzollern sovereign in Berlin. Bohemia, Moravia and the Slovene districts in the south were thus to be subjected to total German rule, their Slav inhabitants reduced to the status of second-class citizens, like the Poles in the Prussian lands (and, indeed, in the Congress Kingdom). The rest of Cisleithania might join the Hungarian Kingdom, an operation which, incidentally, envisaged the transference of nine million Slavs to Magyar rule. To achieve the Linz Programme Schönerer founded a specifically Pan-German political party, the Deutschnationaler Verein, an organization pledged to purge the 'East Mark' of Jewish racial impurities, the compromising treachery of the Habsburgs and the selfish indulgence of big business. A network of 'defensive leagues' was established to safeguard German interests, especially in the Czech lands: the 'German School Union' of 1880, the 'Bohemian Forest League' and the 'North Moravian League' of 1884, and (for the Slovene lands) the 'South Mark' of 1889. By the end of the century there were over a thousand local associations within the Austrian Empire devoting their energies to upholding the purity of German national sentiment; their teaching and influence remained a force in the politics of Central Europe until the collapse of the Third Reich in 1945.

So long as Bismarck was in power, Schönerer and his supporters received no encouragement from within Germany. The alliance he had concluded in 1879 formed the keystone of Bismarck's foreign policy and he had no wish to embarrass his partner by patronizing such fanatical troublemakers. But Wilhelmine Germany knew no such inhibitions. A Pan-German Union, backed by influential members of the Reichstag and linked with the all-powerful Navy League, was set up in Berlin in 1894; and it seems never to have hesitated over interfering in Austrian affairs, to the chagrin both of Francis Joseph and his heir, Francis Ferdinand.

From 1879 to 1893 the prime minister of Austria was a childhood friend of the Emperor, Count Edward Taaffe. His government, a coalition known as the 'Iron Ring,' was not unsympathetic to the Slav peoples of the empire. Taaffe wanted no single nationality to predominate; 'In Austria no one may be squeezed against the wall,' he once declared. At the very start of his ministry he succeeded in persuading the elected Czech deputies to come to Vienna and at last participate in the work of the parliament. The Iron Ring showed its good intentions towards the Czechs in three ways: it issued a series of language decrees permitting the use of either German or Czech in administration and at law within Bohemia; it modified the franchise requirements for elections to the Diet of Bohemia so as to give Czech voters more control; and, most important of all, in 1882 it authorized the division of the University of Prague into two separate institutions, one German and the other Czech. Inevitably the Czech university became an intellectual wellspring for all the Slavs of the empire apart from the Poles (whose academic needs were already met in Cracow); and the presence of Tómaš Masaryk as Professor of Philosophy ensured that while the university might be Czech in spirit it would never be narrowly chauvinistic in scholarship. These concessions to the hated Czechs, coming as they did at a time when the Slav birth-rate was so much higher than the German, infuriated Schönerer and his fractious followers.

Relations between the Czechs and Germans worsened year by year in the last decade of the old century; and the fault was not entirely Schönerer's. In Bohemia a new generation, acutely conscious of the pace and competition of industrial society, was losing patience with the political conservatism of Rieger and the other veterans from the days of Palacký. A 'Young Czech' Party, radical and militant, gradually supplanted Rieger's 'Old Czechs'; and in 1890, after Rieger and Taaffe had worked out a complicated educational and legal compromise (the *Punktationen*), the 'Young Czechs' rejected the plan and went on to win striking successes in the 1891 elections. The 'Young Czechs' responded in kind to Schonerer's provocation. There was so much rioting in Prague that the city seemed on the verge of civil war, especially after a

D*

language decree (promulgated in 1897 and hastily withdrawn in 1899) appeared to concede most of the Czech demands. The Pan-German agitators brought strange undertones to the demonstrations; there was an ugly outcrop of anti-semitism; and a Protestant secession 'Away from Rome' in anger at the alleged anti-Germanism of the Catholic Church – an ironic development in the land of Huss. Nor was violence limited to Bohemia. Even in Vienna the behaviour of the deputies made a mockery of parliamentary institutions: inkpots were hurled about the chamber with the abandon of riotous schoolboys; and there was so much brawling, shouting and singing that the sessions had often to be suspended. 'We have become the laughing-stock of the whole world,' complained Francis Joseph to a Czech deputy in 1900.

This near-anarchy had important consequences on the whole structure of the Dual Monarchy. So long as Taaffe was in power Francis Joseph was forced, almost without realizing what he was doing, to appear as an impartial umpire between the nationalities. The fourteen years of the Iron Ring raised the prestige of the dynasty and of parliament. But when Taaffe fell in 1893 he was followed by a succession of phantom Austrian prime ministers who passed in and out of office with almost French alacrity. There were eight different heads of government in seven years; and none were distinguished in anything more than the resonance of their names and titles. Administration was carried on by making use of paragraph fourteen of the constitution, a provision for the Emperor to rule by decree in an emergency. The first years of the new century saw a slight improvement in political behaviour; and in 1907 an extensive measure of reform, including the introduction of universal suffrage for parliamentary elections (although not for elections to the Diet or in local government), offered a promise of democratic rule; but within a short time Czechs and Germans once again vied with each other in obstructional tactics, paralysing the political administration of all Cisleithania.

Thus by 1908, when Francis Joseph celebrated the Diamond Jubilee of his accession, he had come to despair of parliament and, in particular, of the incessant squabbling of the national groups. The Pan-Germans continued to look for salvation to Berlin; and the 'Young Czechs,' led by Karel Kramář – for Masaryk had repudiated their militancy – drifted into new dependence on Russia, threatening an uprising of the Slav peoples if Austria-Hungary should find herself at war with the Franco-Russian combination. There remained three political parties which were prepared to uphold the territorial form of the Dual Monarchy, although only one was committed to the existing structure. This 'government party', as it were, was the Christian Socialists, clericalist, anti-semitic and petty bourgeois in spirit; they were dominated by the most respected of Vienna's burgomasters, Karl Lueger, and backed by the heir to the throne, Francis

Ferdinand. Their bitterest opponents, the Social Democrats, believed that the Empire was a natural economic unit which would make sense if transformed into a socialist state and freed from the irrelevant middle-class feuding over national rights. And finally there were the Czech 'Realists,' led by Masaryk, who maintained that, despite all the faults of the existing system, a genuinely federalized Austrian Empire was a European necessity in order to hold a balance between the Hohenzollerns and the Romanovs. None of these parties held much appeal for Francis Joseph. In his later years the Emperor inevitably reverted to type. More and more he depended for advice on Crown nominees, not on parliamentary leaders. He listened, as in his youth, to the officer corps and its spokesmen on the general staff. Unfortunately there was no prospect of saner counsels from his ministers in the Hungarian half of the Dual Monarchy.

The spirit of Magyar rule, under the constitution of 1867, was determined by one family. From 1875 to 1890 Kálmán Tisza dominated the Kingdom of which he was prime minister, and even out of office he continued to exert an influence greater than that of any other politician. When he died in 1902, his son, István, succeeded to his father's reputation; and, although he headed governments for a shorter span of time – less than six years in all – he, too, personified in his political life the faults and virtues of the dualist system.

The Tiszas were a Magyar gentry family, not aristocrats, but patriarchs of a small country estate near Debrecen. They were strictly and austerely Calvinist, gaining from their faith a terrifying sense of the righteousness of their mission. Kálmán Tisza founded and led the Hungarian Liberal Party, an organization pledged to maintenance of the Ausgleich and to fiscal reform. There is no doubt that the material prosperity of the Hungarian Kingdom increased remarkably under his direction: the budget was balanced; industry was stimulated, not only in Budapest, but in non-Magyar areas such as Slovakia and Transylvania; the railway network was completed, all the main lines being taken under direct or indirect state control; the value of trade passing through Hungary's one seaport, Fiume, increased twelvefold in fifteen years and there was even a regular transatlantic liner service to New York; while on the Danube the Hungarians gained a potential stranglehold on commercial traffic, especially after the government in Budapest assumed responsibility for constructing the navigation canal to avoid the rapids at the Iron Gates.

Tisza was himself the supreme national salesman. In May 1873 the Viennese had held an ambitious International Exhibition to advertise the new wealth of the Habsburg Empire; but, with a characteristically endearing miscalculation, they chose the very month in which their city –

and all Central Europe with it – was hit by what was at that time an unprecedented economic depression. Yet when Tisza staged an Industrial Exhibition in Budapest twelve years later no shadow of disaster was allowed to fall over the pavilions. Budapest was placed as firmly on the commercial map of Europe as London had been in 1851 or Paris in 1855. The old romantic image of agrarian Hungary as a land of gypsy music and colourful costume was pushed into the background by this pulsating national machine.

Although in parliament Tisza was constantly hounded both by the chauvinistic aristocracy and by the implacable Kossuthists, he was himself convinced of the superiority of Magyar civilization and determined to keep both the Slavs and the Roumanians in a position of servitude. From his first months in office he flagrantly ignored the principles of the Nationalities Law of 1868. Magyarization was promoted as ardently as Russification in Congress Poland, and often with the same weapons; instruction in all state schools had to be in the Magyar tongue; in Inner Hungary (though not until after 1906 in Croatia) all railway workers and postal employees were required to speak Magyar rather than German or the language of one of the subject peoples; and cultural associations, using public funds, promoted the Hungarian way of life in the 'mixed' regions of Slovakia and Transylvania while all Slovak and Roumanian societies were suppressed. Protests by the non-Hungarian members of the Budapest Parliament could make no impression on a man of Tisza's narrow convictions. When a *prečani* Serb deputy challenged the government's right to confiscate funds collected for cultural purposes from the Slovak nation, Tisza replied, 'There is no Slovak nation.' And when a deputy from Transylvania asked Tisza why non-Magyars should not be taught their national history as well as the history of the Hungarian people, he was blandly told that it was impossible for there to be a 'national' history of those who lived in Hungary but were not Magyars.

But Tisza did at least permit the foundation (in 1881) of a Roumanian National Party. His successors were far less tolerant. Roumanian leaders who had sought to present a memorandum of grievances to Francis Joseph were ostracized as though guilty of treachery; and in May 1894 they were arrested on a charge of 'incitement against the Magyar nationality,' put on trial at Kolozsvár (Cluj) before a jury composed exclusively of Hungarians, and duly sent to prison. The Roumanian National Party was thereupon dissolved by order of the Hungarian minister of the interior: but it was allowed to re-constitute itself early in 1906 and the victims of the Kolozsvár verdict subsequently enjoyed a special status among their compatriots, and among liberals throughout Europe, as martyrs for a people's rights.

Croatia was, of course, in a different constitutional relationship to the government than either the Slovaks or the Roumanians of Transylvania. The first five years of the Nagoda had been marked by frequent disturbances in Zagreb and by a mutiny (in October 1871) among Croatian troops along the old military frontier; but in 1873, as a gesture of appeasement, the Hungarian government accepted the appointment as Ban of a Croat, the distinguished scholar and poet, Ivan Mazuranić, and so long as he was in office no attempts were made to impose Magyarization. In 1883, however, there was an outburst of rioting in Zagreb, precipitated in part by the tactlessness of minor officials and in part by the general grievance against heavy taxation and an unfair franchise. Tisza, fearing that the Croats would set an example for the other nationalities, responded with his customary firmness: troops were sent into the streets; the constitution was suspended; and, in place of Ban Mazuranić, he appointed a kinsman, Count Karl Khuen-Hedérváry, a Hungarian magnate with large estates in Croatia.

For twenty years Khuen-Hedérváry governed Croatia with an iron will and an astute appraisal of the strength and weakness of its inhabitants. Like Tisza in Inner Hungary, he saw that the material wealth of Croatia increased: the annual agricultural yield looked impressive and he could rightly claim to have provided the Croats with more schools, better roads and efficient railways (assuming, of course, that the traveller could read Magyar sign-boards and find his way through a Magyar timetable). But any patriotic venture in letters or the arts was muzzled as tightly as the press, despite the opposition of the redoubtable, though aged, Bishop Strossmayer. Khuen-Hedérváry's real power came, however, from the subtlety with which he played off the despised Serb minority against the Croats: concessions were given to the Serbian Orthodox Church; Serbs, and not Croats, filled vacancies in minor administrative posts; and, in the most explosive topic of all, the Serbs were even permitted some independence over educational policy. Much of the Croatian national animus was thereby directed against the Serbs rather than their Hungarian masters, an effective way of stifling the nascent Yugoslav movement. In 1895, while Francis Joseph was on an official visit to Zagreb, Croatian students ransacked Serbian homes and desecrated an Orthodox Church, burning a Serbian flag before passing on to the equally congenial task of ripping up the red, white and green tricolour of Hungary. The seeds which Khuen-Hedérváry had sown with such irresponsible mischief raised a crop of hatred which was harvested between the two wars by the Yugoslav Kingdom.

Yet, in general, the Croats remained loyal to the Habsburg dynasty, believing – like the Roumanians in Transylvania – that redress would come in time from Vienna. Until his tragic death at Mayerling in 1889 they had hopes of Crown Prince Rudolf, whose comprehensive ragbag of intellectual sympathies found room for both the Magyars and the Croats; and, after his death, they turned to Archduke Francis Ferdinand who made no secret of his hostility to everything Hungarian and who was said to be vaguely federalist in sentiment.

Politically, the majority of the Croatian deputies in the Sabor belonged to an organization known as the 'Party of Pure Right,' led from 1897 onwards by Joseph Frank and often called, quite simply, the 'Frankists'. The 'Pure Right' was fanatically anti-Serbian and ostentatiously Habsburg in loyalty; it sought a re-organized monarchy in which all the South Slav areas in the empire (including Bosnia-Herzegovina and Fiume) would be placed on an equal footing with Hungary and the Austrian lands; but – and in this it fell short of Strossmayer's ideal – it vehemently rejected any suggestion that Serbia and Montenegro might be brought into the South Slav brotherhood, though it claimed some overwhelmingly Serbian districts as part of a 'Greater Croatia'. Political consciousness developed slowly in the rural areas until the foundation in 1902 by the brothers Joseph and Stjepan Radić of the Croat Peasant Party, a body specifically designed to safeguard the interests of the agricultural proletariat and reflecting both its suspicion of urban sophistication and its narrowly superstitious Catholicism. The Radić brothers, too, desired the preservation of the Habsburg State; as dutiful Catholics they deplored every concession to the Serbian Orthodox Church – Stjepan Radić had been exiled from Zagreb after the disorders of 1895 – but they were equally opposed to the Magyar supremacy and put forward nebulous schemes for the division of the Empire into no less than five autonomous kingdoms, each owing allegiance to the same Habsburg monarch.

When Khuen-Hedérváry finally left Zagreb in 1903 to serve in the government at Budapest, the strained relations between Croats and Serbs began to ease. The reconciliation of the two national groups was, however, made possible only by the initiative of a couple of convinced believers in the Yugoslav ideal, both of whom came originally from Austrian-administered Dalmatia: Frano Supilo, the son of a stonemason in Dubrovnik who settled in Fiume and edited the Croatian language newspaper in the port; and Ante Trumbić, the mayor of Split. In October 1905 Supilo presided at a meeting in Fiume where forty Croatian deputies passed a resolution seeking the restoration, within the Habsburg Monarchy, of the ancient Kingdom of Croatia, Dalmatia and Slavonia. A few weeks later he induced a Serbian delegation, meeting at Zadar (then known as Zara) to accept the Fiume resolution and to issue a solemn declaration that 'Croats and Serbs are but one people in blood and language.' This historic event made possible the formation of a Serbo-Croat Coalition among deputies both in the Budapest parliament and the Sabor in Zagreb. By 1908 the Coalition had made itself politically so influential that it won a clear majority in the elections for the Sabor, despite the inequitable franchise laws. The Hungarian government then made the mistake of staging in Zagreb a trial similar in character to the disgraceful proceedings in Kolozsvar twelve years previously. More than thirty Serbo-Croat supporters were sent to prison for alleged treasonable links with the authorities in independent Serbia – they had dared to write a letter in the Cyrillic script commenting on the greater democratic freedom enjoyed by the Serbs. The trial became a European *cause célèbre*, and had the incidental effect of linking Masaryk with the Serbo-Croats in joint championship of Slav liberties. The knowledge that there was a specifically Yugoslav group within the monarchy was to have important consequences during the First World War, although Western observers underestimated the following of the Frankists and of the Croat Peasant Party. At heart the Croats continued to distrust the Serbs, both within their frontiers and beyond them; few genuinely shared the fundamentally Yugoslav faith of Supilo and Trumbić or, for that matter, of Ivan Meštrović, the great Dalmatian sculptor whose work won European renown in the last years of peace.

Meanwhile, in Hungary, István Tisza had run into greater difficulties with the hothead Magyar chauvinists than his father had ever experienced. This so-called 'national opposition' had begun by demanding revision of the commercial agreements between the two parts of the monarchy so as to place Hungary in an even more favourable position and went on to seek the protection of tariffs for Hungarian industry and the establishment in Budapest of an independent bank of issue. But the main dispute concerned the Imperial and Royal Army, an institution which – as Tisza knew well – Francis Joseph regarded as virtually a royal prerogative, above the tampering of politicians. Since 1903 the national opposition had demanded that Magyar should replace German as the language of command in the specifically Hungarian (and Croatian) regiments. To counter this threat Francis Joseph announced that he would secure the introduction of universal suffrage for elections to the Budapest Parliament. It was a remarkable piece of political blackmail but it succeeded. The Magyar oligarchs had no wish to see their privileged position challenged by the voice of the masses. The national opposition abandoned its insistence on Magyar in the army; and the proposals for universal suffrage remained mere historical curiosities. The Tisza faction stayed in the saddle, firmly gripping the reins of power up to the death of Francis Joseph in 1916 and, indeed, beyond.

With friction between Czechs and Germans threatening the political stability of the Austrian lands, with the Magyars sulkily maintaining that they had been cheated of their full rights under the Ausgleich, and with the Croats and Roumanians despairing of receiving justice from a sovereign who turned a deaf ear to their grievances, it seemed in those last years of peace as if the Habsburg State had never more deserved its mock title of the 'Ramshackle Empire'. In Vienna foreign observers began to believe that the monarchy would die with the monarch; few had much faith in the odd palliatives emanating from Francis Ferdinand's shadow court in the Belvedere. Perhaps outsiders tended to measure the influence of political leaders by the loudness of their complaints and underestimated the basic conservative loyalty in the rural areas, both of the landowners and the peasantry. Perhaps, too, the critics of the system at home and abroad failed to appreciate the economic advantages given to its peoples by a unified Danubian State. Yet, even so, the Dual Monarchy seemed at the time fundamentally as anachronistic as the stultifying etiquette of the Habsburg palaces; it was a supranational institution in an age of exclusive nationalism, a European necessity running counter to Europe's emotions. And not the least of her misfortunes was the fact that Austria-Hungary, though creaking at every joint, still ranked as a Great Power linked by treaty to the might of the German Reich but bound by both geography and history to respond to the slightest tremor of Balkan politics.

6

To Sarajevo

At the Congress of Berlin and in the years which followed the settlement of the Great Eastern Crisis Bismarck had tacitly assumed that the Balkan lands fell naturally into two spheres of influence: Russia was to control the Eastern Balkans; Austria-Hungary the Western Balkans. It was on this basis of policy that Bismarck encouraged the two empires to join Germany in the renewed Dreikaiserbund of the 1880s. But, even before Bismarck's fall in 1890, the assumption was proved no longer valid by events in Bulgaria, and for the next ten years the Austrians were able to exercise their influence more effectively than the Russians and over a wider area.

Since Belgrade was a frontier town looking out over the Sava to the plains of southern Hungary, the Austrians had more opportunity for intervention in the internal affairs of Serbia than in those of the other Balkan states. In 1881 Milan Obrenović purchased international recognition of his right to call himself king by concluding a far-reaching secret treaty with Austria-Hungary. Serbia bound herself not to make any agreements with other foreign powers and, at the same time, gave an undertaking not to encourage any anti-Austrian agitation in Bosnia-Herzegovina or in Novipazar. Commercial conventions gave the Dual Monarchy so many economic concessions, especially for developing railways, that Serbia seemed for some years to be almost a colonial dependency of the Habsburgs. There was strong opposition from Serbian merchants and the peasantry, as well as resentment among the Orthodox clergy, at this excessive reliance on Austria-Hungary; but it continued for the whole of Milan's reign – he abdicated in 1889, when the scandals of his private life became flagrantly public – and there was little change in the first ten years of the reign of his son, Alexander.

In 1883 the Roumanians, too, moved into the Habsburg orbit when King Carol concluded a defensive alliance with Austria-Hungary and Germany (with which Italy associated herself in 1888). The document was probably the most secret treaty of all, since it was originally known in Bucharest only to the King, to his premier (Ion Bratianu) and to the foreign minister. It was primarily aimed against Russia and was the consequence of resentment at the retrocession of Bessarabia; but Carol seems also to have hoped that, by improving relations with Vienna, he might secure a better status for the Roumanians living in Transylvania and the Bukovina, irredenta of far greater concern to his subjects than the comparatively small area lost to Russia. Technically this treaty, which never became generally known even to the political leaders, was still operative in 1914; by then, however, the Kolozsvár trial and similar instances of Magyar injustice had long since destroyed any real prospect of collaboration between Vienna and Bucharest.

The Austrian link with Bulgaria was more tenuous; it was frequently broken, only to be restored by the next shift of ministerial portfolios in Sofia, for the Bulgars were too cautious to commit themselves irrevocably to either of the rival power blocks. Prince Ferdinand maintained his contacts with the Austrian court and the Magyar aristocracy after he settled in Sofia. For a time he seemed to emphasize his role as a westerner; he married an Italian princess of impeccably Habsburg lineage, and when their son Boris was born in 1893 he even had the child baptized a Roman Catholic, as if to stress the new Bulgaria's independence of Orthodoxy. But for the first seven years of Ferdinand's reign the real master of Bulgaria was the prime minister, Stefan Stambulov, a man who brought to statecraft the sensitivity of a steam-roller: he was unacceptable to Russia, antipathetic to the Austrians, feared in the royal palace and idolized by every Bulgar who had never met him as a political opponent. In January 1894 Ferdinand felt that Stambulov had made sufficient enemies to be dismissed and eighteen months later he was brutally murdered, in a conspiracy of which Ferdinand does not appear to have been entirely ignorant. With his fall, Russo-Bulgarian relations began to improve: little Boris experienced conversion to Orthodoxy at a remarkably tender age; and in 1896 Tsar Nicholas II recognized Ferdinand as ruler of Bulgaria. The immediate objective of Bulgarian policy for the next decade was the formal attainment of complete independence from the Ottoman Empire, for the principality remained technically under the suzerainty of the Sultan. Pro-Russian administrations alternated with pro-Austrian, the inclination of the foreign ministry depending on the attitude of the two rival empires towards the government in Constantinople. Eventually the Austrians were able to strike a better bargain than the Russians; and Ferdinand proclaimed Bulgaria's independence and assumed a royal title ('Tsar of All the Bulgarias') in 1908, at a time when the Austrians needed Bulgarian support for the annexation of Bosnia-Herzegovina.

Potentially the most dangerous problem in the Balkans was the so-called 'Macedonian Question,' the attempt to find a lasting settlement acceptable to all the nationalities of the region for an area with no clearly defined boundary but including the historically-emotive names of Kosovo,

Ohrid, Skopje and Salonika. Most of the area had been promised to 'Greater Bulgaria' by the stillborn Treaty of San Stefano, but it had been left within the Ottoman Empire by the Treaty of Berlin. Promises of reform made by the Sultan's government in 1878 remained unhonoured and it was inevitable that the Balkan States should seek to annex all or part of Macedonia. The racial composition of the area was an ethnographical nightmare in which natural confusion was made worse by the total unreliability of every statistic. A Serbian analysis was published in 1899 and a Bulgarian in 1900: both agreed that there were six main racial groups; the first estimate listed 2,048,320 Serbs and 57,600 Bulgars; the second could find only 700 Serbs but 1,184,036 Bulgars; it is not clear what had happened to the missing 921,194, but they appear to have become 'Turks' or 'Others'.

Ever since the establishment of the Exarchate in 1870 the Bulgars had possessed an advantage over their rivals. There were Bulgarian bishops in the sees of Ohrid, Skopje, Bitolj (Monastir), Veles and Strumica and it is possible that by the turn of the century the Exarchate controlled some nine hundred schools, each of which served as a local propaganda office for the Greater Bulgarian idea. The Serbs, too, maintained more than a hundred schools, although the Turks did not allow the Serbian Orthodox Church to nominate a bishop for the area until 1902. Around the port of Salonika and along the Aegean coast the Greeks had a lead over the Serbs and Bulgars. Even the Roumanians had a school in Bitolj, for there were about a hundred thousand 'Vlachs,' similar in racial origin to the inhabitants of Wallachia, living by some freak of historical continuity along this isolated stretch of the old Roman Via Egnatia. The Roumanians were never serious competitors in the race to partition Macedonia, but they had a certain nuisance value to the principal contestants.

Turkish rule was as oppressive in Macedonia as it had been in Bulgaria and Bosnia-Herzegovina before the revolts of 1875–6. Exasperated by years of misrule, the non-Turks in Macedonia themselves began to demand autonomy. In 1893 an 'Internal Macedonian Revolutionary Organization' (IMRO) was set up in the district between Bitolj and Ohrid to unite all the peoples of European Turkey, irrespective of nationality, in defiance of Ottoman administration. It soon spread throughout the Macedonian lands and was especially strong in Salonika, the most cosmopolitan of all Balkan cities. But in 1896 Macedonian émigrés in Sofia established a 'Supreme Macedonian Committee,' secretly backed by the Bulgarian government in the hope of realizing the cherished frontiers of San Stefano. The Supremists made a takeover bid for IMRO and by 1902 were supplying its district agents with arms. It was the discovery of a cache of such weapons by the Turks that precipitated a new wave of grim repression and bloodshed.

Once again, Europe was shocked at the revelation of Turkish atrocities, while the American public was righteously indignant that a United States citizen, a woman missionary, should have been kidnapped and held to ransom by Bulgarian Supremists. The international situation was, however, very different from that of the 1870s. Neither Austria-Hungary nor Russia was ready for a major crisis over south-eastern Europe; they had agreed in 1897 'to keep the Balkans on ice'. Francis Joseph and Nicholas II, with their foreign ministers, met at Mürzsteg in Styria in October 1903 and produced a programme of reforms, to be carried out under European supervision, which they succeeded in inducing the Sultan to accept. An Austrian civil agent and a Russian civil agent were attached to the Turkish administrative service, a five-nation police force shared protection of the larger towns, and an attempt was made to bring order into the chaotic finances of the region.

Unfortunately this interesting experiment in international cooperation failed to pacify Macedonia: the Turks were unable or unwilling to carry out the proposals of the foreign advisers; and it was impossible to dampen the fires of internecine hatred. Serbian chetniks attacked Bulgarian *comitadji* and were in their turn the victims of retributive raids. Greek *andartes* roamed the mountain valleys around Florina and Edessa, attacking Albanians and destroying Turkish mosques and Exarchate schools in the villages. The Macedonian Question was not solved; it was shelved. Intermittent fighting continued until Macedonia leapt once more into the world headlines during the Balkan Wars of 1912–13. Nor even then was a solution found; the sinister initials IMRO were to acquire still greater notoriety between the two world wars.

The social and political structures of Roumania, Bulgaria and Serbia had much in common: they were all primarily agrarian states, with industry – where it existed at all – developed and owned by foreign capital; they all had a tradition of parliamentary government, even if tampering with the franchise ensured less democratic assemblies than the framers of the constitutions had originally envisaged; they all possessed political parties which were divided from each other by attitudes in foreign affairs rather than over domestic matters; and, since each still thought in terms of national expansion, they all built up armies disproportionate to their size and resources. From these general features, others followed. Because management in industry was in foreign hands, social ambition sought fulfilment in government service or, better still, as an army officer, so that a vested interest was created in the established order; and because constitutional principles were never regarded as sacrosanct, political leaders devised methods of perpetuating control of the spoils of office, and their parties became gluttonous cliques insatiably devouring authority. Moreover, since politicians acted out their life in a remote cuckoo-land of extravagant gesture, the peasantry and the industrial fodder looked elsewhere for ideological inspiration – in the first instance to the fractious offspring of 'Mother Russia'.

There were, however, significant differences between each of the three states. In Bulgaria, for example, the peasantry – some eighty per cent of the population – lived for the most part on small freeholdings; and when in 1900 the Sofia government rashly proposed to take a tithe on every harvest, they formed an Agrarian Party which, under the leadership of Alexander Stamboliisky, showed surprising self-confidence and forcefulness even before the Balkan Wars. By contrast, in Roumania, where three-quarters of the population were peasants, the agrarian problem was more acute but the agricultural proletariat less organized. Nothing was done to help them purchase smallholdings and ownership of estates was almost exclusively in the hands of the old boyar class, most of them absentee landlords. In forty years the annual export of grain had increased six times over, but the peasants remained impoverished and politically of no account. Their discontent boiled over in a fever of destruction during the spring of 1907 when a grim peasant revolt swept through Moldavia and into Wallachia, like an old time *jacquerie*. In three days of repression more than eleven thousand peasants were killed by troops despatched by the minister of war, General Averescu. The ruling-party – the so-called 'Liberals,' led by Ion Bratianu's son, Ionel – promised land reforms which, however, were still incomplete when Roumania entered the First World War.

In all three states popular discontent at times manifested itself in acts of hostility against the commercial classes. In Roumania trade and finance was almost exclusively a monopoly of the Jewish community, a compact and totally unassimilated body of some quarter of a million people. Serious anti-semitic demonstrations, prompted by envy rather than racialist humbug, began in the early 1870s in Moldavia, where most of the Jews had settled. Other outbursts occurred at irregular intervals over the next thirty years and on several occasions attracted the attention of the Great Powers. But if the Jews were the most serious victims of primitive resentment in Roumania, they were not the only source of popular indignation; the money lavished on imposing buildings and grand boulevards in Bucharest irritated taxpayers in the countryside. This distrust of city-life was shared by the Serbs, who tended to fall easy victims to the exorbitant rates of interest of money-lenders, and by the Bulgars, who had a marked distaste for the professional lawyer. The most powerful of pre-war political parties in Serbia, the Radicals, had originated in the 1870s as a protest at the exploitation of the peasantry by the townsfolk;

but by the end of the century the Radicals had themselves come to represent the interests of the business community and new groupings – the Agrarians and the Dissident Young Radicals – were formed to counter the demands of the 'men from the cities'. In Bulgaria Stamboliisky and his Agrarians championed the underdog. When Stamboliisky, in later life, described Sofia as 'a Sodom and Gomorrah, the total disappearance of which I should see without regret,' he was expressing a view of the corrupting influence of urban society already widespread throughout the Balkan lands at the turn of the century.

The peasants were no less suspicious of organized Labour. There were social democratic parties in all three states, each with a Marxist wing, but so long as there were no major industrial enterprises they had little following among the masses. The Roumanian Social Democrats, founded in 1893, disintegrated in ideological confusion seven years later, but re-established themselves in 1910 when the growth of the petroleum industry was changing the face of the country. The Serbian Party was established only in 1903, but a highly individualistic form of Marxism had by then been preached for more than thirty years by the followers of Svetozar Marković, the principal representative of the Balkan peoples in Marx's 'First International,' a socialist considerably influenced by Russian anarchism. Marković's teaching made a deep impression on the students of Bosnia, as well as on their compatriots in Belgrade; he was as outspoken a champion of Pan-Serb unity as any chauvinist radical. Probably the most purely Marxist group was in Bulgaria, where Dimiter Blagoev, a Macedonian peasant expelled from St Petersburg University, set up a Social Democratic Party in 1891. The Bulgarian Marxists were sufficiently strong to encourage a wave of strikes in 1905, in the organization of which a twenty-three year old printer, Georgi Dimitrov, played a considerable part. While the Balkan states were economically backward there was, of course, little likelihood of a socialist revolution, but the close links with the Russian movement were already of some significance; it was no coincidence that the Bulgarian strikes should have occurred at the same time as revolutionary disturbances in Russia. A Panslavism of the Left had come into existence, almost as though by some law of nature, more than a decade before the overthrow of tsarism.

In each Balkan state the monarch continued to exercise great authority. King Carol of Roumania had a right of absolute veto, could appoint or dismiss ministers as he chose and dismiss parliament at will; he had no doubts over the propriety of keeping the secret treaty of alliance with Germany and Austria-Hungary locked up in the private safe of his summer palace. Ferdinand of Bulgaria was no less autocratic, but considerably more devious in his methods. In Serbia the Obrenović dynasty increasingly assumed some of the less estimable qualities of the later rulers of Byzantium. King Milan had abdicated and renounced all his rights in 1889, retiring to Paris with a two million dinar pension from the Russians. But in 1897 he returned to Belgrade, went into residence in the royal palace and induced his son and successor, Alexander, to make him commander-in-chief of the army. For three years Serbia had, in effect, two kings, neither of whom commanded much respect: Milan, who was only in his middle forties, was neurotic and self-indulgent; and Alexander, with all the obsessive tenacity of an essentially weak man, was determined to marry his mistress, Draga Mašin, against the wishes of his father, the Radical Party and the General Staff.

When Alexander announced his engagement to Draga, the ministers all handed in their resignations. Alexander thereupon sought formation of a government of 'King's Friends,' but even so he could not find a single general willing to accept the coveted post of war minister – an ominous portent which the King would have done well to heed. The prestige of the monarchy fell lower and lower: in 1900 Milan finally left Belgrade for Vienna (where he died a few months later) and Alexander celebrated his marriage; in 1901 the press began openly to attack the dynasty; in 1902 members of the General Staff began to complain that their pay was several months in arrears. The end had about it a tragic inevitability. In May 1903 twenty-eight officers of the Belgrade garrison broke into the royal palace and poured thirty shots into the body of the King and eighteen into the body of his Queen before throwing the naked corpses out into the garden. A number of unpopular ministers and relatives of Draga were butchered at the same time.

The assassination shocked Europe: King Edward VII withdrew British recognition of the Serbian government and diplomatic relations between London and Belgrade were broken off for three years; and in St Petersburg the Russian Foreign Minister suggested to the Austro-Hungarian ambassador that Austrian troops might occupy Belgrade and restore order there. For Serbia the murders meant the final extinction of the Obrenović dynasty. The Radicals invited Peter Karadjordjević, grandson of 'Black George' and himself nearly seventy, to accept the crown. It was a wise choice. Peter was naturally tactful and a firm upholder of constitutional government. He had fought for France in the war of 1870 and had assisted the rebels in Bosnia in 1876. He was even said to believe in South Slav unity; as the train bearing him from Geneva to Belgrade passed through Vienna, Yugoslav students from the University hailed him with shouts of 'Long live the King of Croatia!'

Yet Peter's position was an unenviable one. He was overshadowed by the Radical Party and its redoubtable veteran leader, Nikola Pašić; and he well knew that when the military made an entry on the political stage they were rarely content with a walking-on part. Fortunately the King and Pašić, at least in these years, agreed fundamentally over policy and gradually the military conspirators were discreetly dispersed from the capital. In foreign affairs Serbia moved much closer to Russia and an attempt was made to improve relations with Bulgaria; a formal customs union of Serbia and Bulgaria was even considered. But the possibility of a South Slav Zollverein alarmed the Austrians, and so too did a decision to re-equip the Serbian army with French, rather than Austrian, weapons. Goluchowski, the Austro-Hungarian foreign minister, objected to the negotiations with Bulgaria and requested that Serbia should place orders for munitions solely in the Monarchy. When the Serbs rejected his demands, the Austrians in 1906 imposed a prohibitive duty on all Serbian livestock passing across the frontier. Since ninety per cent of Serbia's exports went to, or through, Austria-Hungary and since pigs (alive or dead) formed the largest single item in this trade, the Serbian economy seemed seriously threatened. In the long run, however, Serbia benefited from the 'Pig War': exports were re-routed southwards through Salonika and new markets found in Western Europe. But the bitterness engendered by the dispute brought Austro-Serbian relations to their lowest level for thirty years. And it was at this point that Francis Joseph announced the annexation of Bosnia-Herzegovina to the monarchy.

Since the occupation of Bosnia and Herzegovina in 1878 the Austro-Hungarian administration had considerably improved the material prosperity of the provinces. From 1882 to 1903 they were under the control of Benjamin Kállay, a Hungarian magnate who had once written a history of Serbia (which he now banned in the occupied provinces as a potential source of encouragement to Pan-Serb feeling). Kállay saw to it that a vigorous public works programme was undertaken; effective sanitation was brought to the towns; brigandage put down in the wilder regions. But basically Kállay's policy – and that of his successor, Baron Burian – aimed at the colonization of Bosnia-Herzegovina; their decisions over ecclesiastical affairs, education and the routes to be followed by railways all reflected the needs of the Dual Monarchy. Both territories were included within the commercial framework of the Empire and their inhabitants were conscripted for service in the Imperial and Royal army. The native population was given no opportunity of sharing in local administration; civil servants, all of them good reliable Catholics, were brought from distant parts of the empire and settled in the two provinces. A brewery was established in Sarajevo to supply them with fine quality central European beer; and a spa resort was created in the hills nearby, at Ilidze – a Bosnian Simla for the Habsburg's miniature India.

There were, however, two potentially limiting factors on the Austrian development of Bosnia-Herzegovina: the possibility that resentment among the predominantly Serbian population would lead to outbursts of terrorism; and the threat that a revival of Turkish power might challenge the right of the colonial administration to function in Sarajevo at all, for the two territories were still technically under Ottoman sovereignty and were only legally in Austrian occupation until order was restored. Both dangers seemed nearer realization in 1908 than in earlier years. The change of dynasty in Belgrade had served as a fillip to Pan-Serb enthusiasm in Bosnia, especially among the students; and the revolution of the 'Young Turks' in July 1908, first in Salonika and later in Constantinople, presaged an era of reform throughout the Ottoman Empire. These developments coincided with a change of attitude in Vienna. Francis Joseph was beginning to listen more and more to two men who favoured a vigorous policy in south-eastern Europe to restore the Empire's waning prestige: Aehrenthal, who had succeeded Goluchowski as foreign minister in October 1906; and Conrad von Hötzendorf, who had been appointed Chief of the General Staff in the same year and who believed that the Yugoslav problem within the Monarchy could only be settled by the annexation of both Bosnia-Herzegovina and of the Kingdom of Serbia. The Emperor shrank from giving Conrad a completely free hand, but the news from Constantinople induced him to authorize Aehrenthal to declare the incorporation in the Monarchy of the provinces which had been Habsburg in everything but name for thirty years.

The European chancelleries were formally notified of the annexation of Bosnia-Herzegovina – and, by way of compensation, of the withdrawal of Austrian garrisons from the Sanjak of Novipazar – on 6 October 1908. For the next six months there seemed a strong possibility that the Austrian move would lead to war. The British and French deplored a unilateral breach of the Treaty of Berlin, but they were in general less concerned over Balkan affairs than over Morocco and the increasing tension with Germany. The precipitate independence with which Aehrenthal had acted also angered Berlin; but Germany could not afford to quarrel with her one firm ally and by the beginning of 1909 the German General Staff was able to assure Conrad of military support if mobilization were ordered in St Petersburg. It was the Russian reaction which created the atmosphere of crisis. The Tsar's foreign minister, Alexander Izvolski, was at that moment sounding out the opinion of the Great Powers in the hope of securing revision of the Straits Convention, by which the Bosphorus and the Dardanelles were closed to Russian warships. He had met Aehrenthal at Buchlau only a fortnight before the announcement of the annexation; and he believed that he had reached a verbal agreement that the future status of the two provinces would be determined only after an international conference had discussed the Eastern Question in general.

Izvolski therefore felt deceived by Aehrenthal – whose account of the Buchlau conversations, it should be added, was completely at variance with the Russian version – and a sense of personal affront marred his judgement on international questions for the two years in which he remained foreign minister and for the six in which he was ambassador in Paris. The Tsar and his prime minister, Stolypin, regarded Izvolski as a melodramatic bungler and would willingly have jettisoned him during the crisis; but they could not abandon his policy, for Russian public opinion was aroused by the loss to Habsburg rule of two Slavonic provinces. With scant support from Britain or France, the Russians continued to press for an international conference; but in March 1909 they were brought to heel by a peremptory insistence from Berlin that the annexation should be formally recognized in St Petersburg. Russia bowed to the German demands, for the combined effects of the humiliating defeat by Japan and of the mutinies in 1905 had in reality toppled her from the pedestal of a Great Power. The Germans gained their diplomatic victory; but it proved a costly one. A new note of bitterness entered the relations of the three autocratic empires which was to continue until they found themselves at war in 1914.

Conrad and the military party in Vienna were far from satisfied by the results of the Bosnian Crisis. They sought a 'preventive war' with Serbia, and in February 1909 they nearly succeeded in getting their way. But, though the Serbs mobilized, they knew that they could never risk a conflict with Austria unless certain of Russian support, however angry public feeling might be in the streets of Belgrade. Hence when Russia yielded to German pressure, the Serbs, too, recognized the annexation. Yet they never accepted it at heart. In the first days of the crisis, a Pan-Serb organization had been set up in Belgrade known as the *Narodna Odbrana* (National Defence) to prepare guerrilla resistance both in Serbia and Bosnia-Herzegovina. Even when the tension eased, its supporters continued to foster revolt in the two provinces, despite constant protests from Vienna. Outwardly, it is true, the *Narodna Odbrana* changed its character; training in bomb-throwing and the blowing up of bridges gave way to more innocent pursuits; but there can have been few 'cultural associations' in history whose inner councils contained so many young officers eager for promotion. So far from solving the Yugoslav problem, as Conrad had hoped, the Bosnian Crisis made it acute.

From 1911 to 1914, and even for the first two years of war, the power of the Serbian government was constantly challenged by clandestine military societies, half-masonic in ritual and narrowly nationalistic in character. The most important was *Ujedinjenje ili Smrt* ('Unity or Death'), also known as the 'Black Hand,' which was established in May 1911 to secure the union of the Serbs living within the Austrian and Turkish

Empires with their kinsmen in Serbia proper. The leader of this organization was Colonel Dragutin Dimitrievič (alias 'Apis'), head of Serbian military intelligence and a regicide. The Black Hand, which imposed blood-curdling oaths of obedience and anonymity, operated with such sinister secrecy that its activities remained almost unknown abroad until after the outbreak of war, although Austrian military intelligence soon noted its existence.

The relations between the Black Hand and the radical governments of Pašić and Milovanović were ambiguous. Both groups believed that Serbia should be the 'Piedmont of the South Slavs'; but their interpretations of recent Italian history seem to have been at variance. For, while Pašić worked towards a 'Greater Serbia' (separated from Catholic Croatia by the old religious frontier of Orthodoxy), many of the Black Handers hoped for a unified South Slav state, a 'Yugoslavia' which would not be exclusively Serbian but in which the Serbs would enjoy primacy as the liberators of the nation. It was because the Black Handers had these broader objectives than Pašić and his radicals that they were able to establish links with the widespread revolutionary movement in Bosnia-Herzegovina; but many of these 'Young Bosnians' had political ideas well to the left of Apis and his fellow-officers. Pašić, who was sixty-five years old when in 1910 he became prime minister for the third time, was too set in his ways to welcome cooperation with the 'Young Bosnians' and, though he distrusted the Black Hand, he dared not seek to stamp it out so long as it enjoyed powerful patronage at court. Moreover, while Pašić feared that the Black Hand wished to precipitate a conflict with Austria-Hungary for which Serbia was not yet ready he was prepared to work with it against the Ottoman Empire, particularly if there should be an opportunity to expand in Macedonia or acquire an outlet to the Adriatic by advancing across Albania.

Both these calculations were coming nearer realization in 1911. The 'sick man' looked temptingly weak that summer; the Turkish army was engaged in a muddled colonial war with the Italians in Libya; and the army command in Constantinople was rent by feuds and political conflict. Never before had it appeared so easy for the Balkan peoples to push the Turks out of Europe. If they could overcome their common antagonism there was no reason why King Ferdinand should not gain an Aegean coastline for Bulgaria, the Serbs liberate Kosovo and sweep westwards to the sea, and the Greek flag fly over the valuable prize of Salonika; even King Nikita of Montenegro might mop up a handful of Albanian towns. Once again there was an urgent need for a solution of the Macedonian Question; and the Bulgarian foreign minister hurried to Belgrade for conversations.

In March 1912 the Serbs and Bulgars secretly agreed that, if they defeated the Turks in war, northern Macedonia should be added to Serbia and most of the rest of the province to Bulgaria. It was not by any means a satisfactory settlement – there remained a 'disputed zone' which was to be referred to Tsar Nicholas II for arbitration – but it was a remarkable testimony to the skill of the Russian ministers in Belgrade and Sofia who, acting independently of the foreign minister in St Petersburg, had brought the two governments closer together. There was still, of course, the problem of Greece, but in Athens the prime minister, Eleutherios Venizelos, was no less willing than Pašić and Milovanović to improve relations with Bulgaria; and in May the Greeks concluded a secret anti-Turkish treaty with the Bulgars, while Venizelos went on to make verbal agreements with the Serbs and Montenegrins (who, at the same time, negotiated a military convention with each other).

By the autumn of 1912 there was thus a League of four Balkan states, an alliance created for the most part against the wishes of the Great Powers, who had no desire for anyone to apply a match to the Balkan nationalist fuse. The formation of the League was a development of considerable significance in the evolution of the Lands Between, not so much for what it did, but as a sign of the increased independence of the new nations. The Balkan Crises of 1912–13 were imposed on Europe by peoples who had reached political maturity only in the previous generation. This was, in many ways, a disturbing portent.

At the end of the first week in October 1912, the members of the League declared war, one after the other, on Turkey. It proved to be a short campaign. The Turks were swiftly defeated by the Bulgars at Kirk-Kilisse and Lule-Burgas and by the Serbs at Kumanovo and Bitolj. Nor did the Greeks encounter much opposition: within three weeks they were in Salonika, the Greek army entering the city from the west only a few hours ahead of the Bulgars, advancing from the north. The Turks held out in the old fortress of Adrianople and in the mountain fastness of Janina. They also repulsed Montenegrin attacks on Skutari, in Albania; but the main Turkish army fell back on the Chataldja lines, covering Constantinople itself; and on 3 December the Turkish commanders concluded an armistice with the Serbs and Bulgars.

Military victory created new problems and opened old wounds. The Great Powers were alarmed at the way in which the small Balkan states were tearing up the map of Europe: Russia had no wish to see the Bulgars or the Greeks in triumph at Constantinople; and Austria-Hungary and Italy disliked the prospect of Serbia acquiring a foothold on the Adriatic. A conference of ambassadors in London sought to draw up new frontiers, its chief task being the creation of an independent Albania. Meanwhile, at the end of January 1913, a change of government in Turkey brought to power the more belligerent young officers under Enver. Fearing a resumption of hostilities by the Turks, the Serbs and Bulgars denounced the armistice and war was resumed on 3 February. The Turks fared no better in the new campaign. They lost Janina, Adrianople and Skutari before a second armistice agreement was concluded on 30 May.

The three months which followed this second armistice form a period of unusual complexity, even by Balkan standards. Serbia, finding opinion at the London Conference hardening against her demands for an outlet to the Adriatic, sought more of Macedonia than the original treaty with Bulgaria had assigned to her, including the whole of the 'disputed zone' east of the Albanian mountains. The Bulgars, for their part, were so furious at being 'robbed' by the Greeks of Salonika that sporadic fighting broke out between Greek and Bulgarian troops in the Struma valley. The Bulgarian attitude led Greece and Serbia to conclude a secret military convention on the day after the second armistice was signed; and the two states even made overtures to the Turks. At the same time the Roumanians, who had stood on the sidelines in the earlier campaigns, began to demand compensation from the Bulgars in the southern Dobrudja for the territory which they were going to acquire on the Aegean.

The Bulgars now blundered disastrously. Public feeling in Sofia, seeking tangible prizes for the military victories and suspecting that the government was weak, turned against the ministers. The Supremist IMRO group in the capital intimidated King Ferdinand, and the commander-in-chief of the Bulgarian army, General Savov, presented a virtual ultimatum; only resumption of the advance in Macedonia could save Bulgaria from a military putsch. Savov had his way; and on 30 June 1913 the Bulgars launched a surprise attack on their former allies. There followed a fortnight of humiliation for Bulgaria. The Serbs were victorious in Macedonia, the Greeks overran Thrace, the Turks seized the opportunity to re-occupy Adrianople and the Roumanians crossed the Danube and began to march on Sofia itself. Peace was finally made at Bucharest in August. The treaty left the Bulgars with scant rewards for their sacrifices – a valley in Macedonia, a segment of eastern Thrace and a second-rate harbour, Dedeagatch, on the Aegean. Against these small gains had to be offset the loss to Roumania of the southern Dobrudja. By contrast Serbia and Montenegro doubled the size of their territories and Greece secured western Thrace, including Salonika, southern Macedonia and much of Epirus.

The Bucharest settlement left Bulgaria bitter and frustrated, and her foreign policy for the next three years became almost fanatically revisionist. As early as February 1914 the Bulgars sought an alliance with Austria-Hungary and Germany, but Kaiser William II personally distrusted King Ferdinand, and the Austrians were content to play for time. Ultimately it was resentment at the terms of the Treaty of Bucharest, more than any other issue, which determined the attitude of the Bulgarian political leaders to the rival combatants in the First World War. The Serbs, the Greeks and the Roumanians had succeeded the Turks throughout Bulgaria as objects of patriotic abomination.

The Serbs, too, were not entirely satisfied with the new settlement. Though they carried the frontier to the shores of Lake Ohrid and Lake Doiran and liberated Skopje and Bitolj from Turkish rule and Bulgarian influence, the London Conference had denied them access to the sea. Serbia had, however, been permitted to partition the Sanjak of Novipazar with Montenegro (who, of course, possessed a strip of Adriatic coast) and there were abortive attempts in 1913 and 1914 to merge the two kingdoms, a union which the Austrians threatened to oppose by war, if necessary. But, in general, the Serbs had improved their material position and raised their prestige, ensuring – for good or ill – that they remained Russia's favoured client in the Balkan lands.

Indirectly, however, the Balkan Wars brought to a head the conflict between Pašić and the Black Hand, for the military party now constituted an almost unbearable pressure-group for any civil government. Once Macedonia was liberated, the Black Handers expected the new territories to be placed under military authority. At first there was little that Pašić could do to check their influence, but in October 1913 Dimitrievic and the Black Handers in Military Intelligence induced the General Staff to send troops into a part of Albania which was under Austrian protection. The Austrians despatched an ultimatum to Belgrade, the Russians insisted that Serbia back down, and the army units were withdrawn. This rebuff to Apis Dimitrievic and the Black Hand gave Pašić his opportunity. A formal decree asserted the primacy of civil authority over the military in Macedonia, and known supporters of Apis were transferred to garrison towns where there was less scope for intrigue.

Throughout the spring and summer of 1914 there was a major political conflict between the Serbian Radical Party and the Black Hand. It began with a comparatively trivial incident in April. General Damian Popović, a founder-member of the Black Hand and a regicide, claimed precedence over the Prefect of the Department at the Easter Day celebrations in Skopje, the main city of Serbian Macedonia. Pašić had the general suspended from his duties: his colleagues in the army promptly elected him president of the Officers' Club in Belgrade. Pašić, undaunted, ordered the police to seize the Officers' Club; and in May the newspaper which reflected the views of the military group – it was called, significantly, *Pijemont* – began to make ominous growls recalling how the army had saved Serbia from tyranny in 1903. The parliamentary opposition resorted to a tactic dear to the hearts of every Danubian minority party and absented itself from the Chamber.

King Peter at first kept out of the dispute. But when Marshal Radomir Putnik, a legendary popular idol who had never joined the Black Hand, threatened to resign as commander-in-chief, the King came down on the side of the officers, and the radical government was forced out of office. The King was opposed, however, by his son, Crown Prince Alexander, who distrusted Dimitriević on personal grounds and suspected him of republican ambitions. Under pressure from both the Crown Prince and the Russian minister in Belgrade, the King gave up the struggle: his health was bad and he withdrew to the country, appointing Alexander as regent. Marshal Putnik, whose health was little better than his sovereign's, left Serbia to take the waters at an Austrian spa. The Pašić government was re-instated, apparently victorious. On 24 June parliament was duly dissolved and elections announced for the beginning of August.

They never took place. Four days after the dissolution of the Serbian parliament, while Pašić himself was electioneering in Niš, the Archduke Francis Ferdinand was assassinated at Sarajevo by Gavrilo Princip, a 'Young Bosnian' student who had been supplied with arms from the Serbian Royal Arsenal at Kragujevac by agents of the Black Hand. Within five weeks the domestic squabbles of a small Balkan state were swept aside by the greatest war Europe had known.

The Sarajevo assassination was, of course, the occasion though not the cause of the First World War. A cloud of uncertainty still hangs heavily over the events of 28 June 1914 although no conspiracy in modern times has been described so extensively or so often. We know that the heir to the Austro-Hungarian thrones had many enemies and that his accession was feared by the Pan-Serbs because of his apparent willingness to appease the South Slavs within the Monarchy. We know that the decision to visit the capital of Bosnia on Serbia's national day (Vidovdan) had been treated as an affront by the Serbian people from the moment it was first announced in the press. And we know that chance played a hideous role in the tragedy, for an unexpected change of route forced the Archduke's car to halt only a few yards from where Princip was standing. Some theories we may dismiss as fantasy: but, even so, basic questions remain unanswerable except by prejudiced conjecture. How far, for example, was the Serbian government implicated in the conspiracy? And how far, in the last resort, was Princip acting on his own?

The struggle for power in Belgrade may have prevented either the Black Hand leaders or Pašić from giving the conspiracy the attention it warranted. Princip and his two young associates were in Belgrade at the height of the political crisis and were smuggled back across the frontier into Bosnia on the night of 1/2 June. Pašić was informed of their movements in a long memorandum which he summarized in his own hand soon afterwards: he ordered an inquiry into the activities of Colonel Dimitrievič's Intelligence Department; and he appears to have attempted to use his contacts with the political leaders among the Bosnian Serbs to prevent the assassins from carrying out their plans. His actions seem, however, to have been irresolute and there is no clear evidence that he warned, even indirectly, the Austrian authorities; the Serbian minister in Vienna certainly urged cancellation of the visit, but he did so only on his own initiative and spoke of danger in vague and generalized terms.

The behaviour of Apis Dimitrievič is no less puzzling. The Central Committee of *Ujedinjenje ili Smrt* – the inner circle of Black Hand leaders – was only informed by Apis of the conspiracy a fortnight after Princip had been smuggled back across the frontier. Apart from Major Tankosić, who had supervised the training of the conspirators and was therefore already in the plot, the committee voted against any attempt to assassinate the Archduke. In consequence, Apis tried to halt preparations for the murder; but for once his activities, like those of Pašić, seem half-hearted, although he certainly did not believe that such young and amateurish conspirators would succeed in carrying out their task. It is, of course, possible that Apis was making a reckless political gamble. An abortive plot, with subsequent discovery of weapons bearing the Serbian royal insignia, would lead to a strong Austrian protest to Belgrade. Since Pašić had already shown that he would stop short of military conflict, it was likely that he would have to send a humiliating apology to Vienna. But if Pašić was forced to condemn an act of patriotic protest carried out on Vidovdan, he would discredit the Radical party on the eve of the elections; it would have been the end of his political career. Assuming that there was no invasion of Serbia, Apis and the political opposition had everything to gain from an atmosphere of crisis which involved such emotive concepts as 'national honour' and 'our Serbian brothers under Habsburg tyranny'.

These calculations – if they existed at all – were made irrelevant by the unexpected success of the conspiracy and the violence of the Austrian reaction. Conrad still sought a preventive war in order to destroy the menace of Yugoslav sentiment; as he says, with incredible cynicism in his *Memoirs*, the assassination 'was a godsend, or rather a gift from Mars'; the war-party was given its final justification for the elimination of Serbia. On 23 July the Austrians presented an ultimatum in Belgrade which would have meant the virtual abandonment by the Serbs of their political independence. Yet Pašić accepted the main demands, only refusing to allow Austrian officials to conduct an inquiry into the conspiracy on Serbian soil. This refusal was sufficient to induce the government in Vienna to declare war on Serbia on 28 July.

The war soon spread beyond the Balkans to engulf the whole of Europe. The Serbs appealed for Russian aid: there was hesitation in St Petersburg despite the knowledge that, if Serbia were allowed to be destroyed, Russian influence in the Balkan lands would be at an end. The Russians ordered mobilization. Germany, having assured Austria-Hungary that she would neutralize the effect of Russian support for the Serbs, demanded a halt to all war preparations. When Russia refused, the Germans declared war on 1 August. By the middle of the month five European Great Powers and two of lesser standing (Serbia and Belgium) were locked in battle from the plains of Flanders to the lakes of Masuria.

7

'The Universal War for the
Freedom of Nations'

In the 1830s Adam Mickiewicz, troubled in spirit by the martyrdom of his country, urged his Polish compatriots to pray 'for the universal war for the freedom of nations'. By the beginning of 1918, with tsardom in ruins and the multi-racial democracy beyond the Atlantic involved in Europe's affairs, it seemed as if these supplications might at last receive an answer; for once 'national self-determination' was accepted as the shibboleth of the righteous, a massive struggle for mastery between two armed camps was converted into a revolutionary crusade for the sanctity of treaties and the creation of a new Europe. It would, however, be historically unsound and misleading to antedate the mood of the Fourteen Points. Until the close of 1916 the political leaders of the old Europe thought in terms of a collective security which they had once known and wished to see restored. In 1914 it was assumed in Paris and London and St Petersburg that independent great powers were a European necessity and small powers a historical inevitability; only the over-mighty power was a disaster none could tolerate. Clearly the barriers of the past had proved inadequate and when peace came it would be essential to repair them by adjustment of frontiers, but there seemed no need to cast them aside in radical upheaval. Victory was a programme of action in itself and 'war aims' no more than the cant of journalists. Only when the absence of a military decision had muted the thunder of the guns would the cries of subject peoples for 'freedom from bondage' be taken up in the Entente capitals.

These pleas were so indistinct at the outbreak of war that it is hardly surprising if they passed unheeded. On 20 August 1914 the London *Times* did, indeed, inform its readers of a revolution in Prague, of the river Morava running 'red with Czech blood,' and of the arrest and execution of the Czech political leaders, including Masaryk; but the report was a complete fabrication, typical of the hair-raising rumours which swept across Europe during the early battles. Despite the pre-war threats from the 'Young Czech' party, there was no Slav revolt in Austria-Hungary, and in Prague itself at that time even less evidence of separatist feeling than in the days of Palacký and Rieger. The Imperial and Royal army mobilized without any serious demonstrations in Bohemia-Moravia, although later there were to be incidents in some of the predominantly Czech regiments. Naturally there was much disaffection among the *prečani* Serbs and stern measures were taken against them by the Hungarian authorities, but many of the traditionally dissident nationalities began by supporting the war. In Zagreb, for example, Stjepan Radić as leader of the Croatian Peasant Party gave his blessing to the campaign against the Pan-Serbs of Belgrade; and in Brno Monsignor Sramak – an eventual prime minister of the Czechoslovak government in exile during the Second World War – signed a declaration pledging the unswerving loyalty 'to the state and its exalted monarch' of the Moravian people. Similarly in Cracow the two Polish brigades of General Pilsudski, which had already penetrated across the Russian frontier and raided the town of Kielce, duly took an oath of allegiance to Francis Joseph in the third week of August. From every part of the Monarchy peasants of differing races loyally rallied to the colours. Sergeant-Major Josip Broz (who was to receive the baton of a Marshal of Yugoslavia thirty years later) trudged off with his Croatian Infantry Regiment as a matter of course, first to the Serbian front along the Sava and later against the Russians amid the bitter frost of the Carpathians. It was not until the early battles had ended in deadlock that the nationalities began to grow restive.

There were three regions of war in Eastern Europe in 1914; on the north-western borders of Serbia; in Galicia and the Bukovina; and down the long frontier of eastern Prussia. It was, of course, the third of these areas which produced the most famous of all battles on the eastern front, the rout of the Russians at Tannenberg; but events in the other two sectors had a particular significance by exposing the limited resources of the Austro-Hungarian army and thus emphasizing the extent to which the Habsburg Monarchy was dependent upon German support.

The Austrians assumed when the war began that they would have little difficulty in overrunning Serbia. They had, however, underestimated both the tenacity and the valour of the Serbian army. In August and again in September General Potiorek, the governor of Bosnia, thrust across the river Sava near Sabac, but each time the Austrians could make no progress against the rocky fastness of Mount Cer and were forced to retire to the Srem district. Early in November Potiorek tried once more, this time making good use of his superiority in artillery. The Serbs had to retreat and, after four weeks of heavy fighting, a Magyar cavalry regiment celebrated the anniversary of Francis Joseph's accession by capturing Belgrade on 2 December. But the Habsburg triumph was shortlived. Within a fortnight the Serbs counter-attacked, liberated their capital and threw the invaders back to the swollen waters of the river Kolubara and out of the Serbian Kingdom. It was a resounding defeat for the Austrians, who sustained a hundred thousand casualties in the three abortive offensives. But the Serbs themselves, with few reserves of ordnance and with their towns scourged by typhus, were in no position to carry the war up the Danube. For ten months a silence of frustration settled on the whole Serbian front; it was to be broken only by the arrival of German divisions in the autumn of 1915.

In Galicia the Austrians ran into what was potentially an even greater disaster. An imprudent invasion of Congress Poland brought four Russian armies speeding across the plateau of the river San in a massive counter-offensive towards the Carpathians; and the Austrians fell back some hundred miles. On 3 September General Brussilov captured Lvov (Lemberg), the fourth largest city in the Dual Monarchy, and the fortress of Przemysl was besieged. Farther south Brussilov's advanced cavalry overran the Bukovina, entered Czernowitz and reached the forested slopes of the Carpathians before winter buried all operations in snow. An Austrian counter-attack temporarily relieved the Russian threat to Cracow in the north, but the possibility of an enemy offensive thrusting through the Carpathians and into the granary of central Hungary remained a real threat until the spring of 1915. The Austrians never completely recovered eastern Galicia until after the Bolshevik Revolution of 1917; the Bukovina was caught in a cycle of advance and retreat for three years, and the provincial capital, Czernowitz, changed hands no less than fifteen times.

The initial Russian penetration of the Monarchy was offset by the astonishing German successes in August and September 1914 around Tannenberg and the Masurian Lakes. In East Prussia alone, during the first month of war, the Russians lost a quarter of all the fighting men they had mobilized in July. Yet Tannenberg, staggering victory though it was, did not secure any territorial prize for the Germans; the forests, lakes, rivers and marshes around the Niemen all hampered Hindenburg's communications and made him seek an alternative route to the heart of the Polish lands. At the end of September he therefore sent Mackensen with the German Ninth Army south by rail to assist the Austrians north of Cracow by advancing across western Poland to the Vistula. Within a fortnight Mackensen's left flank was only seven miles from Warsaw itself. A Russian counter-attack, with fourteen divisions, checked the German drive to the east; and by 23 October the Germans had lost most of the land which Mackensen had overrun at the start of the month. Warfare on the eastern front was, however, always far more fluid than in the west; and in November Mackensen was ready to launch yet another attack in the direction of Warsaw. This time the Germans pushed along the river Warta and up the Vistula. For five weeks, despite rain and mud, there was extremely heavy fighting; the Germans captured the textile centre of Lodz and advanced as far as the outer defences of Warsaw; but the Russian line held and, as the full bitterness of the winter clawed at the exhausted armies, the great battle for Poland died away until the following spring.

The ebb and flow of the war determined the attitude of the three auto-cratic empires to the nationalities caught in the battle areas. On 19 August 1914 Grand-Duke Nicolas Nicolaievich, the commander-in-chief of the Russian armies, published two manifestoes addressed to the subject peoples: the first urged all the nationalities of Austria-Hungary to rise against the Monarchy and extend a brotherly arm to their Russian libera-tors; and the second specifically promised the Poles that their nation should be 'born again, free in religion, in language and in self-government' under the protection of the Russian tsar. The Germans had no intention of unfurling the Polish banner in these early months of the war, although they treated the Polish villages and their inhabitants with more sympathy than they showed in the regions through which they marched in Belgium and in France. The Austrians were prevented by the hostility of both the Hungarians and their German ally from issuing any liberal manifesto to the Poles; but they permitted Pilsudski to set up a Supreme National Committee in Cracow which would work for an Austrian solution to the problems of Poland.

At the same time the Russians were encouraging a group of Czech émigrés in the hope that, if their armies broke through the Carpathians, they would be able to establish a secessionist administration in Bohemia and Moravia. A Czech deputation, which consisted mainly of Russophile supporters of Kramář, was received in audience by the Tsar on 20 August and again on 27 September; and there was talk of 'the free and inde-pendent Crown of St Wenceslas' shining 'in the radiance of the Crown of the Romanovs.' But, as the Russian army never penetrated within a hundred miles of the historic Czech provinces, the lustre of this curious diadem reflected no more than the fantasies of the Winter Palace. The Russian foreign minister, Sazonov, certainly had no such extensive re-drawing of the map in mind when he talked to the French ambassador in the middle of September; his new Europe was to include a Tripartite Habsburg Monarchy, with Bohemia given a similar status to Hungary, and a Serbia which would annex Dalmatia and Bosnia-Herzegovina.

The majority of the Czech liberals lacked any confidence in Russian aid and were filled with a sound radical distaste for tsardom. Their relative passivity did not outlast the first battles for, since the Habsburg authorities refused to summon the Vienna parliament, they were denied all open expression of their political views and it was therefore inevitable that they should look for support to Austria's enemies. Masaryk sought contact with the British as early as September 1914 but it was not until December that he finally left Prague and went into exile. Travelling by way of Rome, he settled temporarily in Switzerland. As he subsequently explained in his memoirs, he became convinced that London was the natural political centre of the Allied war effort; and, after four months in Switzerland, he accordingly decided to transfer his activities to Britain. The Czechoslovak State was to be made in the West rather than in the East, as Kramář had hoped.

The British and the French were, however, far slower than the Russians in perceiving the nuisance value of the subject nationalities to their enemies. There were two main reasons for this: years of Pan-Slav agitation had made a crusade of liberation a familiar device in Russian policy; and, in both London and Paris, it was considered that Germany and, after November 1914, Turkey offered a more direct challenge to the vital interests of the Allies than Austria-Hungary. The Russian ambassador in London reported at the end of September that he found both government and opposition leaders reluctant to contemplate the disruption of the Dual Monarchy 'since Austria is fairly generally regarded as a victim of Germany'. By the end of the year, however, opinion was beginning to harden against the continuance of the Habsburg State in its old form. This change of attitude sprang, not so much from contact with the Czech movement, as from the activities of the Yugoslavs, and in particular the arguments of Frano Supilo, the Dalmatian journalist who in 1905 had taken the lead in securing reconciliation between the Serbs and the Croats of the Monarchy.

Supilo's work in awakening Western Europe has never received the recognition it merits, probably because he was to die in September 1917 before it was completed. But in the first eighteen months of the war his influence was far greater than that of any other southern Slav or, indeed, at that time of Masaryk and the Czechs. At the end of September 1914 he contacted the British ambassador in Rome, Sir Rennell Rodd, and endeavoured to win his sympathies for the Yugoslav Ideal. From Rome he travelled to Bordeaux and was received by the French Foreign Minister; and in November he came to London where he put his case to the British Prime Minister, Asquith, and the Foreign Secretary, Grey. Supilo, a forty-four year old volcano of indignation, made a considerable impression: 'He was rough in externals but not lacking a natural peasant courtesy in the formal expression of his views,' declared Rodd quaintly; while Grey found him 'the most interesting and far-sighted politician that I ever met in my dealings with the Middle Europeans'. From London he travelled to Niš, the temporary capital of Serbia, where he induced the redoubtable Pašić to assure him 'with visible emotion' that he was willing, in his own name and the name of Serbia, to do for the Yugoslavs what Piedmont had done for the Italians. And then, indefatigably on to Petrograd where he duly lobbied all the leading ministers, and even Rasputin, but was refused an audience with the Tsar. Back in Paris in May 1915 he joined Ante Trumbić in setting up a Yugoslav Committee to work for the union of the Serbs, Croats, Slovenes and Montenegrins in one Southern Slav State. The most influential members of the committee were, like Supilo himself, Croats from Dalmatia; but the committee also contained a Slovene, a Bosnian Serb and two Croats from Magyar-dominated Croatia proper. The Serbs long remained suspicious of the committee and its programme.

Supilo had more success in London and Paris than in Petrograd or Niš. At heart the Russians disliked the idea of uniting the Catholic Croats and Slovenes with the Orthodox Serbs and Montenegrins; and the Russian General Staff hoped that peace would bring an enlarged Serbia, so much in debt to the Tsar that it would permit the establishment at Kotor of a Russian naval base for an Adriatic squadron. Pašić, too, despite his emotional interview with Supilo, remained a believer in Greater Serbia rather than in Yugoslavia, although he was prepared to accept a formal vote by the Serbian parliament calling for the liberation of their kinsfolk from the Habsburg yoke. But the greatest obstacle to Supilo's policy was in Rome. Italian ambitions ran counter to any programme of South Slav unity, whether on the broad scale of Supilo's ideal or the lesser objectives of Pašić and the Pan-Serbs and, as the Allies sought to entice the Italians into the war against Austria-Hungary, so Supilo's influence gradually declined. By July 1915 Grey could write, testily, that in pre-war Britain 'the concept of Yugoslavia was one which had entered the minds of none but a dozen students.' Supilo's hour had come and gone too early; Allied hopes were centred on Rome.

The British, French and Russians sought Italian participation because they believed that after the indecisive fighting on the western and eastern fronts, only a southern front could open Central Europe to their armies and shift the balance of military strength in their favour. The Italians, however, struck a hard bargain. They were prepared to go to war provided they received by the subsequent peace treaty, not only the last remaining 'Italia Irredenta' under Habsburg rule (the Trentino, Gorizia, the South Tyrol, Trieste and Istria) but concessions in Africa and Asia Minor and a bridgehead into the Balkans as well. After six weeks of negotiations in the spring of 1915 the secret Treaty of London of 26 April promised the Italians most of the territories for which they asked, including Trieste, Istria, the northern Dalmatian littoral, a protectorate over Albania and cession of the Valona region, and all except two of the larger islands in the Adriatic. Some of the the richest prizes along the Dalmatian coast, including the ports of Fiume, Split and Dubrovnik, were not specifically promised to the Italians, but the proposed transfer of territories was a sufficiently hard blow to Southern Slav hopes for the Italians to insist that the Serbs be left in ignorance of the terms of the treaty.

It was, however, difficult to keep the bargain with Italy secret. Supilo accidentally stumbled on the truth during his visit to Petrograd. He informed Pašić, and the subsequent recriminations were so bitter that it was feared at one time in the Allied capitals that Serbia might make a separate peace. Prince Regent Alexander protested to the Russian commander-in-chief that it was inconceivable for so much Slav blood to have been wasted in vain. 'Italy will merely replace Austria as a menace,' Alexander complained; the terms of the treaty would inevitably provoke a new war in the near future. But not even the sentiment of Slav brotherhood could move the Russians that spring; the plain fact was that the Italians appeared capable of launching an offensive against the Austrians, and the Serbs did not. The Italians duly declared war on Austria-Hungary in May 1915 on the assumption that the terms of the Treaty of London would be fulfilled to the letter. In this they were to be disappointed, for before peace was finally made the treaty's violations of the ethnic principle were to incur far stricter censures from President Wilson and the Americans than Alexander, Pašić, Supilo or any other Yugoslav was ever able to voice.

The Austrians themselves expected Roumania, too, to enter the war within forty-eight hours of Italy: official publicists in Bucharest delighted in stressing the Latin links binding ancient Dacia to modern Rome; and, more realistically, the Roumanian government of Ionel Bratianu was determined to secure recognition of its claims to Transylvania, the Bukovina and the Bánát in any future partition of the Habsburg Empire. The possibility that these provinces might also be used as a bait brought sharp protests from Pašić, for the western Bánát was overwhelmingly Serbian in racial composition: 'The Allies are disposing of the Serbs as though they were African tribes,' he complained. As yet, however, nothing came of the negotiations with Roumania, nor of proposals (which were equally objectionable to Pašić) to tempt Bulgaria into the war by promises to revise the Treaty of Bucharest in her favour, especially in Macedonia. Both countries preferred to maintain their neutrality at such an enigmatic stage in the conflict and see which way the battles went in the summer of 1915 before committing themselves. Once fighting begins, Clausewitz's famous dictum is inverted and foreign policy becomes no more than the continuation of war by other means: a military success in Eastern Europe was by now an essential pre-requisite of Allied diplomacy.

Yet throughout 1915 victory remained as elusive as ever. The high hopes of the Dardanelles enterprise turned to bitter disappointment as half a million men failed to seize the commanding ridges of the Gallipoli peninsula. The Italians suffered no less grimly on the lower Isonzo, seeking to reach the fortress of Gorizia, secure on its rocky plateau. But the biggest Allied disasters that summer were in Poland, where on 2 May the Eleventh German and the Fourth Austrian Armies went over to a joint offensive under the command of General von Mackensen. Breaking through the Russian defences on the Dunajec, Mackensen captured the town of Gorlice and pressed on eastwards across Galicia, taking more than 150,000 prisoners in four weeks. By the end of June Lemberg (Lvov) was once more in Austrian hands and Galicia west of the Sereth was freed from the Russian invader. But the thrust through Gorlice was only a preliminary. In July there was a general advance along the whole of the eastern front, towards Kaunas and the Dvina in the north, towards Warsaw in the centre, and northwards towards Lublin from the San valley in the south. 'Russian fortresses were falling like houses of cards,' recalled the Austro-Hungarian foreign minister, Czernin, after the war: Przemysl, Ivangorod, Warsaw and Brest-Litovsk were impressive names in the official communiqués, and with these cities there came over a million Russian prisoners-of-war. It was not until the end of September that the Russians succeeded in stabilizing their front and during the retreat they were forced to abandon most of Lithuania and the whole of the Congress Kingdom. Warsaw itself had fallen as early as 5 August; and when the German advance finally ended, the troops which had entered Warsaw were 200 miles to the east, on the edge of the Pripet Marshes.

Territorial losses are not so decisive in an empire the size of Russia as in the more compact states of Western Europe, but the evacuation of the Polish lands had a disproportionate political significance. Although as yet both the German and Austro-Hungarian governments shrank from committing themselves irrevocably to Polish independence and insisted on treating the Congress Kingdom as conquered territory divided into zones of occupation, the course of the battles had left them with the initiative. A handful of Polish National Democrats, with Dmowski at their head, continued to urge their compatriots to refrain from anti-Russian activities but so long as Russia remained an illiberal autocracy there was little response to Dmowski's appeals and in 1916 he left Petrograd and went to London. Pilsudski, whose brigade had fought resolutely against the Russians in the Bukovina, hastened to Warsaw soon after the entry of German troops but the military authorities, distrusting all political soldiers, regarded him with considerable suspicion and at first even forbade recruiting for his Polish Legion. But, although another year elapsed before the Central Powers accepted the idea of a Polish State, the German military governor in Warsaw, General Hans von Beseler, soon began to make concessions to the Poles in education and municipal administration.

The series of Allied reversals, at Gallipoli and on the Isonzo as well as in Poland, had a considerable effect on the attitude of the remaining neutral states in south-eastern Europe. Roumanian policy became increasingly evasive to an approach from either side. In Athens King Constantine and the Greek army leaders flaunted their pro-German sentiments to the discomfiture of the prime minister, Venizelos, whose sympathies were with the British and French. And in Sofia the Bulgars came down firmly for the Central Powers, despatching an influential colonel on the General Staff for conversations in Berlin during the very week Warsaw fell. These Bulgarian overtures were particularly welcome to the Germans at this stage in the war. Falkenhayn and Conrad, the German and Austrian Chiefs of Staff, were anxious to eliminate the quiescent, but potentially dangerous, Serbian front in order to secure effective cooperation with their Turkish ally; and, if action were to be taken against Serbia, Bulgaria seemingly had little to lose and Macedonia to gain by seeking to avenge her defeat in the Second Balkan War. A secret military convention, signed on 6 September, provided for a Bulgarian attack on Serbia's eastern flank within a week of the launching of a joint Austro-German offensive along the Danube and the Sava. By the end of the month, with the battles in Russia beginning at last to die away, German and Austrian troop trains moved slowly through southern Hungary and Mackensen and his brilliant deputy, Hans von Seeckt, brought to the Balkan peninsula the skills they had perfected in Galicia. On 6 October the guns opened up on Belgrade; and a week later the Bulgars duly marched across their frontier and into southern Serbia.

The Austro-German-Bulgarian threat to Serbia had the indirect consequence of committing Britain and France, for the first time in their history, to a land campaign in the Balkans; for a hastily improvised Anglo-French force landed at Salonika on 5 October 1915 in the hope that it might deter the Bulgars from entering the war and, at the same time, establish links with the Serbs along the Vardar-Morava valleys. But, disliked by almost every military and civilian leader in London and Paris and dependent on the tragi-comic vacillations of Athenian politics for its very existence, the Salonika expedition seemed damned to futility from its earliest days. It turned many Greeks against the cause of the Entente Powers and it failed to save Serbia. Few then, or for long afterwards, could perceive the strategic value of this tenuous foothold on the Balkan Peninsula or foresee the political influence of the inter-allied commander-in-chief of the 'Army of the Orient' in the re-shaping of

Europe. The British, in particular, would have been glad to escape from the Macedonian entanglement at the earliest opportunity.

Meanwhile the Serbs had gone down fighting. Their resistance lasted far longer than Mackensen anticipated; even Belgrade, surprised by the fury of his initial attack, held out for three days, and he had been unable to trap the Serbian army on the field of battle at Kragujevac or at Blace, as he had planned. But the Serbs, short of guns and sick with typhus, could not withstand the onslaught of more than four hundred thousand fresh troops, pouring in from the north, the west and the east. By the third week in November the Serbs were split into four separate contingents, falling back into the inhospitable mountains of Albania, while blizzards and drifting snow checked the invaders. The Serbian retreat claimed as many victims as a pitched battle. Even when the survivors reached the Adriatic coast they could find little sanctuary, for early in January 1916 the Austrians overran Montenegro and began an advance along the Albanian coastal plain. Evvetually French and British naval units evacuated the Serbs from southern Albania to the Greek Island of Corfu, which the French had occupied in the New Year despite sharp protests from King Constantine in Athens. After a period of recuperation on Corfu, the Serbian troops, re-equipped by the French, were transported to Salonika where they joined British, French, Italian and even Russian divisions in the heavily fortified base. But Corfu remained, until the end of the war, the official seat of the Serbian government.

With the Bulgarian alliance and the occupation of Serbia, the Germans and Austrians imposed a military and political unity on Europe and Asia Minor from Brussels to Baghdad; only Roumania stood apart, technically neutral and independent though bound by commercial treaties to supply the Central Powers with the bulk of their corn. Inevitably, proposals were put forward for greater economic integration, and business-men and industrialists followed the soldiers eastwards. Barges began once more to move down the Danube from Vienna and Budapest to the Black Sea within a month of the fall of Belgrade; and in the first weeks of 1916 it became again possible for passengers to travel by Balkan Express from Hamburg to Constantinople. Wilhelm Groener, the Wurttemberger general who emerged as the supreme logistics expert of the war, constructed a special railway at the Iron Gates to tow barges through speedily against the strong Danube currents; and a steady flow of grains, ores and petrol products moved north-westwards by rail and water in an effort to defeat the Allied blockade. The economy of occupied Serbia, of Bulgaria and, such as it was, of Turkey was thus harnessed to the German war effort. There were many writers and publicists in southern Germany and

Austria who wished to see this system perpetuated and who tended to regard the economic unity of the Danubian basin and the Balkan lands as a justifiable war aim in itself, and monthly periodicals appeared in Munich and Vienna to foster these grand designs. The inspiration for this ideal was Pastor Friedrich Naumann, a generous-hearted liberal who, like most prophets, shrank in abhorrence at the excesses of his less far-sighted disciples, especially among the German-Austrians.

Naumann's *Mitteleuropa* was published in Berlin in the first days of October 1915, the same week in which Mackensen opened his offensive to crush Serbia. The book became the academic best-seller of the war. For more than two decades Naumann, a Lutheran theologian and social analyst, had championed the idea of a Germanic Central Europe in which the Hohenzollern and Habsburg empires would be welded together by the indestructible links of a common economy. Some of Naumann's earlier writing is hardly distinguishable from the outpourings of the Pan-Germans but middle age mellowed his sentiments and by 1915 he had become essentially a federalist, insisting that economic and political unity could survive only within an institutional structure which gave constitutional guarantees of national, linguistic and educational auto-nomy. But Naumann was living neither in the age of the Zollverein nor of the Common Market; few of his readers could share such tolerance towards national variation and idiosyncrasy, and his own admiration for Bismarck is at times disconcerting. Moreover, although Naumann held out a slightly patronizing hand to the Poles and to the Czechs, he assumed that Bohemia was an essentially German province and proposed that Prague should be the very centre of his superstate. Hence, to the Slav peoples of the empire and to their friends in the Entente capitals, it seemed as if Naumann was attempting an intellectual apologia for the teutonic regimentation against which they had railed for so long; and paradoxically his book provided the Czech, Yugoslav and Polish exiles in the West with a powerful weapon of ideological warfare. Pirated trans-lations into English, French and Italian were hurriedly made and widely circulated. Naumann's ideals were misunderstood, and often misrep-resented, for many years to come.

Alarm at the apparent implications of *Mitteleuropa* made public figures in both London and Paris more inclined to listen to the exiles from the Monarchy and particularly tó Tómaš Masaryk, whose friendship with Steed, the Foreign Editor of *The Times*, ensured that he had an influential platform for his views. The Czech cause gained a powerful reinforcement with the flight to the west of Edvard Beneš, who became the chief spokesman for Masaryk in Paris. In February 1916 a Czechoslovak National Council was established, of which Masaryk was President, Beneš Secretary and on which a young officer in the French Air Force,

Milan Štefánik, served as the representative of the Slovaks. Contacts with the University of Paris and with King's College, London, enlarged the support which the Czechs were already receiving in academic circles. From October 1916, a weekly periodical *The New Europe* was published from London to champion, with impressive scholarship, the desirability of assuring the peoples of Eastern Europe their national freedom.

There was, as so often, a time-lag between acceptance of Masaryk's general thesis and reiteration of his specific arguments. Until the end of 1916 the Yugoslav Committee, of which Trumbić was President and Supilo the driving force, continued to carry more weight in the counsels of the Allies than the Czechs, especially in London. A Foreign Office memorandum of August 1916 proposed the post-war division of East-Central Europe into national states; but, while it favoured a single South Slav federation and a 'Polish Kingdom under a Russian Grand Duke,' it virtually ignored the Czechoslovak Question, merely recommending 'tacking Bohemia on to the Kingdom of Poland'. This document was, of course, confidential and not binding on any government; it did not even come before the British Cabinet until the following year. But it is instructive to compare its proposals with the first published statement of Allied war-aims, issued to the press in January 1917 in response to a request from President Woodrow Wilson; for the new manifesto avoided specific reference to the Yugoslavs (on the insistence of the Sonnino government in Rome) but called, among other things, for 'the liberation of Italians, of Slavs, of Roumanians and of Czecho-Slovaks from foreign domination' and contained only a guarded comment noting 'the intentions of His Majesty the Tsar of Russia' towards Poland. It is clear that in the five months between the two documents Allied sentiment had begun to move decisively in favour of Masaryk's blueprint for a new Europe, although he had no sympathy for a tsarist solution of the Polish problem. The collapse of the Romanov dynasty was soon to free the Allies from this particular embarrassment; at the same time, it was to elevate still higher Masaryk's status as the mouthpiece of the Slav peoples.

Meanwhile, the war in the east had continued to go badly for the Entente for most of 1916. At midsummer, however, it seemed for a few weeks as if Brussilov's South-West Army Group might even yet carry the Russians to the Carpathian passes. The Austrian Fourth Army and the Austrian Eighth Army collapsed under the momentum of Brussilov's onslaught in early June and fell back sixty or seventy miles in confusion. Fifteen German divisions from the western front and even a Turkish Corps were rushed to Galicia to plug the gap but Brussilov maintained the pressure until the end of September when, with over a million losses and starved of shells by an incompetent administration, the last great offensive of the tsar's armies died away in demoralized exhaustion amid the forested beech slopes of the Bukovina.

The possibility that Austria-Hungary might go down in defeat before Roumania had staked her claim to the spoils appeared so real in the summer of 1916 that Bratianu's government in Bucharest was stirred to a flurry of desperate bargaining. Bratianu himself informed the Entente ambassadors that if their governments did not agree to his terms for entering the war, he would resign and leave the conduct of Roumania's affairs to his pro-German rivals. On 17 August a secret agreement was signed by which Roumania undertook to declare war on 28 August under five conditions: the eventual cession to Roumania of all Transylvania and a section of the Hungarian Plain up to the river Tisza, the Bánát and the Bukovina; equal status at the Peace Conference with Britain, France, Russia and Italy; the immediate launching of an offensive by the armies in Salonika; a continuation of Brussilov's attacks on the Austrians; and the despatch of Russian troops to the Dobrudja so as to safeguard southern Roumania from a Bulgarian invasion. The Allies accepted this very high price for Roumanian cooperation partly because of their hope that it might be possible to cut off the routed enemy forces in the Bukovina but also because the loss of Roumanian grain and oil to the Central Powers would intensify the rigours of the blockade. In the event, the Bulgars stole a march on the Allies by attacking Macedonia within a few hours of the signing of the secret convention, but the Roumanians duly declared war on 28 August and the Salonika armies were able to launch a counter-offensive a fortnight later.

Once again, as in the case of Italy the year before, secret diplomacy failed to bring its expected military reward. The German and Austro-Hungarian High Commands had long anticipated Roumanian intervention on the side of the Entente, although at the actual moment when the Roumanian armies marched on Transylvania General Arz had only twenty-five thousand men to defend the frontier. Mackensen, however, was able to muster an army of Bulgars, Turks and Germans in the Dobrudja and began an advance up the lower Danube in early September. Later in the month Falkenhayn assisted Arz to throw the Roumanians out of Transylvania, and by the beginning of October the Roumanians were everywhere on the defensive. The Russians sent only twenty thousand troops to defend the Dobrudja, many of them Czech and Yugoslav volunteers from the prisoner-of-war camps who were shot as traitors if captured. Constanta and the great bridge across the Danube at Cernavoda fell to Mackensen on 25 October and on 6 December the Germans entered an undefended Bucharest. By the end of the year the Roumanians held only the section of Moldavia east of the Sereth. Three quarters of the Kingdom was occupied by the Central Powers, including all the fertile grain land. Prompt sabotage by a British Member of Parliament, Colonel Norton Griffiths, put the Ploesti oilfields out of action; but the whole campaign was a singular disaster for Allied arms which offset all the gains so dearly won by Brussilov that summer. The success of the Salonika armies in liberating Monastir (Bitolj) seemed small by comparison, though the morale of the Serbs was raised by carrying the war back to a segment of their homeland.

On 21 November 1916 the Emperor Francis Joseph died in the eighty-seventh year of his life, and only eleven days short of the sixty-eighth anniversary of his accession. Although continuing to work at his desk until the very evening of his death, he had long since given up all initiative in political affairs, leaving decisions to the Chief of the General Staff, Conrad, or to the real master of Hungary, Count István Tisza. Francis Joseph never resolved the conflict between dynasticism and the nationality principle which had brought him to the throne in 1848 and yet his personal longevity gave an illusion of stability to the fragile structure of the Dual Monarchy. He was, after all, its one revered institution and his death made it certain that demands for radical change in the character of the empire would no longer be muted by respect for the sovereign as a symbol of cohesion.

The new ruler, his great-nephew Charles, was a young man of twenty-nine who was widely believed to have accepted much of the political testament of his uncle, the murdered Archduke Francis Ferdinand. He had displayed, in private, some sympathy towards the Croats and was critical of Magyar chauvinism in Transylvania; and he was as tired of the war as any of his subjects. But Charles was a prisoner of his great-uncle's system to a far greater extent than he had realized. It would have been difficult for him to throw over the Dualist System in time of peace; during a war it was virtually impossible. Hungarian goodwill was essential, for Hungary alone could ease the food shortage of Vienna and the industrial regions (which had been made especially acute that winter by the breach with Roumania). Tisza insisted on an early coronation in Buda, knowing that once Charles had taken the oath to uphold the constitution and preserve the territorial integrity of the 'Lands of the Holy Crown' the Magyars would be able to veto concessions to the subject peoples within the Hungarian Kingdom (and probably outside it as well). The coronation ceremony was duly held on 30 December, less than six weeks after Francis Joseph's death.

War-weariness and unrest were growing rapidly among every nationality and all social classes within the monarchy; and Charles was made acutely conscious of it every time he passed the queues for bread and for soup in the working-class districts between Schönbrunn and the Hofburg. Administrative incompetence was almost as bad as in Russia, while in Bohemia and Moravia countless arrests had established a regime of oppression, with Magyar regiments policing the provinces as though they were an army of occupation in a conquered land. Charles was determined on some gestures of good intent: he appointed as foreign minister Count Czernin, who was as anxious for peace as the Emperor himself; he replaced the implacable Slavophobe Conrad by Arz von Straussenburg as Chief of the General Staff; he convoked the Austrian Parliament in May 1917 for the first time since the outbreak of war; and, in the same month, finding that Tisza would not accept a broadening of the Hungarian franchise, he dismissed him as head of the government in Budapest. Above all, Charles put out peace feelers to the Allies through his brother-in-law, Prince Sixtus of Bourbon-Parma. But Charles was neither prepared to desert his German partner nor powerful enough to induce him to accept a compromise peace. The contacts with the French delayed any public Allied insistence on the dissolution of the Monarchy, but the negotiations were too confused to bring success; and when a year later Clemenceau, in a fit of temper, revealed that they had taken place, the young Emperor was discredited in the eyes of the ally to whom he had sought to remain scrupulously loyal.

The meeting of the Reichsrat (the Austrian Parliament) at the end of May afforded clear evidence of the discontent among the Slav nationalities; and the change in the attitude of the traditionally conservative Polish deputies was particularly significant. One of the last actions of Francis Joseph in the previous November had been to give his consent to a proclamation, which originated with the German High Command, providing for a Kingdom of Poland 'with a hereditary monarchy and a written constitution' and linked to the two allied powers (Germany and Austria-Hungary). The future frontiers of the Kingdom remained undecided, for the chief reason behind its creation was to provide the Central Powers with a Polish army and premature discussion of boundaries would not help to rally recruits. But once the Reichsrat met, the members of the Polish Club had no hesitation in demanding that the new state was to be fully independent, unified and assured of access to the Baltic. Such an ambitious programme implied the secession of Galicia and Cracow as a minimum concession.

The Czech delegates to the Vienna Parliament were no less outspoken: the monarchy must be converted into a 'federation of free and equal states,' one of which should be specifically Czechoslovak in composition. The Southern Slav members, led by the Slovene priest Antun Korošec, formed themselves into a 'Yugoslav Club' and issued a declaration seeking the union of all Serbs, Croats and Slovenes living within the monarchy in an autonomous entity under Habsburg protection. For the moment Charles could do nothing to satisfy any of these demands but, as a further gesture of goodwill towards the Slavs, he released from prison a number of Czechs who had been convicted of treason, among them the Russophile Kramář. With regional groups associating in political clubs and old enemies stretching loyalty to its limit, the Reichsrat of 1917 began to resemble the States-General of 1789, as Czernin gloomily perceived; and it was disconcerting to find the Emperor mixing obstinacy, weakness and reconciliation as though he were King Louis XVI.

There was, indeed, a scent of revolutionary change in the spring breezes that year. The Romanov dynasty had fallen in Russia at the beginning of March and it rapidly became clear that the authority of the provisional government would not pass unchallenged if it continued to deny the people of Petrograd and the other great cities 'Bread and Peace'. But, though the Russian masses themselves were soon disillusioned with the antics of Prince Lvov and Kerensky, the disappearance of the old autocratic state was immediately interpreted as an important success in the struggle of the subject nationalities of the tsarist empire for recognition and liberation. The Provisional Government sincerely believed in federalization and, within a fortnight of its establishment, issued a manifesto to the Poles, promising the creation of 'an independent Polish State' which was to comprise all provinces in which there were Polish racial majorities. This concession went further than any offer from the Central Powers, but, since most of these territories were in enemy occupation, the proposals remained of largely academic interest. It was followed by gestures towards the Finns and Estonians and by recognition of a Ukrainian Council, although this particular act aroused so much resentment in Petrograd that it split the government and precipitated the replacement of Prince Lvov by Kerensky as chief minister. At the same time, the Russians gave full support to the Czechoslovak movement, permitting Masaryk to organize a Czechoslovak Army Corps; and it was in a speech at a mass meeting in Kiev that he first publicly proclaimed the need to create an independent Czechoslovak Republic.

Polish affairs remained in a state of extreme confusion throughout the summer of 1917. Pilsudski's Polish Legion was already fighting on the side of the Central Powers and Pilsudski himself was a member of the Warsaw State Council, a pre-government for the German- and Austrian-sponsored Kingdom. On 4 July, however, the French announced the formation of a Polish Corps for service with the Allies on the western front and ten days later a Supreme Polish Army Committee was set up in Petrograd, also pledged to the Entente. Meanwhile, Roman Dmowski as leader of the Polish National Democrats was cooperating with the *New Europe* group in London, the great concert pianist Paderewski was influencing the Polish communities in the United States, and a Polish National Committee which claimed the status of a government-in-exile was established in Switzerland. The Committee soon moved to Paris where, with Dmowski as president and Paderewski as American representative, it received recognition in the autumn from all the major Allied Powers. The Provisional Government's manifesto and the entry of the United States into the war against Germany in April 1917 induced Pilsudski to re-assess his policy and he decided that the time had come to break with the Central Powers. In July 1917 he was arrested by the German occupation authorities and interned in fortresses in Prussia for the rest of the war. Pilsudski's activities barely stopped short of treason and no government could have permitted him to remain at liberty but so great was his personal prestige among his compatriots that his imprisonment virtually condemned all Austro-German attempts at Polish reconciliation to failure. Hence, although a puppet Polish government headed by a Regency Council assumed office in Warsaw at the end of the year, the hopes of the Polish people were turning increasingly towards the Entente Powers and their American co-belligerents.

Pilsudski was not the only astute national leader to trim his sails that summer. Prince-Regent Alexander and his prime minister, Pašić, had long depended on the protection of the tsarist state and of their co-religionists at the head of the Orthodox hierarchy; and the first Russian revolution left them politically isolated at a time when there was already serious division in the Serbian High Command, where the survivors of the Black Hand movement were again active. Pašić accordingly determined to strengthen his position in two ways: a trumped-up charge of conspiracy and a court-martial in which there were serious irregularities enabled him to purge the army of Black Hand influence; and contact with Trumbić and the Yugoslav Committee afforded him opportunity of making a gesture towards the national groups seeking secession from Austria-Hungary. As an attempt to court favour in the West Pašić's policy was not entirely successful, for the callous way in which Colonel 'Apis' Dimitrievic was put on trial in Salonika and executed aroused indignation within the influential *New Europe* circle. Nevertheless the agreement with the Yugoslav Committee – the 'Corfu Pact,' as it was called – did indeed have a considerable effect on Southern Slav sentiment within the monarchy and on the attitude of the Yugoslav emigrant groups in the United States. The pact, which was signed on 20 July after five weeks of negotiation, provided for the union of the Serbs, Croats and Slovenes under the Karadjordjević dynasty, with linguistic and religious guarantees and with 'local autonomies in accordance with national, social and economic conditions'. The precise relationship of the various regions to each other and to the central government was left unresolved; all such questions were to be settled in due course by a constituent assembly elected by secret and universal suffrage.

Significantly Supilo (who was to die only a few weeks later) resigned from the Yugoslav Committee when he studied the terms of the Corfu Pact, fearing that Trumbić had been duped by Pašić into a major surrender of principles. At the time, his pessimism seemed excessive even if there were grave defects in the character of the agreement. Since neither the Committee nor Trumbić, its president, had any official status the pact technically had no force in international law; but it clearly imposed on the Serbian government the moral duty to work for a unified Yugoslavia rather than for a 'Greater Serbia'. Trumbić himself had kept in touch with the Croats of the Monarchy through Doctor Barac, the Rector of the University of Zagreb, who met him secretly in Lausanne early in September and assured him of the general support of the Serbo-Croat political leaders, even Radić. Approval of the pact was also given by the Montenegrin National Committee, which had established itself in Paris after the Austrians overran the mountain kingdom. Yet Trumbić and his colleagues were well aware that Pašić still preferred a centralist state dominated by Belgrade to a genuine federation. Much of the tragedy of the inter-war Yugoslavia was foreshadowed by the sharp differences in approach which the vague wording of the pact tried so hard to disguise.

The Bolshevik Revolution of November 1917 made an even wider impact, militarily and ideologically, than the fall of tsardom eight months earlier. It meant the end of all fighting on the eastern front and of the resistance of the Roumanians in Moldavia; it raised the possibility that what Lenin regarded as a conflict between rival imperialisms might be transformed into a civil war involving, not merely the former tsarist lands, but the whole of Central Europe and the Balkans; and, by suggesting a radical basis for the new world order, it stimulated the champions of liberal democracy to public avowal of their own belief in alternative ways of eliminating future wars between the peoples.

The Russians signed an armistice with the Central Powers at Brest-Litovsk on 15 December. Negotiations for a formal peace treaty began there a week later. They were broken off at the end of February 1918 when the Bolsheviks refused to accept a dictated settlement; and hurriedly resumed a few days later when the Germans advanced deeply into the Ukraine and along the Baltic Coast to within fifty miles of Petrograd. The Treaty of Brest-Litovsk was signed on 3 March and the Russians were required to surrender Poland, the Baltic provinces, Finland,

Bessarabia, the Ukraine and the Caucasus. The Bolsheviks were thus deprived of almost all the lands added by successive tsars to their empire since the accession of Peter the Great. All the territory occupied by the Germans and Austrians was subjected to economic controls imposed by the military command and specifically accepted by the Russians in a subsidiary treaty. The Ukraine was declared a separate and independent state with an administration organized by the former tsarist general Skoropadski; the Ukrainian nationalists, of whom there were several different brands, developed ambitions in Eastern Galicia and Ruthenia which were unwelcome to the Austrians and to their Polish clients in Warsaw. But, as Skoropadski's authority rested on German and Austrian arms, the Ukrainian State gave its creators little trouble. An even less genuine freedom was assigned to Lithuania and Estonia.

The Roumanian army, which had fought with valour and enterprise in the eleven months following the fall of Bucharest, was cut off by the Russian armistice, and accepted a separate peace treaty on 7 May 1918. The terms imposed by the Central Powers were relatively generous: the southern Dobrudja was retroceded to Bulgaria and there was a minor adjustment of the frontier in Transylvania, but Roumania was herself permitted to acquire Bessarabia out of the wreck of the Russian State, and only the economic controls were burdensome. The treaty was never ratified by the Roumanian Parliament and its terms were invalidated by the general collapse of Germany and her allies six months after it was signed. The Roumanians, however, contrived to retain Bessarabia in the final settlement.

From the earliest days of the revolution Lenin and the Soviets had made it clear that they believed in the rights of all peoples to complete self-determination and sought a 'Peace without Annexations'. The Brest-Litovsk negotiations – and, for that matter, the activities of the embryonic Red Army in Kiev, Finland and Estonia – suggested that reality was likely to fall far short of this ideal. But the propaganda value of such a message in a war-weary world was considerable and many of the socialist groups in East-Central Europe were prepared to commit themselves to the Leninist programme even though some, in the early days of battle, had been rabidly nationalistic. The number of convinced Marxists was still small but experienced agitators could often find a ready response in communities which had little wish to change the social order. On 1 February 1918, for example, there was a mutiny among the forty vessels of the Austro-Hungarian fleet anchored off Kotor which was led by two Czech socialists serving on the lower-deck of the flagship. Yet, though the seamen who followed them did so under red flags and Bolshevik slogans, many of the mutineers' demands echoed President Wilson's speeches and their main political desires were no further to the left than the programmes of the Slav groups in the Vienna Reichsrat: an end to the war and acceptance of genuine national autonomy. With the return of prisoners-of-war from Russia in the spring of 1918 communist unrest spread rapidly: in May there were mutinies by Slovene units stationed in western Styria, by Ruthenes in Ljubljana and by Czechs at Rumburk in Bohemia, along the Sudeten frontier with Saxony. Each of these disturbances was a demonstration for food, for peace and for national self-determination; they were socially disruptive only in so far as they were aimed against an upper class which depended on the Habsburg dynasty for its privileges. Among the Slav peoples and the Roumanians in the Monarchy national unity and independence had a greater appeal at that moment than social egalitarianism, but the Hungarians were more politically orthodox even in revolution; and it is significant that the first 'school' for foreign communists in Moscow was established in May under the control of the Hungarian-born Béla Kun rather than under a Slav or even a German.

It was on 8 January 1918, while Trotsky was urging the Allies to join Russia at the Brest-Litovsk conference table, that President Woodrow Wilson delivered his famous address to Congress listing Fourteen Points as the 'only possible program' for peace; and the President's words were intended as a moral counter-offensive to the attractive appeal of the Bolsheviks for an immediate end to all fighting. Subsequently, of course, the speech was hailed as a basic charter for freedom among the European peoples. At the time, however, although many agreed with Wilson's general sentiments, his specific proposals had few champions outside the English-speaking nations and some continental liberal democrats felt, not merely disappointed, but positively betrayed by their chosen prophet. Point 13, which proposed an independent Poland 'with free and secure access to the sea' was welcomed by all the Entente governments, but Points 9, 10 and 11 fell short of expectations. The promise to re-adjust Italy's frontiers on lines of nationality was interpreted in Rome as a denial of the Treaty of London, whose terms had recently been revealed by the Bolshevik press although censorship prevented them receiving wide publicity in the West. There was no mention, in Point 11, of Yugo-slav unity but merely of the evacuation of enemy forces from Serbia and Montenegro and of giving Serbia (like Poland) access to the sea. It was, however, Point 10 which caused the most apprehension; for, in assuring the peoples of Austria-Hungary 'the freest opportunity of autonomous development,' the President clearly envisaged the survival of the Habsburg State in the new world order even though he had induced Congress to declare war on the monarchy four weeks before. Since Lloyd George, in an address to the British Trade Unions on 5 January, had gone even further than Wilson and specifically asserted that the dissolution of

Austria-Hungary was not an Allied war aim, the *New Europe* group and the committees of exiles began a campaign of vigorous protest against both statements of policy.

The reluctance of the President and the prime minister to give the Habsburg Monarchy notice to quit sprang in part from a false assessment of the national problem in Central Europe; but they were also influenced by their hope that Austria-Hungary might accept a separate peace, for the Emperor Charles was in contact with the Allies and the Americans by at least four independent intermediaries that winter. By the spring of 1918, however, the official attitude had changed considerably: a wave of strikes in Bohemia and Moravia seemed to confirm the frequent declarations of Masaryk and Beneš that the Czech peoples were devoted to the Allied cause; and the possibility of enticing the Monarchy out of the war lessened with Clemenceau's partial revelations about peace talks and the subsequent tightening of the political and military links between Austria-Hungary and Germany. Even as early as the end of February the British Cabinet authorized its propagandists to launch a campaign to encourage resistance among the subject nationalities; and in the second week of April a 'Congress of Oppressed Peoples' in Rome issued a declaration favouring the establishment of 'completely independent national states' at the end of the war, a move which had special significance since the Congress received backing from the Italian government, which had hitherto been reluctant to support any programme which might encourage the aspirations of the Southern Slavs. It was, indeed, an impressive gathering in the Capitol Hall with representatives of the Czechoslovak, Polish and Yugoslav Committees, spokesmen from the Roumanians of Transylvania and Serbian parliamentarians sitting side by side with such publicists as Wickham Steed and R. W. Seton-Watson and numerous Italian politicians, including the then barely known newspaper editor, Benito Mussolini.

The Czechoslovak cause made rapid progress in the United States during the summer of 1918 after Masaryk arrived in San Francisco at the end of April, for a personal friendship developed between the former professor from Prague and the former professor from Princeton, now resident in the White House. Masaryk was able to supply the State Department with more detailed information on conditions in Central Europe than its own researches had revealed. He did not need to convert Wilson to national self-determination but merely to convince him that autonomous development under the Habsburg aegis was not in itself a sufficient guarantee of the subject peoples' rights. By re-furbishing a contractual theory dear to all American political philosophers Masaryk was able to argue that since the Habsburgs were an elected dynasty on the Bohemian throne, they had forfeited their right to rule in Prague by embarking on a war which was against the interest of the Czech people. Less academically minded Americans were more impressed by the exploits of the Czech Legion in Russia which gave clear proof of its depth of national feeling by fighting its way across Siberia and undertaking a journey of five thousand miles in order to continue the war against the Central Powers.

Masaryk, who remained in the United States until after the final armistices, also made contact with the emigrant Slovak and Ruthene groups: in the so-called 'Pittsburgh Convention' of 30 May he agreed that Slovakia should enjoy autonomy once it united with the Czech provinces; and, after long negotiations with the Ruthenes, he promised them similar rights by the 'Philadelphia Agreement' of 26 October. Neither the Pittsburgh Convention nor the Philadelphia Agreement were legally binding on any future government in Prague since they were concluded with citizens of the United States rather than with delegates from the Slovak and Ruthene people still living in the Old World; but, like Pašić after the Corfu Pact, Masaryk had assumed a moral obligation to place these declarations before accredited representatives of the nationalities after liberation. There is no doubt that Masaryk's willingness to consult the Slovaks and Ruthenes in America increased the sympathy shown by Wilson for the Czechoslovak programme of action. On 3 September the United States formally recognized the Czechoslovak National Council in Paris as a co-belligerent government, a status which was not accorded to the Council by France until five weeks later (although the British had recognized the Council 'as the present trustee of the future Czecho-Slovak government' on 9 August).

Although many units returning from the eastern front were in a state of mutiny, the Austro-Hungarian army facing the Italians along the Piave remained a formidable and well-disciplined force until the late summer of 1918. With German support it had gained an outstanding victory as recently as October 1917, when the Italians were sent reeling back from Caporetto in confusion. Throughout the war the traditional enmity of Italian and Croat ensured a high degree of loyalty among the Southern Slav regiments on this front; and one of the most successful Habsburg commanders was in fact a Serb from the old 'Military Frontier' region, Marshal Svetozar Boroević, whose family had fought for the emperors through many generations. Gradually, however, unrest at home blunted the effectiveness of the army as a military instrument. In June no less than seven divisions were assigned to internal security duties at a time when the High Command was planning one last offensive to break the Italian lines. Despite the frittering away of their fighting power, the Austrians duly attacked on 15 June and lost 150,000 men with few gains. When that night the Emperor Charles heard of the failure to break through the Italian defences he became finally convinced of defeat; and though he authorized desperate experiments in the following months to preserve the integrity of the Monarchy, he sensed that nothing he could offer would counter the persuasive appeals of the National Committees in exile. Within the Monarchy itself representative assemblies of Croats, Slovenes, Poles, Czechs and Slovaks were openly preparing to secede; and in Hungary Count Mihály Károlyi, always a friend of the Entente, was urging his wing of the 'Party of Independence' to take the lead in severing all links with Vienna so as to conclude a specifically Hungarian peace with the Allies. Morale was beginning to crack among the regiments on the Italian front and desertion to thin their ranks. On 14 September the Austro-Hungarian foreign minister, Count Burian, despatched a proposal to Wilson for informal peace talks, but it was rejected: the President was by now firmly resolved on a 'decisive victory of arms'.

The Bulgarian people, too, were heartily sick of war. During six years of intermittent fighting Bulgaria had suffered a higher proportion of casualties than the population of either Germany or France; and her territorial prizes looked insignificant. The economy of the country was exploited by German industrial combines and, with few able-bodied peasants in the fields, famine was imminent, particularly as the harvest of 1917 had been poor. The army fought well in Macedonia, especially in April and May 1917 around Lake Doiran where the British suffered more than five thousand casualties in two night assaults on positions which the Bulgars defended with the tenacity of the French at Verdun. But in June 1918, with the parties of the Left threatening revolution, King Ferdinand dismissed his Germanophile prime minister, Vasil Radoslavov, and appointed as his successor Alexander Malinov, a moderate democrat with Entente sympathies. Malinov was prevented from carrying out his original intention of beginning peace talks by the Bulgarian High Command; but he succeeded in organizing a fairer system of bread distribution and thereby quietened for the moment some of the most dangerous unrest.

The British and French commanders in Macedonia knew that a determined and sustained offensive would 'have more than local effect'; but the Allied governments, particularly the British, were for long reluctant to give consent to operations in a remote theatre of war while vital battles were being fought out on the western front. General Franchet d'Espérey, who took up his appointment as commander-in-chief of the 'Allied Armies of the Orient' at Salonika on 17 June 1918, had ambitious plans for advancing from Macedonia to the Hungarian Plain and beyond; but it was not until 4 September, eleven days before he wished to begin his offensive, that Lloyd George gave approval for British participation.

In London there was far more interest in defeating Turkey than in gaining victories against the Bulgars or the armies of Austria-Hungary; and during the subsequent fighting Franchet d'Espérey was given a free hand to penetrate Central Europe in return for allowing the British Salonika force to swing eastwards on Constantinople. This strategic division of operations into distinctive zones had important consequences in the years of post-war settlement: together with Allenby's successes in Palestine, it ensured that Britain was committed to a positive policy in the eastern Mediterranean and the Levant; and it made it no less certain that France would assume responsibility for keeping watch on the Danube from Bratislava to the sea.

The Macedonian offensive, in which French, British, Serbian, Greek and Italian divisions participated, was a resounding triumph. Within eleven days the Bulgars sued for an armistice, which was signed in Salonika on the night of 29/30 September; and within seven weeks the Serbs had swept back up the Vardar-Morava route to Belgrade while their French allies were 'marching on Vienna, for the first time since 1809,' as Franchet d'Espérey reported with anticipatory hyperbole (for the Austrian capital was, in fact, still 300 miles away).

Meanwhile, the predominantly Italian army along the Piave had gone over to the offensive on 24 October. There was a week of grim fighting but on 30 October the Austrian line was broken at Vittorio Veneto and two days later representatives of the Austro-Hungarian General Staff met the Italian commanders in Padua to work out conditions for an armistice. Fighting ended on the Italian front on 3 November; and since the Turks had signed an armistice at Mudros on 30 October, Germany remained as the sole combatant among the Central Powers. With Bulgaria overrun by the British from Salonika, Allied troops entered Ruse on the lower Danube; and their arrival only forty miles south of Bucharest prompted the Roumanians to declare war on Germany once more on 9 November, even though much of the Kingdom was still occupied by Mackensen's army. Military operations ceased with the German armistice in the West on 11 November; but troop movements with implications for the diplomats long continued throughout the whole of Central Europe.

With an autumn of apprehension passing into another winter of hunger, political change began to outstrip even the fast-moving armies of the Entente; and in its final weeks the great conflict became not so much a 'universal war for the freedom of nations' as a universal scramble for international recognition by local leaders of revolt. Some of the provisional administrations lasted for only a few days of confusion; others merged into larger units after issuing declarations of intent, all too often unfulfilled; and a few became a nucleus around which the political institutions of a new Europe were to develop. At the same time, the revolutionary situation was more complex than in 1848 over all central and south-eastern Europe not only because of the centrifugal attraction of existing national states and of the committees of exiles, but because of the unique respect shown by both the vanquished and the triumphant for the pronouncements of an American President who had never visited their lands and whose lack of expert knowledge was seen as a guarantee of impartiality.

The immediate troubles of Bulgaria were solved with deceptive ease. On 27 September a republic was proclaimed in the small manufacturing town of Radomir with the peasant leader Stamboliisky as president, and some fifteen thousand rebellious soldiers marched on Sofia. There were three days of civil war and a pitched battle was fought at Vladaya, ten miles south of Sofia, in which the old order was defended by German gunners, military cadets and IMRO fanatics under General Protogerov. Republican sentiment was, however, no more than skin deep; the rebels wanted peace first and foremost and, when news reached them of the Salonika armistice, they dispersed to the towns; and nothing more was heard of the republic. On 3 October King Ferdinand abdicated in favour of his son Boris, whose war record was impeccable. Ex-President Stamboliisky went into hiding for ten weeks and joined a coalition government six months later; by October 1919 he was King Boris's premier. An Allied army of occupation kept order in the streets while a wave of communist feeling swept town and country alike; and the new King waited uneasily to see what territories he would have to forfeit for his father's mistaken gamble in 1915.

Polish affairs were more complicated. On 7 October the puppet Polish Regency Council in Warsaw took the initiative by invoking President Wilson's principles of self-determination to proclaim a free and independent Polish State. But, as Austria-Hungary disintegrated, rival authorities sprang up elsewhere: a 'Polish Liquidation Commission' in Cracow and a left-wing 'Provisional People's Government of the Polish Republic' in Lublin. A 'Ukrainian National Council' tried to seize power in Lvov and there was fighting between Poles and Ukrainians in eastern Galicia. Moreover, as revolutionary activity spread through the German regiments, 'Workers and Soldiers Councils' were established in a number of Poznanian towns. The only person with sufficient prestige to check the anarchy and unify the Polish lands was Pilsudski, still imprisoned in Magdeburg when the troubles began. On 10 November, however, he was brought to Warsaw in a German special train; and, although backed by the Lublin socialists and giving their leaders ministerial posts, he

accepted office from the Regency Council, thereby ensuring legal constitutional continuity between the wartime 'kingdom' and the new
republic. On 14 November he became Polish 'Chief of State,' a dignity
enjoyed only once before, by Kosciuszko in 1793. It was another three
months before Pilsudski secured a reconciliation with Dmowski's
committee in Paris, which the Allies and the Americans had recognized
as the true voice of the Polish people.

The Czechoslovak National Council in Paris had long been anxious
to prevent a similar rift with the independence movement in Prague,
and Beneš, who controlled the council's activities while Masaryk was in
the United States, kept in close touch with the *mafie*, the underground
resistance movement in the homeland. A delegation from the Prague
'National Committee' led by Kramář, who still hoped for a constitutional
monarchy rather than a republic, set out for Switzerland on 25 October.
The Austro-Hungarian foreign ministry, anxious to impress Wilson with
its good intentions towards the Slav peoples, supplied the delegation
with passports when it stopped in Vienna on its way to Geneva, where it
met Beneš on 28 October. That same day representatives of the four
Czech political parties in the Prague Committee formally proclaimed 'an
independent Czechoslovak State' and called on their compatriots to be
worthy of their 'liberators, Masaryk and Wilson'.

The transfer of administrative authority to the Czechs went smoothly
and speedily in Bohemia and Moravia, except in the Sudeten towns where
the German population set up national councils and sought to preserve
contact with German-Austria until the end of the year. The claim of the
Czechoslovak National Council or the Prague Committee to speak for the
remanent Slovak politicians, as opposed to Slovak exiles, was questionable
since they had only established links with the Prague *mafie* in May and
these were of the most tenuous kind. There was, moreover, no cooperation as yet between the Czechs and the indigenous Ruthenes in their
isolated valleys 350 miles east of Prague. Both Slovakia and Ruthenia
formed part of the Hungarian Kingdom, which was itself undergoing a
remarkable revolution in these same weeks, and the situation long remained confused. In Vienna, however, there was little doubt over the
character of events in Prague; for as early as 30 October, the last of
Charles's Austrian prime ministers, Heinrich Lammasch, was prepared
to welcome a spokesman of the National Committee as 'ambassador of
the Czechoslovak State'. A Revolutionary National Assembly met in
Prague on 14 November and elected Masaryk as President of the republic.
Kramář, finding little support for his unfashionable monarchism, agreed
to head the first government, with Beneš as his foreign minister.

The Hungarian Revolution came to a head on 17 October when the
veteran Magyar leader Tisza astounded the Budapest parliament by

conceding that Count Mihály Károlyi was correct in maintaining that the war was lost. Three days later the news was received in Budapest that, in reply to proposals from Charles for a peace based on the Fourteen Points, President Wilson had made it clear that 'autonomy' for the subject peoples was no longer a sufficient assurance of satisfaction of their national rights: the Americans had an obligation towards the Czechoslovaks and the Southern Slavs. The full significance of this death warrant on the Monarchy was not immediately perceived in either of its capitals; but in Hungary it clearly strengthened the hand of the Károlyi Independents. Their leader argued that if Hungary broke with the German-Austrians and became genuinely democratic, the nationalities would still choose to remain within a predominantly Magyar state provided that they could be certain of autonomous development. On 25 October Károlyi formed – for it was the fashion – a 'Hungarian National Council' and five days later King-Emperor Charles invited him by telephone to head a new government in the hope that a radical and separatist administration might stave off civil war. Unrest was growing even in Budapest, where an angry mob murdered István Tisza in his own house.

Károlyi remained the King's prime minister for some twenty-four hours. Then, with royal approval, he broke all formal links with Vienna and inclined Hungary for the first time in its history towards a republic (which was duly proclaimed on 16 November). In order to demonstrate his independence of the old order, Károlyi travelled to Belgrade and sought a separate armistice from Franchet d'Espérey. The two men met on 7 November: it was not the happiest of encounters. Károlyi's long statement of democratic principles left Franchet d'Espérey unmoved and Wilsonian attitudes irritated him, for the imperious French general had little sympathy with American idealism. He informed Károlyi that Hungary was a defeated state and handed him the printed conditions of an armistice which authorized the Allied High Command to occupy the whole of the eastern and southern parts of the old Hungarian Kingdom and any other strategic points they might designate. The Hungarians sent a telegram of protest to Clemenceau, without effect; and Károlyi's subsequent appeal to the White House, as from one president to another, seeking 'assistance for the young Hungarian democracy' evoked little response.

The attitude of the Allied authorities made it unlikely that Károlyi's ambitious plans for satisfying the dissident nationalities would ever be put into practice. There is no doubt that when he tore up the Ausgleich he believed he could still preserve the territorial integrity of the 'lands of the Holy Crown'. It was already too late. Croatia had long since determined on a break with Hungary and there was little hope of retaining Transylvania or Slovakia. The Roumanians in Transylvania, ably led by Iuliu Maniu, had set up their National Council at Oradea on 12 October; it passed a solemn declaration in favour of self-determination at Arad on 27 October and contacted Bucharest as soon as it could in November. A Slovak National Council met at Turciansky Svaty Martin on 29 October and in a three day discussion agreed on a declaration which claimed that the Slovaks were members of a single Czecho-Slovak nation, although with a right of free self-determination; and the Slovak political leaders gave a chilly response to Károlyi's 'fraternal greetings' from Budapest. The only local committee to support Károlyi was one which met in Uzhorod, a predominantly Magyar and Jewish town in Ruthenia; but its vote for autonomy within a Hungarian Republic was countered by two other 'Ruthene National Councils,' meeting in Lubovna and Khust, who were uncertain what they wanted but knew it was not union with Hungary. The advance of Allied troops never gave Károlyi a chance of discovering the will of the people of the Voivodina but, as the area around Novi Sad had been a centre of Serbian culture for more than a century, it is unlikely that, even in a free referendum, the Hungarian Republic would have received a majority.

The Yugoslav problem was fundamentally different from all the others: it involved not only the ubiquitous 'National Councils' but the rivalry between Trumbić's 'Yugoslav Committee' and the Serbian government, flushed with the astounding success of its army in Macedonia; and matters were complicated still further by the fate of the Austro-Hungarian navy, which in 1914 had been the fourth most powerful fleet in European waters. On 29 October the Croatian Diet in Zagreb formally proclaimed Croatia-Slavonia, together with Dalmatia and Rijeka (Fiume), as part of an independent 'national and sovereign state of the Slovenes, Croats and Serbs.' Representative bodies in Ljubljana, Sarajevo and other cities issued similar declarations and pledged support to the Yugoslav National Council in Zagreb authorizing it to act as a provisional government responsible for carrying through union with Serbia and Montenegro. The Council was presided over by Antun Korošec, with the *prečani* Serb Svetozar Pribičević as his deputy; and on 31 October it received official recognition from Emperor Charles.

Korošec thereupon set out for Geneva whence he sent a message to Trumbić in Paris empowering the Yugoslav Committee to represent the Zagreb Council in dealing with the Allies. At the time a furious wrangle over the status of the committee was going on between Trumbić and Pašić, who was also in Paris and who was disinclined, now that victory was imminent, to honour the pact made in the dark days on Corfu. Trumbić and Pašić, still at loggerheads, travelled to Geneva and after several days of talks with Korošec issued a joint declaration on 9 November which appeared to concede most of Trumbić's demands: a South Slav union was formally constituted 'from today as an indivisible state-unit'; there would be a coalition cabinet, pending preparations of a new construction. But on returning to Paris, Pašić resigned and declared the agreement null and void.

Events in the northern Adriatic made settlement of these disputes urgent. On the afternoon of 31 October – four days before the Padua armistice – Admiral Miklós Horthy, the commander-in-chief of the Austro-Hungarian fleet, obeyed orders from Vienna to surrender the principal naval base and all the warships to the Yugoslav National Committee in Pula as trustees for the Zagreb Council. The committee, puzzled by their unsolicited gift, sent a radio-telegram to the universal arbiter in Washington inviting President Wilson to despatch US naval units to Pula. They received instead, a visit from an Italian torpedo-boat which, refusing to acknowledge that the fleet was in Allied hands, torpedoed the dreadnought *Viribus Unitis* at anchor, causing considerable loss of life. This dastardly act was clear proof that the Italians would never permit the Yugoslavs to dispose of such a powerful fleet; and on the following day the rest of the squadron put to sea and sailed down the Adriatic to Corfu, where it was handed over to the French for eventual distribution among the Allied states. An Italian task-force seized Pula itself on 5 November and proceeded to occupy other points in Istria and Dalmatia which had been promised to Italy by the Treaty of London.

There was some risk that the Italians might also occupy Ljubljana, the capital of Slovenia. In order to prevent such a blow to Yugoslav hopes Colonel Dušan Simović, the commander of the Serbian advance-guard in Zagreb, sent his men forward into Slovenia; and, at the same time, he pressed Pribičević to reach an agreement with Belgrade, ignoring the slow deliberations taking place in Paris after the breakdown of the Geneva talks. Pribičević, far more conscious of the urgency of presenting a united obstacle to the Italians than either Korošec or Trumbić, secured passage of a resolution by the council in favour of union with the Serbs without any of the safeguards of the Geneva Agreement; and on the evening of 1 December a united Kingdom of Serbs, Croats and Slovenes was formally proclaimed in Belgrade. Although Trumbić subsequently became foreign minister in a coalition of which Korošec was vice-premier, the negotiations of the preceding five weeks left most of the cards in the hands of the Serbian political leaders, a development of ominous significance for the new kingdom.

While almost all his provinces were sprouting the remarkable crop of national councils, the Emperor Charles remained in Vienna, apart from a brief visit to Debrecen, Gödöllö and Bratislava in the fourth week of

October. An imperial manifesto making a final promise to federalize the Austrian lands satisfied no one. Yet, even as late as 20 October, when news of President Wilson's modification of the Fourteen Points reached Vienna, the Emperor still hoped to save something from the wreck. It was only the impact of military defeat on the Italian front that convinced him of the collapse of the dynasty, for the army was the cornerstone on which the imperial structure rested. Technically Charles never abdicated. On 11 November he pencilled his signature to a note acknowledging 'the decision of German-Austria to form a separate state' and relinquished 'participation in the administration of the state'; and two days later he gave a similar renunciation of his Hungarian executive functions to emissaries from Budapest. Eventually he took the inevitable route to exile in Switzerland, but for some weeks he lingered on in the baroque hunting-lodge of Eckartsau, looking out across the misty gloom of the Marchfeld as the imperial insignia were hacked down in city after city of the monarchy.

Curiously enough, ten days after Charles's renunciation of powers, one unit of the Imperial and Royal army duly commemorated the second anniversary of his accession, not knowing that the monarchy had fallen or that the war was over. On 21 November 1918 General Pflanzer-Balltin, whose military career hitherto had been amiably insignificant, took the salute at a march-past of occupation troops in central Albania. The black and gold war standard of Europe's oldest dynasty flew for the last time at a ceremonial parade in the most remote and obscure valleys of the whole continent. It was, perhaps, an appropriate setting for the twilight of the demi-gods.

8

The Making of Peace

Within ten weeks of the German armistice, delegations from the twenty-seven victorious 'Allied and Associated Powers' gathered in the French capital for the most comprehensive of all peace conferences. Technically its sessions lasted for just twelve months, from 18 January 1919 to 21 January 1920; but many problems remained unresolved for a longer period of time and the treaties with Hungary and Turkey were not concluded until after the principal participants had dispersed. Although its decisions were commonly known and frequently abused as the 'Versailles Settlement' most of the detailed negotiations took place at meetings of councils and committees within the city of Paris itself; and only the symbolism of revenge dictated that the treaty with Germany should be signed on 28 June 1919 in the mirrored gallery through which Bismarck's voice had proclaimed an empire less than half a century ago. The other ex-enemy states ceremonially concluded peace in palaces whose past associations bore less heavily on the present: thus the Austrian republicans signed in September 1919 at St Germain, where a Habsburg queen had once given birth to the greatest of French monarchs; the Bulgars in what had been the Pompadour's salon at Neuilly two months later; the Hungarians in the Grand Trianon in June 1920; and the Turks amid the porcelain of Sèvres the following August.

When the conference opened, some delegates were looking to another page of history for instructive parallels. The British Foreign Office had already prepared a handbook on the Congress of Vienna and it was gratifying to see the contrast between that gathering of peacemakers and its successor. In 1815 the princes and aristocrats of Europe had come together to safeguard the principle of legitimism and establish a political equilibrium between their territorial possessions; provinces were bartered with scant regard for the wishes of their peoples. In 1919, on the other hand, there were no hereditary rulers among the major delegates; the only head of state to journey to Paris enjoyed unprecedented respect for the noble ideal he had enunciated so mellifluously on Capitol Hill twelve months before; and the egalitarian doctrine of self-determination carried with it a comforting assurance of righteousness. Yet as the Peace Conference became increasingly immersed in details of negotiation so the difficulty of reconciling Woodrow Wilson's theories with the business of frontier-drawing made distinctions between the two international assemblies more apparent than real. To transact their work efficiently delegates were forced on most occasions to meet in private committees rather than arriving at 'open covenants openly' in plenary session; and in order to cover the large and varied agenda it was necessary to entrust control of procedure to councils which were inevitably dominated by the states with the largest and most varied interests. The organizational structure of the Peace Conference therefore rapidly began to resemble the inner core of the Vienna Congress and the only significant difference was in the composition of the 'Big Four': in 1815 Austria, Russia, Britain and Prussia; in 1919 France, the United States, Britain and Italy. On one important procedural principle it could even be maintained that the Congress had shown a more genuine concern for the future; for, while at Vienna defeated France had been admitted as an equal to the European comity, in Paris defeated Germany and her allies had a right of appeal against the provisions of a treaty only after the victors had secured agreement among themselves over its character. The absence of representatives of the neutrals or of Russia at the Peace Conference gave added weight to the subsequent complaint that the treaties were dictated arrangements forced on a new order out of hatred incurred by the old.

The region separating newly republican Germany from newly Bolshevik Russia had become more truly 'the lands between' than in any earlier epoch. None of the 'Big Four' had long-standing interests in these borderlands, but each hurriedly evolved a policy which would partially fill the power vacuum caused by the absence of the old contenders. Already, in the secret negotiations preceding their entry into the war, the Italians had shown that they possessed ambitions along the Adriatic and in the Balkans; and at Paris they were unwilling to conciliate or compromise. For them the Treaty of London meant far more than all the Fourteen Points. Inspired by the realism of Cavour rather than by the generosity of Mazzini, their obduracy led at times to exclusion from the inner councils, a humiliation which their apparent military weakness made all the easier to inflict and the harder to sustain. The French, on the other hand, enjoyed the advantage of Franchet d'Espérey's army on the Danube, overbearing though its commander tended often to be. The patronage bestowed by successive French foreign ministers on the Serbs, Czechs and Roumanians made willing clients for Clemenceau's ideas on security – and, for that matter, for loans from the Paris Bourse and contracts for arms from Schneider-Creusot (an enterprise which, for a brief period in 1920, also had links with the Hungarians). At first the French were slow to give support to Pilsudski's Poland; they abandoned

F

their hesitancy in March 1919 when they despatched a military mission to Warsaw headed by General Henrys, who had been Franchet d'Espérey's principal deputy in the Balkan offensive.

The Americans and the British were less directly involved in Central and Eastern Europe and were therefore more flexible in their attitudes; and yet there were clear limits to their impartiality. The American delegation – which, it is important to remember, did not contain any spokesmen for the Republicans, the majority party in both Houses of Congress – was well-disposed towards the various Slavonic peoples. No doubt this sympathy reflected in part an awareness of the voting strength of compact emigrant communities within the United States; but there was also a genuine conviction in the justice of a long struggle for self-determination. The United States had never been at war with Bulgaria (or with Turkey) and President Wilson remained suspicious of Allied proposals to settle the problems of Macedonia or Thrace. Lloyd George and the British delegation, on the other hand, had a strong admiration for Venizelist Greece, although there were champions of every Balkan cause among the pamphleteers and publicists of London and each of them was prepared to tender advice to the prime minister on the form the new map should follow. The British government and people cared less about the Danubian and Vistulan basins, apart from doubts over French machinations, especially in Poland. Within the Cabinet a powerful pressure-group was prepared to urge bull-like charges on Red Flags wherever they might be flown; its colour sense at times lacked refined discernment.

Events in Russia inevitably cast a shadow of concern over the deliberations of the Big Four, although it must be admitted one delegation – that of Italy – seems rarely to have perceived it. Both the British and the French hoped that the 'Whites,' whose armies fought vigorously against the Bolsheviks throughout 1919, would 'restore order' in Russia. The British assumed heavier obligations for military intervention than their allies though, even so, their total casualties dead and wounded in northern Russia remained under a thousand. French policy showed greater subtlety: at first the French listened to advice from Russian exiles in Paris, including Sazonov and Prince Lvov; later, as the Soviet government gained in strength, they concentrated on building up a Polish army and in seeking to contain communism by erecting a barrier of states friendly to the West along Russia's frontier, a 'barbed wire curtain' as Clemenceau called it. This notion of a defensive line across Eastern Europe also appealed to President Wilson; it helped to determine policies, not only in Poland, but in Roumania as well.

The procedural arrangements of the Peace Conference provided that each recognized delegation should have the right to present a statement of territorial claims to the 'Big Four' and should, in due course, appear before the Supreme Council to answer criticisms and argue its case. Matters might then be referred to one of the fifty-eight committees or commissions for detailed examination, and subsequently a report would be made and the original delegation summoned for a second session with the council. This method had three main weaknesses: it was cumbersome and slow; it had, over questions involving the defeated states, the appearance of a court-case in which only the evidence for the prosecution was heard; and it placed emphasis on the forensic skill of the heads of the various delegations. Occasionally an experienced advocate would lose favour, especially with President Wilson, by a blustering manner, as happened to Roumania's Ionel Bratianu. Sometimes less professional spokesmen scored unexpected triumphs, such as Paderewski's presentation of Poland's case on east Galicia. The sharpest minds were able to put forward claims so eminently reasonable and propose guarantees so manifestly just that neither the council members nor the specialists on the commission could refute them. In such advocacy Edward Beneš of Czechoslovakia was without an equal; but it is unfortunate that the generous comprehension of his proposal 'to make of the Czecho-Slovak Republic a sort of Switzerland' should hold for the future a promise beyond his powers to fulfil; for in later years disappointment inevitably raised the reproach of deception which undermined much of the respect his statesmanship appeared to warrant. Beneš himself admitted in his memoirs that some of the evidence he submitted to the conference was exaggerated and misleading.

The composition and size of delegations was, of course, a matter for individual governments although the number of plenipotentiaries was prescribed by the organizing secretariat of the conference. Thus Great Britain was permitted five plenipotentiaries and brought a delegation of 207, while the 'Serb-Croat-Slovene Kingdom' – as the Yugoslav State was officially called until 1929 – was represented by four plenipotentiaries and a delegation of ninety-three. At times selection of plenipotentiaries raised questions of general concern. Bratianu's refusal to include his political rival Také Ionescu was a minor disaster for the Roumanian cause; Ionescu had many more contacts in the West and had even taken the initiative in settling some of the problems caused by opposing claims to the Bánát. Pašić, whom Prince-Regent Alexander had insisted on appointing to lead the Yugoslavs (partly to keep him away from Belgrade), was hardly less obstinate than Bratianu: he declined at first to accept the Croat Trumbić as a fellow plenipotentiary or as foreign minister; and the two incompatibles remained on bad terms for much of the conference. There were moments when the Yugoslav delegation seemed to retain cohesion only through the skill of Milenko Vesnić, the Serbian minister in Paris, who had influential social connexions in France and the United States and who had married an American heiress.

Even more serious problems were posed by the claim of other national groups to be heard by the conference, or at least to be represented in the delegation of the state responsible for their future development. Monsignor Hlinka, the leader and founder of the Slovak People's Party, came to Paris and presented a petition to the conference seeking autonomy or a plebiscite in the Slovak lands. The French police, however, discovered that he and his chief political associate, another Slovak priest Doctor Jehlička, had committed a technical offence over passports and both men were sent back to Prague complaining that the Czech delegation had incited the French authorities to intervene: no petition from the Slovak People's Party was received by the official 'Commission on Czechoslovak Affairs'. The Croatian Peasant Party Leader, Radić, did not even get as far as Paris; he was arrested in Zagreb before he had completed a memorandum intended for the conference and urging the establishment of a Peasant Republic in Croatia. A garbled version of his appeal reached the Italian delegation and was used as a somewhat clumsy propaganda weapon against Pašić and Trumbić. Yet a third national group, the Sudeten Germans, had placed themselves at a disadvantage by insisting on being regarded as 'German-Austrians'; their leaders accordingly went to Paris as members of the defeated Austrian delegation to receive, but not to negotiate, the Treaty of St Germain. In retrospect, it seems difficult to reconcile these developments with Wilsonian pledges of self-determination.

There were, on the fringe of the conference, a number of aspiring supplicants with preposterous claims and an underworld of brigandage mocked the sincerity of the peacemakers. Both Clemenceau and Venizelos were wounded in attempts on their life; and that colourful veteran intriguer Essad Pasha, once a Turkish general and now self-styled President of an Albanian government of which the conference refused to take cognizance, was assassinated in the streets of Paris by supporters of one of the other Albanian administrations, also unrepresented and unrepresentative.

The presence at the Hotel Meurice of an embattled King Nikita of Montenegro was a more serious embarrassment. Nikita, who had ruled Montenegro ever since 1860 and celebrated the fiftieth anniversary of his accession by raising his dignity from Prince to King, was the father-in-law of the rulers of both Italy and Serbia; he had fallen from grace but not from favour by his equivocal conduct in the Austrian invasion of 1916. He claimed that his 'prime minister,' Jovan Plamenatz, had a right to sit as an allied delegate even though an assembly in Podgorica had voted for the King's deposition and the union of Montenegro with Serbia.

The Italian delegation supported Nikita's contention. No less than three fact-finding missions were sent from Paris to Montenegro; and they reported that while the Podgorica Assembly had been blatantly packed by the Serbs, there was no doubt that the Montenegrins wished to be included in the Yugoslav State. Protocol was duly observed at the six plenary sessions of the conference by placing a gilt chair behind the table where a white card labelled 'Montenegro' maintained the illusion of representation; but the chair remained empty and the interests of Montenegrins were championed by two relatively junior members of the Yugoslav delegation. Nikita himself lived on in Paris, enjoying a French pension until his death in March 1921.

These problems of procedure and of representation were not trivial, for even their occasional absurdities concealed important matters of principle; they were however, essentially peripheral to the major questions of dispute. Fundamentally the Peace Conference was faced with three overwhelming tasks: the difficulty of reconciling promises of territorial aggrandisement given by wartime secret treaties with the legitimate interests of other states; the drawing of frontiers which made sense in terms of trade and defence but which did not treat the indigenous peoples as 'chattels or pawns in the game'; and the enforcement of decisions taken in Paris which ran counter to arbitrary acts by local zealots. The secret agreements over the Arab lands and over Shantung fall outside the scope of this study and the bargains with Russia on Constantinople and the Straits had been invalidated by the Bolshevik Revolution; but the treaties with Italy and Roumania caused embarrassment and delay throughout the conference and friction for long after, the more especially because the United States had never been a party to them and President Wilson regarded their very existence with abhorrence. The problem of reconciling ethnic claims and of balancing them against economic and strategic considerations was particularly acute in all Central and Eastern Europe. In such cases the conference decided on the evidence of expert commissions, seeking a just settlement but inevitably tending to give the benefit of any doubt to one of the Allied states or new creations rather than to an ex-enemy. If both claimants were on the side of the angels, the decision all too often showed the devastating realism of a Solomon and valley farms were cut off from mountain pastures, villages from markets and even suburbs from towns for which they had been working-class dormitories. It was over disputes of this character that armed detachments of regular troops or auxiliaries sought to pre-judge the settlement, sometimes successfully.

It is hardly surprising that such issues delayed the conclusion of the treaties for many months; some matters were left for ambassadorial conferences or the League of Nations to determine at a later date, while a few were resolved only by hard bi-lateral negotiation. The five Paris peace treaties do not therefore in themselves constitute the peace settlement. There were several instances where political boundaries were clearly delineated at the conference along some sectors of a frontier and left imprecise in others. The most important example of such different standards of map-making was in Poland, for while the conference was very conscious of its responsibilities over the ex-German lands in the West, it regarded the allocation of what had been Russian territory as beyond its competence, contenting itself with advice (which was almost invariably disregarded). Uncertainty over the frontier in the East remained so long as Poland regarded herself at war with Bolshevik Russia; and this in its turn delayed the final settlement of the former Austrian possessions in the south-east, particularly Galicia.

Poland's frontiers in the West were defined, after long disputes between the British and French, in the Treaty of Versailles. The Poles received most of their claim against Germany: Poznania, Pomerania and a corridor to the Baltic which cut off East Prussia from the German State. In two small districts on the East Prussian frontier, Marienwerder and Allenstein, it was agreed that there should be plebiscites; these were duly held in July 1920 and as 96.5 per cent of the population voted in favour of Germany they remained in East Prussia. Since the inhabitants of Danzig were overwhelmingly German the British delegation insisted that the port should be constituted a Free City under the League of Nations and linked by customs union to Poland; responsibility for its foreign relations was to be left with the Poles. When the terms of the treaty were handed to the German delegation early in May 1919, they aroused great bitterness. Poznania was, almost literally, a nursery for the Prussian officer-corps – Poznan itself was the birthplace of both Hindenburg and Ludendorff – and the German High Command even considered denouncing the armistice and resuming hostilities in the East. Such suicidal gestures were abandoned in favour of reasoned protests; and, while the Allies made no modifications over Poznania, they agreed that the fate of the great industrial region of Upper Silesia should be settled by plebiscite. There was, however, a considerable difference between conducting an impartial plebiscite in predominantly rural districts on the borders of East Prussia and in the towns of a mining area, especially as on three occasions local Polish fanatics sought a short cut to a solution by insurrection. When, in March 1921, the vote was taken it gave a majority in favour of Germany but showed that some districts were strongly Polish in sentiment. A committee of inter-allied experts referred the whole problem to the League of Nations which eventually decided in the spring of 1922 to divide the

POLAND 1815-1918

0   200
Miles

LITHUANIA
(Russian)

Vilna

Minsk

EAST
Danzig(Gdansk)
PRUSSIA

POZNANIA
(Prussian)

Berlin

Poznan

RUSSIA

Warsaw
CONGRESS KINGDOM
OF POLAND
(Russian)

Brest-Litovsk

Lublin

PRUSSIA

Breslau
(Wroclaw)

Prague

Cracow

Lvov

GALICIA
(Austrian)

Partitioning Powers: Prussia, Austria and Russia
—·—· Boundary of Polish Republic, 1821
///// "Congress Kingdom"
▓▓▓ Republic of Cracow (1815-1846)

AUSTRIA

POLAND 1919-1939

0   200
Miles

Memel

LITHUANIA

Vilna

U.
S.
S.
R.

EAST
Danzig(Gdansk)
PRUSSIA

Minsk

GERMANY

Berlin

Poznan

Warsaw

Brest-Litovsk

POLAND

Breslau
(Wroclaw)

Lublin

Prague

Cracow

Lvov

Teschen

CZECHOSLOVAKIA

—·—· Boundary 1919-1939
///// Territory seized from Czechoslovakia in 1938
▬▬▬ Russo-German Pact Dividing Line of 1939

ROUMANIA

area between the two contending states, with an international arbitration tribunal ensuring economic and social continuity for a period of fifteen years. Three-quarters of the disputed territory went to Germany but fifty-three of the sixty-seven coal mines were in the area assigned to Poland. It was by no means an ideal solution and was invalidated (drastically) by the events of the Second World War and their aftermath.

In the south the Polish frontiers were drawn entirely through lands which had formed part of the Austro-Hungarian Empire and were therefore surrendered by the Treaties of St Germain and Trianon. In practice their demarcation depended on agreement with the Czechoslovaks, who were neighbours of the Poles along all their southern border, apart from the ninety miles of east Galicia and Roumanian-occupied Bukovina. At first Polish-Czech relations were friendly enough; for when the old Monarchy fell asunder, both nationalities set up committees and these exercised control on either side of a rough and ready boundary, allegedly ethnographical in determination. Tension mounted over two small counties in Slovakia, Orava and Spiš, where the partitioning of Poland had begun exactly 150 years before; but the most serious disputes were in the former Duchy of Teschen which was geographically due south of the contested Germano-Polish area in Upper Silesia.

An Austrian linguistic census had shown the population of the Duchy in 1910 to be approximately 55 per cent Polish, 27 per cent Czech and 18 per cent German. The Czechs wanted Teschen for its coalfields and its position astride one of the few railways linking Bohemia and Slovakia; the Poles claimed the Duchy on ethnic and economic grounds; and neither nationality was prepared to wait for the decision of the Peace Conference nor accept a plebiscite. In December 1918 the Poles announced elections in their zone of occupation for a parliament in Warsaw, and the Czechs replied in the following month by sending their troops north, evicting the Poles after several days of fighting. The problem eluded solution for another eighteen months until a specially constituted inter-allied commission dictated the frontier between the two states at a time when, for differing reasons, both of them were anxious for diplomatic support in the West and were therefore more tractable than in the previous year. The commission left the town of Teschen in Poland but its railway-station and the rich coalfields went to Czechoslovakia; farther east the Poles gained strips of territory in Spiš and Orava but nearly three quarters of these counties were left in Slovakia. The Teschen award was regarded by the Poles as a humiliation and estranged the two Slav peoples for the whole of the inter-war period; and yet even today the frontier follows the demarcation line of 1920, despite Polish incursions southward in 1938–9 and in 1945.

The German minority in the Teschen area hoped, in vain, that the Polish-Czech quarrel might call in question the whole basis on which the Prague government was controlling the frontier districts. In pre-war days Pan-German feeling had been stronger in the old towns on the fringe of Bohemia such as Reichenberg, Aussig and Eger than anywhere else in the Monarchy. The Czechs took over the predominantly German regions of both Bohemia and Moravia before the end of 1918 and administered all of the Sudetenland as though it were enemy territory under occupation. Anti-Czech demonstrations on 4 March 1919 led to shooting and the loss of fifty-two German lives. To draw a frontier separating German and Czech districts would have been difficult because there were numerous ethnic 'islands'; it would also have been economically disastrous, as some German industrialists themselves realized. The Peace Conference therefore determined to accept the historic Austro-German frontier, except for two minor instances: an adjustment at Hultschin, where a predominantly Czech area was surrendered by Germany in the Treaty of Versailles; and a strategic variation at Gmund, where the town was left in Austria and the railway-station ceded to Czechoslovakia.

By maintaining the historic frontier as a boundary the peacemakers made three and a half million German-speaking subjects of the old Monarchy citizens of the Czechoslovak Republic total population, thirteen and a half million). It was over this problem that Beneš informed the Conference in a note on 20 May 1919 that he envisaged the setting up of an 'extremely liberal regime which will very much resemble that of Switzerland,' although in the same document he had already qualified this Swiss analogy by insisting that the new republic would have to take into consideration 'the special conditions in Bohemia'. There is no doubt that, at the time, Beneš was thinking of guarantees of linguistic rights and of wide powers in local autonomy; and these beliefs were reflected in the 1920 Czechoslovak Constitution. It was certainly assumed by the 'Commission on Czechoslovak Affairs' at the Peace Conference that in any Czech 'Switzerland' the Germans and other non-Slav nationalities would be as much a 'People of State' as the Czechs and the Slovaks. The constitution, however, made it clear that the republic comprised Czechs, Slovaks and Ruthenes in partnership; the Germans, Magyars and Poles living within its frontiers were minorities, although assured of equality before the law.

The distinction between these two approaches to the nationality problem became even more important after the demarcation of the frontiers in Slovakia and Ruthenia, when over a million Magyars were included within the new state. Strategic considerations played a far greater part in determining the limits of Slovakia and the fate of Ruthenia than they had

F*

in Bohemia-Moravia. In Slovakia the ethnic boundary followed the foothills of the Carpathians, with the Magyars predominant in the plain although there were Slovak settlements along many of the river valleys and a mixed population in the larger towns. Had this ethnic boundary been established as a frontier it would have made west to east communications through Slovakia virtually impossible and might well have deprived the Czechoslovaks of a Danubian port. The Peace Conference accordingly awarded Bratislava and a small demilitarized bridgehead south of the river to the Czechoslovaks and followed a line well to the south of the ethnic boundary; even so, it left pockets of some hundred and fifty thousand Slovaks in Hungary. Farther east, in Ruthenia, there was a similar pattern of racial settlement and here, too, a strip of plain was included in the area assigned to Czechoslovakia; the Ruthenes were formally assured of 'the widest autonomy compatible with the unity of the Republic'. The thin lizard-tail of Ruthenia was strategically important to the Czechs for three reasons: it gave them a frontier with Roumania; it kept a potentially hostile Poland and a potentially hostile Hungary apart; and it carried the frontier of the most western of Slav states nearer to Mother Russia, a feature which was considered advantageous in those days.

Most of the work of the 'Commission on Czechoslovak Affairs' was completed in Paris by the early spring of 1919 but it was more than a year before the Treaty of Trianon was presented for signature. This delay was caused by political instability within Hungary, which seemed for a few weeks to offer a genuine revolutionary challenge to the character of the whole settlement.

After the conclusion of the Belgrade armistice with Franchet d'Espérey President Mihály Károlyi had been forced to accept in Budapest a representative of the French command, Colonel Vyx, who was ordered to see that its conditions were fulfilled. Thus, while Károlyi endeavoured to secure a number of basic democratic and social reforms, Vyx made certain that Hungarian troops retired from areas claimed by the Allied governments, including the Czechoslovak. When on 3 December 1918 Vyx informed Károlyi that the Czechs had been authorized to occupy the Slovak territories, the Hungarian detachments were duly withdrawn, and a further retreat followed a second peremptory message at the end of the month. On 20 March 1919 Vyx handed Károlyi a note ordering Hungarian troops to fall back in Transylvania so as to allow the Roumanians to advance to a line which was, at its most western point, nearly 250 miles from the pre-war frontier. As Károlyi understood that the area thus occupied would be ceded to Roumania by the peace treaty, he determined to resign rather than accept yet another humiliation to historic Hungary. Power (such as it was) passed into the hands of a left-wing coalition, dominated by the communist Béla Kun. Károlyi, the one totally sincere Wilsonian idealist in European affairs, left Budapest in despair; he later went into an exile from which he returned, fleetingly, only in 1946.

When on 22 March the news reached Paris that there had been 'a Bolshevik revolution in Hungary' the delegates were alarmed, but not surprised. Franchet d'Espérey, who was gathering a considerable force in the Bánát, wanted to march on Budapest at once; he was restrained by Clemenceau, apparently because the Supreme Council had some hopes that it might make contact through Béla Kun with the Soviet government in Moscow. A special mission headed by General Smuts was despatched to Budapest in the first week of April; it found that Kun was not prepared to accept Allied intervention unless the Roumanians retired. Since it also decided that Kun was neither a free agent nor a serious manifestation of Hungary's political will, the mission returned to Paris.

While Kun played grimly with social revolution, the Roumanians continued to advance slowly from the east and the Czechs marched down on Miskolcz from the north. Many former army officers, who had little liking for Kun's theories and even less for the practices of his more notorious associates, were nevertheless prepared to defend Hungarian soil against the Czechs and Roumanians; and accordingly early in June the Hungarian Red Army went over to the offensive, ejected the Czechs from Miskolcz, penetrated the foothills to Košiče and set up a 'Soviet Republic of Slovakia'. Kun himself insisted that his troops should attack the Roumanians, for he came from a Hungaro-Jewish family in Transylvania and detested everything associated with Bucharest. Militarily, action against the Roumanians was disastrous: the Hungarian Red Army was pushed aside and the Roumanians continued inexorably across the Alföld towards Budapest itself, while the Czechs recovered Košiče and eradicated all traces of the Slovak Soviet. Meanwhile, a Hungarian counter-revolutionary regime had been organized in May by members of the old magnate class in Arad, which was under French occupation. Early in June this body established itself at Szeged in Hungary proper; and there it was joined by a 'National Army,' recruited by a thirty-two year old reservist captain, Gyula Gömbös, and commanded by Admiral Miklós Horthy. All three groups – Roumanian, Czech and 'Nationalist' – pressed towards the Hungarian capital, the Roumanians winning the race.

Kun and his leading commissars (including the future Stalinist boss Mátyás Rákosi) fled to Vienna in the first week of August and eventually returned to Russia. Budapest was occupied by Roumanian troops from 6 August to 14 November. When they left, the city was demoralized by the changes of the previous twelve months and desperately short, not only of food, but of many material possessions for there had been wide-spread looting. Horthy made an impressive entry into Budapest on 16 November, but the Allied authorities at first regarded his nationalists with considerable misgiving because of the merciless behaviour of some officers on the march from Szeged. A White Terror replaced the Red Terror of the Kun interlude; among the victims of the Whites were workers' leaders, liberal sympathizers with Károlyi's reforms, and above all, Jews. Yet so marked was the fear in the West of 'Bolshevism' springing up the Danube, that the Allies were prepared to see in the Whites a guarantee of order, provided that the excesses of the embittered wing of extremists could be brought under control. A caretaker administration, not exclusively counter-revolutionary, was established; and in January 1920 elections were held under a wide and secret suffrage in which even women had the vote. No doubt the democratic character of the election impressed the Allies, though one feels that as evidence of a popular mandate its value was offset by the unfortunate circumstance that several thousand socialists were in prison. The new parliament was predictably conservative in spirit and on 1 March 1920 it elected Admiral Horthy as Regent, pending settlement of the final constitutional character of the state. The Paris Conference was by now convinced that Hungary had a stable government; peace terms were at last presented to a Hungarian delegation and on 4 June signed in the Trianon.

The successive Hungarian emergencies of Károlyi, Kun and Horthy had repercussions through Central Europe and beyond. For the Magyars themselves they meant months of bloodshed, destruction and suffering; they hardened the attitude of the Western Powers, making them reluctant to modify any of the terms in the draft treaty; and, by delaying the final conclusion of peace, they lengthened the period of economic blockade. Kun's cumbersome attempt to establish a dictatorship of the proletariat convinced the neighbouring states and propertied classes in the West of the reality of the 'red peril'. To Smuts, who met him, Kun seemed a ridiculous figure; to others from afar he was a terrifying ogre. Yet ultimately the reaction provoked among Kun's opponents in Hungary was more significant than anything attempted by the communists. For the nationalist counter-revolution was the first of all the right radical move-ments to gain any success in the European continent. Horthy himself was a traditionalist who sought throughout his political life to put the clock back to the first years of the century; like the Tiszas he was a Calvinist, sure, as they had been, that what he did was morally right. And yet the men whom he used to come to power (and who used him to retain it for themselves) had none of his restraint or sense of duty, nor did they share with him a respect for past institutions. Moved by both greed for property and social envy, they assumed violence to be a substitute for the rational argument of which they were intellectually incapable; and by perverting a sentimental love of country (which some of them genuinely felt) into a hatred of all other races, they linked the intolerance of Kossuth with the intolerance of Hitler. Men like their leader, Gömbös, were more typical of the inter-war generation of politicians than Károlyi or Kun – or, for that matter, those in the West who sought to salvage Wilson's ideals through the League of Nations.

By the Treaty of Trianon Hungary lost more than two thirds of the territory recognized as within the Hungarian Kingdom when the Ausgleich was concluded in 1867: Slovakia and Ruthenia went to the Czechoslovak Republic; a small segment of the Spiš-Orava counties, less than 250 square miles, was assigned to Poland; the whole of Transylvania, the eastern half of the Bánát and a section of the northern Carpathians in the region of Maramures to the Kingdom of Roumania; and the Voivodina (including the western Bánát) was incorporated in the Yugoslav State, together with Croatia-Slavonia which was not a part of historic Hungary though within the Lands of the Holy Crown. The Hungarians also ceded the port of Fiume (Rijeka) which it was intended should be set up as a Free City similar to Danzig but which became part of Italy. Finally an area of 1,500 square miles of western Hungary, predominantly German in racial composition, was awarded to the new Austrian Republic and subsequently became the province of Burgenland.

The lands lost to Roumania alone were greater in area than the rump of 'Trianon' Hungary, a fact which caused particular resentment in Budapest. In the secret treaty of 1916 Bratianu had demanded a boundary which would have run within a few miles of Szeged and Debrecen: this he did not get, but the final frontier in Crisana ran some distance west of the natural ethnographic line so as to ensure that the road and rail route from the Bánát northwards through Arad and Oradea remained in Roumanian hands. It was, of course, impossible to make a true division on racial grounds at any point in Transylvania because of the Magyar-speaking Szekler communities in the south-east of the province. Further north, in the Maramures, strategic considerations again played a part in the final settlement; the whole region provided a link through Ruthenia (which it much resembled in character) with the heart of the Czechoslovak State. In the south-west the frontier across the Bánát caused considerable friction between Yugoslavia and Roumania and might well, like Teschen, have led to fighting between the two armies had it not been for the presence of French units. Roumania was left with two-thirds of the Bánát including Temesvár, but the Yugoslavs safeguarded the immediate approaches to Belgrade and gained valuable agricultural land. The whole

163

settlement left nearly two million Magyars and Szeklers in Roumania against twenty-five thousand Roumanians still west of the frontier in Hungary. Some seventy thousand Roumanians were also left within Yugoslavia.

Roumania was able to annex other territories apart from these gains made by the Treaty of Trianon. From Austria she acquired, by the Treaty of St Germain, the Bukovina although this territory was recognized as Roumanian only in 1923 after it had been occupied for nearly four years by units of the Roumanian army supported by a local committee in Czernowitz. In March 1920 the Supreme Council accepted the act by which Roumania had secured Bessarabia in the spring of 1918 as Russia was disintegrating in defeat and revolution. Finally, the Treaty of Neuilly stipulated that Bulgaria should return Southern Dobrudja which the Roumanians had originally acquired after the Second Balkan War but lost by the terms of the separate peace of May 1918. The cumulative effect of all these treaties was to secure for Roumania new territories which were larger both in area and in population than the old Regat (the pre-war kingdom). In doubling her size, however, Roumania created a considerable nationality problem for her political leaders: for, whereas in Transylvania and the southern Bukovina the Roumanians formed a a majority, this was far from the case in the northern Bukovina (where the people were Ukrainian) or in the Dobrudja (where they were Bulgarian); and in Bessarabia the Roumanians were the largest single nationality but formed less than half the population. There were, in all, eighteen million people living in the new Greater Roumania; and of these, four and a half million were members of five distinct national minorities (Magyars, Germans, Ukrainians, Russians, and Bulgars). The treaties had also increased the number of Ashkenazi Jews to four per cent of the population; and Roumania's past record of anti-semitism was already so ugly that, on one occasion, at the Peace Conference, it prompted the veteran Dreyfusard Clemenceau to deliver a withering rebuke to Bratianu.

The Treaty of Trianon recognized the outright succession of Croatia-Slavonia as constituted by the Nagoda of 1868 to the Yugoslav union. Although a powerful pressure group in Italy sought to encourage Croatian separatism and made some capital out of the religious differences between Croats and Serbs, there was little likelihood of the conference going against the decisions of the Zagreb National Council. Yugoslav claims to the Voivodina caused more trouble, partly because of the conflict with Roumania over the Bánát, but also because of the Yugoslav desire to include the pocket of *prečani* Serbs living around the town of Subotica within their state. The final frontier in this Bácksa area of the Voivodina ran north of Subotica (a vitally important railway junction) but well south of Baja, a predominantly Magyar town claimed by Pašić in a moment of optimistic exuberance. There were also strange developments over the Baranya triangle, the land between the Danube and the Drava. Serbian troops had crossed the whole of this region in November 1918 and occupied the town of Pécs. The Treaty gave the Yugoslavs a small segment of the Baranya but drew a frontier twenty-five miles south of Pécs; and yet the Serbian troops refused to evacuate Pécs until August 1921, even setting up a 'Republic of the Baranya' which unsuccessfully detitioned the League of Nations to secure not union with the Yugoslavs but autonomy for Pécs within Hungary. The settlement of the frontier in the Voivodina left some 350,000 Germans and slightly more than 400,000 Magyars in Yugoslavia.

It is difficult to establish the size of the minorities left within Croatia after the union with Serbia. The Hungarian census of 1910, while showing the Croats and Serbs as ninety per cent of the population, gave the figure of Magyar-speaking inhabitants of Croatia-Slavonia as 105,948 and of Germans as 134,078; the Yugoslav census of 1921 for the same region showed 70,555 Magyars and 122,836 Germans. The drop in the number of Hungarians may largely be explained by the migration of civil servants and workers on the railways (which during the period of the Ausgleich were controlled from, and staffed by, Budapest) but may also reflect the presence of the floating census-informant, a person whose mother tongue varied for statistical purposes according to the language assumed to be desired by the census-taker. The one demographic statistic necessarily missing for Austria-Hungary and the successor states is the number of floating census-informants; one suspects that they ran into many thousands and were widely scattered.

The Peace Settlement left Yugoslavia with a frontier shared by seven different neighbours, a larger number than any other country in Europe except Germany. The demarcation of each of these boundaries was disputed, apart from the 100 miles shared with Greece. The hardest of all was in the north and west; and here the Serbian army was frequently involved in military operations which were an embarrassment rather than a service to the delegation in Paris.

The original Yugoslav claim proposed a line through Styria and Carinthia running beyond Marburg (Maribor), Klagenfurt and Villach to the old Austro-Italian frontier, which it would then follow southwards to the sea in the Gulf of Trieste. These demands were excessive: all three towns in Styria and Carinthia were predominantly German in character and composition, although much of the adjoining countryside was Slovene; Trieste itself, the third most populous city in Austria-Hungary according to the 1910 census, was fifty-seven per cent Italian and forty-three per cent mixed Slav and German, and acquisition of the port had long been an objective of Italian policy. Moreover, while the former Austrian provinces of Gorz-Gradisca and of Istria were mainly Yugoslav in the east, they were Italian in the west where all the principal towns were situated. A major contest between the Italian and Yugoslav delegates was thus inevitable. The Yugoslav claims clashed with the provisional partition plan of the Treaty of London, not only in these regions but along the coast of Dalmatia and in Albania as well; and the Italians, so far from modifying their demands of 1915, now added Fieum (Rijeka) to the list although it was the natural port for the Croatian hinterland and the population of both the surrounding countryside and the outlying districts was almost exclusively Yugoslav.

Most impartial delegates to the Peace Conference thought the Yugo-slavs had gone too far in asking for Trieste and the Italians in demanding Fiume. As early as the first week in February 1919 Trumbić let Wilson know privately that the Yugoslavs would accept his arbitration should he propose a frontier dividing the Istrian peninsula; but the Italian Foreign Minister, Sonnino, was obdurate. He was under pressure both from embryo-fascist groups in Milan and Venice and also from the Army Staff in Rome; and he appears to have sympathized with much of their Adriatic programme. For, even before leaving for Paris, Sonnino had given written approval to a directive from General Badoglio, the deputy commander-in-chief, outlining direct action to disrupt the Yugoslav union; and from February to April 1919, while the rival claims were under discussion in Paris, the Italian military authorities and their agents did all they could to encourage separatism in Croatia and Montenegro. There were also frequent clashes between Italian and Serbian patrols, which sometimes involved French units as well, in Fiume itself and in Slovenia. After rioting in Fiume in July, during which several French soldiers were killed, the allied command sought to disarm the Italian para-military organizations. On 12 September, however, the city was seized by an air-borne auxiliary task force led by the popular Italian war-hero and roman-tic poet, Gabriele d'Annunzio, acting the part of a right-wing Garibaldi. This absurd escapade – for d'Annunzio's followers really did wear cloaks and carry daggers – delayed a settlement of the Fiume problem for fifteen months. The Allied authorities seemed paralyzed; either they were too peace-weary or too afraid of repercussions in Italy to eject d'Annun-zio; and it was not until after he had gone so far as to declare war on Italy herself, that in January 1921 his city-state of Fiume was re-occupied and its 'unwanted hero' sent into exile.

The Italo-Yugoslav dispute was not resolved by the Peace Conference nor by the Ambassadorial Conference which succeeded it. Wilson's proposed compromise line in Istria remained unacceptable to the Italians although they were prepared to use it as a basis for further bargaining since it seemed to show that the President acknowledged that the Treaty of London had some validity. The Yugoslavs gave up their claim to Trieste and Gorizia (Gorz) and succeeded in making the Italians withdraw their demand for northern Dalmatia although they insisted on the cession of the ancient city of Zara (Zadar, as it was called by the Croats). Nothing, however, could make them change their attitude over Fiume and the growing rift between Wilson and the American people in the summer of 1920 hardened their resolve. Eventually bi-lateral talks between Italy and Yugoslavia led in November 1920 to the Treaty of Rapallo, concluded just one week after the American Democratic Party had lost the Presidential Election. At Rapallo Italy was confirmed in possession of Zara and most of Istria with Fiume constituted a Free City although its suburb, Sušak, was placed within Yugoslavia. Even this agreement did not settle the question: there were renewed disputes over Yugoslav rights in the port area. Further conventions in October 1922 were soon invalidated by Mussolini's advent to power since the Fascists had always shown that they had no respect for the concept of a Free City; and it was only in January 1924 that the Treaty of Rome provided for formal recognition by the Yugoslavs of Fiume's cession to Italy in return for an assurance by Mussolini of 'cordial cooperation.'

Yugoslavia's frontiers with Austria, Bulgaria and Albania were settled far sooner. At the end of April 1919 the Yugoslavs made a determined bid to secure all southern and western Carinthia, crossing the Karawanken Mountains in force and occupying the town of Klagenfurt before the Allies succeeded in imposing a local armistice. The Treaty of St Germain duly gave the Yugoslavs a natural geographical border along the river Mur and the line of the Karawanken, thereby ensuring that most of southern Styria went to Yugoslavia, including the town of Marburg (or Maribor, as it now became). The treaty also stipulated that plebiscites would be held for the disputed area in Carinthia; and for this purpose an inter-allied commission divided the region into a northern zone, comprising Klagenfurt itself and the Wörthersee, and a much larger southern zone. When the plebiscite was held in the southern zone in October 1920 it gave a majority in favour of Austria; and, since this zone was known to contain a higher proportion of Slovenes than its neighbour, no plebiscite was ever held for the Klagenfurt area. Carinthia remained, and remains today, an Austrian province with a Slovene minority.

Over the Bulgarian frontier there was far less trouble, although here, too, the Yugoslavs did not receive all they sought. The Treaty of Neuilly confirmed Serbia's gains of 1913 in Macedonia, adding to them the Strumica salient; it ensured the safety of Niš by ceding the town of Pirot and its outlying villages; and it also secured the railway along the river

Timok from rifle fire, a dangerous pursuit by which the Bulgarian irregular *comitadji* had been known to demonstrate their patriotism. The conference refused to accept Yugoslav claims to the Danubian port of Vidin and to the Dragoman Pass, possession of which would have dominated Sofia. The Bulgars were saved from harsher terms by the sympathy shown for them by President Wilson and Sonnino, an unexpected partnership. But not even Wilson's efforts could save Bulgaria's Aegean coastline, acquired at such cost and frustration in 1912–13. Almost all western Thrace was ceded by the Treaty of Neuilly to Greece, and Bulgaria's hopes of turning Dedeagatch into a major seaport forced into that limbo of lost endeavour where the Powers had cast San Stefano at the Congress of Berlin.

The Albanian settlement was held up by the failure of the Peace Conference to agree over the character of its government and by repercussions of the conflict between Italy and Yugoslavia. A not very general election in January 1920 enabled an Albanian Legislative Assembly to convene in Tirana two months later which, in its turn, appointed a four-man Council of Regency. Rather remarkably, this council secured the admission of Albania to the League of Nations and the withdrawal of Italian troops, even though only a few months earlier it had appeared that Albania might become an Italian mandated territory. Finally in November 1921 the Conference of Ambassadors re-affirmed the provisional frontiers of 1913 with minor modifications; but this settlement was accepted only after the League had threatened action against Yugoslavia for having sent troops into northern Albania and set up yet another impromptu republic.

There were two other major questions which took many years to settle and where peace could be made in the end only after renewed war: the Greek frontier with Turkey; and the Polish frontier with Russia. The 'Greater Greece' ideal of Venizelos sought realization primarily in Asia Minor and is therefore outside the scope of this present study; but as it had repercussions on the balance of interests within the Balkans, it must be briefly noticed. Similarly, although many aspects of the Polish Question concerned regions which are today fully integrated in the Soviet Union and cannot be regarded as part of the 'lands between,' the uncertainties of the post-war decade involved them momentarily in the affairs of East-Central Europe no less than other fringe areas, such as Dalmatia or the Dobrudja; and these events too must be recorded.

The Greek dilemma, although not its disastrous climax, sprang directly from the ambitions of Eleutherios Venizelos. Under his leadership Greece had fought with vigour on the Allied side for the second half of the war, eventually ousting the pro-German King Constantine in favour of his son Alexander in the summer of 1917. Greek demands at the Peace Conference were extensive: Thrace, northern Epirus, the Dodecanese archipelago, the islands in the Aegean, and the heavily Greek-populated region around Smyrna (Izmir) in Asia Minor. The British backed the Greeks and in May 1919 they were given permission by the Supreme Council of the Peace Conference to occupy Smyrna and its hinterland. A year later the Treaty of Sèvres duly confirmed cession of the Smyrna area to the Greeks. It also gave them the whole of eastern Thrace, including the Gallipoli peninsula, and most of the Aegean islands; but the Dodecanese were handed over to Italy for eventual transfer to Greece under a separate convention.

The Treaty of Sèvres was, however, never ratified; its terms stirred up a nationalist revolution among the Turks led by Mustafa Kemal and as dedicated to throwing the Greeks out of Asia Minor as the Balkan League had been to expel the Turks from Europe only a few years earlier. The dynamism of the Kemalist revolt failed this time to kindle a response in Athens. The sudden death of King Alexander from a monkey-bite, the defeat in elections of Venizelos and his liberals, and the return of King Constantine all weakened the position of the Greeks and sapped their resolution. It is hardly surprising that their military venture in Turkey was ineptly led or that the troops were inadequately supplied. A rash penetration of Anatolia led to a Turkish counter-offensive in which the Greeks were thrown out of Smyrna by the end of September 1922. In the following summer a new settlement was negotiated at Lausanne which tore up the provisions of Sèvres.

Territorially Lausanne secured the return to Turkey of all that had been lost to the Greeks in Europe and Asia Minor (although the Dodecanese remained under Italian rule). A separate convention earlier in the year provided for a massive transfer of populations: Moslems were forced to leave Greece; and the last Greeks were forced out of Asia Minor, following the wretched thousands who had already fled the vengeance of the Turks in 1922. By the retrocession of eastern Thrace the Lausanne Settlement ensured that Kemal's new Turkish Republic retained a foothold in Europe. The Turkish presence in Thrace and on the (demilitarized) Straits continued to influence the attitudes of the Balkan States in the inter-war years although in a different way from the opening decades of the century. Under Kemal Turkey became a stabilizing force in the very area in which Ottoman maladministration had for so long imperilled the peace of the continent. The Greeks, on the other hand, had to accept the failure of their 'Great Ideal'; they were forced to concentrate on specifically Balkan problems, safeguarding the lands acquired from Bulgaria by the Treaty of Neuilly. With the exchange of populations the deep hatred of

Greek for Turk began to die away; and the only power in south-eastern Europe to harbour revisionist sentiment through the 1920s and 1930s was Bulgaria.

Just as the triple rivalry of Bulgar, Greek and Turk had long hampered any rational solution of Balkan problems, so the triple conflict of Polish historical rights, Russian Bolshevism and the nationalism of the smaller border peoples delayed a settlement in the East. Pilsudski himself at one time favoured a federation of Poles, Lithuanians and Ukrainians but the Polish authorities were as certain of their racial superiority as the Magyars had been in pre-war Hungary. Pilsudski had to fight for Vilna and the Ukraine; but after successes in Galicia in 1919 he was able to enlist the support of many Ukrainian nationalists against the common enemy, the Red Army. Pilsudski's 'Ukrainian Adventure' reached its zenith in May 1920 when Polish and anti-communist Ukrainian troops entered Kiev. But in the next two months the Russians made spectacular counter-attacks: Budenny's cavalry rolled up the southern front from Kiev to Galicia; and in the north the twenty-eight year old General Tukhachevsky began a 600-mile advance through Vilna and Minsk on Warsaw itself. But Tukhachevsky was not a Bonaparte: no Campo-Formio consolidated the triumphs of the young General. The Poles counter-attacked and by the end of September had thrust the Red Army back across the Niemen; a Polish general, Zeligowski, re-entered Vilna, determined that the Lithuanians should be denied Pilsudski's home city (even though historically it had formed Lithuania's capital). On 18 October the extraordinarily fluid campaign ended with an armistice of near-exhaustion. Direct negotiations began between Poland and Russia and in March 1921 the Treaty of Riga established a frontier following closely along the line on which Polish troops had halted: from the Dvina in the north it ran west of Minsk to the Roumanian frontier on the Dniester. About five million Ukrainians and Byelo-Russians were thus left within the new Poland.

The Supreme Council of the Peace Conference, the later ambassadorial conferences and the League of Nations all made faltering attempts to prevent the Poles from gobbling up more territory in the east than they could digest. The Poles rejected an offer in November 1919 of a twenty-five year mandate for east Galicia in which the Ukrainians would have enjoyed a high degree of autonomy; and they would have nothing to do with the ethnic boundary proposed by the Allied experts and subsequently known as the Curzon Line, for this would have left most of the Ukrainians and Byelo-Russians to the Soviets. In February 1923 the League made one last attempt to secure a Statute of Autonomy for east Galicia, but Polish intransigence ruled out every compromise; and the whole region was left in Poland's unfettered hands. Most Ukrainians, and the Soviet authorities as well, remained unreconciled to the Polish frontiers; but for many years they were powerless to change them. Similarly, though the League recognized Poland's acquisition of Vilna in March 1923, the Lithuanian Republic was never prepared to accept its loss; but by itself Lithuania was far too small to challenge the Polish conquests.

Between the wars disillusioned idealists and the champions of treaty-revision protested that the Peace Settlement made a mockery of the principle of self-determination. Even at the most generous estimate, national minorities constituted nearly a third of the population of Poland and Czechoslovakia, over a quarter of the population of Roumania and almost an eighth of the population of Yugoslavia; and in some of these states it was by no means certain that a majority of the component 'master' nations would have approved of the new structure had they been able to express their will in a completely free vote. Six-and-a-half million Germans were neither citizens of the German Republic nor of Austria, more than five million Ukrainians were outside the Soviet empire, and three million Magyars were beyond the frontiers of Hungary. There were considerable minorities of Albanians in Yugoslavia and, to a lesser extent, in Greece; and a high proportion of Bulgars in Yugoslav and Greek Macedonia and in Greek Thrace. The Yugoslavs in their turn could complain of the Slovenes left beyond the Italian frontier in Istria and the Austrian in Carinthia. Over the whole area of East-Central Europe it is probable that one person in five was a member of a national minority: some accepted their position; some voiced their hostility from the earliest days; and many grew to resent it through years of frustrating inequality.

Critics also attacked the settlement on economic grounds, maintaining that the various treaties had put up tariff barriers within natural trading units so that, for example, Austria-Hungary – which had formed one customs area – was now split between seven economic systems, many of them fiercely competitive rivals. In some regions the settlement produced local, rather than national, economic hardship: Fiume was deliberately allowed to decline so as not to compete with Trieste and the Italian Adriatic ports; and, on a smaller scale, Ismail in Bessarabia suffered for the benefit of the older Roumanian ports along the Danube, Galati and Braila. There were, moreover, a number of instances where the adjustment of a frontier on strategic grounds assigned vital railway junctions to ex-Allied states at the expense of the economic well-being of ex-enemy states. In many cases the loss of old markets harmed both victors and vanquished: thus Hungary suffered from being deprived of Slovakia's timber and ore; but Bohemia-Moravia had to carry the burden of sub-sidizing the depressed Slovak areas (and, of course, even more the backward lands of Ruthenia).

The peacemakers themselves were aware of the imperfections of their work and of the dangers inherent in the settlement. It presupposed the lasting elimination of Germany and Russia from their traditional arena of contest; and much of the diplomacy in the inter-war years sought to retain this rare situation. But there were other possibilities for righting grievances which might lead to a new conflict. The Covenant of the League of Nations was attached to each of the five Paris treaties: and Article 19 provided that 'the Assembly may from time to time advise the reconsideration by members of the League of Treaties which have become inapplicable and the consideration of international conditions whose continuance might endanger the peace of the World'. If no action was ever taken under this Article, the fault hardly lies with the statesmen of Paris. Similarly, the peacemakers sought to protect the minorities by a series of special treaties guaranteeing to them equality before the law, religious freedom and linguistic and cultural rights. Each state in East-Central Europe, whether a new creation, an ex-ally or an ex-enemy, had to sign treaties of this character except for those on the fringe of the area, Russia, Germany and Italy: the Russians were outside the system: the Germans gave a guarantee of this nature for Upper Silesia; and Italy was exempted as a Great Power with traditions of democratic justice who it was mistakenly assumed would grant all her peoples these basic rights as a matter of course.

Attempts were also made to offset the economic malaise created by the settlement. The Czechs were offered special transit rights in Hamburg and Stettin and the Yugoslavs in Salonika. Both the Treaty of St Germain and the Treaty of Trianon included clauses providing for preferential tariffs, over a period of five years, between Austria, Czechoslovakia and Hungary; unfortunately, these arrangements remained inoperative because of the intensity of political feeling in the early 1920s. It is hard to avoid the conclusion that these remedies, such as they were, could never have led to any significant improvement in conditions even had the will to make them function been present at the time.

After half a century it is clear that the Peace Settlement had more enduring qualities than its earlier critics admitted. Paradoxically, the principal destruction to its provisions was caused by the Great Power which made fewest pleas for 'revision' in the inter-war years; but it must be remembered that Russia did, after all, lose more territory than any other state by the events of 1917 to 1921. Apart from Russia's westward thrust in the 1940s and its repercussions on Poland, the frontiers have changed little although nemesis eventually overtook the greed of the Italian chauvinists in the Adriatic. The number of nationalities which benefited from the various treaties was greater than those which suffered, and it is probable that, given the temper of the times and the excessively confused ethnic pattern in the major areas of dispute, no fairer or more equitable system could have been devised by any gathering of victors from a long and bitter war. Yet, in retrospect, the settlement seems less of a historical climacteric than in the period between the wars when it was so widely denounced and violently challenged. The new ordering of Europe too often involved a mere change in management: old complications re-appeared in a fresh setting. It is, for example, ironical that one of the creations of 1918, the Yugoslav State, should have comprised nine nationalities whereas the much-maligned 'Historic Hungary' of pre-war days held only seven; and the difference in attitude between a Serbian nationalist of the 1930s and a Magyar nationalist of the 1900s requires a nicety of distinction which only the most skilful exponent of political semantics could seek to explain. What was re-shaped in 1919–20 was the map of Europe, not the habits of its peoples.

9

Democratic Illusions and Reality

The simultaneous eclipse of both Russia and Germany made the 1920s a decade of opportunity for the states which lay between them. Never before had the Western Slavs or the Southern Slavs or the peoples of the Roumanian provinces been given the opportunity of achieving social cohesion and unity free from external pressure; and it was many centuries since there had been a Vistulan state of such size and potential as the new Polish Republic. Even the defeated Bulgars had the rare prospect of choosing political affiliations by domestic policy rather than by foreign alignment, while if the Magyars could recognize a national purpose which was not aggressively revisionist, they might perceive that Hungary, too, was at last enjoying a genuine, if truncated, independence. It was a period in which constitutional lawyers looked towards the West, and particularly to France, for the blueprint of a parliamentary system; and in each of the six states (except Hungary) deputies were elected on a broad franchise by ballots which, originally, respected individual liberty. At first there was no shortage of political parties, particularly in Czechoslovakia and Poland where systems of proportional representation were written into the constitutions. Seventeen parties sat in the Czechoslovak Chamber of Deputies of 1920 – twenty-two had contested the elections – and fourteen in the Polish Sejm. There were twelve in the Yugoslav Skupstina, nine in the Bulgarian Sobranjie and so many in the Roumanian Chamber that they defy precise classification. All these attempts to consolidate unity on a basis of positive parliamentarianism were sincere in origin and, given the political climate of these years, readily comprehensible. Unfortunately, the grafting of alien institutions on to political bodies of native growth was bound to produce turmoil and facilitate the spread of corrupt practices. Moreover, in each of the states there were influential groups who resented the very existence of the governmental machine and who sought to engineer the collapse of the parliamentary system; and by the end of the decade the democratic ideal seemed irredeemably tarnished everywhere except Czechoslovakia.

The histories of the six countries have much in common in the 1920s: a phase of revolutionary disturbance; a period of democratic experiment;

174

and a period of reaction, in some places blatantly oppressive and in others more deviously exercised. The Czechoslovak Republic conforms to this pattern far less than the others because it inherited a western tradition of liberal democracy and, at least in Bohemia and Moravia, possessed a different social structure. (In Czechoslovakia only a third of the population was dependent for its livelihood on agriculture: over the other five states the proportion was twice as high, rising from fifty-five per cent in Hungary to eighty per cent in Bulgaria). But elsewhere, and including the Slovak and Ruthene areas of the Czech State, the dominant characteristics of the early years of the new era were determined by the experiences of the war and its immediate aftermath.

Veterans returning home to native town or village in 1919–20 differed in political outlook from the youngsters who had flocked to the colours in the first days of battle. They had gained, if not sophistication, at least maturity. For soldiering in mass armies of conscripts has always proved a harsh instrument of social education, as the history of Russia demonstrated for more than a century before the Revolution, and during the five years of war and disorder peasants and workers from the backward regions of Eastern Europe had travelled to more advanced lands, acquiring a restless consciousness of economic privation. They were in consequence prepared to question, as never before, the traditional ways of work and life, seeking a change in agricultural methods and pressing for improved conditions in factory or mine. Nor was this the only effect of military service. Revolutionary beliefs, which could not have spread among scattered rural communities in time of peace, began to evoke a response among conscripted labourers and conscripted peasants, particularly those who passed through prisoner-of-war camps or who deserted in the last weeks of the 'Imperial and Royal Army'. Social unrest, which had already begun to trouble the old order before 1914, increased in intensity alike in the countryside and the towns. Every government had to promise agrarian reform and make agreeable gestures to the workers.

The land reforms barely scratched the surface of the agrarian problem. In Yugoslavia, Roumania and Czechoslovakia a considerable amount of land was, indeed, taken from the large estates and assigned to the peasants, but in the first two instances smallholders found their new plots unworkable and frequently re-sold them to large landowners and sometimes to their former owners. In Poland and Hungary the best estates remained intact and the transfer of land was negligible although each successive government continued to pay lip-service to the principle of reform. Even less was done for the industrial workers. The Czechoslovak government had, of course, inherited a corpus of social legislation from the Austrians, to which in 1924 it duly added comprehensive insurance systems, and the Moraczewski ministry in Poland carried through some progressive measures of factory legislation in 1919. The Yugoslavs, too, introduced an eight-hour day and clarified the status of trade unions. But, in general, working conditions remained primitive and the proletariat drifted naturally towards the Left.

The ruling classes in each of the six countries shared the universal fear of 'Bolshevism,' a bogey made real for Central Europe by the Kun regime in Hungary and the Marxist inclinations of the workers in Vienna. It is difficult to assess the extent of the Communist appeal in the early twenties. There was certainly a powerful Communist party in Bulgaria, which gained a quarter of the votes cast in the 1919 election and which for four years was able to organize Marxist associations with considerable freedom. In Czechoslovakia a separate Communist party only came into being in 1921 with a secession from the largest of Czech parties, the Social Democrats; but, even so, the Communists polled nearly a million votes in the next parliamentary election (1925) and continued to gain substantial support up to the crisis of 1938. The Yugoslav Communists gained dramatic successes in 1919–20, emerging as the strongest party at the municipal elections in Belgrade, Zagreb, Niš and Uzice and winning fifty-eight seats in the Constituent Assembly, where they were the third largest party. They had, however, inherited from such movements as 'Young Bosnia' a terrorist wing and its existence was used as an excuse by the government to issue the notorious *Obznana* decree of December 1920 severely curtailing all Marxist activities. An attempt to assassinate Regent Alexander in June 1921 followed within a month by the murder of the minister who had introduced the *Obznana*, Milorad Drasković, led to the passage of an even stiffer 'Law for the Defence of the State,' which forced the Yugoslav communist movement to go underground. Although there was much social tension in Roumania and a general strike in October 1920, the Roumanian Communist Party never achieved a wide following and was severely repressed soon after its formation and declared illegal in 1924. The Polish communists suffered from the effects of the Red Army invasion in 1920 but gained a limited success in the municipalities for a number of years thereafter. On the other hand, in Hungary there was virtually no organized communist movement after the collapse of the Kun Soviet and the White Terror. When in 1925 the Comintern sought to revive the Hungarian Party and sent two agents to Budapest, both were swiftly arrested and sentenced to long terms of imprisonment. One of the agents was Mátyás Rakoši who was, in time, to gain an even greater notoriety than Béla Kun.

In reality, the Marxist movements never menaced the existing order in any of these six countries between 1920 and the westward thrust of the Red Army in the Second World War. There were isolated acts of terrorism, mutiny and even insurrection but scientific socialism remained funda-

EASTERN EUROPE
1923-38

0 |_____| 300
Miles

SWEDEN

FINLAND

Helsinki

Leningrad

ESTONIA

Riga

LATVIA

BALTIC SEA

Memel

LITHUANIA

Vilna

Minsk

Danzig

EAST
PRUSSIA

U. S. S. R.

Berlin

Poznan

Warsaw

GERMANY

POLAND

Weimar

SAXONY

Breslau

Cracow

Lvov

Prague

CZECHOSLOVAKIA

BUKOVINA

Munich

Vienna

BESSARABIA

AUSTRIA

Budapest

TRANSYLVANIA

Graz

HUNGARY

Cluj

SLOVENIA

ROUMANIA

Trieste

YUGOSLAVIA

CROATIA

Belgrade

Bucharest

Sarajevo

SERBIA

DOBRUDJA

BOSNIA

ITALY

ADRIATIC SEA

Varna

BLACK SEA

MONTENEGRO

BULGARIA

Sofia

MACEDONIA

Istanbul

ALBANIA

International boundaries
Post-war losses of
territory by
    Germany
    Russia
    Bulgaria
    Austria and Hungary
Plebiscite areas

GREECE

TURKEY

AEGEAN SEA

Athens

177

mentally as alien to the character of Eastern Europe in the inter-war years as the democratic guarantees which had been written into the paper constitutions. Potentially the most serious challenge to the bourgeois ruling groups came, not from the Marxist Left, but from the peasant parties which, from modest origins at the turn of the century were swept into positions of astonishing influence by the new mood of the agrarian workers on their return from the wars. The Bulgarian Agrarian Union of Stamboliisky, the Croatian Peasant Party of Radić and the Roumanian National Peasant Party of Mihalache and Maniu conjured up, for a time, the image of a 'Green Rising' in the Balkans in which the workers on the land would defeat the twin evils which the towns sought to impose on them – Big Business and Bolshevism. Nor was this movement limited to the Balkan lands. In Poland the Piast Party of Witos and the Wyzwolenie Party of Dabski, though divided from each other until 1931 by conflicting views on clericalism, maintained a persistent demand for genuine land reforms; and in Czechoslovakia the Agrarian Party under Svehla and Hodža secured an eight-hour day for all agricultural labourers and established links between the producers' cooperatives in the countryside and the consumers' cooperatives in the towns. The Czech Agrarians tended, however, to shed their peasant origin and became associated with the commercial classes and particularly with banking interests. A similar criticism might be made of the Serb Agrarian Party while the Small-holders' Party in Hungary represented only the more prosperous medium-sized landowners – the counterpart to the Russian kulaks – and had little appeal to the peasant masses. Significantly, the 'green' movement could make no progress in the most northern provinces of Yugoslavia where the loyalty of all classes was given to the specifically Roman Catholic organization of Monsignor Korošec, the Slovene Peoples' Party; and to the north of the Danube Monsignor Hlinka kept a no less powerful hold on the political aspirations of his co-religionists among the Slovaks.

The peasant parties were unique to East-Central Europe. They never spread south of the Balkan range to Greece (where less than half of the population gained its livelihood from agriculture) and attempts to form similar political groups in France, Bavaria and Holland came to nothing. Some observers in the West argued that the growth of political consciousness among the rural masses was a major historical event, as momentous as the rise of the middle classes in previous centuries; and they particularly applauded the peasants' rejection of the code of values accepted by industrial society and their soundly pacifist denunciation of armies and armaments. Yet in retrospect the weaknesses of the peasant movement are clearly apparent. The grievances of individual workers on the land are always local and particular, and their enemies unscrupulous landlords, grasping money-lenders or bumbling bureaucrats; their natural sense of independence precludes a comprehensive national policy. As the war receded so their vision became more limited and once their leaders began to concern themselves with broad issues they inevitably cut themselves off from what were, literally, the grass roots of the movement. A wide gulf opened up between the peasantry and its spokesmen. Moreover, village communities are not even in themselves socially cohesive, for the distinction between the wealthy and successful and the wretchedly poor is sufficiently clear to arouse resentment and envy. The peasants fell an easy prey to the tactics of the old ruling classes; they were attacked and exploited by crown, army, lawyers and even by the urban socialists. It was one of the tragedies of the inter-war years that the peasant leaders should have failed to achieve mastery at the beginning of the democratic experiments; only the Czechoslovak Agrarians remained in power for any length of time, and then solely as members of a coalition.

The most remarkable episode of peasant rule was the Stamboliisky government of 1919 to 1923 in Bulgaria. Stamboliisky himself was the archetype of the agrarian leader, combining the demagogy of Danton with the anti-urban invective of Cobbett. He hated the 'verminous parasites' in the towns, irrespective of whether they were members of the bourgeois class or the proletariat; and one of the first acts of his ministry was to pass a law insisting that every citizen should undertake ten days physical labour, compulsory and unpaid, for the state each year. The peasantry was exempted from most taxation while there were severe levies on all capital: price control kept manufactured goods cheap and foodstuffs dear; and only members of the Agrarian Party could be appointed to governmental administrative posts in the countryside. Although Stamboliisky professed respect for democratic liberties and made no attempt to proscribe the communists when they called the railwaymen out on strike in 1920, he showed scant sympathy towards the old political leaders, curbing their parliamentary opposition by the threat of court martial for their wartime incompetence. Yet, although incorrigibly partisan and arbitrary, his rule brought lasting benefit to four fifths of the population: rural education leapt forward; and a land reform severely limiting the size of estates ensured that almost all the peasants in the country cultivated holdings of their own (though, after Stamboliisky's fall, they were made to pay heavily in cash for what they had received).

In April 1923 the Agrarians won 212 of the 245 seats in the Sobranjie and Stamboliisky, unwisely, began to urge the holding of a referendum on the future of the monarchy. But King Boris and the army struck first: on 9 June, while Stamboliisky was out of the capital, there was a bloodless coup in Sofia. For four days there was resistance in the countryside until Stamboliisky himself was captured and murdered with protracted sadism. The communists were prepared to watch their two rivals slaughter each other. When they themselves attempted an insurrection in September, it was suppressed with similar bestiality. Possibly as many as ten thousand Bulgars were killed that summer and autumn; and the reins of power were left firmly in the hands of the officer class and its spokesman, Colonel Volkov. Peasant rule had given way to the politics of murder. It was a pattern other countries were to follow, though never to the same excess.

Stamboliisky's death was, at least in part, a consequence of his faith in international collaboration as a fundamental principle of agrarian philosophy. He had always believed that the surest way of guaranteeing peace in the Balkans was to create a federal South Slav union of which Bulgaria was to be as much a unit as Serbia or Croatia; and, less than a month before his murder, he had reached agreement with the Yugoslav government on joint measures to combat the renewal of IMRO terrorism in Macedonia. Cooperation with Belgrade still seemed treason to King Boris and his officers who, throughout the 1920s, continued to press for abrogation of the Treaty of Neuilly and for international recognition of Bulgaria's claim to primacy in Macedonia. In this intransigent attitude they were, unfortunately, far closer to the general mood of Europe than Stamboliisky; for there were few political leaders who regarded the peace settlement as final and even fewer with the courage to call for reconciliation rather than for revision. Fear and a spirit of revenge dominated the relations of the Eastern European peoples despite all the high hopes of the League idealists in Geneva.

The first combinations between the victorious powers were made even before the Peace Conference had broken up. Roumania and Poland, acutely conscious of the numerical strength of the Red Army to their east, concluded a military convention in 1919 and the Roumanians indicated that they were always prepared to work with the Yugoslavs and the Czechs if there was any risk of a Habsburg restoration in Hungary, which might endanger their hold on Transylvania. At the time it seemed to Beneš that there was a possibility of influential groups on the Paris Bourse inducing the Quai d'Orsay to make Hungary the favoured client of France on the Danube; and it was because of clumsy French intrigues with Horthy's government that in August 1920 the Czechs and Yugoslavs signed a defensive alliance which was operative in case of a Hungarian attack or a Habsburg restoration. A Hungarian journalist scornfully described this combination of two nations whom the Magyars despised as 'the Little Entente'. The name outlasted the derision in which it was originally coined.

The Czech-Yugoslav Alliance was extended to Roumania in the spring of 1921 when the former King-Emperor Charles crossed into western Hungary in an abortive attempt to claim his throne. On that occasion a formal military convention was signed between the three states and the scope of the Yugoslav-Roumanian understanding was extended to a guarantee of the terms of the Neuilly Treaty (for the Yugoslavs already had little confidence in Stamboliisky's ability to voice the true will of the Bulgarian State).

To the north, Polish diplomats too were active. In the face of repeated rumours of secret Russo-German collaboration – a fear which, it is now clear, was amply justified – they were anxious to safeguard the position of their nation between the two fallen giants. In February 1921 Pilsudski accordingly secured a treaty of alliance, including a military convention, with France; and a month later he signed a formal agreement with Roumania guaranteeing the frontiers of the two countries against a Russian attack. But Pilsudski refused to commit Poland to action in case of a Hungarian incursion into Transylvania. He had no quarrel with the Horthy government and, indeed, saw it as a possible ally against the Czechs, for relations between Warsaw and Prague remained bad, even though Beneš made several friendly overtures. The Teschen settlement rankled; and there was a particularly tedious and lengthy dispute over Javorina, a village on the frontier high in the Tatra Mountains, to which both countries attached a disproportionate significance. The rift between Czechoslovakia and Poland continued throughout the inter-war period, despite repeated efforts by the French to secure a reconciliation.

From 1923 onwards the international relations of the whole of Eastern Europe increasingly reflected the growing suspicion and antagonism of two Great Powers peripheral to the area, France and Italy. Originally the French, who thought primarily of security against a revived Germany, were not so interested in the Danubian lands as in the northern sector, finding in Poland both a partial substitute for the old alliance with tsarist Russia and a partner for whose liberties the French people had shown a traditional regard since the days of Kosciuszko. French concern with German reparations delayed the formulation of a clear policy towards the Little Entente Powers. Significantly, the first links were forged with Czechoslovakia, the only one of the three states to possess a German frontier, in the aftermath of the Ruhr crisis: a Franco-Czechoslovak Treaty, providing for maintenance of the *status quo*, was signed in January 1924. It was not until the summer of 1926 that the French were prepared to underwrite the boundaries of Roumania and only in 1927 – on the ninth anniversary of the German armistice – that a treaty of friendship was signed between France and Yugoslavia. Thereafter French political influence was supreme along the Danube until at least 1934 and the French General Staff played a considerable role in organizing the military resources of the Little Entente. There had, in fact, always been a powerful group at the War Ministry which favoured military links with the Successor States, in the Franchet d'Espérey tradition, but its most influential spokesmen tended in the 1920s to find themselves engaged in the affairs of North Africa.

After Mussolini's advent to power in November 1922 the Italians were able to steal a march on the French in Central Europe. Rome disliked the possibility of a Habsburg restoration as much as Prague or Belgrade, and the fascists delighted in emphasizing the alleged historic links with 'Latin' Roumania. A treaty with Yugoslavia in January 1924 pledged 'support and cordial collaboration' and was followed by a similar accord with the Czechs; close contacts were made with the Roumanians in 1926, largely as a result of the admiration shown by General Averescu, the Roumanian prime minister, for the way in which Mussolini was revitalizing the Italian people. As yet Mussolini treated Hungarian overtures with marked coolness, partly because he had no wish to encourage revision in any formerly Habsburg territories but even more because he sensed that patronage of Horthy would drive the Little Entente powers irretrievably into the French camp.

To some extent the advantages won by Mussolini's diplomacy in the Successor States were illusory. There was little enough that Italy could offer them, apart from fair words and bombastic gestures – no commercial or economic ties of any value, no military expertise, no influence at Geneva comparable to that wielded by the French or the British. And, as the prospect of a Habsburg restoration receded, so Mussolini's own ambitions in the Balkans opened up old wounds which had barely healed. His interest in the southern Adriatic, as shown by the bludgeoning treatment of Greece in the so-called 'Corfu Incident' of 1923 – when the Italian fleet bombarded and occupied the Greek island of Corfu to avenge the murder of an Italian general, allegedly by Greek irregulars – and by renewed Italian activity in Albania, necessarily alarmed the Yugoslavs, who had only resigned themselves to the loss of Fiume with a heavy heart. Moreover, Mussolini had begun to encourage the IMRO terrorists even before the downfall of the Agrarian government in Bulgaria: he was almost certainly aware of the plot which led to Stamboliiskys murder; and, by the middle of the decade, IMRO was receiving both arms and money from Rome. By thus stoking the glowing embers of insurrection in Macedonia while intriguing in Albania, Mussolini convinced the Yugoslavs that he was aiming at the dissolution of their kingdom, and they began to press for closer and closer association between the Little Entente and France. The Italians accordingly abandoned their earlier reservation: a treaty of cooperation was signed between Hungary and Italy in April 1927 and the Hungarians were accorded commercial facilities in the port of Fiume, a crowning insult to the Yugoslavs. When, in the following January, Austrian customs officials discovered a consignment of Italian machine-gun parts which were being smuggled into Hungary in defiance of treaty limitations on the Hungarian army, the Czechs too assumed that Mussolini had opted for the revisionist camp. The Duce himself spoke out in support of Hungarian national aspirations in the summer of 1928 and the pattern of the diplomatic game became, at last, sharply defined: France would support those countries which had been satisfied by the settlement of 1919–20; and Italy would champion those with a grievance. It was a division of interests which might have been predicted as soon as the peace treaties were signed.

There were occasional attempts in the 1920s to achieve some understanding between the Little Entente powers and their disaffected neighbour, Hungary. Even as early as December 1920 conversations were held between the Czechs and Hungarians over a possible adjustment of the frontier in Slovakia. Beneš, however, while prepared to retrocede some areas which were almost totally Magyar in composition, insisted as a prime condition of any agreement that Hungary should renounce further claims for treaty revision; and the Hungarian government was far too obsessed with the injustice of the Trianon settlement to consider such an assurance. Neither Horthy nor his ministers felt quite so harshly towards the Serbs as they did towards the Czechs; a treaty of friendship between Hungary and Yugoslavia, proposed by the Magyars in 1926, was, however, never even drafted for the simple reason that when the negotiators began talking they found – though it was several months before they would admit it – that they were anything but friends. There was equally little prospect of reconciliation with Roumania, especially after a Roumanian move in 1927 to expropriate Magyar landowners in Transylvania had called forth the wrath of the newspaper magnate, Lord Rothermere; for it was clear to every right-thinking member of the Budapest parliament that 'Justice for Hungary' by grace of the British press was preferable at any time to a partial accommodation with Bucharest.

The rift between Hungary, on the one side, and Czechoslovakia, Yugoslavia and Roumania, on the other, became wider with each year that passed. Quite apart from the general unwillingness to consider a more equitable drawing of international boundaries, the growth of tariff walls hindered cooperation over economic problems, the field in which it would have been most beneficial to all the Central European peoples. All four countries were members of the League of Nations, with one or other of the Little Entente states allotted a seat on its Council, and few men worked more devotedly for the League than the Czech foreign minister from 1918 to 1935, Edvard Beneš; but, though the Little Entente was willing to incorporate in its own structure all proposals put forward by the League for peaceful collaboration, there was never any attempt made at Geneva for reconciliation with Hungary, still less for implementation of Article 19 of the Covenant, with its provisions for 'reconsideration ... of treaties which have become inapplicable'. It is a gloomy commentary on the dashed hopes of the 1920s that precisely ten years to the month in which this Article was drafted the Little Entente held the first of a series of military conferences to discuss war-plans for operations in the Danube basin should Hungary disturb the peace.

The Little Entente was never as hostile to the Weimar Republic as to Hungary. Neither the Yugoslavs nor the Roumanians had any quarrel with the German democrats and Czechoslovakia was able to maintain good relations with Berlin even though the German press was, from time to time, suspicious of Franco-Czech friendship and tended to revive the old accusation of 'encirclement'. The German authorities cooperated amicably enough with the Czechs over the free port area permitted to them in Hamburg; and they also tried to control the rabidly Pan-German groups that plotted 'Freedom for the Sudetenland' from across the frontier in Saxony. Beneš, for his part, contributed to the lessening of tension in 1925 which was symbolized by the Locarno Pact and, in the following year, he was one of the principal advocates of Germany's entry into the League.

The Czechs would also have liked to secure an understanding between the Little Entente and Russia, but not even Beneš was able to carry his partners with him on this issue: relations between the Roumanian and Soviet governments were hampered by major problems such as the status of Bessarabia and minor irritants such as the retention in Russia of Queen Marie's jewels; and the Yugoslavs flatly rejected all contact with any Bolshevik government because of their sovereign's detestation of the regime which had butchered the Tsar's family. None of the Little Entente countries established diplomatic relations with the Soviet Union until the end of the first decade of peace, and in Belgrade a 'White' Russian Legation was still functioning when the Second World War began.

The largest and most vulnerable of the new nations, Poland, remained on bad terms with no less than four of her six neighbours – Germany, Russia, Lithuania and Czechoslovakia. No foreign minister in the Weimar Republic was prepared to recognize the German-Polish frontier as a final settlement; and the fact that the Locarno Treaties of 1925, which guaranteed the frontiers of Germany in the west, excluded the boundaries along the corridor to Danzig and in Poznania and Silesia was interpreted by the Poles as convincing evidence that Germany would seek recovery of the lost territories in the east, probably in combination with Soviet Russia. Polish and German extremists inflamed passions along the corridor to Danzig and both countries were responsible for a particularly bitter tariff war which led to a chronic economic crisis throughout the region. In December 1927 Pilsudski did, indeed, seek to induce the most conciliatory of German foreign ministers, Gustav Stresemann, to begin negotiations for an understanding between the two states; but Stresemann brushed aside even this tentative overture. Pilsudski's habitual answer to demonstrations of German revisionist sentiment was to order elaborate military manoeuvres along the western frontiers. It was a cumbersome method of keeping the peace, effective only so long as Germany was in the grip of domestic crises and unable to count on Soviet intervention in the east.

Fortunately for Poland tension with Germany and tension with Russia never coincided in this period. There was some risk of another war between Poland and her eastern neighbour in 1927 when the Soviet minister in Warsaw was assassinated by a member of a counter-revolutionary émigré organization towards which the Polish authorities had shown a rash benevolence. On this occasion the Lithuanians supported the Russians because of resentment at Polish treatment of their compatriots around Vilna (which the Russians, in a treaty signed in the previous year, had ostentatiously recognized as Lithuanian territory). But neither of the principal antagonists was prepared to renew the conflict of 1920 and, with Maxim Litvinov gradually taking over responsibility for Soviet foreign policy from Chicherin, relations between Russia and the cordon of states on her western borders began to improve steadily. In February 1929 Poland joined the Baltic States (Latvia, Lithuania and Estonia) and Roumania in adhering to the so-called 'Litvinov Protocol', by which Russia and her neighbours renounced aggressive acts across the Soviet frontiers. Few people believed that general undertakings of this character increased the prospects of a lasting peace, but at least the Protocol afforded its signatories a respite from costly sabre-rattling by putting old causes of friction into cold storage; and in July 1932 the Poles went even further than the terms of the Protocol and concluded a non-aggression pact with Russia.

Throughout the 1920s Polish foreign policy had relied on three basic assumptions: the willingness of the Great Powers to maintain the Versailles settlement; the continued validity of the alliance with France, with its guarantee of military assistance if Russia or Germany launched an unprovoked attack on the Polish State; and the general security offered Poland by membership of the League of Nations. At the end of the decade, with Germany sustained by the Locarno assurances and playing a major role at Geneva, only the French alliance seemed a pillar of support and even that was weakened in Pilsudski's eyes by the constant respect shown in Paris to every wish of Dr Beneš. Inevitably the Poles turned towards more traditional methods of diplomacy, seeking to play off their powerful neighbours against each other rather than be gripped in a vice of their own manufacture. Unfortunately there was little enough the Poles were prepared to offer in return for agreement, and far too much that could be taken away.

The domestic policies of all these six countries both reflected changes in the international balance and helped to upset it, primarily because so much of the tension resulted from problems of national minorities. The least homogeneous state was Czechoslovakia, where the Czechs had to gain the cooperation of the Slovaks and Ruthenes while, at the same time, securing acceptance of the new order by the former master-peoples, the Germans and Magyars; but it was in Yugoslavia that the national issue overshadowed all other matters, whether narrowly political or social and economic. In Poland and Roumania, where there were large Jewish communities as well as national minorities, these questions differed in character; and in Hungary and Bulgaria the humiliation of recent defeats encouraged an artificial stimulation of national pride so that rulers and ruled were distracted from pressing matters of social justice and tempted to interfere in their neighbours' affairs.

Although the Czechoslovak Constitution of 1920 was in most respects a paradigm of democracy, it was fundamentally centralist in character. The old provincial boundaries of the Habsburg Monarchy were abolished so as to emphasize the unitary form of the 'Czechoslovak Nation' and the country was divided into twenty-six administrative districts in each of which it was intended that there should be a council, in part nominated and in part elected. A Statute of Autonomy for Ruthenia was written into the constitution, as Beneš had promised at the Peace Conference. At the same time a Language Law permitted the use of a minority language in the courts, schools and colleges within any area where it was spoken by at least a fifth of the population. Parliamentary deputies might use their native tongue while addressing the Chamber; and the final article of the constitution made 'forcible denationalization' a criminal offence. All these provisions followed closely the stipulations in the Minorities Treaties, although subsequent laws introduced safeguards against separatist conspiracies aimed at the integrity of the state. These measures to preserve the republic were eminently justified: for the Sudeten German leader, Dr Lodgmann von Auen, was prepared to declare in parliament in 1922 that 'He who does not think that the supreme duty of a German Deputy is to commit high treason in this state makes a mistake.'

President Masaryk, an Olympian figure above party strife, was fully alive to the menace implicit in Lodgmann's arrogant speech. In 1919 he had once said, in private, 'The German problem is the most important for us. If we win the Germans for our state we shall win the other nationalities.' Relations between the Czechoslovak administration and the non-

Slav minorities improved rapidly during the 1920s although in the early years there were frequent complaints of discrimination, especially in the application of the Land Reform and in recruitment for employment in the public services. By 1926 the Sudeten German attitude had mellowed sufficiently for one of their parliamentary representatives to join the ruling coalition and, until the growth of the Nazi movement in the thirties, a majority of Sudeten German deputies always thereafter supported the government. The German Social Democrats, in particular, made a distinctive, but positive, contribution to the political life of the republic. The Magyars were less easily reconciled and, indeed, were subjected to far pettier acts of contempt than the Germans. There were never more than ten Hungarian deputies in parliament and some of them were representatives of the Left, as hostile to Horthy's Hungary as to Masaryk's Czechoslovakia.

The Slovak people, especially the peasantry, were far slower in accepting the unitary state than Masaryk, who was himself of part Slovak ancestry, had anticipated during his negotiations with their emigrant brothers in the United States in the spring of 1918. Originally the Slovaks were not so much hostile to the new political order as indifferent and confused; and tactful handling might have won their active support. Unfortunately in May 1919 Milan Štefánik, the air ace who was also chief Slovak spokesman in the *New Europe* circle, was killed when his plane crashed in the Lower Carpathians as he was returning to a hero's reception at Bratislava. In that crucial period no other Slovak leader had both the personality to fire his compatriots and the confidence of Masaryk and Beneš, although in due course the agrarian, Milan Hodža, and the social democrat, Ivan Derer, won wide support in both halves of the republic. But in 1919–20 the Slovaks, astounded by a sudden invasion of administrators, officials and school-teachers from the Czech provinces, turned naturally for advice and political instruction to the few educated members of their community, the men of God. In Protestant towns such as Bratislava, the Lutheran pastors had a long tradition of Czecho-Slovak cooperation and the principle of the unitary state was welcomed, even if there was criticism of its detailed structure; but in the far larger Roman Catholic rural areas the priests were predominantly opposed to rule from Prague and in some districts they were outspokenly pro-Magyar. Particular resentment was caused by the action of the Czech educational authorities in placing the Catholic high schools (*gymnasia*) under state control in order to counter Magyarophil teaching. In the Carpathian foothills the priests were almost local agents for Monsignor Hlinka's 'Slovak People's Party'. There were, of course, a number of villages – mostly in western Slovakia – which delighted in thwarting the Church by voting for the centralist Czecho-slovak parties; but Hlinka's followers consistently polled just under half a million votes at each election from 1925 to 1935 and the People's Party remained the largest single political organization in Slovakia.

Living conditions in Slovakia improved out of all recognition during the 1920s: there was better social legislation, better housing, more schools and cultural institutions and greater freedom of political and religious expression than there had been under Hungarian rule. Nevertheless, one wing of the People's Party cooperated secretly with the enemies of the Czechoslovak State and received both encouragement and money from Hungary and, to a much lesser extent, from Poland. But Hlinka himself, though indignant that Slovakia was not regarded in Prague as 'ripe for self-government,' endeavoured to improve relations between the two main regions of the republic. In 1927 he authorized two members of the party to enter the ruling coalition and they served in the government for a couple of years (although one of these ministers, Father Joseph Tiso, was to achieve later notoriety as Hitler's puppet in Slovakia). A *modus vivendi* was concluded with the Vatican early in 1928 and friction between Czechs and Slovaks was beginning to lessen when in the summer of 1929 one of Hlinka's staunchest supporters, Professor Tuka, was put on trial and sentenced to fifteen years imprisonment for treasonable contacts with the Hungarians. Although there is no doubt of Tuka's guilt – and, indeed, of that of many other members of the party who remained at liberty – the trial exasperated considerable sections of the Slovak community and much of the old bitterness crept back into the relations of the two national groups.

The third national group, the Ruthenes, never gained the autonomous status assured them by the constitution. President Masaryk duly appointed a governor of Carpatho-Ruthenia, as the constitution prescribed, but the Diet to which he was to be responsible failed to meet, presumably because no elections were ever held for it. The Czechs argued that the Ruthenes were not politically conscious, were backward and illiterate and even less suited for self-government than the Slovaks. The League of Nations was informed in 1922 that the elections for the Diet could not be held until the precise boundary between Slovakia and Ruthenia was clearly defined: this, it subsequently appeared, was a matter which required the sanction of the Ruthene Diet. The Ruthenes, of course, voted in the parliamentary elections and, in both 1925 and 1935, the communists gained more support than any of the other nine parties. There was no active hostility shown by the Ruthenes to the Czechs at any time in the 1920s or early thirties; and this is hardly surprising for the Ruthenes had never had such good houses or schools or roads or health services. The Czechs controlled Ruthenia through what was, in effect, a benevolent colonial administration and their twenty-year experiment was unique in the history of Central Europe. The merits of the experiment were considerable and the Ruthenes enjoyed greater freedom and a higher standard of living than their compatriots beyond the frontiers, in Poland or Roumania or the Soviet Ukraine; but it was not precisely what had been envisaged at the Peace Conference. Beneš' vision of the Czechoslovak Republic as 'a sort of Switzerland' seemed even less appropriate at the end of the 1920s than at their beginning.

The 'Kingdom of the Serbs, Croats and Slovenes' was, despite its cumbersome title, an even more centralized administrative unit than the Czechoslovak Republic. Although the Corfu Pact and the intricate negotiations in the last weeks of the war had held out some prospect of genuine Yugoslav union, the new state was dominated by Pašić and the Serbian Radical Party and every one of its nine nationalities was ruled directly from Belgrade. During the twenty-three years of the Yugoslav Monarchy there was only one interlude of five months when the government was headed by a non-Serb (the Slovene priest, Korošec, in 1928). Similarly, a Serb was always minister of the army and navy; and, once Trumbić had resigned as foreign minister in November 1919, this portfolio too remained in Serbian hands. Key diplomatic posts and the high military commands were only given to Serbs, almost all of whom came from the territory of pre-1912 Serbia. Slovenes, Croats and Moslems from Bosnia sat in the various governments – of which there were twenty-four in the first ten years of the Kingdom – but they were rarely trusted with the more important departments.

The position of the non-Slav nationalities was grim throughout the 1920s and, indeed, beyond. It was assumed from the earliest days of the Kingdom that all Bulgaro-Macedonians were already second-class Serbs and that the Albanian Shqiptar community was of similar lowly status and anxious to be Serbized. Accordingly no national freedom was bestowed on the Macedonians and only a few religious liberties on the Moslem Shqiptars. The Roumanians in the Bánát were, at first, severely repressed with the result that most of their teachers and priests fled across the frontier, their property (which included not only schools and convents but church lands) being sequestered for the benefit of the Serbs. Considerations of foreign policy led, in time, to a more enlightened attitude and, by the end of the twenties, negotiations had begun between Belgrade and Bucharest for re-opening Roumanian schools and recovering some independence for the Roumanian Orthodox Church; but it was not until 1933 that a convention was signed permitting these trifling concessions.

Since Roumania was, after all, a friendly neighbour and a partner in the Little Entente, it may be imagined how badly the 'ex-enemy' Hungarian minority fared. It was, perhaps, inevitable that land reform should impose a heavy burden on the Magyar minority because of the size of the Hungarian-owned estates, especially in the Voivodina. But repression went much further, hitting the poorer Magyar labourers and peasants rather than the former gentry class (most of whom migrated northwards). Every attempt was made to restrict the use of the Magyar tongue, in administration, in commerce and, so far as possible, in private life. A limited number of Magyar-speaking classes were permitted in some schools but the majority of teachers were Serbs or Croats, with an imperfect knowledge of the language. The German minority (who numbered about half a million, slightly more than the Magyars) were treated less severely, partly because in the days of the Weimar Republic they did not seem such a security risk as the Magyars. A German National Party contested the 1923 elections and gained eight parliamentary seats, although it was dissolved a year later when its leaders fell foul of Pašić. Characteristically, the next change of government ensured that the party could be re-constituted and it continued to be represented in parliament throughout the 1920s. But neither the Magyar nor the German minorities were ever reconciled to the Yugoslav State; and their accumulated venom was unleashed with particular savagery in the Second World War.

The parliamentary history of Yugoslavia began, as it was to continue, with chaos bordering on confusion; for the political structure of the Kingdom was determined by a constitution which was approved by a gratifyingly large majority in an Assembly from which two fifths of the members had absented themselves in protest. The constitution was adopted, appropriately but unwisely, on Vidovdan, the national day of the Serbs, 28 June 1921. The Croats and Slovenes, having pressed in vain for a federal system, refused to register any vote on a document of which they strongly disapproved; and both nationalities continued to demand decentralization throughout the inter-war period. The constitution was, however, a fundamentally democratic instrument of government, with a single-chamber parliament elected by manhood suffrage and with the principle of ministerial responsibility firmly established. Moreover, Prince-Regent Alexander (who only succeeded to the throne on King Peter's death in August 1921) honestly desired to act as a constitutional monarch serving as trustee for all his peoples. Unfortunately Alexander was a soldier through and through, and a Serbian soldier at that. To him factious opposition implied sedition and mutiny. Hence the structure of the state could not be modified by threats or by violence, but only by changes subtly insinuated and not invested with the formal finality of constitutional amendment. The Slovenes perceived this: the Croats did not.

The Slovenes gradually achieved a high degree of autonomy in the state, partly through the skill of their chief spokesman, Korošec, and partly through the good fortune of their national characteristics. So long as Slovene was recognized as one of the 'languages of state,' local affairs were bound to remain in their own hands, for no Serb official was going to learn another language in order to cajole nine per cent of the population when the remaining ninety-one per cent could be bullied in good, plain Serbo-Croat. The Slovenes, too, had another advantage. As even the Serbs admitted, they were more efficient than their fellow South Slavs and had often had administrative experience under the Austrians; and hence it is not surprising that in a kingdom where more than half the population was illiterate, they were frequently appointed to high posts in the civil service or in banking and similar professions. 'The Slovenes are our Czechs,' declared the Serbs grudgingly: 'The Slovenes are our Jews,' said the Croats, in an interesting variation. Serbian domination never caused the resentment in Slovenia that it did in Croatia. Conscripts from the Serbian regions guarded the Slovene frontier and garrisoned its towns while young Slovenes were sent to police the Balkan territories; and the Cyrillic script appeared unfamiliarly beside the Latinized Slovene of public hoardings; but these were minor irritants. There was never any powerful separatist movement in Slovenia.

No lasting accommodation seemed possible between the Croats and Serbs, although many attempts were made at reconciliation. In part their differences lay far back in history and in part they sprang from immediate grievances, such as Croatian resentment at high taxation imposed by a government which was taking trade away from Zagreb to Belgrade; but they were exacerbated, above all, by a conflict of personalities. The most powerful figure in Yugoslavia until his death in December 1926 was undoubtedly Nikola Pašić who had learned everything and forgiven nothing from almost half a century of Balkan politics; and opposing him at every turn in Zagreb was Stjepan Radić, the temperamental and heavily-blinkered mule on whom the peasants of Croatia had loaded the burden of their discontent. Neither man understood or trusted the other; and their mutual antipathy was both transmitted to and fed by the hostility of their supporters.

In 1923 the Peasant Party won such striking successes in Croatia in elections for the Skupština that Radić contemplated a complete breach with Belgrade. But, after refusing to permit the newly elected deputies to participate in any parliamentary deliberations, he slipped across the frontier on a false passport and began a grand tour of revolutionary Europe to win foreign sympathy for the Croatian cause. His most startling achievement was in Moscow, where in July 1924 he suddenly announced that his party would join a Peasant International, planned by the Comintern as one of the earliest 'Common Front' organizations. Since most of the Croatian peasants were good Catholics, this development caused some consternation at home, although Radić's views on the Church were always mildly idiosyncratic and he had been known to open meetings with the invocation, 'Praise be to Jesus and down with the clergy!' From Russia Radić sent glowing reports back to his newspapers in Zagreb: 'The new Russia is the same as our humanitarian and republican Croatia except that Soviet Russia is much, much bigger,' his readers were informed; and he succinctly described his impressions of Europe with poetic rhapsody – 'In Moscow the sun shines, in Vienna there is moonlight, in Budapest darkness.' Similar sentiments publicly expressed with even more fire on his return from exile led Pašić in December 1924 to seek the dissolution of the Peasant Party as a Bolshevik movement and landed Radić and four other deputies in prison.

Yugoslav politics remained disconcertingly individualistic. Approaches to Pašić by Radić's nephew had remarkable consequences: the Peasant Party was permitted once more to function openly; and, in the summer of 1925, its incorrigibly perverse leader was not merely freed from jail but brought into Pašić's government and inaptly appointed Minister of Public Instruction. But although Radić tempered his advocacy of separatism with respectful gestures to King Alexander, he could never understand notions of collective responsibility and was so unversed in the niceties of parliamentary etiquette that he even stood up in the chamber and denounced his cabinet colleagues as swine. On 1 April 1926 the minister of Public Instruction duly resigned, and the Peasant Party moved into total opposition. For two years the Croatian deputies did all they could to hamper measures proposed by the Serbs or any other nationality. There was, perhaps, an inevitability about the climax of these disputes: on 20 June 1928 a Montenegrin deputy pulled out a revolver in the Skupština and shot two of the Croatian Peasant members dead, gravely wounding three others including Radić. When he died seven weeks later the whole Yugoslav union seemed about to disintegrate.

King Alexander was genuinely horrified at these events. He appointed Korošec as prime minister, hoping that a Slovene might reach some agreement with the Croats where any Serb would certainly have failed. But the peasants wanted more than mere political change: there was a bad harvest that year, and they believed the state owed them compensation for the failure of their crops; and it was over this issue rather than the nationalities question that Korošec's government fell in December. There was no obvious successor. In the first week of the New Year the King had two long interviews with the new leader of the Croatian Peasants, Vladko Maček: nothing but a federal re-organization of the country would satisfy the Croats; and this the King refused to concede. On 6 January 1929 Alexander announced that he would assume responsibility for the political direction of the kingdom: the Constitution of 1921 was abolished; all existing political parties were dissolved; restrictions imposed on the press; and executive powers shared by the King and a council of ministers headed by General Petar Zivković, a close friend of Alexander ever since the conflict with the Black Hand in 1913–14. In the following October decrees were issued drastically changing the administrative system of the kingdom (which, on this occasion, was officially called 'Yugoslavia' for the first time). All the old provinces and departments were abolished and such dangerously evocative words as 'Serbia,' 'Croatia,' 'Slovenia' etc., were replaced by regions (*Banovine*) which were mostly named after rivers. The boundaries of six of the nine *Banovine* were so drawn that they included a majority of Serbs, an administrative arrangement which demonstrated clearly enough the true spirit of the royal dictatorship, even though later decrees removed the specifically Serbian regimental colours from the army and deprived Vidovdan of its status as the major national festival.

The royal dictatorship was unashamedly anti-democratic, but it was not necessarily unpopular for that; the political game had become tediously vexatious. Moreover, the two summers which followed the King's coup brought good harvests and there was at the same time a short-lived economic boom, especially in the fledgling textile industry.

But the measures employed by the Yugoslav police to stamp out political activity were monstrously brutal and both the Peasant Party and the Communists were grimly persecuted. Inevitably those who avoided arrest sought escape from the country. Some fled to Geneva and prepared a memorandum on the condition of Croatia which they submitted to the League; and public opinion in the West was shocked by the evidence it provided of imprisonment without trial and of the use of torture. Others determined to secure aid for Croatia from Yugoslavia's natural enemies, Hungary, Bulgaria and Italy. Among those who settled in Italy was a former Croatian Peasant deputy, Ante Pavelić, who on the day after the King's coup, founded in Zagreb a secret society whose members were pledged to fight for an Independent Croat State. Pavelić's followers, who called themselves *Ustaše* ('Rebels') had no use for the liberal pacifism of Radić and Maček; they were convinced that only violence and terror would destroy Serbian domination. The royal dictatorship, so far from solving the national question, merely ensured that when it was renewed the struggle would be fought with even greater bitterness; and the shots which had rung through the Skupština that evening in June 1928 were to echo for almost twenty years through the valleys and forests of the South Slav lands.

Technically Yugoslavia was the first of the new nations of Eastern Europe to rescind a democratic constitution. It was not, however, the first to establish a dictatorship; for in Poland the parliamentary era ended abruptly in the spring of 1926, although in this instance the deputies were allowed to perform the charade of government for another four and a half years before the prisons filled with the leaders of opposition.

Polish democracy perished, not from some conflict of nationalities, but because of the impatience of one man with its weaknesses. For, paradoxically, the Polish Republic was dominated from its foundation by an autocrat more powerful than any Balkan monarch – Jozef Pilsudski, on whom the nation had bestowed the dignity of Marshal in March 1920. In retrospect, the essence of Pilsudski's magic eludes those who seek it: he was an able military commander, but no Sobieski; he had courage, but little foresight; he declined political office and chafed explosively when others exercised authority; he turned against old comrades and raised an army against the very republic he claimed to have brought into being. Yet, if the pedestal of his reputation is too frail for his stature, the quality of greatness is there, none the less: it rings through his proclamations and resounds with the confidence of one who knew he was custodian of the national will to exist. If he was the first of the post-war Bonapartes, he was also the last of the Polish romantics – perhaps that is where his secret lies.

The record of the Sejm, the Polish parliament, from 1919 to 1926 is consistently unimpressive, partly because proportional representation made for weak compromises and partly because its members had been trained in the markedly different schools of the three fallen empires. The largest single party was formed by the Piast Peasants of Witos, originally from Galicia, who was well to the left of the landowners from the ex-Russian territories and the aristocracy of Poznania but far more conservative than the agrarian leaders of the Danubian basin. Land reform was disgracefully half-hearted and the protracted tariff war with Germany encouraged a natural tendency towards inflation so that the country was faced both in 1923 and 1925 by rising prices and an alarming growth in unemployment. When Witos tried to relate wages to prices there were strikes, riots and even a one-day Soviet in Cracow; and subsequent panic measures introduced by the national democrat, Stanislaw Grabski, failed to save business ventures and banks from collapse. Only severe cuts in governmental expenditure and the imposition of heavy taxation seemed capable of giving the republic a financial breathing-space; and when in April 1926 the coalition government proposed these measures, it was faced with a threat of revolt from the social democrats and from the industrial workers in general.

The marshal had held no governmental post since December 1922 when he surrendered his powers as 'Chief of State' to the first of the figure-head presidents envisaged by the constitution, Professor Narutowicz (who was, in fact, assassinated two days later and succeeded by the cooperative movement leader, Wojciechowski). Pilsudski remained Chief of the General Staff for another five months and then retired to his estate at Sulejowek, suspicious of the Sejm and angry that the constitution should have imposed so weak an executive on the country.

For three years Sulejowek was to Pilsudski what Colombey-les-Deux-Eglises became to his young admirer, Charles de Gaulle, from 1946 to 1958. From time to time the marshal gave unsolicited advice to President Wojciechowski on checking parliamentary extravagance, but with little apparent effect. At last, on 11 May 1926, he published a thunderous attack on the Sejm in general and the Piast Party in particular; and the following day troops loyal to Pilsudski seized a suburb of Warsaw. Significantly, the workers supported the marshal – who had, of course, begun his career as a revolutionary socialist – and a railway strike prevented the government from bringing troops to the capital from Poznania. There was severe fighting for several days and perhaps as many as a thousand casualties; but during the night of 14/15 May the President and government resigned, leaving all power once more in Pilsudski's hands.

At first Pilsudski still declined office, preferring to nominate his personal friends for president and prime minister, but he agreed to head governments from October 1926 to March 1928 and briefly in 1930; and he insisted on being made Inspector-General of the Army, a post equivalent to commander-in-chief. In reality, his titular position was an irrelevancy for his views prevailed on every question of foreign and domestic policy until his death in 1935, on the ninth anniversary of the coup. The Sejm remained in being and elections were even held in 1928 and 1930 but legislation greatly strengthened the authority of the executive and government was conducted by administrators who bore only a formal responsibility to parliament. On paper, the Polish economy prospered: Pilsudski appeared a sound rampart against Bolshevism, and foreign loans, especially from America, helped balance the budget; industry recovered from the effects of the wars; and the construction of Gdynia enabled Poland to free her foreign trade from dependence on the heavy port taxes of Danzig. But inevitably Poland was closely tied to the American stock market; and the Wall Street Crash of 1929 was to send tremors through the banks of Warsaw and Cracow.

The problem of national minorities was posed acutely in the Pilsudski era, and little was done to solve it. In Poznania and Pomorze (the 'Polish Corridor' to the Baltic) there had, from the first, been conflicts between the authorities and the German population over educational policy, and once Germany entered the League the complaint that there were not enough German-language schools was taken up at Geneva. Pilsudski in no way modified the 'polonizing' tendencies of his predecessors and economic pressure was applied to the German minority in the hope that its members would emigrate to the Reich (as many did). Although Upper Silesia enjoyed a degree of autonomy under the protection of commissioners from the League, Pilsudski appointed as regional governor Michal Grazynski, a fanatical Polish nationalist, who permitted intimidation in the elections not only against Germans but against Polish-speaking champions of genuine autonomy. In the east the Ukrainian minority, far larger than any other in Poland, was denied any form of local self-government and had more reason than the Germans to complain of 'polonization' in the schools. The Ukrainians became so desperate that they formed a secret revolutionary organization, the Ukrainian Liberation Organization (UWO), which was responsible for a series of terrorist attacks on Polish officials and landowners in the summer of 1930. Pilsudski regarded the disturbances as a major revolt and sent cavalry through the villages of eastern Galicia, establishing a regime of terror which won for the Polish troops a notoriety similar to that accorded to the British 'Black and Tans' in Ireland ten years previously. The Pilsudski government kept neither the spirit nor the letter of the Minorities Treaty imposed in 1919; and, indeed, in the autumn of 1934 it openly repudiated all such obligations.

The one minority to benefit from the marshal's veiled dictatorship was the Jewish community, which was larger in Poland than in any other country in the world apart from the United States. Anti-semitism had deep roots in the Polish lands, especially in the regions which had been subject to the crude discriminatory legislation of the last two tsars. One of the first problems to be settled by the Pilsudski government of 1926 was an appeal by a Jewish mayor whose election had been declared invalid by a Polish official on the ground that it contravened a Russian statute of 1890; and it was only in 1931 that Pilsudski ensured the final abrogation of all tsarist restrictions on Jewish liberties. More positively, the marshal secured the passage of legislation protecting the religious rights of Jewish believers and continued the policy already begun by Grabski of accepting the need for independent Jewish educational institutions. Nevertheless, many lower officials in the civil service remained fundamentally anti-semitic and deeply envious of the key positions held by members of the Jewish community in commerce and banking. Even before Pilsudski's death old habits had begun to re-assert themselves and no serious attempts were made to assimilate the Polish Jews during the last years of the republic; they survived a series of gross affronts to their liberty only to pass under a far more hideous tyranny in the Second World War.

Roumanian internal politics between the wars suffered from chronic dyspepsia. This is hardly surprising, for the new territories absorbed in 'Greater Roumania' were larger in area and in population than the old pre-war kingdom (the Regat, as it was called). They were, moreover, richly profuse in ethnic and social variations. But if Roumania had changed, the Bratianus and Averescus had not; and much of the stress of these years sprang from the reluctance of the old political oligarchs in Bucharest to accept the fact that they were living in a new country, and not merely a bloated Regat. Political progress was also impeded by absurd palace scandals which tended to eliminate the dynasty as a unifying force. With fertile wheat-lands and rich oil deposits, Greater Roumania possessed potentials denied to the other Eastern European states; but none frittered away its resources with such feckless abandon. The general standard of living over the whole country was actually lower on the eve of the Second World War than it was in the Regat in 1914.

Although the new Roumanian Constitution was not drafted until 1923, King Ferdinand honoured a wartime pledge to widen the franchise as soon as peace was formally concluded and the elections held for the unified kingdom in November 1919 were genuinely representative and free from the chicanery which so often accompanied the Roumanian electorate to the polls. Neither of the traditional parties satisfied the voters: the Conservatives were regarded as pro-German; and the Liberals as a mere extension of Bratianu's ego. The greatest success was won by the (Transylvanian) National Party, which for nearly thirty years had championed the Roumanians against intimidation from Budapest; its leader, Vaida-Voevod, formed a coalition ministry of which the second string was to be Ion Mihalache, whose Peasant Party was another novelty in Roumania's political life.

There seemed at last some prospect that the agrarian reforms, first promised by Bratianu before the Balkan Wars and re-affirmed by both King Ferdinand and by parliament in 1917 and 1918, might be put into effect; but the King and the old political leaders became alarmed at what they had unleashed by permitting so free an election. The thought of what Lenin was doing to the north of them and Stamboliisky to the south sent shivers down the tinselly bourgeois boulevards of Bucharest. After only four months of office Vaida-Voevod was peremptorily dismissed by the king. A new government was formed by Roumania's principal war-hero, General Averescu, who had established a 'People's Party' for just such an occasion. He duly won a majority in elections which either showed the extent of his popularity or demonstrated that Roumania's police and petty officials were still as good manufacturing craftsmen as any in the country.

Averescu, who had suppressed the *jacquerie* of 1907, was politically heavy-handed: dissident workers found themselves called to the colours and placed under military discipline; and trade-union organizers were arrested and imprisoned as Bolsheviks. But Averescu was also a son of the peasantry; he knew that land reform, if properly controlled, would serve as a safety-valve; for once the peasants were made masters of their own soil, they would become tenacious property-owners who would have no truck with the political Left. Hence in July 1921 the Land Reform Act duly became law: the extent of redistribution varied in the different provinces and was greater among the foreign-owned estates of Transylvania than in the Regat; but the general effect was to expropriate about one third of the total arable land in the kingdom from the boyar-gentry class and assign it to the peasant proprietors (who now became the largest single element in Roumanian society). Socially and politically the Act was a success; but economically it was a disaster, for the disruption of the large estates led to a decline in standards of cultivation. Lack of agricultural knowledge kept the annual yield of crops depressingly low. In some instances peasants sold their strip-holdings to larger farms and migrated to the towns, but there was still a severe problem of rural over-population throughout the kingdom.

In December 1921 the Averescu government ended as abruptly as had Vaida-Voevod's when the finance minister, Titulescu, courageously proposed a property-tax and the general himself indiscreetly delivered a speech unpleasing to the king's ear. Elections followed in March 1922. It was now the turn of the liberals to romp home: they increased their representation from 17 in 1920 to 260, and Averescu's party fell from 209 to 11. This was such an astounding swing in twenty-two months that all the opposition members promptly challenged the validity of the returns, and then walked out of parliament in disgust. But the absence of an opposition hardly embarrassed Bratianu. He proceeded to prepare a new constitution, the publication of which brought his opponents back to the Chamber although they were powerless to amend it.

The 1923 Constitution remains a sad commentary on the moral decay of a great political party. It began uncompromisingly with the assertion, 'The Kingdom of Roumania is a unitary and indivisible state'; and centralism was the fundamental principle in the whole document. There was no vestige of local autonomy. Despite the protests of the 'new Roumanians' the old provinces were swept aside in favour of Departments administered from Bucharest. The Chamber was elected by an ingenious, and blatantly unscrupulous, method of proportional representation which required further legislation in 1926 to demonstrate precisely how 'bonus seats' were to be awarded to the successful party. Universal suffrage with secret ballot was guaranteed to men and promised to women when parliament had settled the conditions under which they might exercise their voting rights, a task which was presumably too taxing for the deputies since female suffrage was not conceded until 1946. The crown retained considerable powers: the king had an absolute veto on legislation, the right to dissolve the Chamber at will, and the right to appoint and dismiss ministers without deference to parliament's wishes. The constitution did, indeed, give assurances of the traditional civil and political liberties, but not if they endangered 'state security,' a vague phrase which was subsequently given a broad interpretation and applied particularly to check the growth of trade unionism. In general, the constitution was a backward-looking document for which no one outside the Liberal Party felt an iota of respect. It was a device by which an ageing party sought to perpetuate its political grip on the kingdom, and it lasted just as long as the liberals themselves – until King Carol II decided to give his dictatorship the force of constitutional law in 1938.

The centralist constitution was followed, as might have been expected, by a period of self-assertive internal nationalism. The Magyar minority in Transylvania and the Bánát and the Bulgarian majority in the southern Dobrudja were regarded as irreconcilable opponents of the Roumanian national state and their political activities were watched with suspicion; but the Magyars, at least, enjoyed better educational facilities than in Yugoslavia. The German community gave little trouble; it was tolerated and even petted by the government in Bucharest which, while accepting that its ways were too foreign for assimilation, was anxious to prevent its members from listening to the revisionist sirens on the middle Danube. On the other hand, the Ukrainian minority in Bessarabia suffered considerably, partly because the Roumanians believed that the province was riddled with communism and partly because, when not under martial law, it tended to serve as a repository for the more error-prone petty officials. There was a serious, and genuinely communist-inspired, rising in the village of Tatrabunary (midway between Ismail and Odessa) in 1924 and frequent disturbances elsewhere which were put down with ominously casual police brutality. The Ruthenes in the Bukovina were treated with as little consideration as their Ukrainian brethren but with less overt repression.

Roumanian nationalism was concerned, not so much with the eradication of extraneous cultural influences, as with ensuring economic mastery. By Vintula Bratianu's 'Nationalization Laws' of 1924 companies with non-Roumanian directors were placed under the control of nominees from Bucharest. These measures, aimed primarily at securing control of expanding industry in Transylvania and the Bánát, aroused protests both from the minorities and from some of the new Roumanians who resented the showering of favours on men from the old Regat. The Jewish community, with its great hold on pre-war commerce, might well have suffered from these laws, had it not been for the established convention by which businesses threatened with hostile legislation could secure immunity by paying substantial sums to those who mattered in the party or the state. In time, the richer German and Magyar firms used a similar 'protection racket' to take the sting out of the legal restraints, and their burden fell almost exclusively on the smaller companies. It may be added here that one of the most important side-effects of this xenophobic financial policy was the discouragement of foreign investment, thus hampering the growth of undertakings which would have bolstered the Roumanian economy.

In Moldavia, and to a lesser extent elsewhere, the young generation lacked sympathy with the easy pragmatism by which their elders would mellow national zeal at the drop of a cheque. These young men, many of them students, possessed a curiously warped idealism which affected to believe that Roumanian purity had been corrupted by the Jews; and it was in this climate of anti-semitism that the only mass movement of fascism in the Balkan lands took root and flourished. The 'Iron Guard' was founded by Corneliu Codreanu, then in his early twenties, at the University of Jassy in 1923 and by 1928 it had become so powerful that it attracted the attention of the League of Nations for violent acts perpetrated against the Jews in Cluj, Oradea, Hunedoara and other Transylvanian towns. The Guard chose victims from among the minorities as well as the Jews; and not least among its terrifying features was a fanatical religious mysticism, for Codreanu claimed that, while in prison in 1923, he had been granted a vision of the Archangel Michael who had summoned him to achieve the moral regeneration of the Roumanian people.

The parliamentary scene in Bucharest remained, for the most part, singularly unedifying. Election returns still bore a marked numerical similarity to cricket scores although the outcome of the contest was always more predictable: Averescu notched up 292 in 1926 and Bratianu 298 in 1927. It was, however, the last of Bratianu's triumphs, for he died later in the year and was succeeded as leader of the Liberals by his brother, Vintula. Death also removed King Ferdinand who had forced his eldest son, Carol, to renounce the throne as he was scandalized by his private life. Since King Michael, Ferdinand's grandson, was only six years old, the royal prerogatives were exercised by a Council of Regency which, in 1928, broke recent tradition by permitting free elections. As in 1919, victory went to a combination of the Transylvanian Party and the agrarians, organized jointly as the National Peasant Party and led by that incorruptible and ascetic veteran of the pre-war Budapest parliament, Iuliu Maniu.

For two years Roumania enjoyed, for the only time in her history, genuine parliamentary government. Maniu and Mihalache, who took the portfolio of agriculture, did much for the peasantry: the burden of taxation was eased, and administration was decentralized, with elected communes permitted to exercise responsibility over local affairs. The restrictions on foreign capital were lifted and an international loan enabled Roumania at last to balance her budget. Everywhere there was a sense of nation-wide cooperation, not merely of formal constitutional unity. Conditions improved, even in the mire of Bessarabia. But in the summer of 1930, Maniu made a grave tactical error: believing that a long regency would be dangerous for the Roumanian people, he negotiated with the thirty-six year old Prince Carol in exile. On 6 June Carol stole the headlines of Europe's newspapers by flying back dramatically to Bucharest and seizing his throne. All the arrangements for Carol's return had been made by Maniu; the only condition on which he insisted was that Carol should abandon his mistress, Magda Lupescu. Once on the throne, however, Carol did not feel bound by a verbal agreement made by private emissaries in Paris. On 4 August Lupescu slipped back to Roumania: on 6 October Maniu resigned in protest.

It was not the end of the National Peasant Ministry; but, in a sense, it was the end of National Peasant government. The party struggled on until the spring of 1931 under colourless leadership, but political life became dominated more and more by Carol II and his personal entourage. Unfortunately, the King lacked the qualities of statesmanship, and his private affairs could hardly add to his stature. For the Lupescu entanglement was not some Racine drama of insatiable passion; it was a Feydeau farce in which the red-haired daughter of a provincial chemist became the source of patronage and advancement. The image which Carol created had more of the seedy playboy than the Grand Monarch in its composition. It is hard to escape the feeling that Bucharest society got the ruler it deserved; but Bucharest society was not Roumania.

The two defeated states, Hungary and Bulgaria, were of course fundamentally different from each other in social structure and history; but the very fact that they had been forced to accept a peace settlement imposed by the victorious powers gave a rare similarity to their grievances in the inter-war period. The treaties reduced them to approximately the same size although Hungary, the smaller of the two, had a population more than half as large again as that of Bulgaria. Both were overwhelmingly one-nation states, both were revisionist, and both tended to regard the acute revolutionary unrest of the immediate post-war years as a trauma on the body politic. Yet the way in which each country reacted to its wounds emphasized once more the essential distinction between the habits of Central Europe and the Balkans: Hungary, in crisis, looked for firm government from its traditional ruling class; Bulgaria, unsure of itself and uncertain of its course, perpetuated feuding and murder.

Hungary's policy from 1920 to 1931 was shaped by two dominating personalities, Regent Horthy and the conservative aristocrat whom he eventually appointed prime minister in April 1921, Count István Bethlen. At first, Horthy had moved cautiously. Elections held in the summer of 1920 resulted in the Smallholders' Party emerging as the largest single group in parliament but, since it was unthinkable for a party as radical as Sir Robert Peel's Tories to rule in Trianon Hungary, the Smallholders were induced to take minor offices in a coalition presided over by one of the most noble-minded magnates, Count Pál Teleki. A 'first instalment' of Land Reform, involving about one twelfth of the agricultural area of Hungary, was duly promulgated: the 'second instalment,' though promised, was never carried out. Once this minimal measure of Land Reform had discharged their debt to the electorate, the bulk of Small-holder deputies merged with the aristocratic 'Christian Union' to form the 'Party of Unity,' in which the guiding spirit was Bethlen.

Bethlen, even more than Horthy, was a political anachronism in the democratic twenties. He had too much of a sense of duty to be a tyrant and too high a regard for the Hungarian parliamentary tradition to be a dictator; but he had an almost eighteenth-century concept of aristocratic responsibility which made him confine Hungarian politics within an authoritarian strait-jacket for the ten years in which he headed the government. Significantly, one of his first political acts was to reduce the proportion of the population entitled to vote from the already low figure of forty per cent in 1920 to a mere twenty-seven per cent. At the same time, he restricted balloting in secret to municipalities which were sufficiently long established to possess charters: in the countryside and in the newer urban communities 'open' elections were the practice. It is, perhaps, not surprising that the Party of Unity won the election of 1922 and that its successors (which bore an interesting variety of names but were generally known as the 'Government Party') won every contest in Hungary until the arrival of the Red Army in 1944; although it should be added that before the Whitsun election of 1939 the principle of secret ballot was extended to the whole country.

During all these years Hungary was a kingdom which lacked a king, ruled by an Admiral who lacked a fleet (apart from the Danube flotilla). The mystic territorial symbolism associated with the 'Holy Crown' made it essential that Hungary should remain a monarchy; and the solemn procession which bore the crown through the streets of the capital each year on St Stephen's Day was an impressive exercise in revisionist pageantry. On two occasions in 1921 Hungary's legitimate sovereign, Charles, sought 'to come into his own again'; but Admiral Horthy was not a General Monk. The regent showed a marked disinclination to surrender his powers and, during the second attempt, even checked the King's advance on Budapest by force of arms. A Habsburg restoration would certainly have caused consternation in the Successor States and might well have led to war, but the anger of Hungary's neighbours was, perhaps, not displeasing to her regent who found it difficult to envisage what a Habsburg might do that a Horthy could not do better. Under pressure from abroad, the Hungarian Parliament passed a Dethronement Act in November 1921 solemnly abrogating all of King Charles's rights. With a vacant throne, the 'Free Electors' among Hungary's natural royalists could play the delightfully irrelevant game of hunting for a candidate; and by the end of the decade there were said to be some who were praying for Lord Rothermere. But Regent Horthy was still in the great palace on Buda Hill when the Red Army broke through the Carpathians.

Horthy, Bethlen and indeed every Hungarian who believed he possessed social standing had one supreme political objective – the complete revision of the Trianon settlement and the restoration of Historic Hungary. This obsession permeated public instruction and the mass media of the times; the Magyars were no more allowed to forget their former territories than the citizens of the Third French Republic to accept the loss of Alsace-Lorraine after 1871. Inevitably, archaic customs were cherished and pressing social problems left unresolved. The Bethlen government did, indeed, improve working conditions in the factories; but it did nothing for the three million peasants, virtually landless and living in wretched poverty. Bethlen encouraged ethnic Hungarians to go into business for the first time in large numbers; but they found that the best positions in industrial management and in banking were already in the hands of Hungarian Jewish families; and the growth of this state-sponsored capitalism merely stimulated the latent anti-semitism of the new Magyar middle-class.

There is no doubt that Bethlen's concern for financial reconstruction, and in particular the loan he negotiated through the League at the end of 1923, checked inflation and secured vital international credit for the kingdom. But, like Poland, Hungary became ultimately dependent on the maintenance of American prosperity; and her main exports were still agricultural, especially wheat. Hence when in 1929 the Wall Street Crash coincided with a fall in the world price for cereals, the slim basis of the Bethlen system became rapidly apparent. Bethlen himself resigned in August 1931; within fifteen months the anti-semitic reactionary Gömbös was in power. The accumulated prejudices of 'Right Radicalism' had triumphed in Hungary even before Hitler became Chancellor of Germany.

Bulgaria had no period of Bethlen-type reconstruction, for its economic structure was more primitive and its political problems grimly unsophisticated. The nation's leaders were as anxious for treaty-revision as Hungary's, but they lacked the will to pursue it through sympathizers in the West and they were themselves unable to control the violence of the Macedonian irredentists.

For eight years after the 1923 coup and the death of Stamboliisky Bulgaria was theoretically governed by two coalition ministries, headed by Tsankov until January 1926 and then by Liapchev, who was eventually defeated in the elections of June 1931 by a combination of liberals and moderate agrarians. For most of that period, however, real power rested with the war minister, Volkov, who at the time of the coup had been political boss of the Officers' League. Very little was done during these years to improve the standard of living in the country although Liapchev secured a loan from the League in 1927 to relieve the quarter of a million refugees from Macedonia and Thrace whom the Bulgarian economy could not absorb. Political life revolved around three main issues: the threat from the communists; the perpetual menace from the super-terrorists of IMRO; and control of the Officers' League.

Indiscriminate persecution of 'Bolsheviks' and their sympathizers continued throughout 1924 and 1925. The extremists among the communists, apparently acting against the official party line, resorted to assassination. On 14 April 1925 they murdered a member of the government and, during his funeral service two days later, a bomb exploded in the roof of the Sveta Nedyela Cathedral in Sofia which wrecked the building and left more than a hundred dead in the rubble. Among those killed were the Chief of Police, the Mayor of Sofia and no less than fourteen generals. In the following four months death sentences equalling the number butchered in the cathedral were imposed on alleged communists, and many more were killed without the apparatus of a formal trial. The Inter-Allied Control Commission, responsible for ensuring that the Bulgarian army did not exceed the 20,000 regulars permitted by the Treaty of Neuilly, authorized the recruitment of ten thousand volunteers to 'restore order'; but there were protests at government brutality by intellectuals in Western Europe and the United States. No attempt was made, however, to silence the parliamentary opposition and 'socialists' continued to win successes in local elections until 1933. The official Communist Party functioned clandestinely and was ably directed from Moscow by Georgi Dimitrov, who had escaped to Russia in 1923 but one of whose brothers perished in prison during this 'White Terror'.

The flood of refugees who had swept into the country at the end of the war destitute and disillusioned were natural recruits for IMRO, which renewed its activities in the second year of the Stamboliisky government.

But in 1924 the movement split into two groups: the faction of Alexandrov and Protoguerov favoured an autonomous or even independent Macedonia within a Balkan federation; and the 'Centralist' faction of Mihailov sought the union of all the Macedonian lands under the rule of the Sofia government. The two wings of IMRO fought each other with as much bitterness as they fought the Yugoslavs and Greeks over the frontier. Alexandrov was murdered by the centralists in 1924 and Protoguerov suffered a similar fate four years later. IMRO terrorism extended well beyond the borders of Bulgaria: one victim was killed in Milan, and another was shot during a performance of *Peer Gynt* in the Vienna Burgtheater. But the main activities of IMRO were directed to embarrassing the Greek and Yugoslav governments along the Vardar and Struma valleys; and in 1925 the Greek army actually invaded southern Bulgaria in the hope of halting these attacks.

There were plenty of officers in Sofia who sensed that IMRO provocation would bring down on Bulgaria the wrath of the other Balkan states; they feared that a new Balkan war would be a disaster and rule out any possibility of treaty revision by consent; and they also thought that the IMRO terror within the country was no more tolerable than the anarchy which had followed the World War. It was, however, clear that Mihailov enjoyed the protection of the minister of war and a new Officers' League formed behind Colonel Damian Velchev to oust its former president, General Volkov, from the ministry. In 1928 the Bulgarian ruling military clique was therefore split just as the Serbian army 'establishment' had been in 1913–17: all really depended on whether King Boris was prepared to assert himself as Prince-Regent Alexander had done on that occasion.

It was difficult then – and it is no easier now – to discover the attitude of Boris; for, to safeguard his person and throne, he had cultivated a charming, if abstracted, boredom over any subject more controversial than the mechanics of clocks and locomotives. IMRO terrorism was nevertheless alien to his character, for assassins were not always scrupulously selective; and in his customarily devious way he began to take action against the Mihailovists and their protectors. While not prepared to dismiss Volkov, he was willing early in 1929 to send him as minister to Rome; and, while unable to have Mihailov arrested, he had no objection to a trial *in absentia*, although it might well have been foreseen that Mihailov would be acquitted for lack of evidence. Boris had no intention of being a mere political cipher, but he was not going to commit himself irrevocably to any one side in a contest until he had a strong conviction that it would win. In time, he was to use this shrewd approach as a guide in foreign policy as well as domestic affairs.

Gradually Bulgaria seemed to be moving towards democracy – and this at the very time when her neighbours were resigned to authoritarianism. The elections of June 1931, which brought back to office the liberally-minded Malinov, showed a rejection of the old coalitions of the Right. People were becoming tired of the Macedonian Question; they were seeking a reformist government. Yet, unfortunately for the Bulgars, the change in Sofia was more apparent than real. IMRO activity along the frontier kept tension with Greece high until 1934; and though Malinov had the best intentions, he could not cleanse the bureaucratic stable of Volkov's nominees. Parliamentary government was as much a façade in Bulgaria as in the rest of Eastern Europe; and, with the West already under the shadow of the World Depression, it was anyone's guess how long this vestigial democracy would survive.

10

Right Incline

The Depression of the early 1930s, which destroyed people's savings in Britain and the United States, ravaged Eastern and Central Europe like some medieval epidemic. Its effects were far more than economic, for it brought not only personal tragedies but a lowering of standards of communal behaviour in an area where they had never reached the highest level. Cancerous cells, already diagnosed in the political body, throve on its depredations. In the end it claimed the very concept of a liberal society as its victim and the soul of Europe lay exposed to new ideologies of violence and inhumanity.

The pattern of disaster is grimly clear. Throughout the last quarter of 1929 all six countries in the region were increasingly affected by an agricultural recession which was intensified early in 1930 by the impact of the American financial crisis on investment and banking. The fall in commodity values had begun modestly enough in 1928, when Russian competition caused a drop in the price of timber which hit the exports of Czechoslovakia, Poland and Yugoslavia, although not disastrously. But in the following year the over-production of wheat in Canada and the American Mid-West came as a far more serious blow for it forced down the world price of the basic crop of all the agrarian lands. Peasants and agricultural labourers, faced with small returns for their work, virtually abandoned money and relied on a primitive system of barter or satisfaction in kind for services rendered by the non-farming classes in rural districts. Smallholders and the larger landowners sought two remedies for their immediate poverty: they borrowed from the banks, so long as that was possible; but, more and more, they isolated themselves within a narrowly local economy which was essentially an extension of the methods already practised by the peasantry. As prices fell even lower and lower in 1930, 1931 and 1932, so everyone who depended for his livelihood on the land ceased to be a consumer of products from the towns and factories. This drastic revolution within the countryside led in turn to the collapse of industry and to mass unemployment in the urban areas. And when, as an indirect consequence of the Depression, the Viennese Creditanstalt failed to meet its obligations in May 1931, bankruptcy stalked through all the Danubian States, for the Austrian financial house was sufficiently large and respected to have had links with smaller enterprises in many cities of the old empire. Inevitably, men whose savings melted away began to look for scapegoats and to listen to the diatribes from the Right Radical politicians.

At first the governments of the six countries made some attempt to meet the great economic crisis by abandoning the foolishly exclusive nationalism which had hampered cooperation in the preceding ten years. Two agrarian conferences were held in July 1930 in Bucharest and Sinaia at which representatives from Hungary sat beside experts from Roumania and Yugoslavia to discuss their common problems; and other meetings followed during each of the next three months in which the Poles, the Bulgars and the Lithuanians participated as well as the Little Entente countries. Genuine proposals were put forward for lowering tariffs and for fixing a general level on the price of cereals. Plans for an even broader European Union were also outlined by the French Foreign Minister, Briand, and discussed in detail by a League Committee.

Unfortunately every scheme presented for consideration eventually encountered the opposition of one or other of the states, jealous for its independence, or ran into hostility from the Great Powers who saw their own trading agreements endangered by new combinations. The old division between an Italian-dominated group and a French-dominated group was widened by these conflicts. The project for an Austro-German Customs Union in March 1931, which could have been the first step in dismantling tariff walls, aroused furious opposition from France and the Little Entente; and, indeed, by prompting the French to withdraw their funds from the Creditanstalt, it precipitated the worst phase of the whole crisis. Conversely, the French suggestion of an exclusively Danubian Customs Union – the so-called 'Tardieu Plan' of March 1932 – was opposed by Italy and her clients who, significantly, were joined by the Germans because of their insistence on close economic links with Austria. A final conference of fifteen countries at Stresa in September 1932 failed to overcome the political suspicions of the rival factions; and Europe was already split into two hostile camps before the Nazi revolution in Germany ruled out all prospects of cooperation within the existing framework of nation-states.

As conflict continued at the conference tables so the more aggressively irredentist groups in each country began to assert themselves, looking for support across the frontiers. In Czechoslovakia, for example, the Sudeten Germans knew that they could count on Hitler for encouragement even before 1933: the banning by the Czech government of Nazi uniforms in 1931 was an ominous sign of future strife; and so, too, was a treason trial at Brno of seven members of the Nazi Youth Movement which dragged on from the summer of 1932 through inconclusive evidence to a weak verdict in the autumn of 1933. A more immediate threat to peace arose from the encouragement given by Mussolini and some Hungarians to the Croatian *Ustaše*. A training centre for terrorists was established at Janka Puszta in south-western Hungary with the approval of the authorities in Budapest; and in June 1932 the *Ustaše* planned to take advantage of a mutiny in the Yugoslav army stationed in Dalmatia to foster a general revolt in Croatia and proclaim an Independent Croatian State (which Mussolini would at once recognize). This ill-conceived venture was countered by vigorous action from King Alexander, including a stern warning to the Italians. But Croatian separatist activity remained a serious menace: an understanding existed between the *Ustaše* and IMRO for combined terrorist activity to free Croatia and Macedonia from 'Serbian domination'; and a secret military convention was drawn up by the Italians and Hungarians, with Croatian representatives as 'consulting parties,' which provided for joint military action if a Croatian revolt led the Yugoslavs to take punitive measures against their neighbours. There were so many hypothetical circumstances attached to the convention that it was probably of little importance in itself: what mattered was that Maček's Peasant Party, and not merely the *Ustaše*, had been involved in the negotiations which led to its conclusion.

During the years of the Depression the threat of political and social unrest led to a strengthening of the government's hands in the two countries which were already under authoritarian regimes, Poland and Yugoslavia; and the effective rulers of both Roumania and Hungary also inclined towards the right, although with some hesitancy. In Poland Pilsudski had some seventy members of the Sejm arrested in the summer of 1930, including such well-known figures as Witos and Korfanty (the leader of the Silesian autonomists). Many of the politicians were imprisoned under conditions of particular brutality in the old citadel of Brest-Litovsk; and while they were suffering this humiliating incarceration, Pilsudski held an election which ensured his hold on the puppet parliament.

In Yugoslavia, the king promulgated a new constitution in September 1931 which provided for the establishment of a bi-cameral parliament but restricted the responsibility of ministers solely to the crown and, by insisting on oral voting in public, hampered the creation of a free opposition. Since all political associations remained forbidden, the subsequent elections had little interest: voters were presented with a list of approved candidates. There was, of course, much boycotting of the elections in Croatia and even in some predominantly Serbian districts. Three days before the elections the students of Belgrade University staged a series of anti-monarchist demonstrations and the authorities reported increased communist activity in a number of areas, notably Slovenia. In the following spring there was, indeed, a curious communist conspiracy at Maribor where a dozen junior officers and sergeants planned to seize control of the town; but, since the affair was reported to have ended with two lieutenants in flight to the frontier with regimental mess funds, it is possible that the motives of some of the participants were not exclusively political. There was, nevertheless, serious trouble in Slovenia and peasant unrest in Dalmatia; and it was against this background that the leading 'opposition' spokesmen issued a vigorous manifesto of protest from Zagreb urging a return to popular sovereignty on a federal basis. The King responded – much as Pilsudski would have done – by casting into prison for a few months Maček, Korošec and other non-Serbian political leaders. The principal Marxists were, of course, already serving far longer sentences in widely separated parts of the kingdom: Josip Broz – not yet code-named 'Tito' – was in a former Habsburg jail at Lepoglava, between Maribor and Zagreb; others, including Aleksander Ranković, were in prison in Old Serbia and the Vojvodina. The organizational secretary of the communists, Djaković, had been shot by Yugoslav police on the Austrian border in April 1929; and he was by no means the only victim of an increasingly brutal gendarmerie.

Carol of Roumania was less autocratic by nature than King Alexander and, as yet, he was not prepared to establish the full apparatus of a royal dictatorship. He was, however, a master of intrigue and in the first years of the thirties he succeeded in splitting all the old parties and acquired an ascendancy through the sheer incompetence and confusion of the parliamentary leaders. From April 1931 to June 1932 Roumania was governed by the King's former tutor, Nicholas Iorga, a historian of considerable repute and even greater self-esteem. The King himself presided over cabinet meetings each week: the economic situation deteriorated, not least because Carol refused to cut the salaries of government officials; and a press campaign developed against the administration, and, since it dared not attack the king directly, against the unfortunate Magda Lupescu. A brief interlude of short ministries followed Iorga's resignation. There were serious strikes but the country secured a loan from Swiss bankers; and the civil servants (of whom there were far too many) received their pay regularly enough. By the end of 1933 the King had managed to create a stable administration consisting for the most part of a rump of the old Liberal Party, under Tatarescu. But by now the strongest political group in the country was the Iron Guard, whose violence ruled almost unchecked; and there were also smaller anti-semitic organizations which sought to emulate them. Carol himself, never a good judge of men, had developed a considerable admiration for Mussolini;

and his speeches began to echo, in a slightly ridiculous way, the Duce's flamboyant bombast. For the moment, however, Roumania remained loyal to the Little Entente, to the French alliance, and to the League of Nations, which rendered the country financial support. Titulescu, who was foreign minister from 1932 to 1936, was as strong a believer in the League as Dr Beneš.

The Depression was particularly severe in Hungary, partly because of the importance of wheat-prices to the landowners of the Great Plain and partly because of financial connexions linking the banks with the Creditanstalt. In 1931 and 1932 the Hungarians had to seek monetary protection from the League of Nations, which insisted on drastic economies and ruthless taxation. Inevitably, the smallholders turned against the government, and at the end of September 1932 the regent decided to break with the old conservative aristocracy and to entrust power to the noisiest spokesman of the middle classes, Gyula Gömbös. In 1919 Gömbös had organized the 'National Army' which brought Horthy to power and in October 1921 it had been his troops which defeated Charles Habsburg's attempts to recover his Hungarian throne, but during the twenties the political views of Gömbös had been at once too 'radical' and too far 'right' for the regent's tastes. Horthy insisted on vetoing his new prime minister's first list of cabinet appointments and continued to keep a restraining hand on his domestic policy during the three years he was in office. There was accordingly no drastic solution of the 'Jewish Question,' as Gömbös had threatened in true Nazi fashion; and with Hungary in considerable debt to foreign bankers, it would have been difficult for any demagogue to live up to the anti-semitic venom of his speeches. But in 1928 Gömbös' impressionistic mind had conjured up a vision of what he was the first to term 'a Berlin-Rome Axis': the nationalism of Germany and of Italy, supported by a 'Hungarian renaissance' would re-shape the map of Europe. And, within a month of his appointment as head of the Hungarian government, he hastened to Rome to flatter and be flattered by Mussolini. Hungary's tent was pitched securely enough in the Italian camp.

The most startling effects of the general economic crisis were in Germany, outside the area with which this present book is directly concerned. In three years German industrial production was halved, German unemployment trebled and the membership of the Nazi Party doubled. There were, of course, many reasons why Hitler became chancellor on 30 January 1933 – not least among them the political ineptitude of his opponents – but the legend that the German people had thrust the Nazis into office in a mood of despair and frustration seemed so plausible to contemporaries faced with a similar collapse of the 'bourgeois order' that other nationalities beside the Germans were encouraged to look to their parties of the Right for salvation. The blatant Nazi rejection of traditional liberal values appealed to peoples already shaken by chronic uncertainty over the virtues of personal freedom and equality of rights. Hitler's revolution did not introduce the intolerance of authoritarian government: it made it the norm of political life.

At first, however, it seemed unlikely that Hitler would stay in office long enough to translate his extremism into action. His appointment as chancellor immediately aroused apprehension in the two states of East-Central Europe which had already experienced subversive Nazi agitation, Czechoslovakia and Poland. Beneš, in particular, had for several months feared a Nazi-Fascist combination, not unlike the 'Axis' of Gömbös's imagination; and it was no coincidence that, less than three weeks after Hitler's success, the Little Entente countries should have signed a pact which renewed their common treaty obligations and transformed their loose cooperation into what was virtually a diplomatic federation, organized into a Permanent Council, an Economic Council and a Secretariat.

The Polish reaction was even more hostile than that of the Czechs. Pilsudski was so infuriated by demonstrations organized by Nazi fanatics in Danzig that on two occasions in March and April 1933 he urged his French allies to support him in military action against the new German government: with French backing, the Poles would occupy Danzig, East Prussia and the German Silesian regions and would retain these territories until Hitler had resigned and the chancellor appointed to succeed him had given guarantees to maintain the Versailles settlement. (Pilsudski was even inclined to maintain a garrison in Danzig indefinitely). The French, however, with problems of their own at home, were unwilling to accept the risks involved in such a policy. They restrained Pilsudski, and the opportunity for a preventive war against the Nazi administration passed, never to return. Early in May Hitler himself assured the Polish ambassador that he would respect the existing Germano-Polish frontier, and the enthusiasm of the German Danzigers for the Fatherland was duly muted, presumably on orders from Berlin.

Throughout 1933 all the running in the Danubian States and the Balkans continued to be made by Italy and France, with Mussolini setting a pace which the four short-lived governments of that year in Paris found impossible to attain. It is true that the Duce's favourite idea of destroying the Little Entente by achieving treaty-revision through a Four Power Agreement of Britain, Germany, France and Italy was too subtle to succeed; but his contacts with Bulgaria remained close, and he was able to interest the Roumanians and even the Yugoslavs in amicable discussions. His greatest triumph came early in 1934, thanks largely to the indefatigable Gömbös; for in February the so-called 'Rome Protocols' created a Danubian bloc of Italy, Hungary and Austria which not only countered the Little Entente, but bolstered up the semi-fascist regime of Dollfuss in Vienna at a time when it was under pressure from Hitler's Germany. In retrospect, it seems as if the spring of 1934 marked the zenith of Italian influence in central and south-eastern Europe; for by the following winter Mussolini had weakened his position by over-indulgent patronage of the *Usta^ve* and IMRO; and by 1935 Germany was in the ascendant.

Meanwhile, the French appeared to be losing their foothold on the Vistula, for the Nazis achieved a spectacular success in January 1934 by concluding a ten-year non-aggression pact with Poland. The agreement followed several months of negotiations in which Rauschning, the newly-elected president of the Danzig Senate, had served as a valuable inter-mediary. The practical effects of the pact were, however, limited: Hitler formally abandoned support of the German minority in Pomorze and ordered the Nazi leaders to lie low; and Pilsudski refrained from sabre-rattling along the frontiers with East Prussia. Neither side was convinced of the other's honesty of purpose; and each believed it had scored a diplomatic victory. The Germans were anxious to make a gap in the French wall of encirclement and hoped to widen the breach by encouraging Polish hostility towards Czechoslovakia; and in this they succeeded. The Poles, piqued by the cool reception given to Pilsudski's earlier proposals for military action against Germany, believed that the pact would remind the French of the need to conciliate Warsaw no less than Prague; and perhaps it did. There is no doubt that Colonel Beck, Poland's foreign minister from November 1932 until the disasters of 1939, hated the Czechs and resented, largely on personal grounds, the patronage of France: and the pact seemed to him to possess the virtues of a declaration of independence, for he was a remarkably vain and foolish man. Pilsudski knew better. He insisted that Beck should complement the German Pact by a similar understanding with Soviet Russia in May 1934. But the marshal was by now a spent force, at the start of his last year of life; and, from the following spring onwards, Beck had full responsibility for Poland's external affairs, a task calling for more breadth of vision than he had ever possessed.

The French were alarmed at Hitler's success, although the Poles had taken the precaution of letting them know that a non-aggression pact was being negotiated. Louis Barthou, who became foreign minister of France in January 1934, planned a grand alliance against Germany which would embrace, not only the Little Entente states, but Italy and Soviet Russia as well; and conversations which were intended to bring about a reconciliation between the Rome Protocol Powers and the Little

Entente began in the following March. Four months later it seemed as if they had achieved a success; for when Austrian Nazis murdered Chancellor Dollfuss as a first step towards union with Germany, both Italy and Yugoslavia responded by concentrating powerful divisions along the Austrian frontier. The abortive Vienna *putsch* had the incidental effect of worsening the personal relations of the Führer and the Duce, for Mussolini was indignant that Dollfuss should have been assassinated by Nazi thugs at a time when Frau Dollfuss and her family were his private guests in Italy. If Hitler's immediate objective was a political Anschluss, then he had been thwarted by the firm action of two states hitherto mutually hostile; and Barthou believed that his policy of containment was vindicated.

Yet, in reality, the Germans were extending their influence along the Danube and into south-eastern Europe by far more effective methods than Barthou's traditional network of alliances. For Germany was ready to trade with Hungary and Yugoslavia and Roumania; and to countries still wallowing in the wake of the Depression, a Great Power which was prepared to modify its economic policy to their benefit was a more attractive partner than a Great Power which talked only of security and the need to preserve the European Order. A secret commercial treaty between Germany and Hungary was signed in February 1934, and the Germans thereafter began to receive almost a quarter of Hungary's total exports, mostly livestock, bauxite and raw materials for industry; and Hungary, in turn, imported from Germany manufactured products and coal and coke, or their derivatives. The economies of the two countries became so interlocked that had there been an interruption in the supply of machinery or spare parts from Germany, the Hungarian factories would once more have faced disaster. A similar, although less extensive, treaty was signed between Germany and Yugoslavia in May 1934; and within two years German investment in Yugoslav industry increased remarkably while trade between the two countries almost doubled. A further barter agreement was signed in May 1936 and when the Second World War began Germany was receiving more than half of Yugoslavia's exports and was supplying almost as large a proportion of her imported requirements.

Naturally the Germans did not help the Danubian States to solve their economic problems out of sheer kindness of heart. A German Foreign Office memorandum of June 1934 (which is printed in the relevant volume of German Diplomatic Documents) records that both the Hungarian and the Yugoslav agreements 'had political significance above their actual commercial content' and were 'designed to create in Hungary and Yugoslavia two points of support for German policy in the Danube region, and above all to counteract French and Italian policy directed

Belgrade, 1806: The Serbs under Karadjordje attack the Turkish citadel

Poland, 1863: Polish patriot troops passing the Abbey of Czenstochow

The Danube at Pest, 1846

Lajos Kossuth (1802-94)

Prague in the 1840s

(*Above and opposite*) Invaders of the
Balkans: Russian troops crossing the
Danube on pontoons at Braila, 1877

(*Opposite*) Marshal von Mackensen
and his staff watch German troops
crossing the Danube at Sistovo, 1916

(*Above right*) Tómaš Masaryk (1850-
1937)

(*Right*) Josef Pilsudski (1867-1935)

Budapest, December 1916: The Coronation Oath of King Charles

Balkan Royalty, June 1922: King Ferdinand of Roumania (*centre*); King Alexander of Yugoslavia (*on his left*); the future King Carol II of Roumania (*on his right*)

Yugoslav Partisans, early in 1944: Marshal Tito on the right

Bucharest, 1941: Marshal Antonescu (*centre*) with King Michael (*on his left*)

The Statue Toppled;
Budapest, October
1956

Prague, August 1968

against German policy there'. It is significant that when, only three weeks after the Yugoslavs had struck their bargain, the Roumanians sought a commercial agreement, they were told by the German Foreign Minister that Germany 'could make sacrifices only in favour of those states which did not support our opponents politically, as was the case with Roumania'. In the event, the Roumanians had to wait until May 1935 for their treaty, although in the end they did well out of the settlement, securing from Germany a price for wheat which was well above the general world market value and restricting the quantity of oil sold to Germany so as not to hamper Roumania's existing commitments in the West. Bulgaria, too, concluded commercial agreements with Germany in 1935: the Germans bought Bulgarian tobacco and paid well for it, supplying Bulgaria in return with armaments (for which the country appeared to have an inordinately large appetite).

The double effect of the Depression and of the re-entry of Germany into the eastern arena led to changes of attitude, if not of heart, among the Balkan States. The French – and, in so far as they did anything at all, the British – were anxious to seal up the old Balkan cockpit. Titulescu of Roumania spent much of the autumn of 1933 in journeys through south-eastern Europe, drafting non-aggression treaties and suggesting an even bigger treaty which would guarantee the Balkan frontiers. Alexander of Yugoslavia preferred a direct approach to Bulgaria in the first instance and had two meetings with Boris (in Belgrade and Varna) before proceeding to Istanbul and Athens to exert his personal magnetism on the Turks and the Greeks. Boris, too, was more forthcoming: he paid an official visit to Belgrade in December 1933 and to Bucharest in January 1934. But Bulgarian revisionism ran too deeply for Boris to associate himself with an international order based on the existing post-war settlement; and the other Balkan leaders went ahead without him. Early in February 1934 the two 'eastern' Little Entente Powers, Yugoslavia and Roumania, joined Greece and Turkey in acceptance of a Balkan Pact which guaranteed the frontiers of the four countries within the Balkan zone and pledged the signatories to consult together before taking action against another Balkan state (presumably Albania or Bulgaria). Before the end of the year these four states broadened the scope of the pact, creating a 'Balkan Entente' which had a Permanent Council and which succeeded in holding a series of conferences until the early months of 1940. Although it never had the military associations of its Danubian prototype, it was a step towards independence in international affairs. Quite clearly, it was a rebuff to Italy but it also avoided subservience to the French.

The Balkan Pact did not immediately send the Bulgars in search of a counter-alliance. There was, in fact, a remarkable development in Bulgaria's domestic affairs that spring; for on 19 May King Boris found that he was faced, as he had been eleven years previously, by a military coup. Once again the Officers' League had struck, this time under Damian Velchev. Boris was induced to appoint as prime minister General Kimon Georghiev, the leader of a group which called itself Zveno (The Chain) and which had as its main programme the political cleaning up of the Bulgarian State. The methods by which Zveno were to achieve this laudable purpose bore a startling resemblance to those already undertaken by Dollfuss and Mussolini; but Velchev's apologists have always insisted that his ideas, although authoritarian, were non-fascist. Certainly in foreign affairs Bulgaria turned against the Italian connexion and continued to seek a reconciliation with Yugoslavia. All political parties were dissolved, but so too was IMRO; Mihailov was expelled from the country and in June Georghiev announced that the military authorities in south-western Bulgaria had confiscated from IMRO terrorists no fewer than 10,938 rifles, 7,767 hand grenades, forty-seven machine guns and an ample supply of ammunition. If cleaning up Bulgaria implied the destruction of IMRO and nothing else, then the Zveno did its work well; but other problems proved less tractable and the Zveno administration was so top-heavy in brass-hat officers that it had no room for a mere economist.

There were many aspects of the Zveno philosophy (if such it may be called) which appealed to Alexander of Yugoslavia, and at the end of September 1934 he paid a return visit to Sofia to promote Bulgaro-Serbian friendship. He was, at the time, moving away from dependence on France and was anxious to strengthen the links between Yugoslavia and Germany: Hitler had himself spoken, somewhat patronizingly, of the fighting qualities of the Serbs, and there had recently been some friendly talks between the King and General Hermann Goering. The French, for their part, could not afford a breach with Alexander on top of their rebuff from Pilsudski and Beck. Barthou was, indeed, still hoping that he could reconcile the Italians and Yugoslavs and bring them both into his united camp against the new Germany. In June Barthou visited Belgrade and found that the King was not entirely hostile to his proposals: Alexander was willing to offer Mussolini economic concessions, especially supplies of timber, in return for political guarantees. But there were, of course, limits to his policy and, in order to make certain that the French understood his views, Alexander accepted an invitation to undertake a State Visit to Paris in October 1934, his fifth royal progress abroad in thirteen months. This time, however, he failed to reach his objective; for he had barely left the quay at Marseilles when a Macedonian assassin shot him dead, killing Barthou at the same time.

The Marseilles murders thrust Central Europe into its most dangerous crisis since Sarajevo. The assassin was an experienced IMRO gunman who had been seconded to Pavelić's *Ustaše* by Mihailov. The plot was apparently hatched in Italy but investigations showed that the responsibility for harbouring and encouraging the Croatian terrorists lay with Hungary. The new French Foreign Minister, Laval, was even more anxious for a general agreement with Mussolini than Barthou had been; and nothing was done to censure Italy for her championship of the *Ustaše* cause or for the sanctuary she had given to known murderers. The debate at the League of Nations in December duly denounced Hungary, with Anthony Eden as the voice of British conscience delivering a particularly impressive list of Hungarian sins of neglect. No decisive action was taken, although the Italian authorities imprisoned, for a short time, the leading *Ustaše* members on their soil. Pavelić was sentenced to death *in absentia* by a French court but was never handed over by the Italians, who allowed him eventually to settle in a small house on the outskirts of Florence. The question of his extradition does not appear to have been taken up by Laval in a visit he made to Rome less than a month after the League debate; but Mussolini agreed to make gestures of appeasement towards the Little Entente in return for French cooperation to forestall a Germano-Austrian Anschluss.

In Yugoslavia itself the death of Alexander led to the accession of his eleven-year-old son, Peter II. The dead King's will provided for a regency which was intended to be legally effective until Peter reached his eighteenth birthday (September 1941). The chief regent was Prince Paul, Alexander's cousin, a man of considerable culture with a deep sense of responsibility and no taste for Balkan politics. In many ways Paul was more truly a Yugoslav than Alexander, for he distrusted narrowly Serbian nationalism and delighted in escaping from Belgrade to the Alpine peace of Slovenia. Since he regarded himself as a temporary custodian of the crown, he was not prepared to make radical changes in the constitutional structure of the kingdom, but he deplored the militaristic centralism of the royal dictatorship and believed that his own disinterestedness might enable him to win over the Croats. After experimenting with three different prime ministers in nine months, the regent appointed in June 1935 a former Serbian radical, Milan Stojadinović, who had been recommended to Prince Paul by the British minister in Belgrade and who had the twin virtues of knowing something about economics and of being prepared to sit down at the same table as a Croat. His banking connexions with the City of London seemed to Whitehall a sure guarantee of Stojadinović's respectability. From the British point of view, however, it soon became unfortunate that – like the Regent – he should have found General Goering so sympathetic, so generous and so understanding.

By the beginning of 1935 it was clear that the German Reich had recovered much of its traditional influence over the Eastern European lands even though its claim to mastery was now challenged by two newcomers, France and Italy, rather than by the massive rival of old, Russia. As yet the Soviet State remained a wounded Titan, impressively parading tanks and guns each May Day but sheltering behind the paper guarantees of the Litvinov Protocol. Yet Litvinov himself had no illusions about Hitler's intentions, and slowly Russia began to play a positive role once more in European diplomacy. The Germans had walked out of the League of Nations in October 1933; the Russians joined the League just eleven months later and proceeded to work as earnestly for collective security as any of their fellow member-states. But Litvinov was prepared to go even further to contain Germany: he revived the traditional policy more than a palisade, the British and French continued to be impressed with Beneš and Titulescu.

A formal pact of mutual assistance was concluded by France and the Soviet Union in May 1935 which not only confirmed the obligations of both signatories under the League Covenant but also provided for immediate aid should either of them be the victim of an unprovoked attack. Within a fortnight a similar treaty was concluded with the Russians by Czechoslovakia, although on this occasion it was explicitly stated that military help would be given only provided that France, too, offered armed support to whichever country was attacked. No pact was signed between Russia and Roumania but a secret understanding was reached between Litvinov and Titulescu by which the Roumanians agreed to permit the Red Army to pass across the Bukovina and into Ruthenia in order to assist the Czechs to repel an invasion. Few Roumanians were as sure of Russian goodwill as Titulescu, and official relations remained far behind the private undertakings of the foreign ministers. It was not until the middle of October 1935 that the railway bridge crossing the Dniester between Bendery and Tiraspol, closed in 1920, was re-opened for traffic, and life along the Bessarabian-Ukrainian frontier began to enjoy four and a half years of abnormal 'normalcy'.

The Franco-Soviet Pact was never as serious a diplomatic instrument as the Dual Alliance which had linked the Third Republic to the Tsarist Empire before 1914. No military conversations defined the scope of the new agreement as they had the old. Laval had so low an opinion of the Soviet Union that he did not even submit the pact for ratification and, since the Russians refused to ratify before the French, its terms did not become binding until March 1936, two months after Laval had fallen from grace (and from office) over the Ethiopian war. At heart, Laval despised Litvinov and distrusted Stalin; he preferred collaboration with Mussolini, and his ideal was attained at Stresa in April 1935 when the French, Italians and British solemnly condemned Hitler's abrogation of the disarmament clauses imposed at Versailles and re-affirmed their determination to prevent any forcible re-drafting of the political map of Europe.

This united 'Stresa Front' was soon seen to be no more than a passing illusion. The French and Italian chiefs-of-staff spent much time that summer planning joint operations to save Austria from Germany; and General Gamelin of France even tried to interest the military leaders of the Little Entente in the project, without conspicuous success. It was all in vain. In the next eighteen months the successive crises over Ethiopia and over Spain led to cooler relations between France and Italy than had ever existed during the rivalry of the twenties, although it was characteristic of the confused thinking of the day that a powerful lobby in the French Chamber still preferred the Duce's braggadocio to the remonstrances of Geneva. But the empty weapon of sanctions half-applied forced Mussolini into the Axis which Gömbös had predicted; and the cost of friendship between Italy and Germany was abandonment of the watch on the Danube which he had assumed in 1934 to protect Dollfuss's Austria. Inevitably the states of central and south-eastern Europe had to adjust their policies to the new conditions; and most of them, noting with relish the evidence of the trade figures, willingly acquiesced in the new-found primacy of Germany.

The events of March 1936 increased their doubts over the value of a French alliance. For it was in that month that Hitler re-occupied the Rhineland, justifying this breach of Locarno by complaining of the menace to Germany implicit in the newly ratified Franco-Soviet Pact. France thus became separated from her eastern allies by a wall of German steel, which in time became a line of fortifications. Russia and Czechoslovakia both gave assurances that they would back up the French in military counter-measures, and Beck appears to have given qualified support from Poland, although since his hatred of Russia was exceeded only by the bitterness of his feud with the Czechs, it is a little difficult to imagine the three powers working in harness. The French, of course, did nothing, partly through their own internal political weakness and partly because of the uncooperative isolationism of Britain. The German army established itself along the middle Rhine without a single reservist being called to the colours in any of Germany's western neighbours. Her eastern neighbours observed what had happened, and made their own calculations.

Outwardly the Little Entente remained united and loyal to its French connexion. An impressive communiqué stressing their solidarity 'against all the European forces of international anarchy' was drafted by Titulescu and signed by the three foreign ministers in conference during the first week of May. Militarily, too, the Little Entente was in accord with Paris. The three General Staffs set up a joint intelligence service and agreed on methods by which telegraphists might cooperate with the French army using a common code. In May they discussed standardization of equipment and in June they even broached the possibility of a joint military commander. They also drew up contingency plans for dealing with a Habsburg restoration should Austria summon Archduke Otto to his father's throne: the Czechs would march on Vienna from Brno; the Yugoslavs would meet them at the gates of the city, having advanced from Maribor, by way of Graz; and the Roumanians would keep watch on Hungary. No doubt it was a jolly little war game with which to pass a summer's evening. It was also, as it happened, the last. The Little Entente was falling apart. At the end of August King Carol replaced Titulescu by Victor Antonescu as foreign minister, and the Roumanian line hardened against the French and the Russians. Stojadinović had followed the Czechs and Roumanians with the greatest reluctance and now began to dig in his toes. By the autumn of 1936 both Roumania and Yugoslavia were seeking an understanding with Germany.

In foreign affairs Stojadinović was essentially a neutralist. He believed that Yugoslavia should pursue an independent policy, breaking away from the leading-strings of the French and reaching a natural and realistic accord with the Germans, and for that matter with those old rivals, the Bulgars and the Italians. In the closing quarter of 1936 he stood out against any broadening of the links between France and the Little Entente. At the same time he reached an informal agreement with Germany by which, if Hitler could persuade the Bulgars and Italians to settle their problems with Yugoslavia, then Stojadinović would slowly drop out of the French alliance into a genuine neutrality and hoped that he might carry Roumania with him. At the end of January 1937 Bulgaria and Yugoslavia duly signed a treaty which promised, a little optimistically, that 'indivisible peace and sincere and perpetual friendship' should exist between the two countries. In March a no less remarkable treaty between Yugoslavia and Italy was signed in Belgrade: the two kingdoms undertook to settle their differences without resort to war and agreed to respect their common frontiers; neither would permit terrorist conspiracies to be organized on its soil against the other; both would seek to preserve the existing regime in Albania (which, in fact, had been virtually an Italian colony since March 1936, although still nominally independent); both governments would seek to increase their mutual trade; and the Italians would make cultural concessions to the Slovene population of Istria. Even more impressive than the terms of the treaty was its timing. The Italian foreign minister, Ciano, came to Belgrade for the formal signature of the pact precisely one week before the Little Entente was due to hold one of its periodic conferences in the city, and just twelve days before Beneš – who was by then President of Czechoslovakia – was expected in the Yugoslav capital for an official visit. It is hardly surprising that Stojadinović again refused to strengthen the connexion of the Little Entente, as a whole, with France. 'We must be as wise as a serpent and as gentle as a dove,' he wrote to Prince Paul.

Roumania, for the moment, did not take such an independent line as Yugoslavia partly because there were personal and commercial links binding King Carol and his entourage to Paris, and partly because Roumania's rearmament still depended on the steady arrival of supplies from the Czechoslovak Skoda works at Plzeň (in which the French firm of Schneider-Creusot had a considerable interest). The Roumanians did, however, back up Stojadinović in his defiance of the Franco-Czech line at the two conferences. Moreover, they informed the Russians that under no circumstances would the Red Army be permitted to cross Roumanian soil in the event of war – a complete reversal of Titulescu's unofficial policy. But the Roumanians could not make any concessions to Hungary, and both the Germans and the Italians insisted that an understanding between Roumania and Hungary over Transylvania was an essential first step towards any general agreement with what was now termed 'the Rome-Berlin Axis'.

The third of the Little Entente states, Czechoslovakia, was increasingly isolated from her two partners and, at the same time, weakened by internal dissension. Tómaš Masaryk resigned as President in December 1935 when he was eighty-five years old. He lived on in retirement until September 1937 sadly watching as the shadows seemed to lengthen around his friend and successor, Edvard Beneš. The principal menace to the integrity of the state came from the Sudeten German Party (originally known as the Sudeten German Home Front) which was organized by a former gymnastics instructor, Konrad Henlein, and which received subsidies from Berlin even though it was not a specifically Nazi organization. All the older German democratic parties in Czechoslovakia crumbled before the electioneering tactics of Henlein in 1935 and he won votes, not only in the smaller towns of predominantly rural areas but in the industrial centres of northern Bohemia which were traditionally left-wing in sympathy. At one moment it seemed as if Czechs and Germans might reach a political accord. Early in 1937 the prime minister, Milan Hodža (who was a Slovak), proposed a settlement which would have permitted the Germans a considerable share in the administration of the predominantly German-speaking areas. Henlein, however, interpreted this offer as a sign of weakness and pressed for recognition of the right of national groups within Czechoslovakia to form themselves into separate autonomous 'corporations'. This programme, which was totally unacceptable to the government in Prague, appealed to the Slovak Clericals of Hlinka and Tiso, and Czech centralism was firmly assailed by the Germans in the north-west and the Slovaks in the east. Since the Ruthenes, too, were restless and the Polish and Hungarian governments fomented unrest among their minorities within the republic, it seemed unlikely that Masaryk's state would long outlive its creator. When in October 1937 a Czech policeman in the town of Teplitz proved unable to resist the temptation to arrest and beat up the most arrogant of the Sudeten spokesmen, Karl Frank, the whole of the Nazi propaganda machine in Berlin launched a violent verbal offensive against Czechoslovakia. For the next eleven months the Germans consistently maintained that their Sudeten kinsfolk were being intolerably oppressed by the Czech administration.

Beneš remained in charge of Czechoslovak foreign policy until the end of 1935 and subsequently intervened in matters of international concern to a greater extent than his predecessor. Until the incorporation of Austria into the Reich in March 1938 he continued to regard a Habsburg restoration as potentially the gravest threat to the existing order: better even Hitler in Vienna than Archduke Otto. It was a curious error of judgement for so experienced a statesman. No doubt it sprang in part from the memory of political battles in his youth, but it was also true that while the pact with Russia and the alliance with France offered some assurance against a German invasion, there were many anti-Nazis in the West who would have welcomed Otto as an obstacle to revolution from the Right. Beneš himself was fully prepared to seek an understanding with Germany. As he once reminded the British Foreign Secretary, he had worked well with Stresemann and the Czech State had no frontier dispute with Hitler's Germany (as it had, of course, with France's other ally, Poland).

There were two occasions on which the Czechs contemplated adjustments of their foreign policy. From October 1936 until the end of January 1937 there were some unofficial conversations between Beneš and two German emissaries. The initiative seems to have come from the German side, although not from the Nazi establishment. Hitler approved of the talks as a way of weakening the Russo-Czech connexion (and, possibly, as a means of sowing discord in Russia). The Czechs appear to have offered 'to refrain from adopting a pro-Russian foreign policy' in return for a specific guarantee by the Third Reich of Czechoslovakia's frontiers. It is, however, doubtful if these talks were meant as a serious contribution to the diplomacy of the period. Their vagueness and imprecision suggest that they were primarily manoeuvres in which the two sides tested each other's reactions. Later in 1937 an attempt was made by Hodža to bring Austria and Hungary together with the Little Entente into a 'Danubian Pact'; but although conversations dragged on through the summer, the proposals had come far too late. The Magyars could see nothing to gain from propping up a tottering Little Entente at this stage.

Kánya, the Hungarian foreign minister, tended to look to Berlin over such matters, and, since Hitler was prepared to assure him personally that he recognized Hungary's claims on Slovakia and Ruthenia, a Danubian pact could have been no more than an empty form of words.

Menaced by the Poles to the north and uncertain of the fate of Austria, the Czechs were left to build up their defences and hope that the treaties with Russia and France would deter the hostile forces encircling them. Work began on constructing a fortress barrier along the frontier with Germany in the summer of 1936. Plans were made to transfer the Skoda arms works from Plzeň, which was only forty miles from the German border, to central Slovakia. The airfield at Užhorod in western Ruthenia was enlarged so as to accommodate Soviet bombers, if they came.

It was not only in foreign affairs that the peoples of East-Central Europe turned to Berlin. There had been political movements favouring authoritarian romantic myths even before the Depression, although only the Iron Guard in Roumania became a mass organization as opposed to a minority cult. During the 1930s the fashion was to follow Nazi rather than fundamentally fascist forms. Thus in Budapest Ferencz Szálasi founded a Hungarian National Socialist Party in 1937 which was far too radical and anti-semitic for Regent Horthy and the old-fashioned Magyar aristocrats; and in Roumania the poet Octavian Goga led a 'National Christian Party' in which hostility towards the Jews dominated every action. The 'National Radical Camp,' which split off from the Polish National Democrat Party in 1934, had a similar ideology and won support from the younger generation through the 'Union of Young Poland'. There was a small Nazi-type group in Serbia, headed by Dimitrije Ljotić, but within the Czechoslovak Republic the only out and out anti-semitic organization was Henlein's Sudeten German Party. Since there were no more than fifty thousand Jews in Bulgaria, King Boris was spared the embarrassment of this particular form of Right Radicalism. When, in the spring of 1938, a Nazi-inspired movement known as the Radnitsa sought to become a mass organization Boris swiftly ordered its dissolution.

Only one of these exotic pocket führers held office for any period between the wars: Goga was prime minister of Roumania for forty-four days at the start of 1938. There was, none the less, a distinct swing towards the extreme Right in all the countries of East-Central Europe, except Czechoslovakia, during the mid-thirties. In most cases existing governments merely sought to refurbish conservatively-minded regimes with the trappings of fascism in order to give an appearance of modernity. Thus Pilsudski introduced a constitution for Poland in April 1935 which finally reduced the Sejm to a consultative body and set up the strong presidential regime for which the marshal had always hankered. Officially Poland was neither a Nazi nor a Fascist state but a 'conducted democracy,' but the freedom allowed to socialist or agrarian groups was minimal. Pilsudski himself died on 12 May 1935, the ninth anniversary of his *coup d'état*. In the four years following his death, the 'conducted democracy' lacked its essential pre-requisite, decisive leadership at the top. The effective ruler of the nation was not Moscicki, who remained titular President, but the inspector-general and commander-in-chief of the armed forces, General Rydz-Smigly. As if to emphasize the continuity between Pilsudski and Rydz-Smigly, he was duly elevated to the rank of Marshal in November 1936. Yet, although Rydz-Smigly was a brave soldier and an impressive figure on any saluting-base, he had none of his predecessor's legendary authority. He knew little about politics and despised politicians. He had personal charm and his horsemanship showed commendable elegance, but his military gifts were limited and quaintly old-fashioned. It is characteristic of the man and of his environment that when war came in 1939 Poland had the most impressive cavalry regiments in the world. The Polish State of Rydz-Smigly, Moscicki and Beck was a social and military anachronism: swords and lances make little impact on armoured divisions.

By contrast the Yugoslav army stood outside politics, allowing the civilian ministers to stage ideological fancy-dress parades so long as the real power of the Serbian High Command was left unchallenged. The Stojadinović government inclined more definitely towards the example of Mussolini rather than of Hitler. 'Stojadinović is a fascist,' wrote Ciano after visiting Belgrade in 1937. 'If he is not one by virtue of an open declaration of Party loyalty, he is certainly one by virtue of his conception of authority.' His party, the Yugoslav Radical Union, used the fascist salute and referred to him as '*Vodja*' (Leader); its members wore green shirts of orthodox right-wing cut. When, however, Prince Paul questioned the character of the Radical Union, he received a reassuring reply from his chief of police: the greenshirts' salute could not possibly be confused with its Roman prototype if observed 'from the time of raising the arm until the time of lowering it.' Prince Paul, being an intelligent man, was not convinced; but there were, perhaps fortunately, few Yugoslavs prepared to take the green-shirted *Vodja* seriously. Since, however, his statecraft was considerably superior to his essays in demagogy it was not until February 1939 that Prince Paul was able to dispense with his services.

In Hungary, Gömbös, whose ideology was more sincerely akin in origin to that of Hitler, died in October 1935 without ever having persuaded the regent to authorize enactment of his earlier tenets; and it was not until the Imrédy ministry of 1938 that legislation limited the activity of the Jewish community in the professions and commerce. There was, nevertheless, widespread anti-semitism in the Hungary of this period, especially among the middle-classes, and most strongly in those communities which were not themselves ethnically Magyar. It was from these groups that Szálasi found his leaders, both for his National Socialist Party and for the broader and more self-consciously Hungarian fascist movement, the 'Arrow Cross,' which he directed from 1938 to 1945. In time, he was able to recruit unskilled workers from the newer industries to his organization, partly because of a sense of social inferiority in comparison with the older crafts, with their long-established habits of trade unionism.

The swing to the political Right in both Bulgaria and Roumania took a different form from the rest of south-eastern Europe, largely because King Boris and King Carol pushed it as they themselves desired. The Zveno dictatorship of 1934 was weakened by dissension among the officers who led it and much of the political life of Sofia in the summer and autumn of 1935 consisted of a tussle between Boris's nominees and those officers who were still loyal to the original reforming zeal of Velchev. It is probable that Velchev and Georghiev were, even at this stage, republicans by nature; and Boris used all his considerable talents of intrigue to destroy their position. By November 1935 Boris felt sufficiently sure of his position to entrust the government to a personal friend who had served as minister in Belgrade and had no political past, Georgi Kiosseivanov. Velchev was thrown into prison on a charge of treason and the Officers' League dissolved. The Zveno movement was broken up. It had, however, taught Boris that there was no need to rule through parliaments. From March 1936 until his death in August 1943 the King was dictator of his country in everything but name. Elections, with a suffrage which even gave the vote to married women, were held early in 1938; but, since all the old parties were still proscribed and as the reconstituted Sobranjie was a purely consultative body, King Boris was not unduly concerned with their outcome. He did not bother to create an image of himself as the guardian of the nation; and, perhaps for that very reason, he was by no means unpopular with his subjects.

Carol of Roumania also established a royal dictatorship, but unlike Boris he was determined to appear as the state's first demagogue. Unfortunately for Carol that role had already been assumed by Codreanu and the Iron Guard, with its simple slogan of 'One man, one acre,' attracted support from the peasantry as well as from the traditional centres of anti-semitism in the towns. Carol distrusted Codreanu and was blatantly jealous of him. It is possibly for this reason that the King invited Goga to form a government in the last days of 1937, even though his party had polled less than nine per cent in the recent election. Goga's brief spell of eccentric extremism discredited the whole Right Radical movement in Roumania, including the Iron Guard; and Carol was able to substitute what might be described as a 'Right Royalist' movement in its place. On 8 February 1938 a 'Cabinet of National Concentration' was sworn in, headed by the Patriarch of the Roumanian Orthodox Church. Less than three weeks later a new constitutional law gave all essential powers to the King. Political parties were suppressed and a carefully managed plebiscite approved Carol's action with that near-unanimity so characteristic of the Roumanian electoral machine. And while socialist and peasant leaders abroad were condemning the King's fascist experiment, Carol himself prepared to direct a major attack on the strength of Iron Guard sympathies in the country and, in particular, on the hated Codreanu.

At the time, however, this conflict between the Roumanian King and the Iron Guard attracted little attention in the European press; for the pace of international relations quickened suddenly at the beginning of 1938. There had long been political uncertainty in Vienna. The situation had been tense ever since the proclamation of the 'Rome-Berlin Axis' in November 1936 virtually deprived the Austrian semi-fascist regime of its one effective protector, Mussolini. Provided that there was no Habsburg restoration (which the Nazis feared no less than Beneš), Hitler was pre-pared to wait for Austria to join Germany of her own volition, confident that the Austrian President would eventually appoint an Austrian Nazi administration even as President Hindenburg had entrusted him to form a government in 1933. It was the Austrians themselves who forced Hitler to move in 1938. Chancellor Schuschnigg, conscious that Nazi propaganda was undermining his position, staked his political future on a plebiscite in which the people were invited to vote for or against 'a free and German, independent and social, Christian and united Austria'. Had a vote been taken over this form of words Schuschnigg would inevitably have gained a considerable majority and the case for union with Germany would have suffered a serious setback. As soon as he heard of the plebiscite, Hitler ordered mobilization. There was a flurry of political intrigue in Vienna, much of which seems in retrospect totally irrelevant. On 12 March the German army crossed the Austrian frontier and Hitler was welcomed in the land of his birth. Next day Austria was formally proclaimed 'a pro-vince of the German Reich'; and the Anschluss, which the treaties of Versailles and St Germain had explicitly forbidden, became a reality.

No foreign power was surprised; some protested, but all accepted the new political order. German troops mounted guard along the borders of four of the six countries of Europe's central belt; only the Roumanians and Bulgars were deprived of the sight of a swastika flag at their frontier-posts. Czechoslovakia, the arsenal of the successor states, had become a beleaguered bastion of democracy. No one believed that its territory would remain inviolate for more than a few months unless there was a major change in Czechoslovak policy. It was an open question that spring whether any government was prepared to face war in order to uphold the integrity of the republic.

11

The German Tide

In the three and a half years which followed Hitler's triumphant entry into Vienna, the Germans surged eastwards to the shores of the Black Sea and the Aegean and to the reedy shallows of the Gulf of Finland. Other East European problems seemed puny and other issues irrelevant compared with the growing threat from Germany; and, indeed, most internal changes of this period were indirect responses to the chronic external crisis. The shadow of the swastika lay heavily over the whole area.

The chief instrument in the accomplishment of these remarkable conquests was, of course, the German army with its brilliant contingency planning, imaginative use of armoured columns and ruthless employment of tactical air power. But final military success depended on three preliminary circumstances: the ability of the German foreign service to exploit old resentments, distracting potential enemies by playing off rival neighbours against each other; the appeal of racial unity and superiority to the six million *Volksdeutschen,* the German-speaking and German-thinking minority groups living beyond the borders of the Reich; and the trade treaties which, ever since 1934, bound the smaller states of central and south-eastern Europe closer and closer to Berlin, offering genuine economic benefit to countries which otherwise lacked secure markets. Greater German primacy was thus already established in the Danube basin and the Balkans before the first panzer-divisions moved against Poland in September 1939.

Hitler's ultimate objectives in the East changed little over the years, probably because they were essentially ill-defined. He wanted to secure for the German people *Lebensraum,* living space in Europe's eastern marchlands and especially in the Ukraine. He envisaged a Greater German Reich which would embrace all the racially Germanic communities except those whom he considered fortunate enough to live under the enlightened rule of Mussolini in the South Tyrol. The other peoples of East-Central Europe – Poles, Lithuanians, Ukrainians, Hungarians and perhaps even the Czechs – might exist as subordinate vassals, permitted a degree of local government but bound to the Reich economically and politically. Yet Hitler had no rigid timetable of conquest and no detailed

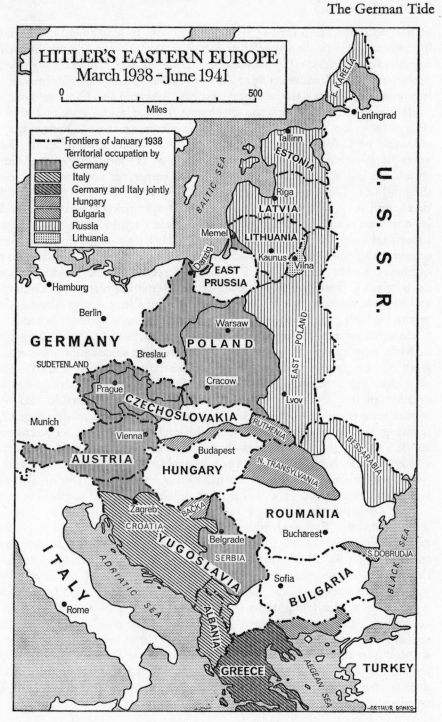

HITLER'S EASTERN EUROPE
March 1938 – June 1941

0   500

Miles

Frontiers of January 1938
Territorial occupation by
- Germany
- Italy
- Germany and Italy jointly
- Hungary
- Bulgaria
- Russia
- Lithuania

U. S. S. R.

Leningrad

E. KARELIA

Tallinn

ESTONIA

BALTIC SEA

Riga

LATVIA

Memel

LITHUANIA

Kaunus

Vilna

Danzig

EAST PRUSSIA

Hamburg

Berlin

Warsaw

POLAND

EAST POLAND

GERMANY

SUDETENLAND

Breslau

Prague

CZECHOSLOVAKIA

Cracow

Lvov

Munich

Vienna

RUTHENIA

BESSARABIA

AUSTRIA

Budapest

HUNGARY

N. TRANSYLVANIA

Zagreb

BACKA

CROATIA

YUGOSLAVIA

Belgrade

SERBIA

ROUMANIA

Bucharest

ITALY

ADRIATIC SEA

S. DOBRUDJA

BLACK SEA

Sofia

Rome

ALBANIA

BULGARIA

GREECE

AEGEAN SEA

TURKEY

-ARTHUR BANKS

229

plan of administration for his 'new order'. From time to time he lectured his military and civilian chiefs on future policy, always leaving himself considerable freedom to manoeuvre. Thus in the famous four-hour prolation of 5 November 1937 (the so-called 'Hossbach Conference') he committed himself to the incorporation of Austria and Czechoslovakia in the Reich as essential first moves against Russia; but he gave no indication of the order of events, or of their character, or even of their timing although he insisted that the operation must be completed before the years 1943-5. His one rule of action was that favourable opportunities should be seized whenever they presented themselves and created when they did not. The German armed forces were to be ready to move at all times; and yet it was not always certain what their next destination would be nor who were their friends and who their enemies. There is thus a superficial clarity of purpose and intent in Hitler's foreign policy which obscures the swift variations of emphasis that so increased the uncertainty of these months of tension. The detailed record of the Czechoslovak crisis of 1938 affords ample evidence of the alternating phases of hesitancy and impetuosity which underlay his handling of foreign affairs; and so it was to be with each international emergency of the years that followed.

Hitler had always disliked and despised the Czechs as a people, although he had a passing regard for the Slovaks in his more sentimental moments. Both of these prejudices sprang from his Austrian childhood; and to them was added, in time, a political hatred of the Czechoslovak Republic as a creation of the 'Versailles system'. It was therefore predictable that he would seek to destroy the Czech State at the earliest possible moment, securing the annexation of Bohemia-Moravia to the Greater German Reich. A fortnight after the Anschluss Henlein was summoned to Berlin and instructed to put forward a progressively exacting series of demands on behalf of the Sudeten Germans, which the Czechs would always refuse to grant. Henlein was told that he should regard himself as the Führer's representative among the three and a quarter million *Volksdeutschen* in the Sudetenland and other frontier districts. It was his responsibility to ensure that Czechoslovakia would be weakened by turmoil and political discord. The Germans, too, made preparations: in the third week of April the General Staff was instructed to draw up a war-plan for action against the Czechoslovak Republic; and approaches were made to the Hungarians (and by them to the Poles) so as to encourage Czechoslovakia's other neighbours to demand a share of the spoils. But as late as the first week in May Hitler was willing to wait several years before making military moves against the Czechs, shrewdly calculating that the protracted disintegration of the republic would demonstrate to other small states the worthlessness of the French system of alliances.

Henlein duly took up the position which was expected of him at the Sudeten German Party's annual congress in the town he called Karlsbad and the Czechs Karlovy Vary. On 24 April he rejected, before it was even drafted, a proposed 'Minorities Statute' which the Prague government was prepared to put forward as a conciliatory gesture. He demanded full self-government for the German minority with guarantees of 'freedom to profess German nationality and the German world outlook'. Autonomy of this character would have destroyed the whole democratic basis of the republic, and the Czechs refused to consider his demands. They were, however, under pressure from the French and more especially from the British (for Henlein twice visited London and made a favourable impression, even on Winston Churchill). There is no doubt that Henlein had the bulk of the German-speaking population behind him. His party had numbered three-quarters of a million members at the time of the Anschluss: another half a million joined in the following two months. The Sudeten German Social Democrats, who remained loyal to the concept of a Czechoslovak State, also pressed for recognition by the Prague authorities of the special rights of the German minority. The Czechs were induced to extend the original concept of a 'Minorities Statute' into a more comprehensive 'Nationalities Statute' which would have given a higher degree of autonomy within the existing political structure. The minister of the Interior even authorized the establishment of a Sudeten German Defence Force which policed some of the predominantly German towns on the eve of local elections (which were due to be held on 22 May). The republic was falling apart, as Hitler wished.

At the end of the third week in May a sudden war scare sharpened the intensity of the crisis. It is probable that the activities of the Sudeten Defence Force, coupled with rumours of German troop movements, prompted Beneš to believe that Czechoslovakia was about to be invaded. France, Britain and the Soviet Union all warned Hitler that precipitate action along the frontiers could well lead to a general war. The Czechoslovak government ordered partial mobilization. Nothing happened. There is still no evidence that the German army moved even a single division that week, and the parachutists whom the Czechs saw in the sky over Prague were certainly the products of over-stretched nerves. The British and French governments were displeased; they had been forced to commit themselves to a positive statement of purpose and were indignant that Beneš should (as they saw it) have manoeuvred them into such an uncharacteristic act. Even more pressure was put on Beneš to reach agreement with Henlein, and it was decided that the British would send out an 'unofficial mediator' to reconcile the Czechs with the German minority. In July Chamberlain, the British prime minister, announced that this mission would be undertaken by Viscount Runciman, an elderly Liberal shipping magnate who had been an effective President of the Board of Agriculture and Fisheries a quarter of a century before. Lest it was thought that Lord Runciman knew nothing of the background to this task, he was photographed reading Miss Wiskemann's *Czechs and Germans,* hot from the press, on the train to Prague, his face a study in bland incomprehension.

It is hardly surprising that Runciman failed to solve the problems of 'this accursed country,' as he was calling Czechoslovakia after fully four weeks in Prague that August. In general he sympathized with the Sudeten leaders and wrote testily of Beneš' 'slow movements and dilatory nego-tiations'. It made little difference. Hitler had already made up his mind. He had been angered by the May war-scare: a crisis manufactured outside Germany was not part of his reckoning; and he was incensed by claims made in the Czech and French press that the warnings from Paris, London and Moscow had forestalled a German invasion. On 20 May he had dic-tated a military directive which began: 'It is not my intention to smash Czechoslovakia by military action in the immediate future without provo-cation. . . .' Precisely eight days later he changed the phrasing so that the directive declared, uncompromisingly, 'It is my unalterable decision to smash Czechoslovakia by 1 October at the latest.' He did not believe that there would be a general war but he was prepared to take the risk.

In the following months the Germans made a genuine attempt to convince the Western Powers, especially Britain, of the justice of the German cause. The British government and press was by no means un-sympathetic, and the French were content to follow the lead of London. Politically the French were in full retreat from the comprehensive under-takings of Briand and Barthou. Bonnet, the French Foreign Minister, ignored a suggestion from Moscow that the time had come for military conversations between the General Staffs of France, Czechoslovakia and the Soviet Union. And the German ambassador in Paris reported to Berlin a conversation he had held with the French prime minister on 22 May in which Daladier spoke of his desire to save Europe from a new culture carried westwards into 'depopulated and war-devastated terri-tories' by 'hordes of Cossacks and Mongols.' With this curious commen-tary on the Franco-Soviet Pact to hand, it is not difficult to see why Hitler was optimistic over the chances of avoiding a European war.

Soviet policy throughout the summer of 1938 was an enigma and remains so, even in retrospect. The alliance with Czechoslovakia became effective only if the French gave military support to the Czechs. Documents published by the Novotny government in 1958 suggest that Stalin and Litvinov were prepared to fulfil the Russian commitment. Thus in May 1938 the Czechoslovak ambassador in Moscow telegraphed to Prague:

'If requested, the USSR is prepared – in agreement with France and Czechoslovakia – to take all necessary measures relating to the security of Czechoslovakia. She disposes of all necessary means for doing so.' But did she? The Western Powers were acutely aware of Russia's apparent weakness that summer. These months coincided with the climax of the *Yezhovshina,* the great purge of Old Bolsheviks and of Soviet military leadership which numbered among its victims three marshals of the Soviet Union (including Tukachevsky, the Chief of the General Staff) and 400 of the 700 generals in the Red Army. It was reasonable to doubt the efficacy of the Soviet military machine. Moreover Czechoslovakia and Russia shared no common frontier and neither Poland nor Roumania would grant the passage of Soviet troops, although the Roumanians (whose statements of foreign policy remained monumentally devious) might conceivably have failed to notice if Russian aircraft flew across the Northern Bukovina to Užhorod.

Finding little comfort from its French ally and uncertain of its Russian, the Czechoslovak government as a last resort endeavoured in August to animate the Little Entente. If it was impossible to halt the Germans then at least the threat from Hungary might be neutralized. The Hungarian minister in Belgrade was invited to attend a meeting of the foreign ministers of the Little Entente countries held amid the melancholy beauty of the Slovenian lakes at Bled. There an agreement was concluded by which the Hungarians renounced the use of force against any member of the Little Entente in return for recognition of the right to rearm and the promise of statutes improving the position of the Magyar minorities within the three states. Horthy and Kánya, his foreign minister (who were on a visit to Germany at the time) insisted that the agreement completed the isolation of Czechoslovakia since it ensured that Beneš would receive no assistance from the Roumanians and Yugoslavs. The Germans, on the other hand, suspected that they had been double-crossed and never thereafter trusted the Hungarians. It is, however, clear that the Czechs were, indeed, the losers and that the Bled meeting marked the effective end of the Little Entente. King Carol sent a message to Hitler at the height of the September crisis assuring him of Roumania's desire for closer relations with Germany; and although Stojadinović approved a partial mobilization of the Yugoslav army, he maintained unofficial contact with Goering and subsequently expressed to the German minister in Belgrade 'his boundless admiration' of the way in which Hitler had incorporated the Sudetenland in the Reich. The Czechs were friendless in an alien world.

The Czechoslovak crisis came to a head in the first week of September when Beneš received two of the Sudeten German leaders in Prague and offered them virtual autonomy, similar to the demands made by Henlein at Karlovy Vary in April. The proposal embarrassed Henlein, who had left the country for the Nazi Party rally at Nuremberg intent on secession. But three days after Beneš' offer a riot in the small town of Morava-Ostrava gave the Sudeten Germans their excuse for breaking off all negotiations. All seemed ready to erase the Czechoslovak State from the map.

On 12 September Hitler denounced the 'intolerable conditions' in Czechoslovakia from the rostrum at Nuremberg. There were ugly scenes in the Sudeten towns that night with mobs smashing Czech and Jewish shops, and the Czechs called up reservists next day, establishing martial law in the disaffected regions. It was against this background that Chamberlain flew from London to meet Hitler at Berchtesgaden on 15 September. On his return he induced the British Cabinet and the French government to put pressure on the Czechs for the transfer of the Sudetenland to the Reich in return for an Anglo-French guarantee of the rump of Czechoslovakia against unprovoked aggression. He flew once more to Germany on 22 September and at Godesberg informed Hitler that the Czechs would cede the German areas. But Hitler wanted the full disintegration of Czechoslovakia. In the intervening week he had made contact with the Poles and Hungarians and he had sent an emissary to Slovakia to encourage Tiso (Hlinka had died in August). At Godesberg Hitler accordingly presented Chamberlain with a memorandum which sought satisfaction of the claims of the non-German nationalities as well as transference of the Sudetenland.

It seemed briefly as if Hitler had made a miscalculation. The British and French rejected the Godesberg Memorandum. The Hungarians limited their claims to the ethnically Magyar fringe and the Slovaks indicated that they would be content with a federal reorganization of the state. Only the Poles did all that Hitler expected of them, brushing aside French attempts at restraint. Czechoslovakia did not fall apart; and for a few days there was a greater risk of a general conflict than Hitler had anticipated. But none of the Great Powers was militarily prepared for war, and Italian mediation led to the famous conference at Munich on 29 September between Hitler, Chamberlain, Daladier and Mussolini. The Munich Agreement recognized transference of the predominantly German areas to the Reich and provided for a four-power guarantee of the remainder of Czechoslovakia against an unprovoked attack on the understanding that the question of the Polish and Hungarian minorities should be speedily settled. On 1 October German troops moved into the Sudetenland, most of which was in Hitler's hands by the time he made a triumphal crossing of the old frontier on 3 October. President Beneš resigned on 5 October and shortly afterwards left Prague to settle eventually in the United States.

The Poles occupied some 400 square miles of the area around Teschen on 2 October but it took longer to determine the new frontier with Hungary, partly because Hitler was still angry with Horthy and Kánya both over the Bled Agreement and their subsequent insistence that Hungary was too weak to take part in military operations should there be a general war. Eventually, however, Hungary's claims were settled by a Germano-Italian arbitral pronouncement – the 'First Vienna Award' of 2 November 1938 – which assigned the predominantly Magyar-inhabited fringe of southern Slovakia and Ruthenia, including the important racially-mixed towns of Košiče and Užhorod, to Hungary but left Bratislava in Slovakia and denied the Hungarians a common frontier in Ruthenia with Poland (as both Kánya and Beck had wished). Hungarian troops moved into the retroceded areas – the Felvidék, as they were called – later in the same week. On 11 November Regent Horthy, astride the inevitable white horse, rode into Košiče (or Kassa, as it now once more became) at the head of a procession of all the government dignitaries and there was considerable public rejoicing in Hungary at this victory for revisionism. The Felvidék comprised some 5,000 square miles with a population of 850,000, three quarters of whom were indisputably Magyar or Magyar-speaking.

The Munich Agreement and the First Vienna Award reduced the size of the Czechoslovak State by rather less than a third; the truncated republic was still greater in extent than Austria before the Anschluss and was only slightly smaller than the enlarged Hungary. But the Czechs had lost all their defences, most of their industries in Bohemia and Moravia, half of their towns and their richest coalfields. Economically Czechoslovakia became a satellite of Germany, a process emphasized by the agreement reached between the Prague government and Hitler at the end of November by which the Germans were authorized to construct a strategic highway across Moravia to Vienna and to begin work on a navigable canal between the Oder and the Danube. Politically, too, the republic inclined more and more towards the German fashion. Both Slovakia and Ruthenia were given full autonomy: but Tiso, who became prime minister of Slovakia, suppressed all political parties other than the 'Slovak National Front' at the end of October and depended for the maintenance of his authority on a specially recruited paramilitary organization, the 'Hlinka Guard'. The pattern of events was similar in Ruthenia, or as it was now called 'Carpatho-Ukraine,' but since the administrative capital was no more than a swollen village (Khust) the political life of the whole region was pathetically absurd. The Ruthene leader, Father Vološin, sought to follow the example of Monsignor Tiso and there was a 'Sič Guard' to defend Ukrainianism against Magyar incursions. 'Carpatho-Ukraine' concluded its own economic treaty with

Germany, handing over to Berlin all mineral rights in the mountain region.

Bohemia and Moravia never became so blatantly authoritarian as the Slovak and Ruthene areas. Emil Hacha, an elderly and distinguished jurist with little political experience, succeeded Beneš as President and the former Agrarian leader, Rudolf Beran, formed a government. Both Beran and his foreign minister, Chvalkovsky, favoured cooperation with Germany. All political groups of the centre were linked in a new 'Party of National Union' which was opposed by an umbrella organization of the left, the 'National Labour Party'. At first the Communist Party was tolerated and won many recruits since it was believed that the Soviet Union, unlike France, would have stood by the republic in the September crisis, and no Russian delegation had flown to Munich. But, by the end of the year, the Communist Party became a proscribed organization; and the proceedings of the parliamentary assembly in Prague were little more than an empty charade.

Even after Munich there were still nearly a quarter of a million *Volksdeutschen* in Bohemia and Moravia (and almost as many in Slovakia and Ruthenia). The textile and engineering centre of Brno had sixty-thousand German inhabitants and there were fifty thousand in Prague itself. It was part of Hitler's policy to see that this minority was advanced to key positions in the state and their political spokesman, Kundt, was by Christmas demanding privileges from Hacha and Beran with even greater arrogance than Henlein had shown towards Beneš. In reality Hacha had as little freedom of initiative as the burgomaster of a German city; but he failed to perceive the limitations on his independence and fondly believed that he could guide the republic into a new position among the European nations, associated with Germany but apart from the administration of the Reich and serving as a bridge between Teutons and Slavs. Within six months of taking office he was to be sadly disillusioned: in Hitler's new order the Czechs ranked as vassals, not partners.

Munich was a historical climacteric for all the peoples of central and south-eastern Europe. To states taught to regard the principles of the League Covenant as sacrosanct, it seemed a cynical negation of the Geneva spirit. In reality none of the countries in the region had a clear conscience over this matter (except, perhaps, Bulgaria where King Boris had shrewdly contrived not to notice what was happening). Moral self-righteousness ill-suited the signatories of the Bled Agreement or the Poles, whose gobbet of Silesia had a predominantly Czech population. It was, however, the French and the British who lost most face by Munich; their decline in influence seemed confirmed by their subsequent absence from the conference-table which decided the boundaries of the Felvidék. France's treaty obligations were assumed to exist only on paper and Daladier and Bonnet were seen as weak, ineffectual and indecisive. But it was the British prime minister who became a particular object of scorn. In his broadcast to the nation Chamberlain had said: 'How horrible, fantastic, incredible it is that we should be digging trenches and trying on gas-masks here because of a quarrel in a far-away country between peoples of whom we know nothing.' Most of his listeners would have agreed with him, even though the areas in dispute were nearer to London as the bomber flies than the main base of the British Home Fleet. Yet, if a good case may be made for Chamberlain, the rhapsodic Little Englander iso-lationism of 'Peace in our Time' was hardly calculated to raise British prestige in other 'far-away countries'. If London and Paris believed in appeasement, then it was logical for it to be the mood of Belgrade and Bucharest and Budapest. The small states swung through 'neutralism' towards the Axis giants.

The German successes also influenced the domestic policies of the remaining independent countries in the area. In Hungary the gradual worsening of the Czech crisis during the summer and autumn of 1938 had coincided with a series of anti-semitic measures introduced by Béla Imrédy, whom Horthy had asked to form a government in May. A quota system limited the proportion of Jews permitted to participate in certain professions to twenty per cent. After Munich the quota was reduced to six per cent and the definition of a Jew was made more comprehensive. It was then discovered by his opponents that Imrédy's great-grandmother, born in 1807, had been a Jewish believer for the first seven years of her life. Such a grave reflection on the purity of his ancestry was refuted by Imrédy in a lengthy speech which does not appear to have convinced all those who heard him. Horthy, who disliked Imrédy personally and who always insisted that there were good Hungarians who happened to be Jewish, seized the opportunity to force Imrédy's resignation; and Count Pál Teleki, the moderate conservative prime minister of 1920, took his place. Although Teleki favoured contacts with the West, he believed that German influence was so strong in Central Europe that he could not make a dramatic break with Imrédy's policy. He accordingly retained Imrédy's foreign minister, Count Csáky, who was convinced of the need to cooperate with the Axis Powers. He also permitted the anti-Jewish laws to complete their passage through parliament. On the other hand, Teleki dissolved the 'Arrow Cross' organization – its leader, Szálasi, had already been cast into prison by Imrédy – and unobtrusively extinguished a 'movement' created by Imrédy on the lines of Stojadinović's greenshirts.

In Roumania King Carol continued to move cautiously along the political tight-rope. He had already arranged to pay state visits to London and Paris in the autumn of 1938 and he dutifully fulfilled these obligations.

Although he tried some brisk salesmanship in the interlude between cere-monial engagements, neither the City of London nor the Paris Bourse responded to his blandishments. He decided that it would, perhaps, be diplomatic to break his return journey in Germany and on 24 November he was received at Berchtesgaden by Hitler, who plied him with soft words and declared himself in favour of closer economic links between Roumania and the Reich. At the same time Hitler spoke sympathetically of Codreanu, who had been imprisoned for ten years on a charge of treason in the previous April. It was therefore unfortunate that six days after the King's interview with the Führer, the vigilance of the Roumanian prison authorities resulted in the shooting of Codreanu and thirteen other Iron Guard leaders 'while trying to escape'. But so anxious was Hitler to secure Roumanian oil and wheat that even this affront was not allowed to delay the negotiation of a new trade treaty, which was duly signed on 10 December. And, as if to prove that he was at least as good a fascist as Codreanu, the king promptly created a single-party 'Front of National Rebirth' which received the approval of the Roumanian people at an election held by open ballot and with no list of opposition candidates. Hitler was not, however, impressed by Carol's political performance and had no intention of supporting him. The Iron Guard survived Codreanu's murder and took its revenge in September 1939 by assassinating Carol's pliant prime minister, Calinescu.

There was no change in the internal affairs of Bulgaria and only minor modifications in her foreign policy. All decisions continued to be taken by King Boris and his friend Kiosseivanov, the prime minister; but parliamentary debates were permitted in the Sobranjie and there were occasional dissenting voices in the press, although it should be added that these criticisms tended to come from the political right rather than from any liberals. At the end of July 1938 an agreement was concluded in Salonika between Bulgaria and the Balkan Entente (Greece, Turkey, Roumania and Yugoslavia) formally recognizing the right of Bulgaria to rearm and recording the decision of all five states to abstain from the use of force against one another. But, so far from drawing Bulgaria into the Balkan Entente, the Salonika Agreement stimulated a new outburst of revisionist sentiment in Sofia for it was argued that, if the disarmament clauses of the Treaty of Neuilly could be erased at the stroke of a pen, so too could the most unacceptable aspects of the territorial settlement. Since there was no *Volksdeutsch* minority in the country, it was this spirit of revisionism which provided the Germans with their most effective induce-ment for winning over the Bulgarian governing class to an Axis policy. But Boris, who had family connexions in Germany and had married an Italian princess, knew both the strength and the limitations of Hitler and Mussolini. While his royal neighbour in Roumania was prepared to move forward along the tightrope, Boris preferred to observe such political acrobatics from a distance, glancing apprehensively at the chasm beneath the performers.

The most extensive changes in the Balkan lands during this period took place in Yugoslavia. Prince-Regent Paul became increasingly disillusioned with Stojadinović in the months following Munich. In internal affairs he had achieved little: no reconciliation with Maček and the Croats: abandonment, under pressure from the Serbian Orthodox Church, of a Concordat with the Vatican; and alienation of the older radicals and Serbian *prečani*. Although he had improved Yugoslavia's relations with her neighbours, Prince Paul distrusted the growing friendship between Stojadinović and Ciano, rightly suspecting that Stojadinović was involved in an intrigue which would have permitted Italy to annex Albania. Stojadinović, however, failed to perceive that his position was becoming weaker. He secured the dissolution of the Skupština and held elections shortly before Christmas 1938.

Voters opted either for a government list (consisting of Stojadinović's 'Yugoslav Radical Union,' Korošec's Slovenes and a Muslim party) or for the opposition list (which was headed by Maček's Croatian Peasants but included Serbian democrats and agrarians and even some of Pašić's one-time followers). The government received fifty-nine per cent of the votes and the opposition forty-one per cent, despite pressure and intimidation. More than a quarter of a million more votes were cast against the government list than in the previous election of May 1935. In a total electorate of two million and with the existing political system, this was virtually a vote of no confidence. But Stojadinović was unrepentant: it was, he explained to Prince Paul, all Korošec's fault that the election had gone so badly, for the Slovene priest had so far neglected his duties as minister of the interior as to allow all state employees to vote according to their consciences. Korošec resigned and there followed six weeks of complicated political intrigues in Belgrade. On 3 February Stojadinović's minister of forests and mines lost his temper in parliament and declared that only those Serbs who had stormed up Kajmakcalan in 1916 had a right to determine the policies of the nation. This was a supremely tactless remark: the number of veterans of the courageous assault by the Serbian army was by 1939 necessarily limited, and the regent had himself been at the time in Paris. On 4 February Stojadinović was dismissed from office.

The new government was headed by Dragiša Cvetković, a competent mayor of Niš in a bleak period. He brought to international problems the limited vision of a civic dignitary in a provincial railway-junction but his understanding of Yugoslavia's domestic weaknesses was sound. He had already established good personal relations with Maček. Negotiations aimed at giving Croatia a degree of autonomy continued from March to August in 1939. They were long and difficult, not only because of Maček's intransigence – for he knew that he was the real master of Croatia even as Radić had been before him – but because the Serbian opposition groups feared that Cvetković would perpetuate the existing authoritarian government by winning over the principal advocate of change. At one time Prince Paul himself refused to accept all Maček's demands and representatives of the Croatian Peasant Party once again contacted the Italians. There was even a risk that Italy might march into Yugoslavia in April to impose a settlement (from which of course Pavelić, rather than Maček, would have been the chief beneficiary). But on 23 August an agreement (Sporazum) was duly signed; and three days later Maček became vice-premier.

The Sporazum merged two of the *Banovine* established in 1929, adding to them certain border districts of Bosnia, Slavonia and Dalmatia so as to create a single administrative unit known as 'Croatia,' which was to have a governor and a Diet of its own and was to enjoy considerable powers of local self-government. There was a close parallel between the new constitutional structure and the old Croatia-Slavonia of the Dual Monarchy. All responsibility for defence, foreign policy, commerce and communications rested with the central government in Belgrade, just as it had once depended on Budapest and Vienna. The gendarmerie in Croatia was trained by the Yugoslav War Ministry but controlled by the provincial governor. The Sporazum was supposed to benefit all the peoples of Yugoslavia: it was agreed that there should be a new electoral law so as to ensure a fairer system of representation; and the Yugoslavs were promised a return of political liberties. Yet neither the Slovenes nor the majority of Serbs were satisfied by the terms of the Sporazum even though Cvetković and Maček gave assurances that, in time, the federal principle would be extended to the whole kingdom. Little progress was made in the following eighteen months, partly because Prince Paul was reluctant to authorize a constitutional revolution in the last two years of his regency but even more because both he and the government genuinely feared that any open move towards a democratic system would invite intervention from Yugoslavia's Axis neighbours. The settlement of the Serbo-Croat dispute thus remained incomplete: it had come too late to save the kingdom from disaster.

It was in March 1939 that Hitler finally abandoned his earlier claim to be seeking the unity of exclusively German-dominated regions and proceeded to destroy the rump of Czechoslovakia. A military directive for the occupation of Prague and the rest of Bohemia-Moravia had been issued in Berlin only three weeks after the signature of the Munich Agreement. Once again, however, the timing was ultimately determined by the internal affairs of the republic, as the Anschluss had been in the previous year. A dispute over the amount of money allocated to Slovakia by the central government led to a serious breach between Prague and Bratislava at the end of February. At the same time, in 'Carpatho-Ukraine,' Vološin's Sič Guard made trouble for anyone or anything considered Czech, Polish, Jewish or Magyar in origin. At the end of the first week in March President Hacha and the Beran government plucked up courage and ordered a Czech general to assume control of Ruthenia. Soon afterwards Hacha dismissed Tiso's Slovak administration and, on the morning of 10 March, sent Czech troops into Bratislava.

These events gave Hitler his opportunity. Tiso was fetched to Berlin and advised to summon the Slovak Diet and proclaim Slovakia's independence under German protection: this was done on 14 March. That night President Hacha also flew to Berlin and, in the small hours of the morning (15 March), was informed by Hitler that German troops would enter the Czech provinces at six o'clock. Goering, attendant in an anteroom of the chancellery, added the information that Prague was to be destroyed by bombing. Hacha fainted. Two hours before the invasion he signed a communiqué 'confidently placing the fate of the Czech people in the Führer's hands'. Hitler entered Prague that evening and on the following day Bohemia-Moravia was incorporated in the Reich as a German protectorate. Slovakia retained nominal independence, under German protection with German troops garrisoning her towns. Tiso became president of a one-party state whose activities were strictly coordinated with the Reich and whose economic development was regulated in Berlin.

Vološin, following Tiso's example but without Hitler's backing, proclaimed the Carpatho-Ukraine an independent republic on 14 March. It was now the turn of the Hungarians to move, fearing that if they did not seize Ruthenia it would be overrun by the Poles or Roumanians or both. Vološin's tiny republic never had a chance. It existed for precisely twenty-four hours. There was some shooting between the Hungarians and the Sič Guard before Khust fell but little organized resistance. By 17 March the Hungarians had occupied all Ruthenia, establishing at last a common frontier between Hungary and Poland. Fighting also broke out in the west of Ruthenia when the Hungarian army tried to advance to the Dukla Pass, which was held by Slovak units. Slovakia's German protectors peremptorily ordered the Hungarian column to halt only a few miles over the Ruthene border. The whole province of Ruthenia, which was in area slightly larger than the English county of Devon or half the size of the American state of Connecticut, was thereafter incorporated in Hungary as part of the Felvidék.

Although the destruction of the Czechoslovak State was not technically a breach of the Munich Agreement, since German troops had been 'invited' to assume the role of protectors, the events of March 1939 led to a reversal of British and French policy. Appeasement was abandoned in favour of a series of guarantees, liberally offered to states threatened with invasion by Germany or Italy but not always accepted. The Poles received assurances of support from London and Paris on 31 March but negotiations were also held with the Roumanians, whose representative in London believed that his country faced an imminent German invasion in the third week of March. Even when the threat failed to materialize, some members of the British foreign service continued to press for a united front of Balkan nations, bolstered up by the West and perhaps even guaranteed by Russia. It was a period of confused thought, both in Whitehall and the embassies abroad.

Yet that Easter a Balkan alliance system seemed momentarily a necessity. Mussolini, anxious for the sake of his personal prestige to achieve a spectacular success, occupied Albania on 7 April and incorporated it in the Italian kingdom a few days later, its former ruler (King Zog) passing hurriedly into exile and out of active politics. The loss of Albanian independence was in many ways a political technicality, since the country had been an Italian satellite state for over a decade. But Mussolini's move was interpreted in the West as evidence of an Axis forward policy; and Greece, as well as Roumania, was given a guarantee on 13 April. Subsequently, the Turks too accepted an Anglo-French guarantee but the Bulgars and Yugoslavs preferred to keep their hands free and were determined not to offend the Axis partners.

Italo-German solidarity was emphasized in May by the signature of the 'Pact of Steel,' a portentously worded political and military alliance; but it became clear in the early summer that the Germans, rather than the Italians, continued to pose the real threat to peace in Eastern Europe and that the principal region of contention was Poland. Hitler had always distrusted the Poles even though, until after his occupation of Prague, he maintained the illusion of good relations based upon the non-aggression pact of 1934. Even as late as January 1939 the Germans would have been prepared to cooperate with Poland provided that the Poles agreed to the transference of Danzig to the Reich (in return for certain rights in the port) and the granting to Germany of an extra-territorial passage across Pomorze to East Prussia. The Poles were also required to subscribe to the Anti-Comintern Pact, the agreement originally signed by Germany and Japan in 1936 as a gesture against Bolshevism with which Mussolini subsequently associated Italy in November 1937. But Beck, the Polish foreign minister, feared that acceptance of these terms would have made Poland a German pensionary; and nothing came of the German proposals.

There is no doubt that Beck exaggerated both his own statesmanship and the military strength of the Polish nation. Since Poland was the largest state in Eastern Europe he believed that he possessed a freedom of movement denied to other smaller powers. He thought in terms of a 'Third Europe' of Poland, Hungary, Roumania and Yugoslavia which would balance the partnership of Britain and France and the Axis alliance. When in Berlin he emphasized that the Third Europe was a barrier against Russian expansion; and when in London or Paris he explained it as a wall to contain Germany in the east. No one, except perhaps the Hungarians, took him seriously; but whereas Hitler sensed that the barrier was no more than a palissade, the British and French continued to be impressed by the Polish army.

Hitler was surprised by the British guarantee of the Polish State. Four days after it was announced he gave orders for preliminary planning to be undertaken by the High Command for a Polish campaign. Beck, visiting London, emphasized that he had come to negotiate a reciprocal treaty of alliance (which was, in fact, only signed on 25 August) although Chamberlain was doing all he could to persuade the Poles to act with moderation, especially over the Danzig problem. Hitler allowed himself to be convinced by the visit to London that there was an Anglo-French conspiracy to use Poland as a means for encircling Germany. He accelerated down the road to war. Serious military planning for the invasion of Poland began in earnest on 11 April and seventeen days later Hitler formally denounced the Germano-Polish Non-Aggression Pact. Press attacks on the Poles for their treatment of the German minority in Pomorze and Poznania mounted ominously day by day until the end of May. But throughout June and most of July there was an air of restraint in German public pronouncements. Little was seen of Hitler, and it began to appear that the whole episode had been a false alarm, a shock reaction to the occupation of Prague. The crisis flared up again at the end of July with Polish complaints at the treatment of customs-officers by Germans in Danzig; and throughout August the German press and radio carried examples of Polish intimidation of *Volksdeutschen* in the frontier districts.

Neither the British nor the French were able to render direct military assistance to the Poles in the event of war. Talks between General Gamelin, the chief of the French General Staff, and senior Polish staff-officers were held in Paris in the middle of May but they merely emphasized Poland's geographical isolation. The most Gamelin would concede was the promise of a diversionary offensive to be launched against Germany in the west on the seventeenth day of military operations. Clearly the only power capable of giving Poland effective support in a war with Germany was Soviet Russia.

Throughout the spring and early summer of 1939 desultory conversations were held in Moscow between representatives of Britain and France and the Russians. No progress was made towards an alliance: the Soviet Union wanted a reciprocal assurance of support whereas the British were hoping to secure a Russian unilateral pledge; and, even had the Russians been prepared to give an undertaking of military assistance, the Poles made it clear that they would not permit the Red Army to enter Galicia or the Vilna area in order to establish a front with the German enemy. It may be doubted if Chamberlain's government ever really wanted the Soviet Union as an ally; and, when Molotov succeeded Litvinov as Soviet foreign commissar on 3 May, it began to look as if the Russians certainly did not want any contact with the West. There was, after all, still a Franco-Soviet Pact in being and little enough was ever done to implement it. Each side profoundly distrusted the other. The only value of the talks was as a deterrent to Germany. But even this proved ineffective, for while the British and French press made the western approach to the Soviet Union public knowledge, private contacts between Russia and Germany made much greater progress. The last abortive meeting of the western negotiators with the Russians broke up on the morning of 21 August: that evening it was announced that the German foreign minister, Ribbentrop, had been invited to Moscow.

Ribbentrop and Molotov signed the Nazi-Soviet Pact on 23 August. Its published terms comprised pledges to refrain from mutual aggression and assurances of neutrality in case either Germany or Russia were involved in war. Like the non-aggression pact with Poland, which Hitler had denounced four months previously, its provisions were to be valid for ten years. Secret clauses prove the extent to which Russia and Germany were once again the real masters of Eastern Europe: the Soviet Union was to have a free hand to settle territorial problems in Finland, Estonia, eastern Poland and Bessarabia; but the Germans reserved the right to dispose of Lithuania – from whom in March they had already secured retrocession of the port of Memel – and the remainder of Poland, west of the rivers Narew, San and Vistula. The pact publicly isolated Poland while privately preparing the way for a fifth partition of the Polish State, although not necessarily for its total extinction.

The Nazi-Soviet Pact was a major diplomatic triumph for Germany. Hitler knew that he could now dismember Poland at will and he sought assistance in his forthcoming campaign only from the newest of his European clients, Slovakia. It is probable that he believed the pact would indicate to the British and French the folly of supporting Poland and when Chamberlain despatched a Swedish intermediary on a peace mission to Berlin he assumed, not unreasonably, that the first steps had been taken towards another Munich conference. His reactions to the sequence of events in the first week of September show that he was not anticipating a general European war, even though the Anglo-Polish Treaty of Mutual Assistance was finally signed only two days after Ribbentrop's agreement with Molotov. Mussolini duly proposed a conference eleven months to the day after the meeting which he had sponsored at Munich, and he continued to put forward proposals for mediation until 3 September. There seemed to him no reason why the problems of Danzig and the Polish Corridor should not be solved as the Sudeten Question had been settled in 1938. But this time Chamberlain remained at Westminster.

Mussolini had, as so often, misjudged the mood of the West; and, if Hitler thought of a localized war, he too had blundered or been misinformed. The Polish campaign began, without a declaration of war, at 4.45 in the morning of Friday, 1 September, with incidents on the outskirts of Danzig and a German advance across the frontiers into Pomorze and Poznania. Seventy minutes later the first German bombers appeared in the sky over Warsaw. On Sunday Britain and France honoured their obligations to Poland and surprised Europe, and themselves, by going to war over Danzig.

The invasion of Poland began on a Friday. By the following Tuesday evening the Polish defences had been shattered and their main armies in the field were menaced by German armoured columns wheeling in two massive pincer movements. The campaign was virtually over in eighteen days, although isolated Polish garrisons held out in Warsaw, Lvov and on the tip of the Hela peninsula, near Danzig. The Germans had made full use of their air superiority and of their tank formations, but they were assisted also by the disruptive activities of the German minority and by the outmoded Polish defensive strategy. The Polish army was spread thinly along hundreds of miles of frontier instead of being concentrated along the river barriers. On the night of 16 September the Russians informed the Polish government, which had fallen back on eastern Galicia, that the Red Army would occupy the White Russian and Ukrainian areas of Poland so as to afford their population a protection which the Polish State could no longer give. And on 17 September the Polish authorities crossed into Roumania, where they were interned. Western Poland was formally incorporated in the Greater German Reich on 19 October with the predominantly Polish areas administered by a 'General Government' based on Cracow. Polish territories east of the line of the rivers Narew, Bug and San were annexed by the Soviet Union.

The fate of Poland shocked the remaining independent states of Eastern Europe in three distinctive ways: they were appalled at the rapidity with which a comparatively large country had been militarily defeated; they were disturbed at the failure of Britain and France to render the Poles effective assistance, for the promised French offensive in the West became no more than a gentle probing towards the Saar; and they were thrown into a near-panic at the westward surge of the Red Army, with the evident connivance of the author of the Anti-Comintern Pact. Throughout the winter of 1939–40 it was this threat from Moscow which seemed most immediately to menace the general stability of the eastern marchlands. The Russians followed up their incorporation of eastern Poland in the Ukrainian and Byelo-Russian Soviet Republics by demanding bases in two of the Baltic States, Estonia and Latvia. There were complicated negotiations between Molotov and Ribbentrop over Lithuania, which had originally been assigned to the German sphere of influence but which was transferred to the Soviet sphere when the Germans extended their line in Poland to the banks of the Bug. The Russians ceded Vilna to Lithuania but insisted on military and naval bases in various parts of Lithuania. The Russians also sought concessions from the Finns, who rejected them. On 30 November 1939 Russia invaded Finland, without a declaration of war, but the Finns held out for fifteen weeks before surrendering the bases Stalin required. The long Finnish resistance won the admiration not only of the British and French but of countries more closely linked with the Germans, such as Italy and Hungary. The 'Winter War' with Finland also led the League of Nations to take its first decisive act for five years (and the last it was to make). The Soviet Union was solemnly expelled from membership in December 1939.

The League's anathema brought no relief to the Finns and only scant comfort to Russia's other western neighbours. Each of the states in south-eastern Europe took pains to make itself appear more indispensable to Germany, assuming that Hitler's veto would check any Russian threat to invade. The Yugoslavs were prepared to sell to Germany their total output of copper and virtually all their yield of lead and zinc in return for 100 Messerschmitt aircraft (which never came) and 370 guns from the Skoda arms-works, now under German management. The Roumanians had even more to offer: oil from Ploesti, maize and wheat from the Wallachian Plain; and Hitler was, indeed, determined to keep war away from Roumania, for he had no wish to see the oilfields wrecked by bombing or the wheatlands churned over by tank-tracks. In successive agreements signed in December 1939 and January 1940 the Roumanians made to Germany the most far-reaching economic concessions ever granted up to that date; and, though the Germans did not encourage the Roumanians to hope that Bessarabia might be held against Russian demands, Ribbentrop did dampen down revisionist sentiment in Hungary and Bulgaria. Boris, having little to offer Germany, exercised political caution, declining Turkish attempts to bring Bulgaria into the Balkan Entente, rejecting Russian feelers for an anti-Roumanian alliance, and appointing as prime minister in February 1940 the pro-German Bogdan Filov as successor to his faithful amanuensis, Kiosseivanov.

The Soviet menace hardened while the great battles were being fought in Belgium and France in the early summer of 1940. As the German tanks thrust through to the Channel, so the Russian press was reporting 'anti-Soviet activities' in Lithuania; and, as the armoured columns entered Paris, Stalin was advancing his frontier to the river Niemen. Latvia, Lithuania and Estonia were all compelled to accept Communist Front governments in the middle of June 1940; and each was admitted as a member republic of the Soviet Union in August.

In the last week of June the Russians tabled their demands on Roumania. Originally Molotov had sought, not merely the restitution of Bessarabia, but the cession of the former Habsburg Crownland, the Bukovina. The Germans, informed in advance of Molotov's intentions, protested at this enlargement of the Soviet sphere, for the Bukovina had not figured in the secret bargain struck by Ribbentrop and Molotov in the previous August. The Russians accordingly limited their requirement to Bessarabia and the northern Bukovina, where the population was predominantly Ukrainian. A twenty-four hour ultimatum was presented by the Soviet minister in Bucharest on 26 June. King Carol, whose speeches had so often resounded with warlike patriotism, considered resistance. The Germans advised acceptance and so did the Italians; the British could do nothing to help; and the French had themselves fallen from their pedestal. Carol gave way; and the Red Army reached the Pruth and the Danube.

It was, of course, intolerable for the Hungarians and Bulgars to watch the Roumanians handing territory over to the Soviet Union without conceding their revisionist claims. The Hungarians behaved correctly; they did not send an ultimatum to Bucharest. Teleki and Csáky merely presented Hungary's claims to the German and Italian Foreign Office, indicating that if Germany and Italy could not secure their demands in Transylvania by peaceful means the Hungarians would have to take it for themselves by force. Hitler found that King Carol was resolutely opposed to giving way over Transylvania, but that he was prepared to satisfy the Bulgars in the southern Dobrudja. At the urgent insistence of both Hitler and Mussolini the Roumanians and Hungarians agreed to hold conversations on the Transylvanian Question in August at Turnu-Severin. After three days the talks broke up, in some disorder. A week later, a second attempt was no more successful; and the Hungarians began to call up reservists. Hitler was furious, not least because the Russians were adopting a threatening attitude on the borders of Moldavia. Ten German divisions were hurriedly moved eastwards, for Hitler had no intention of permitting the Russians to reach the oilfields. At the same time, Ribbentrop and Ciano summoned the Hungarians and Roumanians to a conference in Vienna. But when the delegations arrived from Budapest and Bucharest they found that the Axis foreign ministers had decided to impose, rather than negotiate, an arbitral award. Rather more than two fifths of Transylvania was retroceded to Hungary by the 'Second Vienna Award' of 30 August 1940 with a population of over two and a half million, fifty-two per cent of whom were reckoned as Magyar in the subsequent census. The line of demarcation ran from north-west to south-east, giving the Hungarians such important towns as Kolozsvár (Cluj) and Nagyvarad (Oradea), but with Roumanian salients to the east of Kolozsvár where a German industrial concern, the Hermann Goering Works, controlled the methane gas deposits by grace of trade treaties already negotiated with the Roumanian government. Both Hungary and Roumania were required to sign agreements protecting their German minorities; the Hungarian protocol was a truly remarkable document, for it allowed the *Volksdeutschen* to enlist under German colours rather than carry out their military service in the Hungarian army.

The agreement with the Bulgars was signed at Craiova a few days later. It returned the southern Dobrudja, with its overwhelmingly Bulgarian population, to the Sofia government, thus at last rectifying the injustice of 1913. In the course of eleven weeks King Carol had lost for his people Bessarabia, the nothern Bukovina, almost half of Transylvania and the Southern Dobrudja. There was a violent reaction in Roumania, stimulated by Carol's old enemies in the Iron Guard. On 6 September Carol abdicated in favour of his son, Michael (who had already been titular sovereign, under a regency, from 1927 to 1930). Carol thereupon fled the country, as precipitately as he had returned ten years previously. An authoritarian regime, predominantly Iron Guardist in character, was set up under the leadership of General Ion Antonescu who decreed that, if Germany flourished under a Führer and Italy under a Duce, then Roumania should recognize him as the 'Conducator'.

The Germans decided that, rather than allow a protracted crisis to endanger their economic hold on Roumania, they would tighten their political and military grip on the country. Antonescu was informed at the end of September that Hitler had resolved to protect Roumania's industrial centres and oilfields with German troops. The Hungarians were asked to allow the passage of aircraft and infantry from the Reich to Roumania. By October six trains a day were carrying German troops eastwards through Hungary and a large German military mission established itself in Bucharest in the middle of the month. Roumania was left with little more independence than Slovakia.

Ironically the arrival of the Germans led to the final dissolution of the Guardists. The first three months of Antonescu's government saw bestial pogroms in the provinces and a number of atrocities in Bucharest itself. The Iron Guard murdered not only Jews, but many liberals and former supporters of King Carol. On 21 January 1941 they tried to overthrow Antonescu who had already sought to control their excesses. For three days the Roumanian army wrestled savagely with the Iron Guard fanatics while the Germans supported Antonescu. The Guard was virtually wiped out; and on 27 January the Conducator set up a new government, which was almost entirely military in composition. All political life ceased in the country for three years: Antonescu, the army and the Germans controlled the kingdom.

In the autumn of 1940, Germany, Italy and Japan concluded a portentously worded alliance pledging themselves to political cooperation, the 'Tripartite Pact'; and much of Ribbentrop's foreign policy in the following months was concerned with securing adherence by Germany's clients to this document. Hungary, Roumania and Slovakia all subscribed in the fourth week of November 1940. In Bulgaria King Boris characteristically procrastinated for as long as he dared, alleging when he visited Hitler that same month, that although he sympathized with those countries which sought to establish a New Order, he could not put his name to a pact which might push his Turkish neighbour into the arms of Germany's enemies. But, by the middle of January 1941, Hitler had become impatient with Boris, partly because the reports of his ambassador in Ankara convinced him that Turkey would not make any dangerous moves. On 8 February, a military agreement was signed between representatives of the German and Bulgarian General Staffs and on 1 March the Bulgars, too, adhered to the Tripartite Pact. The German Twelfth Army was invited to take up protective positions within Bulgaria on the following day. Of the six independent states of East-Central Europe in the inter-war period, only Yugoslavia had not as yet been swamped by the German tide.

The Italians posed a more serious threat to Yugoslavia than the Germans. Italo-Yugoslav friendship had not survived the fall of Stojadinović and, when Mussolini annexed Albania at Easter 1939, Italian troops mounted guard along more than 300 miles of Yugoslavia's frontiers, in the south as well as the north-west. The Italian fleet menaced the long Dalmatian coastline and Yugoslav agents knew that Mussolini was still encouraging Pavelić's *Ustaše* and other Croatian separatist movements. And for many months in 1940 it was uncertain whether the Italians would seek a prestige victory at the expense of Greece, as Foreign Minister Ciano wanted, or of Yugoslavia, as Mussolini himself preferred. On 28 October 1940 Ciano had his way: an ill-prepared Italian army moved against Greece.

The Italian attack on Greece raised acute problems for Yugoslavia. The Greeks were old allies and the port of Salonika had served for more than twenty years as the principal outlet to the sea of the specifically Serbian areas of the kingdom. The Yugoslavs enjoyed special treaty rights in Salonika; if the city fell into Italian hands, Mussolini's stranglehold would tighten. There were some senior members of the Yugoslav High Command – including General Milan Nedić, the minister of war – who wished to invade Greek Macedonia and seize Salonika before the Italians could reach the port. Prince Paul, however, would have nothing to do with this project and such Yugoslavs as heard of it tended to regard it as a virtual act of treason, including the then minister in Berlin, Ivo Andrić (who, abandoning diplomacy for literature, was to gain a Nobel Prize in 1961). The immediate threat to Salonika receded as the Greeks repulsed the initial Italian attack and subsequently thrust the invaders back into the grim snows of Albania. But Italy's embarrassment seemed to Hitler to emphasize the need for Yugoslav collaboration within the Axis camp; and the bait with which he hoped to tempt the Cvetković government was the prospect of securing Salonika. On 27 November, just three days after Roumania had signed the Tripartite Pact, Hitler received Aleksander Cincar-Marković, the Yugoslav foreign minister, at Berchtesgaden and urged him to commit Yugoslavia to the new European order.

The Cvetković-Maček government was heart and soul neutralist to a man; and so, for that matter, was Prince Paul although his personal sympathies were with the West. But the government was unpopular with many sections of the Yugoslav public: with the students of Belgrade University, who had rioted at the end of 1939; with the Serbian army veterans over whose mental horizon loomed the shadow of Kajmakcalan; with the Orthodox Patriarch who disliked the Sporazum and who, incongruously, viewed the Axis as a weapon of political Catholicism; and with the small businessmen of Serbia, who cared little for foreign politics, but who blamed Cvetković for 'selling out' to the Slovenes and Croats. Zagreb and Ljubljana were reasonably content but rumours of a possible *putsch* swept through Belgrade: they were noted by the diplomatic corps and reported to London and Washington and Berlin. The Cvetković government had to move with caution.

Cincar-Marković, though hardly an inspiring figure, was an adroit diplomat, as evasive as King Boris in neighbouring Sofia. For three months he played for time. Partly as an act of re-insurance and partly to placate Hitler he induced the government to accept an offer from Hungary for a non-aggression pact. Nothing was said in the agreement of Hungary's revisionist claims against Yugoslavia, although it was understood during the negotiations that these might be raised at a later date.

With excessive optimism or anticipatory irony, Cincar-Marković insisted that the principal clause in the treaty should read: 'Constant peace and eternal friendship shall prevail between the Kingdom of Hungary and the Kingdom of Yugoslavia'; and it was in this form that the pact was duly signed on 12 December 1940. The Yugoslavs hoped that the agreement would serve as a substitute for adhering to the formal Tripartite Pact and would therefore allow them some freedom to negotiate with Britain and the United States and even with the Soviet Union, for they had been in touch with Moscow for several months. But the pact was interpreted abroad as a sign that the Yugoslavs were creeping into the Axis camp, although Hitler remained anxious for a more precise declaration of Yugoslav support.

Both the British and the Americans encouraged Prince Paul to take a firm stand against Hitler; he received personal messages from Churchill, Roosevelt and King George VI. The Yugoslavs were not unimpressed by these attentions and sought definite pledges of support. The British, however, had little to spare from their commitments in Africa and the Americans could promise only arms at some future date. With good reason Prince Paul complained to the American minister, Arthur Bliss Lane: 'You big nations are hard. You talk of our honour but you are far away.' And, as Bulgaria fell into line, the Germans increased their pressure to induce Yugoslavia to sign the Tripartite Pact. Cvetković and Cincar-Marković were summoned to meet Hitler in Salzburg on 14 February and Prince Paul made the journey to Berchtesgaden two and a half weeks later. He returned to Belgrade on 5 March convinced that Yugoslavia must accept the German terms or face an invasion; and, unless the Allies could give military assistance, he was certain that Yugoslavia would be overrun within a fortnight.

There were a number of contacts that March between the Yugoslavs and the British, for neither Prince Paul nor Cvetković wished their country to slip into the clutch of the Germans. The most curious of these negotiations concerned the ex-premier Stojadinović. Suspecting a conspiracy aimed at bringing to power a political leader favourable to the Axis, the Cvetković government arranged to have Stojadinović escorted across the frontier into Greece where he was arrested by British representatives and subsequently interned in Mauritius. Other contacts were more orthodox but less successful. Secret military talks were held in Athens between a senior Yugoslav staff officer and British and Greek commanders; and in Split Maček himself had conversations with a British spokesman at the home of Mestrović, the great sculptor who had championed the South Slav ideal even before the First World War. The Allies, however, made it clear that there was no hope of sending an expeditionary force up the Vardar before it was cut by the Germans;

all they could propose was an invasion of Albania, where there were stocks of Italian arms lightly defended.

On 19 March the Germans informed the Yugoslavs that they had five days in which to sign the pact or accept the consequences. There were agonizing councils in the regent's palace outside Belgrade. Reluctantly it was decided to sign the pact, though three members of the government resigned in protest. Fearing the temper of the capital, Cvetković and Cincar-Marković slunk away to Vienna from a suburban railway-station on the evening of 24 March. Next day they signed the pact at a ceremony in the Belvedere Palace: Hitler, who was not the most sensitive of men, complained that the atmosphere was funereal.

British agents had for several weeks been in touch with dissident factions in Belgrade, particularly among the members of the Reserve Officers Club. On the night of 26 March a broadcast was made in the overseas service of the BBC by a member of Churchill's government, Leo Amery, in which he appealed specifically to the Serbs 'to keep the national spirit alive'. A few hours later, at 2.20 in the morning of 27 March, the Belgrade garrison and the air force commanders in neighbouring Zemun rose in revolt. By dawn the radio was proclaiming the end of Prince Paul's regency and the resignation of the government. The prince, who was at the time in Zagreb, returned to the capital and after formally surrendering his powers followed Stojadinović into exile and British internment.

The Belgrade coup, a 'lightning flash illuminating a dark background' as the *New York Times* called it, was planned and led by General Bora Mirković; but the new government was headed by his senior commander in the air force, General Dušan Simović (who as a Colonel in 1918 had led the Serbian troops into Slovenia). There was considerable rejoicing in the squares and streets of Belgrade, for the Serbian people had never understood Prince Paul's devious politics and had distrusted Cvetković and his colleagues. They were also far more obstinately independent than their eastern and northern neighbours and had resented the bullying and hectoring technique of the Germans (who, for example, had sought to intimidate the people of Belgrade by a special gala performance of the propaganda film, *Victory in the West*). The mass of the people were, however, more resolute than Simović and his colleagues. The new government declared its acceptance of all Yugoslavia's foreign commitments; it denied any desire to change the country's relationship with the Axis partners. Privately Simović made it clear to the British that he could not accept a visit from Eden, the foreign secretary, who was then in Athens. The chief of the Imperial General Staff did, indeed, fly secretly to Belgrade but on his return he was unable to give Churchill any assurance of Yugoslav cooperation.

Hitler refused to believe the first reports of the Belgrade coup. When the news was confirmed, he became intensely angry and no protestations of friendship from the Simović government could save the Yugoslavs from his wrath: he ordered 'the destruction of Yugoslavia militarily and as a national unit'. The German General Staff was already prepared to march into Greece early in April and rescue the Italians from their embarrassing series of military reversals. Preparations for the Balkan campaign were hastily modified, and less than fifteen hours after Mirković's men had made the first moves, Hitler signed a general plan of operations against Yugoslavia and Greece. The Italian, Hungarian and Bulgarian governments were invited to satisfy their territorial ambitions and it was assumed that the pliant Roumanian Kingdom would also serve as a base for the German invaders.

The Hungarians proved less cooperative than Hitler had expected. Horthy at first welcomed the German proposal, believing that it was a way to secure a seaboard for Hungary, one of his cherished personal ambitions. But Teleki, who had always believed in contact with the British, sought to avoid war by pointing out to the regent that military action would be contrary to the 'Friendship Pact' which he had signed four months before. A Ministerial Council agreed that the Hungarian army would advance into the Voivodina only if Yugoslavia disintegrated or if the Magyar minority was in danger. It was, however, difficult to hold back the Hungarian General Staff; and in the small hours of 3 April Teleki, seeing that the army leaders were pushing him into a disastrous war, shot himself rather than accept such a reversal of policy. 'Out of cowardice, we have allied ourselves with scoundrels,' he wrote in a last message to Horthy. His death saved his honour but not Yugoslavia, nor ultimately Hungary.

German divebombers struck at Belgrade out of a lavender blue sky early on 6 April. There was no declaration of war, merely wave after wave of Stukas flying in across the plains beyond the Danube. And while bombs fell on the city for two days with only brief intermissions, the German Twelfth Army thrust westwards from Bulgaria on Skopje while armoured columns struck southwards towards Salonika and the heart of Greece. On 8 April two more German divisions and a Bulgarian division headed across the frontier on Niš and Belgrade itself; and on the next day the main German Second Army entered Slovenia from southern Austria and Croatia from the Hungarian plain. Yet another German corps crossed the Bánát from Temesvár on 11 April, the day on which the Italians and Hungarians decided that they, too, could move forward. After a campaign lasting less than a week the invading columns converged on Belgrade, which passed formally under German control on 13 April. Organized resistance was virtually over. Four days later the unfortunate Cincar-Marković, discovered as a refugee in Bosnia, was flown back to Belgrade by the Germans to add his signature to that of a captured general on an armistice agreement. In German eyes he was a representative of the last legal Yugoslav government; it was only three and a half weeks since he had put his name to another document in the Führer's presence in Vienna.

It was a strange campaign in which less than 170 Germans died in battle and a quarter of a million Yugoslav soldiers passed into prison-camps. On paper the Yugoslavs had possessed twenty-eight infantry and three cavalry divisions, but when the Germans attacked, they were spread out along more than 1,000 miles of land-frontier. Only five infantry and two cavalry divisions participated in the fighting. The Yugoslav defeat was as much political as military. The kingdom fell apart. The German-speaking minority had seized key positions in the Yugoslav rear with arms smuggled across the frontier; they secured the centre of Maribor and the principal bridges across the Drava. Three Croatian regiments deserted without firing a shot and some units openly turned against the Serbs. The *Ustaše* followed in the wake of the invaders and on 10 April proclaimed Croatia a 'free and independent state' in German-held Zagreb. Six days later Ante Pavelić, the leader (*Poglavnik*) of the *Ustaše*, nominated himself as prime minister of the 'first Croatian national government'. Maček, refusing to seek flight with the other Yugoslav leaders, called on the Croats to accept the new dispensation, although he withdrew from political life himself. The young King Peter II, having shown much of his father's and grandfather's courage in the disastrous days of battle, left an exiled government to quarrel bitterly in Cairo and that autumn became an undergraduate at Cambridge, studying international law.

By the end of April Hitler had decreed the partition of the Yugoslav lands. Germany annexed northern Slovenia, the southern third passing to Italy. Mussolini also acquired Montenegro, the Kosovo region and the Dalmation sea-coast southwards from Split. *Ustaše* Croatia became a kingdom under the Italian Duke of Spoleto (who never got round to visiting his domains); it included Bosnia, Herzegovina and small sections of the coast. Hungary had hoped for an autonomous Croatia and a strip of Dalmatian littoral – and believed it had been promised to her by Hitler – but she received only a small area in the north-west of Croatia and half of the Voivodina. The Bánát was disputed by Hungary and Roumania and remained under German administration. Bulgaria occupied most of Yugoslav Macedonia but the Germans refused to permit Boris to annex it outright. The rump of Serbia remained under strict control by the German army although a shadow 'government' was set up in Belgrade in the following August, with General Nedić, the former minister of war, as its nominal head, and with the Serbian Nazi Ljotić as the chief colla-borator. Yugoslavia had, indeed, been destroyed 'as a national unit'.

By 23 April Greece, too, had passed under Axis occupation and the swastika flag flew across Eastern Europe from the Acropolis of Athens to the port of Memel. Since the entry of Hitler's troops into Roumania in October 1940 the German army had mounted guard along a frontier of more than nine hundred miles with the Soviet Union, and the unusual amity of the Nazi-Soviet Pact wore thinner and thinner during the winter months. The first rift came as early as September with the continued Russian threats to Roumania, but there was a slight improvement in the following weeks and Molotov was received with some warmth by Ribbentrop in Berlin during November even though the Germans were, at the time, already strengthening their position in another of Russia's neighbours, Finland.

Hitler regarded an eventual war between Germany and the USSR as inevitable; he wished it to be fought at his timing rather than at Stalin's. Initial planning for a German offensive in the east began immediately after Molotov's return from Berlin to Moscow. The famous 'Decree No. 21,' a directive 'to crush Soviet Russia in a quick campaign' was signed by Hitler on 18 December and secret preparations for 'Operation Barbarossa' (as the war with Russia was called) were pressed steadily forward in the following three months. By the end of February 1941 there were 680,000 German soldiers and airmen in Roumania alone. When, in the first week of March, German troops crossed into Bulgaria as well, Molotov protested at the way in which Hitler was extending Germany's hold on the Black Sea coast. The Russians did not, however, believe that war would come to them so soon.

Inevitably, a worsening of German-Soviet relations had repercussions on all the other states of the area. To counter the German political initiative, the Russians sought to strengthen their links with Hungary and Yugoslavia in the early months of 1941. The Hungarian approach never went much farther than the formal return to Horthy's frontier-guards in Ruthenia of more than fifty flags captured by Tsar Nicholas I at Vilagos in 1849. But the Yugoslav contacts were more serious. Russia ostentatiously courted both the Cvetković and Simović governments. Less than five hours before the Germans began the destruction of Belgrade, a Non-Aggression Pact was signed in Moscow between the Soviet Union and Yugoslavia. In writing to Mussolini, Hitler even used the threat of Soviet interference in Yugoslav affairs as a pretext for his Balkan campaign and it is possible that he genuinely feared a Russo-Yugoslav military convention, an object for which Simović was certainly working though Stalin was far too cautious to commit himself by such a gesture.

In reality there was nothing which Russia could do, or refrain from doing, which would have altered Hitler's decision to invade. After

Yugoslavia's rapid collapse Stalin belatedly made a series of amicable gestures to the Germans. They had no effect. The Belgrade coup had postponed Operation Barbarossa, which was originally fixed for the middle of May. At an army conference on 30 April it was decided that the invasion should begin on 22 June. Privately Hitler said that he expected Moscow to be in German hands by 15 August and that Russia would sue for peace before October. The German satellites were assigned appropriate roles in the crisis. Antonescu was told on 23 May that Germany was preparing 'to defend Roumania against a possible attack by Russia'; and on 12 June he was summoned to Munich and informed of Hitler's plans. The Roumanians began a partial mobilization, determined to use the new campaign as a means of recovering the Northern Bukovina and Bessarabia. Other pieces fell rapidly into place. The Slovaks were alerted, for Tiso could always be relied upon to despatch his limited forces at a fitting distance behind the German tanks. No cooperation was sought from Bulgaria, apart from the concentration of troops along the Turkish frontier in case the Ankara government should seek to take advantage of Germany's preoccupation with the Red Army to march into the Balkan lands.

As so often, Hungary posed a problem. Hitler had no wish for her participation, partly because of the low quality of the Hungarian army – an armoured column entering the Voivodina that April had run out of petrol after covering only thirty miles – and partly because he distrusted Hungarian security plans. A group of German generals and most of the Hungarian General Staff were anxious for Hungary to enter the war. Teleki's successor as prime minister, László Bárdossy, wanted to have the best of both worlds, preferably without actually fighting. As a compromise to the military party, it was agreed by a Ministerial Council that if Hitler wanted Hungary to march, she would accept his request. But all that Hitler asked was that Hungary should protect the line of the Carpathians against a Russian counter-offensive at the German flank.

Russia was invaded on 22 June. Hitler defended his action by maintaining that he had forestalled a treacherous attack by the Red Army on an unsuspecting Germany although there is no evidence that anything so positive had entered Stalin's mind. Italy, Roumania and Slovakia duly declared war and Finland formally allied with Germany on 24 June. The Hungarians wavered until 26 June when planes, alleged to be Russian, bombed the town of Košiče and a railway-line in the vicinity, and Bárdossy used this incident as an excuse for announcing that Hungary considered herself to be at war with the Soviet Union. No one knows to this day the identity of the planes that bombed Košiče: they appeared to be German in design and to carry Axis markings; and it is possible that they were Slovak rather than Russian. The question is largely academic in character; for Hungary could not long have stood out of a crusade against Bolshevism, especially one in which Tiso and Antonescu were on the side of the righteous. The German tide was in flood across the limitless steppe-land; the small states of Eastern Europe were no more than its flotsam.

I2
Divided Loyalties

'Barbarossa' was a military operation without precedent in the history of warfare. Nine million men were engaged in battle that summer along a land front which was more than eleven hundred miles in extent. In the north, the Finns, assured this time of foreign support, declared war on the Soviet Union on 24 June and 'resumed' the campaign of 1939–40. Along the main sector of the front, from the Gulf of Finland to the Black Sea, the opposing forces were mobilized in what was, on paper, equal strength, with 160 divisions on either side. The northern group of German troops was commanded by von Leeb and had Leningrad as its main objective. The centre group under von Bock struck towards Smolensk and Moscow along the route followed by Napoleon in 1812; it captured three hundred thousand prisoners in the first two and a half weeks of the campaign. The southern group, which included a large Roumanian contingent, an Italian army corps and a Slovak expeditionary force was commanded by von Rundstedt; it headed for Kiev and the Don basin. After reeling under the initial surprise impact of the assault, the Red Army was also organized in three main groups: Voroshilov opposed Leeb; Timoshenko opposed Bock and Budenny opposed Rundstedt. By the autumn it was clear that, though the Russians had sustained heavier casualties than in any previous war, their tenacity and ruthlessness were denying the German armoured columns a decisive triumph.

As in 1812 the Russian commanders determined to take advantage of the great extent of their homeland in order to entice the invaders to destruction. Their strategy was to retreat across the steppe, 'scorching the earth' as they fell back, but rallying in defence of major towns or railway junctions so as to delay the enemy's advance and inflict heavy casualties without counting the cost to themselves. They were, however, prepared to concentrate on retaining the principal cities for purposes of prestige until the frost and snow came to their rescue. Hitler was deluded by this policy, as Napoleon had been before him. On 3 October the Führer announced in Berlin that 'the enemy is clearly broken and will never rise again.' At precisely the same moment in Napoleon's campaign, the Emperor had informed his entourage that the Russians would sue for peace within a fortnight. On 8 December – it was the anniversary of the day on which the Grand Army crawled back into Vilna – Hitler declared the campaign of 1941 officially at an end. He had achieved on paper far more than Napoleon, for his troops were over six hundred miles east of the Russian frontier and Kiev, Smolensk, Kalinin and Orel were in German hands. But the Red Flag still flew over Leningrad and Moscow and Sebastopol, the war had not as yet reached the Volga, and the invaders had been thrown back from the lower Don. The winter proved grimmer than any within living memory and the Russians gave the enemy no more respite than their ancestors had done in 1812. For the first time a German *blitzkrieg* had failed to bring an enemy to his knees and it is significant that Hitler took pains to explain to his foreign visitors in November that the concept of a lightning-war was invented by Anglo-Jewish propagandists to denigrate German triumphs. By Christmas there were rumours in both Rome and Tokyo of peace overtures from Germany to Russia. It is hardly surprising that doubts over the infallibility of German arms began to spread among Hitler's eastern allies. The unity of the Tripartite Pact barely survived the first Russian winter; it was to be broken beyond repair on the great arc of the Volga before the second spring.

At first the dramatic canvas of 'Barbarossa' effectively concealed the different attitudes to the war of Hitler's three principal partners in the east, Bulgaria, Hungary and Roumania. Of the three, Bulgaria gave Germany least assistance and least trouble, apart from friction with her Italian ally over delineation of the Albanian-Macedonian frontier. On the other hand, the hostility between Hungary and Roumania constantly disturbed the German High Command, even at times threatening a possible war within a war.

King Boris was convinced that his country had nothing to gain and everything to lose from a Russian campaign. He was prepared to congratulate Hitler on his successes against the Bolsheviks and to afford the German army and navy use of Bulgarian bases, but he explained frequently and with some skill that the traditional Panslavism of the Bulgarian people made it undesirable for there to be an open conflict of arms with the Soviet State. Russian diplomats remained in Sofia and enjoyed considerable freedom of movement, despite the presence of German units in the country. Boris's premier, the archaeologist Bogdan Filov, assured the German minister on 25 September that Bulgaria would be pleased if all contact with Russia came to an end but 'she would not do the Russians the favour of breaking off relations of her own accord.' This dubious argument seems, for the moment, to have satisfied the Germans; Bulgarian non-belligerency kept the army intact for occupation duties in the Balkans and provided Hitler with a possible means of direct communication with the Soviet authorities should they sue for peace. Boris, for his part, demonstrated his loyalty to the Tripartite Pact by readily declaring war on both Britain and the United States in December 1941, an act which exposed his countrymen to little immediate inconvenience.

When Hungary went to war with Russia it was assumed in Budapest that the campaign would be over in a matter of weeks. A Mobile Corps of twenty-four thousand men joined in the initial advance to the Dnieper. It fought with courage, suffered comparatively light casualties and, to the consternation of both Horthy and the General Staff, succeeded in having most of its equipment destroyed within two months of the start of the operations. The regent was anxious for his men to be returned to Hungary before the winter and he was supported by Bárdossy, his prime minister. On 6 September he dismissed the pro-German Chief of Staff and appointed as his successor General Ferencz Szombathelyi, an outspoken man who failed to see the value for Hungary of losing her best troops in the endless Russian plains. No sooner had Szombathelyi taken office than he set off, with Horthy and Bárdossy, for a meeting with Hitler at field headquarters in East Prussia. As Halder, the Chief of the German Army General Staff, wrote at the time, Szombathelyi 'takes the selfish view that what matters is to preserve Hungary's forces in consideration of her task in the Balkans.' Horthy himself asked for the return of the Mobile Corps to the homeland and it was apparently agreed that the troops should be withdrawn at the end of the current operations although the Germans assumed that Hungary would furnish replacements. There followed long negotiations between the two military staffs, the practical consequence of which was the total disappearance of all Hungarian units from the Russian front although a token force remained on occupation duty in the Ukraine. When Hitler next received Bárdossy at headquarters (on 28 November) he spoke to him rather pointedly of the splendid military record of the Finns. Hungary had fallen from grace.

The Roumanians participated in the early battles with enthusiasm. Antonescu despatched thirty divisions to the front, anxious to recover Bessarabia and the northern Bukovina. Both provinces were in Roumanian hands by the end of July. On 5 August the Roumanians cut off the great seaport of Odessa although it was not until 16 October that, with German support, they were able to overcome stubborn Russian resistance in the city. The Conducator himself bathed in the reflected glory of Roumanian arms: Hitler personally awarded him the Knight's Cross on 6 August, adding to it for good measure the Iron Cross, first and second class; King Michael elevated him to the rank of marshal on 21 August; and when later in October he annexed the south-western Ukraine, he was pleased to decree that Odessa should henceforth be known as 'Antonescu' in his honour.

There were, however, already signs of disaffection in Roumania. Public support for the war had come at first not only from Antonescu and his entourage but from the old leaders of the Liberals and Peasants, Constantin Bratianu and Iuliu Maniu. It was assumed that if Roumania proved herself a more reliable ally than Hungary, Hitler would revise the second Vienna Award and give back northern Transylvania. The Roumanian people did not hide their feelings. On 8 November there was a victory parade in Bucharest at which Field Marshal Keitel represented the German High Command. As the Roumanian troops marched past the Triumphal Arch, a section of the crowd began to chant, 'Give us back Transylvania.' Sebastopol, the next objective of German strategy, meant little to the Roumanians; Cluj was the prize they sought.

Tension between Hungary and Roumania mounted in the last weeks of 1941 over both Transylvania and the Bánát. The Germans and Italians endeavoured to calm the two sides and at least prevented an open clash, although Antonescu insisted that Hungarian and Roumanian troops should never be employed side by side in the Russian campaign 'in order to avoid incidents.' By the beginning of 1942 influential groups in Bucharest were as anxious as their Hungarian rivals for disengagement in Russia. In January Maniu and Bratianu sent a joint letter to the Conducator complaining that 'the country is suffering a long and continuous haemorrhage' and urging him 'to withdraw troops from Russia.' Significantly they asked Antonescu if he had any guarantee from Hitler that 'lost Transylvania' would be restored to Roumania in the peace settlement.

Antonescu sought to impress Roumania's case on Hitler and Ribbentrop by personal visits in both February and March 1942. He was still one of the Führer's favourite clients, lauded for his 'fanatical nationalism' and so efficient in rounding up Jews that it was necessary to urge him to temper his zeal because of the harm anti-semitism was doing to the German-controlled Roumanian economy. But nothing would induce the Germans to re-open the Transylvanian Question, not even the presentation of a high Roumanian order of chivalry to the Reich foreign minister. As Roumanian outbursts against Hungary became louder and more frequent, the High Command seriously considered placing Transylvania under German protection. The Hungaro-Roumanian frontier was partly closed in April 1942, a curious circumstance for two nominally allied countries in the crusade against Bolshevism. There was even a momentary echo of the Little Entente, for the Roumanians induced the Slovaks and Croats to put pressure on Hungary, though with little effect. In both Berne and Lisbon the diplomats of Roumania and Hungary indulged in a flurry of conspiratorial excitement, secretly denouncing each other to the German Intelligence Service for contacts with the Western Allies – accusations not entirely groundless. It was hardly surprising if the Germans found their partners exasperating.

Yet, tiresome though they were, Hitler needed the cooperation of both Hungary and Roumania. He required their cereals and their petroleum (for the Hungarians, too, were developing oilfields although Roumania's output was four times as great). Above all, as the Russian winter took its toll of the German army, Hitler needed manpower for the summer campaign of 1942. Both countries were required to contribute substantially, despite the growing unpopularity of the war in the cities and in the countryside. In June the Roumanian army suffered heavy casualties in the Crimea; in July the Hungarians met a grim resistance along the river Don. Worse was to follow. Fifteen Roumanian divisions participated in the thrust to the Volga and shared, with the German Sixth Army, the privations and defeat of Stalingrad in January 1943. And in the same month the Hungarian army suffered what was proportionally an even greater disaster at Voronezh, losing half of the country's trained soldiers and almost all of its tanks and modern equipment.

Stalingrad and Voronezh were catastrophes of such magnitude that both countries were forced to retire from active participation in the campaign within Russia. At the same time they abandoned their own quarrel. Horthy's prime minister Miklós Kállay (who had replaced Bárdossy in March 1942) assumed that Germany would be defeated and began to foster links with the British and Americans in the hope that Hungary could be saved from an eventual Russian invasion. Antonescu and other Roumanian groups made contact with the West in a similar effort to save what they had gained from the Russians. By the summer of 1943 the main pillars of Hitler's Empire in the East were beginning to crumble. It could not then be seen that they would take so long to fall to the ground.

The smaller Axis satellites had not, as yet, suffered so heavily from the Russian campaign but they, too, were becoming disillusioned with the New Order by the first months of 1943. The earliest of these creations, the 'Protectorate of Bohemia and Moravia,' was indeed, never reconciled to totalitarian rule; for, though the protectorate was technically autonomous and preserved the fiction of an administration until the end of the war, all Czech resources were unscrupulously exploited by the nominated representatives of the Reich, K. H. Frank (the former Sudeten-German demagogue) and the notorious SS leader, Reinhard Heydrich. The war with Russia completed the alienation of the Czech peoples. The Germans even found it necessary to execute their puppet head of government,

General Elias, for alleged contacts with exiles in London. And when Heydrich was assassinated in the early summer of 1942 the subsequent reign of terror surpassed all previous repressive measures of the Nazi authorities; nearly 1,300 Czechs were executed in seven weeks and two whole villages (Lidice and Ležaky) were wiped out. No attempts were made in the last two years of the war to conceal Hitler's decision to eliminate the Czechs as a nation; and, despite the formal existence of the 'Protectorate,' they were treated as badly as the Poles, over whom Hitler had never created a substitute native government.

By contrast, conditions in the neighbouring Protectorate of Slovakia were remarkably good. Repressive laws were laxly administered in the first years of the war. Food was plentiful outside the towns and not difficult to obtain inside them on the black market. Communications were improved by the German army, for strategic reasons; and industry, so long neglected, was developed as never before, although three-quarters of Slovakia's trade was with the Reich. But during 1942 the Germans began to make heavier demands on Tiso and his ministers for Slovak labour, and by the spring of 1943 a quarter of a million Slovaks were working in the Reich as inferior industrial animals. Almost as many Slovaks were serving in the armies on the Russian front, although at first their lack of military training and their suspected Panslav sympathies kept them on garrison duties well behind the lines. Resentment at German exploitation, anger at the Tiso government for going to war with the United States (the earthly paradise for so many Slovak families in the past) and a shrewd conviction that the disaster of Stalingrad would prove a mortal wound to Hitler's system – all these motives convinced the Slovak people that Tiso's protectorate would not long survive. In the summer of 1943 Slovak patriots with little love for the Czechs of the old republic began to put out feelers to the United States and even to the exiled Beneš. At the same time the Slovak hierarchy, which had for so long served as a spiritual power house for Tiso and his followers, began to take a firm stand against Jewish persecution. There was not, as yet, any strong resistance movement in Slovakia but the popularity of Tiso, which had been high in the prosperous days of 1940–41, was on the wane.

If Slovakia was to Germany the 'model protectorate' of the New Order, the Independent State of Croatia seemed a political shambles for which most of Hitler's civil and military officials felt nothing but contempt. The Ustaše State was organized by its Poglavnik, Ante Pavelić, on the fascist model but it lacked the veneer of efficiency with which the Duce's creation had deluded foreign observers for many years. As early as 9 July 1941 General Glaise von Horstenau, the old Austrian Nazi who commanded the German troops in Croatia, complained to Pavelić at the excesses committed by the Ustaše against the Serbian minority; and there were other protests at these 'intolerable incidents,' although the German military authorities felt unable to intervene since, as Glaise wrote back to Berlin, 'Croatia was an independent state belonging to Italy's sphere of influence.' Massacres of Serbs and Jews and the forceful conversion of members of the Orthodox Church to Catholicism continued despite the German protests. The only beneficiaries of *Ustaše* rule were the Muslims of Bosnia-Herzegovina whom Pavelić considered reliable allies against the Jews and Orthodox. They were rewarded by the construction in Zagreb of a mosque although it is difficult to see for whom it was intended as a place of worship, for the nearest Muslim community was more than seventy miles away.

Ustaše sadism and maladministration prevented Pavelić from winning any of the popularity which Tiso enjoyed for a time in Slovakia. In the late summer of 1942 the peasants were especially infuriated by a decree of the *Poglavnik* peremptorily requisitioning the harvest of that year. Although bureaucratic corruption was hardly alien to Croatia, Pavelić's officials sank to a record level of venality. Even his own minister of defence, General Slavko Kvaternik (whose family had served in the Habsburg armies for generations), complained to the Germans of Pavelić's incompetence, but an attempt in October to oust Pavelić in his favour was countered by the Italians, who bitterly resented all German influence in Zagreb. Kvaternik was retired to Slovakia and Pavelić re-organized his government. It made little difference. By the spring of 1943 so much of Croatia was in the hands of resistance groups that the *Poglavniks'* authority barely extended to the outer suburbs of Zagreb itself. Yet ironically, as the war dragged on, Pavelić became essential to the Germans; for most of his political colleagues sought contacts with the Western Allies, posing as champions of Christendom against the Bolshevik hordes. It was a role which convinced no one; and the Roman Catholic Church, which had at first supported Pavelić, became lukewarm and belatedly critical of his methods.

The other areas of Yugoslavia never achieved the same degree of nominal independence as Croatia. Hitler would not admit the existence of a Slovene nationality and no attempt was made to create a puppet regime in Ljubljana, although in 1943 the Germans allowed General Rupnik, one of the few Slovenes to have held a high command in the Yugoslav army, to organize a local militia for action against the partisans. In Serbia a rump government was established by the local German military authorities without reference to the Foreign Ministry in Berlin; and when, at the start of September 1941, Ribbentrop accepted the need for a specifically Serbian administration to restore order, he administered a sharp rebuke to his representatives in Belgrade for allowing the army such a free hand. Subsequently Nedić's 'Government of National Salvation' was permitted to raise a small auxiliary force, but Berlin continued to regard the revival of political life in Serbia with misgiving, fearing that the Nedić administration would, in Ribbentrop's words, 'turn against Germany in its mental attitude and conduct.' It was a just suspicion, for Nedić remained at heart a narrowly Serbian patriot; but, like so many of his generation, he preferred to collaborate with the old enemy rather than see the society in which he lived succumb to communism.

The entry of the Soviet Union into the war posed major problems of policy for the members of the anti-German coalition. Britain's position was clear enough; for, eighteen hours after the German guns opened up on the eastern front, Churchill declared uncompromisingly, 'Any State who fights Nazism will have our aid . . . . We shall give whatever help we can to Russia.' It was, however, difficult for the spokesmen of the smaller nations of Eastern Europe to see the situation in such simple terms. Old quarrels, suspicions and disappointments made the governments-in-exile distrust their newly found Soviet ally. Each of the governments was seeking to organize the resources of its nationals who had sought refuge abroad or who were already living in other lands when their country was attacked; and each also claimed the allegiance of its compatriots under enemy occupation. From midsummer 1941 the exiles found that, while there was a broadening of the scope of revolt in the homeland, its character was changed by a social revolution antipathetic to many of the old political leaders. Moreover, the authority of the refugee governments was increasingly challenged by new committees established by the patriot insurgents themselves or by communists who had sought sanctuary in the Soviet Union. In time, these developments affected the future policy towards Eastern Europe of the greater allies, Britain and the United States.

The most intractable problems concerned the future of Poland. The rift between Poles and Russians ran as deeply in 1941 as at any time in the nineteenth century. To the Polish exiles the Soviet Union was no less a despoiler of their homeland than the German Reich. For nearly two years the Poles had made considerable efforts to build up a new republic in embryo and the sudden change in status of Stalin's government in the eyes of the other allies seemed to threaten much that had already been prepared. The events of 1939–40 cast a heavy shadow over the later years of the war.

When the Polish government fled to Roumania at the end of September 1939 its members were interned by order of the authorities in Bucharest. President Moscicki thereupon resigned on the grounds that he was unable to carry out his duties. He handed over the presidential prerogatives to the Speaker of the Senate, Raczkiewicz, who had fled to Paris. Although President Raczkiewicz was a former supporter of Pilsudski, he took the opportunity of carrying through what was virtually a political revolution; he invited the dead marshal's most formidable opponent among the Polish officer-corps, General Wladyslaw Sikorski, to head the government-in-exile. Sikorski established at Angers a 'National Council' consisting of representatives of all the pre-war opposition parties except the communists. His government was recognized by Britain, France and the United States; and when the French army collapsed in 1940, Sikorski transferred both the government and the National Council to London. It is significant that when President Raczkiewicz arrived at Victoria Station on 21 June 1940, he was received by King George VI with the honours due to a head of state.

The prestige of the Polish exiles continued to grow throughout 1940 and 1941. Polish soldiers fought in Norway, France and Greece; Polish warships served with the Royal Navy in the Atlantic and the Mediterranean; and Polish airmen particularly distinguished themselves in the Battle of Britain. Nor was this all. Sikorski's government also organized a 'Home Army', originally designed to carry out acts of sabotage and secure information for the Allied intelligence overseas; and, side by side with the Home Army, an underground civilian authority was set up to challenge the occupation regime. By June 1941 the Home Army numbered some seventy thousand men and was still growing. The existence of this formidable force, owing allegiance specifically to the exiles in London, seemed to Sikorski a trump card in his dealings with the Soviet Union in the months following Hitler's invasion.

Seven weeks after Hitler's invasion of Russia there was an apparent reconciliation between the Poles and the Russians. On 30 July 1941 an agreement was signed in London by Sikorski and the Soviet ambassador, Maisky, which formally cancelled the Ribbentrop-Molotov partition of 1939, restored Russo-Polish diplomatic relations, and provided for the formation on Soviet territory of a Polish army. Subsequently, Polish military prisoners-of-war were liberated from Soviet camps and organized in specifically Polish units attached to the Red Army but commanded by General Wladyslaw Anders, a former tsarist colonel who had shown considerable ability during the Pilsudski era. A visit by Sikorski to Stalin in December 1941 had moments of frigid cordiality; but most of the released Polish prisoners-of-war hated the Russians as much as they did the Germans, and few Poles believed that the Soviet forces would resist the invaders for many more months.

The limited understanding of Poles and Russians could not last. A series of incidents in 1942 led to a rapid deterioration of relations: the Russians arrested and subsequently shot two Polish socialists who were seeking to create separate Jewish units in the Anders army; the Poles complained that they were being kept on short rations by the Soviet authorities; and the Russians, in their turn, accused the Poles of being unwilling to fight the Germans. The disputes dragged on for several months until, in the spring and early summer, Anders was allowed to transfer his army, with Stalin's grudging consent, to Persia and eventually to North Africa. It had become clear to the Russians that Anders was too formidable a personality to serve their political interests and his departure tightened the grip of the Russians on the remaining Polish communities which had been forcibly transported to the Soviet Union. One of Anders' officers, Lieutenant-Colonel Zygmunt Berling, remained in Russia and in May 1943 undertook the formation of a 'Kosciuszko Division' to fight on the eastern front with the Red Army under Soviet-imposed commanders.

Armed resistance to the Germans grew considerably within the old Polish territories during 1942 and the early months of 1943. Differences in the character of the countryside prevented guerrilla operations on a Balkan scale but there were a number of skirmishes between the Home Army and SS units in the forested regions of the South. But the Home Army looked with suspicion on the Partisan leaders parachuted into Poland from the USSR as the vanguard of a 'People's Guard'. And both the Home Army and Partisans failed to give effective support to a specifically Jewish militant organization which was established in October 1942 to resist the atrocious policy of extermination enforced by the Nazis. For more than a week in April 1943 there was severe fighting in the Warsaw ghetto, as a hundred thousand Jewish survivors offered armed defiance of the Germans in a last gesture of pride. The Home Army made some diversionary raids and supplied arms; but, for the most part, the Jewish population of Warsaw died as they had lived – in isolation. The ghetto rising was a noble chapter in the history of the Jewish people but it is part of the Polish tragedy that their sacrifice should have left little mark on the attitude of the government-in-exile or on the Soviet authorities. It is, however, possible that the courage of the Warsaw ghetto and the smaller revolts five months later by the Jews incarcerated in the ghettoes of Vilna and Bialystok did much to soften, for a few years, the old anti-semitism of the Polish people themselves.

The destruction of the Warsaw ghetto coincided with the moment at which relations between the Sikorski government and the Russians sank to their nadir. On 13 April 1943 the Germans announced that they had found a series of mass graves of thousands of Polish officers who had been massacred by the Russians in 1940 and buried in the forest of Katyn, near Smolensk. Since the Russians had refused to account for the disappearance of ten thousand Polish soldiers captured in 1939 the Sikorski government asked the International Red Cross to investigate the Katyn revelations. Stalin insisted that such a move was tantamount to collaboration with the Germans; and on 25 April diplomatic relations were broken off by the Russians with the Polish government-in-exile.

Less than a fortnight after the official breach with Sikorski, the Russians announced the formation of a 'League of Polish Patriots'. The League, with Berling's 'Kosciuszko Division', formed a basis for the future communist liberation committee, a body which increasingly challenged the authority of the 'London' Poles. Almost at the same time, the government-in-exile suffered a great and unexpected blow: on 4 July 1943 General Sikorski was killed in an air accident at Gibraltar. President Raczkiewicz appointed the peasant leader, Stanislaw Mikolajczýk, to succeed him as prime minister and General Sosnkowski, who was once a close friend of Pilsudski, took over his responsibilities as military commander-in-chief. Mikolajczýk was respected in the West as a moderate and democratic leader but he had two great disadvantages: he lacked experience of diplomatic negotiations; and he did not enjoy the prestige of Sikorski among the soldiers nor, indeed, among the Allied statesmen. By Sikorski's death the hold of the government-in-exile on the Polish nation was lessened at the very moment when the tide was turning militarily on the eastern front.

Sikorski had always hoped for a westward-looking Polish State. His death ruled out such a possibility. Although the Polish army in Italy was to win great distinction in 1944 and the Home Army stage a rising in Warsaw itself, the initiative no longer lay with the old Polish leaders. Once the Germans began to fall back in Russia, all the political advantages were held by the Polish communists. In November 1943 a reconstructed 'Polish Workers' Party' was established under the direction of Boleslaw Bierut and its new secretary-general, Wladyslaw Gomulka. Victory against the invader in the East foreshadowed a specifically Russian solution of the Polish question, as in the days of Napoleon and Alexander I. The future lay with Bierut and Gomulka rather than with the better-known figures in the West; and their authority depended on the power of the Red Army and the whim of their patron in the Kremlin.

None of the other émigré governments experienced such difficulties with the Soviet Union as the Poles. This is hardly surprising, for none had already lost territories to the Russians. By contrast, it could even be argued that the position of Beneš and the Czech exiles in the West was actually improved by the invasion of Russia; for, although a Provisional Czechoslovak government was established in July 1940, Beneš continued to be treated with some coolness in London and it was not until 18 July 1941 that his government received full recognition from the British. This was the very day on which it also established diplomatic relations with the Soviet Union.

At times Beneš saw himself as an arbiter and an interpreter of East to West. During the inter-war period he had always shown more sympathy towards the Russians than Tómaš Masaryk or any of the older generation of Czech politicians. Now he was determined to work as closely as possible with Stalin and his military commanders while remaining on good terms with the British and Americans. Since he believed that Czechoslovakia would be liberated from German occupation by the armies on the eastern front, it was natural that he should seek his own agreements with the Russians and with the Moscow-trained Czechoslovak communists. This independence was regarded with some suspicion in both Washington and London.

In December 1943 Beneš visited Moscow and signed a twenty-year treaty of alliance between Czechoslovakia and the Soviet Union. At first his communist compatriots, led by Klement Gottwald, were highly critical of Beneš; they blamed him for having given way to western pressure in the autumn of 1938 rather than relying on alleged assurances of support from Stalin. The Russians themselves were, however, less interested in old reproaches than in present realities. They knew that Beneš still enjoyed considerable prestige at home and abroad. The evident sincerity of his admiration for the Soviet military achievement ensured close cooperation between the Czechs and the Russians in the final phases of the war. No attempt was made by the Russians to set up a satellite Czechoslovak administration.

Beneš' success in Moscow enabled a Czechoslovak Army Corps to be raised in the Soviet Union. Its commander was General Ludwig Svoboda, a forty-eight year old veteran of the First World War who, after serving as instructor in Magyar at the Czechoslovak Staff College, escaped to Poland in 1939 and was subsequently interned by the Russian authorities. Unlike his Polish contemporary, General Anders, Svoboda respected the Red Army commanders, especially Marshal Tolbukhin and Marshal Koniev and his feelings were reciprocated. Czechoslovak units were thus able to play a considerable part in the liberation of their country from the Germans. Although a communist-led Ruthene National Council was set up in 1944, the authority of Beneš and his prime minister, Monsignor Sramek was not challenged by the Russian commanders. Eventually a coalition government was established in liberated Košiče in March 1945 under the man whom Beneš had selected as his emissary in Moscow, Zdenek Fierlinger.

Russian policy had a less direct bearing in 1942 and 1943 on the future of Greece and Yugoslavia than on Poland and Czechoslovakia, and there was little direct contact between the two Balkan exile governments and

Moscow. In August 1942 the Soviet Union did, indeed, give the Yugoslav Kingdom an apparent vote of confidence by raising the status of its diplomatic representative in Moscow from the rank of minister to ambassador but it was a gesture of little significance, a token of re-assurance at a time of growing communist activity within the occupied territories. The truth was that the disasters of April 1941 had rocked the social fabric of the two countries more than the émigrés appreciated. The Yugoslavs became aggressively and exclusively Pan-Serb in character and cut off from their compatriots under enemy occupation. The Greek exiles too behaved as if the old order would survive the war in its entirety. The royalist politicians were so confident of the future that they even concluded with the Yugoslav government an agreement to serve as the basis of a new Balkan Union once the kings were back in Belgrade and Athens.

This optimism was unjustified. To outsiders it seemed increasingly improbable that either country would restore its monarchical institutions when the invaders were thrust out. The Greek royal family, with its traditional predilection for Germanic authoritarianism, held little appeal for the junior officers abroad or for the resistance leaders in the mountains; and in Serbia the old attachment to the Karadjordjević dynasty was severely strained by tales from London and Cairo of petty feuds among the émigré soldiers and politicians and of injudicious acts by the young King himself. Naturally these reports were much magnified by Peter's enemies at home but his published statements were not always calculated to improve his image. The loyalty of both the Yugoslav and Greek armed forces in the Middle East wavered on several occasions in 1942 and 1943 and there were minor mutinies among the units stationed in Egypt.

The future pattern of government depended, however, not so much on what the émigrés wished as on the character of the resistance movements and the patronage given to them by the major allies. Risings against the Germans and Italians began in various regions of Yugoslavia within three months of the Axis invasion and spread into Albania the following winter. A Greek resistance sprang up at the same time among the university students of Athens and in the remoter mountain villages but it was not until November 1942 that the Greek guerrillas achieved their first important work of sabotage, the destruction of a vital railway viaduct at Gorgopotamus. The political significance of these developments was considerable but by no means uniform. If, as in Yugoslavia, a patriot hero emerged from the guerrilla forces and was accepted by the occupation authorities as a dangerous adversary, it was hard for any exiled body to assert its will against the reality of his power, irrespective of its political inclinations. Communism in Yugoslavia was not based on an exclusive concept of nationality or an exclusive religious creed; it served as a unifying element in contrast to the narrow particularism of the inter-war political parties. Much the same is true of the Albanian movement, though on a smaller scale and without the complication of royalist sentiment (for none of the Albanians wanted Zog to return). In Greece, on the other hand, where the communist-led front (the EAM) failed to produce any single dominant personality and where the idea of unity was linked historically with the Orthodox Church, it was possible for British troops to maintain the Greek government on its return from exile until it was able to whittle down the support felt for the EAM in many regions of the country. Greece's geographical position on the southern fringe of eastern Europe permitted a degree of British commitment impossible in the other Balkan states.

It was perhaps inevitable that Yugoslavia should provide the archetype of Balkan resistance movement, for the mountains and forests of Serbia and Bosnia were naturally suited to a war of this character. Originally, in the late summer of 1941, two politically distinct groups of guerrillas emerged to oppose the occupying powers: the chetniks of Colonel Draža Mihailović, steeped in the legends of Serbia and looking back to a romantic past of warrior saints and bearded hajduk heroes; and the partisans who, from the first, sought to accomplish social revolution through a war of national liberation. The conflict between these two movements deepened the tragedy of the South Slav peoples, one in ten of whom perished in the four years of war.

Mihailović's followers were reported in action against the Germans in September 1941, long before news reached the West of the partisan revolt. The government-in-exile understandably built Mihailović and his chetniks up until they were accepted as resistance heroes by the Allied governments and by the press in London and New York. The Yugoslav government insisted that the chetniks were members of the regular army and promoted Mihailović to the rank of general, even appointing him as an absentee minister of war in January 1942. British officers were parachuted into the chetnik areas of southern Serbia in the winter of 1941–2. But Mihailović was in many ways a political anachronism. He was able to give generous protection to Allied airmen shot down over Serbia but his contribution to the defeat of Hitler was limited by a highly individualistic assessment of his country's needs. He hated the Croats; he hated even more the 'communist bandits'; he believed that his task was to harbour his resources for a rising in support of an Allied landing in the Balkans; and he was unable, or unwilling, to prevent his subordinate commanders from collaboration with the Germans and Italians against the partisans. Ultimately there was little difference between his policy and that of Nedić but, although there was growing evidence that the chetniks were doing little to hamper the common enemy, it was not until January 1944 that

271

Churchill halted supplies to Mihailović. The British military mission
was only withdrawn in the following May.

Partisan resistance began in Serbia on 7 July 1941 and by the end of the
month had spread to Montenegro, Slovenia, Croatia and Bosnia. There
was a rising in Serbian Macedonia in the second week of October. The
Germans mounted a major offensive against the partisans in November
and, using aircraft and tanks, forced them out of the town of Uzice and
into the mountainous borderland between Serbia and eastern Bosnia.
A second offensive was undertaken by the Germans and the *Ustaše* in
January and February 1942 but the partisans escaped encirclement and
established themselves in the small town of Foca on the upper reaches
of the river Drina. Here they experienced a three-month respite from
serious German attacks and it was during this interlude that Josip Broz-
Tito, the forty-nine year old Croat who had been appointed secretary
general of the Yugoslav Communist Party at the end of 1937, emerged as
a strategist of revolt and a champion of Southern Slav unity.

By midsummer 1942 enemy pressure had become so strong that Tito
decided to move his centre of operations 180 miles to the west across
Bosnia to the area around Bihać. There he established an administration
for the towns and villages liberated by the partisans. A representative
assembly, the Anti-Fascist Council for the National Liberation of Yugoslavia, was convened in Bihać on 26 November 1942 under the presidency
of Ivo Ribar, a non-communist who had been Speaker of the Constituent
Assembly in 1920. The council passed resolutions guaranteeing the
Yugoslav peoples 'true democratic rights' and affirming the 'inviolability
of private property'. An assembly of this character held in occupied
Europe forced the greater Allies to take note of the remarkable developments within Yugoslavia. No such statements of democratic principles
had come from Mihailović and his chetniks (though eventually, in
January 1944, Mihailović did indeed summon an assembly, the 'Congress
of St Sava', in the Serbian town of Ba). There was still confusion both in
Moscow and in London over events in Yugoslavia. Thus as late as April
1943 Churchill persisted in regarding the partisans as a specifically
Croatian resistance movement and it was not until the first British officers
were parachuted into the Tito-controlled areas of Yugoslavia at the end
of May that the Allies began to understand the full significance of the
National Liberation Movement.

Desperate efforts were made by the Germans and their allies to smash
the partisans in the early months of 1943 and the Yugoslavs suffered
heavy casualties. They were, however, aided considerably by the fall
of Mussolini and the subsequent withdrawal of Italy from the war in
September 1943. Meagre supplies could be replenished from depots in
such centres as Split, a city which the partisans were able to hold for

three weeks that autumn before German pressure forced a withdrawal into the mountains once more. At the end of November 1943 a second session of the Anti-Fascist Council was convened. On this occasion it met at Jajce and its political decisions were far more radical than at Bihać twelve months before. The National Liberation Council declared itself the 'supreme executive and legislative body of the Yugoslav State' and proclaimed that post-war Yugoslavia would be a federation 'ensuring full equality for the nations of Serbia, Croatia, Slovenia, Macedonia, Bosnia and Herzegovina'. The future of the monarchy would be settled after the liberation of the country. On a motion proposed by the delegates from Slovenia, the Jajce Congress formally bestowed on Tito the title of 'Marshal of Yugoslavia'.

These revolutionary acts reduced the standing of King Peter and the Yugoslav government-in-exile. But Tito had every right to claim a voice in the future of his country. At the time of the Jajce Congress the partisans were tying down no less than nineteen German divisions and 160,000 other Axis troops. The Germans were forced to concentrate specially trained units in the mountains of Bosnia and bring an airborne task force in the hope of routing out the partisans. With the Germans falling back in the east towards the Danube and in the south-west up the Italian peninsula, Tito's strategic significance was far greater than his material strength. His forces were operating midway between the Red Army as it impinged on the Balkans and the Anglo-American troops across the Adriatic. It is not surprising that Hitler took the Partisan movement so seriously. As he suspected, Churchill too had sensed the potential value of Yugoslavia as an avenue to Central Europe (although he was opposed, for differing reasons, by both the Americans and the Russians).

Throughout 1943 the Germans and their satellites in south-eastern Europe seemed held by a gradually tightening pincer. The last major German attack came to a halt east of Kharkov at the end of March and from July onwards the Russians moved relentlessly westwards. Orel and Kharkov were liberated in August and seven Russian army groups swept down on the Dnieper. On 24 September Marshal Rokossovsky's advance units sighted the towers of Kiev across the river while, on the following day 300 miles to the north, Marshal Sokolovsky entered Smolensk. By the first week in November Kiev was in Russian hands and the Red Army across the Dnieper at several points. The frost hardened the marshy ground to the west and, by the end of the year, the Russians were approaching the pre-1939 Polish-Soviet frontier and were less than a hundred miles from the border with Roumania. At the same time, the British and Americans were thrusting northwards up the Italian peninsula and, with

Brindisi in their hands, seemed able to launch an invasion of the Balkans across the Adriatic. The Italian collapse in September 1943 had repercussions throughout south-eastern Europe where mini-Mussolinis had strutted so blatantly in the inter-war years. Momentarily there seemed some prospect that Roumania and Bulgaria might desert the German cause and Hungary, too, conclude a separate peace.

Hitler had been aware of the possible disintegration of his New Order ever since the spring. In April he took up residence at Schloss Klessheim, near Salzburg, and summoned there King Boris, Marshal Antonescu, Admiral Horthy, Tiso and Pavelić for a succession of angry interviews which were intended to prove to them that there could be no future for their states outside a total German victory. Boris, as usual, appears to have held his own in the verbal disputes with Hitler. The Roumanians and Hungarians were bitterly assailed for their attempts to contract out of the war. Hitler particularly upbraided Antonescu for the freedom he permitted a critic such as Maniu. 'I killed my political opponents,' said Hitler: 'I did not,' replied Antonescu, laconically. Horthy, in his turn, was accused of sheltering too many Jews and was told that his prime minister, Kállay, was 'a political adventurer and enemy number one of the German people'. The regent angrily refused to dismiss Kállay at German dictation and he also resisted attempts to make him sign a declaration of Hungary's intention to continue the fight 'against Bolshevism and its Anglo-Saxon allies' until final victory. Although the German press releases ignored Horthy's scruples and insisted on the unity of all Germany's partners, Hitler was left in no doubt of Hungary's real intentions.

The Klessheim conversations made little impression on Hitler's visitors except, perhaps, for the wretched Pavelić. In August Kállay concluded an agreement with the British by which it was understood that if the western Allies should reach the frontiers of Hungary, they would find the Hungarian armed forces prepared to surrender unconditionally. Nor was Kállay alone in seeking to be numbered among the saints. The Roumanian foreign minister, Mihai Antonescu – who was not related to his namesake, the marshal – was also in touch with sympathizers in London and indirectly with Beneš. There was, of course, no collaboration between the Hungarians and the Roumanians: the Transylvanian Question, though dormant, still kept them apart and, indeed, influenced their calculations.

Bulgaria was in a different position from any of the other members of the Tripartite Pact. The Bulgars were neither willing partners of Hitler nor active opponents. Nazi-style anti-semitic decrees were promulgated in 1942 but ineffectually administered, except in the foreign territories occupied by Bulgarian troops. The communist bogey was, from time to time, conjured up in the press and on the radio, especially when there were a number of assassinations in the capital and the suburbs. In June 1942 General Zaimov, who had been a respected member of Velchev's military circle in the mid-thirties, was executed as an alleged Russian agent. The charge satisfied no one and it was generally assumed that Zaimov had been plotting a military coup. But, apart from these alarms, Bulgaria remained strangely isolated from the main conflict. The Bulgars had not, as yet, fared badly from the war. Considerable areas of Macedonia and Thrace were under Bulgarian control from the spring of 1941 and these territories were actually enlarged after the Italian collapse in 1943. Russia and Bulgaria were still at peace. There was a risk of air raids on Sofia and other centres as the Balkans came more and more within the range of Allied bombers but it was not until January 1944 that an intensification of the air offensive led to partial evacuation of the capital. Only a few thousand Germans were stationed in the country. Conditions were far better than they had been in the First World War.

King Boris remained a popular figure with his subjects. Despite the high political crime rate in Bulgaria he continued to walk openly in the streets of Sofia, as befitted a great-grandson of Louis Philippe, the 'citizen King' of France. But on 28 August 1943 Boris died suddenly, three days after returning from a visit to Hitler at his East Prussian headquarters. As Boris was only forty-nine and had shown no obvious signs of ill-health there were rumours that he had been murdered by the Germans: some said he had been shot on the plane returning from East Prussia; and others that he had been poisoned. Probably he died from natural causes.

With Boris's death the Bulgarian governing class lost an astute spokesman whose natural gifts for statecraft had been sharpened by a quarter of a century of varying fortunes. Since his son and successor, Simeon, was only six years old, the royal prerogative was exercised by a Regency Council which was nominally headed by Boris's brother, Prince Cyril, but on which the most influential member was the former premier, Bogdan Filov. The regents were still able to keep the country out of the Russian campaign but as the Red Army approached the Balkans there was a growth of Panslav sentiment in the land. Dissident officers, agrarians, social democrats and genuine communists banded together in a 'Fatherland Front,' an underground political opposition. Partisan groups began operations in the Rhodope Mountains and a resistance movement gradually emerged in Bulgaria; but it never reached the same pitch of intensity as in Yugoslavia.

With the defeat of Italy and with the Red Army liberating the Ukraine it was clear to the Allied statesmen that the war in Europe had swung in their favour. Yet, although there had been meetings of foreign ministers and bi-lateral discussions between Churchill and Roosevelt and between Churchill and Stalin, no major conference had gathered to determine the final military spheres of operations or to prepare for a post-war settlement. A summit meeting of Churchill, Roosevelt and Stalin had long been predicted in the press. It opened at last in Teheran on 28 November 1943, thus coinciding with Tito's revolutionary congress at Jajce. Its consequences were momentous for the whole of Eastern Europe.

To the British and Americans the Teheran Conference was primarily a means of securing strategic coordination against Hitler's Germany and eventual Soviet entry into the war against Japan; and as such it was a success. For Stalin the conference had a dual purpose of a somewhat different character. Militarily it enabled him to stress to his allies the Russian desire for a determined effort to be made in the forthcoming 'Second Front' in France and dissuading them from sideshows along the Adriatic or in the Aegean. It was also an opportunity for him to ensure that the Red Army would act as the sole gendarme of Russia's borderland, free from Anglo-American interference in Poland, Roumania, Bulgaria and even along the middle Danube. The military agreement of 1 December was precise and to the point: joint support for Tito's partisans; joint offensives across the Channel and on the eastern front in May 1944; encouragement of Turkey to become a co-belligerent by promising that Russia would declare war on Bulgaria if the Bulgars launched an offensive against the Turks; and an understanding that there would be further collaboration between the military staffs over the details of later operations. By contrast the political questions raised at the conference were left vague and ill-defined. Stalin declined to give a clear statement of Russia's territorial demands. It was agreed that Poland's frontiers should be 'moved' westwards to the Oder, with the formerly Polish lands to the east of the Curzon Line restored to the Soviet Union, in which they had been incorporated in 1939; but Stalin seems to have accepted, with some gratitude, Churchill's formula that 'the actual tracing of the frontier line requires careful study and possibly disentanglement of population at certain points.' Over Roumania little was said. Stalin had already maintained on several occasions during the war that the cession of Bessarabia and the northern Bukovina was final, and the British and Americans clearly regarded the two provinces as falling within a Russian sphere of military interests. Many highly placed Roumanians seem to have been convinced that Anglo-American forces would, by some mysterious means, arrive in the kingdom and negotiate an armistice before the descent of the Red Army. But the time for such illusions was gone. After Teheran there could be little doubt in London or Washington who would be the master of all the East European marchlands although it was not foreseen how far to the west his power would extend.

Some of the provisions of the Teheran Conference remained academic and some received, in practice, considerable qualifications: Turkey could not be tempted into the war at this stage and it was therefore not necessary for the Russians to send an ultimatum as yet to Bulgaria; and although the Russians sent a military mission to Tito in February, they left the task of supplying him with material to the British, who were able to open a base in Bari. But the course of the military campaigns ensured that the two areas in which the Russians were at that time particularly interested, Poland and Roumania, would soon serve as testing grounds for the Teheran decisions.

The Red Army crossed the old inter-war Polish-Soviet frontier at Sarny, a railway junction on the southern edge of the Pripet Marshes, on 4 January 1944. The Polish Question was acutely poised. Some units of the Home Army were willing to assist the Russians to expel the Germans while others found themselves from the start fighting against the Red Army, not always from their own choice. The Mikolajczýk government in London proposed that the Home Army should give tactical support to the Russians so long as they accepted Polish sovereignty west of the inter-war frontier. At the same time negotiations continued between Mikolajczýk and Churchill in the hope that the Poles and Russians might come to some general agreement over future boundaries. In February the Polish government-in-exile offered as its maximum concession, and one to which the military party agreed with the greatest reluctance, a 'temporary demarcation line' running immediately east of Vilna and Lvov and leaving both cities within the Polish State. Since Stalin insisted that the ethnographically correct frontier was the Curzon Line (and Churchill fundamentally agreed with him) there was no hope whatsoever of securing Soviet acceptance of this proposal. The Russians continued to support Boleslaw Bierut and his newly-formed 'National Council of Poland' despite attempts by Roosevelt and Churchill to heal the breach with the government-in-exile; and, as the Red Army approached the 1941 frontier, Bierut's National Council was entrusted with executive responsibilities for the territories soon to be liberated west of the Curzon Line. General Bulganin – the later Soviet premier – was appointed as Stalin's representative with this acting administration. In August Bierut and Bulganin established a 'Committee of National Liberation' in the town of Lublin which it declared to be the Polish capital so long as Warsaw remained in German hands.

Roumania, too, was threatened by the arrival of Soviet troops that spring. The British and Americans persistently refused to conclude any separate agreement with the Roumanians, even though emissaries from Mihai Antonescu and from Maniu were active in Madrid and Ankara. Marshal Antonescu himself was anxious to take Roumania out of the war and he, too, had secret contacts with the Allies. Soon after the Teheran Conference an envoy of the marshal's, Florian Nano, met in Stockholm a Bulgarian who was peddling introductions to Soviet diplomats and second-hand jewellery. Through this singularly unorthodox salesman Nano was able to hold conversations with the Russians for over three months and in April Molotov publicly announced that, while the Soviet Union intended to retain Bessarabia and the northern Bukovina, Roumania's territorial integrity would not otherwise be impaired and the Russians would not seek to change the 'existing social structure' in the country. By now the Red Army had reached the Bukovina and conversations were being held in Ankara with more urgency than in Stockholm. The Roumanians were given to understand that they would be expected to declare war on Germany and that, in the final settlement, all Transylvania would be restored to Roumania. At this point all negotiations were suspended, ostensibly because of Antonescu's indignation at heavy American air-raids on Ploesti and other centres but more probably because of events in Hungary.

Despite Hitler's harsh remarks to Horthy about Kállay in the previous August, the regent declined to make any major changes in the Hungarian government and even presented Kállay with a high decoration on the second anniversary of his appointment as prime minister. Kállay, for his part, continued throughout the last months of 1943 to seek assurances of support from the Allies. His range of contacts was remarkable: he was able to secure an indirect link across the Atlantic with the head of the House of Habsburg, Archduke Otto (who had three interviews with Roosevelt and a meeting with Churchill); and, at the other end of the scale, he arranged a private truce, of more practical value than the archduke's proposals, with Marshal Tito. Yet Kállay failed in his grand design. He wanted a British and American military mission to be parachuted into Hungary so as to prepare for an airborne landing by Anglo-American forces: he had in mind some twenty thousand men (about twice as many combatants as were dropped at Arnhem in the following September). Kállay also proposed to withdraw all Hungarian troops behind the Carpathians and disengage entirely from the Russian campaign, apparently hoping that he could make with the Red Army a similar arrangement to his truce with Tito. Kállay argued that by these means Hungary would remain the one stable political unit in Central Europe, a pillar of the West against Bolshevism.

It is hard to believe that these plans were ever seriously entertained by responsible public figures for they bore little relationship to the political and military balance of 1944. Yet the rumours that Anglo-American troops would fly in with the spring birds spread widely and 20 March, the fiftieth anniversary of Kossuth's death, was a favourite date for their arrival. The rumour was duly reported to German headquarters where, on the strength of some of Kállay's intercepted messages, it was given a certain credence. In the last week of February Hitler decided on a military operation to discipline the Hungarians and discourage such treachery among his other partners. Horthy was summoned once more to Schloss Klessheim.

Horthy reached Salzburg on 18 March. There was a series of angry interviews in which Hitler charged the regent with Kállay's 'treacherous intrigues'. He insisted that Horthy must either cooperate with Germany under a government in which the Germans had confidence or face the occupation of Hungary as an enemy state, not only by the Germans but by the Slovaks, Croats and Roumanians as well. Horthy accepted the German demands believing that so long as he remained regent he might still retain some influence. But the Germans saw to it that Horthy was virtually their prisoner. The train in which he returned from Salzburg to Budapest was deliberately delayed so that it took fifteen hours to cover the 320 miles between the two cities and neither he nor his companions were able to telephone Kállay and inform him of what had happened. While the regent was being shunted round the suburbs of Vienna, politically isolated, the Germans proceeded to occupy Hungary from four different directions and sent parachutists to seize all airfields and strategic points in Budapest itself. There was no resistance and by the time Horthy at last reached the capital, in the late morning of 19 March, a German Guard was mounted in the station and in front of the palace. Ominously, the notorious SS General Ernst Kaltenbrunner was in obsequious attendance on the regent.

For the next four and a half months the Germans were the masters of Hungary and the full terror of the Nazi machine was employed against those suspected of undermining the 'New Order'. Kállay, who found diplomatic sanctuary in the Turkish Legation, was replaced as prime minister by a weak and pliant general. The heaviest burden of all fell on the Jews. A third of a million Hungarian Jews perished, mostly in the gas-chambers of Auschwitz: possibly as many as another quarter of a million suffered the horrors of deportation and incarceration but survived. Although individual Hungarians gave protection to certain Jewish families, there were many cases of brutality by non-Germans and the attitude of Horthy and his ministers to the deportations was equivocal. The regent seems to have believed, somewhat naively, that once the Jews were removed from the kingdom the Nazis would follow them; but he intervened to prevent the deportation of the more prosperous Jews of Budapest, a community of importance to the Hungarian economy.

The German occupation of Hungary had important international repercussions. It bolstered up the puppet regimes in Slovakia and Croatia, for both Tiso and Pavelić believed that they would benefit from the apparent disgrace of Horthy; and it had a double effect on Antonescu. While the Roumanians were alarmed at the speed with which the Germans had taken control of their neighbour, they had hopes that Transylvania would be restored to them in its entirety. Hitler actually said to Marshal Antonescu in the last days of March that 'for him, the Vienna Award no longer existed.' At that time, the Russians were advancing in Bessarabia and approaching the Carpathian foothills, which they reached on 31 March. It must have been clear to Antonescu that Hitler would not be in a position to dispose of Transylvania unless the Russian offensive was checked. But in the spring of 1944 a deceptive lull came in the fighting on the borders of both Hungary and Roumania. Along the southern sector of their front the Russians concentrated all their efforts at clearing the Germans from Odessa, which was liberated on 10 April, and from the Crimea, where they re-entered Sebastopol on 9 May. Meanwhile, the arc of the Carpathians remained inviolate; and optimists in both Hungary and Roumania began to feel that the Russians might be halted.

Marshal Antonescu himself seems to have hoped that the new line of fortifications would so delay the Red Army that Stalin would be prepared to negotiate a 'reasonable' settlement. The Conducator argued, as he had in 1941, that if the Roumanians remained loyal to the German alliance in this crisis they would show their superiority to the treacherous Magyars and gratitude would ensure the retrocession of Transylvania once mutual exhaustion had forced the Nazis and the Soviets to negotiate their compromise peace. This mood of confidence did not last long in Bucharest: Maniu and the 'tolerated' opposition were in contact with the British again by mid-June and Antonescu with the Russians in July; but the momentary euphoria delayed the collapse of Roumania by several months and, in consequence, the Red Army did not enter the Danubian basin until after the harvest had been gathered in.

By the spring of 1944 the British were becoming alarmed at the probable extent of Russian penetration in south-eastern Europe. Churchill's fertile mind conjured up projects for landings in Greece or along the Dalmatian coast but neither his chiefs-of-staff nor the Americans liked such diversions; and indeed his earlier schemes for operations in the Balkans had been defeated at Teheran. But Churchill was never prepared to give up a strategy which he felt to be justified by later events; and in May and June 1944 he continued to urge the desirability of exploiting the Italian campaign north-eastwards so as to secure an Anglo-American hold on the middle Danube before the Red Army poured over the Carpathians. He proposed a landing in Istria, union with Tito's forces, a thrust through the Ljubljana Gap and thence to Vienna by way of Graz and the Semmering Pass. The plan did not appeal to Roosevelt's military advisers (who, rather oddly, seem to have persisted in regarding it as a 'Balkan venture') but, with modifications, it remained in Churchill's mind throughout that summer and contributed to his desire 'to bring order out of chaos' in the political feuds of Yugoslavia. It is significant that when at last Churchill met Tito at Naples in August 1944 one of his first concerns was how far the partisans would cooperate in securing a route for British troops through Ljubljana and Maribor to Graz.

Tito's military and political fortunes varied considerably in the course of 1944. On 24 May he was nearly captured by a brilliantly planned German airborne attack on partisan headquarters at Drvar; he even lost his marshal's uniform, which was displayed in Vienna as a trophy of war. But his importance to the British ensured that he was soon able to establish a new centre of operations from the island of Vis, where he could be protected and supplied by British naval craft before crossing to the mainland and carrying the partisan attacks into Serbia. Politically, some agreement was at last reached between Tito and the royalist government-in-exile. In June King Peter was induced by the British to dismiss his prime minister, Bozhidar Purić, and replace him by Ivan Šubašić, the first Croat to be entrusted with the formation of a Yugoslav government. For many months Purić had been striking Serbian chauvinist attitudes which would not have disgraced his father-in-law, Pašić, a quarter of a century previously; but Šubašić was prepared to meet Tito and at the end of August induced King Peter to recognize publicly that Tito was the sole military commander of the Yugoslav resistance. Attempts to arrange a meeting between Tito and King Peter failed; but Tito's own prestige had soared to remarkable heights. In August he discussed strategy with Churchill in Naples; and in September he negotiated with Stalin in Moscow an agreement for military collaboration between the Red Army and the partisans, stipulating that all liberated areas should be under Yugoslav administration. Tito, as an individual commander and as a legend, seemed essential to both East and West; and he was shrewd enough to take full advantage of his position.

The Poles, too, produced a brilliant resistance leader that summer. General Count Tadeusz Komorowski, who was generally known by his code-name 'Bor,' was a regular officer in one of the crack cavalry regiments before the war; but in July 1943 he took command of the Home Army on orders from London. Unfortunately, he became the victim of misunderstandings between Mikolajczýk and the Allies in the West. It is also possible that his own career and aristocratic heritage were against him. Originally it was intended that the Home Army should harass a retreating German enemy along its line of communications;

but Bor, with the approval of the government-in-exile, planned a rising in Warsaw according to the traditions of 1794 and 1830. Had it succeeded, representatives of the old order in Poland would have been in a strong position to bargain with the Red Army and the Polish communists in its baggage-train. Its failure destroyed the only powerful anti-communist force in Eastern Europe. Politically this was an inestimable advantage to Stalin. It confirmed that Poland would remain under Soviet influence in the post-war world. There is, of course, no proof that the Russians deliberately allowed the Germans to suppress the national resistance in order to save themselves the necessity of doing so; but such cynicism would not have been out of character in the Stalinist era.

The epic of the Warsaw rising is deceptively simple to narrate. It began on 1 August 1944. By 4 August two-thirds of the city was in the hands of the Home Army. The Germans, however, brought up SS reinforcements and besieged the insurgent districts. The Home Army was split into small groups able to contact each other only through the labyrinth of sewers. After waiting in vain for outside help, shortage of food forced them to capitulate on honourable terms on 3 October. They had been in revolt for nine weeks and had suffered fifteen thousand casualties, while inflicting something like two-thirds of that figure on the enemy.

Bor and his men were objects of widespread admiration, not least among their German adversaries. British, South African and Polish airmen, flying in from Italy, dropped supplies, but on a small scale and with high casualties; in the third week of September, American planes also brought assistance which was parachuted to the defenders. The Red Army, however, did little to help. It is true that Marshal Rokossovsky, the commander in this sector, had advanced nearly four hundred miles in less than five weeks and that his supply line was heavily taxed. Moreover it could be argued that the Soviet strategic master-plan provided for a halt on the Vistula and consolidation before making a further leap to the west; for the Russians always tended to move forward systematically from one great river to the next, and Warsaw was a difficult bridgehead for a weary army. Yet it is significant that Mikolajczýk, who was himself in Moscow when the rising began, was refused Soviet support by Stalin in person unless he agreed to accept the Curzon Line frontier and to cooperate with Bierut and the communists in a joint government. It is also ominous that, after appeals from Churchill and Roosevelt, the Red Army was indeed able to launch an assault on the city. By then, however, it was the middle of September and far too late to be effective. More than six weeks had passed since the initial rising and although the 'Soviet Poles' (Berling's 'Kosciuszko Division') were able to seize the Praga district on the east bank of the Vistula, they were unable to establish a bridgehead across the river.

The Red Army did not enter the ruins and glory that was Warsaw until 17 January 1945 – fifteen weeks after Bor's surrender.

The tragedy of the Polish rising imposed a severe strain on the relations between the Soviet Union and its western allies. There was little understanding of Russia's military problems, only a deep suspicion of her political intentions. The Poles had always been the victims of their geographical position, isolated between Germany and Russia. In 1944 the alarming novelty seemed to be the ease with which the Russians could observe the next round in the contest before the present one was concluded, and the inability of Britain and the United States to do anything about it. By that autumn it was even more apparent than at Teheran that in future the Lands Between would be little more than a field of manoeuvre for the Red Army.

The main military effort of the Russians in August and September of 1944 was concentrated far to the south of the Vistulan basin along the three-hundred mile sector between the Carpathians and the Black Sea. The line was held by twenty-seven German divisions and twenty war-weary Roumanian divisions. The Germans had no reserves so far south, for the earlier Russian offensive towards Warsaw had drawn the more mobile divisions northward in an effort to ensure that the Russian drive towards Berlin was halted on the Vistula. The Russians gained remarkable successes. Their offensive began on 20 August. Within three days they were across the Pruth and in Jassy, their armoured columns thrusting deeply into Moldavia. It seemed unlikely that any defensive line could be constructed north of the Danube.

Maniu and the opposition leaders had abandoned such hopes as they had ever held of persuading the Conducator to abandon the German alliance. They believed that, in this crisis, Roumania should follow the example set in 1943 by Italy. King Michael shared their convictions; and when on 23 August both the Antonescus sought an interview with him in the palace at Bucharest, he seized the opportunity to have them arrested, detaining them in the specially ventilated safe constructed by his father for the royal stamp-collection. The King then appointed his military adviser General Sanatescu as prime minister of a ministry of all the talents. Sanatescu's four deputy premiers were Maniu, Bratianu, a prominent socialist (Patrescu) and a communist (Patrascanu). The Roumanians ceased fighting against the Russians on that same day; and on 24 August King Michael declared war on Germany.

The rapidity with which the Roumanians changed sides brought considerable advantages to the Soviet commanders. There was virtually no destruction of railways, harbour installations or oilwells. By 30 August the Russians were not merely in occupation of Constanta but were using its port facilities for the landing of reinforcements and equipment shipped in from Sebastopol. On the following day they were welcomed in Bucharest as liberators. The whole of the German flank in south-eastern Europe was turned within ten days.

The Roumanian transformation encouraged the Finns, who had long despaired of victory, to seek peace; and a Soviet-Finnish armistice was announced over Helsinki radio on 5 September. It had an even more dramatic effect on the Bulgars. In Sofia the three regents sent for any opposition leader they could find and invited him to form a pro-Western government. The mandate, if such it could be called, was accepted by Stamboliisky's nephew, Muraviev. The Fatherland Front refused to take any notice of the regents' overtures or, for that matter, of Muraviev. But pro-Western sentiments were not enough. On 5 September the Russians declared war on Bulgaria and prepared to cross the Danube and enter the Dobrudja. But Muraviev showed remarkable dexterity: he asked for an armistice on the same day and followed this up, within a few hours, by announcing that Bulgaria had declared war on Germany. The Russians crossed into Bulgaria in force on 8 September and met with no resistance. That night, Velchev and Georghiev – those veterans of military coups – seized power in Sofia in the name of the Fatherland Front. The new government was headed by Georghiev and, rather un-expectedly, had strange echoes of the Zveno ministry of 1934, but it included two communists and the agrarian Nikola Petkov. The Fatherland Front was supported by demonstrations of workers in the cities and by partisan celebrations in the mountain villages. When the Red Army reached Sofia on 16 September it was, once again, welcomed as a body of liberators. The regular Bulgarian army and the partisan units fought with the Russians and with Tito against the German occupation troops in Yugoslavia and Hungary. At times, however, there was some friction with the Yugoslavs over the future of Macedonia.

Most German units had already left Bulgaria proper before Muraviev's *volte-face*. There had never been many German troops in the country and Hitler had decided that Roumania's defection necessitated withdrawing all German divisions from the Balkans proper so as to establish a new defensive line for Central Europe. Yugoslav, Greek and Bulgarian partisans all harassed the Germans as they began to pull out of Greece and Macedonia and there was severe fighting along the main lines of communication and especially in the Vardar-Morava valleys. The German retreat was orderly but slow and many units found that the great westward sweep of the Russian armies had cut them off. Behind them came the British, who landed on the Greek mainland at Patras and Nauplion in the first week of October, entering the Piraeus and Athens on 14 October.

It was not until the end of the month that Greece was finally cleared of German troops.

The main Russian armies paused only briefly in Roumania and Bulgaria before wheeling south-westwards in Wallachia during the third week in September. By the beginning of October they were pressing forwards through the Transylvanian Alps to the border with Hungary. Further south Marshal Tolbukhin's Army Group crossed the Yugoslav frontier in two columns, one coming from the Roumanian Bánát and the other from south-east of the Iron Gates. On 4 October Russian units linked up with Tito's partisans in the Morava Valley. Both the Russians and the partisans entered Belgrade on 20 October, the Germans having decided to hold the line of the river Tisza as a winter dyke against the Russian surge. Tolbukhin's troops had advanced more than 450 miles in less than two months. Their arrival on the central Danube posed an entirely new threat to Germany, similar to Franchet d'Espérey's in 1918 although supported by far more fire-power.

There was one veteran of the collapse of 1918 who was still in a position of high authority twenty-six years later, Miklós Horthy. Then he had surrendered the Austro-Hungarian fleet to the Southern Slavs and watched from his estate as men whom he despised sought a separate peace for Hungary and an armistice which would save her from occupation by the minority nationalities for whom most Magyars felt contempt. Now he found himself in a not dissimilar situation. German political pressure on Budapest was relaxed during the Roumanian crisis weeks and Horthy took the opportunity of dismissing his ineffectual Germanophile premier, Sztojay, and replacing him by the more solidly reliable General Lakatos. Although Horthy had scruples about deserting his German ally, he believed that the war was lost. Slowly, for he was in his seventy-seventh year, the regent convinced himself that Hungary must make peace but only if the western Allies could save the kingdom from the horrors of a Soviet occupation (and preferably from the indignities of Yugoslav, Czech or Roumanian occupation as well). During September many approaches were made to the West – even by means of Archduke Otto, who was again received by President Roosevelt – and a secret mission was flown out to British headquarters in Italy on 22 September. But all requests to the West elicited the same response: an armistice could only be negotiated with the Soviet Union. Preliminary contacts had indeed already been established with the Soviet High Command in Slovakia and an armistice delegation was flown to Moscow on 1 October. Churchill and Eden arrived in Moscow on 9 October to discuss Polish and Balkan questions with Stalin and Molotov; and the British were therefore aware of Hungary's attempts to secede from the German alliance. A provisional agreement was signed by the Russians and Hungarians on 11 October:

Hungarian troops would retire to the 1920 frontiers and, in due course, turn against the Germans. The Russians assumed that these events would take place immediately but Horthy did not. At the right moment he intended to have an announcement of an armistice broadcast over the radio, as the Finns had done. It was a misleading precedent, for Helsinki was outside the main battle-zone and Budapest was astride one of the principal routes into southern Germany.

Meanwhile, the Germans had gathered what was happening and had taken precautions. They had always kept in reserve the fanatical Arrow Cross leader, Ferencz Szálasi. They also had, in the suburbs of Budapest, the specialist troops of Major Skorzeny (who had rescued Mussolini from imprisonment in September 1943). Early in the morning of 15 October Skorzeny kidnapped the regent's son as he was holding conversations with an alleged representative of Tito. When later that Sunday a proclamation was read over Budapest radio in which Horthy announced that Hungary was concluding an armistice, the Germans were able to take swift action to counter the regent's move. They seized Horthy himself, forced him to declare his armistice proclamation 'null and void' and, using his son as a hostage, induced him to abdicate and appoint Szálasi as prime minister. Horthy was then taken to Bavaria and placed under detention; and his son was eventually sent to Dachau concentration camp. The whole episode was a sad example of mistiming, confusion and uncertain loyalties. The Hungarians were forced to fight on beside the Germans for another six months of grim destruction while the Szálasi regime fed its warped and frustrated patriotism on bestial anti-semitism.

All attempts by the Germans and Hungarians to halt the advance of the Russians and their allies were unsuccessful until the coming of the winter frosts. Marshal Malinovsky advanced on Budapest from the east but the main threat came from Tolbukhin's forces who, at the end of November, forced a crossing of the Danube in the swampy wastes near Mohács and struck northwards towards the capital and eastwards to Lake Balaton. Budapest was encircled at Christmas but the natural citadel of Buda held out until the middle of February and the whole city suffered almost as much devastation as Warsaw. The Germans fought with determination along the shores of Lake Balaton and even mounted a surprise counter-offensive near Székesfehérvár in March. It was not until 4 April 1945 that the last German troops pulled out of Hungary and into Austria. No campaign since the coming of the Turks had wrought such havoc to the Hungarian Kingdom.

At the end of December 1944 a provisional government of Hungary was established, under Soviet auspices, in Debrecen. It was headed by General Miklós and included representatives of the agrarian parties and the social democrats as well as the communists. On 21 January 1945 its emissaries formally concluded an armistice with the Allies in Moscow and on 14 April the government returned to Budapest with the melancholy responsibility of converting a shell-shocked people into the champions of a democratic republic.

Through October, November and December of 1944 there were no major advances on the Polish front. This apparent stalemate was in part caused by difficulties in communication: the regions behind the Russian lines had been devastated and direct railway links were hampered, not only by destroyed tracks, but also by the difference between the standard European gauge and the wider Russian gauge. By the end of the year all was ready; and on 12 January 1945 the Red Army launched a massive offensive on the upper Vistula along the eighty-mile sector between Cracow and Sandomierz. Five days later Zhukov struck on the centre of the Polish front, around Warsaw; and Rokossovsky penetrated into East Prussia, heading for Danzig. Since the Russians enjoyed a six-to-one superiority in men and armoured vehicles their advance was as rapid as the German attack had been in the early days of 'Barbarossa'. The front line was carried 100 miles to the west within a week. By the beginning of February most of pre-war Poland had been occupied by the Red Army and, though the Germans still held two-thirds of Czechoslovakia, all western Hungary and a sector of the Croatian plain, Hitler's hold on Eastern Europe had been finally loosened. At the same time the British and the Americans (with the support of the other allies in the West and General Anders' Poles) had crossed the Rhine into Germany and reached the Arno in Italy. Such was the military situation in Europe when Churchill, Roosevelt and Stalin met for their second summit conference of the war, at liberated Yalta in the Crimea from 4 February to 11 February 1945.

Yalta was not, as has sometimes been said, a remarkable diplomatic triumph for the Russians over a tired British Prime Minister and an ailing American President. While Roosevelt showed a far more acute consciousness of the balance of power than he had at Teheran, Churchill continued with his realistic policy of asserting a right to be heard in an area where all decisions rested ultimately on the overwhelming strength of Russian arms. Already in October 1944 Churchill had struck his famous 'percentage' bargain with Stalin which accepted that Russia should have an almost free hand in Roumania and Bulgaria in return for Stalin's recognition of Anglo-American predominance in Greece and of equality of Soviet and Anglo-American influence in the future of Hungary and Yugoslavia. At Yalta he sought to ensure a 'Western' share in the new

Poland even though the Russians had recognized the Lublin Committee as the legitimate government while London and Washington continued to acknowledge the émigré institutions. He duly secured a compromise, both over the form of the Polish government and the future of Poland's frontiers; and Roosevelt, for his part, was able to induce Stalin to accept a 'Declaration on Liberated Europe' which provided for 'free elections of governments responsive to the will of the people'. The concessions made by Stalin looked more impressive on paper than they were in reality but at least they held out the hope that, once the military emergency had eased, there would be an opportunity of establishing a democratically elected assembly.

At Yalta more time was spent on the Polish Question than on any other topic but no final solution was reached. By now it had been accepted that the frontier in the west would follow the Curzon Line, with minor adjustments, but the Russian demand that the western frontier of Poland should follow the Oder and the western branch of the Neisse was shelved. It was announced that 'Poland must receive substantial accessions of territory in the North and West,' but that 'final delimitation of the western frontier' should await a peace conference. Similarly, though it was accepted that the Lublin Committee should form the basis of a 'Provisional Government of National Unity,' it was stated that the new administration would contain democratic leaders from the Poles abroad. When it was, at last, established at the end of June 1945 'National Unity' was seen to imply sixteen 'Lublin' Poles, three 'London' Poles (including Mikolajcýk) and two other members. This was not the compromise for which Churchill had hoped: all would depend on how the 'Declaration on Liberated Europe' was interpreted; and this, of course, was as true of all the Eastern European lands as of Poland.

The fighting continued in Europe for another twelve weeks after the Yalta Conference had dispersed. The Anglo-American forces and the Russians raced for Berlin. The city fell to Zhukov's army advancing from the Oder but Americans to the south-west were little more than fifty miles from the capital and had penetrated more than 100 miles into the occupation zone provisionally assigned to the Russians at Yalta. It was the Russians, too, who entered Vienna although with the collapse of German resistance in northern Italy the British were able to seize Trieste and advance into southern Austria. In Carinthia they took into custody several thousand *Ustaše* troops fleeing from Tito's partisans who, like the Serbs in 1919, crossed the Karawanken so as to reinforce Yugoslavia's persistent claim to the Klagenfurt basin.

The Germans surrendered unconditionally at Eisenhower's headquarters in Rheims on 7 May and, on the following day, the people of Western Europe and the United States celebrated the end of the war in Europe. Yet there remained one prize to be won, one capital city still rocked by the explosion of shells and bombs even after the surrender was ratified by the German High Command in Berlin on 9 May. The Czech provinces were not so suited to partisan warfare as the Balkan lands or Slovakia, where a formidable resistance movement had hampered the Germans and their puppets as the Russians approached the Carpathians at the end of 1944. But Prague, like Warsaw, had traditions of defiance deep in its past; and on 5 May 1945 the people of Prague rose against their Nazi oppressors. They met fierce resistance, however, for the local SS troops were fanatics and the Sudeten German Nazis had nothing to lose but their lives. For several days Prague experienced some of the horrors of Warsaw and Budapest.

When the revolt broke out, General Patton's American Third Army was in Plzeň forty-five miles to the south-west and Marshal Koniev's Army Group (which included General Svoboda's Czechoslovak Corps) was no more than seventy miles away on the borders of Moravia. Although Patton's tanks could have reached Prague within a day and although Eisenhower requested the Soviet chief of staff to permit them to press forward, the Russians insisted that they should halt on a line running from Karlovy Vary through Plzeň to Česke Budejovice, on the upper Vltava. The Red Army, which had freed Ruthenia and Slovakia. wished for the sake of prestige to liberate the most westerly Slav city in Europe. Prague thus became the victim of a tragic episode in rival power politics. Even when the first Russian troops arrived on 9 May they were unable to silence the Nazi resistance. It was not until 11 May, when Marshal Koniev himself entered the city, that the last of the German sharpshooters were rounded up and the Czechs free to display the enthusiasm for the Soviet soldiery which they genuinely felt at that time. Five days later President Beneš, who had flown from London to Moscow in March and followed Svoboda's men from Košiče to Brno, returned to the castle on the Hradschin above the battered city. He was the one pre-war statesman restored by the grace of the Red Army and the will of his people.

13

The Soviet Impact

The process of peacemaking after the Second World War differed in form and character from the lengthy deliberations of 1814–15 or of 1919–20. Although the leading statesmen at Vienna and Versailles suspected each others' motives and doubted the sincerity of each others' ideals they were bound together by traditional concepts of order and an accepted form of diplomatic idiom. But in 1945 this was no longer the case. Such words as 'fascism' and 'imperialism' and such phrases as 'democratic rights' and 'free elections' had different connotations for the Russians and for the British and Americans. Failure to understand the intentions of rival spokesmen led to resentment and accusations of bad faith; and all too frequently these charges seemed proven by a clumsy exercise of military power. The Soviet Union brought to international affairs a new and compulsive method, described by Pokrovsky, the principal Russian historian of diplomacy, as 'the scientific dialectic of the Marx-Lenin formula'. In practice the technique was as cumbersome as its definition; and being compounded in equal parts of hostility and dissimulation, it formed no basis for a constructive peace. Nor was it meant to be. To many of the younger Red Army commanders and to some of the older Bolsheviks it seemed as if the Revolution was once more on the march. There would be no single comprehensive Peace Congress this time.

Yet Stalin himself was too experienced to be the slave of party jargon. At the last of three wartime summit meetings he was more interested in consolidation and security than in carrying the Red Flag further still. When he met Churchill, Attlee and Truman on 17 July 1945 at the start of the Potsdam Conference he had two clear objectives in Eastern Europe. Knowing that the governments established with Russian patronage in Roumania, Bulgaria and Hungary had little popular backing, he sought Anglo-American diplomatic recognition as a sign of stability; and conscious that the Poles were already settling their people in the former German lands east of the Oder and western Neisse, he sought final confirmation that these territories were to be under Polish sovereignty. It was, at times, a stormy conference.

The Russians encountered strong opposition from Churchill and, after the Labour government had taken office, from the new Foreign Secretary, Ernest Bevin. It proved easier to agree on the military administration of the German economy than on the affairs of Eastern Europe and much was left for future settlement by the Council of Foreign Ministers. But, after sixteen days of intermittent wrangling, the final communiqué showed that some progress had been made. Recognition of the new governments was postponed until preparatory work was completed on a series of peace treaties with the former Axis satellites. Poland was authorized to 'administer' the area east of the Oder-Neisse Line but Poland's frontiers in the west would only be settled when a peace treaty was concluded with Germany.

The most controversial section of the Potsdam Declaration concerned the German minorities in the Eastern European lands, many of whom had been atrociously treated in the immediate aftermath of the war. It was accepted at Potsdam that racially Germanic inhabitants would be expelled from the newly restored states and from the areas under Polish administration. The declaration hoped that such expulsions would be 'orderly and humane' and would be suspended until the Allies had jointly arranged for the refugees to be properly received in Germany. These conditions were not fulfilled. At least 6,000,000 Germans were ejected by the Poles, many of them in a shamefully brutal manner. The Czechs, in the course of 1945 and 1946, expelled some 3,000,000 Germans from the Sudetenland. Although the Czechoslovak government sought to control the exodus after the Potsdam Declaration, there had already been local excesses and cases of maltreatment in certain areas. To describe this demographic transformation as the nemesis of nationalism may explain the tragedy but can never justify it. The hatred of German and Slav was perpetuated for yet another generation; and Poland and Czechoslovakia, who had expelled these unfortunate peoples from their homes, were bound to become militarily dependent on the Soviet Union if, at some future date, there was to be a powerful revisionist sentiment among the dispossessed Germans from across the frontiers. With these expulsions were sown the seeds of the Warsaw Pact, and much else besides.

The Potsdam Conference authorized the Council of Foreign Ministers (of the Soviet Union, the USA, Britain, France and China) to meet from time to time in order to 'do the necessary preparatory work for the peace settlements' and to consider other urgent matters referred to it by agreement of the five member governments. The council thus became a regular source of international quarrelling from its first meeting in London in September 1945 until it finished its nominal task in December 1947. Bevin and the American Secretary of State, James E. Byrnes, consistently urged the Soviet authorities to permit 'democratic governments' to be established in the Eastern European countries; and Molotov countered by charges of Anglo-American interference in the domestic concerns of Poland and Roumania, and of capitalist plots to restore the old regime. Bevin certainly, and probably Byrnes as well, wished to encourage good relations between the Soviet Union and the Balkan and Vistulan states for the sake of European security; but there was an odd reluctance in London or Washington to see that disillusionment with their Russian liberators would have led to the return of anti-Soviet governments if free elections were permitted in Poland, Roumania or Hungary; and that this development would have been as unacceptable to the Russians in 1946–7 as the freely voted union of Germany and Austria had been to the victorious allies after the First World War. Although the Russians were depressingly uncooperative at the meetings of foreign ministers and at the early assemblies of the United Nations, there was a tendency in the West to expect the Soviet Union to conform to unrealistically high standards of international behaviour; and this aggravated the division of Europe into opposing camps. Slow progress was made on the preparation of the peace treaties.

Two questions which had given considerable trouble in the inter-war period were settled by the Soviet Union before the council had even begun its work. On 20 June 1945 the Polish and Czechoslovak governments were requested to send representatives to Moscow where Molotov decreed that Polish troops were to withdraw from Teschen (which they had occupied in the middle of June) and that the frontier of 1920 was to be re-established in the area. At the same time the Russians induced the Czechoslovaks to cede Ruthenia to the Soviet Union thus ensuring that all Ukrainians would henceforth be united within Stalin's empire and that the Red Army would command the vital passes through the Carpathians. This territorial adjustment seemed ethnographically justifiable so long as it was assumed that Russians and Ukrainians were linked in a common political state. Tómaš Masaryk himself had taken it for granted in 1915 that, once the Habsburg Monarchy collapsed, Ruthenia would naturally become a Russian possession; and between the wars it had been an economic liability for the Czechoslovak State. Now, however, 'Sub-Carpathian Ukraine' was strategically of major importance for it gave the Soviet Union seventy miles of common frontier with Hungary.

In the early summer of 1946 limited agreement was reached at the Council of Foreign Ministers on the peace treaties with Italy, Finland, Roumania, Hungary and Bulgaria. A twenty-one nation peace conference met in Paris from 29 July to 15 October and thrashed out detailed drafts of the treaties. There was strong opposition from the Soviet Union and from the Yugoslav, Polish and Czechoslovak delegations to a number of proposals, notably those which might have perpetuated western economic links in south-eastern Europe. The drafts were eventually forwarded to a meeting of the Council of Foreign Ministers in New York early in November. Once again Molotov delayed acceptance, seeking concessions until after a month it seemed as if there would be endless deadlock. Yet, in the end, rather than have no settlement at all, the Russians gave way over most points. Four of the peace treaties were signed in Paris on 10 February 1947; and the fifth – with Italy – four days later.

The territorial changes embodied in the treaties were few in East-Central Europe. The Roumanians and Bulgars had, after all, fought beside Soviet troops for the last eight months of the war. Thus, although Roumania had sacrificed half a million men in Hitler's Russian campaign, she lost another 150,000 in the advance through the Carpathians and up the Danube. Similarly the Bulgarian army participated in Tolbukhin's offensives in Yugoslavia and by May 1945 had crossed into Austria where they linked up with British troops from the Italian front in Klagenfurt; and thirty-two thousand Bulgarian soldiers were killed in these operations. The treaties duly restored Bulgaria's frontiers of January 1941, thereby permitting the Bulgars to retain their inter-war territories intact and with the addition of the Southern Dobrudja, which had been ceded by Roumania in September 1940. Roumania received all Transylvania but the Soviet Union retained Bessarabia and the northern Bukovina. The Hungarians fared badly from the settlement. Although a high-powered mission had visited Moscow, London and Washington in the spring of 1946 to demand justice for Hungary in the predominantly Magyar regions of Transylvania, the delegates to the Peace Conference – with a lone dissentient American voice – insisted on the Trianon frontier, which had already been provisionally restored by the Soviet-sponsored armistice of 1945. The Hungarians also had to cede to the Czechs a small segment of territory across the Danube from Bratislava, but the Yugoslavs were content with the Trianon boundaries and showed no desire for expansion in the Baranya triangle or the Bácksa. Their ambitions lay elsewhere.

The only beneficiaries in Eastern Europe from the Italian Peace Treaty were the Greeks, who gained the Dodecanese Islands, and the Yugoslavs who acquired Zadar, the Italian islands in the Adriatic and most of the Istrian Peninsula, including the ports of Rijeka (Fiume) and Pula. The future of Trieste was left unresolved by the treaty. The Yugoslavs had hoped to obtain the great port, for the hinterland was predominantly Slovene. The partisans were fighting in the suburbs of Trieste at the beginning of May 1945 when its German commander surrendered to a New Zealand division advancing from Venetia. For nearly two months there was much tension between the Yugoslav forces and the British Commonwealth troops; but in June it was agreed that the city itself and the railway route to Monfalcone and Venice were to be administered by the Allied Command in Italy, while the southern zone of the disputed region would be controlled by the Yugoslavs. The Italian Peace Treaty established Trieste as a 'Free Territory' but this solution pleased neither the Yugoslavs nor the Italians. It was proposed that Trieste should be governed by a nominee of the United Nations Security Council and, until he was appointed, the two military zones established in June 1945 were to remain in being. The Security Council, however, could never agree on who was to be governor of Trieste. Friction continued for several years between the Italians and Yugoslavs and the commerce of the port suffered. Eventually, in October 1954, it was agreed that the Anglo-American zone should be handed back to Italy and the southern zone, with minor adjustments of the line of demarcation, incorporated in Yugoslav Slovenia. Geographically, Trieste was thus left in a similar position to Fiume between the wars but there was none of the tension which had existed between the old Yugoslavia and Mussolini's Italy. The final settlement, though little more than a despairingly pragmatic compromise, worked well.

The Trieste dispute did not arouse especially strong feelings among Russian deplomats although in retrospect it is interesting that even in 1946 they tended to support the Italians rather than the Yugoslavs, presumably to please the increasingly influential Italian Communist Party. The Soviets made their greatest impact on the new map of Europe in the north and in the Danubian basin. On paper they benefited most from the treaty with Finland, which ceded the Petsamo area and granted the Russian fleet the lease of a naval base at Porkkala on the northern approaches of the Gulf of Finland. Ultimately, however, the Russian gains along the Danube were of more lasting significance. By confirming the incorporation of Bessarabia in the Ukrainian Soviet Republic, the USSR became the only riparian Great Power, able to control all commerce on the river from Linz to the sea. The treaties did, indeed, contain clauses guaranteeing freedom of navigation and equal treatment for every country on the Danube but the military position of the post-war decade made these assurances virtually meaningless. Russian primacy was consolidated in the following year when an international conference, meeting in Belgrade, revised the statutes of the Danubian Commission so as to exclude from membership any country which did not have territories touching the river. These provisions, together with the heavy reparations from Hungary and Roumania assured to the Soviet Union by the armistices and the peace treaties, made it certain that Moscow would dictate the economic life of the area, seeking to determine the character and volume of foreign trade as Germany had done in the Hitler period.

In finally accepting the treaties, Molotov appeared to have made some concessions to the West. Each treaty contained a guarantee of fundamental human rights and liberties for the citizens of the country with which it was concerned; but it was difficult to see how nations far distant from the region could ensure that these obligations were carried out and there was a complete difference between the Russian and the western interpretations of what these liberties implied. Moreover, although the settlement provided for the evacuation of Allied troops from Hungary, Bulgaria and Roumania, it was stipulated that the Soviet Union might retain garrisons in Hungary and Roumania so as to ensure communications with the Russian zone in Austria. The Red Army withdrew its occupation forces from Bulgaria in the third week of December 1947; but as the Council of Foreign Ministers failed to make any progress towards a peace settlement with Austria, it seemed as if the Soviet authorities would have a legal right of military passage along the Danube indefinitely. With Russian troops also stationed in Poland, to protect communications with the Soviet zone in Germany, the Red Army continued to advertise its presence in Eastern Europe during the years of political and economic readjustment. The Czechoslovaks, however, were in a slightly happier position than their immediate neighbours. All foreign troops were withdrawn from the republic at Christmas 1945, the Americans evacuating western Bohemia and the Russians the rest of the country; but with the Red Army along all her frontiers, except in Bavaria, Czechoslovakia's independence in foreign affairs was largely illusory.

Communism had never been a powerful force in any of the Eastern European countries before the Second World War. It was too urbanized and dogmatic for predominantly peasant lands, too sophisticated for simple rural communities whose ways of life had been moulded over the centuries by the Churches and a feudalistic structure of society. The traditional radical parties in these areas were agrarian rather than communist in form, while in the towns the workers turned more naturally to the Social Democrats than to revolutionary socialism. Apart from Yugoslavia and Albania, where communist leaders were recognized as national heroes, the principal Marxists were alien figures with no popular following (although Georgi Dimitrov had acquired a legendary reputation in Bulgaria for his ridiculing of the Nazis in the Reichstag Fire Trial at Leipzig in 1933). Many lesser personalities had spent years in the Soviet Union; out of touch with the problems of their homeland, they tended to think first of specifically Russian interests. Some, like Rákosi of Hungary, 'had liberated their country by flying in afterwards, smoking a pipe,' as Tito was later to remark acidly in a phrase that was, perhaps, also intended to apply to Dimitrov. Others, such as Bierut in Poland, had participated in the campaign against the Nazis but under the aegis of the Soviet High Command, moving westwards with the Red Army. Before the communists could secure exclusive control of the apparatus of government in any of the East European states, they had to build up the party machine and climb to power on the shoulders of discredited representatives of the older political organizations. There were coalition cabinets, in which communists and all parties left of centre had representatives, in Roumania, Poland, Hungary, Bulgaria and Czechoslovakia. Even in Yugoslavia, the provisional government of 1945 at first included a former member of the Croatian Peasant Party and the pre-war leader of the Yugoslav Democratic Party, although both resigned within six months of taking office. The coalitions survived for a rather longer period elsewhere.

Russian control was firmest in Bulgaria. There were three main reasons for this: the character of the Fatherland Front coalition; the personality of Dimitrov; and the willingness of the Bulgars to accept the forms of government that satisfied their fellow-Slavs in Russia. The Fatherland Front was not openly communist-dominated for over two years after its creation. Established by Velchev's coup of September 1944 it was led until the autumn of 1946 by Kimon Georghiev, who had also been premier of the Zveno government of 1934–5. The leaders of the Agrarian Union, which with its traditions of peasant mastery still had a considerable following in Bulgaria, and the leaders of the Social Democrats supported the Fatherland Front until the summer of 1945. Attempts by the communists to control the police and to curb all political criticism made the principal agrarian and social democrat spokesmen break with the Fatherland Front, but there remained lesser figures in both parties who were prepared to continue serving Georghiev in the Front government. Some were little more than opportunist time-servers.

Dimitrov arrived back in Sofia by air from Moscow on 8 November 1945, precisely twelve days before the holding of a long postponed General Election. He was given an enthusiastic reception but wisely decided to remain in the background until he had acquainted himself with the political trends in the country from which he had been exiled for twenty-two years. His return boosted the morale of the communist wing of the Front who saw in him the Bulgarian Lenin, but no one can say what effect his presence had on the election. It was, in time, announced that three quarters of the electorate had turned out to vote in support of a single government list, for the opposition officially boycotted the contest. British and American observers, unused to the peculiar habits of Balkan polling, protested that the election was preceded by intimidation and followed by blatant falsification of results. They were probably right: it made no difference. The Fatherland Front assumed that it possessed popular support and proceeded to purge all the leading figures of the

COMMUNIST-DOMINATED EASTERN EUROPE

0   500

Miles.

- ---·--- Frontiers of January 1938
- Incorporated in the Soviet Union, 1945
- States which became Communist between 1945 and 1948
- Allied Control Zones in Germany
- Allied Control Zones in Austria, 1945 to 1955
- Anglo-American occupation, May 1945. Subsequent withdrawal of forces
- Ceded by Italy to Yugoslavia, 1947

FINLAND

Viborg

Leningrad

ESTONIA

Pskov

Riga

LATVIA

LITHUANIA

Memel

Königsberg

EAST PRUSSIA Annxd. by Poland

Vilna

Minsk

Danzig

Bremen (U.S.A.)

Szczecin (Stettin)

Berlin

British

Russian

Annexed by Poland

Poznan

Warsaw

U. S. S. R.

Pinsk

Erfurt

POLAND

Wroclaw (Breslau)

Prague

Cracow

Nuremberg

American

CZECHOSLOVAKIA

Lvov

Fr.

U.S.A.

Russian

Vienna

Czernowitz

French

British

Uzhgorod

Budapest

Kishinev

HUNGARY

Trieste

ROUMANIA

Pola

Bucharest

YUGOSLAVIA

Belgrade

ITALY

ADRIATIC SEA

BULGARIA

Sofia

BLACK SEA

ALBANIA

AEGEAN SEA

GREECE

TURKEY

—ARTHUR BANKS—

old regime. The former regents, Prince Cyril, Professor Filov and General Mihov, had already been tried and executed. Several hundred high-ranking officers now followed their fate. Possibly the government feared an army *putsch* for it began to seek evidence against Velchev (the minister of war) but, protected by Georghiev, he survived and in the summer of 1946 was appointed Bulgarian minister in Berne, a discreet passage to exile. A referendum held in the autumn of 1946 showed that ninety-two per cent of the Bulgarian people were opposed to the institution of monarchy and the Coburg dynasty in particular. The boy king Simeon and his mother left the country; and Bulgaria was duly proclaimed a 'People's Republic' on 15 September.

These radical political changes took place against a background of more cautious land reform. The early agrarian policy of the Fatherland Front owed much to the changes proposed by Stamboliisky a quarter of a century earlier. It favoured cooperative development rather than collectivization. 'Working peasants' could retain their holdings provided they did not exceed forty-eight acres in extent; and the Orthodox Church was permitted to keep much of its property belonging to those admirably cooperative institutions, the monasteries. Yet, though the Fatherland Front spokesmen took pains to emphasize that the peasants were still owners of their land, even in a cooperative, the reforms seemed too advanced for many peasants and the government had to slow down the pace of change in the countryside. It is difficult to assess the popularity of the Georghiev government's measures. An election held in October 1946 is no true guide, as there had been the usual interference in campaigning including the arrest and imprisonment of many agrarian and social democrat politicians. Although the communists and their allies in the Front gained 364 out of the 465 seats, Dimitrov himself subsequently admitted that a million electors had voted against the Front's candidates. The Front government was thereupon re-organized, with Dimitrov becoming prime minister and communists holding nine of the most important posts. By the start of 1947 Dimitrov was as much the dictator of Bulgaria as Boris had been four years previously.

It took longer for the communists to secure a complete hold on Roumania, not least because of the vigorous resistance of King Michael. His initiative in toppling the Antonescus in August 1944 had won widespread admiration in the country; and for a time he was regarded with favour by the Soviet authorities, who even awarded him the Order of Victory. For seven months after the royal coup the government was headed by generals appointed by the king from among members of a group known to be anti-German but by no means sympathetic to communism. It was only in March 1945, under pressure from the Soviet Deputy Foreign Minister Vyshinsky, that King Michael appointed a 'National

Democratic Front' coalition and another two and a half years elapsed before the King conceded a full victory to the communists.

The National Democratic Front was a bastard offspring of dissident agrarianism and Moscow-trained communism. The authority of the government in the winter of 1944–5 did not extend into the more distant rural areas. There the peasants began to support the 'Ploughmen's Front', a left-wing agrarian movement which was founded as long ago as 1933 in southern Transylvania and headed by Petru Groza, who had held office under Averescu in 1920 and 1926. Such support as there was for the communists in the industrial centres was shared between Ana Pauker and Gheorghe Gheorghiu-Dej. Ana Pauker was a handsome Jewess in her early fifties who had survived fifteen years of intermittent imprisonment to become the principal broadcaster to Roumania on the Russian radio. Gheorghiu-Dej was a 'home-grown' communist who had not been indoctrinated in Moscow and whose hyphenated surname was testimony to the many years he had spent incarcerated in the prison of the town of Dej. Far less flamboyant than Ana Pauker, he was responsible for the organizational network of communists in the factories and in later years claimed credit for the coup of August 1944, an assertion which is not substantiated by such facts as we possess. Behind Pauker and Gheorghiu-Dej was the powerful but unknown figure of Emil Bodnaraş, a man of mixed Ukrainian and German descent. Bodnaraş, who had served as an officer in the Roumanian army and experienced an almost Pauline conversion to communism on the way to Stalingrad, became a Soviet citizen and returned ahead of the Red Army to build up and control the paramilitary formations of the Communist Party. His powers of political survival are considerable for in 1969 he was still listed as a member of the Communist Party Presidium and a vice-president of the republic.

King Michael appointed Groza as prime minister of the National Democratic Front Government, a post he held for more than seven years. At first the communists took only three portfolios, the Interior, Justice and National Economy (which went to Gheorghiu-Dej). Rather surprisingly, the Ministry of Foreign Affairs went to Tatarescu, who had led one of the more reactionary wings of the Liberal Party in the 1930s and served King Carol as prime minister from December 1933 to December 1937. Relations between Groza and King Michael were so strained that the King for several months absented himself from Bucharest and refused to give the royal assent to any governmental measures. The most important reform, a decree re-distributing all land holdings of more than 120 acres in extent, was put into effect before the royal strike began. When in January 1946 Groza brought into the government a representative of the National Peasant Party and of the less malleable wing of the liberals, the King resumed his duties; and the British and Americans accorded the government diplomatic recognition.

The three most distinguished veteran leaders of Roumania were scorned, and to some extent feared, by the Groza government. Maniu, Mihalache and Constantin Bratianu found their activities hampered by organized bands of slogan-shouting hooligans who, despite their political allegiance, might almost have been Iron Guardists (and probably were, in earlier years). Under these circumstances the election of November 1946 was hardly calculated to give a fair estimate of popular feeling. 348 seats went to the 'National Democratic Front,' thirty-two to Maniu and Mihalache's Peasant Party, and three to Bratianu's brand of liberalism. Another twenty-nine seats went to a Hungarian minority party, communist in inclination but not technically within the coalition. The significance of the election was the distribution of votes for the Front candidates: eighty-one to the Social Democrats, seventy-two to the Tatarescu Liberals, seventy to Groza's Ploughmen, and sixty-seven to the Communists. Only one deputy in six in the Roumanian parliament of 1946–7 was a member of the Communist Party, but Groza and his ministers seemed little more than communist puppets.

Maniu himself had, over the years, flourished on opposition, from his days of baiting István Tisza in the Budapest parliament to his critical memoranda to the Conducator during the Russian campaign. He belittled the threats of the Groza government, holding its nominal president in withering contempt. When the Antonescus were put on trial for war crimes in May 1946, Maniu insisted on shaking hands with both the former marshal and the former foreign minister after he had given evidence; it was a gesture not appreciated by the National Democratic Front. The Antonescus were condemned to death and shot. Maniu remained politically active for another year. In June 1947 Mihalache was arrested and charged with conspiracy; Maniu suffered a similar fate in the following month, and so did some 100 members of his National Peasant Party. There was evidence that a few supporters of the party had talked rashly about armed resistance to communism with American agents. Although neither Maniu nor Mihalache were directly implicated, plans had been made to bring them by air out of Roumania. In November 1947 they were brought to trial, the presiding judge having been an administrator of prisons and detention camps under Antonescu. Maniu defended himself with dignity, insisting that he regarded the Groza government as illegal because it had broken those clauses in the Peace Treaty which guaranteed political freedom. Both Maniu and Mihalache were sentenced to solitary confinement for life. Their conviction came seven weeks after the execution in Sofia on trumped-up charges of treason of the Bulgarian peasant leader, Nikola Petkov. Together the two verdicts shocked opinion in the non-communist world. Later trials were to make such mockeries of human rights a familiar feature of the post-war decade.

The arrests of Maniu and Mihalache were used by the communist members of the Front as a means for tightening up 'internal order'. The National Peasant Party was dissolved, and Tatarescu induced to resign as foreign minister in favour of Ana Pauker (the first woman anywhere in the world to hold such a post). King Michael was allowed to leave Roumania immediately after the end of the Maniu trial in order to attend the wedding of Princess Elizabeth in London. Perhaps it was hoped that he would not return. He became engaged to Princess Anne of Bourbon-Parma, went back to Bucharest, found the government did not approve of a royal wedding in Roumania (for it would have increased even more the popularity of the twenty-six year old monarch), and was confronted with a demand for his abdication, which he duly signed on 30 December 1947. Subsequently, in exile, he maintained that the abdication act was invalid since it had been obtained under duress.

In the spring of 1948 Roumania became a 'People's Republic' and adopted a constitution based on the Soviet 1936 model. The ruling coalition changed its name from 'National Democratic Front' to 'People's Democratic Front'. It also increased the hold of the communists on the principal posts in the state. General Bodnaraş was made minister of defence and Gheorghiu-Dej assumed responsibility for long-term planning of the economy, another importation from the Soviet Union.

The methods by which the communists established control in Hungary and Poland were basically similar to their takeover bids in the two defeated Balkan states, except for the incidental circumstance that there was no royal family to be sent on its travels in either country. Hungary's anachronistic claim to be a monarchy was ended abruptly on 1 February 1946 with the proclamation in the Budapest parliament building of a republic; but it had really ceased on 27 March 1945, when the 'Holy Crown of St Stephen' was solemnly conveyed by its guard commander, Colonel Paytás, across the Austrian frontier and eventually handed into the custody of the American Third Army. The Polish State, for its part, claimed direct legal continuity with the republic proclaimed in 1918 but, following the fashion, changed its title to 'Polish People's Republic' in July 1952.

The 'Provisional National Government of Democratic Hungary,' set up under Soviet auspices at Debrecen in December 1944 and transferred to Budapest four months later, was a remarkably conservative body. As prime minister it had General Béla Miklós who, only twelve months previously had been head of Horthy's Military Chancellery and who was a personal friend of the fallen regent. General János Vövös, a former Chief of the General Staff and another member of Horthy's inner circle, became minister of defence; and Count Géza Teleki was minister of cults and education. None of the other members of the government were such distinguished figures, even in their own parties. Zoltán Tildy, the former Calvinist minister who led the Smallholders' Party, had been considered for office and rejected; and the Smallholders, who over the years had become more progressive in outlook than they were during the Depression, were represented by two insignificant spokesmen. As yet there was no sign of the best-known of the Moscow Hungarian communists, Mátyás Rákosi, but his deputy, Ernö Gerö acted as kingmaker in the formation of the government, though declining office himself. One, who became minister of trade, was of no importance. The other, the minister for agriculture, achieved more renown than anyone, least of all Gerö and Rákosi, expected. He was an expert on soil-conservation, a genial thick-set man with pince-nez so that he looked like a caricature of an earnest continental academic. His name was Imre Nagy; he had, like Tito, been captured by the Tsar's armies and witnessed Lenin's revolution as a newly released prisoner-of-war; and he was to have his month of triumph and tragedy in 1956.

Imre Nagy was responsible for the most important legislative act of the provisional government, a land reform decreed in March 1945 and immediately put into effect in liberated territory. The great Hungarian estates and the extensive monastic lands were divided up into holdings, most of which were smaller than 100 yokes (140 acres). The reform was not completed until the autumn of 1946, by which time it was calculated that 642,000 people had acquired the right to own land in a period of eighteen months. The provisional government also gave assurances of democratic rights and of respect for private property although it indicated that there would, in time, be a plan for nationalization of the major industries.

This was a Smallholders' Party programme rather than a socialist revolution. Genuinely free elections (excluding only the reactionary parties of the Right) were held in November 1945; and it is hardly surprising that the Smallholders won sixty per cent of the parliamentary seats and that the communists and socialists only gained seventeen per cent each. The result of the election naturally entailed the supercession of the provisional government. But what was to take its place? A political crisis of the first magnitude had arisen. The head of the Allied Control Commission in Hungary, Marshal Voroshilov, had no intention of permitting the communists to be pushed into a parliamentary opposition. He had insisted, even before the election, that the government would still have to be a coalition; but he was prepared to allow the victorious

Smallholders half the seats in the cabinet. Zoltán Tildy duly became prime minister with Rákosi and the socialist leader, Szakasits, as his deputies. The communists also ensured control of the police, for Imre Nagy became minister of the interior.

The Hungarian election of 1945 taught the Russians two lessons of general importance for all the Eastern European countries: land reform won support for agrarian or smallholder policies rather than for communism with its dogma of agricultural collectives; and genuinely free voting afforded an opportunity for protest against the enormities of the 'liberators' and any Marxists who might have been in their baggage-train. There were no more free elections in any of the Eastern European states so long as they were under Soviet military domination.

Within two years the Smallholders' Party in Hungary was reduced in standing from an independent movement of enterprise and initiative to a mere auxiliary of the communist Front. Tildy himself was prime minister for only three months; for, as soon as the republic was proclaimed, he was elected President. The new government continued to be headed by a member of the Smallholders' Party, Ferenc Nagy (who was no relation of his communist minister of the interior, Imre Nagy). Unlike Tildy and most of the Smallholders' Party spokesmen in the Horthy era, Ferenc Nagy was himself a member of the class he claimed to represent. He had no intention of bowing to unreasonable Soviet pressure nor of accepting a policy dictated by Rákosi; but he knew the faults and virtues of his own followers and when one of the veteran smallholder deputies, Desider Sulyok, delivered a speech in March 1946 critical of the Slovaks, the prime minister was prepared to accept Soviet complaints of 'chauvinist revisionism' on one wing of the Smallholders' Party. Sulyok and twenty-one other deputies were expelled from the party but remained in parliament and attracted considerable notice for another twelve months by campaigning as a 'Freedom Movement' both in the Chamber and, so far as communist toughs would permit, in the country at large.

Rákosi used the Sulyok episode to have Imre Nagy replaced as minister of the interior by a more ardent revolutionary, László Rajk (whose political beliefs were shaped at a Hungarian university and in the Thirteenth International Brigade in Spain rather than at the Moscow finishing-school). It was Rajk who, with Gabor Peter, organized the sinister and sadistic Security Police, the AVO, whose victim he was himself to become three years later; but for the rest of 1946 and for much of 1947 its attentions were concentrated on discrediting the Smallholders' Party. It had valuable allies in a special corps of frontier police, organized by the ministry of defence, which also came under communist control for the first time in the spring of 1946. General Sviridov, who succeeded Voroshilov as head of the Control Commission in April, was adept at

303

discovering potential centres of disaffection and requiring Ferenc Nagy to take action against them. By this means that 'dangerous nest of reaction,' the Boy Scout movement, was dissolved; and so too were the Roman Catholic youth movements. Nagy rejected several complaints but he agreed to warn the prince-primate of Hungary, Cardinal Mindszenty, that clerical attacks on the Red Army and on Hungary's liberators must cease. It was a sign of future storms, for when Mindszenty was installed as primate in October 1945 he had been lauded by the provisional government, and even by communist spokesmen, as the anti-Nazi bishop who, when arrested by Szálasi's men, had insisted on going to prison in full canonicals.

The main attack on the Smallholders' Party came in the early months of 1947. In the last weeks of the previous year, the communist-dominated security services discovered a nationalist conspiracy, alleged to have as its objective the re-establishment of the Horthy regime as it had existed before the German occupation of Budapest in March 1944. The military leader of the plot was General Lajos Veress and among the civilian conspirators were members of the Smallholders' Party. The AVO began to investigate the activities of several parliamentary deputies, despite the protests of Ferenc Nagy and President Tildy; and on 26 February the Russians intervened, claiming that Béla Kovács, the secretary-general of the Smallholders' Party and a close friend and associate of the prime minister, had carried out espionage against Red Army installations. General Veress had to face a seven week trial and was condemned to death, but reprieved: Béla Kovács was not brought into a court of law. It made little difference. They were deported to Siberia and long presumed dead, though both emerged after eight years in a Soviet prison camp and were in Budapest during the October turmoil of 1956.

Ferenc Nagy himself, in bad health and considerably alarmed by the fate of his friend, went on holiday to Switzerland. While he was there, the communists alleged that they had evidence that he, too, was linked with a conspiracy. He resigned office without returning to Budapest. An amiable nonentity succeeded him and it could still be said that the prime minister was a non-communist. But all real power now rested with Rákosi. A three-year plan on the Soviet model was announced in August 1947. It was followed by a general election, as fraudulent and oppressive by western standards as any in Hungary's history to that date. The Smallholders' Party was splintered into factions. All the communists needed to do in the following year was to set one faction against the others, and, at the same time, to bring the remaining social democrats into an alliance of death with the Moscow Marxists. In January 1948 communists and socialists were fused into a 'United Workers' Party'; and seven months later President Tildý was forced to resign in favour of the new party's chairman, Szakasits. Hungary became a 'People's Republic,' dependent on Stalin and his prophet, Rákosi. With unintentional irony the communist-controlled coalition re-named itself, 'National Independence Front'.

The communists and their political allies were more strongly organized in Poland at the end of the war than in any other East European state. They were, however, in no sense popular. Bierut, the Moscow nominee for leadership (and from February 1947 formal president of the republic), was an unknown figure with none of the legendary reputation of other Moscow-trained communists such as Dimitrov in Bulgaria or even Rákosi in Hungary. Gomulka, who had participated in the resistance struggle at home enjoyed a certain reputation as a pre-war trade unionist and an anti-German left-wing patriot; and so, too, did his friend Marian Spychalski, the most successful Polish partisan commander. The socialists were better known, especially Josef Cyrankiewicz who had been widely active among the students at Cracow before 1939 and who emerged from the concentration camps of Auschwitz and Mauthausen to become secretary-general of the Socialist Party in July 1945. But the only man who had any real following in the country was Mikolajczýk, who returned from London to serve as vice-premier in the 'Government of National Unity'. He became leader of the Peasant Party when its aged founder, Witos, died in October 1945. Three months later the Peasant Party claimed to have six hundred thousand registered members, a remarkable tribute to his compatriots' belief that Mikolajzcyk would find a specifically Polish solution for the problem of peasant participation in government, a compromise between 'western' parliamentary traditions and 'eastern' authoritarianism. It is significant that even as early as July 1945 Gomulka could describe Mikolajczýk as a 'symbol of all anti-democratic elements, the enemy of democracy and of the Soviet Union'.

Yet by the end of 1947 Mikolajczýk was back in exile and Poland no less communist-dominated than the Danubian republics; for the close links between the Soviet military command and the 'Polish Workers' Party' ensured that, from the start, the communists controlled all the means of internal security and therefore reduced much of the activity of the Peasant Party. The Government of National Unity only contained six communist (Workers' Party) members but, as in Hungary, they held the posts that mattered. Home affairs were shared by two ministries, Public Administration and Public Security. The minister of public administration was a member of the Peasant Party but his responsibilities were limited to normal civil service duties; and a separate department, the 'Ministry of Regained Territories' [sic], was established to settle affairs in the former German lands. Gomulka himself handled these matters, a source of considerable communist patronage giving the party a hold over the western regions not unlike that of the Tammany tiger over New York City in the heyday of immigration. The minister of public security, Stanislaw Radkiewicz, was a Soviet-trained communist and he controlled, until 1954, an armed security corps greater in numbers than the military forces.

The Government of National Unity implemented a decree of the Lublin Committee which provided for expropriation of large estates and their redistribution among the peasants. This measure carried further agrarian reforms initiated during the inter-war period; and, for the moment, it left Church lands intact since the government had no wish to fall foul of the influential Catholic hierarchy. In January 1946 all industries employing more than forty men were nationalized; but it was another twelve months before Poland adopted a three-year plan to increase agricultural and industrial output and Soviet long-term planning was not introduced until July 1950, by which time the Polish and Russian economic systems were closely interlocked. During the last months of 1945 and the first half of 1946 the government sought financial aid towards recovery from the United States, using Mikolajczýk as an intermediary, but the failure of the Poles to carry out the Yalta and Potsdam Declarations induced the American government to withdraw all support by mid-summer 1946.

At the time of the Potsdam Conference the Polish provisional government had given assurances that a free election would be held within a year. It was, however, postponed until January 1947, allegedly because of the internal migrations caused by the new frontiers, and even when it was held the electoral procedure shocked western observers into protests. An electoral law, passed four months earlier, gave proportionately higher representation to the ex-German areas in the west which, under the benevolent eye of Boss Gomulka, might be expected to reflect gratitude to the Workers' Party. Every effort was made to discredit and disrupt the Peasant Party, ranging from disqualification of candidates to trials designed to show the links between Mikolajczýk and the British and American intelligence services. Subsequently Mikolajczýk calculated that a hundred thousand of his party members were imprisoned during the campaign. The combined communist-socialist bloc won 394 seats, the Peasant Party 28 and splinter groups sympathetic to the government 22. The socialist Cyrankiewicz became prime minister in February and an interim constitution basically of Soviet design was promulgated only a month after the election. Mikolajczýk, hounded and abused, determined to leave the country before he was silenced. And in October 1947, avoiding the fate of Petkov and Kovács and Maniu, he escaped to the West. The Polish socialists remained technically independent from the

POLAND SINCE 1945

0   200
Miles

EAST
Danzig(Gdansk)
PRUSSIA

Stettin
(Szczecin)

EAST

Berlin   Poznan   Warsaw

GERMANY

Oder

Neisse

Breslau(Wrocław)   Lublin

Prague

Cracow

CZECHOSLOVAKIA

Vilna

Minsk

U.

Brest-Litovsk

S.

S.

R.

Lvov

—·—· Boundary since 1945
Polish Administered Lands since 1945 (formerly German)
Territory ceded to Russia in 1945

communists for another fourteen months but in December 1948 the two organizations coalesced in the 'United Workers' Party,' which has ruled Poland ever since.

The resurrected Czechoslovak State was in an entirely different situation from her neighbours to north and south. The Red Army remained in Prague for only seven months and there was no Soviet military interference in the internal affairs once the Teschen problem had been settled and the cession of Ruthenia acknowledged. Almost all the political leaders had participated in the parliamentary life of the republic before 1938. This was as true of the principal communists Gottwald, Siroky and Zápotocky as of the far better known 'bourgeois' spokesmen, Beneš and Jan Masaryk, the president-liberator's son who had become foreign minister of the government in London in July 1940. The coalition government announced in October 1945 that it would undertake considerable nationalization of industries and carry out extensive land reforms. These measures were not so much concessions to the Left as decisions reached by Beneš and his associates in the cool reflection of exile. They were seen as logical steps after the disruption of Czech industry and agriculture by the German occupation and the developments in Slovakia.

In May 1946 parliamentary elections, with an unfettered campaign and a scrupulously secret ballot, gave the Communist Party 114 of the 300 seats in the Assembly. The communists polled 38 per cent of the votes, the 'National Socialists' (the Beneš-Masaryk party) gained 18 per cent, the People's Party (Roman Catholic) 16 per cent and the Social Democrats 13 per cent. In Slovakia the Beneš-Masaryk tradition had little following and the voting was 61 per cent for a Slovak Democrat Party and 30 per cent for the communists, a remarkably high figure for a predominantly rural area. The president duly sent for Klement Gottwald, the communist leader, and invited him to form a coalition government. His cabinet contained twenty-six ministers, only nine of whom were communists. Jan Masaryk remained foreign secretary but the communists controlled two key posts, the Interior and Information.

The coalition worked well until the summer of 1947. In foreign affairs Czechoslovakia tended to support the Soviet Union but at home there was genuine parliamentary freedom and a lively and critical press. The most serious internal crisis concerned the fate of Monsignor Tiso, the former puppet president of Slovakia. He was tried for treason in the spring of 1947 and was found guilty. The communists insisted on his execution, but the Slovak Democrats and the People's Party favoured clemency, both because he was a Slovak and because he was a priest. Beneš, however, refused to interfere with the law, and Tiso was hanged. There continued to be widespread dissatisfaction in Slovakia and the old complaints against Czech dominance and the tyranny of Prague were made again in Bratislava and even more in the strongly Catholic districts among the Carpathian foothills.

On 4 June 1947 the American Secretary of State, George C. Marshall, made his famous offer of United States 'aid to improve the economic health of the world'. A conference to consider the form of what became known as Marshall Aid was arranged in Paris in the following month. The Poles and Hungarians at first indicated their wish to attend, but subsequently refused. The Czechoslovak government accepted the invitation to send representatives to Paris, announcing its decision on 7 July. Next day a Czech delegation, which happened to be in Moscow and which included Gottwald and Jan Masaryk, was told by Stalin that Czechoslovak participation in the Marshall Plan 'might be interpreted as a blow to the friendly relations between her and the Soviet Union'. On 10 July the Czechoslovak government officially reversed the decision made three days earlier: Marshall Aid was to be a recovery programme for Western Europe alone.

Some commentators have maintained that this episode induced Stalin to prepare for the total absorption of Czechoslovakia into the Soviet system, an argument which receives powerful backing from the narrative of Dr Hubert Ripka, minister of foreign trade in Prague at that time and a warm supporter of Beneš. There were, however, other reasons for the sudden intensification of Soviet pressure on the Czechs. With the division of Europe into two mutually suspicious armed camps, the west-to-east geographical axis of Czechoslovakia was of paramount strategic importance, a corridor 370 miles long between American-garrisoned Bavaria and Carpatho-Ukraine and separating the Red Army on the Vistula from the Red Army on the Danube. Even without the Marshall Plan it was likely that Czechoslovakia, under her democratic constitution, would soon strengthen her links with the West; for elections were due in May 1948 and popular sentiment was hardening so much against individual communist bosses that it was improbable Gottwald's party would gain the most votes on this occasion. Gottwald, however, retained one advantage; his party colleague, Nosek, was minister of the interior, a post which enabled him to pack the police with reliably 'progressive' officials and to discover anti-democratic conspiracies, notably in Slovakia.

The crisis of February 1948 was provoked by the non-communist members of Gottwald's cabinet. All protested at Nosek's attempt to pack the police, and at a cabinet meeting on 12 February demanded that he should no longer dismiss experienced officers loyal to the state, a practice which was causing great indignation in Prague, where eight senior police commandants had been replaced in the preceding weeks. Neither Nosek nor Gottwald took any notice of the protests; and on 21 February all members of the government who belonged to the National Socialist, Peoples' and Slovak Democrat Parties resigned from office. The Socialists, however, remained in the government, even though they had joined in the earlier protest at Nosek's action. With their support, Gottwald still had a parliamentary majority.

For a week Prague seemed on the verge of revolution. The Workers' Militia flocked out into the streets from the factories, and action committees took over government administrative buildings and university faculties. The minister of defence, General Svoboda, took no action. He was a non-party man and his duty was to keep the army neutral unless the president, as commander-in-chief, ordered it on to the streets to maintain order. Svoboda did his duty; and so, within the strict letter of the constitution, did President Beneš. He had hoped to reconcile the communists and the secessionists, but Gottwald's position was so strong that he had no desire for compromise. Although a high-ranking Soviet envoy came to Prague, no Red Army units entered the country. Gottwald had the support of the militia and of Nosek's police; and the communists had made sure that the radio stations and printing-presses were in their hands. Beneš was persuaded to retain Gottwald as prime minister of a coalition in which all key posts were in the hands of the communists and left-wing socialists but with a member from each of the other parties nominated by Gottwald rather than by their own leaders. As an apparent concession, Jan Masaryk was invited to remain foreign minister and accepted, no doubt hoping that he could delay the transformation of his father's creation into a Soviet satrapy. On 25 February 1948 Gottwald's new government took office: on 10 March, exactly a fortnight later, Jan Masaryk was found dead in the courtyard of the Czernin Palace, the Foreign Ministry building. It remains uncertain whether he was murdered or whether, finding himself a lone dissentient in a council of fanatics and time-servers, he committed suicide.

The election was held in May, as the constitution had prescribed, but not according to democratic methods. There were no opposition candidates: the voters decided for or against an official list, chosen from the communists and social democrats. Gottwald gained a striking victory, for what it was worth: ninety per cent of the Czechs and eighty-six per cent of the Slovaks registered their approval. It was too much for Beneš. He was already a sick man but when he resigned on 6 June he made it clear to Gottwald, his successor, that he was leaving the Hradschin for political reasons. He died within three months and his memory was scorned by his country's new rulers.

When Gottwald became President, he was succeeded as prime minister by Antonin Zápotocky, the communist chairman of the Czechoslovak Trade Unions, an organization of considerable power with a larger membership than the Communist Party itself. Vladmir Clementis, the most prominent Slovak communist, became foreign minister. The political development of the republic followed a familiar pattern. Universities and the civil service were purged of 'reactionary elements,' the churches were subjected to abuse and intimidation, and forced labour camps established as corrective institutions for those who held erroneous political views. In January 1949 a five-year plan was announced, placing an emphasis on heavy industrialization and on closer links with the Soviet Union. Despite the absence of Russian troops, Czechoslovakia was as tightly bound to the Soviet political and economic system as her neighbours to north and south although her peoples continued to enjoy a higher standard of living and greater sophistication. The independence recovered with such agony in the spring of 1945 was cast aside by the Czech workers almost casually less than three years later.

For three years after the end of the war it seemed to the British and Americans that Yugoslavia was the most reliable ally of the Soviet Union among all the communist states. On numerous occasions at international conferences and at the United Nations the Yugoslavs gave public support for Soviet policy, often in terms more extravagantly phrased than any Russian delegate would have used in the soberly negative Molotov era. Thus as soon as the Marshall Plan was put forward in the summer of 1947, the Yugoslavs denounced it with the wrath of a six-teenth-century Protestant invited to receive a Jesuit mission. And when, in the following September, a meeting of communist parties announced the formation of a 'Communist Information Bureau' (or 'Cominform'), it seemed natural that the new body should have its headquarters in Belgrade; for the purpose of the Cominform was to educate the peoples' democracies so that they thought and behaved in a 'fraternal spirit of comradely unity' with the Soviet Union. If this was the task demanded of them, then there could be no better model in 1947 than Tito's Yugoslavia.

The Yugoslavs had accomplished most of the stages by which the party created a monolithic structure in the state before the end of 1945, and were therefore more than two years ahead of the Roumanians, Poles and Hungarians. The circumstances of the war had given the partisans and their communist political committees control of the National Libera-tion Front, which was re-named 'People's Front' in August 1945. The period of nominal cooperation with 'bourgeois' parties was short-lived: Šubašić left the government in September 1945 and the representatives of the other political groups withdrew at the same time (apart from the People's Peasant Party leader, Dragoljub Jovanović, who remained a supporter of Tito until July 1946). Elections in November 1945, with a single 'National Front' list, showed that ninety-and-a-half per cent of the voters approved the choice of candidates. A new parliament, meeting at the end of the month, proclaimed Yugoslavia a 'Federal People's Repub-lic' on the second anniversary of the Jajce resolutions. Ivo Ribar was elected President and a new constitution, introduced in January 1946, emphasized the federal character of the republic and contained clauses which embodied the basic principles of a socialist economy.

State security in Yugoslavia was organized by Aleksander Ranković, a Serbian partisan leader of particular distinction. The secret political police and its network of spies and informers surpassed in efficiency the pre-war security under which Ranković himself had suffered. In March 1946 they hunted down Draža Mihailović, the chetnik leader, in the mountains of north-east Bosnia. He was charged with raising an army against the partisans and with committing war crimes. Twenty-three other enemies of the communist system were put on trial with Mihailović in June; eleven defendants, including Mihailović, were sentenced to death. There were protests in Britain and the United States, although it is unlikely that Mihailović expected any other fate, and he defended his actions with fatalistic courage. He was shot on 17 July. Two months later, the security police arrested Archbishop Stepinac, the head of the Roman Catholic Church in Croatia. He was accused of having collaborated with the *Ustaše* and was sentenced to sixteen years imprisonment (although he was released in 1951 on condition that he served as a village priest and did not resume his archiepiscopal functions). He was the first senior Church dignitary to be imprisoned by an East European communist government. There was a feeling among foreign observers that Stepinac was condemned, not for his wartime contacts with Pavelić, but for his public denunciation of the way in which the Yugoslav authorities were infringing the traditional rights of the Roman Catholic Church in education and were confiscating Church property. The militant anti-clericalism of the Yugoslav Marxists was far more unbridled than in the other Eastern European republics. Once again the Yugoslav Party gave proof of its advanced doctrinal orthodoxy.

Yet, from Stalin's point of view, the Yugoslav communists enjoyed too much independence and initiative. Tito had two advantages over the other communist leaders: genuine popular support; and the geographical position of his country, for, while Yugoslavia was strategically valuable to Russia, the long Adriatic sea-coast ensured that at no point was the republic gripped in the Soviet vice which held Poland, Czechoslovakia, Roumania and Hungary so securely. Tito was able to determine his own policy towards isolated Albania (where the resistance leader Enver Hoxha had established a communist government in November 1945) and to decide on the form and extent of the assistance he would give to the Greek communists, who began to wage a civil war against the restored monarchy in the summer of 1946. He believed that he could also reach agreement with Dimitrov over specifically Balkan problems; and it was on this issue that the first major clash came between the Russians and Yugoslavs.

After the establishment of the Fatherland Front in Bulgaria genuine attempts had been made by the two countries to avoid friction over Macedonia. An uneasy compromise decided that the Macedonians on either side of the frontier should receive cultural and linguistic rights. Subsequently, a Macedonian People's Republic formed one of the six constituent federal units in Tito's Yugoslavia; and Dimiter Vlahov, one-time district commissioner for King Ferdinand of Bulgaria and later an IMRO terrorist with Marxist proclivities, became a vice-premier of Yugoslavia with special responsibilities for the Macedonian region. Projects were even discussed, at various times between 1944 and 1947, for a Greater South Slav Federation reaching from Trieste to the Black Sea, an interesting reversion to ideas which were more than a hundred years old. There was, however, a significant difference between the attitudes of the

Yugoslavs and the Bulgars; for while the Yugoslavs assumed that Bulgaria would enter the federation as a seventh constituent unit, equal in standing to Croatia or Serbia or Macedonia, the Bulgars favoured a dual republic of Yugoslavia-Bulgaria. In August 1947 Dimitrov travelled to Bled and there signed an agreement with Tito promising close political, cultural and economic cooperation between the two states.

In the autumn of 1947 Tito visited most of the East European capitals, much as King Alexander had done in the early 1930s. The marshal was greeted by large crowds in Prague, Warsaw, Sofia, Budapest and Bucharest. In Sofia on 27 November he told the Bulgars, 'We shall establish cooperation so general and so close that federation will be a mere formality'; and nine weeks later Dimitrov, in Bucharest, spoke hopefully of an eventual federation which would include all the peoples of south-eastern Europe. Stalin was alarmed at such evidence of independence from the Balkan communists. Dimitrov hastened to Moscow, duly penitent. Tito declined a Russian request to make the journey to the Kremlin: he was represented by his principal theoretician, Kardelj, and the Montenegrin leader, Milovan Djilas. More intellectually gifted than Dimitrov, they argued the Yugoslav case: there were no serious differences between Moscow and Belgrade. Stalin and Molotov were not convinced. In the small hours of 12 February 1948 Kardelj was induced to sign an agreement that Yugoslavia would consult the USSR over all future issues in foreign affairs. Yugoslav national pride does not easily forget humiliation.

There had been other disputes between Tito and Stalin in the previous three years: complaints over the scandalous behaviour of the Red Army liberators in Belgrade; protests at Russian recruitment of Yugoslavs as secret agents; and the refusal by Tito to accept a joint Soviet-Yugoslav bank, headed by a director nominated by Stalin. Now the Russians proposed to intervene in Balkan affairs in a way unparalleled since the fall of the tsars: the Soviet Union would establish a new Balkan State, a federation of Bulgaria and Yugoslavia to which Albania could be added and which would have a specially devised name of its own. At a meeting of the Yugoslav Party Central Committee on 1 March, Tito rejected all Russian proposals. At the end of the month all Russian military experts and civilian construction engineers were withdrawn from Yugoslavia. A series of letters was exchanged between Belgrade and Moscow, in which the enormity of his heresy was brought home to Tito: he was even reminded of the fate of Trotsky. But Tito refused to recant, and only one member of the Central Committee took the Soviet side against the marshal.

On 28 June 1948 a Czechoslovak communist newspaper announced that the Cominform, meeting in Bucharest, had expelled Yugoslavia from the family of fraternal Communist Parties. Stalin assumed that the

Yugoslav Party would overthrow its leaders. There were a few defections from the foreign service, Yugoslav diplomats living in other Cominform states, but unity at home was hardly broken, partly no doubt because of the efficiency of Ranković's secret police. Yet, on the night of 11/12 August a frontier patrol happened, allegedly by chance, to intercept and shoot dead the chief of the Army Staff, General Arso Jovanović, as he was escaping into Roumania. It is not clear if he intended to become leader of an anti-Tito government-in-exile or whether he was seeking to establish contact with Red Army commanders as a first stage towards a military coup in Belgrade which would coincide with Soviet action on the frontier. His abortive flight was the only serious manifestation of dis-affection in Yugoslavia.

Stalin believed that economic blockade by the Cominform countries would cause so much distress in Yugoslavia that Tito would be over-thrown. By cutting off all credit and stopping all materials to build steel mills and power stations the Russians were dealing a heavy blow at the five-year plan for industrialization which the Yugoslavs had adopted in April 1947. At the same time, Yugoslavia's foreign trade was disrupted, for more than half of it had been with the so-called Soviet bloc. Eventually Tito sought and obtained aid from the West but it was more than a year before this could be of assistance to the Yugoslav economy, partly because of mutual suspicion and partly because several Western European governments insisted on undertakings for eventual compensation for pre-war foreign assets nationalized since 1945. Although the Yugoslavs re-assessed their policies, shaking off some Russian preconceptions, the basic intention of building up an independent socialist state was never abandoned, and in time the existence of this alternative to the Stalinist model gave Yugoslavia particular eminence to men of the Left, especially in Africa and the Middle East.

A more immediate effect of the break between the Soviet Union and Yugoslavia was the cessation of support from Tito for the Greek com-munists. In October 1949 the last Greek partisan bands were rounded up and a bitter civil war ended. There were other reasons for the defeat of the Greek communists than the closing of the Yugoslav frontier after the Cominform's denunciation, but it made a considerable difference, not least because Stalin was always uninterested in Greek affairs and dis-trusted the loyalty of all Greek adherents to Marxism.

Tito had established economic mastery over Albania, to the chagrin of Enver Hoxha and most of his supporters, who feared that their country would be absorbed by its much bigger neighbour. The Albanians accordingly welcomed the dispute between Belgrade and Moscow as a means of securing release from the Yugoslav yoke. The Russians them-selves took over the Yugoslav enterprises in Albania and for the rest of his life the Albanians were Stalin's favoured clients in south-eastern Europe. Within two years of the breach with Tito, three thousand Soviet experts had settled in Albania, building up the primitive industries of the state, and encouraging the irredentist activities of the Shqiptar Albanian minority across the Yugoslav frontier. No one could denounce the 'Tito clique of Trotskyist Turkish terrorists' quite so vehemently or comprehensively as Hoxha; and for six or seven years the violence of his abuse was sweet music to the Russians. Moreover, though Albania had no resources of its own, its geographical position enabled the Red Fleet to maintain its patrols in the Adriatic and the Gulf of Otranto, for there were good naval bases near Vlonë and Durrës (Valona and Durazzo, as they were called in other times). Unfortunately for the Russians, they could no more understand Enver Hoxha than they had Tito; and when it became necessary for there to be a reconciliation between Yugoslavia and her communist neighbours, they were astounded to find that Albania continued its campaign of denunciation against 'the would-be colonizers of Belgrade,' adding to them (for good measure) the 'colonizers of Moscow'. Eventually the Russians had to evacuate their fleet from Vlonë and break off diplomatic relations with Enver Hoxha; but by then Stalin had been dead for eight years. In the early 1950s Hoxha's Albania was as much under Soviet influence as Zog's Albania had been under Italian influence twenty years previously; but it is curious that while in the end Italy threw out Zog, on this occasion Hoxha remained and it was the Russians who departed.

The expulsion of Yugoslavia from the Cominform was a decisive turning-point for all the lands of Eastern Europe under communist rule. Stalin lived for another four and three-quarter years after the breach with Tito but he was constantly suspicious of all his principal lieutenants in the 'Peoples' Democracies'. The clash of 1948 had come because ultimately both the Soviet and Yugoslav leaders thought in national terms. Stalin was so accustomed to identifying Russian nationalism with the spread of international Marxism that he genuinely expected all non-Russian communists to subordinate their individual loyalties to the cause of the 'Soviet Fatherland,' a concept created in the 'Great Patriotic War' of 1941–5. Tito's defiance had the effect of inducing Stalin to begin a witch-hunt among communist leaders outside Russia for any who favoured local nationalism rather than the 'interests of world communism' as they were interpreted within the Kremlin walls. 'Titoism' was the new dirty-word of the Marxist inquisition and it was applied, not merely to those who believed in national communism, but to others who, from time to time, thought independently rather than accepted uncritically the domination of the Soviet Party. There were two great waves of purges in these last years of Stalin: in 1949-50 the victims were mainly 'home' communists, who had never been trained in the Moscow school of dialectic; and in 1952 they were principally Jewish intellectuals, for in his final months Stalin became the complete Great Russian nationalist, releasing a torrent of anti-semitism over lands where, in the past, it had flooded too often and too easily.

No one knows the number of victims of these purges. Not all were executed and some later returned to public life, often bearing on their bodies and in their spirit the scars of past torment. Occasionally official figures were issued of expulsions from the party: the Bulgars announced on All Fools Day, 1950 that 92,400 members had been thrown out in the preceding twelve months; and in the following July the Roumanians gave their total of expulsions as 192,000 over the previous two years. Some of the prominent figures were placed on trial and their faults made public; others merely withdrew into obscurity or oblivion. The purges left considerable gaps in the central committees and new figures emerged to shape their party's policy along lines which they assumed Stalin approved.

Technically the purges began in Albania with the condemnation and execution of the 'Titoist' minister of the interior Koçi Xoxe on 11 June 1949 but the first trial of a major political personality opened in Budapest on 16 September. László Rajk, who had been shifted from the Ministry of the Interior to the Foreign Ministry in August 1948, was arraigned with seven 'accomplices' and charged with conspiring 'to overthrow by violence the democratic State order'. Rajk was alleged to have been a traitor to Hungarian communism for eighteen years and to have planned a coup in Budapest by arranging with Ranković for Yugoslav troops in Hungarian uniforms to enter the country and install Rajk as a puppet prime minister. The evidence was manifestly fabricated although had the geographical and strategic position of Hungary made it possible for there to be a Titoist show of independence, then Rajk was its most probable leader. All the accused confessed to their 'crimes': Rajk and two former members of the Party Secretariat were sentenced to death and hanged on 27 September; the other defendants were imprisoned. Other prominent Hungarian communists were dismissed, and in some cases jailed, over the following eighteen months: among them were the former socialist president, Arpád Szakasits, and Rajk's successor as minister of the interior, János Kádár (who was subjected to bestial tortures by the AVO, and spent many months in solitary confinement at Vác).

Seven weeks after Rajk's death a 'show trial' opened in Sofia in which Traicho Kostov and ten other Bulgarian communists were accused of nationalist agitation and left-wing sectarianism. Kostov was arrested in

June, at a time when he was a deputy prime minister. A week after Kostov's arrest it was announced that Dimitrov had died while receiving medical treatment in Moscow. There is no doubt that Kostov's trial was connected with the power-struggle of the Bulgarian communist party leadership, which had at times an almost Byzantine quality of ruthlessness. Kostov, like Rajk, was alleged to have planned a *coup d'état* in association with the Yugoslavs; he was accused of being a British agent; and with 'thwarting the fulfilment of the State Plan'. He refused to confess to these crimes but was found guilty and hanged; his co-defendants were sentenced to long terms in prison. His execution took place at the height of the contest for political supremacy in Sofia for Dimitrov had been succeeded by an elderly veteran of the 1923 communist insurrection, Vassil Kolarov, whose health was bad when he took office and who died at the end of January 1950, only five weeks after Kostov's execution. The succession now fell to Vulko Chervenkov, Dimitrov's brother-in-law, a thorough 'Muscovite' who slavishly copied Stalin, even when delivering a funeral oration for a dead leader. Chervenkov proceeded to secure the expulsion of seven possible rivals from the Communist Party directorate (the Bulgarian Politburo) for being linked with 'members of the Kostov gang'. His own deputy prime minister, Anton Jugov, confessed his errors to the Party Congress of 1950, but was graciously permitted to remain in office. The deaths of two of the Old Guard and the whole Kostov bogey had enabled Chervenkov to climb to a position of authority in Bulgaria which, so long as Stalin survived, seemed as secure as Rákosi's in Hungary.

The purge in Poland was less dramatic but gave the Russians even greater control over the country. Three weeks before the Cominform's expulsion of Yugoslavia Gomulka, as secretary-general of the Workers' Party, delivered an address on 'the historical traditions of the Polish labour movement' which, in the atmosphere of 1948, was interpreted as nationalistic. He subsequently repented at a Polish Politburo meeting and his willingness to withdraw into the background may have saved him from a public trial. In December he was dismissed from the government and in 1951 taken into protective custody where he was detained until the autumn of 1955. Other 'home' communists were purged at the same time as Gomulka and Bierut was confirmed by the Russians as their trusted delegate in Warsaw. The Red Army was, however, suspicious of political activities among the Polish officers and, largely as a result of the growing tension between east and west in Germany, Stalin insisted that Russia should have a firm hand on the Polish armed forces. The war minister, Zymierski (once an officer in the Pilsudski Legion) was dismissed and so too was his deputy, Spychalski, Gomulka's friend and colleague of the resistance. On 6 November 1949 Marshal Rokossovsky was appointed minister of war and six months later he was made a member of the Polish Politburo. Although Rokossovsky was of Polish descent, his military career had been spent entirely in the Red Army and, at the time of his appointment, he was commander of the Soviet units on Polish soil. For the seven years in which he was master of the Polish army Warsaw was as much under Russian control as it had been in the days of the Grand-Duke Constantine.

At first, the purges had little effect on the higher posts in Roumania and Czechoslovakia. Lucretiu Pátráşcanu, a distinguished intellectual, had been expelled from the Roumanian Party in February 1948 and subsequently imprisoned for exercising a narrowly nationalistic supremacy over the Magyar minority in Transylvania, a cause of disgrace unique among Bucharest politicians; he was executed in April 1954. There were many shifts of office in 1948–9, most of them apparently aimed at the advancement of Ana Pauker (who was an outspoken critic of Tito) and Vasile Luca. Pauker remained foreign minister and Luca became finance minister: both were made deputy premiers. The main change in Roumania occurred in the spring of 1952 when Gheorghiu-Dej, who had been content to keep party administration and control of the national economy, asserted himself: both Pauker and Luca fell from grace. Petru Groza, after seven years as nominal head of the government, received titular promotion and became nominal head of state. Gheorghiu-Dej became prime minister in June 1952. He purged the government of all Pauker and Luca supporters, many of whom were Jewish (as indeed was Ana Pauker herself). It is possible that Gheorghiu-Dej struck first in order to safeguard his position; but the disappearance from the Roumanian Party of a number of Jews would have been pleasing to Stalin at this time for he had become obsessed with the menace of 'Zionism' and the 'bourgeois' state of Israel. Luca, however, was by no means sympathetic to the Jews; and conversely one Jew, Josif Chisinevschi, remained a prominent member of the Roumanian Politburo until 1957.

Yet if anti-semitism was only a side issue in the Roumanian purges, it appears to have been in the forefront of the Czechoslovak convulsions of 1952. There had been a number of arrests of minor figures in 1949 and a massive change in personnel in the Defence Ministry and the High Command. A former socialist deputy was tried and executed in the summer of 1950. It was, however, not until November 1952 that fourteen leading communists, the majority of them Jewish, were put on trial. Among them were Rudolf Slansky, who had been party secretary from the time of Tito's disgrace until September 1951, and Clementis, the foreign secretary of the period 1948–50; both were Jewish intellectuals and Clementis enjoyed considerable support in Slovakia, where he was born and educated. Collectively the accused were charged, in the indictment, with being 'Trotskyist, Titoite, Zionist, bourgeois nationalist traitors ... in the service of American Imperialists'. Eleven of the accused were sentenced to death and hanged; the remaining three, comparatively minor 'offenders', were given long prison sentences. Once again, new party-members came rapidly to the forefront, although Gottwald, as President, kept both the state and party machines under control for the rest of his life. Among the communists in the ascendant was Antonin Novotny, who secured much of the party patronage formerly exercised by Slansky and used it with more discretion. The trial, and its ramifications, created more of a shock in Czechoslovakia than any of the earlier purges in neighbouring states, partly because its proceedings were broadcast day after day but also because such an evident mockery of justice was alien to a people as westernized as the Czechs. It created a sense of fear, but also of revulsion for a regime which depended for its mystique of government on informers and abject confessions.

It would, of course, be misleading to represent the Eastern European states as entirely concerned in these years with the struggle for power within a narrow oligarchy of party members. Genuine attempts were made to increase industrial production and to implement the long-term economic plans adopted in imitation of the Stalinist models. Through devices such as 'joint' companies the Soviet Union increased its hold on the trade of the Danubian countries, especially Roumania. Major projects were begun which aimed at the construction of valuable canals, hydro-electric plants, the modernization of railways, the extension of textile industries and the improvement of communications between states (as exemplified by the construction, under Soviet auspices, of the strategically vital rail and road bridge across the Danube, linking Giurgiu in Roumania to Ruse in Bulgaria). In Poland much progress was made on large-scale undertakings, such as the development of an entirely new industrial centre near Cracow and known as Nowa Huta, but consumer goods became rarer and rarer in the towns. Similarly in Hungary there was an increase in heavy industry but many of the products were unsuited to Hungary's resources, being manufactured from raw materials imported from Russia and subsequently sent back to Russia for consumption. Since the arrangements for exchange were to the advantage of the Soviet Union, it was not clear what long-term benefits Hungary gained from this process. All states dutifully sought to encourage the peasants to accept collectivization, but with little success. The agricultural yield remained below expectations.

The greatest resistance to communist ideology came from the Christian churches. In Bulgaria and Roumania it was found possible for the government and the Orthodox Church to exist without serious conflict, partly because the Orthodox clergy and episcopate were prepared to accept regulations denying them the right of political activity and threatening action against any religious demonstration disturbing public order. The Protestants fared less well: the Lutheran churches were traditionally politically committed; and the Calvinists, in Hungary, had too many associations with the Horthy era and even with the Tiszas in earlier days. But it was the Roman Catholic Church, with its international obligations and its links with the old regimes, that ran into the greatest conflict with the state. Archbishop Beran in Prague had no hesitation in condemning the Catholic Action Committee, set up in 1949 with Government encouragement, to rid the Church of reactionary clergy and bishops. Cardinal Hlond of Warsaw and the later Cardinal Wyszynski tried to keep the peace in Poland, but the authorities introduced measures curbing church rights in political affairs and education as soon as there were any large scale religious demonstrations. The most famous incident of conflict between the Church and the communists was the arrest in December 1948 – on the Feast of the Holy Innocents – of Cardinal Joseph Mindszenty, the primate of Hungary.

Mindszenty behaved with splendid courage, showing both the fortitude and the obstinacy of a Becket. He denounced the government, admitted that he thought a third world war probable and that, under those circumstances, he would be prepared to serve as provisional head of state should the existing regime collapse. He also described a long conversation he had held with Archduke Otto in Chicago when the Ferenc Nagy government permitted him to visit the United States in 1947. The Cardinal did not attempt to hide his hostility to the communists and his basically Habsburg legitimist beliefs. Perhaps he courted martyrdom. If so, in the accepted form, it was denied him. He was sentenced to penal servitude for life. An appeal was dismissed by the Supreme Court on the grounds that he had 'deserved the death penalty'.

To many Hungarians who, under a more liberal government, might have found the cardinal's views unbearably repressive and socially conservative, Mindszenty became a symbol of resistance against communism and the Soviet occupation in general. Although rumours went round, from time to time, that he was dead or dying, they sensed that he had not as yet said the final word. He became, despite himself, a popular hero; there were few of them in Eastern Europe in the early fifties. Ironically, his only peer was the man who had imprisoned Archbishop Stepinac of Zagreb, Marshal Tito.

14

Toppling the Statue

The cult of personality was at its zenith throughout East-Central Europe in the early 1950s. Except in Yugoslavia, the name of Stalin was omnipresent in each of the people's democracies. Brasov, the second largest city in Roumania, appeared on the map as 'Orasul Stalin'. Verna, the chief Bulgarian seaport, and Kucove, remote in the Albanian uplands, were both known officially as 'Stalin', unadorned. The Polish industrial town of Katowice became 'Stalinograd' and in Hungary rural Dunapentele lost its character and identity as the iron and steel centre of 'Sztalinvoros'. The Czechoslovaks, though prepared to perpetuate President Gottwald by changing the name of Zlin, were too cautious or too sophisticated to import a foreign statesman into their gazetteer; but the East Germans thought that Stalinstadt was an appropriate designation for a new steel town near the Polish frontier and ensured that the generalissimo whose tanks had penetrated Unter den Linden should be honoured in the streetnames of Berlin. With portraits in the factories and massive sculpted figures in the public places a liberated proletariat in six lands was unlikely to forget all that was owed to 'Great Stalin'. It was many centuries since a European ruler had fostered his apotheosis in this way.

On 5 March 1953 the god was found to be mortal and four days later he was interred in the mausoleum beside Lenin. He was, in many ways, fortunate in the timing of his death. Despite the tyranny of his own secret police and the agents of his main lieutenants in the peoples' democracies, discontent had begun to show itself in the last months of his life. There were strikes in Czechoslovakia, demonstrations in Plzeň, unrest in Poland. The standard of living had not increased and, indeed, in Czechoslovakia had declined. There was marked resentment in the Danubian lands at enforced collectivization of agriculture. The communist leaders looked to Stalin for advice, but it was clear that he was an old man, obsessed with ghostly shadows of past conspiracies. Nor was the international situation any easier. In 1949 the Russians had created in their zone of occupation in Germany a political entity which they called the 'German Democratic Republic,' placing at its head Walter Ulbricht who had been a communist deputy in the Reichstag in pre-Hitler times and had returned to Berlin as a Red Army colonel in 1945; but by 1953 the republic was already a political and economic liability for the Soviet Union and its communist partners. It was not as yet permitted full political sovereignty, for the Russians still hoped that the Ulbricht regime was only a provisional administration which could be abandoned once a German peace treaty was signed with the West. The East German government was so un-popular at home that it had to undertake constant repression while, at the same time, lacking the resources to carry out the programme of heavy industrialization assigned to it by the Russians. On 17 June 1953 there were riots in east Berlin and several other towns. Ulbricht could not control the situation and had to appeal to the Russians to restore order. The Red Army, originally reluctant to intervene, moved in tanks and armoured vehicles: it was the first, but not the last, occasion on which such heavy-handed methods were employed to keep a communist regime in being. The Berlin riots had important consequences on Soviet policy, for the Russians felt unable to negotiate over a Germany unstable and militantly hostile towards communism. Six years later Ulbricht admitted that he had expected his masters in the Kremlin to abandon him on the death of Stalin. But there was no one else to take his place.

In Russia itself Stalin's death was followed by an immediate struggle for power among the surviving members of the Politburo, with Malenkov successfully defending his position against Beria, the head of the security services, who was purged in June and executed in December. All the East European leaders seemed in secure positions. The only immediate change was in Czechoslovakia, for President Gottwald caught pneumonia at Stalin's funeral and died three days after returning from Moscow. He was succeeded by Antonin Zápotocky, whose genial earthiness made him highly popular with the Czechoslovak workers. President Zápotocky never wielded the authority of Gottwald and the new premier, Viliam Siroky, had no political stature for he was a Slovak despised by the Czechs for his origins and by his compatriots for having 'sold himself to Prague'. The chief beneficiary from Gottwald's death was Novotny who consolidated his position within the party by becoming first secretary, at the age of forty-eight. Novotny knew and understood the workings of the party machine better than the chief functionaries of the communist organizations in any of the other people's democracies. He was primarily a political engineer, a supreme example of what the Russians call an *apparatchik*, a bureaucrat trained narrowly within the party administration and lacking personality or imaginative sympathy. In the post-Stalin reaction more and more *apparatchiki* were to assume effective control in the East European states and in the Soviet Union itself, leaving dramatic gestures to a few veterans of the more spacious revolutionary era.

For a few months in 1953 it seemed as if Hungary might liberate herself from the tyranny of Rákosi and the AVO. Conditions in Hungary had worsened, mostly because of incompetent planning and maladministration. In August 1952 Rákosi himself had taken over the government and instituted a policy of deportations from the towns to the countryside, a procedure which enabled him to reward loyal and indigent party members by providing them with accommodation in confiscated apartments in Budapest. But this policy, which might almost have been copied from French Jacobin legislation of 1794, was no more successful in solving economic difficulties under Rákosi than it had been under Robespierre. The harvest of 1952 was excellent, but mismanagement made the food shortage of the following winter and spring abysmal. Rákosi, incorrigible in his dogmatism, prepared a new five-year plan. Courageously the rest of the Politburo, led by Imre Nagy, opposed him; and so too did Malenkov in Moscow. Rákosi, Nagy and two other members of the Hungarian Politburo were summoned to the Kremlin and advised to embark on a 'new course'. Nagy replaced Rákosi as premier in July 1953: he promised an end to the artificially false development of heavy industry and he held out the prospect of greater political freedom, of more consumer goods, of relaxation of agricultural collectivization. Unfortunately, Imre Nagy's tolerance extended to the old Stalinists. Rákosi was spared a Thermidor that summer: he remained in control of the party machine. Although the standard of living improved under Nagy and there was even a return to private enterprise in some undertakings, the structure of AVO terrorism remained in being and none of the criticisms of past errors mentioned Rákosi by name. With considerable contradictions in public statements, it seemed at times as if the 'new course' was inadequately charted.

There were no important changes in Poland, Bulgaria or Roumania in the two years which followed Stalin's death. Bierut's control of Poland remained unchallenged despite increased anti-Russian feeling among intellectuals in Warsaw and Cracow. Chervenkov, exaggerating his hold on the Bulgarian administration, ignored the growing threat to his position from Todor Zhivkov who became first secretary of the party in March 1954 and whose career and personal characteristics resembled Novotny's. Gheorghiu-Dej continued as Roumanian prime minister and party secretary until April 1954 when he allowed his post in the party to go to a trusted follower, Gheorghe Apostol. But in October 1955 Gheorghiu-Dej, seeing that real power came from the party administration rather than the state, resigned as premier and ousted Apostol from the post he had given him eighteen months previously. In reality, his grip on the party machine was relaxed since, unlike Chervenkov, he took care to see that his own nominees were advanced to the principal organizational posts. Chief among them was Nicolae Ceausescu who, on the liberation of Roumania in 1944, had been given the important task of building up the Communist Youth Movement. He became a candidate member of the Roumanian Politburo in April 1954, when he was thirty-six years old.

On 8 February 1955 Malenkov resigned as Soviet premier and was succeeded by Bulganin although the real power was held by Khrushchev, who had become Communist Party Secretary in 1953. Malenkov's fall appears to have been caused primarily by internal feuds but, as he had become identified with a policy of moderate reform in the East European states, it was inevitable that the change of leadership should have repercussions across Russia's western frontiers. At first, it seemed as if there might be a reversion to unadulterated Stalinism. Within eleven days of Malenkov's resignation Rákosi had replaced Imre Nagy as head of the Hungarian government by the more pliable Hegedus. If the Soviet Union was preparing to withdraw its armed forces from Austria, it was essential to have a strong ruler in Hungary so as to safeguard the strategically vital route up the Tisza river to the Carpathian passes. Nagy appeared in Russian eyes to be a weak man who, in the previous year, had encouraged the formation of a movement known as the 'Patriotic Popular Front,' a non-party body. Hence Khrushchev preferred to reinstate a nominee of Rákosi although insisting that excessive repression should be kept in reserve as a threat rather than be imposed in such a way that it produced a violent upheaval. Imre Nagy was politically disgraced and, in the following November, expelled from the party because he would not admit his errors. There was, however, no trial or execution either because the new communist management wished to dissociate itself from past purges or because it was known that his health was bad and it seemed likely that he would soon die and be forgotten. He was allowed to withdraw into private life and he remained a popular figure in Budapest, mingling openly with the crowds in the cafés and the theatres and other places of public entertainment.

The first year of the Khrushchev era saw remarkable changes in Soviet policy. With the convening of the first summit conference since Potsdam at Geneva in July 1955 there seemed a relaxation of tension between East and West. It had been preceded by two unexpected gestures by the Russian leaders. In the early spring they had suddenly withdrawn all the objections made by Soviet governments over the preceding nine years to the conclusion of an Austrian peace treaty; and in May it was announced in Moscow that Bulganin and Khrushchev would pay a visit 'in the near future' to Yugoslavia.

The Austrian State Treaty was signed by the foreign ministers of

Britain, France and Russia and by the American secretary of state at the Belvedere Palace in Vienna on 15 May 1955. The Austrian Republic became a fully independent state, pledged to permanent neutrality: it would never permit a Habsburg restoration or union with Germany. Occupation forces withdrew from their respective zones, the last Red Army units crossing into Hungary during the fourth week of October. The Russians safeguarded their military position in Central Europe by negotiating an Eastern European Mutual Assistance Treaty which was signed in Warsaw on the day before the Austrian State Treaty. The 'Warsaw Pact,' as it is generally called, was concluded by representatives of the Soviet Union, Albania, Bulgaria, Czechoslovakia, Eastern Germany, Hungary, Poland and Roumania. While asserting the need for friendship and cooperation, it provided for the establishment of a unified military command for the armed forces of all the member countries. It could thus justify the retention of the Red Army and Air Force in Hungary and Roumania once the pretext that they were stationed there to safeguard communications with the Soviet zone of Austria had ceased to be valid. At the same time the pact provided for greater intervention by the Soviet Union in the internal management of the military affairs of its allies. The pact was not specifically an instrument of communist collaboration: Article 9 stated that other countries might accede to the treaty 'irrespective of their social and state systems'. When, in the following September, the Russians announced their intention of withdrawing from the naval base of Porkkalla in Finland, they invited the Finns to join the Warsaw Pact; but Finland preferred neutrality, and the Russians appeared to be satisfied with a mere Treaty of Friendship.

Less than a fortnight after the Austrian State Treaty was signed, the Russian leaders flew to Belgrade and publicly expressed regret at the events of 1948, repudiating the denunciations of Marshal Tito made by Stalin and others at that time. Tito himself, who had assumed the presidency of the Federal People's Republic early in 1953, was no more prepared than the Finns to become a Soviet ally once more. He made every effort to whittle away the remaining traces of Stalinist repression among his neighbours and eventually, in the following April, he secured the formal dissolution of the Cominform. He was, however, unable to persuade Khruschev that security in Central Europe would be best served by the retirement of Rákosi, towards whom he felt a particular antipathy. In March 1956 Rákosi, in a speech at Eger, announced that Rajk (whom he had condemned as a Titoist in 1949) had been posthumously rehabilitated by the party and that his trial had been a miscarriage of justice. If this cynical gesture was intended to placate Tito, it failed. He continued to press for Rákosi's dismissal when he visited Moscow later that summer.

Attempts were also made by the Russians from 1955 onwards to strengthen the economic links between the communist countries. In January 1949 a Council for Mutual Economic Assistance ('Comecon') had been established to provide an Eastern European counter-organization to the growing interdependence of the Western European economy. So long as Stalin was alive, Comecon was permitted little initiative and he seems to have regarded it as primarily an institution for enforcing the economic boycott of Yugoslavia. But Mikoyan, who was Soviet deputy premier in 1955 and had been foreign trade commissar when Comecon was set up, succeeded in gaining acceptance for the principle that the council should hold regular meetings at which ministers from the Eastern European countries were able to work out a common economic policy and adjust the pattern of trade. At a ministerial meeting in Budapest in 1955 it was agreed that commissions should be established to decide on appropriate industrial specialization among the member states. Progress, however, was slow: the members showed marked suspicion of each other and, indeed, of the Soviet Union; and it was not until 1960 that Comecon was sufficiently organized to publish its basic statutes and decide on its principles of cooperation. Ultimately the whole project caused more friction among the communist states than any of the military issues involved in the Warsaw Pact.

The Twentieth Congress of the Communist Party of the Soviet Union took place in February 1956. Subsequently it became famous for the long and secret denunciation of Stalin and condemnation of his methods made by Khruschev and published by the United States intelligence services in a 'leaked' version four months later. Yet the philippic was not merely an exercise in sustained invective. It embodied the three principles which other speakers amplified at the congress: the need for co-existence; the acceptance of 'different roads to socialism'; and the fundamentally anti-socialist character of the cult of personality. Such ideological revision inevitably had profound consequences in each of the Warsaw Pact countries: for some it proved a dangerously heady wine.

The effects of 'de-Stalinization' were felt first in Poland, partly because of the accidental circumstance that Bierut, like Gottwald three years earlier, succumbed to the Russian winter. He died in Moscow only seventeen days after the congress had ended. It was not easy to find a successor as party boss, for Bierut had held power for twelve years and had removed most of his rivals from positions of authority. Khruschev himself helped the Poles choose their new first secretary, Edward Ochab, on 20 March. Ochab was an old Stalinist with little following in the country. He was, however, related by marriage to Gomulka and throughout the next five months he sought Gomulka's advice, though he did not always accept it. The political situation was full of anomalies. Thus, although Gomulka had been a free man since the previous October, his release from protective custody was not made public until the first week in April and he was not formally re-admitted to the party until August. Similarly the prime minister was still the ex-socialist Josef Cyrankiewicz who was head of the government when Gomulka was dismissed and had every intention of remaining in office, despite the disappearance of his old Stalinist patrons. Hence, on 23 April 1956 Cyrankiewicz was able to make an enthusiastic speech welcoming the 'creative search for a new policy and the great debate in which practically all of us are participating'. He has continued to serve as prime minister ever since.

The remaining Stalinists in the Polish Government were removed from office during April and May: survivors of the purges were re-habilitated; and new names figured in the lists of office-holders. It was, for example, in the government re-shuffle of 27 April that the former socialist, Adam Rapacki, became foreign minister, a post he was to hold for over twelve years. But political changes only scratched the surface of Poland's problems. Consumer prices had increased by some fifty-five per cent in the previous five years and the new government's offers of wage increases seemed inadequate and delayed by bureaucratic bumbling. On 28 June the workers in the engineering works at Poznan – ironically named after Stalin – went on strike against their low wages. While marching to the centre of the town the strikers were joined by other citizens with grievances and attacks were made on public buildings. Sporadic rioting continued until the evening of the following day. Troops were called in so as to restore order speedily. Fifty-three people were killed. But, although Bulganin and Marshal Zhukov flew to Warsaw to induce Ochab and Cyrankiewicz to take a strong line against the rioters, the Poles insisted that the strikers had legitimate complaints. Wages were increased and only light sentences imposed on those who had been arrested.

The Poznan riot was followed by other demonstrations, more peaceful in character, during July and August. Popular sentiment transformed Gomulka into a Polish Cincinnatus who would be brought into the government to save the republic from the machinations of its enemies. There was also a significant gathering at Czestochowa on 25–6 August when more than half a million people attended the tercentenary of a re-ligious festival which had placed the Polish nation under the protection of the Virgin Mary at a time of prolonged conflict with the Russians. The climax to the political agitation came in the middle of October, when the central committee of the Workers' Party was due to meet and elect its new officers. There were rumours of Soviet troop movements and of

327

Russian intervention to thwart the Gomulka faction. Khrushchev, Mikoyan and other Soviet dignitaries arrived in Warsaw on the first morning of the committee meeting. Marshal Rokossovsky advised the Russian delegation that armed intervention against Gomulka would lead to the permanent alienation of the Polish people. The election was a triumph for Gomulka and his reformers. Khrushchev was assured that the Poles did not intend to break links with the Russians and turn their state into a Vistulan Yugoslavia. Marshal Rokossovsky was replaced as commander-in-chief and minister of war by General Spychalski, but Poland stood loyal to the Warsaw Pact and there was no interference with Russian communication lines to Germany.

Gomulka's return to power was welcomed throughout the country as a specifically national victory. He became first secretary of the party at the age of fifty-one; Ochab accepted his own relegation to the ministry of Agriculture with dignity and loyally cooperated with the new administration. Gomulka's idea of socialism was strangely old-fashioned, strict and austere: it lacked the enthusiasm of those of his supporters who had hailed his victory as 'Spring in October'. Some were soon disillusioned when the reality fell short of the vision. Yet Gomulka remained loyal to two basic principles: acceptance that Poland could shape her own form of socialism; and the certainty that the security of Poland within her post-war boundaries necessitated a common defence policy with the Soviet Union. If these ideals fell short of the liberal revolution envisaged by his admirers, at least they had the merit of practical common-sense. Gomulka was, and is, a pragmatic conservative Marxist inclined in moments of impatience to hanker for authoritarianism, but prepared to see in limited reform a safety-valve for angry hotheads. His statecraft saved Poland from the tragedy which fell on Budapest.

The aftermath of the Twentieth Party Congress led to a major change of government in Bulgaria but had little effect on either Roumania or Czechoslovakia. In Sofia Chervenkov was blamed by the Party Central Committee for indulging in 'the personality cult' and in April 1956 he was replaced as prime minister by a Macedonian, Anton Yugov, although the real victor in the power struggle was Zhivkov, the first secretary of the party. At the same time the Bulgarian Politburo announced a series of reforms which were intended to raise living standards. Chervenkov was not entirely disgraced: he remained a vice-premier. Gheorghiu-Dej had already rid the Roumanian Party of its Muscovite Stalinist wing in 1952; and his report to the Roumanian Party Congress in December 1955 anticipated the doctrines of peaceful co-existence and of national variations in socialism which Khrushchev was to put forward in Moscow two months later. The Czechoslovaks were reasonably content politically and economically, and latent national antagonism towards the Magyars and Poles made them unresponsive to the ferment across their frontiers. Nevertheless, Novotny could not afford to ignore the Twentieth Congress entirely. He secured the dismissal of the unpopular minister of defence, Alexei Cepicka, and a few minor bureaucrats shared his disgrace; but the workers were well pleased with an administration which raised pensions, limited the length of the working-day and introduced price cuts as evidence that the years of hardship were over. Revolts do not spring from such conditions, as Novotny well knew.

It was otherwise in Hungary. Hegedus, Rákosi's puppet prime minister, condemned the cult of personality at the end of March and followed up his broadcast by an announcement of widespread price cuts. But the unrest in Budapest was far more historical and patriotic in sentiment than in any of the other communist states. Agitation continued throughout the spring and summer in a society originally intended for young intellectuals within the party and called, significantly, the Petöfi Circle. Demands were made for freedom of the press and for a more specifically Hungarian policy, less subservient to Moscow. Rákosi himself prepared another purge: he was alarmed by the way in which the intellectuals were turning Imre Nagy into a Magyar Gomulka. But the Russians wanted no more purges, particularly as they were trying at that moment to complete negotiations with Tito. Mikoyan flew to Budapest and delivered the Kremlin's verdict of 'no confidence' to Rákosi. On 18 July Rákosi resigned and left Hungary for Yalta and obscurity.

Rákosi was replaced as first secretary by Ernö Gerö, the former Stalinist who had assisted in the formation of the provisional government at Debrecen in 1944. To appease the more radical elements, Gerö was to share his party responsibilities with János Kádár, who had been imprisoned as a Titoist in 1949 and released by Imre Nagy in 1954. The new Politburo promised 'further democratization' but tension mounted through the autumn days and into a wet October. Unrest was increased by two familiar concomitants of revolution: a bad harvest and shortage of fuel (caused in this instance by a breakdown in the supplies of Polish coal). As another concession to public demand, Imre Nagy was reinstated as a party member early in October, but the press openly urged that he should be brought back as head of government. Nagy himself left Budapest for Badacsony, near Lake Balaton, where he was principal guest at a wine festival on 22 October. On the following afternoon university students and factory workers from Csepel Island demonstrated in the streets of Pest in favour of political concessions and genuine independence for Hungary. At half-past nine that night the massive statue of Stalin was toppled from its pedestal in the centre of the city park and dragged by

street-cleaning trucks to the National Theatre. The gesture faithfully
caught the spirit of the hour. Unfortunately, his boots remained firmly on
their plinth: and that too was symbolic.

The Hungarian Revolution which began on 23 October 1956 ended in
failure on 4 November. It was, from the start, more extensive and deep-
rooted than the wave of feeling which had swept Gomulka to power in
Poland. The first demands of the Budapest students and workers on 23
October reflected their innate sense of continuity with the historic past
of Hungary: for, alongside an insistence on the withdrawal of Soviet
troops and the restitution of basic freedoms, their programme proposed
the replacement of alien insignia by 'the old Hungarian arms of Kossuth'
and recognition of 15 March as a national holiday in memory of the
struggle of 1848–9. The verse of Petöfi was as much an inspiration in 1956
as it had been in the earlier revolution, and the demonstrators laid wreaths
on his monument and at the foot of the memorial to General Bem, the
Polish exile who had fought for Hungary against the Russians in 1849.
Ultimately these historical associations may have harmed the revolutionary
cause by convincing the Soviet rulers that the movement was aggressively
nationalistic and anti-Slav rather than primarily patriot-reformist, as in
Warsaw (where there was no blatant evocation of 1830 and 1863). The
Hungarian Revolution increased in momentum until, by the second week,
its objectives seemed to the Russians more dangerously 'reactionary' than
they could tolerate.

On the second and third days of the Budapest rising the Soviet authorities believed that they could work with a new government and party
administration in Hungary as in Poland. Imre Nagy replaced Hegedus
as premier on 24 October. Gerö was edged out and Kádár took over as
sole first secretary on the following day. Mikoyan and Suslov, the
Russian Politburo specialist on East-Central Europe, were in Budapest
to supervise the transition. An agreement was negotiated by Mikoyan
with Nagy and Kádár for the withdrawal of the Red Army from Hungary
and it is probable that the Russians were sincere in their efforts at cooperation until the very end of the month. But the removal of restrictions
released a wave of political feeling: all the old political parties of 1945–6
reappeared overnight; a force of Hungarian militia brought back Cardinal
Mindszenty to the primate's palace in Buda and, on the evening of 31
October, he broadcast to the Hungarian people. Nagy had taken into his
coalition the former smallholders' leader, Béla Kovács, the ex-President
Zoltán Tildy (another smallholder) and the courageous social democrat,
Anna Kethly; but there was a danger that these representatives of the
moderate Left and Nagy himself would be swamped in a flood of irrational
nostalgia for the old order. On the night of 1/2 November János Kádár
disappeared from Budapest after a day in which reports came into the

capital that Soviet troops had halted their movement to the frontier and were moving westwards, with new columns of the latest tanks.

Nagy appealed for help to the United Nations and, announcing Hungary's withdrawal from the Warsaw Pact, sought recognition of Hungary as a neutral state, similar to Austria and Switzerland. There was no response from the major powers of the West, for on 31 October the British and French began bombing Egyptian airfields in their ill-conceived plan to solve by force the problems of the Suez Canal and the Middle East, contrary to the policy of the United States and the will of world opinion. Hungary was left isolated. Kádár, in eastern Hungary, proclaimed the establishment of a 'revolutionary government of peasants and workers' which would save the republic from the 'Horthyite fascist revolutionaries' in Budapest. The Soviet tanks moved into the boulevards of the capital on 4 November while heavy artillery shelled Buda and the waterfront from the promontory of the Gellert Hill where the Freedom Monument bore witness to the agony of the city and its people. Nagy and his ministers sought sanctuary in the Yugoslav Legation, Mindszenty in the Legation of the United States. The return of the Russians was resisted with magnificent heroism by the people of the city, many thousands of whom were killed. A General Strike by factory workers and miners continued even after Kádár re-established control in the capital. Some two hundred thousand refugees flocked to the West. No one knows how many Hungarians were transported to the East.

Kádár remains an enigmatic figure. At the time, he was reviled in the West and among some of his fellow-communists as a traitor to Nagy. Yet he never restored the full terrors of the Rákosi era and he permitted greater freedom in Hungary from 1959 onwards. It is possible that he was genuinely alarmed at the speed with which Hungary was changing its political character during the second week of the revolution. There is much, however, that can never be condoned: the arrest and subsequent execution of General Pál Maleter, despite a safe-conduct from the Soviet military authorities; and the transportation, trial and execution in June 1958 of Imre Nagy after he had emerged from the Yugoslav Legation with assurances from the Kádár government on 22 November 1956. There are some who believe that Kádár was not a free agent in these matters and that, within a decade, Hungary achieved under his guidance all the principles he had accepted as one of Nagy's colleagues, except the withdrawal of Russian troops from the frontier area. Kádár has certainly won a popularity in Hungary which seemed impossible in the immediate aftermath of 1956. Time heals more speedily than history forgives.

15

From Budapest to Prague

From 1956 to 1968 the communist states of Eastern Europe gradually obtained greater freedom of manoeuvre, despite the appalling tragedy in Hungary. The pace of de-Stalinization slackened for two years after the October revolutions but the process was never completely reversed. It was helped by external circumstances, notably the growing interest of the Soviet Union in the Middle East and Africa and the tendency of Russia and America to confront each other on a global basis rather than specifically in the chosen arena of Eastern Europe. Even the crisis over Berlin in 1961 and the construction of the hideous wall across the city had few repercussions among the other Warsaw Pact states: this, it was felt, was primarily a contest between the two Great Powers and their German clients. On the other hand, the East European governments were more directly concerned with the chronic uncertainties in Sino-Soviet relations from 1959 to 1964, and some of the communist leaders were able to use to advantage a natural aptitude for bargaining by threatening the rulers in Moscow with a shift of allegiance to the new pope in Peking. The Russians themselves showed less interest in the Balkans than they had in the previous decade. Apart from propping up that anachronistic relic of old antagonisms the so-called 'German Democratic Republic,' Khrushchev was mainly anxious to promote a supranational economic order and most of his disputes with his communist partners were caused by decisions of the Comecon committees.

So long as Khrushchev was in power the other communist states followed their own 'paths to socialism,' sometimes falteringly but ultimately towards the goal of greater autonomy. Only when he was succeeded by Brezhnev and Kosygin in October 1964 were these 'new courses' called seriously in question and even then concessions continued to be won at the international communist party conferences. It remained uncertain, by the end of 1968, if these developments foreshadowed a genuine independence or were merely an interlude in the long struggle of external powers to dominate East-Central Europe.

Throughout this period Yugoslavia remained the least conformist of the communist states and the only one totally independent of the Soviet Union in foreign affairs. The breach with Stalin in 1948 allowed experiments to be made with the organization of economic enterprises and in decentralization of government. Foreign aid enabled industrial production to leap ahead in the middle of the 1950s and the export of manufactured goods more than doubled between 1953 and 1960. From 1953 onwards peasants were allowed to withdraw land and livestock from agricultural cooperatives although retaining cooperative undertakings for the provision of machinery and the more sophisticated aspects of farming, and there thus remained a 'private sector' in Yugoslav agriculture. The most interesting reform in terms of political theory was the handing over of management in factories and other institutions to the workers themselves, a process made possible by a decree of June 1950 providing for the election of bi-annual Workers' Councils. When in 1953 the Yugoslav Constitution was extensively revised, these Workers' Councils were given recognition by the establishment of a second chamber of parliament which was to be elected by the workers in the state enterprises through their councils. Ten years later the third Constitutional Law of the Tito era extended this process of representation even further by setting up four Producers' Councils to form one half of the parliament, the other house being composed of directly elected deputies and delegates nominated by the six constituent republics within Yugoslavia. There is no doubt that growth of workers' management and the remarkably complicated constitutional structure of the central government gives Yugoslavia its unique standing as an example of a socialist state.

The economic changes in Yugoslavia were accompanied by increased liberty of expression and by monetary encouragement to work overtime or to take more than one job of work. Competition was introduced between various enterprises, and in consequence life in Yugoslavia changed remarkably between 1952 and 1961. There were few political prisoners and little sign of the security services. Nevertheless there were limits to the political reforms: no organized oppositional groups were tolerated, although non-party members were elected to parliament; and when the former vice-president, Milovan Djilas, urged the growth of a westernized form of democratic government, he was condemned by the party and in 1957 sent to prison for four years for subversive activity. (Subsequently, Djilas's further published criticisms led to another trial and prison sentence in 1962 from which he was released in December 1966 and allowed to go to Western Europe and the United States in the summer of 1968.)

Tito himself remained firmly in control of state and foreign affairs throughout the 1950s and beyond. His principal lieutenants were Edvard

Kardelj, a Slovene and the chief theorist in the party, and Aleksander Ranković who remained responsible for internal security from 1945 to 1966. In November 1952 the party was changed in name to 'League of Yugoslav Communists' while four months later the scope and influence of the mass organization from which it recruited its members was extended and its title, the 'Peoples' Front,' changed to 'Socialist Alliance'. There were occasional conflicts between the Alliance and the League, and for a time it looked as if the Alliance might reduce the hold of the old partisan leaders on the communist structure. Ranković regarded the Alliance with suspicion and when in 1960 he succeeded Kardelj as general secretary of the Alliance it lost much of its independence. In 1966 the Alliance's Congress attacked the stiflingly archaic attitudes of the League. Tito supported these critics and, finding that Ranković was employing security procedure to spy even on the President himself, began a brief but effective purge in the structure of the League. Complaining that Ranković's chief political ally Stefanović had used his position as minister of the interior 'to wire-tap his way into the lives of people at every level,' Tito dismissed both men from public office on 1 July 1966. Both Ranković and Stefanović were allowed to defend themselves publicly and their statements were openly printed in the Yugoslav press. It is a significant commentary on the degree of personal freedom achieved in Yugoslavia that neither man was subjected to criminal proceedings.

There remained, however, a sinister shadow behind the Ranković affair of 1966: both victims of the purge were accused of having given preferential treatment to Serbs at the expense of other nationalities. The national antagonisms of the inter-war period have by no means totally disappeared in Yugoslavia. Both the Croats and the Slovenes showed at various times, and especially in the early sixties, that they resented the extent to which the north was subsidizing the backward areas of southern Serbia and Macedonia, and less impoverished regions in Bosnia-Herzegovina for that matter. In 1967 a group of prominent Croatian intellectuals published a declaration in Zagreb complaining that the purity of the Croatian language was being ruined by excessive importation of specifically Serbian words and usages. Nevertheless these expressions of regional patriotism have been harmless in comparison with the feuds of the twenties and thirties. The existence of six regional parliaments has given an outlet for narrowly nationalist sentiment and the republic has moved more and more towards the confederation of peoples envisaged by Trumbić and Supilo in the First World War. The worst conflicts of 1968 arose through resentment among the million Shqiptar Albanians living primarily in Kosovo-Metohija and Macedonia at alleged injustices perpetrated by the predominantly Serbian bureaucrats in local administration. There were similar outbreaks in Kosmet, as the region is generally known, in 1957 and they were certainly instigated at that time from across the frontier in Tirana. The 1968 disturbances, which involved serious rioting in two towns, may have been encouraged by the indefatigable Enver Hoxha but it is possible that, with the coming to manhood of the first well-educated Shqiptar minority, social divisiveness is feeding latent national animosity. The Magyar minority in the Voivodina, which numbers more than half a million has been treated with good sense and permitted a wide linguistic freedom as well as participating in the auto-nomous administration for the area established in Novi Sad; and there has been no serious conflict with the authorities in Belgrade.

Yugoslav foreign policy has shown considerable flexibility. During the period of total estrangement from the other communist states, Yugo-slavia inevitably drew closer to the West; and in 1953 even concluded a Balkan Pact with Greece and Turkey, both of whom were members of NATO. But, in general, Yugoslavia has sought to avoid alignments with clearly defined Power blocs and has played a considerable role in the United Nations. As relations between Greece and Turkey worsened over the Cyprus question, the Yugoslavs were prepared to let the provisions of the Balkan Pact fall away, and although there were military staff talks of the three countries in Belgrade as late as April 1955, the pact gradually became as much a historical curiosity as its predecessors of the inter-war period. The Yugoslavs preferred to emphasize their neutrality by colla-borating with the 'uncommitted nations' of Asia and Africa, notably in an impressive international conference of heads of state held in Belgrade in September 1961 and attended by representatives of more than two dozen countries. At the same time, the Yugoslavs have concentrated on improving trade links with the underdeveloped states although they have sent observers to the meetings of the EEC (Common Market) in Brussels and from late 1964 onwards participated in certain agencies of its Soviet-sponsored rival, Comecon.

Even after the interchange of visits between Khrushchev and Tito in 1955–6 there were occasional strained relations between Yugoslavia and her communist neighbours to the north and east while there was never any real improvement in her contacts with Albania. From the last months of 1957 until the spring of 1962 Belgrade and Moscow eyed each other with considerable suspicion partly because of the intense opposition of the Chinese communists, with whom the Russians were still nominally friendly, to everything Yugoslav. This attitude, it should be added, was not entirely caused by Peking's disapproval of Yugoslavia's ideo-logical waywardness, for China and Yugoslavia were also political and trading rivals in the emergent states of south-eastern Asia and particularly in Indonesia. The growing estrangement of Russia and China, openly demonstrated at the 22nd Communist Party Congress in Moscow in

October 1961, facilitated another rapprochement between Khrushchev and Tito. There were close relations between Yugoslavia and the Warsaw Pact countries from September 1962, when the Soviet president paid a State Visit to Yugoslavia, until the fall of Khrushchev in October 1964. During that period Tito himself was once more received in Moscow and exchanged visits with the leaders of Hungary, Czechoslovakia and Roumania. When Khrushchev resigned, Tito risked offending Russia's new masters by speaking out openly in defence of the fallen premier's policy. There was, however, no marked breach on this occasion: a Soviet delegation attended the Congress of the League of Yugoslav Communists in December 1964 and Tito made the journey to Moscow yet again the following June. Events in Czechoslovakia in 1968 imposed the severest strain on Soviet-Yugoslav relations since the death of Stalin. When the five countries of the Warsaw Pact intervened in Czechoslovakia in August 1968 President Tito, who had been in Prague only ten days previously, reacted with angry words: 'The entry of foreign troops without the legal government's invitation . . . and the trampling of a communist country's sovereignty,' he declared, were serious blows against 'socialist and progressive forces in the world'. For some months there were disquieting rumours of troop movements in southern Hungary and Bulgaria.

Albania, a country rather less than a third the size of Scotland, has remained stubbornly isolated from all her neighbours since 1948. Enver Hoxha has retained all the appurtenances of Stalinism, controlling the party as an inflexible first secretary although permitting Mehmet Shehu, the chairman of the Council of Ministers, some initiative in routine administration. Albania's external policy has depended mainly on her latent conflict with Yugoslavia. Thus, the rapprochement between Tito and Khrushchev in 1955 marked the beginning of a deterioration in Russo-Albanian relations which became rapidly worse when the Albanians accepted the Maoist interpretations of Marxist-Leninist doctrines and executed a number of pro-Soviet party-members in the course of 1961. The complete severance of all contacts with the Soviet Union in that year was followed in 1962 and 1963 by intensive Chinese patronage. In September 1968 the Albanian parliament passed a law formally withdrawing from the Warsaw Pact since its members had shown by their 'treacherous' attitude to Czechoslovakia that they were 'real fascists'. Suspicions that the Bulgars were reviving old claims to all the Macedonian lands, as delineated at San Stefano in 1878, led to an exchange of mutual insults between Tirana and Sofia in the course of 1968; but there was no sign of a corresponding reconciliation with Yugoslavia or with Greece, both of whom would be affected even more than Albania if IMRO rode the Balkan range again. Old passions have continued to smoulder in Albania, a country which has remained backward and poverty-stricken even under communism. In any major conflict the Albanian people would have little to lose but their chains.

Throughout the fifties and sixties Yugoslavia and Albania consistently represented opposite extremes in the extent to which their concepts of socialism tolerated personal and economic freedom. It is far harder to place Poland accurately on any such scale of values. The Polish election of January 1957 permitted the voters to show their feelings far more than was customary in any of the Warsaw Pact countries: for the electorate could strike out the names of candidates from the Workers' Party, and rejected them in some instances in favour of representatives from other groups. The electoral regulations still ensured a majority for the party, but the new Sejm had a larger opposition than its predecessors and among the deputies were former members of the old peasant parties and of the Roman Catholics, now again permitted to organize into political clubs. This cautious approach to liberal democratic practice was characteristic of the limited reforms undertaken in the first five years of the Gomulka period; but by 1962 a halt had been called to such experiments and by the summer of 1963 Gomulka seemed in full retreat from the programme which had brought him to power less than seven years earlier.

The changes of 1956–7 were impressive, and some have shown qualities of permanence. In agriculture, for example, the hated system of collectivization was modified extensively and private ownership of land was confirmed as the system of farming most natural for Polish conditions: more than four fifths of the arable land in Poland has remained in private hands throughout the Gomulka era. Moreover, restrictions on the powers of the secret police led to a genuine relaxation of the old system of prying and repression in 1957 and 1958. When there were signs of its revival in 1965 Gomulka personally intervened by placing the internal-security troops under military discipline, and in July 1968 he sought to check another phase of police persecution by a change in administrative personnel at the Ministry of the Interior. But the Polish 'road to socialism' is littered with reforms discarded by the wayside. Cultural freedom and literary initiative, briefly restored in the 'October spring,' were considerably curtailed by the end of 1957. Gomulka has frequently attacked progressive intellectuals for spreading false and insidious doctrines, notably in 1963–4 and in the early summer of 1968 after student riots in the spring in Warsaw and the university towns of Cracow, Lublin and Poznan.

Yet it was the religious issue which caused the most dramatic conflicts. In December 1956 Cardinal Wyszynski, the Polish Primate, brought his considerable moral prestige to the support of Gomulka at a time when extremist religious feeling might have imperilled the delicate relationship between a 'new look' administration and the Russians, as it had in Hungary. In return, the Polish episcopate was permitted an influence unparalleled in any communist country, with free pastoral activity in the schools and even the army. By the summer of 1960 the government appears to have become alarmed at the extent of clerical influence. Special taxation was imposed on buildings used for ecclesiastical purposes and the Sejm passed laws re-asserting the secular character of the schools. Disputes over birth control, favoured by the State and condemned by the Church, led to a campaign in which the communists sought to portray Wyszynski as a reactionary, lagging behind some of his fellow bishops and priests.

It was, however, in the winter of 1965–6 that conflict reached its height, with the despatch of a letter by the Polish hierarchy to the West German episcopate inviting a number of bishops to attend the millenary celebrations of Polish Christianity in May 1966 and expressing a desire to forgive, and be forgiven for, all that happened in the war. Gomulka insisted that this letter was interference by the Church in external affairs; and all visas were refused for foreigners wishing to come to Poland for the celebrations, a petty act of spite which effectively prevented the proposed visit by Pope Paul. The majority of Poles supported the Church dignitaries and several hundred thousand believers participated in the religious observances although the communists organized counter-millennium demonstrations and their propaganda represented Wyszynski as a pro-German advocate of 'the slave philosophy of forgiving your enemies'. The effect of the dispute was to enhance the popularity of the cardinal. In contrast to Gomulka's obsessive concern with the German question, Wyszynski appeared as a man who, though socially conservative by nature, was uninhibited by the recent past.

The change in Gomulka's attitude to 'liberalization,' which became evident in 1962, was caused by two inter-related events: severe economic difficulties, resulting in part from a rejection by the Politburo in 1957 of proposals for Yugoslav-type decentralization; and the growth of a formidable neo-Stalinist and anti-semitic faction within the party. The leaders of this new group were Ryszard Strzelecki, an ex-resistance fighter who had worked his way up through the party administration and General Mieczyslaw Moczar, a former NCO in the professional army of the thirties who retained in politics much of the harshness of a barrack-square. Their supporters, who were known as the partisans, were rallied by demagogic outbursts which reviled 'Jews, liberals and revisionists,' called for 'strong action' against student demonstrators and exuded waves of Polish national sentiment. The rise of the partisans coincided with an increase in the number of unemployed which had reached a quarter of a million by the spring of 1964. Most of the workers without occupation were young men, the chance victims of a population bulge and enforced contraction of the economy. There were more echoes of the last days of Weimar Germany than were healthy in a socialist state.

Gomulka was better able to deal with the personal challenge from Moczar and the partisans than to solve the economic malaise. Early in 1964 Strzelecki entered the Politburo and Moczar was made minister of the interior; but Gomulka countered this increased influence by reducing the effective authority of the minister and by virtually ignoring Strzelecki's proposals. Moczar remained influential throughout 1966 and at the main conference of the Workers' Party in May 1967 delivered a blistering attack on the 'spies and imperialist agents' who were over-running Poland. Anti-semitism was so rife in the first quarter of 1968 that it provoked dissension at the party central committee session in the following July, and Gomulka managed to manoeuvre Moczar off the Politburo and out of the Ministry of the Interior, although both Moczar and Strzelecki became members of the eight-man Workers' Party Secretariat, which was still headed by Gomulka. In April 1967 Marshal Spychalski, long the friend and colleague of the first secretary, was elected President in succession to the colourless Ochab, who had held the office since August 1964; but since the presidential prerogatives in socialist Poland are no stronger than they were in the inter-war republic, Spychalski's elevation made little effective difference to the standing of the Gomulka faction. The struggle for power continued longer in Poland than in any other communist state and it is possible that the eventual victor may be neither Gomulka nor Moczar but Gierek, the party boss of Silesia.

The Polish economy remained unstable from 1963 to 1968 despite reforms urgently introduced in 1964 which gave factories greater freedom in running their own affairs within the general plan, but Poland's productive capacity had to be buttressed increasingly by the other Comecon states, especially the Soviet Union, an obvious limitation on the country's independence of action. The possibility of further unemployment continued to cause alarm in the Sejm: by 1966 almost a million young people were completing their formal education each year and seeking work which the existing industrial structure could not provide; and there seemed no solution for these problems apart from emigration (which was frowned on in both Warsaw and Moscow) or a massive 'back to the land' campaign.

Internal problems have limited the earlier independence shown by the reformed Polish administration in foreign affairs. Rapacki, the Polish foreign minister, put forward a suggestion at the United Nations General Assembly in October 1957 for the creation of an atom-free zone covering Poland and the two Germanies, a proposal subsequently supported by

Czechoslovakia. The 'Rapacki Plan,' as it was called, was welcomed by the British Labour Party and a number of American intellectuals showed interest in it as a first step towards 'disengagement'; but its champions in the West were all the spokesmen of the political opposition at that time and, when the Russians needed to bolster up East Germany in 1961, the plan was shelved and soon forgotten. Thereafter Poland pursued a foreign policy identical with the wishes of its Soviet ally and Rapacki seems to have followed Gomulka's ideas closely until he left the Foreign Ministry in the autumn of 1968. Gomulka himself had two fixed beliefs on the world situation: the conviction that Germany was a dangerous revisionist power, anxious to thrust Poland out of the lands acquired in 1945; and the assumption that American policy over any question was double-faced and injurious to Poland, an attitude of mind that may date from his childhood, since his father had returned to Galicia from the United States as a disillusioned emigrant shortly before Gomulka was born. It is not clear whether it was fear of Germany, fear of a massive regiment of American spies or traditional Polish Czechophobia which induced Gomulka and Rapacki to support the Warsaw Pact intimidation of Czechoslovakia in the summer of 1968. The action emphasized the extent to which Poland had bound herself once more to the Soviet Union: it was in striking contrast to the gestures of defiance of the 'October spring' of 1956.

Poland's retreat from the reform programme of 1956 was in complete contrast to what happened in Hungary under Kádár. Until the Hungarian Party Congress of November 1959 Kádár's regime was basically on the defensive although Kádár was anxious to win popular support and always resisted the temptation to reimpose a police terror. After the congress, criticism of party methods was once more allowed and writers, who collectively had been regarded with deep suspicion since 1956, were permitted greater freedom of expression. In 1961 even more artistic freedom was conceded when cultural links were re-established with the West and more Hungarians began to travel abroad than at any time since the war. A general amnesty in March 1963 led to the release of several thousand political prisoners and non-party members began to participate in the running of state enterprises. The tendency to break away from the narrow confines of the old party continued even after the fall of Kádár's friend and supporter in Russia, Khrushchev. An Electoral Reform Act in 1966 permitted voters to choose from several members for a constituency rather than accept the party list despatched on a national basis; but all candidates for election had to be members of the 'Patriotic People's Front,' the umbrella association which included the party and all social and cultural organizations. Subsequently, Kádár appeared genuinely disappointed that the electoral campaign of 1967 had been conducted in an atmosphere of wide indifference and that most voters were apathetic over political matters. But strict precautions were taken to prevent any commemoration in October 1966 of the tenth anniversary of the abortive revolution, and it seemed ominous that soon afterwards a senior police official, Mihály Korom, should have been appointed minister of justice.

If many Hungarians withdrew from active politics in the 1960s, as Kádár complained in March 1967, then the reason was partly to be found in the events of the previous decade and partly in the 'get rich quick' materialism which swept through all sections of the community when consumer goods re-appeared on the market in plenty towards the end of 1963. The economic changes introduced by Kádár from 1959 onwards followed the example of the Yugoslavs in encouraging competition and in decentralization; but they were also backed by solid support from Russia. The five-year plan of 1960–65 emphasized the importance of heavy industry, particularly chemicals, but also allowed for the manufacture of furniture, shoes, clothes, public transport vehicles and even non-essential luxuries. Less progress was made in agriculture and it was a sad commentary on the early years of collectivization that cereals had to be imported from Russia throughout the Khrushchev era. Kádár extended the principle of cooperative management to almost all the remaining farms but, in contrast to the methods of Rákosi, the peasants were tempted into the cooperatives by assurances that they could hold small plots individually and sell produce in the traditional manner on a free market. The agricultural yield increased during the middle of the 1960s but the system remained vulnerable, and a severe drought in the spring of 1968 made Hungary again dependent on the Soviet Union for supplies of cereals at a time when Russian policy was hardening against manifestations of social-liberalism in Central Europe.

Kádár himself retained control of policy throughout the twelve years which separate his return to power from the Soviet invasion of Czechoslovakia. He never had the party difficulties which plagued Gomulka. On two occasions he served as head of the government as well as chief party functionary: his first ministry, from November 1956 to January 1958, was primarily concerned with the suppression of the strike movement which had followed the failure of the revolution; his second ministry, from September 1961 to June 1965, was a period of economic and political reform in which every effort was made to reconcile potential enemies. An agreement was even concluded in 1964 with the Vatican, enabling the Roman Catholic Church to function with some latitude despite the continued presence of the prince-primate of Hungary in the American Legation. When Kádár resigned the premiership, he was

succeeded by Gyula Kallai who had been a member of the Social Democratic Party in the 1930s and, with Rajk, had taken an active part in
opposing the war in 1942–3. Kallai was a close political associate and
friend of Kádár: he had been arrested by the AVO in 1951 and sentenced
to death but was released after two years in the condemned cell when Imre
Nagy became premier for the first time. Kallai had no liking for police
methods and appears to have restrained the less liberal members of his
government. In April 1967 he became Speaker of the Hungarian Parliament, handing over the premiership to Jeno Fock, an economist who had
long advised Kádár on labour relations. The Fock government immediately introduced economic reforms, implemented at the start of 1968:
they permitted the closure of enterprises seen to be working at a loss, and
they encouraged further decentralization and greater diversity within
industry. The threat of a price rise and of unemployment in some regions
of the country led to criticism of Fock's proposals; and throughout
1968 he had to rely heavily for support on Kádár, who remained at fifty-
six a popular father-figure in the party, a leader who by then had managed
its administration for a longer period than even Rákosi.

Neither Bulgaria nor Roumania was greatly affected by the events of 1956
in Hungary and Poland, although the Roumanians played a sinister role
in the suppression of the Hungarian revolution by detaining Imre Nagy
and his associates between the moment they were arrested by the Russians
and the preparation of an indictment against them in the early summer of
1958. But both Balkan states responded, with diplomatic skill and
ingenuity, to every vibration of Sino-Soviet discord even though it may be
doubted if either of them had much sympathy with Mao Tse-tung's
ideological pretensions.

Bulgarian internal politics from 1956 to 1961 were a curious mixture of
drastic economic reforms, announced with a bravura flourish in the
Sobranjie as a 'great leap forward,' and a triangular power game involving
Zhivkov, Yugov and Chervenkov. Although Chervenkov had been
forced to resign as prime minister in the spring of 1956, he retained a
considerable influence for the following five years. In 1958 he visited
China and was much fêted in Peking and on his return Bulgaria adopted a
policy of rapid industrialization, imitating on a small scale the vast and
diversified plans which were, at that moment, transforming the Chinese
economy. The Bulgarian policy failed dismally since it proved impossible
to reach even the first targets of development; and it seemed that the
country would have to resign itself to the role of 'country cousin' imposed by the Comecon meeting of May 1958 when it was assumed that
Bulgaria's only industry was agriculture. Politically the failure of 'the

great leap forward' led to a further decline in Chervenkov's fortunes and the dismissal of some of his nominees from ministerial posts. So long as there seemed some possibility that the programme might be completed, there was no more forward-leaping spokesman than Zhivkov but when the Bulgarian economy was seen to lack the athletic prowess demanded by the metaphor, Zhivkov absorbed himself in party administration and left Yugov to dispose of Chervenkov, who disappeared from the political scene at the end of 1961. The Russians were alarmed at the rumours that China might begin to assist the Bulgars in their difficulties and, in consequence, the Soviet Union began to bolster the Bulgarian economy by investments and to strengthen Zhivkov, a proven 'anti-Maoist', against all his rivals. Yugov was induced to resign in November 1962, precisely a year after the final fall of Chervenkov, and Zhivkov thereupon became prime minister himself, while retaining his post as first secretary.

Although Zhivkov's pending resignation was rumoured frequently for the following six years, he continued to keep both offices in his own hands. Khrushchev used him as a non-Russian spokesman for what were essentially Soviet policies and he acquired a particular value in testing the reactions of other communist parties to ideological statements in the contest with China. After Khrushchev's fall, Zhivkov performed the same service for Brezhnev, notably at the Bulgarian Communist Party Congress of 1966 when he also extended a distinctly heavy hand of reconciliation to an unresponsive Enver Hoxha. In home affairs Zhivkov began with fashionable gestures towards liberalization: political prisoners were released; and press comments on administrative bungling showed a rare acidity. Within six months Zhivkov was attacking all aspects of 'liberalism' in culture and political life and the country soon became almost Stalinist in rigidity. The secret police discovered a military conspiracy in April 1965 which would have established a fundamentally national communist administration far more independent of Moscow and resembling, in its general policy, the decentralized government of Yugoslavia. It is hard to estimate the degree of dissatisfaction in Bulgaria: an election in the following February showed that 99·85 per cent of the voters approved of the single 'Fatherland Front' list presented to them, a figure which seems so artificially inflated that it suggests Zhivkov had little genuine following of his own. Three weeks after the election the party's chief ideological theorist, Mitko Grigorov, followed Chervenkov and Yugov into the political limbo; and Zhivkov made a speech in which he claimed a remarkable jump of 97 per cent in foreign trade within one year.

By the beginning of 1968 Zhivkov was echoing other communist leaders in condemning the apathy of the post-war generation towards politics. Yet his proposal that young Bulgarian communists should take

M

pride in their country's heritage had unfortunate consequences; for historical nationalism chose to celebrate the ninetieth anniversary of the Treaty of San Stefano with assertions of the Bulgarian character of the Macedonian lands, and there was a sharp rejoinder from Belgrade (and, as was mentioned earlier, from Tirana). Relations between Bulgaria and her Yugoslav neighbour remained tense throughout the year, increasing markedly when Zhivkov showed his loyalty to the Soviet alliance by despatching tank and infantry units to Slovakia, by way of Varna and Odessa. So long as the Russians continued to buttress the Bulgarian economy, there seemed no reason why Zhivkov should not keep the country tightly tied to the Warsaw Pact and dutifully denunciatory of the Marxist apologetics of Peking.

Roumania was for long the last bastion of orthodox communism in the Danubian lands. It would not be true to regard Gheorghiu-Dej as a Stalinist, for until 1962 he was as amenable to Khrushchev's ideas as he had been to those of his predecessors. But under Gheorghiu-Dej the Roumanian Workers' Party was built up as the powerful 'cadre of revolution' foreseen by Lenin as essential to the achievement of socialism: the party was never popular as an institution, and its teachings had little appeal to the Roumanians in general, but it was tightly knit and – after the purge of 1952 – remarkably united around its leaders, unlike the Polish and Bulgarian parties.

During the Stalinist period Roumania was ruthlessly exploited by the Russians: joint Soviet-Roumanian companies took over the concerns which, before the war, had depended on foreign capital; and Roumania's oil and cereals were sold to Russia at peppercorn rates. The Red Army remained in the country, bolstering the security forces. By 1957 Roumania seemed a cowed and obedient satrapy; and in June 1958 Khrushchev felt so sure of Gheorghiu-Dej's continued support that all Soviet troops were withdrawn, either across the Pruth to Bessarabia or westward into Hungary.

Gheorghiu-Dej believed, as a prime article of communist faith, in industrialization; and in 1960 he proposed a six-year plan which would have developed the mineral resources of Transylvania and increased the hydro-electric power in the south-west of the country. Pride of place was given to a large metallurgical combine at Galati, where Gheorghiu-Dej had worked as a tramway mechanic in his early twenties, and to an aluminium factory at Slatina, eighty-five miles west of Bucharest. The plan had the personal approval of Khrushchev who was present when Gheorghiu-Dej announced it at a Party Congress and who applauded with all his customary fervour at the end of the speech. But at a Comecon meeting in Moscow in September 1962 the Russian leader proposed supra-national economic planning for Eastern Europe, by which both Roumania and Bulgaria were to concentrate on agriculture, leaving industrial production to countries in which it already formed the major part of their economy, such as Czechoslovakia and East Germany. The Roumanians were furious at such dictation from their Comecon partners: it made nonsense of the six-year plan and the money and labour already devoted to it; it ignored the fact that the growth rate of Roumanian industry was already higher than in any other communist state in Europe; and it neglected natural resources, still untapped, and capable of turning Roumania into an industrial state as productive as Czechoslovakia by the early 1980s. The Comecon proposals were fought tooth and nail by the Roumanian delegates to the various commissions; and by the autumn of 1963 they appeared to have been substantially modified, and perhaps even abandoned, by their Soviet and Czechoslovak patrons.

The Roumanians, however, continued to show independence of the Soviet Union even after their substantial victory over the Comecon plan. Economic links were strengthened with the United States and with Western Europe, especially Germany and France; and various anti-Russian pinpricks in education and culture, and even in names of streets and places, were encouraged within the country – a slightly childish series of gestures, but very popular. More seriously, the Roumanians cultivated the Chinese communists and their Albanian puppets in Europe: they expanded trade with China, at a time when the other Comecon members were reducing all contacts with Peking; they published all the major doctrinal attacks made by Mao and Chou En-lai on Khrushchev; and in 1964 the Roumanian prime minister visited Peking, a courtesy returned by Chou En-lai in June 1966. The threat of Chinese influence at Bucharest induced Khrushchev and his successors to accept rebuffs from the Roumanians which would have been unthinkable in earlier years. An apparent attempt by Khrushchev in 1963 to encourage General Bodnaraş to overthrow Gheorghiu-Dej and set up a pro-Soviet regime met with no response: Bodnaraş headed a diplomatic mission to Belgrade and Peking and showed no inclination to revert to his earlier role of a Russian hench-man.

The definitive statement of Roumania's ideological position was issued by the Central Committee of the Party at a meeting in April 1964: it condemned the supra-national economic plans of Comecon, reiterated the national sovereignty of each communist state and the equality of all communist parties, and insisted that no one party should have its policy dictated by others. This strongly independent attitude led to criticism of both the Warsaw Pact and the attempts by the Russians to secure a unified policy in opposition to China. It was in accord with the 1964 declaration for Ceausescu to condemn every attempt to discipline Czechoslovakia in 1968; for, as he said in a speech on 15 July of that year, 'Not for a moment, ever, did we think of the Warsaw Treaty as a reason to justify interference in the internal affairs of other states.' Subsequently he visited Prague and, after the Soviet invasion, denounced the 'flagrant violation of the sovereignty of a fraternal state' in uncompromising terms.

Ceausescu had succeeded to the post of secretary-general of the party on Gheorghiu-Dej's death in March 1965. The transition meant little change in policy, for Ceausescu had long been a supporter of the dead leader and the government continued to be headed by Ion Gheorghe Maurer, who had become prime minister in March 1961. Ceausescu consolidated his position rapidly, defeating another clumsy attempt to create a pro-Soviet faction, headed by the chief of the security services, Alexandru Draghici. In December 1967 Ceausescu was elected President, thus resuming the practice followed in the last four years of his life by Gheorghiu-Dej of combining the posts of party leader and head of state. Ceausescu and Maurer were anxious to counter the repressive reputation of the Roumanian state machine and in April 1968 a Central Committee meeting posthumously exonerated Pátrásçanu, who had been executed in 1954, and rehabilitated some earlier victims of what were euphemistically described as 'imaginary confessions'; but the party remained reluctant to commit itself to more positive measures of liberalization.

During Maurer's premiership earlier restraints on the Roumanian sense of national pride were removed, at first almost imperceptibly. The revised 'Constitution of the Socialist Republic of Roumania,' adopted in 1965, showed significant changes from its predecessor of 1952 over the status of the minority nationalities; the Magyar Autonomous Area, which had been guaranteed in the earlier constitution, lost its special mention in the later version. In reality it had already been deprived of much of its independence in 1960 and attempts had been made to merge the Hungarian University in Cluj with its Roumanian counterpart. At a lower level a number of minority language schools were closed, as being 'no longer necessary'. The old Latin characteristics of the Roumanian people were again stressed in the press and the bonds linking Paris and Bucharest received a rhapsodic benediction from President de Gaulle on a state visit in the spring of 1968. In October 1967 a new administrative structure was established for the whole country which replaced the regional subdivisions of the People's Republic with some four dozen counties, bearing a close resemblance to those existing under King Carol II and involving the total disappearance of any autonomous Magyar districts. On the other hand, the seven deputy premiers included one ethnic Hungarian, János Fazekas, and there remained constitutional guarantees of 'the free use of their mother tongue' by resident nationalities. In 1968 the Magyar

minority appeared less oppressed than forty years previously, but sufficiently underprivileged for the issue to be raised in Budapest at times
when the whole policy of communist Roumania was questioned by her
Warsaw Pact neighbours.

There was another side to the revival of Roumanian nationalism.
Resentment at the loss of the northern Bukovina and more especially
Bessarabia came into the open. In December 1964 the Roumanian Academy of Science published a neglected and hitherto unedited manuscript
of Karl Marx attacking the Russians for having annexed Bessarabia in
1878 and establishing there a repressive regime; and, although the target
for Marx's invective was tsarist tyranny, its practices seemed almost
embarrassingly familiar to Russia's communist partners more than eighty
years later. Official care was taken to avoid overt revisionism: thus, when
Ceausescu delivered a long address on the history of the Roumanian
Communist Party on 7 May 1966 he deplored the calls made for the dis-
memberment of inter-war Roumania by the old Communist International
and the 'unjust conditions' under which Roumania ceded part of Transylvania to Hungary by the Vienna Award; but he left it to his listeners to
decide whether a similar injustice had deprived Roumania of the territories lost to the Soviet Union at the same time and confirmed in Russian
possession after the war. By insisting at the end of his speech that peoples
'who had fought for centuries to throw off the yoke of foreign oppression,
dreaming of freedom and national independence' would not willingly
'give up these sacred prerogatives,' Ceausescu made it clear that he was
no less a Roumanian patriot than Maniu and the Bratianus had been.
He had come a long way since 1944, when his Union of Communist
Youth greeted the Soviet troops as a revolutionary vanguard liberating
Bucharest from chauvinist reactionaries.

There were few changes among the political personalities in Czechoslovakia in the ten years after Gottwald's death. Novotny remained leader
of the party and became President of the republic on the death of Zápotocky in November 1957. Siroky was prime minister throughout the
decade. But for the Czechs and Slovaks politics mattered less than economics. Even before the war Czechoslovakia, alone of the countries of
East-Central Europe, was a heavily industrialized state, and the factories
of Bohemia and Moravia had suffered comparatively little damage from
either aerial bombardment or invasion. Gottwald and his successors
continued the policy, begun during the war and accepted as beneficial
by Beneš, of bringing industry to the Slovak highlands as well. When the
first five-year plan was promulgated in 1949 an official directive decreed
that, 'in keeping with the principles of proletarian internationalism,'

Czechoslovakia was to become 'the machine works for the entire socialist camp'.

For the first twelve years of the communist regime Czechoslovak industry flourished and the economy was a model of stability. The Soviet Union supplied the Czechs with most of the raw materials they needed and the finished articles were re-exported to the Russians and their Comecon partners. Statistics showed a steady growth in production, even if the figures lagged behind the optimistic assumptions of the five-year plans. The standard of living was higher than in neighbouring communist states: no serious food shortages were reported and rationing was abolished in the summer of 1953. There was rioting over currency reform in June of that year but at no time in the fifties did the Czechoslovaks offer serious resistance to communism. To outside observers their attitude seemed compounded of political apathy, a silent contempt for bureaucratic maladministration and a strong element of national complacency. Anti-Russianism was never far below the surface, but it was kept well under control.

The Czech bubble burst in 1961, although it was not until the intensively cold winter of 1962-3 that the full effects of economic crisis were felt in the country as a whole. Machines which had become old and overstrained failed on a massive scale; cuts in electric power lowered production and caused domestic hardship, food was short, for there had been a disappointing harvest in the previous year, and its distribution was hampered by breakdowns in the transport system. The reasons for this sudden drop in living standards went back many years: there had been so much investment in heavy industry that the lighter manufacturing processes, which had been a speciality of Bohemia and Moravia, were ignored and fell into decline; and excessive central control stifled regional variations and initiative so that commitments for underdeveloped countries outside Europe led to the neglect of essential works of repair, maintenance and modernization at home. As later critics of the system emphasized, there were far too many administrative officials and not enough skilled workers, for it is doubtful if the management of some industries – particularly textiles – ever adequately replaced the German-speaking artisans expelled from the Sudetenland in 1945-6. Agriculture was in as bad a state as industry: collectivization imposed a uniformity in farming methods for which many regions in the country were unsuited; and it is significant that the productivity of the small private holdings, which farmers were still permitted to cultivate, was relatively higher than the yield from the collectives. The peasantry showed an obstinate reluctance to cooperate in the agricultural plans, especially in Slovakia.

Yet, despite all these shortcomings, Novotny stayed in power and survived the economic crisis. In February 1962 he announced that the former Stalinist minister of the interior, Rudolf Barak, had been arrested on charges of 'abuse of office' and embezzlement, and he was subsequently sentenced to fifteen years imprisonment. Other lesser officials were also stripped of political authority. But jettisoning such ballast hardly satisfied the Czechoslovak workers, many of whom felt disillusioned by the contrast between the reality of living conditions and the high promises made by the official party press as recently as July 1960, when a new constitution marked the completion of the revolutionary era and the title of the state was changed to 'Czechoslovak Socialist Republic'. The students, more volatile than the workers, demonstrated at the end of 1962 against the hard-core Stalinists still in the government and criticisms from writers began to penetrate the screen of censorship.

The most serious unrest of 1962–3 was in Slovakia. For this, there were both economic and political reasons. The farmers were not satisfied with the workings of the collectives and there was particular resentment among the workers when it was decided to close a number of superfluous and inefficient factories established in Slovakia during the first five-year plan. Political discontent sprang from the failure of the central government to allow the Slovaks any real degree of autonomy, for by the 1960 Constitution the legislative powers permitted to the 'Slovak National Council' were limited to strictly local affairs, and from the continued imprisonment of two Slovak 'bourgeois nationalist revisionists,' Laco Novomesky and Gustav Husak, who had been condemned soon after Novotny became leader of the party and while Stalinism was still in vogue. The Slovaks were far from gratified at having a compatriot as prime minister, for they considered Siroky as too willing to rubber-stamp Novotny's decisions; and most of the party members had little regard for Karol Bacilek, their first secretary in Bratislava, another Novotny nominee.

Throughout 1963 President Novotny was on the defensive. He had abandoned the third five-year plan in 1962 and sought to increase production by a more flexible system, running the economy on a year-to-year basis and hoping that Czechoslovak industry might be shored up by Comecon. At the same time, he made further political concessions. Novomesky and Husak were quietly released and allowed to resume their activities within the Communist Party in Slovakia. Bacilek was dismissed in April 1963 and Siroky in the following September. Jozef Lenart, chairman of the Slovak National Council, was summoned from Bratislava to succeed Siroky as prime minister in Prague; he was forty years old and had worked his way up to the Party Central Committee in 1958 after serving as an organizer in the former Bata shoe-factories. It was assumed that he would prove less pliable in Prague than Siroky. Bacilek's successor was Alexander Dubcek, a year older than Lenart and educated in the Soviet

Union in the thirties. Since Dubcek had returned to Moscow for a three-year course in Marxist studies from 1955 to 1958 he was regarded as a good Khrushchev supporter; but, though Novotny himself was heavily backed by Khrushchev in 1963, Dubcek was as critical as most Slovaks of the president and his policies. Yet in November 1964 Novotny still had a sufficient command of the Party *apparatchiki* to secure re-election as president for another seven years of office.

The changes in political leadership were accompanied by a trend towards liberalization. Professor Ota Sik, the country's most distinguished economic theorist was in September 1963 permitted to publish an article in the principal ideological monthly of the party calling for a radical re-assessment of the economic structure, and there were many who agreed with him. Outside Prague there were signs of political change. In May 1964 the powers of the Slovak National Council were broadened and the system of executive commissioners, which had functioned in Slovakia until 1960, was restored. The new critical spirit was expressed most openly in the Slovak literary reviews. Bratislava recovered some of the cultural prestige enjoyed by the city at the end of the eighteenth century as an outpost of the enlightenment; and in the summer of 1967 the numerous bookshops in the old town offered a remarkably wide selection of reading, a licence in odd contrast to the watch-towers and wire along the heavily guarded frontier with Austria a few miles upstream. Some of the ideas in circulation among Slovak intellectuals were too advanced for the party pundits; and when, in March 1965, Eugen Loebl wrote an article in a Slovak cultural review suggesting that in a socialist state the individual had rights superior to those of the corporate community, he was criticized for a false sense of values. He was not only a Slovak but a Jew, who had been imprisoned in the aftermath of the Slansky affair; and he wrote from the heart as well as the mind.

Novotny hoped to ride the tide of indignation by encouraging Ota Sik to formulate the 'new economic model' (NEM), designed to give more flexibility to the Czech economy. With a return to prosperity and wage stability it appears that Novotny intended to clamp down once more on the new freedom of the writers and intellectuals. The NEM proposed that individual enterprises should be left to organize themselves within a general coordinating trust. Central control would be reduced to a minimum, the preparation of long-term plans of a general nature. Some prices were to be freely determined, others were to vary according to market conditions through the agreement of the trusts, and some basic products were to sell at a fixed price stipulated by a central administration. Incentive payments would supplement wages and salaries in highly productive undertakings. The reforms were approved in January 1965 but two years were to elapse before the NEM became operative in all sections of the economy. Professor Sik complained in the party press that implementation of the reforms was delayed by the deliberately conservative attitude of the ministerial bureaucrats. Progress in 1966 was much slower than expected and, at the end of the year, Eugen Loebl joined Sik in criticizing the authorities for their reluctance to encourage free competition; but output rose in general by some seven per cent over the whole year. Prices, however, went up more sharply than the planners had anticipated and in May 1967 the Central Committee of the party had to take deflationary measures, sweetening the pill by slight increases in social security benefits and by vague promises that in the following two years efforts would be made to establish a basic forty-two hour week, spread over five working days. The economic crisis continued to throw its shadow over the whole country: the 'Socialist Republic' might well have been a capitalist state.

The first serious unrest in Prague came during the May Day celebrations of 1966 when the students tore down political slogans and hurled abuse at the police. A fortnight later the *Majales*, the students' own spring festival, was turned into a major political demonstration; 'Long live the Soviet Union – but on its own resources' ran one of the slogans. Novotny used the occasion of the Thirteenth Party Congress at the start of June to denounce the students, blaming irresponsible writers in the cultural magazines for the erroneous political ideas which young people were daring to put forward. Stern warnings were issued to intellectuals who encouraged the spread of a 'bourgeois ideology'. The warnings had little effect. Another broadside from Eugen Loebl in September 1966 jolted the ministerial 'dogmatists' without either dislodging them or bringing vengeance from the authorities. There was an uneasy and suspicious truce in the winter of 1966–7 with demands being made for further inquiries into past injustices and for the rehabilitation of alleged traitors. By April Novotny seemed sufficiently secure for an international communist conference to be held at Karlovy Vary. It could agree on nothing except the evils of the Americans and West Germans. The 'united political front of all progressive forces' was seen to have worn very thin, and Novotny's attempts to rally support for a neo-Stalinist uniformity had the air of a plaintive and desperate swansong.

From June until September 1967 there was constant tension between the party and the Czechoslovak Writers' Union, who were indignant at attempts by the authorities to ensure that all cultural activities conformed to an ideologically correct policy. Linked with this clash was renewed anti-semitism, for many of the writers were Jewish and, while the party itself supported the Arabs in the Middle East conflicts, public opinion in general sympathized with the Jewish cause and admired the achievements of the State of Israel. Yet it was a protest over material living conditions rather than a major political demonstration which began the Czechoslovak liberal revolution. On the evening of 31 October students from a university hostel marched into the centre of Prague carrying candles and demanding 'We want light.' They were complaining about a totally inadequate electrical supply to their hostel, but their procession coincided with press reports of a Central Committee meeting at which there had been 'very animated discussion of the position and role of the party'. The students were attacked by the police, who then entered the hostel and beat up those who had not even joined the march. Inadvertently, the burning candles had caused a major political explosion.

Intellectuals throughout the republic supported the students. A government inquiry conceded that the hostel's heating and lighting installation was inadequate and regretted that the police had used 'unduly harsh measures'; but it excused their behaviour on the grounds that the situation was 'confused' at that time. No one was satisfied and rumours began to circulate that the party itself was split over its future. The NEM had brought disappointing returns in production, trade and price-levels: its opponents blamed Sik and the reformers; its champions argued that the party dead-heads had never meant it to succeed. The Central Committee met again from 20–22 December, a few days after publication of the official report into the police actions against the students and of a review of an economic policy. Another session was summoned within a fortnight and on 5 January 1968 it was announced that President Novotny had resigned as first secretary, surrendering office to the forty-six year old Slovak leader, Alexander Dubcek.

Novotny clung to the presidency for another eleven weeks, but by surrendering his party post he had allowed the new post-Stalinist communists to take over the administration. Throughout February and March criticism of the President coincided with demands for the restoration of political rights and the abolition of censorship. On 25 February it was confirmed that Novotny had sought to preserve his hold on the party by asking the Czechoslovak army to march on Prague and that the professional officers had refused to intervene in political affairs. The new Party Committee purged its minor officials, of whom it was calculated that there were some quarter of a million in the country, and, following the demands of the trade unionists, began in March to re-organize the government. Novotny resigned on 22 March and, at the end of May, was suspended from the party.

The new President was General Svoboda, the seventy-two year old veteran commander of the Czechoslovak troops on the eastern front in 1943–5 and minister of defence from the liberation until 1950. He was held in high esteem by the Russians and he numbered among his decorations the Order of Lenin and the insignia of a Hero of the Soviet Union.

By a tradition dating back to Masaryk and Beneš, the presidency has always carried more prestige and authority in practice than the Czechoslovak constitutions have stipulated and, in an era of political transformation, it was essential that the head of state should be no mere puppet on a reformist string. Svoboda assured continuity to the republic: he had been a member of the Czechoslovak Legion in 1918, even before the achievement of independence; half a century later, as President, he was to insist that tributes should be paid to Masaryk and Beneš at their graves for the first time in twenty years.

One of President Svoboda's first acts was to accept the resignation of Lenart as prime minister, for he had supported Novotny in the December tussle within the party and had thus sacrificed the popularity he had earlier enjoyed as a Slovak liberal among the communists. He was succeeded by Oldrich Cernik, a Czech and former deputy premier. Among his deputies, Cernik included Ota Sik and Gustav Husak. He appointed the progressive liberal, Jiri Hajek, as foreign minister. The most vehemently outspoken critic of Novotny in the preceding months, Josef Smrkovsky, was elected Speaker of the National Assembly.

The chief task of the Cernik government was to translate an 'action programme' of democratic reform, which had been accepted by the Central Committee at the end of May, into legislative reality. The programme proposed freedom of the press, of assembly, of the right to travel abroad; and it attacked excessive concentration of power in the party administration. It was relatively easy for the Assembly to ensure that the apparatus of censorship was dismantled, and attempts were made to secure retrospective justice by the passage of a Rehabilitation Bill which would give compensation to people unjustly sentenced for political offences between 1953 and 1965. At the end of June a Federalization Bill was approved providing for Slovakia to have equal status with Bohemia-Moravia, although the Assembly rejected a proposal that the republic should become a triple rather than a dual political entity, with Moravia-Silesia sharing administrative independence with Bohemia and Slovakia. The difficulty for Cernik as prime minister and Dubcek as first secretary was how to reduce the totalitarian character of the party without permitting it to abdicate the prime position it held in the state. Dubcek was adamant that there should be no multi-party system, knowing from the earliest days of the reform that the Soviet Union and other communist parties would not accept a return to a western-style democratic constitution.

Throughout the summer of 1968 Dubcek and Cernik were subjected to pressure at home and abroad. Meetings in both the Czech lands and Slovakia wanted a speedy reformation of the whole party system and not merely a purge of the despised *apparatchiki*; and Dubcek countered these demands by promising the holding of an extraordinary Communist

Party Congress in the autumn at which such matters could be thrashed out. It was far harder to satisfy the party leaders of the other Warsaw Pact members, several of whom could not believe that a state could remain 'socialist' if it permitted non-communists to criticize the wisdom of the party's decisions. From May onwards the Soviet and East German press and radio began to denounce 'the Czechoslovak nationalists': correspondence was exchanged between foreign party leaders and the Czechs on the dangerous liberty permitted to Czech newspapers. The Russians were worried and sent members of their Prague Embassy staff to tour the factories and encourage any orthodox Marxists they might find. It appears to have been a difficult task.

The Russians had two methods of disciplining the Czechoslovaks, monetary and military. They sought to delay the grant of a loan requested by the Cernik government to relieve problems caused by half-hearted transition to the NEM; and they insisted on holding Warsaw Pact manoeuvres within the republic's territories. Military exercises by the combined armies had always antagonized the Czechs because of their expense and the dislocation they caused to industry, transport and farming. In September 1966, for example, the largest manoeuvres since the war had been held in southern Czechoslovakia with the Warsaw Pact armies repelling a simulated NATO attack. Cernik and Hajek negotiated with the Russians in May 1968 and secured a partial victory: the manoeuvres were limited to communication troops and staff exercises, but they showed the mobility of the Warsaw Pact armies and the extent to which they still held Czechoslovakia in a strategic vice.

The foreign crisis began in earnest on 14/15 July when the leaders of the Soviet Union, Bulgaria, East Germany, Hungary and Poland met in Warsaw and sent a letter to the Czechoslovak Party calling for 'Marxist-Leninist unity' and threatening intervention: 'Peace and security of nations are maintained above all by the strength, cohesion and unity of socialist countries,' it declared 'and a determined struggle for the preservation of the socialist system in Czechoslovakia is not only your task but ours as well.' The Czechs replied with a calm statement of loyalty to the socialist cause, reminiscent of the replies sent by Tito to Stalin twenty years previously. While the Russians ostentatiously carried out military exercises along the Czechoslovak frontier, it was agreed that there would be a meeting between the Russian and Czechoslovak leaders at Cierna-nad-Tisou, a small Slovakian village between Košiče and Transcarpathia. The meeting lasted from 29 July to 1 August and was followed two days later by talks in Bratislava between the Czechoslovaks and the participants in the meeting which had taken place at Warsaw in mid-July. Statements by Dubcek, Smrkovsky and President Svoboda indicated that at Cierna and Bratislava agreement had been reached on implementation of the reforms and assurances had been given of Czechoslovakia's loyalty to the Warsaw Pact. Momentarily the crisis eased.

At ten o'clock on the night of 20 August 1968 Russian tanks entered Czechoslovakia accompanied by token forces of occupation from Poland, Hungary, East Germany and Bulgaria. By the following day there may have been as many as a quarter of a million foreign soldiers in the Republic and a week later the Czechoslovak Minister of Defence maintained that 650,000 troops had occupied the country, one soldier for every thirteen members of the adult population. Dubcek was arrested and taken hand-cuffed to Moscow. The President was isolated in the Hradschin Castle but he was able to broadcast to the nation calling for restraint. There was no open military resistance although acts of defiance were undertaken by civilians in some towns, especially Prague. There were demonstrations, token general strikes of limited duration, and a number of fires were started. A Russian attempt to establish an alternative government failed, partly because the presidential executive, the government and the party were able to have a joint statement broadcast within four hours of the invasion deploring the illegality of the action and emphasizing the unity of the people and the party. President Svoboda behaved with great dignity over the following days, heading a six-man delegation which negotiated in Moscow and secured the release and return of Dubcek and others arrested with him. But, although the invasion did not lead to a repetition of the tragedy and destruction in Budapest twelve years before, it demonstrated that the Russian leaders were once more determined to impose limits on the independence shown by their communist neighbours. The reasons why the Warsaw Pact countries decided on such drastic action after the apparent compromise at Bratislava remain obscure: possibly they had convinced themselves that the Dubcek-Cernik administration was the vanguard of counter-revolution; and perhaps the Soviet leaders were alarmed at the effect of liberalization on the Ruthenes and the Slovak minority across the frontier in Carpatho-Ukraine. The enthusiastic welcome given to President Tito in Prague on 9–10 August and to President Ceausescu of Roumania on 15 August may have suggested an anti-Soviet Little Entente, a deviation unacceptable alike to orthodox party theorists and military strategists. Whatever the motives behind the invasion, the effect was to stifle the growth of the partially open society which seemed, in the early months of 1968, as if it would be Czechoslovakia's contribution to the further evolution of Marxist ideology.

When, at the end of October 1968, the Czechoslovaks celebrated the fiftieth anniversary of national independence most of the objectives of the 'action programme' had necessarily been abandoned. Public Order Acts, a Press Law, the banning of non-party political associations, and the partial re-introduction of censorship suggested a return to the dreary restraints of the Novotny era. Hajek was dismissed from office, Ota Sik forced into exile and Smrkovsky's liberty as Speaker of the Assembly limited. But all did not appear lost. The Central Committee still contained a majority of progressive liberals. The Russian hope of establishing a puppet regime had not as yet succeeded: even the fallen Novotny had protested at the invasion. Work was proceeding on the Federalization Law so as to ensure separate administrations for Slovakia and Bohemia-Moravia by the beginning of 1969. The courage and ingenuity of the Czechoslovak people prevented a full political retreat in domestic matters. Even though Russian troops remained in the outskirts of most towns and cities, Christmas was celebrated openly as it had not been for twenty years.

As 1968 ended, doubts remained. In September Smrkovsky had stressed the need for unity: it was, he said, 'an arch from which not a single stone must be allowed to fall'. Yet was Smrkovsky's arch any surer in its foundations than Beneš's bridge from East to West? Arches, like bridges, may be undermined and blown up; and demolition engineers were not lacking, even on the Central Committee. With the economic situation of the country deteriorating rapidly, there seemed little prospect that the 'Prague Spring' would ever blossom into full summer.

Notes On Sources

For fuller details of the books and articles listed below, see the Bibliography. In these notes and in the Bibliography I have used the following abbreviations:

AHR   *American Historical Review* (Washington)
IA   *International Affairs* (London)
JCEA   *Journal of Central European Affairs* (Boulder, Colorado)
JMH   *Journal of Modern History* (Chicago)
SEER   *Slavonic and East European Review* (London)

1 Borderlands of Europe

This chapter relies primarily on a number of standard works and on personal observation. The most useful geographical accounts have been: H. G. Wanklyn, *Eastern Marchlands of Europe*; P. George and J. Tricart, *L'Europe Centrale* (two volumes); A. F. A. Mutton, *Central Europe* (for the Czech lands only). General histories used for this chapter and for later ones include: L. S. Stavrianos, *The Balkans since 1453*; C. A. Macartney, *Hungary, A Short History*; R. W. Seton-Watson, *A History of the Roumanians* and *A History of the Czechs and Slovaks*; O. Halecki, *The Limits and Divisions of European History*; Stephen Clissold (ed.), *A Short History of Yugoslavia*; R. J. Kerner (ed.), *Yugoslavia*; W. F. Reddaway (ed.), *Cambridge History of Poland*, volume 2; Huertley, Darby, Crawley and Woodhouse, *A Short History of Greece*. See also, C. A. Macartney, *National States and National Minorities*. For specific areas of dispute, see the pamphlet by R. W. Seton-Watson, *Transylvania: A Key-Problem* and compare the treatment of the subject in C. A. Macartney, *Hungary and her Successors*; and on Macedonia see E. Barker, *Macedonia, its place in Balkan Power Politics* and H. R. Wilkinson, *Maps and Politics*. There are a number of stimulating essays on East-Central Europe in L. B. Namier, *Facing East*; and a controversial study of the misuse of history in Walter Kolarz, *Myths and Realities in Eastern Europe*. F. B. Singleton, *Background to Eastern Europe* is a valuable introductory summary.

2 The Congress of Vienna and the first National Revolts

The general histories cited above are also useful for this chapter. To them may be added H. Nicolson, *The Congress of Vienna*; Bertier de Sauvigny, *Metternich and his Times*; Golo Mann, *Secretary of Europe*, a life of Friedrich von Gentz. On the growth of national feeling see H. Tiander, *Das Erwachen Osteuropas*; Hans Kohn,

Panslavism; Ferdo Sišić *Jugoslovenska Misao*. See also the three articles by F. Zwitter, 'Illyrisme et sentiment yougoslave,' in *Le Monde Slave* for April, May and June 1933. I have used the American edition of Obradović's autobiography, edited and translated by G. R. Noyes, *The Life and Adventures of Dositej Obradović*. Dame Rebecca West's *Black Lamb and Grey Falcon* is a highly evocative study of Serbia's past, not always strictly accurate but written with exquisite artistry. D. Loncar, *The Slovenes: a Social History* is tantalizingly brief. Two articles of use for this period are: J. Hának, 'Slovaks and Czechs in the early Nineteenth Century,' *SEER*, April 1932; and V. Corović, 'Vuk Karadzić,' *SEER*, April 1938.

On the Serbian revolt see E. Haumant, *La Formation de la Yugoslavie*, which is valuable for the whole of the nineteenth century and for the first two decades of its successor. I prefer Haumant's narrative to G. in der Maur, *Die Jugoslawen einst und jetzt*, a comprehensive reference work but written in the Germany of the mid-thirties. H. W. V. Temperley's *History of Serbia* is also dated. G. Yakchitch, *L'Europe et la résurrection de la Serbie* remains a minor classic. Vašo Cubrilović, *Istorija Politicke Misli u Srbiju* puts the revolt in its general ideological context although with less marked a breach with earlier non-Marxist 'romantic historians' than one might have expected. See also the review article by W. S. Vucinich on 'Marxian interpretations of the First Serbian Revolt,' in *JCEA* for April 1961. For the background to the Greek revolt, see the introductory chapter of C. M. Woodhouse, *The Greek War of Independence* and the article by D. Dakin on 'The origins of the Greek revolution of 1821,' in *History* for October 1952. M. S. Anderson, *The Eastern Question*, surveys the problem from 1774 to 1923.

3   The Years of the Barricades

For Polish affairs in the mid-nineteenth century the *Cambridge History of Poland* may be supplemented by W. J. Rose, *The Rise of Polish Democracy* and R. Dybowski *Outlines of Polish History*. Russian policy is described in detail by Professor Hugh Seton-Watson, *The Russian Empire, 1801–1917*, chapters 5, 9 and 10. The most exhaustive treatment in English of the Polish Question during this period is contained in the two studies by Professor R. F. Leslie, *Polish Politics and the Revolution of November 1830* and *Reform and Insurrection in Russian Poland* (primarily on the revolution of 1863). Some of the literature of the Polish expatriates, such as Mickiewicz and Krasinski, may be read in English in T. M. Filip, *A Polish Anthology*.

At the time I wrote this chapter there were no detailed and scholarly works on the revolutions of 1848 in the Habsburg lands. The publication in February 1969 of C. A. Macartney's *The Habsburg Empire* remedied this defect, as it did so many others. In its absence, I relied on L. B. Namier's Raleigh Lecture in History for 1944, *1848: the Revolution of the Intellectuals*, which contains a few pages on Galicia in 1846, rather more on Poznania in 1848 and devotes about a quarter of its length to Bohemia and Moravia. The lecture was originally printed in the *Proceedings of the British Academy, 1944*, and I cite from this version (p. 276) the report of the Governor of Bohemia on the Prague Congress (quoted on

p. 58) and, from pages 246–7, the debate in the Frankfurt Parliament on Poland (see above, pp. 59–60). Further essays by Sir Lewis Namier on the events of 1848 are included in his *Vanished Supremacies*; they may be supplemented by P. Tabori and J. Eastwood, *Forty-eight; the Year of Revolutions* and R. J. Rath, *The Viennese Revolution of 1848*. In the *Actes du Congres Historique du Centenaire de la Révolution de 1848*, I used the articles by Francis Eckhart on 'La Révolution de 1848 en Hongrie et la cour de Vienne,' by Professor Gasiorowska on 'Le Problème Sociale en Pologne en 1846–1848,' and by J. Macurek on 'L'Année 1848 et la Moravie'. An article in *JCEA* for April 1942 by J. C. Campbell on 'The Transylvanian Question in 1849' throws an interesting light on the growth of Roumanian sentiment.

For the Magyar literary revival see the primarily non-political studies of Eötvös and Petöfi in D. M. Jones, *Five Hungarian Writers*. The whole of the October 1960 issue of *JCEA* was devoted to Szechenyi, with articles by George Bárány, B. G. Ivanyi and Francis S. Wagner. Palacký's literary work is discussed in an article by Joseph F. Zacek on 'Palacký and his History of the Czech Nation,' in *JCEA* for January 1964 (the last number before it ceased publication).

There are no modern biographies of Kossuth. His *Speeches in England* are still a significant self-revelation. Edward Crankshaw's *Fall of the House of Habsburg*, although a delightful book to read, seems at times exceptionally hostile to Hungary and to Kossuth in particular. The first four chapters of A. J. P. Taylor's *Struggle for Mastery in Europe* emphasize the continuity in international affairs from the revolutions of 1848 to the Crimean War. T. W. Riker, *The Making of Roumania* remains the most detailed study of the subject in English.

4 Ferment down the Danube

Arthur S. May's *The Hapsburg Monarchy, 1867–1914* is a balanced and comprehensive analysis, while A. J. P. Taylor's *The Habsburg Monarchy* is highly readable. Both have now, to some extent, been superseded by Macartney's *Habsburg Empire*. Louis Eisenmann's *Le Compromis Austro-Hongrois de 1867* remains a first-rate study, rather broader in scope than its title suggests. Wickham Steed's *The Habsburg Monarchy* is an analysis of the structure of the State as it appeared to *The Times* correspondent in Vienna from 1902 to 1913, but it contains considerable historical background and has some brilliantly perceptive comments, even though in retrospect it seems strangely optimistic. R. W. Seton-Watson's *The Southern Slav Question and the Habsburg Monarchy* champions the Croatian cause and is particularly valuable as a source on Strossmayer. There is a seven hundred page collection of forty-four different articles on the history of Fiume entitled *Rijeka: Zbornik*, and edited by Jakša Ravlić. It is a rich source of information and, although written in Serbo-Croat, each article is summarized in English. The Czech problem from 1868 to 1870 is discussed in the general histories listed above and received detailed attention in two articles in *JCEA*: 'The Prague Slav Congress of 1868,' by Stanley B. Kimball, *JCEA*, July 1962; and 'Russia and Czech National Aspirations,' by Otakar Odložilík, *JCEA*, January 1963. The opening chapters of Professor Wiskemann's *Czechs and Germans* include a survey of the attempts to reach a compromise between these nationalities in Bohemia-Moravia during this period.

I have used information on the early history of Bulgarian industry from I. Sakazov, *Bulgarische Wirtschaftgeschichte* and from the introductory chapters of J. Rothschild, *The Communist Party of Bulgaria*. The most recent treatment in English of the Serbian Omladina is in Vladimir Dedijer's *Road to Sarajevo*, pp. 48–50. There is a particularly brilliant analysis of the early South Slav movement sent to the French Foreign Office by Engelhardt, the Consul-General at Belgrade, in February 1872 and printed in *Documents Diplomatiques Françaises*, 1st series, vol. 1, pp. 127–130. The Serbian movements and the unrest in Bulgaria are discussed in much detail in B. H. Sumner's *Russia and the Balkans, 1870–1880*, a magnificent work of scholarship which one would like to see re-published. On Bulgarian affairs see, also, the article by C. E. Black, 'The Influence of Western Political Thought on Bulgaria, 1850–1885,' in *AHR* for 1943 and compare Charles Jelavich, *Tsarist Russia and Balkan Nationalism*, and the article by Peter Sugar, 'The Southern Slav Image of Russia,' in *JCEA* for April 1961. The massive study of D. Harris, *A Diplomatic History of the Balkan Crisis of 1875–78*, does not, despite its title, go beyond 1876 but is useful for the first period of international tension. R. W. Seton-Watson, *Disraeli, Gladstone and the Eastern Question* and M. D. Stoyanovich, *The Great Powers and the Balkans* supplement Sumner's classic. There are detailed bibliographies in W. L. Langer's *European Alliances and Alignments*. Chernyaev's activities in Serbia have been described in an article by D. Mackenzie entitled 'Panslavism in Practice,' *JMH*, 1964. There is a short article by R. Rosetti on 'Roumania's Share in the War of 1877,' in *SEER*, March 1930. The extract from the Tsar's speech of 11 November 1876 (quoted above, p. 85) is taken from Sumner, p. 227. For subsequent events see especially C. E. Black, *The Establishment of Constitutional Government in Bulgaria*.

5 The Heyday of Nationalism

For events in Poland I used the standard works cited above, supplemented by R. W. Tims, *Germanising the Prussian Poles*. On Schönerer and the Taaffe Era see May's *Hapsburg Monarchy*, chapter 9, and Wiskemann's *Czechs and Germans*, chapter 5; and compare Hitler's remarks on Schönerer in *Mein Kampf* (English translation, pp. 93–4). For Tisza I relied on the works by May and Macartney (*Hungary*), supplemented for Transylvanian questions by R. W. Seton-Watson, *History of the Roumanians*. Other books by Dr Seton-Watson are, in themselves, part of the history of this period and cannot possibly be ignored: *Racial Problems in Hungary* is mainly concerned with the Slovaks and contains details of political trials; *Corruption and reform in Hungary* includes detailed examination of particular elections and an account of the Szakolcza Election of 1910; and *Absolutism in Croatia* which is no less anti-Magyar but primarily an extension of Dr Seton-Watson's *Southern Slav Question*. For Croatia see the markedly right-wing work of Rudolf Kiszling, *Die Kroaten*. On the Southern Slav movement in general see, in addition to works on the Yugoslav idea cited above, Ante Smith Pavelić, *Dr Ante Trumbić*.

6   To Sarajevo

The first volume of I. Albertini, *The Origins of the War of 1914* and Bernadotte Schmitt, *The Coming of the War*, supplement the works of May, Taylor and Stavrianos, already cited. For specific topics, see W. S. Vucinich, *Serbia between East and West, 1903–1908*; D. Dakin, *The Greek Struggle in Macedonia, 1897–1913*; and Bernadotte Schmitt, *The Annexation of Bosnia, 1908–9*. On IMRO see, J. Swire, *Bulgarian Conspiracy*. The Roumanian *jacquerie* of 1907 is analysed by D. Mitrany, *The Land and the Peasant in Roumania*. For Blagoev and the Bulgarian Marxists, see Rothschild, *Bulgarian Communist Party* (already cited). The most detailed account of unrest in Bosnia between 1908 and 1914 is contained in V. Dedijer, *The Road to Sarajevo* (with an extensive bibliography). E. C. Helmreich, *The Diplomacy of the Balkan Wars, 1912–1913*, has never been superseded although it was published more than thirty years ago. For the events of June and July 1914 see, also, Joachim Remak, *Sarajevo*, and Hans Uebersberger, *Österreich zwischen Russland und Serbien*; and the article by S. Gavrilović on 'New Evidence on the Sarajevo Assassination,' in *JMH* for December 1955. Conrad von Hötzendorf's memoirs, *Aus meiner Dienstzeit*, seem to me to constitute a more formidable indictment of Austrian policy than any work by a sympathizer of the Entente: this is particularly true of volume 3. A. F. Pribram's *Austrian Foreign Policy, 1908–1918* is a useful corrective. I find it hard to accept the judgements of Professor Arthur J. May on the responsibility of the Serbian government given in the first part of volume 1 of his otherwise excellent study, *The Passing of the Hapsburg Monarchy*; the evidence he uses does not seem to be any more conclusive than in earlier blatantly polemical works.

7   'The Universal War for the Freedom of Nations'

As well as the standard histories, I have used: Z. A. B. Zeman, *The Break-Up of the Habsburg Empire, 1914–1918*; J. C. Adams, *Flight in Winter*; T. Komarnicki, *The Rebirth of The Polish Republic*; T. G. Masaryk, *The Making of a State*; E. Beneš, *My War Memoirs*; W. W. Gottlieb, *Studies in Secret Diplomacy*; Albert Pingaud, *Histoire diplomatique de la France*. For Russo-Czech relations in 1914 see A. Popov, 'The Czechoslovak Question and Tsarist Diplomacy' (in Russian) in *Krasny Arkhiv*, vols. 33, 34. I have also made use of a number of documents from the Russian archives printed in *Mezhdunarodnye Otnosheniya v Epokhu Imperializma* (ed. M. Pokrovsky), 3rd Series, vols. 6, 7, 8: detailed references to most of these are included in the footnotes to Macartney and Palmer, *Independent Eastern Europe*, chapter 2. On Supilo and the Yugoslav Committee see: Josip Horvat, *Supilo* (in Serbo-Croat); P. D. Ostović, *The Truth about Yugoslavia*; Rodd, *Social and Diplomatic Memories*; Mlada Paulova, *Jugoslavenski Odbor*, (in Serbo-Croat but a very important work of scholarly honesty); and Ante Mandić, *Fragmenti za Historiju Ujedinjenja*. There are many interesting documents on the Serbo-Italian disputes in P. H. Michel, *La Question de l'Adriatique, 1914–1918*. For Serbia's role in the war and for the activities of the inter-allied army in Macedonia, see Alan Palmer, *The Gardeners of Salonika* (with bibliography).

Notes On Sources

For Naumann and his ideas the best study is H. C. Meyer, *Mitteleuropa in German Thought and Action*, supplementing Meyer's article on German economic relations with south-eastern Europe from 1890 to 1914 in *AHR* for 1951–2. The shaping of the British attitude to Central Europe may be traced in Harry Hanak, *Great Britain and Austria-Hungary in the First World War*; but see, also, R. W. Seton-Watson, *Masaryk in England*. For the policy of the United States and the influence of Woodrow Wilson, see V. S. Mamatey, *The United States and East Central Europe, 1914–1918*. Professor May's two volumes on *The Passing of the Hapsburg Monarchy* see these problems in a world perspective.

On particular topics, see the article by Z. Szász, 'The Transylvanian Question; Roumania and the Belligerents, July to October, 1914,' *JCEA* for January 1954; and the article by Charles Jelavich, 'Nikola P. Pašić, Greater Serbia or Yugoslavia?,' in *JCEA* for July 1951. On the Emperor Charles see E. von Glaise-Horstenau, *The Collapse of the Austro-Hungarian Empire* and A. C. Polzer-Hoditz, *The Emperor Karl*. Gordon Brook-Shepherd's *The Last Habsburg* uses some of the private archives of the dynasty and includes passages from the Empress Zita's diaries, but Reinhold Lorenz's *Kaiser Karl und der Untergang der Donaumonarchie* is more comprehensive, though suffering from the absence of an index. Sir Lewis Namier's 'Downfall of the Habsburg Monarchy,' originally written for the *History of the Peace Conference of Paris*, was reprinted nearly forty years later in *Vanished Supremacies*. The two autobiographical works of Count Mihály Károlyi, *Fighting the World* and *Faith without Illusion* are full of moving reminiscence. The curious status of the South Slav National Councils is discussed by I. Lederer, *Yugoslavia at the Peace Conference*.

8   The Making of Peace

The most entertaining and academically stimulating book about the Peace Conference is still Sir Harold Nicolson's *Peacemaking* while the semi-official *History of the Peace Conference of Paris*, edited by H. M. W. Temperley, is a study which cannot be ignored (volume 4 contains most of the relevant sections on East-Central Europe). In this chapter, and the three which follow it, I have used some of the same sources as in Macartney and Palmer, *Independent Eastern Europe*, and I shall not cite here every work consulted since that book has a lengthy bibliography of its own. I shall, however, list recent books and articles and all really important studies.

I found four books on the policy of individual countries at the Peace Conference of especial value: Lederer's *Yugoslavia at the Peace Conference*, already cited; Albrecht-Carrié's *Italy at the Paris Peace Conference*; F. Deák's *Hungary at the Peace Conference* (which should be contrasted with the defence of Trianon in the article by Temperley, 'How the Hungarian Frontiers were Drawn,' *Foreign Affairs*, April 1928); and Professor S. D. Spector's *Roumania at the Paris Peace Conference*, a brilliant study of Bratianu and written in a particularly lively style. A. J. Mayer, *The Politics and Diplomacy of Peacemaking*, is remarkably detailed on specific questions, notably the attitude of the Allied and American governments towards Bolshevism in Russia and Hungary, but it is not so much a study of diplomatic bargaining as of the pressure groups which shaped (and at times distorted) the policy of the major victorious Powers. Rudolf Tokés, *Béla Kun and the Hungarian Soviet Republic* traces the origins of the Hungarian communist movement and examines the form of the communist-socialist alliance, but it ignores the support given to Kun as an apparent champion of 'historic Hungary' by members of the middle classes and fails to see the significance, then and for the future, of Kun's Jewish origin. C. A. Macartney's *Hungary and Her Successors* is peerless for Slovakia and Ruthenia as well as for Transylvania. Professor Wiskemann's *Czechs and Germans* gives a fairer assessment of Beneš than Seton-Watson's *History of the Czechs and Slovaks* (or, indeed, than many other writers). E. Schramm von Thädden, *Griechenland und die grossen Mächte, 1913–1923*, although written nearly forty years ago, has not been surpassed. For the economic questions raised at the end of the chapter, see F. Hertz, *The Economic Policy of the Danubian States* and A. Basch, *The Danube Basin and the German Economic Sphere*.

9 Democratic Illusions and Realities

The Royal Institute of International Affairs' *Surveys of International Affairs*, with the corresponding volumes of *Documents*, are indispensable for the inter-war periods; I have used them extensively. I have also gained much from specific national histories including, in addition to those already mentioned: Roos, *History of Modern Poland*; H. L. Roberts, *Roumania: Political Problems of an Agrarian State*; and C. A. Macartney's *October Fifteenth* which, although primarily a history of Hungary from 1929 to 1945, has five chapters of the first volume devoted to the earlier period. Hugh Seton-Watson's *Eastern Europe between the Wars* remains a stimulating introduction and is particularly good on events in Roumania. Three works by D. Mitrany are important: *The Effect of the War on South-Eastern Europe* is a social and economic analysis: *Land and Peasant in Roumania* is a minor classic; and *Marx against the Peasant* is an interesting study in the conflict of agrarianism and communism over the whole region. There is additional information on the international peasant movement in the memoirs of M. Hodža, *Federation in Central Europe*. J. Tomasevich, *Peasants, Politics and Economic Change in Yugoslavia*, delves deeply into the sociological problems of a Balkan peasantry and its political affiliations. The chapter by H. L. Roberts on 'Politics in a small state: the Balkan example,' in C. and B. Jelavich, *The Balkans in Transition*, is an interesting general essay on the dynamics of south-east European politics. On Stamboliisky see Swire, *Bulgarian Conspiracy* and Rothschild, *Bulgarian Communist Party*. The first volume of Avakumović's *History of the Communist Party of Yugoslavia* contains a wealth of material on all aspects of Yugoslav internal politics from 1918 to 1941 and I found its use of contemporary newspaper cuttings from the Croatian press particularly valuable in trying to understand the extraordinary appeal of Radić.

The history of the Little Entente in the 1920s may be studied in R. Machray, *The Little Entente*; see also F. J. Vonoraček, *The Foreign Policy of Czechoslovakia*. For material on the military conferences see Rudolf Kiszling, *Die militarischen Vereinbarurzen der Kleinen Entente 1929–1937*. For Polish foreign policy: J. Korbel, *Poland between East and West, 1919–1933*; R. Debicki, *Foreign Policy of*

Poland, 1919–1939; and the articles on Polish-Czechoslovak relations between 1918 and 1926 by Z. J. Gasiorowski in *SEER*, December 1956 and June 1957. P. S. Wandycz, *France and her Eastern Allies, 1919–1925*, deals with the filling of the power vacuum in East-Central Europe.

10   Right Incline

Many of the books mentioned in the notes to chapter 9 are equally informative on the period covered by this section. Hertz's *Economic Problems of the Danubian Basin* and Basch's *Danube Basin and the German Economic Sphere* may be supplemented by the League of Nations study on *The Course and Phases of the World Economic Depression*; and by chapter 6 of volume 1 of C. A. Macartney's *October Fifteenth*. Dr Macartney's great work has a considerable store of material on Roumanian and Yugoslav policy as well as on Hungary and its political personalities. M. Szinai and L. Szücs (eds.), *The Confidential Papers of Admiral Horthy*, have included some important documents for this chapter and its successor, notably on Gömbös. Maček's memoirs, *In the Struggle for Freedom*, are selective but, so far as they go, illuminating. King Carol is treated kindly by A. L. Easterman, *King Carol, Hitler and Lupescu* and King Alexander is romanticized by Stephen Graham, *Alexander of Yugoslavia*. There are useful studies of the origins of the right-wing movements in Hungary, Roumania and Poland in S. J. Woolf (ed.) *European Fascism*. For the effect of Hitler's advent to power on Pilsudski, see the article by Zygmunt Gasiorowski on 'The German-Polish Non-Aggression Pact of 1934,' in *JCEA*, April 1955 and Hans Roos, *Polen und Europa*, pp. 65–78. On the later phases of Little Entente cooperation, see R. Machray, *The Struggle for the Danube and the Little Entente, 1929–38*. The first volume of Series C of the *Documents on German Foreign Policy* is especially valuable on the German attitude to Poland and Czechoslovakia in this period. On the Zveno movement in Bulgaria, see Swire, *Bulgarian Conspiracy*. For the effects of Alexander's murder on Yugoslav foreign policy during the regency, see J. B. Hoptner, *Yugoslavia in Crisis, 1934–41*. Dr Hoptner's article, 'Yugoslavia as Neutralist, 1937,' in *JCEA*, July 1956 is also of interest. There is some material on Stojadinović in Nevile Henderson's *Water under the Bridges* and in King Peter's, *A King's Heritage*. J. F. Montgomery's *Hungary, the Unwilling Satellite* also contains information on Yugoslav affairs, Gerhard Weinberg's article on 'Secret Hitler-Beneš Negotiations in 1936–37' in *JCEA*, July 1960 includes material unavailable elsewhere. Gordon Brook-Shepherd's *Anschluss: The Rape of Austria* sees the event in its Central European setting. A. J. P. Taylor's *The Origins of the Second World War* scrutinizes many orthodox opinions and finds them lacking in logic.

11   The German Tide

The thirteen volumes of Series D of *Documents on German Foreign Policy*, covering the period from the autumn of 1937 to 11 December 1941, are an indispensable source for this chapter, although of course several are primarily concerned with other parts of the world. The 'Hossbach Memorandum' will be found in vol. 1, pp. 29–39. One of the most valuable sources for military matters is the *Kriegstage-buch* of Colonel-General Franz Halder, daily notes written by the Chief of the German General Staff from mid August 1939 to September 1942: volume 2 of Halder's diary, covering the period from June 1940 to June 1941, is especially good on Balkan affairs. For the activities of the *Volksdeutsche* minorities in the period 1938–41, see L. de Jong, *The German Fifth Column in the Second World War*.

I have continued to rely for Sudeten affairs primarily on Professor Wiske-mann's *Czechs and Germans* but it may be supplemented by Dr J. W. Bruegel's *Deutsche und Tschechen* and by the contentious study by Wenzel Jaksch, *Europas Weg nach Potsdam*. Dr Bruegel's article 'German Diplomacy and the Sudeten Question before 1938,' in *IA* for July 1967 is primarily a study of the reports from Prague of successive German ministers; it shows that, even as early as 1934, Henlein had support from Czech groups politically hostile to Beneš. The most recent study of the Munich crisis is Dr Keith Robbins, *Munich 1938*, but the fullest treatment of the subject is still to be found in Boris Celovsky, *Das Münchener Abkommen von 1938*. J. A. Lukacs, *The Great Powers and Eastern Europe* is particularly good on Russo-Czech relations, but his account should be supplemented by V. E. Klocho (ed.), *New Documents on the History of Munich* and by the article (with a similar title) by W. V. Wallace in *IA* for October 1959, which includes material from the Prague archives. For British policy and public opinion see Gilbert and Gott, *The Appeasers*. Sir Charles Webster's Stevenson Memorial Lecture of 1960, 'Munich Reconsidered,' printed in *IA* for April 1961, is a judicious retrospective survey.

Dr Hoptner's *Yugoslavia in Crisis* and Macartney's *October Fifteenth* include considerable material, unpublished elsewhere, on the policies of Yugoslavia and Hungary for the whole of the period covered by this chapter. M. Winch, *Republic for a Day*, although written within weeks of the events it describes, is still a first-rate book on the Ruthene question.

On Polish policy see the (incomplete) memoirs of Beck, *Dernier Rapport*, and the more useful chronicle of a former Polish Under-Secretary, J. Szembek, *Journal 1933–39*. The papers and memoirs of the Polish ambassador in Berlin, Josef Lipski, *Diplomat in Berlin, 1933–39* emphasize the degree to which Polish foreign policy was under the personal direction of Beck, with his deep hostility towards the Czechs and their supporters in the West. Professor Anna Ciencala's defence of Beck in *Poland and the Western Powers, 1938–39* – see, especially, her remarks on p. 241 – does not seem to me convincing, but it emphasizes how closely Beck's political outlook coincided with the views of Poland's foreign enemies; he even put out feelers for the cession to Poland of a mandated colonial territory, to be settled principally by Polish Jews. I fear that I am equally unimpressed by the favourable picture given of Beck in Dr Bohdan Buduro-wycz's *Polish-Soviet Relations 1932–1939*, a work which incidentally confirms that militarily 'the Eastern frontier enjoyed a high priority' to the neglect of the border with Germany.

For Roumanian policy, see Hillgruber, *Hitler, König Carol und Antonescu* and Gafencu's *Last Days of Europe*. Mario Toscano's *The Origins of the Pact of Steel* is a revised translation of the original Italian edition and includes many useful documents on the events of 1938–9.

The wartime series of the *Survey of International Affairs* (edited by A. and V. Toynbee) follows a different pattern from the earlier volumes. It begins with *The World in March 1939* and continues with *The Eve of War* and *The Initial Triumph of the Axis* (September 1939 to December 1941); all three volumes have been of considerable value in writing this chapter. Jean Blairy's *Crépuscule Danubian* conveys the atmosphere of Bucharest and Belgrade in the first years of war; but it should be supplemented by the extremely interesting and partly autobiographical article of K. St Pavlowitch, 'Yugoslavia and Rumania, 1941,' in *JCEA*, January 1964. Volume 12 of Series D of the *Documents of German Foreign Policy*, covering the period February to June 1941, is particularly rich on Balkan affairs; and, while the reputation of Antonescu and the Roumanians is not enhanced by the German record, Prince Paul and the Yugoslav ministers appear to have offered far more resistance to Hitler than earlier commentators were prepared to admit (cf. Churchill, *The Second World War*, volume 3, chapter 9). The prince also emerges well from the reports of Bliss Lane, the American minister to Belgrade, printed in *Foreign Relations of the United States 1941* (volume 2). The most recent study in a Western language of the Belgrade coup of 1941 is Dragiša Ristić's, *Yugoslavia's Revolution of 1941* but it fails to answer all the questions about the revolt and it lacks the high quality of Dr Hoptner's book. No one seeking to understand the events of 1941 can possibly ignore the dramatic chapters at the end of volume 1 of Dr Macartney's *October Fifteenth*.

12 Divided Loyalties

I have used the personal records of the Russian campaigns, such as Alexander Werth's *Russia at War 1941–45*, Guderian's *Panzer Leader* and Halder's *Kriegstagebuch*, volume 3, rather than more recent historical narratives of 'Barbarossa'. The R.I.I.A. Survey, *Hitler's Europe*, and its accompanying volume of documents are sources of prime importance; they contain, for example, a translation of the letter from Maniu to Bratianu of January 1942. Volume 13 of Series D of the *Documents on German Foreign Policy* prints some important despatches from Budapest, Sofia and Bucharest and I have drawn on these extensively for the first section in the chapter. The German Documents also cover the establishment of the Nedić government in Belgrade and include criticisms of the Pavelić regime in Croatia by Glaise von Horstenau and others. The only serious and impartial study of the 'Independent State of Croatia' is Ladislas Hory and Martin Broszat's *Der Kroatische Ustascha-Staat, 1941–45*; it is far more critical than the relevant sections of Kiszling's *Die Kroaten*.

There are no entirely satisfactory studies of the tragic history of Poland in these years, although Hans Roos, *History of Modern Poland*, provides a good summary and the chapters by Sidney Lowery in *Hitler's Europe* and its successor, *The Realignment of Europe* are the most judicious assessments. Colonel Stanislaw Bieganski, and others, edited two volumes of *Documents on Polish-Soviet Relations 1939–45*: vol. 1 primarily covers the period from August 1939 to April 1943, and vol. 2 covers May 1943 to August 1945, with a few supplementary items from the earlier years. I have also used Mikolajczýk's *The Pattern of Soviet*

Domination, Woodward's *British Foreign Policy in the Second World War* and Churchill's *Second World War*. M. K. Dziewanowski's *The Communist Party of Poland* is an impressive piece of scholarship which covers the years from the Russian Revolution to September 1958; more than a fifth of the book consists of bibliography. Chapters 6 and 7 of Hugh Seton-Watson's *The East European Revolutions* are of value as a summary of what happened in Poland and other states in the area. The *Memoirs* of Dr Beneš are an important source for this period although necessarily more selective than his reminiscences of earlier diplomatic battles. Lukacs, *Great Powers and Eastern Europe* and R. Lee Wolff, *The Balkans in Our Time* are sound and comprehensive general surveys, with Lukacs especially good on Central Europe and Wolff on Roumania.

For Yugoslav affairs see Stephen Clissold, *Whirlwind*, V. Dedijer, *Tito Speaks* and the two books by Fitzroy Maclean, *Eastern Approaches* and *Disputed Barricade*. The abridged English translation of the war memoirs of the later Yugoslav Vice-President, Rodoljub Čolaković, *Winning Freedom*, deserves to be better known; the book is particularly interesting on events at Jajce in 1943. Books sympathetic to Mihailović include D. Martin, *Ally Betrayed*, and C. Fotitch, *The War We Lost*.

Kállay was one of the few survivors from the Axis states to have written his memoirs, *Hungarian Premier*; the book is fuller than Regent Horthy's *Memoirs*. I have followed Dr Macartney's *October Fifteenth*, volume 2, closely for the events of March and October 1944. Although Miss Barker's *Truce in the Balkans* is mostly concerned with Bulgaria and Roumania in 1946, it includes retrospective sections on the war years. Chester Wilmot's *The Struggle for Europe* remains an impressive work, even if dated by publication of later material.

13   The Soviet Impact

For this chapter I have used many of the books mentioned in the immediately preceding note, especially Hugh Seton-Watson's *The East European Revolutions*. The section in *The Realignment of Europe* on 'The Peace Settlement in Eastern Europe' by Sidney Lowery is a first-rate summary of events. Other books which I found useful were Ferenc Nagy, *The Struggle behind the Iron Curtain*; E. Halperin's *The Triumphant Heretic* (principally concerned with Yugoslavia from 1945 to 1956); and Ghiţa Ionescu, *Communism in Roumania 1944-1962*. Doreen Warriner's article 'Economic Changes in Eastern Europe since the War,' in *IA* for April 1949 is a perceptive assessment of the first attempts at Soviet-type planning in the region. Elizabeth Wiskemann's *Germany's Eastern Neighbours* discusses the Oder-Neisse line and the problems of the Czech frontier with Germany.

A brief research monograph by Professor Morton Kaplan, *The Communist Coup in Czechoslovakia*, provides an able analysis of events from 1945 to 1948. I find it easier to accept Kaplan's thesis that the coup was essentially unpremeditated than Josef Korbel's *The Communist Subversion of Czechoslovakia 1938-1948*, the title of which is an epitome of its argument. Korbel's book does not seem to me to appreciate the dilemma of the Czechoslovak army officers, notably General Svoboda. Hubert Ripka's *Czechoslovakia Enslaved* is a particularly valuable source as it was written by a democratic member of the Gottwald government. Taborsky's *Communism in Czechoslovakia 1948–1960* is a sober and sobering study. Gordon Shepherd's *Russia's Danubian Empire* is able journalism covering the period of the trials and purges.

14 Toppling the Statue

When the original edition of Hugh Seton-Watson's *East European Revolutions* was published the narrative closed in the early months of 1950; but the revised edition of 1956 carries the story down to the start of the Khrushchev era. Roos's *History of Modern Poland* is especially good on Gomulka, perhaps a little over-optimistic. There have been many books and pamphlets on Hungarian affairs. I have used: George Mikes, *Hungarian Revolution*; Tibor Meray, *Thirteen Days that Shook the Kremlin*; and the UNO *Report of the Special Committee on Hungary*. A study of the new course entitled *Imre Nagy on Communism* appears to have been written in 1955 and smuggled to the West after Nagy's arrest.

15 From Budapest to Prague

I have relied extensively for this chapter on contemporary newspaper reports, principally from *The Times* and *The Guardian*, and I am grateful to the Chatham House Press Library for its services. I have also found *Keesing's Contemporary Archives* of value.

There is one excellent book covering the Khrushchev era in these lands: J. F. Brown, *The New Eastern Europe*. Some sections of Kurt London (ed.), *Eastern Europe in Transition*, reach a high standard in objectivity; and the chapter by George A. Schöpflin on 'National Minority Problems under Communism' ably condenses a mass of detailed information. R. Barry Farrell's *Jugoslavia and the Soviet Union, 1948–56* prints seventeen documents, preceded by an introduction summarizing the main exchanges in diplomacy up to December 1955. In *Yugoslavia*, a brief introductory survey for the 'Modern World' series of paperbacks, I included a diagrammatic analysis of the structure of Yugoslav government under the Constitutional Law of 1963. Ghiţa Ionescu's *The Break-Up of the Soviet Empire in Eastern Europe* emphasizes the doctrinal differences of the communist parties in the period 1948 to 1964. Dr Ionescu's larger work, *The Politics of the European Communist States* is a more profound analysis of variations on the Marxist theme. Vaclav Beneš, Andrew Gyorgy and George Stambuk, *Eastern European Government and Politics* is a country-by-country commentary on continuity and change in the twenty years following the Second World War; but it is unfortunate that the book excludes Bulgaria from its terms of study.

At the time I wrote this chapter there were no books on events in Czechoslovakia in 1968 and I had to depend on newspaper reports and on personal observations during a brief visit to Slovakia in the previous year. Soon after I completed the manuscript two good books appeared on the subject: Z. A. B. Zeman's *Prague Spring* and the study of 'reform, repression and resistance' by Philip Windsor and Adam Roberts, *Czechoslovakia 1968*, a paperback which includes the text of ten important documents relating to the crisis.

Bibliography

I Documentary Sources

I have used only a few volumes of the official collections of diplomatic documents in writing this present work. Details of those cited in the notes are as follows:

Documents Diplomatiques Françaises (1871–1914), 1st Series, 1871–1900, volume 1 (Paris, 1929 ff.).

Documents of German Foreign Policy (1918–1945), Series C, 1933–7, 6 volumes; Series D, 1937–41, 13 volumes (London, 1948–64).

Foreign Relations of the United States, 1941, vol. 2 (Washington, 1958).

Pokrovsky, M. (ed.), *Mezhdunarodnye Otnosheniya v Epokhu Imperializma*, 3rd Series, 1914–16, volumes 6, 7, 8 (Moscow, 1930 ff.).

Other collections of documents cited:

Bieganski, Stanislaw (and other editors for the General Sikorski Historical Institute), *Documents on Polish-Soviet Relations, 1939–1945*, volume 1, 1939–43 (London 1960, and New York); volume 2, 1943–5 (London 1967, and New York). Klochko, V. E. (ed.), *New Documents on the History of Munich* (Prague, 1958).

Michel, P. H., *La Question de l'Adriatique, 1914–1918* (Paris, 1938).

Szinai, M. and Szücs, L. (eds.), *The Confidential Papers of Admiral Horthy* (Budapest and Wellingborough, Northants, 1966, and New York).

II Diaries, Memoirs and Speeches

Beck, J., *Dernier Rapport: Politique Polonaise, 1926–1939* (Neuchatel, 1951).

Beneš, E., *My War Memoirs* (London, 1928).
> *Memoirs of Dr Eduard Beneš: From Munich to New War and New Victory* (London and Mystic, Conn., 1954).

Colaković, Rodoljub, *Winning Freedom* (New York, 1962).

Conrad von Hötzendorf, Franz, *Aus meiner Dienstzeit, 1906–1918*, volume 3 (Berlin, 1924).

Guderian, Hans, *Panzer Leader* (London, 1952; New York, 1967).

Halder, Franz, *Kriegstagebuch*, 3 volumes (Stuttgart, 1962–4).

Henderson, Nevile, *Water under the Bridges* (London, 1945).

Hitler, A., *Mein Kampf* (unexpurgated English edition, London, 1939, and New York).

Hodža, M., *Federation in Central Europe* (London, 1942).

Bibliography

Horthy, N., *Memoirs* (London 1956, and New York).

Kállay, N., *Hungarian Premier* (New York, 1962).

Károly, M., *Fighting the World* (London, 1925).
                    Faith without Illusion (London, 1956).

Kossuth, L., *Kossuth: his speeches in England, with a brief sketch of his Life* (London, 1852).

Lipski, Josef, *Diplomat in Berlin, 1933–1939* (New York, 1968).

Maček, Vladko, *In the Struggle for Freedom* (New York, 1957).

Maclean, Fitzroy, *Eastern Approaches* (London, 1949).

Mandic, Ante, *Fragmenti za Historiju Ujedinjenja* (Zagreb, 1956).

Masaryk, T. G., *The Making of a State* (London, 1927).

Mikolajczýk, S., *The Pattern of Soviet Domination* (London, 1948).

Nagy, Ferenc, *The Struggle behind the Iron Curtain* (London, 1949).

Nagy, Imre, *Imre Nagy on Communism: In Defence of the New Course* (New York, 1957).

Noyes, G. R. (ed.), *The Life and Adventures of Dositej Obradović* (Berkeley, 1953).

Obradović, Dositej, see immediately above.

Peter II, King of Yugoslavia, *A King's Heritage* (London, 1955).

Szembek, J., *Journal 1933–39* (Paris, 1952).

III   Other Secondary Works

Adams, J. C., *Flight in Winter* (Princeton, 1942).

Albertini, I., *The Origins of the War of 1914*, volume 1 (Oxford and New York, 1952).

Albrecht-Carrié, R., *Italy at the Paris Peace Conference* (New York, 1938).

Anderson, M. S., *The Eastern Question* (London and New York, 1966).

Avakumović, I., *History of the Communist Party of Yugoslavia* (Aberdeen, 1964).

Barker, Elizabeth, *Truce in the Balkans* (London, 1948).
                    Macedonia, its Place in Balkan Power Politics (London, 1950).

Basch, A., *The Danube Basin and the German Economic Sphere* (New York, 1943).

Beneš, V., Gyorgy, A., and Stambuk, G., *Eastern European Government and Politics* (London and New York, 1966).

Black, C. E., *The Establishment of Constitutional Government in Bulgaria* (Princeton, 1943).

Blairy, Jean, *Crépuscule Danubian* (Paris, 1946).

Breugel, J. W., *Deutsche und Tshechen* (Stuttgart, 1967).

Brook-Shepherd, Gordon, *The Anschluss* (London, 1963).
                    The Last Habsburg (London, 1968).

Brown, J. F., *The New Eastern Europe* (London, 1966, and New York).

Budurowycz, Bohdan, *Polish-Soviet Relations, 1932–1939* (London and New York, 1963).

Celovsky, Boris, *Das Münchener Abkommen von 1938* (Stuttgart, 1958).

Churchill, Sir Winston S., *The Second World War*, 6 volumes (London, 1948–54, and New York).

Ciencala, Anna, *Poland and the Western Powers, 1938–1939* (Toronto, 1968).

Clissold, Stephen, *Whirlwind: an account of Marshal Tito's Rise to Power* (London, 1949).

⸻ (ed.), *A Short History of Yugoslavia* (Cambridge and New York, 1966).

Crankshaw, Edward, *The Fall of the House of Habsburg* (London and New York, 1963).

Cubrilović, Vaso, *Istorija Politicke Misli u Srbija* (Belgrade, 1958).

Dakin, Douglas, *The Greek Struggle in Macedonia, 1897–1913* (Thessaloniki and Chicago, Ill., 1967).

Deák, F., *Hungary at the Paris Peace Conference* (New York, 1942).

Debicki, Roman, *The Foreign Policy of Poland, 1919–1939* (New York, 1962; London, 1963).

Dedijer, Vladimir, *Tito Speaks* (London, 1953).

⸻ *The Road to Sarajevo* (New York, 1966; London, 1967).

Dybowski, R., *Outlines of Polish History* (New York, 1931).

Dziewanowski, M. K., *The Communist Party of Poland* (London and Cambridge, Mass., 1959).

Easterman, A. L., *King Carol, Hitler and Lupescu* (London, 1942).

Eisenmann, Louis, *Le Compromis Austro-Hongrois de 1867* (Paris, 1904).

Farrell, R. Barry, *Jugoslavia and the Soviet Union, 1948–1956* (Hamden, Conn., 1956).

Filip, T. M., *A Polish Anthology* (London, 1944).

Fotitch, C., *The War We Lost* (New York, 1948).

Gafencu, G., *The Last Days of Europe* (London, 1947).

George, P. and Tricart, J., *L'Europe Centrale*, 2 volumes (Paris, 1954).

Gilbert, Martin and Gott, Richard, *The Appeasers* (London and New York, 1963).

Glaise-Horstenau, E. von, *The Collapse of the Austro-Hungarian Empire* (London, 1930).

Gottlieb, W. W., *Studies in Secret Diplomacy* (London and New York, 1957).

Graham, Stephen, *Alexander of Yugoslavia* (London, 1938).

Halecki, O., *The Limits and Divisions of European History* (London, 1950; Notre Dame, Indiana, 1962).

Halperin, E., *The Triumphant Heretic; Tito's Struggle against Stalin* (London, 1958).

Hanak, Harry, *Great Britain and Austria-Hungary during the First World War* (Oxford and New York, 1962).

Harris, D., *A Diplomatic History of the Balkan Crisis, 1875–78: the First Year* (Stanford, 1936).

Haumant, E., *La Formation de la Yugoslavie* (Paris, 1930).

Helmreich, E. C., *The Diplomacy of the Balkan Wars* (London, 1937; New York, 1938).

Hertz, F., *The Economic Problems of the Danubian States* (London and New York, 1947).

Heurtley, W. A., Darby, H. C., Crawley, C. W., and Woodhouse, C. M., *A Short History of Greece, from early times to 1964* (Cambridge and New York, 1965).

Hillgruber, A., *Hitler, König Carol und Antonescu* (Wiesbaden, 1954).

Bibliography

Hoptner, J. B., *Yugoslavia in Crisis, 1934–41* (London and New York, 1962).

Horvat, Josip, *Supilo* (Zagreb, 1922).

Hory, L. and Broszat, M., *Der Kroatische Ustascha-Staat, 1941–1945* (Stuttgart, 1964).

Ionescu, Ghiţa, *Communism in Roumania, 1944–1962* (Oxford and New York, 1964).

  The Break-Up of the Soviet Empire in Eastern Europe (London and New York, 1965).

  The Politics of the European Communist States (London and New York, 1967).

Jelavich, Charles, *Tsarist Russia and Balkan Nationalism: Russian Influence on the Internal Affairs of Bulgaria and Serbia, 1879–1886* (Berkeley, 1958).

  (with Jelavich, B.) (eds.), *The Balkans in Transition* (Berkeley, 1963).

Jones, D. M., *Five Hungarian Writers* (Oxford and New York, 1966).

Jong, L. de, *The German Fifth Column in the Second World War* (London, 1956).

Kaplan, Morton, *The Communist Coup in Czechoslovakia* (Princeton, 1960).

Kerner, R. J. (ed.), *Yugoslavia* (Berkeley, 1949).

Kiszling, Rudolf, *Die Kroaten: Der Schicksalsweg eines Sudslawensvolkes* (Graz and Cologne, 1956). *Die militarischen Vereinbarurzen der Kleinen Entente, 1929–1937* (Munich, 1959).

Kohn, Hans, *Panslavism: its History and Ideology* (New York, 1953).

Kolarz, Walter, *Myths and Realities in Eastern Europe* (London, 1946).

Komarnicki, T., *The Rebirth of the Polish Republic* (London, 1957).

Korbel, Josef, *The Communist Subversion of Czechoslovakia, 1938–1948* (London and Princeton, 1959).

  Poland between East and West, 1919–1933 (London and Princeton, 1963).

Langer, W. L., *European Alliances and Alignments, 1871–1890* (revised edition, New York, 1950).

(League of Nations Study), *The Course and Phases of the World Economic Depression* (Geneva, ? 1945).

Lederer, I., *Yugoslavia at the Peace Conference* (London and New Haven, 1963).

Leslie, R. F., *Polish Politics and the Revolution of November, 1830* (London and New York, 1956).

  Reform and Insurrection in Russian Poland 1856–1865 (London and New York, 1963).

Loncar, D., *The Slovenes, a Social History* (Cleveland, 1939).

London, Kurt (ed.), *Eastern Europe in Transition* (London and Baltimore, 1966).

Lorenz, Reinhold, *Kaiser Karl und der Untergang der Donaumonarchie* (Vienna, 1959).

Lukacs, J. A., *The Great Powers and Eastern Europe* (New York, 1953).

Macartney, C. A., *National States and National Minorities* (Oxford, 1934; New York, 1968).

  Hungary and her Successors (Oxford and New York, 1937).

  October Fifteenth: a History of Modern Hungary 1929–1945, 2 volumes (Edinburgh, 1957).

  Hungary, a Short History (Edinburgh, 1962 and Chicago, Ill.).

  The Habsburg Empire, 1790–1918 (London, 1969).

(with Palmer, A. W.), *Independent Eastern Europe* (London and New York, 1962).

Machray, R., *The Little Entente* (London and New York, 1929).

        The Struggle for the Danube and the Little Entente, 1929–1938 (London, 1938).

Maclean, Fitzroy, *Disputed Barricade* (London, 1957).

Mamatey, V. S., *The United States and East-Central Europe, 1914–18* (Princeton, 1957; Oxford, 1958).

Mann, Golo, *Secretary of Europe, the life of Friedrich Gentz, Enemy of Napoleon* (New York, 1947).

Martin, D., *Ally Betrayed, the uncensored story of Tito and Mihailovitch* (New York, 1946).

Maur, Gilbert in der, *Die Jugoslawen einst und jetzt*, 3 volumes, (Leipzig, 1936–8).

May, Arthur J., *The Hapsburg Monarchy, 1867–1914* (London and Cambridge, Mass., 1951).

        The Passing of the Hapsburg Monarchy, 2 volumes (London and Philadelphia, 1966).

Mayer, A. J., *The Politics and Diplomacy of Peacemaking* (London and New York, 1968).

Meray, Tibor, *Thirteen Days that Shook the Kremlin: Imre Nagy and the Hungarian Revolution* (London, 1959).

Meyer, H. C., *Mitteleuropa in German Thought and Action, 1815–1945* (The Hague, 1955).

Mikes, George, *The Hungarian Revolution* (London, 1957).

Mitrany, D., *The Land and the Peasant in Roumania* (Oxford, 1930).

        The Effect of the War on South-East Europe (New Haven, 1936)

        Marx versus the Peasant: a Study in Social Dogmatism (Chapel Hill, N.C., 1951; London, 1961).

Montgomery, J. F., *Hungary, the Unwilling Satellite* (New York, 1947).

Mutton, A. F. A., *Central Europe* (London and New York, 1961).

Namier, L. B. (Sir Lewis), *Facing East* (London, 1947, and New York).

        Vanished Supremacies (London, 1958, and New York).

Nicolson, Harold, *Peacemaking* (London, 1933 and New York, 1965).

        The Congress of Vienna (London and Magnolia, Mass., 1946).

Palmer, Alan, *The Gardeners of Salonika, the Macedonian Campaign 1915–18* (London and New York, 1965).

Palmer, A. W., *Yugoslavia* (Oxford and New York, 1964).

Paulova, Mlada, *Jugoslavenski Odbor* (Zagreb, 1921).

Pavelić, Ante Smith, *Dr Ante Trumbić, Problemi Hrvatska-Srpsih Odnosi* (Munich, 1959).

Pingaud, Albert, *Histoire Diplomatique de la France pendant la Grande Guerre*, 3 volumes (Paris, 1938–41).

Polzer-Hoditz, A. C., *The Emperor Karl* (London, 1930).

Pribram, A. F., *Austrian Foreign Policy, 1908–1918* (London, 1923).

Ravlić, Jaksa (ed.), *Rijeka Zbornik* (Zagreb, 1953).

Rath, R. J., *The Viennese Revolution of 1848* (Austin, Texas, 1957).

Reddaway, W. F. (ed.), *Cambridge History of Poland*, volume 2 (Cambridge, 1941).

Bibliography

Remak, Joachim, *Sarajevo* (London and New York, 1959).

Riker, T. W., *The Making of Roumania, a Study of an International Problem, 1856–1866* (Oxford, 1931).

Ripka, H., *Czechoslovakia Enslaved* (New York, 1950).

Ristić, Dragiša, *Yugoslavia's Revolution of 1941* (London Park, Penn., 1966; London, 1967).

Robbins, Keith, *Munich, 1938* (London, 1968).

Roberts, H. L., *Rumania, Political Problems of an Agrarian State* (London and New Haven, 1951).

Roos, Hans, *Polen und Europa: Studien zur polnischen Aussen-politik, 1931–9* (Tübingen, 1957).
> *A History of Modern Poland* (London and New York, 1966).

Rose, W. J., *The Rise of Polish Democracy* (London, 1944).

Rothschild, Joseph, *The Communist Party of Bulgaria, Origins and Development, 1883–1936* (London, 1959; New York, 1962).

Sakazov, I., *Bulgarische Wirtschaftgeshichte* (Berlin, 1929).

Sauvigny, Bertier de, *Metternich and his Times* (London, 1962, and New York).

Schmitt, Bernadotte E., *The Coming of the War*, 2 volumes (New York, 1930).
> *The Annexation of Bosnia, 1908–9* (Cambridge, 1937, and New York).

Schramm von Thadden, E., *Griechenland und die grossen Mächte, 1913–1923* (Göttingen, 1933).

Seton-Watson, Hugh, *Eastern Europe between the Wars* (Cambridge, 1945; Hamden, Conn., 1962).
> *The East European Revolutions* (revised edition, London, 1956 and New York).
> *The Russian Empire*, 1801–1917 (Oxford, 1967).

Seton-Watson, R. W., *Racial Problems in Hungary* (London, 1908).
> *The Southern Slav Question and the Habsburg Monarchy* (London, 1911).
> *Corruption and reform in Hungary: a study of electoral practice* (London, 1911).
> *Absolutism in Croatia* (London, 1912).
> *Disraeli, Gladstone and the Eastern Question* (London, 1933; New York, 1962).
> *A History of the Roumanians* (Cambridge and Hamden, Conn., 1934).
> *A History of the Czechs and Slovaks* (London, 1943, and Hamden, Conn.).
> *Transylvania, a Key-Problem* (Oxford, 1943).
> *Masaryk in England* (Cambridge, 1943).

Shepherd, Gordon, *Russia's Danubian Empire* (London, 1954).

Singleton, F. B., *Background to Eastern Europe* (Oxford and Long Island City, N.Y., 1965).

Sišić, Ferdo, *Jugoslavenska Misao* (Belgrade, 1937).

Spector, S. D., *Roumania at the Peace Conference* (New York, 1962).

Stavrianos, L. S., *The Balkans since 1453* (London and New York, 1958).

Steed, H. Wickham, *The Hapsburg Monarchy* (London, 1911; New York, 1914).

Stoyanovich, M. D., *The Great Powers and the Balkans, 1875–1878* (Cambridge, 1939).

Sumner, B. H., *Russia and the Balkans, 1870–80* (Oxford and Hamden, Conn., 1937).

Swire, J., *Bulgarian Conspiracy* (London, 1937).

Tabori P. and Eastwood J., *Forty-eight, the year of revolution* (London, 1948).

Taborsky, E., *Communism in Czechoslovakia, 1948–1960* (Princeton, 1961).

Taylor, A. J. P., *The Habsburg Monarchy* (revised edition, London, 1951, and New York).

　　　　　The Struggle for Mastery in Europe, 1848–1918 (Oxford and New York, 1954).

　　　　　The Origins of the Second World War (London, 1961; New York, 1962).

Temperley, H. W. V., *History of Serbia* (London and New York, 1917).

(ed.), *History of the Peace Conference of Paris*, 4 volumes (Oxford, 1920).

Tiander, H., *Das Erwachen Osteuropas* (Vienna and Stuttgart, 1934).

Tims, R. W., *Germanising the Prussian Poles, the H-K-T Society of the Eastern Marches, 1894–1914* (New York, 1941).

Tokes, Rudolf, *Béla Kun and the Hungarian Soviet Republic* (London and New York, 1967).

Tomasevich, J., *Peasants, Politics and Economic Change in Yugoslavia* (Stanford, 1965).

Toscano, Mario, *The Origins of the Pact of Steel* (3rd revised edition, Baltimore, 1967).

Toynbee A. and Toynbee V. (eds.), *Survey of International Affairs, 1939–1946*, 11 volumes including *The World in March 1939* (London, 1958);

　　　　　The Eve of War (London and New York, 1958);

　　　　　The Initial Triumph of the Axis (London and New York, 1958);

　　　　　Hitler's Europe (London and New York, 1954);

　　　　　The Realignment of Europe (London and New York, 1955).

Uebersberger, Hans, *Oesterreich zwischen Russland und Serbien* (Cologne-Graz, 1959).

(United Nations General Assembly), *Report of the Special Committee on the Problem of Hungary* (London and New York, 1957).

Vondraček, F. J., *The Foreign Policy of Czechoslovakia* (New York, 1937).

Vucinich, Wayne S., *Serbia between East and West, 1903–1908* (Stanford, 1954).

Wandycz, P. S., *France and her Eastern Allies, 1919–1925* (Minneapolis, 1962).

Wanklyn, H. G., *Eastern Marchlands of Europe* (London, 1941).

Werth, Alexander, *Russia at War, 1941–45* (London and New York, 1964).

West, Rebecca, *Black Lamb and Grey Falcon*, 2 volumes (London, 1942, and New York).

Wilkinson, H. R., *Maps and Politics, a Review of the Ethnographic Cartography of Macedonia* (Liverpool, 1951).

Wilmot, Chester, *The Struggle for Europe* (London, 1952, and New York).

Winch, M., *Republic for a Day* (London, 1939).

N

Bibliography

Windsor, Philip and Roberts, Adam, *Czechoslovakia 1968 – Reform, Repression and Resistance* (London, 1969).

Wiskemann, Elizabeth, *Czechs and Germans* (Oxford, 1938; New York, 1967).
    Germany's Eastern Neighbours, Problems relating to the Oder-Neisse Line and the Czech Frontier Regions (Oxford, 1956).

Wolff, R. Lee, *The Balkans in Our Time* (London and Cambridge, Mass., 1956).

Woodhouse, C. M., *The Greek War of Independence: its historical setting* (London, 1952).

Woodward, Sir Llewelyn, *British Foreign Policy in the Second World War* (London, 1963; New York, 1967).

Woolf, S. J. (ed.), *European Fascism* (London, 1968).

Yakchitch, G., *L'Europe et la résurrection de la Serbie, 1804–1934* (Paris, 1907).

Zeman, Z. A. B., *The Break-Up of the Habsburg Empire, 1914–1918* (Oxford and New York, 1961).
    Prague Spring (London, 1969).

IV Articles in Journals and Periodicals

Bárány, George, 'The Szechenyi Problem,' *JCEA* (Boulder, Colorado), vol. XX, no. 3 for October 1960, pp. 249–67.

Black, C. E., 'The Influence of Western Political Thought on Bulgaria, 1850–1885,' *AHR* (Macmillan, New York) vol. XLVIII for April 1943, pp. 507–20.

Breugel, J. W., 'German Diplomacy and the Sudeten Question before 1938' *IA*, (RIIA, London) vol. 37, no. 3 for July 1961, pp. 323–31.

Campbell, J. C., 'The Transylvanian Question in 1849,' *JCEA* (Boulder, Colorado), vol. II, no. 1 for April 1942, pp. 20–34.

Corović, V., 'Vuk Karadzić,' *SEER* (London), vol. XVI, no. 48 for April 1938, pp. 667–77.

Dakin, D., 'The Origins of the Greek Revolt of 1821,' *History* (London), vol. XXXVII, no. 131 for October 1952, pp. 228–35.

Eckhart, Francois, 'La Révolution de 1848 en Hongrie et la cour de Vienne,' *Actes de Congrès Historique du Centenaire de la Revolution de 1848*, hereafter cited as *Actes . . . de 1848*, (Paris, 1848), pp. 229–39.

Gasiorowska, N. 'Le Problème Social en Pologne en 1846–1848,' *Actes . . . de 1848*, pp. 177–83.

Gasiorowski, Z. I., 'The German-Polish Non-Aggression Pact of 1934,' *JCEA* (Boulder, Colorado), vol. XV, no. L, for April 1955, pp. 15–45.
    'Polish-Czechoslovak Relations, 1918–1926,' *SEER* (London), vol. XXXV, no. 84 for December 1956, pp. 170–87 and no. 85 for July 1957, pp. 340–61.

Gavrilović, S., 'New Evidence on the Sarajevo Assassination,' *JMH* (Chicago, Ill.), vol. XXVII, no. 4, for December 1955, pp. 410–14.

Hanak, J., 'Slovaks and Czechs in the early Nineteenth Century,' *SEER* (London), vol. X, no. 30 for April 1932, pp. 588–601.

Hoptner, J. B., 'Yugoslavia as Neutralist, 1937,' *JCEA* (Boulder, Colorado), vol. XVI, no. 2 for July 1956, pp. 156–76.

Ivanyi, B. G., 'From Feudalism to Capitalism; the Economic Background to Szechenyi's reforms in Hungary,' *JCEA* (Boulder, Colorado), vol. XX, no. 3 for October 1960, pp. 270–88.

Jelavich, Charles, 'Nikola P. Pašić: Greater Serbia or Yugoslavia?', *JCEA* (Boulder, Colorado), vol. XI, no. 2 for July 1951, pp. 133–52.

Kimball, Stanley B., 'The Prague Slav Congress of 1868,' *JCEA* (Boulder, Colorado), vol. XXII, no. 2, for July 1962, pp. 174–99.

Mackenzie, D., 'Panslavism in Practice; Chernaiev in Serbia,' *JMH* (Chicago, Ill.), vol. XXXVI for 1964, pp. 279–97.

Macurek, J., 'L'Anneé 1848 et la Moravie,' *Actes . . . de 1848*, pp. 203–9.

Meyer, H. C., 'German Economic Relations with South-Eastern Europe,' *AHR*, (Macmillan, New York), vol. LVII, for 1952, pp. 77–90.

Namier, L. B., '1848, the Revolution of the Intellectuals,' *Proceedings of the British Academy for 1944* (London, 1948), vol. XX, pp. 161–282. (Also published as a separate pamphlet by the Oxford University Press.)

Odložilík, Otakar, 'Russia and Czech National Aspirations,' *JCEA*, (Boulder, Colorado), vol. XXII, no. 4, for January 1963, pp. 407–39.

Pavlowitch, K. St, 'Yugoslavia and Roumania, 1941,' *JCEA*, (Boulder, Colorado), vol. XXIII, no. 4, for January 1964, pp. 451–84.

Popov, A., 'The Czechoslovak Question and Tsarist Diplomacy' (in Russian), *Krasny Arkhiv* (Moscow, 1929), vol. 33, pp. 3–33 and vol. 34, pp. 31–8.

Rosetti, R., 'Roumania's Share in the War of 1877,' *SEER* (London), vol. VIII for March 1930, pp. 548–51.

Sugar, Peter F., 'The Southern Slav Image of Russia,' *JCEA* (Boulder, Colorado), vol. XXI, no. 1 for April 1961, pp. 45–52.

Szász, Z., 'The Transylvanian Question, Roumania and the Belligerents, July to October 1914,' *JCEA* (Boulder, Colorado), vol. VIII, no. 4 for January, 1954, pp. 409–35.

Temperley, H. W. V., 'How the Hungarian Frontiers were Drawn,' *Foreign Affairs* (New York), vol. 6 for April 1928, pp. 432–47.

Vucinich, W. S., 'Marxian Interpretations of the First Serbian Revolt,' *JCEA* (Boulder, Colorado), vol. XXI, no. 1 for April 1961, pp. 3–14.

Wagner, Francis S., 'Szechenyi and the Nationality Problem in the Habsburg Empire,' *JCEA* (Boulder, Colorado), vol. XX, no. 3 for October 1960, pp. 287–309.

Wallace, W. V., 'New Documents on the History of Munich,' *IA*, (RIIA, London), vol. 35, no. 4 for October 1959, pp. 447–54.

Warriner, Doreen, 'Economic Changes in Eastern Europe since the War,' *IA* (RIIA, London), vol. 25, no. 2 for April 1949, pp. 157–67.

Webster, Sir Charles, 'Munich Reconsidered,' *IA*, (RIIA, London), vol. 37, no. 2 for April 1961, pp. 137–53.

Weinberg, Gerhard, 'Secret Hitler-Beneš Negotiations in 1936–37,' *JCEA* (Boulder, Colorado), vol. XIX, no. 4 for January 1960, pp. 366–74.

Zacek, Joseph F., 'Palacký and his History of the Czech Nation,' *JCEA* (Boulder, Colorado), vol. XXIII, no. 4, January 1964, pp. 412–23.

Zwitter, F., 'Illyrisme et sentiment yougoslave,' *Le Monde Slave* (Paris), April 1933, pp. 39–71; May 1933, pp. 161–85; June 1933, pp. 358–75.

377

Index

Index

Apponyi, György, Hungarian 'Progressive Conservative', 50, 51

Arabs, communist support for, 367

Arad, Hungarian counter-revolutionary regime at, 161

armaments, French, supplied to Serbia, 110, and to Czechoslovakia and Roumania, 151; German, supplied to Bulgaria, 215; Czechoslovak, supplied to Roumania, 221

armies, Austro-Hungarian, 101, 121, 149; of Balkan countries, 106; conscription for, in Bosnia-Herzegovina, 110; conscript, as instrument of social education, 175; Polish, 224, 243; German, 228, 262, 263

Arpád dynasty, Hungary, 19

Arrow Cross, Hungarian fascist movement, 225; suppressed, 237

Arz von Straussenberg, General, 132; chief of Austro-Hungarian General Staff, 134

Asia, 'uncommitted' nations of, 335

Asquith, H. H., British prime minister, 124

Attlee, C., British prime minister, 290

Auen, Dr Lodgmann von, Sudeten German leader, 186

Ausgleich (Compromise) between Austria and Hungary (1867), 71, 73–4, 101; end of (1918), 146

Austria (province of Empire or Dual Monarchy), constituent assembly for (1848), 52, 64; railways in, 71

Austria-Hungary, Dual Monarchy of (1867), 71–4, 102, 133, 146; Poles in, 92–3; Czechs in, 95–6; secret treaty between Serbia and (1881), 103; promotes railways in Balkans, 80; agreements on Balkans between Russia and, 85, 86, 106; presents ultimatum to Serbia (1913), 116, (1914), 118; battles between Serbs and, 121–2, 128–9, between Russians and, 122–3, 127, 131; war-weariness in, 133; meeting of Parliament of (1917), 134–5; dissolution of, not an Allied war aim, 139–40; battles between Italians and, 141–2; seeks armistice (1918), 143; parts with Bohemia and Moravia, 145; and Hungary, 146; fate of navy of, 147, 148; split into 7 economic systems, 171

Austrian Empire (before Ausgleich), 12, 20, 21; proclaimed as Empire (1804), 27; at Congress of Vienna, 24–7; Sardinia-Piedmont declares war on (1848), 52; Hungarian war with (1848–9), 61–3; bureaucratic administration of, 64; occupies Danubian Principalities during Crimean War (1854–7), 65; and Polish rebellion against Russia (1863), 68; industrial development in, 71–2; transformed into Dual Monarchy (1867), 71–4; see further Austria-Hungary

Austrian Republic ('German Austria'), peace treaty with (1919), 150; Yugoslav frontier with, 167; project for Customs Union of Germany and (1931), 208; in Danubian bloc of Rome Protocols (1934), 213; Anschluss with Germany (efforts to prevent), 217, 219, (effected by Hitler, 1938), 226; British troops advance into (1945), 288, 293; peace settlement with, 295, 323–4; Russian forces withdrawn from, 324, 325; neutral state, 324, 331

Avars, 6

Averescu, Marshal, suppresses peasant revolt, 107; Roumanian prime minister, 182, 197–8, 299

Bacilek, Karol, secretary of Slovak Communist Party, 349

Bácska region of Vojvodina, 8, 293

Badoglio, General, Italian commander, 166

Baja, town in Vojvodina, 164

Balkan League (1912), 114, 169

Balkan Pact (1934), later Balkan Entente, 215, 246; Salonika Agreement between Bulgaria and, 238

Balkan Pact (1953), 335

Balkan mountains, 13

Balkan wars (1912–13), 114–15

Balkans, 13–17, railways in, 15, 16, 79, 80; agreements between Austria-Hungary and Russia on (1877), 85, 86, (1903), 106

Baltic Provinces, surrendered by Russia (1918) to become Baltic States, 137

Baltic States, adhere to Litvinov Protocol (1929), 185; to Russia in Nazi-Soviet Pact (1939), 244; incorporated in Soviet Union, 247; see also Estonia, Latvia, Lithuania

Bánát region of Vojvodina, 8; Roumanian claims to (1915), 126; promised to Roumania by secret treaty (1916), 132; divided between Yugoslavia and Roumania at peace conference, 153, 163; repression of minorities in, 189, 199; under German occupation (1941), 254

Baptists, in Transylvania, 12

Barac, Dr, Rector of University of Zagreb, Croat leader, 137

Barak, Rudolf, Czechoslovak minister of the interior, 349

Baranya region of Vojvodina, 8, 165, 293

Bárdossy, Lászlo, Hungarian prime minister, 256, 260

Barthou, Louis, French foreign minister, 213, 216, 232; assassinated, 216

Basarab family, Wallachia, 10

Bashi-Bazouks, Turkish irregular troops, 85–8

Index

Index

Bulgaria, 13, 14, 16, 17, 80; linguistic revival in, 29, 81; Russians occupy (1828-9), 81; first railway in (1866), 79; national awakening of, 81-2; Exarchate established in (1870), 82, 105; Turks suppress rising in (1876), 83-4; Austrian patronage of, 83, 84-5; in Russo-Turkish war (1877), 85; new autonomous state of, 86-7; crisis in (1885-6), 88-9; proclaimed independent of Turkey (1908), 104; Agrarian Party in, 107, 178, 179; Social Democratic Party in, 108; in Balkan wars, 113-14, 114-15; seeks alliance with Austria-Hungary and Germany (1914), 115; maintains neutrality (1914), 126; enters war on Austro-German side (1915), 128; war weariness in, 142; armistice with (1918), 143; post-war disorders in, 144; peace treaty with, 150, 167-8; revisionist sentiment in, 170, 186, 238, 246; political parties in, 174; percentage of population in agriculture, 176; communists in, 176, 204; army coup in (1923), 179-80; communist rising suppressed, 180; domestic policies in, 204-6; Officers' League in, 205, 216, 225; contacts of Mussolini with, 212; German trade treaty with (1935), 215; and Balkan Entente, 215, 238, 246; move to right in, 216, 225; treaty with Yugoslavia (1937), 220; Nazi-inspired movement in, suppressed, 223; Roumanians cede Dobrudja to (1940), 247-8; adheres to Tripartite Pact, German troops enter (1941), 249, 255; joins in attack on Yugoslavia, 253; occupies most of Macedonia, 254; non-belligerent in attack on Russia, 259-60; isolated from main conflict, 274-5; Fatherland Front in, 275, 284, 296; new government declares war on Germany, and Russians enter Sofia as liberators, 284; Russia to have free hand in, 287, 290; in peace settlement, 293; Red Army withdraws from (1947), 295; coalition government in, 296; communists come to power in, 298; relations of, with Yugoslavia and Albania over Macedonia, 312-13, 336, 344; purge of communists in, 316; internal politics in (1950-61), 342-4; agriculture regarded by Comecon as sole industry of, 342, 345

Bulgarians, 17; in the Dobrudja, 164; in Greece, 171; in Yugoslavia, 171, 189; in Roumania, 199

Bülow, Prince von, German Chancellor, 93

Buol, Count Ferdinand, Austrian foreign minister, 65, 66

bureaucracy, Prussian, 59; Austrian, 64, 79

Burgenland, transferred from Hungary to new Austrian Republic (1920), 163

Burian, Count Stephen, administrator of Bosnia-Herzegovina, 110; Austro-Hungarian foreign minister, 242

Byelo-Russians, in Poland, 4, 170

Byrnes, James E., U.S. Secretary of State, 291, 292

Byzantium, Byzantine Empire, 16-17

Calinescu, Anton, Roumanian prime minister, assassinated by Iron Guard, 238

Calvinism, in Transylvania, 12; of Tiszas, 97; of Horthy, 162; and communists, 320

Capodistrias, John, 24; Russian joint foreign minister, 36; first President of Greece, 37-8

Caporetto, Italian defeat at (1917), 141

Carinthia, 29, 30; Yugoslav claims in, 165, 167; plebiscite in southern part of, 167; remains Austrian, 167; *ustaše* troops flee from partisans into, 288

Carniola, 29, 30, 74

Carol I of Roumania, 87; makes secret treaty with Austria-Hungary and Germany (1883), 103, 108

Carol II of Roumania, 199, 200, 201, 220; echoes Mussolini, 210-11; linked with France, 221; dictatorship of, 225-6; and Hitler, 233, 238; visits Paris and London, 237; considers resistance to Russia, 247; agrees to session of territory, 248; abdicates, 248

Carpathian mountains, 1, 6, 9, 11

Carpatho-Ukraine (independent Ruthenia), 235-6, 241, 355

Castlereagh, Viscount, British foreign secretary, 23, 24, 25, 26

Catholic Church, in Poland, 4, (under Russia), 45, 68, 92, (under Prussia), 46, 92, (under communists), 306, 337-8; in Croatia-Slavonia, 17, 54, 56, 100, 264; in Czechoslovakia, 96, 187; in Slovakia, 263; in Hungary, 304, 320, 341; in Yugoslavia, 312

Caucasus, 87, 138

Cavour, Count di, 70

Ceausescu, Nicolae, Roumanian communist, 323-4; President, 346, 347; welcomed in Prague (1968), 355

censuses, linguistic and racial; in Macedonia, 105; in Teschen, 158; in Croatia-Slavonia, 165

Cepicka, Alexei, Czechoslovak minister of defence, 329

Cernavoda, bridge over Danubian marshes at, 79, 132

Cernik, Oldrich, Czechoslovak prime minister, 353, 354

Cetinje, old capital of Montenegro, 15, 83

Index

Chamberlain, Neville, British prime minister, sends intermediaries to Hitler (1939), 231, 244; meets Hitler, 234; on Czechoslovakia, 237; and Poland, 243

Charles, Emperor of Austria and King of Hungary, 133, 142, 146; in contact with Allies, 134, 140; abdicates (1918), 148–9; makes abortive attempts to reclaim throne, 181, 202, 211

Charles of Hohenzollern-Sigmaringen, chosen as prince of Roumania (1866), 80; in Russo-Turkish war, 85; becomes king (1881), 87; *see further* Carol I

Charles IV of Holy Roman Empire, 5

Charles V of Holy Roman Empire, 5

Chernaev, General, Russian commander in Bulgaria (1876), 84

Chervenkov, Vulko, Bulgarian prime minister, 317, 323, 328, 342

Chicherin, Georghi, Russian foreign Commissar, 185

China, relations of: with Russia, 332, 335, 343, 344; with Yugoslavia, 335; with Albania, 336; with Bulgaria, 342; with Roumania, 345

Chisnevschi, Josif, member of Roumanian Politburo, 318

Chlopicki, General Jozef, head of Polish provisional government (1830), 42

cholera, epidemics of: in Poland (1831), 43; in Italy (1849), 53

Chou En-lai, visits Roumania (1966), 345

Churchill, Winston, impressed by Henlein, 231; and Czechoslovakia, 251, 252, 272, 273; prime minister, broadcasts after attack on Russia, 265; at wartime conferences with Stalin, (Teheran), 276, 277, (Moscow), 285, (Yalta), 287; meets Archduke Otto, 278; plans Anglo-American hold on Danube, 280–1; at Potsdam Conference, 290

Chvalkovsky, František, Czechoslovak foreign minister, 236

Ciano, Count, Italian foreign minister, 220, 224, 239, 248, 249

Cierna-nad-Tisou, meeting of Russian and Czechoslovak leaders at (1968), 354

Cincar-Marković, Aleksander, Yugoslav foreign minister, 250–1, 252, 253–4

Circassian irregular troops (Turkey), 84

Cis-Leithania (non-Hungarian part of Austria-Hungary), Pan-Germanism in, 94–5

cities, Balkan distrust of, 107–8

Clausewitz, General, 45–6, 126

Clemenceau, Georges, French prime minister, 134, 146, 151, 152, 154, 161, 164

Clementis, Vladimir, Czechoslovak foreign minister, 310; executed, 318–19

Cluj (Kolozsvár, Klausenberg), chief city of Transylvania, 12; trial of Roumanian leaders at (1894), 98, 104; to Hungary by Vienna Award (1940), 248; Roumanian desire for, 261; Hungarian and Roumanian universities in, 346

coal mines, in Duchy of Teschen, 158

Codreanu, Corneliu, founder of Roumanian Iron Guard, 200, 225, 226, 238

collective security, 120

collectivization of agriculture, 319, 321, 337, 348

'Comecon' (Council for Mutual Economic Assistance of East European countries), 326, 332; and Yugoslavia, 335; and Bulgaria, 342, 345; and Roumania, 345; and Czechoslovakia, 347

Cominform, 311, 313; dissolved (1954), 325

Comintern, 176, 191; Pact against, 242, 246

communists, in Austria-Hungary, 139; in Hungary, 161, 302–5; in Yugoslavia, 176, 193, 295, 311–14; in Bulgaria, 176, 204, 295, 298; in Roumania, 176, 298–301; in Czechoslovakia, 176, 236, 307–10; in Albania, 295, 314–15; in Poland, 295, 305–7; in Greece, 312, 314; purges of, 316–20

Conrad von Hotzendorf, Franz, chief of Austro-Hungarian General Staff, 111, 112, 128, 133, 134; on Sarajevo assassination, 118

Constanta, Black Sea port, 11, 79; taken by Germans (1916), 132; Russians in (1944), 284

Constantine, Grand Duke, brother of Tsar Alexander I, 42, 43

Constantine, King of Greece, 128, 169

Constantinople, 80; Young Turks in, 111; British Salonika force turns towards (1918), 143

constitutions: Bulgarian (1879), 88; Czechoslovak, (1920), 186, (1960), 349; Yugoslav, (1921), 190, 193, 194, (1931), 209, (1946), 311, 333; Roumanian, (1923), 197, 198–9, (1948), 301, (1952, 1965), 346; Polish (1935), 223–4

cooperative societies, in Czechoslovakia, 178

Coraes, Adamantios, Greek nationalist, 35–6

Corfu, French garrison in, 22; Serbian government in, 129; Pact of, between Serbs and Yugoslav National Committee (1917), 136, 189; Italians bombard and occupy (1923), 182

Cracow, city of Vistulan basin, 2, 25, 77, 95; 10-day Republic in (1846), 47; demonstrations in (1848), 58; one-day Soviet in (1925), 194; student riots in (1968), 337

Index

Index

Georghiev, General Kimon, Bulgarian prime minister, 216, 225, 284, 296, 298

German Confederation, under Habsburgs, 27, 54

German National Assembly, Frankfurt (1848), 54, 57, 59

Germanos, Archbishop of Patras, 37

Germans, in East Central Europe, 4–5, 7, 11, 12, 17; spread of nationalism among, 41, 94, 95; in Czech lands, 48, 54; promote railways in Balkans, 80; in Czechoslovakia, 159, 186–7 (*and see* Sudetenland); in Yugoslavia, 165, 190; in Roumania, 164, 199; outside Germany and Austria (Volksdeutschen), 171, 228, 248; in Poland, 196; ejected from Poland and Czechoslovakia (1945–6), 291, 348

Germany, riots in (1830), 41, secret treaty of King Carol of Roumania with (1883), 103, 108; and Austrian annexation of Bosnia-Herzegovina, 111; supports Austria-Hungary and declares war (1914), 119; in 1914–18 war, 127, 128; and Balkans, 129–30; peace treaty with, 150, 151; Little Entente and, 184; on bad terms with Poland, 184–5; economic crisis; Hitler comes to power in, 211–12; makes 10-year non-aggression pact with Poland (1934), 213, (denounced) 243; extends influence into Balkans, 214, 218, 219; proposed Customs Union of Austria and, 208; Anschluss of Austria and, (efforts to prevent), 217, 219, (effected by Hitler, 1938), 226; reoccupies Rhineland (1936), 219; destroys Czechoslovakia, 230–6, 240–2; makes Pact of Steel with Italy, 242; pact with Russia (1939), 244; in Tripartite Pact (1940), 249; relations with Russia, 255–6; invades Poland, 245–6; occupies Roumania (1940), 247–9, 255; occupies Bulgaria (1941), 249; invades and partitions Yugoslavia (1941), 251–4; invades Russia (1941), 256; occupies Hungary (1944), 279; pulls out of Balkans (1944), 284, and Hungary (1945), 286; surrenders, 288

Gerö, Ernö, secretary of Hungarian Communist Party, 302, 329, 330

Gheorgiu-Dej, Gheorghe, Roumanian communist, 299; minister for planning, 301; prime minister, 318, 323, 328, 344–5

Gierek, E., Communist Party leader in Polish Silesia, 339

Gladstone, W. E., 76, 84

Glaise von Horstenau, General, commander of German troops in Croatia, 263, 264

Gmund, Austria, frontier adjustment at (1919), 159

Gneisenau, General, and Prussian Poland, 45–6

Godesberg, meeting of Hitler and Chamberlain at, 234

Goering, Hermann, and Yugoslavia, 216, 217, 233

Goga, Octavian, leader of Roumanian National Christian Party, 223; prime minister for 44 days, 225

Goluchowski, Count A., Austro-Hungarian foreign minister, 110

Gömbös, Gyula, Austro-Hungarian 'Nationalist' leader against revolution, 161, 162; prime minister, 203, 211, 224

Gomulka, Wladyslaw, Polish communist, 268, 305, 306; dismissed, 317; re-admitted to Communist Party, 327; returns to power, 328, 337

Gorchakov, Prince Alexander, Russian Chancellor, 82, 85, 86

Görgei, Arthur, Hungarian general, 62, 63

Gorgopotamus, Greece, railway destroyed by resistance forces at, 270

Gorizia (Gorz), Italian claim for (1915), 125; fighting for, 127; Yugoslav claim for, 166, 167

Gottwald, Klement, Czechoslovak communist, 269, 307; prime minister, 308, 309–10; President, 310, 319, 321, 347; death of, 322

Grabski, Stanislaw, leader of Polish National Democrats, 194, 196

grain, Roumanian, 79, 197, (supplies Central Powers, 1914–18), 129, 132, 133, (Hitler and), 215, 238, 246, 262, (Russia and), 344; Hungarian, 203, 341; American overproduction of, 207; conference on price of, 208

Graz, Slovene studies at, 30

Grazynski, Michal, Polish governor of Upper Silesia, 196

'Great Stalin', 321

'Greater Bulgaria', 86, 105

'Greater German Reich', 228, 245

'Greater Germany', 91

'Greater Greece', 168

'Greater Moravian Empire', 5

'Greater Roumania', 91, 197

'Greater Serbia', 91, 113, 125

'Greater South Slav Federation', 312

Greece, 13, 14, 16; Albanians in, 18, 171; struggle for independence of, 35–8; secures Thessaly, 87; in Balkan wars, 114, 115; in 1914–18 war, 128, 168–9; Britain and, 152; at peace conference, 169; occupies Smyrna; ousted by Turks (1922), 169; percentage of population in agriculture in, 178; tension with Bulgaria over IMRO, 205, 206; British and French guarantee to, 242; Italy attacks,

Index

Index

Kosovo, battle of (1389), 19, 104; region round, acquired by Italy (1941), 254

Kosovo-Metohija (Kosmet) region of Yugoslavia, 334

Kossuth, Lajos, Hungarian orator and journalist, 50-1, 52, 91; as ruler of Hungary, 57, 61, 62; in exile, 63, 64; and Croats, 76; memory of, 330

Kostov, Traicho, Bulgarian deputy prime minister, 317

Kosygin, A. N., succeeds Khrushchev (1964), 332

Kotor, naval base, 27, 125, 138

Kovács, Béla, of Hungarian Smallholders' Party, 304; in Nagy's government, 330

Kramár, Karel, Young Czech leader, 96, 123, 124, 135, 145; first prime minister of Czechoslovakia, 145

Krasinski, Count Valerian, Polish poet, 44

Kresimir, Peter, Croatian hero, 19

Kulturkampf, 92

Kun, Béla, Hungarian communist, 139; head of short-lived government, 161

Kundt, Erich, spokesman of Germans in remnant of Czechoslovakia, 236

Kutchuk-Kainardji, Treaty of (1774), 20

Kvaternik, General Slavko, Croatian minister of defence, 264

Lakatos, General, Hungarian prime minister, 285

Lammasch, Heinrich, last Austro-Hungarian prime minister, 145

land reform, 175; in Poland, 194; in Roumania, 197, 198, 299; in Hungary, 202, 302; in Bulgaria, 298; in Czechoslovakia, 307

Langiewicz, General Marjan, Polish leader, 68, 69

languages, and consciousness of nationality, 28-31

Latin America, Polish refugees in, 44

Latvia, adheres to Litvinov Protocol (1929), 185; incorporated in Soviet Union, 247

Lausanne, Treaty of (1923), 169

Laval, Pierre, French foreign minister, 217, 218

Lazar, Prince of Serbia, 19

League of Nations, 163; Danzig to be Free City under, 156; Albania admitted to, 168; recognises Polish acquisition of Vilna (1923), 171; convenant of, attached to peace treaties, 172; Little Entente seat on Council of, 183; and Roumania, 211; and Hungary, 211, 217; Germany leaves (1933), 218; Russia joins (1934), 218; Russia expelled from (1939), 246

Ležaky, Czech village, 263

Leeb, General von, German commander against Russia, 258

Lelewel, Joachim, Polish historian and councillor (1830), 43, 44

Lenart, Jozef, Czechoslovak prime minister, 349, 353

Lenin, 137, 138, 321

Leningrad, 258, 259

Leopold II of Holy Roman Empire, 29

Liapchev, Andrij, Bulgarian prime minister, 204

Liberated Europe, Declaration on (1945), 288

Lidice, Czech village, 263

Linde, Samuel Bogomil, Polish Dictionary of, 28

Linz Programme, for Pan-Germanism, 94

List, Field-Marshal Wilhelm, 6

Lithuania, Polish claims for, 43, 67; Russian repression in, 69; falls to Germans (1915), 127; declared independent (1918), 138; loses Vilna to Poles 170, 171; adheres to Litvinov Protocol (1929), 185; in agrarian conferences, 208; to Germany in Nazi-Soviet Pact, 244; Russia insists on bases in, 246; incorporated in Soviet Union (1940), 247

Lithuanians, in Poland, 4, 92

Little Entente, of Czechoslovakia, Yugoslavia, and Roumania, 180; France and, 181, 219-20, 221; conferences of neighbour states with, 208; renewed (1933), 212; Mussolini and, 213, 217; Czech attempts to reanimate (1938), 233; Roumanian echo of, 261

Litvinov, Maxim, Russian foreign commissar, 185, 218, 244

Litvinov, Protocol (1929), 185, 218

Ljotić, Dimitrije, leader of Serbian Nazi-type group, 223, 254

Ljubljana (Laibach), Slovene capital, 9, 29, 30, 147, 264

Lloyd George, D., British prime minister, 139-40

Locarno Pact (1925), 184, 185, 219

Lodz, Poland, 93, 123

Loebl, Eugen, Slovak writer, 350, 351, 352

Lombardy, annexed by Austria, 27; rising in (1848), 52-3

London, Convention of (1832), on Greek independence, 38, 40; conference of ambassadors in (1912-13), 114, 115; secret treaty of (1915), 125-6, 151, 166, (published by Bolsheviks), 139

Lovcen, Black Mountain of Montenegro, 13

Lublin, temporary Polish government at (1944), 277, 288; student riots in (1968), 337

Luca, Vasile, Roumanian finance minister and deputy prime minister, 318

Index

Index

Index

Rapacki, Adam, Polish foreign minister, 327; proposes 'atom-free zone', 339–40

Rapallo, Treaty of (1920), between Italy and Yugoslavia, 167

Rasputin, 125

Rauschning, Hermann, President of Danzig Senate, 213

Reichstadt, Austro-Russian secret agreement on Balkans at (1876), 85

resistance movement, in Croatia against *Ustaše* rule, 264; in Slovenia, 264; in Poland, 266, 267, 268, 281–3; in Yugoslavia, 270, 271–3, 281; in Greece, 270–1; in Bulgaria, 275; in Czechoslovakia, 289

Rhineland, Hitler reoccupies (1936), 219

Rhodope mountains, 13, 15, 275

Ribar, Ivo, president of Anti-Fascist Council for National Liberation of Yugoslavia (1942), 272; President of Yugoslavia, 311

Ribbentrop, Joachim von, German foreign minister, 244, 246, 247, 255, 261

Rieger, František, Czech politician, 77, 78, 95

Riga, Treaty of (1921), establishes Russo-Polish frontier, 170

Rijeka, *see* Fiume

Ripka, Dr Hubert, Czechoslovak minister of foreign trade, 309

Ristić, Joven, Serbian prime minister, 84

Rodd, Sir Rennell, British ambassador in Rome, 124

Rokossovsky, Marshal, of Red Army, 273, 282, 287; appointed Polish minister of war, 318–19, 328

Romanovs, 97, 131, 135

Rome, Congress of Oppressed Peoples in (1918), 140; Treaty of (1924), between Italy and Yugoslavia, 167; Protocols of (1934), agreed by Italy, Hungary, and Austria, 213

Rome-Berlin Axis, 212, 219, 221; proclaimed (1936), 226

Roosevelt, President, 251, 276, 287, 288; Archduke Otto and, 278, 285

Rothermere, Viscount, newspaper magnate, and Hungary, 183, 203

Roumania, 8, 10–13, 17 (*and see* Danubian Principalities); Crimean war and, 65; first official use of name, 80; in Russo-Turkish war, 85, 86; independence recognized (1878), 86, 87; secret treaty of Austria-Hungary and (1883), 103; peasant revolt in (1907), 107; Social Democrats in, 108; Allies negotiate with (1915), 126, and sign secret treaty with (1916), 132, 155, 163; peace treaty with (1918), 138; declares renewed war on Germany, 143; France and, 151; occupies Transylvania and advances to Budapest (1919), 161; territorial gains of, 163; minorities in, 164, 171, 199; political parties in, 174, 197; agrarian reform in, 175; communists in, 176; military convention of Poland and, 180, 181; Little Entente extended to, 180–1; French treaty with, 181; Italy and, 182; Hungary and, 183; Russia and, 184; adheres to Litvinov Protocol, 185; domestic policies in, 197–201; in agrarian conferences, 208; move to right in, 209, 210–11, 225–6; Mussolini and, 212; German trade treaties with, 215, 246, 248; seeks understanding with Germany (1936), 220; secret pact with Russia, 218, (repudiated), 221; Rome-Berlin Axis and, 221; National Christian Party in, 223; refuses passage to Russian troops, 221, 233; and destruction of Czechoslovakia, 233; Front of National Rebirth in, 238; British and French guarantee to, 242; Polish authorities interned in, 247, 265; Russia occupies territories of, 247, 255; cedes Dobrudja to Bulgaria, 247, 248; Iron Guard government in, 248; Germany and, 247–9; German troops in, 248, 255; subscribes to Tripartite Pact, 249; declares war on Russia, 256; in attack on Russia, 260, 261, 262; makes contacts with West, 262, 274; Teheran Conference and, 276, 277; Britain and U.S. refuse to conclude separate agreement with, 277; changes sides, 283–4; Russia and, 287, 290, 292, 293; in peace settlement, 293, 294; Russian garrisons in, 295; coalition government in, 296; communist government in, 298–301; 'Ploughmen's Front' in, 299; purge of communists in, 316, 318; development of industry in, 319; exploited by Russia, 344; de-Stalinization in, 328; and Hungarian rebellion, 342; Russian troops withdrawn from (1958), 344; and Czech rebellion (1968), 346, 347

Roumanian National Council, 146–7

Roumanians, 11, 17, 18, 60; in Transylvania, 11, 12, 61, 75, 104; language of, 28; and Hungarian nationalism, 49, 50, 56; national feeling among, 66; school for, in Bitolj, 105; in Hungary, 164; in Yugoslavia, 164, 189

Rudolf, Austrian Crown Prince, 99

Rumelia, Eastern, 15, 87, 88

Runciman, Viscount, emissary to Czechoslovakia, 232

Rundstedt, General von, German commander against Russia, 258

Rupel Pass, 15

Rupnik, General, organizes Slovene militia against partisans, 264

Index

Index

Index

Uzice, Yugoslavia, communists in, 176; partisans forced out of (1941), 272

Vaida-Voevod, Alexander, leader of Roumanian National Party, 197
Varna, Black Sea port, 11, 79; British troops land at (1854), 65; renamed 'Stalin', 321
Vatican Council (1870), Strossmayer at, 76
Velchev, Col. Damian, head of Bulgarian Officers' League, 205, 216, 225; seizes power in name of Fatherland Front (1944), 284, 296; minister in Berne, 298
Veles, Bulgarian bishopric of, 105
Venetia, annexed by Austria, 27; rising in, 53
Venetian Republic, recognizes Hungary (1849), 63
Venice, and Dalmatia, 16; embryo fascist groups in (1919), 166
Venizelos, Eleutherios, Greek prime minister, 114, 128; wounded at peace conference (1919), 154; 'Greater Greece' ideal of, 168; electoral defeat of, 169
Veress, General Lajos, alleged conspirator in Hungary, 304
Versailles, peace treaty with Germany signed at (1919), 150
Vesnić, Milenko, Serbian minister in Paris, 153-4
Via Egnatia, 15, 105
Vidin, Danube port, 168
Vienna, Turkish armies defeated at (1683), 20, 21; Napoleon in, 21-2; Congress of (1814-15), 23-7, 150; riots in (1848), 51, 53; second rising in (1848), 57, 62; slums of, 71; disorders in Parliament of, 96; International Exhibition in (1873), 97; French army marches on (1918), 143; communists in, 176; Creditanstalt fails in (1931), 207, 208, 211; abortive Nazi *putsch* in (1934), 214; Russians enter (1945), 288
Vienna Awards to Hungary, First (1938), 235; Second (1940), 248; Roumania hopes for revision of, 261, 280, 347
Világos, capitulation of Hungarians at (1849), 63
Villach, Yugoslav claim to, 165
Vilna (Wilno), 4; university of, 42, 45; taken by Poland from Lithuania (1919), 170, 171; Polish-Lithuanian antagonism over, 185; Russia takes, and cedes to Lithuania (1939), 246; rising of Jews in (1943), 267; Polish claim to, 277
Vis island, centre of partisan operations, 281
Vistula river, axis of Polish nation, 1-2, 128, 282, 287
Vittorio Veneto, Italian victory at (1918), 143
Vlachs, in Macedonia, 105

Vladaya, Bulgaria, civil war battle at (1918), 144
Vladimirescu, Tudor, Wallachian leader, 36
Vlahov, Dimiter, Yugoslav deputy prime minister, 312
Vlonë (Valona), Albania, as base for Red Fleet, 315
Vodnik, Fr Valentin, and Slovene language, 29, 30
Vojvodina region, 8; centre of Serbian culture, 30-1, 34, 56; Serbs escape to, 33; Hungarian war in, 62; in 1918, 147; to Yugoslavia (1920), 163, 164; Magyar minority in, 165, 190, 335; in partition of Yugoslavia (1941), 254, 256
Volga, German and Roumanian thrust to (1942), 262
Volkov, Ivan, Bulgarian war minister, 204, 205
Vološin, Fr, Ruthene leader, 235, 241
Voronezh, Hungarian losses at (1943), 262
Vörös, General János, Hungarian minister of defence in provincial government (1944), 302
Voroshilov, Marshal, Russian commander against Germans, 258; head of Allied Control Commission in Hungary, 302
Voulgaris, Archbishop of Kherson, 35
Vyshinsky, A., Soviet deputy foreign minister, 298
Vyx, Col., representative of French command at Budapest, 160

Wachock, Polish insurrection based on (1863), 68
Wallachia, *see* Danubian Principalities
Warsaw, 2, 44, 45, 60, 67; Napoleon's Grand Duchy of, 22, 24; Tsar Nicholas I crowned at, 42; falls to, Germans (1915), 127; Russian minister assassinated in (1927), 185; Germans bomb (1939), 245; Poles hold out in, 245; rising and resistance of Jews in (1943), 267; Home Army rising in (1944), 268, 282-3; student riots in (1968), 337
Warsaw Pact, seeds of, 291; signed (1955), 325; Yugoslav relations with countries of, 336; Albania withdraws from (1968), 336; Roumania and, 345; armies of, manoeuvre in Czechoslovakia, 354, threaten intervention in Czechoslovakia, 354, invade, 355
Warsaw State Council, pre-government for German- and Austrian-sponsored Poland (1917), 135
Warta river, 2, 123
Wenceslas, St, King of Bohemia, 5
White Mountain, battle of (1620), 19, 20
White Russians, in Poland, 4, 170

404